The Guinness Book
of
Sitcoms

CONTENTS

DON'T TELL FATHER (BBC)
DON'T WAIT UP
DOOGIE HOWSER MD
DORA
THE DORIS DAY SHOW
DOUBLE BEDLAM
DOUBLE CROSS
DOUBLE FIRST
THE DOUBLE LIFE OF HENRY PHYFE
DOWN MANGEL STREET
DOWN OUR STREET
DOWN THE GATE
DREAM ON
DREAM STUFFING
DRIVE INN
DROP ME HERE, DARLING
DROP THE DEAD DONKEY
DUET
DUFFY'S TAVERN
THE DUKES OF HAZZARD
THE DUSTBINMEN
DUTY FREE
E.R.
EAST END – WEST END
EASY STREET
EDUCATED EVANS
EDUCATING ARCHIE
EDUCATING MARMALADE
THE EGGHEADS
EIGHT BELLS
EL C.I.D.
THE EMBASSY LARK
EMNEY ENTERPRISES
EMPIRE
EMPIRE ROAD
EMPTY NEST
THE ENCHANTING WORLD OF HINGE AND
    BRACKETT
ENSIGN O'TOOLE
EVENING SHADE
EVER DECREASING CIRCLES
EVERY SILVER LINING
EXECUTIVE STRESS
THE FAINTHEARTED FEMINIST
FAIRLY SECRET ARMY
THE FALL AND RISE OF REGINALD PERRIN
FAMILY AFFAIR
THE FAMILY BRANDON
FAMILY CRACKERS
FAMILY TIES
THE FAMOUS TEDDY Z
FANCY WANDERS
FARRINGTON OF THE FO
FASTEN YOUR SEATBELT
FATHER CHARLIE
FATHER, DEAR FATHER
FATHER KNOWS BEST
FATHER MATTHEW'S DAUGHTER
FATHER OF THE BRIDE
FATHER'S DAY
FAWLTY TOWERS
FEET FIRST
THE FENN STREET GANG
FFIZZ
FIDDLERS THREE
FILTHY RICH AND CATFLAP
A FINE ROMANCE
FINKEL'S CAFE
FIRE CRACKERS
FIRST OF THE SUMMER WINE
FISH
FLOGGIT'S
FLYING BLIND
THE FLYING SWAN
FLYING THE FLAG
FOLLOW THAT DOG
FOLLOW THAT MAN
FOOLS' PARADISE
FOR BETTER OR FOR WORSE
FOR THE LOVE OF ADA
FOREIGN AFFAIRS
FOREIGN BODIES
THE FOSDYKE SAGA
THE FOSSETT SAGA
THE FOSTERS

FOUR IDLE HANDS
FOXY LADY
FRANK STUBBS PROMOTES
FRANK'S PLACE
FRASIER
THE FRED ALLEN PROGRAMME
FREDDIE AND MAX
FREEBIE AND THE BEAN
FRENCH FIELDS
FRESH FIELDS
FRESH PRINCE OF BEL-AIR
FROM A BIRD'S EYE VIEW
FROM THE TOP
THE FRONT LINE
FULL HOUSE
FULL STRETCH
FURTHER ADVENTURES OF LUCKY JIM
THE FUZZ
THE GAFFER
GALLOPING GALAXIES!
A GENTLEMAN'S CLUB
GEORGE AND MILDRED
GEORGE AND THE DRAGON
THE GEORGE BURNS SHOW
GERT AND DAISY
GET BACK
GET SMART
GET SOME IN
THE GHOST AND MRS MUIR
THE GHOSTS OF MOTLEY HALL
GILLIGAN'S ISLAND
THE GINGERBREAD GIRL
THE GIRL WITH SOMETHING EXTRA
GIRLS ABOUT TOWN
GIRLS ON TOP
GIVE US A BREAK
THE GLAMOUR GIRLS
GLORIA
THE GLUMS
GLYNIS
THE GNOMES OF DULWICH
GOING STRAIGHT
GOLDEN GIRL
THE GOLDEN GIRLS
GOLDEN PALACE
THE GOLDEN PARROT CLUB
GONE TO THE DOGS
GONE TO SEED
GOOD EVENING, EACH
GOOD GIRL
THE GOOD GUYS
THE GOOD LIFE
THE GOOD LIFE (USA)
GOOD PULL-UP FOR CYCLISTS
GOODBYE MR KENT
GOODNIGHT AND GOD BLESS
GOODNIGHT SWEETHEART
THE GOON SHOW
THE GOVERNOR AND JJ
GRACE AND FAVOUR
GRANDAD
THE GRAVY TRAIN
THE GRAVY TRAIN GOES EAST
GREEN ACRES
GRINDL
GROWING PAINS
THE GROWING PAINS OF ADRIAN MOLE
THE GROWING PAINS OF PC PENROSE
GROWING RICH
GRUEY
THE GRUMBLEWEEDS IN . . .
GRUNDY
GUESTWARD HO!
HAGGARD
HAIR IN THE GATE
HALLELUJAH
HANCOCK
HANCOCK'S
HANCOCK'S HALF HOUR
THE HANDY GANG
HANGIN' WITH MR COOPER
THE HAPPIDROME
HAPPILY EVER AFTER
THE HAPPY APPLE
HAPPY DAYS

HAPPY EVER AFTER
HAPPY FAMILIES
HAPPY HOLLIDAY
HARDLUCK HALL
HARDWICKE HOUSE
HARK AT BARKER
HARRY AND THE HENDERSONS
HART OF THE YARD
THE HATHAWAYS
HAVE I GOT YOU . . . WHERE YOU WANT ME?
HAVING A WONDERFUL CRIME
HE AND SHE
HE'S A WONDERFUL WIFE
HEAD OF THE CLASS
HEALTH AND EFFICIENCY
THE HELLO GOODBYE MAN
HELLO PLAYMATES
HELL'S BELLS
HELP!
HELTER SHELTER
HEMSLEY'S HOTEL
HER MAJESTY'S PLEASURE
HERE COME THE DOUBLE DECKERS
HERE WE GO AGAIN
HERE'S ARCHIE
HERE'S HARRY
HERE'S LUCY
HEY JEANNIE
HI-DE-HI!
HIGH AND DRY
HIGH ST BLUES
HILARY
HIS AND HERS
HIS LORDSHIP ENTERTAINS
HITCH HIKE
THE HITCH-HIKER'S GUIDE TO THE GALAXY
HMS PARADISE
HOGAN'S HEROES
HOGG'S BACK
HOLD THE FRONT PAGE
HOLDING THE FORT
HOLIDAY LODGE
HOLMES AND YOYO
HOME AGAIN
HOME AND AWAY
HOME IMPROVEMENT
HOME JAMES
HOME TO ROOST (BBC RADIO)
HOME TO ROOST (YTV)
HONEY FOR TEA
THE HONEYMOONERS
HONOLULU BEACH
HOOP-LA!
HOPE AND KEEN'S CRAZY HOUSE
HOPE IT RAINS
HOT METAL
HOTEL MAJESTIC
HOUSE CALLS
HOUSE OF WINDSOR
HOW NOW, BROWN?
HOW'S YOUR FATHER? (BBC RADIO)
HOW'S YOUR FATHER? (GRANADA)
HOW'S YOUR FATHER? (YTV)
HUDD
HUGH AND I
HUGH AND I SPY
HULBERT HOUSE
ITMA
I DIDN'T KNOW YOU CARED
I DREAM OF JEANNIE
I LOVE LUCY
I, LOVETT
I MARRIED JOAN
I OBJECT
I THOUGHT YOU'D GONE
I WAS KITCHENER'S TREBLE
I WOKE UP ONE MORNING
IF IT MOVES – FILE IT
IF THE CROWN FITS
IF YOU SEE GOD, TELL HIM
I'M DICKENS . . . HE'S FENSTER
I'M KEN, HE'S BILL
IN FOR A PENNY
IN LOVING MEMORY
IN SICKNESS AND IN HEALTH

THE INCREDIBLE ADVENTURES OF PROFESSOR BRANESTAWM
THE INCREDIBLE MR TANNER
INSIDE GEORGE WEBLEY
INSIDE OUT
IRISH HALF HOUR
IT AIN'T HALF HOT MUM
IT STICKS OUT HALF A MILE
IT TAKES A WORRIED MAN
IT'S A CRIME
IT'S A DEAL
IT'S A FAIR COP
IT'S A GREAT LIFE
IT'S A LIVING
IT'S AWFULLY BAD FOR YOUR EYES, DARLING
IT'S GARRY SHANDLING'S SHOW
IT'S YOUR MOVE
THE JACK BENNY SHOW
JACK OF DIAMONDS
JACK'S DIVE
JACKSON PACE: THE GREAT YEARS
JEEVES AND WOOSTER
JENNINGS
JIM THE GREAT
THE JIMMY STEWART SHOW
JOAN AND LESLIE
JOANIE LOVES CHACHI
JOEY
JOHN BROWNE'S BODY
JOINT ACCOUNT
JOKING APART
JOLLYOLIDAY
JOSSY'S GIANTS
JULIA
JULIE
JUST A GIGOLO
JUST DENNIS
JUST FANCY
JUST GOOD FRIENDS
JUST JIMMY
JUST KIDD-ING
JUST LIZ
JUST OUR LUCK
JUST PERFICK
JUST THE JOB
JUST WILLIAM
KYTV
KATE AND ALLIE
KEEP IT IN THE FAMILY (THAMES)
KEEP IT IN THE FAMILY (YTV)
KEEPING UP APPEARANCES
THE KIDS FROM 47A
A KIND OF LIVING
KINDLY LEAVE THE KERB
KING STREET JUNIOR
KINVIG
KIT CURRAN
THE KIT CURRAN RADIO SHOW
KNIGHT AND DAVE
KNOW YOUR PLACE
L FOR LESTER
THE LABOURS OF ERICA
LADIES' MAN
THE LADY IS A TRAMP
LAME DUCKS
A LANCASHIRE LAD IN LONDON
LANCE AT LARGE
LAND OF HOPE AND GLORY
LANGLEY BOTTOM
THE LARKINS
THE LAST OF THE BASKETS
LAST OF THE SUMMER WINE
THE LAST SONG
LATE EXPECTATIONS
THE LAUGH TRAIL
LAURA AND DISORDER
LAVERNE AND SHIRLEY
LAW AND DISORDER (BBC RADIO)
LAW AND DISORDER (CENTRAL)
LAZARUS AND DINGWALL
LEAVE IT TO CHARLIE
LEAVE IT TO ME
LEAVE IT TO THE BOYS
LEAVE YOUR NAME AND NUMBER
LEAVING
LEGACY OF MURDER

LEGAL, DECENT, HONEST AND TRUTHFUL
LENIN OF THE ROVERS
THE LENNY HENRY SHOW
LES AND ROBERT
LES DAWSON – MAN OF FICTION
LES GIRLS
LET THERE BE LOVE
THE LIFE AND TIMES OF HENRY PRATT
LIFE BEGINS AT FORTY
LIFE IS WHAT YER MAKE IT
A LIFE OF BLISS
THE LIFE OF RILEY (GRANADA)
THE LIFE OF RILEY (USA)
LIFE WITH FATHER
LIFE WITH LORD CHARLES
LIFE WITH THE BURKES
LIFE WITH THE LYONS (BBC)
LIFE WITHOUT GEORGE
THE LIKELY LADS
LIL
LITTLE ARMADILLOS
A LITTLE BIG BUSINESS
A LITTLE BIT OF WISDOM
THE LIVER BIRDS
LIVING IT UP
LIVING WITH BETTY
LOLLIPOP LOVES MR MOLE
THE LONELYHEARTS KID
LOOKING FOR TROUBLE
LORD TRAMP
THE LOSERS
LOVE AND KISSES
THE LOVE OF MIKE
LOVE, SIDNEY
LOVE THY NEIGHBOUR
LOVEJOY
LOVELY COUPLE
THE LOVERS
LUCK'S WAY
LUCKY FELLER
THE LUCY SHOW
LUV
M*A*S*H*
McHALE'S NAVY
McKAY THE NEW
MAGGIE AND HER
THE MAGNIFICENT EVANS
MAID MARIAN AND HER MERRY MEN
MAJOR DAD
MAKIN' IT
MAKING FACES
MAKING OUT
MALCOLM
MAMA MALONE
MAN ABOUT THE HOUSE
THE MANAGEMENT
MANN'S BEST FRIENDS
THE MANY WIVES OF PATRICK
MARBLEHEAD MANOR
MARJORIE AND MEN
MARRIAGE LINES
MARRIED
MARRIED WITH CHILDREN
THE MARSHALL CHRONICLES
MARY
THE MARY TYLER MOORE SHOW
MAUDE
MAY TO DECEMBER
ME AND MY GIRL
ME AND THE MISSUS
ME MAMMY
ME, YOU AND HIM
MEET CHRISTOPHER BLAZE
MEET THE CHAMP
MEET THE HUGGETTS
MEET THE REV
MEET THE WIFE
MELLORS AND SELLERS
MELODY AND CO
MEN BEHAVING BADLY
THE MEN FROM THE MINISTRY
MEN OF AFFAIRS
MEN OF THE WORLD
MERRY-GO-ROUND
THE MERRYMART
MESS MATES

MICKEY
MIKE AND ANGELO
MIKE AND BERNIE
MIND YOUR LANGUAGE
MIND YOUR OWN BUSINESS
MINDER
THE MISFIT
MISFITS
MISLEADING CASES
MISS JONES AND SON
MRS MULLIGAN
MRS THURSDAY
MR AITCH
MR AND MRS NORTH
MR BIG
MR DEEDS GOES TO TOWN
MR DIGBY, DARLING
MR DON AND MR GEORGE
MR ED
MR JOHN JORROCKS
MR MUDDLE – PRIVATE DETECTIVE
MR MUDDLECOMBE JP
MR WILLOW'S WIFE
THE MISTRESS
MIXED BLESSINGS
MIXED DOUBLES
MOG
MOLESWORTH
THE MOLLY WOPSIES
THE MONKEES
MONKEY
MOODY AND PEG
MOONLIGHTING
THE MORE WE ARE TOGETHER
MORK AND MINDY
MORRIS MINOR'S MARVELLOUS MOTORS
THE MOST LIKELY GIRL
MOTHER AND SON
MOTHER'S RUIN
THE MOTOR WAY
THE MOTORWAY MEN
MOVING
MOVING STORY
MUCH-BINDING-IN-THE-MARSH
MUD
MULBERRY
MUM'S BOYS
THE MUNSTERS
THE MUNSTERS TODAY
MY BROTHER'S KEEPER
MY DEAR DAD
MY FAVOURITE MARTIAN
MY GOOD WOMAN
MY HERO
MY HONOURABLE MRS
MY HUSBAND AND I (A-R)
MY HUSBAND AND I (YTV)
MY MAN JOE
MY MOTHER THE CAR
MY NAME IS HARRY WORTH
MY OLD MAN
MY SAINTED AUNT
MY SISTER AND I
MY SISTER EILEEN
MY SON REUBEN
MY THREE SONS
MY TWO DADS
MY WIFE AND I
MY WIFE JACQUELINE
MY WIFE NEXT DOOR
MY WIFE'S SISTER
MY WORLD AND WELCOME TO IT
9 TO 5
NANNY AND THE PROFESSOR
NATHANIEL TITLARK
THE NAVY LARK
NEAREST AND DEAREST
NELSON'S COLUMN
THE NESBITTS ARE COMING
NEVER A CROSS WORD
NEVER MIND THE QUALITY, FEEL THE WIDTH
NEVER SAY DIE (C4)
NEVER SAY DIE (YTV)
NEVER THE TWAIN
NEVER TOO LATE
NEW ATTITUDE

THE NEW DICK VAN DYKE SHOW
THE NEW PHIL SILVERS SHOW
THE NEW STATESMAN (BBC)
THE NEW STATESMAN (YTV)
NEWHART
NEWS AT TWELVE
THE NICK REVELL SHOW
NIGHT BEAT NEWS
NIGHTINGALES
NIGHTS
NINETEEN NINETY-FOUR
THE NINETEENTH HOLE
NO APPOINTMENT NECESSARY
NO COMMITMENTS
NO FRILLS
NO – HONESTLY
NO JOB FOR A LADY
NO PLACE LIKE HOME
NO PROBLEM
NO SOAP, RADIO
NO STRINGS (BBC)
NO STRINGS (YTV)
NO – THAT'S ME OVER HERE
NO TIME FOR SERGEANTS
NOBODY'S PERFECT
NORMAN
NORTHERN EXPOSURE
NOT IN FRONT OF THE CHILDREN
NOT ON YOUR NELLIE
NOT WITH A BANG
NOW AND THEN
NOW LOOK HERE . . .
NOW, TAKE MY WIFE
NURSE DUGDALE TAKES THE AIR
NURSES
THE NUTT HOUSE
THE ODD COUPLE
ODD MAN OUT
OFF THE RACK
OFFICE HOURS
OH, BROTHER!
OH, FATHER!
OH HAPPY BAND
OH MADELINE
OH MOTHER!
OH NO! IT'S SELWYN FROGGITT
OLD BOY NETWORK
THE OLD CAMPAIGNER
OLD MOTHER RILEY
THE OLDER WOMAN
ON THE BUSES
ON THE HOUSE
ON THE ROCKS
ON THE UP
ONCE UPON A TIME IN THE NORTH
ONE FOOT IN THE GRAVE
ONE MAN'S MEAT
ONE OF THE BOYS
ONLY FOOLS AND HORSES
ONLY WHEN I LAUGH
OPEN ALL HOURS
THE OTHER 'ARF
THE OTHER ONE
OUR DORA
OUR ELIZABETH
OUR HOUSE (ABC)
OUR HOUSE (BBC)
OUR KID
OUR LES
OUR MAN AT ST MARK'S
OUR MAN HIGGINS
OUR MR MEREDITH
OUR SHED
OURS IS A NICE HOUSE
OUT OF THIS WORLD
OUTSIDE EDGE
OVER THE GARDEN WALL
OVER THE RAINBOW
OVER TO YOU
PC 49
PACIFIC STATION
PALACE HILL
PAPER MOON
PAPERS! PAPERS!
PARADISE ISLAND
PARDON MY GENIE

PARDON THE EXPRESSION
PARENTHOOD
PARSLEY SIDINGS
PARTNERS
THE PARTRIDGE FAMILY
THE PARTY PARTY
THE PATTY DUKE SHOW
THE PAUL LYNDE SHOW
PEOPLE LIKE US
PERFECT SCOUNDRELS
PERFECT STRANGERS
PET PALS
THE PETER GOODWRIGHT SHOW
PETTICOAT JUNCTION
PHENOM
THE PHENOMENON SQUAD
THE PHIL SILVERS SHOW
PHONEY ISLAND
PHYLLIS
PIE IN THE SKY
THE PIG AND WHISTLE
PIG IN THE MIDDLE
THE PIGLET FILES
PINKERTON'S PROGRESS
PLAZA PATROL
PLEASE SIR
PLEASURE BEACH
THE PLUMS
POLICE SQUAD
POOR LITTLE RICH GIRLS
PORRIDGE
PORTERHOUSE BLUE
POTTER
POTTER'S PICTURE PALACE
A PRESENT FOR DICKIE
PRESS GANG
THE PRINCE OF DENMARK
PRIVATE BENJAMIN
PRIVATE SCHULZ
PRIVATE SECRETARY
A PROPER CHARLIE (1956)
A PROPER CHARLIE (1985)
THE PRUITTS OF SOUTHAMPTON
PUBLIC FUTILITIES
PULL THE OTHER ONE
PULL UP AT DAVE'S
PUNCH DRUNK
PUNKY BREWSTER
QUANTUM LEAP
QUEEN OF ROMANCE
QUEENIE'S CASTLE
RAB C NESBITT
RADIO ACTIVE
RADIO BOOST
RADIO CARS
THE RAG TRADE
RANDALL AND HOPKIRK DECEASED
THE RANDOM JOTTINGS OF HINGE AND
  BRACKETT
RAY'S A LAUGH
RED DWARF
THE REFUGE
REGGIE
RELATIVE STRANGERS
THE RELUCTANT ROMEO
RENT
RENTAGHOST
REP
THE RETURN OF SHELLEY
RHODA
RICH TEA AND SYMPATHY
THE RIFF RAFF ELEMENT
RINGS ON THEIR FINGERS
RISING DAMP
THE RITZ
THE RIVER
ROBBING HOOD
ROBERT'S ROBOTS
ROBIN'S NEST
ROGER DOESN'T LIVE HERE ANYMORE
ROLL OVER BEETHOVEN
THE ROLLING STONES
ROMANY JONES
A ROOF OVER MY HEAD
ROOM AT THE BOTTOM (ITV)
ROOM AT THE BOTTOM (BBC)

ROOM SERVICE
ROOT INTO EUROPE
ROOTS
ROSEANNE
ROSIE
THE ROUGH WITH THE SMOOTH
ROUND AND ROUND
ROUND THE TWIST
ROY'S RAIDERS
RUDE HEALTH
RULE BRITANNIA
RUN BUDDY RUN
RUNNING THE HALLS
RUNNING WILD
RUTLAND WEEKEND TELEVISION
SADIE, IT'S COLD OUTSIDE
SALE THIS DAY
ST ELSEWHERE
SAM AND JANET
SAVED BY THE BELL
SCOTT FREE
SCREAMING
SCULLY
SEAVIEW
SECOND THOUGHTS
SECOND TIME AROUND
SECONDS OUT
THE SECRET DIARY OF ADRIAN MOLE
  AGED 13¾
THE SECRET LIFE OF KENNETH WILLIAMS
SEINFELD
SELWYN
SEMI-CIRCLES
SEND FOR DOCTOR DICK
SEND FOR SHINER
SEPTEMBER SONG
SERGEANT BILKO
SERVICE WITH A SMILE
SHARE AND SHARE ALIKE
SHARON AND ELSIE
THE SHARP END
A SHARP INTAKE OF BREATH
SHELLEY
SHILLINGBURY TALES
SHINE A LIGHT
SHINE ON HARVEY MOON
SHIRLEY'S WORLD
THE SHUTTLEWORTHS
SIDE BY SIDE
SILK, SATIN, COTTON, RAGS
SIMON'S BUG
SINGLES
SINK OR SWIM
SIR YELLOW
THE SIT-CROM
SITTING PRETTY
THE SKYLARKS
THE 'SLAP' MAXWELL STORY
SLINGER'S DAY
SLOE COACHES
THE SMALL INTRICATE LIFE OF
  GERALD C POTTER
A SMALL PROBLEM
THE SMALL WORLD OF SAMUEL TWEET
SNAKES AND LADDERS
SNIBSON'S CHOICE
SO HAUNT ME
SO I'LL TELL YOU
SO YOU THINK YOU'VE GOT TROUBLES
SOAP
SOB SISTERS
A SOFT TOUCH
SOLO
SOME MOTHER'S DO 'AVE 'EM
SOMETHING TO SHOUT ABOUT
SON OF CLICHÉ
SON OF THE BRIDE
SORRY
SORRY, I'M A STRANGER HERE MYSELF
SORRY I'M SINGLE
SOUTH OF THE BORDER
THE SPAMFRITTER MAN
SPARE A COPPER
SPATZ
SPLIT ENDS
SPOKEN IN JEST

INTRODUCTION

here were situation comedies before anyone had coined the phrase. The earliest
written reference that I have seen is in an
article by Gale Pedrick titled 'Laughter
In The Air' and published in the BBC
Year Book for 1948. In that article Pedrick refers to
the 1938 show BAND WAGGON, which starred
Arthur Askey, describing it as 'the first important
manifestation of American influence. Askey himself broke new ground by exploiting "situation
comedy" in the (Jack) Benny manner. Listeners
really believed that he and "Stinker" (Richard
Murdoch) shared a flat on top of the BBC. Here was
a new radio framework.'

From this we can see that sitcom as we now
know it began in America and probably with THE
JACK BENNY SHOW. Prior to Askey's innovation, comedy on the British wireless was usually
provided by veterans of the variety stage telling
jokes and anecdotes in the clinical cold of a bare
studio. Norman Long, 'A Song, A Smile, And A
Piano', is generally credited with being the first
entertainer to be heard on British wireless. In 1922
he went into a studio in Marconi House, London,
where he found the necessary piano and also the
tubular bells on which whoever was suitably placed
was expected to chime the passing hours of the
clock. The earliest example that I have included in
this book of what we might now recognise as sitcom
is THAT CHILD from 1926.

So, what is a sitcom? I must freely confess that
some of the entries in this book are neither instantly
nor easily slotted into the pigeon hole so marked.
There are grey areas all around. The dividing line
between soap and sitcom is often a wavy one. The
dividing line between sitcom and all the intensity
that the word drama invokes can be equally waver-
ing. There will be some dramatists upset at being
included in these pages. There may be some writers
who set out to amuse but I missed their purpose and
they are consequently excluded. The reader will
have his or her own thoughts and opinions as to
which side of those wobbly lines some shows should
have been categorised. I welcome suggestions for
future editions.

My approach throughout the compilation of
this book has been to identify all those programmes
broadcast terrestrially which satisfied my own personal definition of situation comedy. I looked for

continuity of situation and/or character in a work
that intended to amuse through either. I believe
that characters outweigh situations in importance
and in the finest examples the characters are so rich
and well drawn that they could have been located
anywhere. That STEPTOE AND SON were rag
and bone men was good and appropriate but the
middle-aged son, yearning to escape from his dirty
old dad, knowing he never would, could have been
set in a strip club, on a farm or at Crewe station and
still have worked. In similar vein one might argue
that THE GOLDEN GIRLS could have been set in
Brighton rather than Miami. So they could if that
was where they had originated. But to take an
established and loved show and try to relocate it
with new faces is not the brightest of ideas.

Rarely does the USA take our creations in their
original form. We, on this side of the Atlantic, seem
to me to be mugs. We buy their stuff off the peg and
true, some is brilliant. But they buy ours, format
only, then rewrite it, re-situate it, re-characterise it
and generally Americanise it out of all recognition.
Then, blow me down, we buy it back! DEAR
JOHN: USA for example or ALL IN THE FAM-
ILY were, to this author, not a patch on our origi-
nals. There is another striking difference between
our two sitcom-producing countries. Most of the
best of British is the work of one or two writers
who, naturally, have a limit to their creative output
and consequently deliver series of six, seven or
occasionally thirteen episodes. The American networks buy by the metre and vast teams of writers
are hired and fired in the quest to deliver hundreds
of shows. The mortality rate of writers on
ROSEANNE is frightening. At least we in Britain
nurse and nurture our writers because without
them, there is no beginning.

If I sound parochial I apologise but I believe the
joy of laughter is worth more than pounds or
dollars. I respect fun and I was brought up in a
house that positively rocked with laughter. My
parents took me at the tender age of six to the Palace
Theatre, Manchester, to see Albert Modley dressed
as a schoolboy tormenting his dad as the latter tried
to read the paper. I have vivid memories of Norman
Evans in his guise as Fanny Fairbottom doing OVER
THE GARDEN WALL behind my grandmother's
piano in Gorton Street, Heywood. I recall early
years at Sedgeley Park Rugby Club where a sausage

factory proprietor named Al Read reduced the toughest of men to painful hysterics with his everyday stories. Man is the only animal that laughs and this God-given gift is the greatest catharsis for our emotional trials. Indeed, we even laugh at death itself.

Within this book are the names of writers, actors and producers to whom society owes an enormous debt. Yet, we only cover the best part of 70 years. Shakespeare gave us sitcom and today, market forces would see us at least on A Midsummer Night's Dream 6! There has not been space enough for me to attempt critical appraisal of the entries and I freely confess there are several which I have never seen nor heard. However, my tireless editor, Charles Richards, to whom I express my gratitude, has said that I may make my own choice of personal favourites within this brief introductory passage. He also added that nobody ever reads introductions anyway!

I was thrilled when Jimmy Perry agreed to write the foreword; thrilled because DAD'S ARMY has to be my number one selection. The reason is something to which he alludes in the foreword; the best of sitcom is achieved by a marriage between great writing, inspired casting, virtuoso acting and creative direction. When those four factors come together a gem is being forged. My British top five thus join DAD'S ARMY because they correspond to this elusive formula and they are: A BIT OF A DO, STEPTOE AND SON, TILL DEATH US DO PART, ONLY FOOLS AND HORSES and FAWLTY TOWERS, although the last mentioned copped out after only twelve editions and we will never know whether or not it could have sustained its excellence for longer.

As far as the American efforts are concerned, my top five begins with SERGEANT BILKO and continues with THE BEVERLY HILLBILLIES, CHEERS, ROSEANNE and a tie for fifth place between THE COSBY SHOW and FRESH PRINCE OF BEL-AIR.

So, where do we go from here? We have a plethora of sitcoms as desperate networks believe they are the key to ratings. What lessons are there for would-be sitcomers to learn? Well, unless a show is located in the obviously surreal or outer space like THE MUNSTERS, MORK AND MINDY or RED DWARF, the characters and situation must have some base in credibility. The much maligned HONEY FOR TEA is a good example. The viewer was first of all asked to believe that Felicity Kendal was American. We had known and

Rod Taylor is a Northwesterner, born, bred and educated, and, apart from three years at Nottingham University reading law, has lived all his 51 years in Lancashire and Cheshire. He began his career with Granada Television in 1964, has since produced and directed programmes for all four channels, and his greatest love is comedy. Rod has two sons, Benjamin and Dominic, and an actress daughter, Samantha Jane.

loved her too long to accept that. Then we were asked to believe that a college at Cambridge University would have a Master as ludicrous as the one portrayed by Leslie Phillips and would give an undergraduate place to a nincompoop like Jake. I apologise to all involved for singling this out and it is in no way the worst of a bad crop. All those involved are talented and Kendal, Phillips and writer Michael Aitkens have delighted on so many past occasions.

The market is satiated and we should be looking to eliminate the stinkers. Probably Michael Grade put his finger on the root of the problem in Edinburgh a few years ago when he said, 'Those entrusted with commissioning new ideas wouldn't know a good one if it hit them in the face.' There have been changes and there must continue to be changes and those who believe that the only path to laughter necessitates obscenities, expletives and bodily functions must be discouraged. Comedy is not a cheap commodity and must be treated with respect. I hope the contents of these pages bring some memories and once more tickle the chuckle muscle.

FOREWORD BY JIMMY PERRY, OBE

What is it about sitcoms that people love so much? The entire British public seems to consider itself expert on the subject. The mortality rate is very high; critics leap on a new sitcom and more often than not devour it. But for every show that fails, another springs up to take its place.

Quite often the one who gets it in the neck is the poor writer. Complete strangers accost them with the words, 'I saw your show last night and I will be quite frank with you . . .' But in spite of all this, every once in a while a show takes off and captures the heart of the whole nation. And when this does happen, it's magic.

Doing sitcom is so very hard. There are so many pitfalls, so many things that can go wrong. A brilliant script can be ruined by bad casting and direction. Sometimes good actors can salvage a not-so-brilliant script, but when the right actors meet the right script and director the result is pure gold. Harry H Corbett and Wilfrid Brambell in STEPTOE AND SON, Warren Mitchell in TILL DEATH US DO PART and those four wonderful women in THE GOLDEN GIRLS are just a few examples of teamwork at its very best.

Strange that sitcom seems to be a purely Anglo-American art form. Apart from the fact that the Dutch enjoy our shows – and I believe the Germans once did their own version of STEPTOE AND SON – the rest of Europe is totally uninterested. Perhaps the answer is that we British like to laugh at ourselves and our sacred institutions. Indeed we are the only country in the world that finds vicars funny.

But there are countless examples in this massive catalogue of comedy. Old ones, new ones, loved ones, blue ones – they're all here.

Jimmy Perry

HOW TO USE THE BOOK

The entries in this book are arranged alphabetically by title with the broadcaster who originated or commissioned the work listed alongside. Abbreviations requiring clarification are: A–R (Associated Rediffusion), YTV (Yorkshire Television) and LWT (London Weekend Television). Unless an entry specifies radio, it is a television programme.

As far as credits are concerned I have tried to identify the writers and producers wherever possible and in many, but not all cases, the term producer includes director.

First transmission dates, particularly for ITV, can vary from region to region and, indeed, there are some purchased American programmes which certain regions have never shown at all.

In cases where a title has been screened on more than one channel it is the first broadcaster who is credited.

Where a programme title is in capital letters in the text, this indicates that it has its own entry in the book.

AJ WENTWORTH BA

THAMES. First broadcast: 12 July 1982

Basil Boothroyd adapted the stories of 'Punch' writer HF Ellis which were set at Burgrove School in the 1940s. AJ Wentworth (Arthur Lowe) was a benevolent, old-fashioned maths teacher who was weak on discipline but strong on dignity. He was rather prone to disaster and had many a brush with Matron (Marion Mathie). The headmaster was portrayed by Harry Andrews. Other characters in the series of six included Miss Coombes (Deddie Davies), Rawlinson (Ronnie Stevens) and Gilbert (Michael Bevis). Wentworth's chief tormentor in Class 3A was Mason (Marcus Evans). The shows were recorded shortly before Arthur Lowe died on 15 April 1982.
Producer: Michael Mills.

A.L.F.

NBC (AMERICA) PRESENTED BY ITV.
First broadcast (UK): February 1988

A.L.F. (Alien Life Force) was a wise-cracking 'thing' from another planet which was adopted by a middle-class American family, the Tanners, after its spaceship crashed through their garage roof. The Tanners were Willie (Max Wright), Kate (Anne Schedeen), Lynn (Andrea Elson) and Brian (Benji Gregory). Their neighbours were Trevor and Raquel Ochmonek (John La Motta and Liz Sheridan). More than 50 episodes were sprayed around the ITV regions.

ABIGAIL AND ROGER

BBC. First broadcast: 4 July 1956

This 13-week series of 20-minute episodes was written and produced by Kevin Sheldon as the 1956 summer replacement for *The Grove Family*. Abigail (Julie Webb), aged 21, and Roger (David Drummond), aged 26, were an engaged couple living in separate bedsits in the Gloucester Road area of West London. They found London life exciting, they wined and dined and went to the pub but always returned to their respective rooms. They never even kissed on screen as Sheldon considered such activity to be improper. Abigail was intelligent and practical but had no special training and had to find jobs based on her personality. Easily bored, she was prone to leaving jobs prematurely. Roger worked in the City, planned for the future and kept himself fit.

Other regular characters were Shirl (Rosina Enright), an Australian double-bass player, Abigail's landlady Mrs Moloch (Grace Denbeigh-Russell) and Clive (John Stone), a chap with no visible means of support but a friend of the young couple. Abigail's mother was played by Maud Long.

ABSOLUTELY FABULOUS

BBC. First broadcast: 12 November 1992

Every so often a sitcom comes along that shakes up the genre by its very originality. So it was with this creation of Jennifer Saunders which duly swept the awards field, notably picking up an American Emmy. Saunders herself played Edina Monsoon, a neurotic single mother – though twice married – who thought she was hip and worked in public relations. Teenage daughter Saffron (Julia Sawalha) rebelled against her mother's crazy lifestyle and was a goody-goody. Edina's best friend was Patsy (Joanna Lumley), an unmarried fashion editor who seldom attended her office. Edina and Patsy clung to their 1960s images and values of all things superficial, supported by their addiction to cigarettes, alcohol and fashion. While Saffron worked hard at her studies and sipped Coca-Cola, contemplating the serious issues facing the world, Edina and Patsy would be falling down drunk after worrying themselves about keeping up with the very latest fashion trend. At work Edina had a totally incompetent personal assistant, Bubble (Jane Horrocks), and at home her mother was played by veteran comedy actress June Whitfield. There were six episodes in the first series with seven further editions beginning on 27 January 1994. The shows made much use of guest stars who, in the wake of its enormous popularity, were queueing up to appear.
Director: Bob Spiers. Producer: Jon Plowman.

Maureen Lipman in AGONY – as newspaper columnist Jane Lucas (Photo: LWT)

THE ADDAMS FAMILY

ABC (AMERICA) PRESENTED BY ITV.
First broadcast (UK): 18 March 1965

This black comedy was based on the creations of *New Yorker* cartoonist, Charles Addams. It centred around the everyday lives of a macabre family and their cobwebbed Gothic home. They considered themselves normal but the outside world viewed them differently. The head of the family was a lawyer, Gomez (John Astin), who harboured a pet octopus called Aristotle. He was married to Morticia (Carolyn Jones), whose pastimes included the cultivation of a man-eating plant. They had two children, daughter Wednesday (Lisa Loring) whose pride and joy was a headless doll, and son Pugsley (Ken Weatherwax) whose playroom contained an electric chair and a gallows. Former child star Jackie Coogan portrayed Uncle Fester, a deathly-looking toothless ghoul with a cackle of a voice and the ability to light up bulbs in his mouth. Blossom Rock was the actress who played the grumbling Grandmama but perhaps the most memorable character was the butler, Lurch, played by almost 7ft-

tall actor Ted Cassidy. Lurch relaxed by playing the harpsichord and, when summoned by the family, would inquire in a long, grunted drawl: 'You rannng?' Cassidy had a second role to play as the dismembered hand of the family servant, Thing, who emerged from various unexpected places.

The theme song set the tone:

> They're creepy and they're kooky
> Their life is kinda spooky
> They're altogether ooky
> The Addams Family.

The show ran to 64 episodes and was produced by David Levy.

THE ADVENTURES OF AGGIE

USA PRESENTED BY ITV.
First broadcast (UK): 17 September 1956

Joan Shawlee starred as fashion buyer and expert Aggie whose assignments took her on a series of adventures to Paris, Cairo, Venice, Tangier and other exotic locations around the international world of haute couture. More than 50 episodes were screened.

THE ADVENTURES OF HIRAM HOLLIDAY

USA PRESENTED BY BBC.
First broadcast (UK): 18 July 1961

This was the first sitcom to be 'stripped' in Britain. Stripping, that is to say playing episodes on a daily rather than weekly basis, was a regular practice in the States, but Hiram Holliday found himself so scheduled as the summer replacement for the serious *Tonight* programme and slotted in on three or four nights a week. Gangly, bespectacled Wally Cox starred as the inoffensive, mild, small-time newspaper reporter Hiram, whose character was based on a creation by Paul Gallico. As a reward for eliminating a libellous misprint in his paper, Hiram was sent on a world tour during which he encountered all sorts of dangers and pulled off some miraculous feats. Armed with only an umbrella, he fought and talked his way out of improbable situations through 26 episodes.

THE ADVENTURES OF PC 49

BBC RADIO. First broadcast: 24 October 1947

Spanning ten series and more than 100 editions to the last broadcast on 26 May 1953, the adventures

of Police Constable Archibald Berkeley-Willoughby (Brian Reece) engaged and amused listeners of all ages. He was despatched on his missions by Divisional Det. Inspector Wilson (Leslie Perrins) and Det. Sgt Wright (Eric Phillips) with the command: 'Out yer go, 49.' PC 49 was bright and courageous and brought all his cases to a satisfactory conclusion. His own catch-phrase was 'Oh, my Sunday helmet!' He had a fiancée, Joan Carr, who was portrayed by Joy Shelton. Producer Vernon Harris justified Archie's lack of promotion by saying, in 1951, that though the show had been on for four and a half years, the 78 episodes to that date represented only 18 months in the service of the Metropolitan Police Force.
Writer: Alec Stranks

THE ADVENTURES OF TOMMY TROUBLE
BBC RADIO.

See WELSH RAREBIT.

AFTER HENRY
BBC RADIO. First broadcast: 17 April 1985

Writer Simon Brett's creation began on the radio almost three years before Thames would launch the format on television. Thirty-four editions were broadcast between then and 7 March 1989. Prunella Scales was Sarah, widowed in her early forties following the death of husband Henry, and left to cope with teenage daughter Clare (Gerry Cowper) and her demanding mother Eleanor (Joan Sanderson). The owner of the bookshop where Sarah worked was Russell (Benjamin Whitrow). For the final series, Clare had gone to Australia with a boyfriend, much to Eleanor's disgust, so her contributions to domestic friction were then limited to letters and phone calls.
Producer: Pete Atkin

THAMES. First broadcast: 4 January 1988

Following the success of this series for BBC radio, creator Simon Brett wrote 30 episodes for television.

The generation gaps still accounted for all manner of misunderstandings, with Sarah stuck somewhere in the middle. While Eleanor was dependent on Sarah, Clare (Janine Wood) craved her independence as she grew through her adolescent years. Eleanor spent much of her time trying to keep up with or get the better of neighbour Vera Poling

(Peggy Ann Wood). Russell was played by Jonathan Newth. The final edition was seen on 31 August 1992.
Producers: Peter Frazer-Jones, Bill Shepherd.

AGONY
LWT. First broadcast: 11 March 1979

Maureen Lipman starred as newspaper and radio agony aunt Jane Lucas in this series created by Len Richmond and Anna Raeburn. Raeburn was herself one such real-life journalist. In the shows Jane was surrounded by a clutter of oddballs who gave her more problems than those members of the public who solicited her advice. She was Jewish with a dominant mother, Bea (Maria Charles), and she was married to a non-Jewish psychiatrist, Laurence (Simon Williams). Her editor was a dragon, Diana (Jan Holden), while her secretary Val (Diana Weston) was a paragon of virtue hard to live up to. Her neighbours and friends were a couple of homosexuals, Rob and Michael (Jeremy Bulloch and Peter Denyer), while at the radio station she had as colleagues a mad disc-jockey, Andy (Peter Blake), and a transvestite, Mr Mince (Robert Gillespie). During the first run of 13 shows, her marriage began to collapse as Jane struggled to find the same glib answers to her own troubles that she found for those of her correspondents or phone-in callers.

By the second run of seven, beginning 13 April 1980, Jane was estranged from Laurence and there were two new characters at the radio station, the bumptious Vincent Fish (Bill Nighy) and her unspeakable but handsome new producer, Junior Truscombe (Robert Austin), who forced her into resigning. She continued to work at *Person* magazine. In the final series of seven, beginning 18 January 1981, she was pregnant, though still separated, and gave birth to a son. When the baby was born, there was a conflict over which religion he should be brought up to follow, a conflict which involved Bea and Jane's in-laws (Geoffrey Chater and Phyllida Law).
Writers: Len Richmond and Anna Raeburn, Stan Hey and Andrew Nickolds. Producer: John Reardon.

AIN'T MISBEHAVIN'
BBC. First broadcast: 20 March 1994

Writer Roy Clarke set this series in Harrogate. Clive Quigley (Peter Davison) was a happy man who loved his wife Melissa (Lesley Manville), had

a small business, MC Office Supplies, and an unseen doting mother who called him frequently on his mobile phone to be reassured of his devotion. All was well until he was contacted and, incidentally, knocked down in the street by Sonia Drysdale (Nicola Pagett), a tough, no-nonsense owner of a hairdressing salon. She broke the news to Clive that Melissa was having a steamy affair with her husband Dave Drysdale (John Duttine). After much fainting, to which Clive was prone, and a suicide attempt interrupted by one of his mother's calls, he was persuaded by Sonia to join her in a plan to destroy the relationship between Melissa and Dave without their being aware that their partners even knew of the liaison. By the second episode, viewers – but not Clive and Sonia – realised that the affair was far from steamy and Dave's every effort to get Melissa into bed was thwarted. Casting a sceptical eye over the ensuing events was Clive's dutiful assistant Mrs Wales (Polly Hemingway), who herself had the hots for Clive. By the sixth and final episode there was a suggestion that a romantic liaison might be on the cards for Sonia and Clive. The famous 1929 song of the title was sung by Paul Jones.
Producer: Tony Dow.

ALBERT

YTV. First broadcast: 25 April 1972

In this extension of DEAR MOTHER – LOVE ALBERT, Albert Courtnay (Rodney Bewes) still worked at the factory where his boss was Mr AC Strain (Garfield Morgan), and was still engaged to Doreen Bissel (now played by Cheryl Hall), whose mother Ada (Amelia Bayntun) was ever present. The only perceptible difference was that when this series began, Albert had grown his hair long.
Director: Bill Hitchcock. Writers and producers: Rodney Bewes and Derrick Goodwin.

ALBERT AND ME

BBC RADIO. First broadcast: 6 November 1977

Richard Beckinsale starred in a series of eight programmes as Bryan Archer, father of baby Albert. His girlfriend, the baby's mother, had run off with the electrician and left Bryan to raise Albert as a single parent. Bryan's mum was played by Pat Coombs, who also made the requisite noises for Albert, while John Comer was Bryan's dad. Although Beckinsale died in 1979, the series was revived on 16 March 1983 for eight more editions

with Robert Lindsay as Bryan and Pat Coombs again as his mother and Albert.
Writer: Jim Eldridge. Producer: John Fawcett Wilson.

ALBERT AND VICTORIA

YTV. First broadcast: 13 June 1970

Reuben Ship created and wrote these stories of a Victorian family, the Hacketts. The series returned for a second run the following autumn. When Great Aunt Agatha died, she left all her wealth to her niece, Mrs Victoria Hackett (Zena Walker in 1970, Barbara Murray for the first two episodes in 1971. When she was forced to quit by her own pregnancy complications, Frances Bennett took over). There were several strings attached to the will before Victoria and her husband Albert (Alfred Marks) could lay their hands on the money. They had three children living at home, Emma (Kika Markham 1970, Gay Hamilton 1971), Lydia (Petra Markham) and George (John Alkin). Albert was actually responsible for the upkeep of nine children. The family had a building firm, but, much to Albert's irritation, young George showed little interest in the business.
Producers: John Nelson Burton, Quentin Lawrence.

ALCOCK AND GANDER

THAMES. First broadcast: 5 June 1972

From two rooms and a toilet over a Soho strip club, Mrs Marigold Alcock (Beryl Reid) ran her late husband's business empire with her partner, failed student Richard Gander (Richard O'Sullivan) and their sole employee, old retainer Ernest (John Cater). The ashes of the late Mr Alcock stood on the mantelpiece. The empire embraced various activities including Flybynight Tours, the Mary Peabody Marriage Bureau, Tom O'Thimble Lucky Pixies, Capt. Sotheby's Racing Service and Alcock's Swiss Elixir, in a series of six programmes by Johnnie Mortimer and Brian Cooke.
Producer: Alan Tarrant.

ALEXANDER THE GREATEST

ATV. First broadcast: 15 April 1970

The Alexander of the title was the 16-year-old, rebellious Alexander Green (Gary Warren). He felt ready to quit his bourgeois home and school and leave his cosy middle-class existence behind him. His parents Joe and Fay Green (Sydney Tafler and Libby Morris) had other ideas. Theirs was a good Jewish family, living in Golders Green with an established furrier business. The Greens also had a daughter, Renata (Adrienne Posta), who toed the line with a good Jewish boyfriend, Murray (Peter Birrel). In order to sway Alexander back on course, Joe and Fay moved mountains to understand and please him. Alexander sat back and wallowed in the attention.

The show began with a six-week run and returned for one further series in March 1972 when the part of Fay was played by Stella Moray.
Writer: Bernard Kops. Producer: Shaun O'Riordan.

ALF AND HIS COSTER PALS
BBC RADIO. First broadcast: 20 October 1942

Cockney musician and funny man Leon Cortez starred in this short series as Alf Hawkins ('Awkins). The stories and excuses for music and song were fashioned around the doings of Alf's devil-may-care family, his wife Fanny (Doreen Harris), his son Alfie (Sydney Brigden) and his brother 'Arry (Harry Loman). Other characters, as and when required, were portrayed by Horace Percival, Ewart Scott and Thea Wells. Billy Ternent conducted the BBC Dance Orchestra.
Producer: Tom Ronald.

ALICE
USA PRESENTED BY CHANNEL 4.
First broadcast (UK): 3 September 1984

This show owed its origins to the 1975 movie *Alice Doesn't Live Here Anymore* which starred Ellen Burstyn. In the TV version which ran to a staggering 209 episodes, Linda Lavin played 35-year-old widow Alice Hyatt, who headed for California with her 12-year-old son Tommy (Philip McKeon). She had aspirations to a future as a singer and actress but became financially stranded near Phoenix, Arizona. She took a job in a café owned by Mel (Vic Tayback), where her fellow waitresses were the loud-mouthed but big-hearted Flo (Polly Holliday) and the rather dim and quiet Vera (Beth Howland). There Alice stayed to raise her son. When Polly Holliday left late in the run, a new waitress came in, Belle, played by Dianne Ladd who ironically had played Flo in the movie. Vera later married police officer Elliot (Charles Levin). All the girls enjoyed a love–hate relationship with Mel.
Creator: Robert Gretchell. Producer: David Susskind for Warner.

ALL ABOARD
First broadcast: 6 December 1958

The SS *Adriana* set sail from Liverpool and by the time she sailed off into an Adriatic sunset after 26 programmes on 30 May 1959, she had completed four transatlantic crossings to New York and a Mediterranean cruise. There was a more or less permanent crew on board but the passengers changed with each voyage. Arthur Lowe starred as steward Sydney Barker, with Avril Angers as stewardess Joan Harrison. The assistant purser was Janet Fraser (Susan Shaw), the radio officer was Mark Rogers (Richard Coleman) and the ship's Romeo was 3rd officer Peter Norton (John Gale) who scanned the embarking passenges in each port for vulnerable young females. The chief officer was Bill Stafford (Charles Morgan), 2nd officer was John Caldwell (Richard Thorp) and the bellboy was portrayed by Peter Greenspan. Among the passengers were Ronnie Hughes (Richard O'Sullivan) who sailed to New York to meet up with his mother; Alastair Robbins (Gordon Jackson) and Gwen Wilson (June Jago) who developed a shipboard romance; Austin Carter (Leslie Sands), Penelope Ann Smith (Elizabeth Wallace), Fenton (Gerald Flood); Alice Sheldon (Susannah York) who fell for young violinist Ian Ashworth (Murray Hayne); Sir John and Lady Gilbert (Julian Somers and Georgina Cookson) with their daughter Imogen (Mary Webster); and Alan Rogers (Terence Alexander).
Writers: Gerald Kelsey and Dick Sharples, John Jowett. Directors: Guy Verney, Anthony Finigan. Producer: Guy Verney.

ALL AT NO. 20
THAMES. First broadcast: 10 February 1986

Richard Ommanney created and wrote this situation in which Sheila Haddon (Maureen Lipman), a widow of 18 months' standing, faced a huge mortgage and financial insecurity because her husband had failed to take out any life insurance. Sheila had a daughter, Monica (Lisa Jacobs), to support, but her independent spirit refused to call in help from obvious sources like old family friend Richard Beamish (Gary Waldhorn) or her close girl-friend Carol (Gabrielle Glaister). She took on part-time employment and took in lodgers, the first of which were Chris (Gregory Doran), newly arrived in London in search of the bright lights, and Hamish (David Bannerman). The second series of six, which featured new lodgers Candy (Carol Hawkins) and

Henry (Martin Clunes), ended on 1 December 1987.
Producer: Peter Frazer-Jones.

ALL CHANGE
YTV. First broadcast: 15 November 1989

In this children's series, Uncle Bob (Frankie Howerd) continued to dominate the lives of two families from the grave. He had died and left fortunes to each family on condition that they swapped existences. The Londons were an upmarket family who lived well in London. The Oldfields ran a greasy cafe somewhere up North. The Londons were Fabia (Maggie Steed), Julian (William McGillivray), Charles (David Quilter) and Polly (Lisa Butler). The Oldfields were Brian (Tony Haygarth), Maggie (Pam Ferris), Vicky (Donna Durkin) and Nathan (Robert Ellis). A first series of six was followed by six more episodes, ending 12 March 1991. Aunt Fanny (Peggy Mount) joined the second run.
Writers: Chris England and Morwenna Banks, John Stevenson. Directors: Graham Dixon, Garth Tucker. Producers: Peter Tabern, Greg Brennan.

ALL GAS AND GAITERS
BBC. First broadcast: 31 January 1967

This much-loved series first came to life as a *Comedy Playhouse* presentation with the title 'The Bishop Rides Again' on 17 April 1966 before writers Edwin Apps and Pauline Devaney turned it into a TV series. There were 32 episodes over five seasons ending on 17 June 1971. The hallowed cathedral of St Ogg's was presided over by the Bishop (William Mervyn). His Chaplain was the Rev. Mervyn Noote (Derek Nimmo) and the Dean was portrayed by John Barron. The Archdeacon was played by Robertson Hare. The shows were among the first to permit comedy at the expense of the Church, although the fun was poked very gently.
Producers: Stuart Allen, John Howard Davies.

BBC RADIO. First broadcast: 5 January 1971

The same writers scripted two radio series. The first ran for 13 episodes with the same cast as the television shows and the second ran for 20 editions from 24 July 1972 but without Derek Nimmo. Jonathan Cecil portrayed the new Chaplain.
Producers: David Hatch, John Dyas.

ALL GOOD THINGS
BBC. First broadcast: 14 May 1991

Brenda Blethyn starred as Shirley Frame in this six-part comedy drama by Lesley Bruce. Shirley was approaching 40 and had just had a new baby. She already had two sons, Anthony and Paul (Paul Reynolds and Timothy Stark), and a good if long-suffering husband Phil (Warren Clarke). Shirley was overwhelmed by her obvious good fortune and had an uncontrollable urge to share it with other people, whether or not they wanted her help. Phil was understanding, even when her meddling in other lives proved dangerous.
Director: Sharon Miller. Producer: Lynn Horsford.

ALL IN GOOD FAITH
THAMES. First broadcast: 30 December 1985

John Kane created and wrote these stories of a caring vicar, Reverend Philip Lambe (Richard Briers), who was comfortably installed in a wealthy rural parish with a flock of parishioners who made his life both pleasant and easy. It came as a shock to all, but especially to his wife Emma (Barbara Ferris) and his son Peter (James Campbell), when he was struck by a middle-age crisis of conscience and sought a transfer to a troubled inner-city appointment. It took all six programmes of the first series to execute the move. The new life for the Lambes got into full swing in the second run of six beginning 26 February 1987 and ground to a halt after yet seven more episodes on 23 May 1988.
Producer: John Howard Davies.

ALL IN THE FAMILY
CBS (AMERICA) PRESENTED BY BBC.
First broadcast (UK): 8 July 1971

Johnny Speight sold his format for TILL DEATH US DO PART to America where writer and producer Norman Lear transposed Alf Garnett into Archie Bunker. When Bunker first hit the American screens in January 1971 he released a television time-bomb. Social comment, bad language and ethnic humour were new to the American viewer and within the first three months the show had tackled homosexuality, miscarriage, race, cohabitation, menopause and impotency, thereby changing the entire face of American television. ABC had rejected the idea as too dangerous but CBS president Robert Wood took the gamble

The Bunkers lived in the Queens district of New York. They were Archie (Carroll O'Connor) and his wife Edith (Jean Stapleton), their daughter Gloria (Sally Struthers) and son-in-law Mike Stivic (Rob Reiner). After several years of success the younger characters left the show, as did Jean Stapleton, but after 160 editions Archie continued his tirades in ARCHIE BUNKER'S PLACE. See also GLORIA.

ALL OUR SATURDAYS
YTV. First broadcast: 14 February 1973

In this series of six programmes set in Yorkshire's West Riding, Diana Dors starred as Di Dorkins, known as 'Big Di'. She ran a large textile business, Garsley Garments, and the firm had an amateur rugby league team. They regularly found themselves at the foot of the local league table until Di took over as manager and proved that she was tougher, rougher and fitter than the lads who played. The characters included Ken Hicks (Tony Caunter), Stan Maycock (Norman Jones), Frank Bosomworth (Anthony Jackson), Ronnie Rendell (Doug Fisher) and Wilf (John Comer).
Writers: *Stuart Harris, Oliver Free. Director: Roger Cheveley. Producer: Ian Davidson.*

ALL QUIET ON THE PRESTON FRONT
BBC. First broadcast: 4 January 1994

Set in the Lancashire town of Roker Bridge, twinned with Aix-en-Availle, this comedy drama was in six parts, each of 50 minutes, written by Tim Firth. It followed the lifelong friendship, often strained, of Dave 'Hodge' Gadd (Colin Buchanan) and Eric Dislay (Paul Haigh) who spent their weekends as part-time soldiers with the Territorial Army. Hodge worked in a garden centre and lived in a caravan. All his involvements with the opposite sex ended in disaster. Eric, whose real name was Wayne, lived at home with his dutiful mother (Joan Campion) and his chair-bound vegetable father (Gordon Langford Rowe). The weekends were controlled by rival corporals Polson (David MacCreedy) and Lennox (Sam Graham). Regular characters were student teacher Dawn Lomax (Caroline Catz); solicitor's wife Ally (Kate Gartside); leisure club assistant Carl Rundle (Keiran Flynn), who had a running battle with Polson; Lloydy (Adrian Hood) and petrol-station owner Diesel (Tony Marshall). The garden centre was owned by Mrs Ruddock (Matyelok Gibbs) where a man who always complained about the dummy heron which he had bought was played by former comedian Freddie Davies. Another pal of the two boys was Spock, who was portrayed by Stephen Tompkinson. It later transpired that Hodge had a daughter in Blackpool, the product of his encounter at the age of 17 with a 36-year-old woman.
Director: Brian Farnham. Producer: Chris Griffin

'ALLO 'ALLO
BBC. First broadcast: 7 September 1984

Nine series and 83 episodes later, this creation by Jeremy Lloyd and David Croft finally bowed out on 14 December 1992. It trod what might have been highly sensitive ground by spoofing the French Resistance, the German occupation of France and the British all within the confines of the four walls of a café, but it got away with it, mainly by ridiculing all sides equally. There was no pretence of wartime realism and the storylines remained thin and, one was almost tempted to forget, based on the attempt to repatriate two British airmen, Flying Officers Fairfax and Carstairs (John D Collins and Nicholas Frankau) who had been shot down.

The principal characters, however, were French café owner René Artois (Gorden Kaye) and his

'If you say no, René, I will sing' – Carmen Silvera and Gorden Kaye as Edith and René in 'ALLO 'ALLO (Photo: Copyright © BBC)

wife Edith (Carmen Silvera), who would burst into atonal song to torture the ears of all assembled. While the main storyline hung by a thread, the many sub-plots were quite complicated and inter-woven. Extra-marital affairs, disguised spies, forg-ers and underground workers merged with German lechers and Resistance subterfuge. To keep the viewer abreast, René would often talk furtively to camera.

The characters were many and given their own individuality through catchphrases and eccentric behavioural patterns. They included Michelle (Kirsten Cooke) of the Resistance who would say 'Leesten very carefully, I will say zis only once'; Crabtree (Arthur Bostrom), the disguised British agent with fractured French producing another catchphrase, 'Good Moaning'; Yvette (Vicki Michelle), one of the objects of René's lust; Maria (Francesca Gonshaw); Monsieur Alfonse (Kenneth Connor); Monsieur Leclerc (Jack Haig, later Derek Royle, later Robin Parkinson); Lieutenant Gruber (Guy Siner); Captain Hans Geering (Sam Kelly); Colonel Von Strohm (Richard Marner); General Von Klinkerhoffen (Hilary Minster); Herr Flick of the Gestapo (Richard Gibson) and his sidekick Von Smallhausen (John Louis Mansi); Fanny (Rose Hill), who eventually married Leclerc; Mimi (Sue Hodge); Helga Geerhart (Kim Hartman) and Cap-tain Bertorelli (Gavin Richards, later Roger Kitter). *Writers: Lloyd and Croft, Ronald Wolfe and Ronald Chesney, John Chapman and Ian Davidson, Paul Adam. Directors included: David Croft, Martin Dennis, Susan Belbin, Robin Carr, Mike Stephens, Richard Boden, John B Hobbs and Sue Longstaff. Producers: David Croft, Mike Stephens, John B Hobbs.*

AMEN

USA PRESENTED BY CHANNEL 4.
First broadcast (UK): 30 January 1988

Set in a small church in Philadelphia where Deacon Ernest Frye (Sherman Hemsley) hired a new minis-ter, Rev Reuben Gregory (Clifton Davis) in an attempt to improve church attendance. The Dea-con's daughter was Thelma (Anna Maria Horsford) and the new Reverend's flock included Casietta and Amelia Hetebrink (Barbara Montgomery and Roz Ryan) and Rolly Forbes (Jester Hairston). In the very first of the 26 episodes the role of Lorenzo was taken by Little Richard, but subsequently it was played by Franklyn Seales.

AMOS 'N ANDY

CBS (AMERICA) PRESENTED BY BBC.
First broadcast (UK): 22 April 1954

Writing now in the 'politically correct' 1990s, it is hard to believe that this series ever drew breath. Yet it garnered a huge following, particularly on Ameri-can radio where it began in 1928. Two white men, Freeman Gosden and Charles Correll, acted out, in comedy, the exploits of two black men and their families and familiar circles. The blacks were stere-otypes, caricatured with dialects that recalled the Christy Minstrels. Amos was portrayed as hard-working and trusting while Andy was depicted as lazy and a product of the depression. It is estimated that a staggering 40 million people listened to the radio show in the USA in the 1930s.

It is a moot point as to when sitcom was created and there are those who would point to Amos 'n Andy as being the source. However, when one first encountered the characters in Britain, much had changed. With the transition to television, Gosden and Correll must be credited with unusual percep-tion, for they chose to relinquish their roles as actors and become producers of the television shows. In their wisdom they cast black actors Alvin Childress and Spencer Williams Jr with Tim Moore playing The Kingfish, a minor star in the radio series but elevated to co-stardom on TV, as was Sapphire, portrayed by Ernestine Wade. One other element of the series that was new to British viewers was the sound of laughter and applause which came from a studio audience watching edited episodes.

AN ACTOR'S LIFE FOR ME

BBC RADIO AND TELEVISION.
First broadcast: 20 January 1989

John Gordon Sinclair starred as struggling actor Robert Wilson, who was prepared to do absolutely anything just to get work. He had a vivid imagina-tion and considerable vanity. There were 13 radio broadcasts over two series ending on 18 March 1990. The format then moved to television where Robert became Robert Neilson in a six-part series beginning on 14 November 1991. On 5 January 1993, the series reverted to radio for six further broadcasts. Throughout, Robert had an agent, Desmond Shaw (Gary Waldhorn radio, Victor Spinetti television) and a girl-friend, Sue Bishop (Caroline Quentin, later Gina McKee). *Writer: Paul Mayhew-Archer. Radio producers: Paul Spencer, Diane Messias. TV producer: Bryan Izzard.*

AND MOTHER MAKES FIVE

THAMES. First broadcast: 1 May 1974

The continuing story of Sally and David Redway (Wendy Craig and Richard Coleman), married at the end of AND MOTHER MAKES THREE. With Sally's children Simon and Peter (Robin Davies and David Parfitt) and David's daughter Jane (Maxine Gordon) they now had a houseful. Sally's auntie (Valerie Lush) was installed in a flat. Over the ensuing four series the children inevitably grew up and by 1976 Sally was convinced that her entire family was besotted with sex. In the final two seasons the Redways had new neighbours, Joss and Monica (Tony Britton and Charlotte Mitchell).
Writers: Richard Waring, Jonathan Marr, Johnnie Mortimer and Brian Cooke. Producer: William G. Stewart.

Sally (Wendy Craig) and family showing how MOTHER MAKES THREE (Photo © Thames Television)

AND MOTHER MAKES THREE

THAMES. First broadcast: 27 April 1971

Created by Richard Waring, this series starred Wendy Craig as attractive young widow Sally Harrison, left with two children, Simon (Robin Davies) and Peter (David Parfitt), a cat and a goldfish. She got a job as secretary to the local vet, Mr Campbell (George Selway) and invited her auntie (Valerie Lush) to move in and help with the family. During the second series, which began towards the end of the same year, Mr Campbell retired and his practice was acquired by a newcomer to the neighbourhood, David Redway (Richard Coleman), who had a daughter, Jane (Miriam Mann). Sally and David fell in love, met each other's parents – Mrs Redway (Lally Bowers) and Sally's mum and dad (Gwen Nelson and Keith Marsh) – and became engaged. Their courtship continued through a third run. By the fourth series, David was running a book shop and plans were afoot for the wedding. They were married on 13

June 1973 and Auntie moved into the flat above the book shop. That was not to be the end of the story: see AND MOTHER MAKES FIVE.
Theme music: Johnny Hawkesworth. Writers included Richard Waring, David Cumming and Derek Collyer, Peter Buchanan and Peter Robinson. Producer: Peter Frazer-Jones.

ANDY CAPP
THAMES. First broadcast:22 February 1988

The newspaper comic-strip creation of cartoonist Reg Smythe was dramatised by Keith Waterhouse and starred James Bolam in the beer-guzzling, hen-pecked title role, with Paula Tilbrook wielding the rolling pin as the harridan wife Flo. Other regular characters in the small world of the Capps included Jack (John Arthur), Shirley (Collette Stevenson), Percy (Keith Marsh), Walter (Kevin Lloyd), Chalkie (Keith Smith), Ruby (Susan Brown), the bookie (Mike Savage), the pawnbroker (Richard Tate), the vicar (Ian Thompson), Mr Watson (Philip Lowrie) and Andy's mother-in-law (Shirley Dixon). Six episodes were shown.
Producer: John Howard Davies.

The picture of innocence, Miss Brahms (left, Wendy Richard) doesn't seem to convince Mrs Slocombe (Mollie Sugden) in ARE YOU BEING SERVED? (Photo: Copyright © BBC)

ANY BLOKE
BBC RADIO. First broadcast: 6 October 1993

This story in six parts was written by Gary Brown. Jim Sweeney starred as Phil who worked as a supply teacher but when daughter Sophie (Nadine Ballantyne) became of school age, his wife Sarah (Caroline Quentin) was offered an exciting new job and encouraged by Fay (Shirley Stelfox) to take it. Swingeing changes were afoot and Phil feared plots were being hatched behind his back.
Producer: Ann Jobson.

ANY MORE
BBC RADIO. First broadcast: 7 September 1940

Frank Randle starred in his variety stage persona of the Old Boatman in this excuse for a variety show subtitled 'Who's For a Sail?' which ran for a six-week season. The harbour master was portrayed by both Malcolm Graeme and Wilfred Pickles.
Producer: Richard North

ARCHIE BUNKER'S PLACE
CBS (AMERICA) PRESENTED BY CHANNEL 4.
First broadcast (UK): 4 July 1983

Johnny Speight's British creation, TILL DEATH US DO PART, was transposed into an American situation in 1971 as ALL IL THE FAMILY in which Alf Garnett became Archie Bunker. After 160 episodes of that show, Archie (Carroll O'Connor) found himself alone without his family when this first series of thirteen episodes was made. He opened a bar in partnership with Harry Snowden (Jason Wingreen). When Archie wished to expand the operation by taking over the next door restaurant, Harry sold his half-interest to Murray Klein (Martin Balsam), the last man in the world that the bigoted and prejudiced Archie could tolerate. He continued his tirades against the world through a second series of 13 episodes which ran from 29 April 1986.
Producer: Norman Lear.

ARE YOU BEING SERVED?
BBC. First broadcast: 14 March 1973

Writers Jeremy Lloyd and David Croft relied on honest vulgarity and blatant innuendo for most of the laughs in this series which ran for 64 editions to 1 April 1985. Set in Grace Brothers department store, the Chairman was Young Mr Grace (Harold

Norman Rossington (seated), Bernard Bresslaw (left) and Alfie Bass at the very first rehearsal for THE ARMY GAME (Photo: NR)

Bennett), the Manager was Mr Cuthbert Rumbold (Nicholas Smith) and the Floor Walker was Captain Stephen Peacock (Frank Thornton). The Head of Ladies' Fashions was Mrs Slocombe (Mollie Sugden) who spent much time worrying about her pussy, and her assistant was Miss Brahms (Wendy Richard). Head of Men's Wear was Mr Grainger (Arthur Brough) whose Senior Sales Assistant was the camp Mr Humphries (John Inman). Humphries took every opportunity to measure inside legs and created the catchphrase 'I'm free'. Junior Sales Assistants were Mr Lucas (Trevor Bannister) and, later, Mr Spooner (Mike Berry). The porter was Mr Harman (Arthur English). Later characters to emerge included Miss Belfridge (Candy Davis), the Canteen Manageress (Doremy Vernon), and Mr Goldberg (Alfie Bass). See also GRACE AND FAVOUR.

Directors: David Croft, Ray Butt, Bob Spiers, Martin Shardlow, John Kilby. Producer: David Croft.

THE ARMY GAME

GRANADA. First broadcast: 19 June 1957

To begin with, this well-remembered show was transmitted live from Granada's London studio at the Chelsea Palace in King's Road. The setting was a Surplus Ordnance Depot and transit camp at Nether Hopping, somewhere in the middle of nowhere in rural Staffordshire. The stories revolved around the shower who occupied Hut 29. Sid Colin created a set of characters that was instantly recognisable to a nation which still had conscription and where memories of the war were just twelve years distant. Colin and producer Peter Eton employed the services of a military adviser Major John Foley, in developing the stories.

Command at Nether Hopping was initially in the hands of the pig-keeping Major Upshot-Bagley (Geoffrey Sumner) and passed successively to Captain Pilsworth (Bernard Hunter), Major Geoffrey Gervaise Duckworth (CB Poultney) and Captain Pocket (Frank Williams) before Upshot-Bagley returned in 1960. Trying to extract a little discipline from the men were the brutal RSM Bullimore (William Hartnell, who left in the second season to go and play another sergeant in the first Carry On film, Carry On Sergeant) and the exasperated Sergeant Claude Snudge (Bill Fraser), whose plots to outwit the occupants of Hut 29 knew no bounds.

The wide-boy of the hut was Corporal Springer (Michael Medwin), who brought his endemic Cockney ability as a scrounger into the Army. The other occupants were Private Hatchett (Charles Hawtrey), known as the 'Professor', whose hobbies included knitting; Private 'Popeye' Popplewell (Bernard Bresslaw), tall and gormless with the catchphrase 'I only arsked'; Private 'Cupcake' Cook (Norman Rossington), a Scouser who acquired his nickname from the number of food parcels he received from his mother; and Private 'Excused Boots' Bisley (Alfie Bass), who slouched around in a pair of plimsolls.

Some strange casting decisions were made by Granada in 1958, when Rossington received a letter telling him he was fired. He was briefly replaced as 'Cupcake' by Keith Banks but such was the public outcry that Rossington was swiftly reinstated. Granada made two further failed attempts to replace characters at that time, with Jack Allen playing Upshot-Bagley and Keith Smith the 'Professor'. By the end of 1958, only Bisley and Snudge remained of the original cast. The new intake continued the show's success with Harry Fowler as Corporal 'Flogger' Hoskins, another Cockney fly-boy to replace Medwin. The gormless 'Popeye' was replaced by Lancashire comedian Ted Lune as the equally gormless Private Bone. Others included Privates Dooley (Harry Towb) and Billy Baker (Robert Desmond) and, in 1959, Lance-Corporal Ernie Merryweather (Mario Fabrizi) and Private Chubby Catchpole (Dick Emery). At the end of that season, Alfie Bass and Bill Fraser left to begin their own spin-off series, BOOTSIE AND SNUDGE. After 157 episodes, THE ARMY GAME came to an end on 20 June 1961. The theme music was written by one-time Granada floor manager, Patrick Knapper. *Writers included Sid Colin, David Climie, Barry Took and Marty Feldman, Larry Stevens, Maurice Wiltshire. Producers: Peter Eton, Eric Fawcett, Max Morgan-Witts, Milo Lewis.*

THE ARTFUL DODGER

BBC. First broadcast: 28 September 1959

Veteran radio star Dave Morris wrote this television vehicle for himself with Frank Roscoe. As the dodger, he was the life and soul of the labour exchange. His two interests were the avoidance of all forms of work and supporting Manchester City. He schemed to obtain money without having to graft and was always trying to divert the suspicious

eye of his wife, played by Gretchen Franklin. His mild-mannered pal was portrayed by Joe Gladwin in the six editions of the show.
Producer: John Ammonds.

THE ARTHUR ASKEY SHOW

ATV. First broadcast: 11 March 1961

Radio and stage star Askey was equally at home on television but was better seen as a stand-up patter comic or in sketches than in sitcom. This seven-programme series by Dave Freeman was set in 1910 but there was little else to single it out from the standard domestic situation. Askey played Arthur Pilbeam, married to the rather snobby Emily (June Whitfield). She was genteel but managed to transpose her aitches to where they did not belong. The obligatory neighbours, the Rossiters, were portrayed by Arthur Mullard and Patricia Hayes.
Producer: Josephine Douglas.

AS GOOD COOKS GO

BBC. First broadcast:28 January 1970.

Variety legend 'Two Ton' Tessie O'Shea starred in these six programmes as Blodwen O'Reilly, a Welsh–Irish cook whose job took her to a different location to cook a banquet or a simple dinner each episode. There were no other regular characters.
Writers: John Warren and John Singer. Producer: John Howard Davies.

AS TIME GOES BY

BBC. First broadcast: 12 January 1992

Bob Larbey created and wrote this comedy of the rekindled flame of romance which starred Judi Dench as widow Jean Pargetter and Geoffrey Palmer as divorcé Lionel Hardcastle. Thirty-eight years previously they had been lovers who each mistakenly thought the other had dropped them. In the intervening years they had both married someone else but had never forgotten their passion from all those decades ago when Jean was a nurse and Lionel was in the Middlesex Regiment. They came to meet again when Lionel, who had spent most of those years in East Africa, went to Jean's secretarial agency for help in typing the manuscript of his book, My Life in Kenya. Help was forthcoming in the form of Jean's daughter Judith (Moira Brooker), whom Lionel dated. It was only when he escorted Judith home that he and Jean saw each other.

Jean (Judi Dench) has laid down her burden,
Lionel (Geoffrey Palmer), here by the riverside
in AS TIME GOES BY
(Photo: Copyright © BBC)

Over the course of three series and 24 episodes
to 6 March 1994, their renewed acquaintance blossomed into love, not always smooth, and Lionel
eventually moved in with Jean and Judith. Other
principal characters were Lionel's literary agent
Alistair Deacon (Philip Bretherton) who dated
Judith, made passes at all other females and irritated
Lionel by calling him Li. Jean's agency had the
benefit of the highly efficient Sandy (Jenny Funnell),
and when the time came to open a second branch it
was to Sandy that Jean turned to run it rather than
Judith. However, Sandy turned down the opportunity and the job went to Sally Curtis (Fiona
Mollison), known to one and all as Miss Ice Cubes.
Lionel was rather dull and reserved in his manner,
rarely displaying enthusiasm for anything, in sharp
contrast to his ebullient father Rocky (Frank
Middlemass) who, with his life drawing to an inevitable close, married country and western loving
Madge (Joan Sims).

The original idea for the series came from Colin
Bostock-Smith and the 1931 song which inspired
the title was sung over the credits by Joe Fagin.
Producer: Sydney Lotterby for Theatre of Comedy.

ASTRONAUTS

ATV. First broadcast: 26 October 1981

Graeme Garden and Bill Oddie created Britain's
first space mission and set it aboard a skylab
codenamed Piglet. The all-British crew was led by
Commander Malcolm Mattocks (Christopher
Godwin), a former RAF officer who had no flair
for handling people. The technical officer was David
Ackroyd (Barrie Rutter) and completing the crew
was Dr Gentian Foster (Carmen Du Sautoy) whose
duties included the welfare of them all as well as
conducting a series of biological experiments. A
dog named Bimbo joined them on the voyage.
Cooped up in their capsule, they found it difficult
to get on with each other. The American ground
controller was former astronaut Beadle (Bruce Boa).
The series ran for seven shows.
*Director: Douglas Argent. Producers: Tony Charles
and Allan McKeown.*

AT THE BLACK DOG

BBC RADIO.

First heard nationally on 23 December 1937, though
there had been a few prior broadcasts on the Empire
Service, this series ran to its 100th edition on 5 April
1940. The setting was the Black Dog pub where
mine host was William Wilkes (Cyril Nash),
assisted by his wife Aggie (Sunday Wilshin). Much

interplay was made between them and their most regular customer, Howard Marshall (as himself). There were weekly visitors who entertained the customers.

Writer: SE Reynolds. Producers: Roy Speer, CF Meehan.

AUF WIEDERSEHEN PET
CENTRAL. First broadcast: 11 November 1983

Dick Clement and Ian La Frenais created this much praised series from an idea by Franc Roddam. There were two runs of 13 one-hour programmes and the last was transmitted on 16 May 1986.

Three Geordies left girlfriends and wives behind in Newcastle where unemployment was at a desperate level. They headed for Germany and found jobs as brickies on a Dusseldorf building site. The three were the philosophical Denis (Tim Healy), Neville (Kevin Whately) who missed his wife Brenda (Julia Tobin) fretfully, and Oz (Jimmy Nail), an ignorant, violent slob with bigoted opinions. All hoped for a big tax-free pay packet for different reasons. Once in Dusseldorf they were joined by, and shared a hut with, Cockney carpenter Wayne (Gary Holton), Bristolian former wrestler Bomber (Pat Roach), Moxey (Christopher Fairbank) from Liverpool and boring Barry (Timothy Spall), an electrician from Birmingham. Other important characters in the first series included Dagmar (Brigitte Khan), with whom Denis cheated on his wife; Christa (Lysette Anthony), who won Wayne's heart; Irish labourer Magowan (Michael Elphick); Grunwald (Michael Sheard), Pfister (Heinz Bernard) and Ulrich (Peter Birch).

The second series was set four years after they had left Germany. Moxey had been in prison, Wayne remained in Germany to get married, Oz and Barry joined a building gang in the Falklands, Bomber had tried wrestling once more, Neville had returned to Newcastle and he and Brenda had a child, while Denis had acquired gambling debts and was forced to be general dogsbody for the ruthless Ally Fraser (Bill Paterson). Barry had a fiancée, Hazel (Melanie Hill), and Denis a girlfriend Christina (Madelaine Newton), having split with his wife Vera (Caroline Hutchinson). Oz was also apart from his wife Marjorie (Su Elliott), who was raising son Rod alone. Barry, meanwhile, had set up his own business and employed the lads to help build his dream home. Then gangster Ally Fraser had them work on a mansion in Derbyshire before coercing them all to Marbella on the Costa Del Crime to work on his ill-gotten villa. Wayne had rejoined the gang as his marriage split after a few months.

Writers: Clement and La Frenais, Bernie Cooper, Stan Hey, Francis Megahy. Directors: Roger Bamford, Baz Taylor, Anthony Garner. Theme music: 'That's Livin' Alright' sung by Joe Fagin. Producers: Martin McKean, Allan McKeown.

AUNTIE RIDES AGAIN
BBC RADIO. First broadcast: 11 May 1955

Len Fincham and Lawrie Wyman wrote this series in eight parts which starred Athene Seyler as Amelia Grimly-Bracewell, managing director of G-B Motor Works. The manager was Charles Todmarsh (Hubert Gregg) and the staff included Pamela Scott (Mary Mackenzie) and Bert Crocker (Leslie Dwyer). *Producer: Vernon Harris.*

B AND B

BBC. First broadcast: 6 November 1968

Canadian married couple Bernard Braden and
Barbara Kelly starred as themselves, each with a
separate career and struggling to cope with the
threats of a new teenage society which encom-
passed marital infidelity, drug addiction and the
sexual liberation of the young. The series of seven
programmes began with a repeat of the original
pilot which had been screened in the summer of
1968 as a one-off *Comedy Playhouse*. The children
were Sally (Kim Braden) and Johnny (Mark
Griffith).
Music: John Dankworth. Producer: Michael Mills.

BACHELOR FATHER

BBC. First broadcast: 17 September 1970

Ian Carmichael starred for 13 editions as wealthy
bachelor Peter Lamb, whose jaded life had been
one round of romantic failures. He had always
loved children and hit upon the idea of becoming
a full-time foster parent, thus acquiring an
instant family without the bother of a woman. The
story was prompted by the real-life experience of
Peter Lloyd Jeffcock who fostered 12 children as a
bachelor. Lamb fostered five: Anna (Briony
Roberts), Ben (Ian Johnson), Donald (Roland
Pickering), Jane (Beverley Simons) and Mandy
(Angela Ryder).
*Theme music: Eric Rogers. Writer: Richard Waring.
Producer: Graeme Muir.*

BACHELOR PARTY

BBC RADIO. First broadcast: 4 July 1935

This series was originally called *Stag Party* but the
Reithian authority of the day insisted on the change
of title after just a few editions. The idea was the
conception of, and starred, violinist and comedian
Stanelli. It was really an excuse for music and
variety but, nonetheless, it did have a situation and
three regular comedy characters. It was ostensibly
set in Stanelli's London flat where his batman from
the 1914–18 war, Jim Emery (Jack Wynne), was

installed as his domestic servant with the
catchphrase, 'More sandwiches, Mr Stanelli, sir?'.
The third original member was Norman Long,
known in this series as 'Old Teeth and Trousers'.
The party was broadcast haphazardly until a regular
run got underway on 21 February 1940 when the
three regulars were joined by Hutch (Leslie A
Hutchinson) and Mario 'Harp' Lorenzi.
*Writer: Stanelli. Producers: Bill MacLurg, Michael
North.*

BACKYARD FOLLIES

BBC RADIO. First broadcast: 31 December 1941

Diminutive variety star 'Wee' Georgie Wood, 4ft
9in tall, wrote this rare wireless series for himself in
collaboration with Bert Lee. As he had always done
on the stage, Wood played small boy Georgie
Robinson and his long-time theatre partner Dolly
Harmer portrayed his mother Ethel. In this particular series, which ran for six editions, Georgie ran
concerts from the family backyard, the price of
admission being anything that would contribute to
the war effort. The location was an industrial town
near a large steelworks whose owner Alec McLeod
(Ian Sadler) had instructed his foreman Tom
Leatherbarrow (Tom Moss) to erect a roof over the
yard so the Follies could play to friends and factory
workers in all weathers. Mounting the concerts was
not made easy by the Robinsons' awkward neighbours, Harry Townsend (Charles Harrison) on one
side and Ada Curtis (Gwen Lewis) on the other.
The owner's daughter Carrie (Karina) was always
on hand to sing and harmonica player Arthur Dudley
(Arthur Tolcher) was a stalwart member of the
troupe.
Music: Charles Shadwell. Producer: Harry S Pepper.

BAD BOYES

BBC. First broadcast: 15 September 1985

This children's serial was written by Jim Eldridge
and his son Duncan. Bryan Arthur Derek Boyes
(Steven Kember) was the brightest brain but also
the artful dodger of his school. He used his talents
to trick teacher Mr Wiggis (Gregory Cox), the

Headmaster (Christopher Owen) and his parents (Susan Jameson and Dean Harris). Boyes further used his ability to defeat the school bully, Edward 'the Slug' Slogg (Warren Brian). Boyes' school pal was Bernetta Vincent (Nicola Greenhill). A first series of six was followed by ten more editions running from 20 October 1988.
Producer: Jeremy Swan.

BAGDAD CAFE
USA PRESENTED BY CHANNEL 4.
First broadcast (UK): 12 September 1991

This 13-part series was based on the 1988 Percy Adlon movie of the same title. Whoopi Goldberg starred as the short-tempered Brenda who ran a run-down diner and motel in an isolated outpost of California's Mojave Desert. Cut off from civilisation, she was also separated from husband Sal (Cleavon Little) who blew in and out of her life at will. Brenda had a son Junie (Scott Lawrence) who was himself a single parent, and a daughter Debbie (Monica Calhoun) who had taken up with a local biker. Just when Brenda thought she had hit rock bottom, into her life walked warm-hearted Jasmine (Jean Stapleton) who had just abandoned her own husband while driving through the desert. They got off to a bad start but soon became friends and began to transform the café.

THE BAILEYS OF BALBOA
CBS PRESENTED BY ITV.
First broadcast (UK): 26 April 1965

Balboa was a luxurious yachting area in southern California where widower Sam Bailey (Paul Ford) owned a valuable island and a fishing boat which he chartered. Sam was a battler against all forms of establishment and authority and his principal antagonist was Cecil Wyntoon (John Dehner), the commodore of the upper-crust yacht club. Wyntoon's aims were to have Sam evicted from his land and have his boat, the Island Princess, removed from the waters. Unfortunately for Wyntoon, a romantic relationship developed between his daughter Barbara (Judy Carne) and Sam's son Jim (Les Brown Jr, son of bandleader Les Brown). Sam's practical seawear contrasted with Wyntoon's immaculate blazer, cap and white trousers. Sam considered Wyntoon a bore and the symbol of stupidity. Helping Jim crew Sam's boat was Buck Singleton, played by Sterling Holloway. Two other regular characters were Hans (John

Banner) and Stanley (Clint Howard). The series ran weekly on ITV until 19 July.
Producer: Robert Sweeney.

BALLYSKILLEN OPERA HOUSE
GRANADA. First broadcast: 6 January 1981

Although this series of six programmes was really an excuse for a variety show, it did have a scripted situation and regular characters, headed by Frank Carson as Frank O'Grady, the fiddling manager of a rundown Irish theatre where he also kept a bed for his own use. His staff were box-office girl Theresa Halligan (Anna Manahan), electrician and general dogsbody Seamus Maguire (Charlie Roberts) and barmaids Kathleen and Mary (Bernadette Short and Angela Catterall). The part of Father Hennessy was played by Terry Iland.
Writer: Linda Thornber. Director: David Liddiment. Producer: Stephen Leahy.

BAND WAGGON
BBC RADIO. First broadcast: 5 January 1938

In the annals of British broadcasting history, BAND WAGGON is a radio classic. It stemmed from the original idea of the BBC's then head of variety, John Watt, to establish Arthur Askey as the BBC resident comedian and to give him a 12-week series – a thing unheard of previously at the Corporation. Never before had a comedy show been placed on a regular day at more or less a regular time. He was paired with Richard Murdoch, and the rest of the team comprised eight-piece band Phil Cardew and the Bandwaggoners, and vocal trio Miff Ferrie and the Jackdauz (George Crow and Terry Brown).

The first edition was not a success, and neither were the second and third shows. At this point John Watt cut the run from twelve to six programmes and it was also at this juncture that Askey declared that if he were tagged the 'resident comedian', he should live on the premises. So, from the fourth programme, he and Murdoch were installed in an imaginary flat on top of Broadcasting House. This was the result of a panic script-assembly with the two stars and writer/producers Gordon Crier and Vernon Harris. By the time they got to the sixth show, John Watt had removed his threat to axe the series and increased the original commitment from 12 to 18.

Askey became nationally known as 'Big-Hearted'

'Big-Hearted' Arthur (Askey) and Richard 'Stinker' Murdoch revolutionised radio comedy with BAND WAGGON in 1938 (Photo: © BBC)

Arthur and Dickie Murdoch, equally popular, as 'Stinker' Murdoch. Listeners came to believe they really did live in the flat with Lewis the goat and two pigeons, Lucy and Basil. For a while there was even a camel named Hector in residence. Then it was decided they should have a char and Askey saw a van in London bearing the name 'Diploma Bagwash'. So Mrs Bagwash was born and she had a daughter Nausea who was never heard but who became Arthur's fiancée. Mrs Bagwash herself only gave the occasional grunt on the air while Nausea always fainted and all that was heard was a thud. Lewis the goat was written in when it was decided that it was too far to go down 49 stairs and then descend seven floors in a lift just to collect the milk. This gave rise to the joke: 'A goat in the flat – what about the smell?' 'Oh, he'll get used to it!'

BAND WAGGON spawned numerous catchphrases. Askey began saying 'I thank you' (pronounced Aythangyow) which he had picked up from a London bus conductor. Murdoch would deride Askey as 'You silly little man'. Askey would proclaim 'Doesn't it make you want to spit' and 'Don't be filthy'. One of the regular features was 'Mr Walker Wants to Know', presided over by comedian Syd Walker whose own closing line, 'What would you do, chums?' also caught on with listeners. The imaginary flat produced several sur-

prises. They discovered the chimney went straight down to the Director General's office where a fire was always lit. Hence they were able to lower a kettle and boil a couple of eggs. The flat was also conveniently close to the 'announcers' bathroom. Subsequent series of BAND WAGGON took the total tally to almost 50 but it all came to an end with the escalation of war and Murdoch leaving to join the RAF. On 13 November 1947 there was broadcast a one-off Jubilee revival show with all the original cast except Syd Walker who had died. His part was taken by Fred Yule.

Throughout the life of BAND WAGGON it was BBC policy never to credit the writers, as they wanted the public to believe that Askey and Murdoch made it all up as they went along.
Producers: Gordon Crier, Vernon Harris, and Harry S Pepper.

BARKER'S FOLLY
BBC RADIO. First broadcast: 4 March 1959

The title was the name of the house in which lived Eric Barker and his wife Pearl Hackney in the imaginary village of Duxborough. Each week for 13 weeks, their domestic troubles and strife were interrupted by visitors, the most unwelcome of whom was probably John Lawley (Deryck Guyler), Eric's bank manager, and his wife Mary (Denise Bryer). Others who turned up out of the blue included Eleanor Summerfield, Leonard Sachs, Kenneth Horne, Gilbert Harding, Ian Carmichael and Fay Compton.
Writer: Eric Barker. Producer: Charles Maxwell.

BARNEY MILLER
ABC (AMERICA) PRESENTED BY ITV.
First broadcast (UK): 18 May 1982

Danny Arnold and Theodore J Flicker created and produced these shows which were set in the 12th precinct of the New York Police Department. There was total racial integration, with most minorities represented. Detective Barney Miller (Hal Linden) worked alongside Det. Phil Fish (Abe Vigoda), Det. Sgt Chano Amenguale (Gregory Sierra), Det. Wojohowicz (Max Gail), Det. Yemana (Jack Soo) and Det. Harris (Ron Glass). Although the shows were essentially comedy, they treated New York crime realistically, often touching on tragedy. The shows were made in the USA in 1975 but did not begin their British run until seven years later.

BARNEY IS MY DARLING

BBC. First broadcast: 9 December 1965

Bill Fraser and Irene Handl starred in six episodes as Barney and Ramona Pank, who married in 1940 but had been separated for most of their married life. In middle age, they were all but strangers to each other. He had been away in the Merchant Navy as Chief Steward aboard the SS Addis which worked the Tasmania to Sumatra route. Ramona had learned to manage without his presence and was well set in her ways. She ran a hairdressing salon in Willesden. When Barney returned after 12 years they had to try to adjust to married cohabitation once more, a task made all the more difficult for Barney by Ramona's Pekingese dog Scampi with whom he shared a mutual hatred and contempt. At work Ramona had an assistant Cissie Ludgrove (Angela Crow) and at play she had a confidante to whom she could unload her burden, Miss Hobbitt (Pat Coombs).

Music: Max Harris. Writers: Barry Took and Marty Feldman. Producer: James Gilbert.

BATMAN

ABC (AMERICA) PRESENTED BY ITV
First broadcast (UK): 21 May 1966

POW! WHAM! KRUNCH! were words flashed onto screens when Bob Kane's 1939 comic strip was spoofed into a television series. Wealthy Bruce Wayne (Adam West) and his teenage ward Dick Grayson (Burt Ward) lived in Wayne Manor, a grand house where the resident butler was Alfred (Alan Napier). When their help was called for on the Batphone, they made for a hidden door at the back of the bookcase, slid down poles to the Batcave where they metamorphosed into Batman and Robin, and chased villains in their converted Lincoln known as the Batmobile. Occasionally they were assisted by Batgirl, librarian Barbara Gordon (Yvonne Craig), daughter of Police Commissioner Gordon (Neil Hamilton). Others ever-present were Police Chief O'Hara (Stafford Rep) and the Manor housekeeper Mrs Cooper (Madge Blake).

Batman, known as the caped crusader, and Robin went in pursuit of a glittering array of star villains including the Riddler (Frank Gorshin), the Joker (Cesar Romero), Queenie (Nancy Kovak), the Penguin (Burgess Meredith), Mr Freeze (George Sanders, later Otto Preminger), Zelda the Great (Anne Baxter), Catwoman (Julie Newmar), King Tut (Victor Buono), the Bookworm (Roddy McDowall), Shame (Cliff Robertson), the Black Widow (Tallulah Bankhead), Fingers (Liberace), Ma Parker (Shelley Winters), the Siren (Joan Collins), the Archer (Art Carney), the Minstrel (Van Johnson), the Egghead (Vincent Price), Lola Lasagna (Ethel Merman) and Minerva (Zsa Zsa Gabor). There were 120 editions.

Producers: Howie Horwitz and William Dozier.

THE BED-SIT GIRL

BBC. First broadcast: 13 April 1965

Sheila Ross (Sheila Hancock) was the bed-sit girl of the title, a muddled, disorganised person who aimed for sophistication but usually found catastrophe. She was a typist, rather bored at work and in some awe of the life of neighbouring bed-sitter Dilys (Dilys Laye), an air hostess and her rival when it came to men. Both were unmarried but wished to change that status. By the second six-episode series running from 18 April 1966, Dilys had flown and Sheila had a new neighbour, eligible bachelor David (Derek Nimmo) with whom romance developed though not easily or smoothly. Sheila found a friend in Liz (Hy Hazell), an older and wiser woman who had the best room in the house.

Music: Mike Sammes. Writers: Ronald Wolf and Ronald Chesney. Producers: Duncan Wood, Graeme Muir.

BEGGAR MY NEIGHBOUR

BBC. First broadcast: 13 March 1967

This series originated as a single *Comedy Playhouse* presentation on 24 May 1966. Writers Ken Hoare and Mike Sharland turned it into 22 episodes which spanned three series ending 26 March 1968. Gerald Garvey (Peter Jones, later Desmond Walter-Ellis) and his wife Rose (June Whitfield) lived in Muswell Hill where their next-door neighbours were Harry and Lana Butt (Reg Varney and Pat Coombs). Rose and Lana were sisters, which might have made for a very comfortable arrangement had it not been for the fact that the Garveys were chronically broke while the Butts were rolling in it and led an opulent lifestyle. The state of affairs led to open warfare, with the Garveys determined never to lose face.

Theme music: Alan Roper. Producer: David Croft.

BEHIND THE BIKE SHEDS

YTV. First broadcast: 8 January 1985

Jan Neadle and Tony Slattery wrote this children's series of nine programmes set at Fulley Comprehensive School, where a gaggle of unruly kids tormented Headmistress Megan Bigge (Val McLane) who was affectionately known as Megapig. She had a passion for jelly babies. Other adults in the line of fire were Whistle Willie (Ken Jones), Trolly Molly (Sarah Mair-Thomas) and, occasionally, Joe (Tony Slattery).

Producer: Peter Tabern.

BENSON

ABC (AMERICA) PRESENTED BY ITV.
First broadcast (UK): 22 January 1981

Susan Harris, the creator of SOAP, took one of her characters from that series, the black butler Benson Dubois (Robert Guillaume), and set him up as butler to incompetent State Governor Gatlin (James Noble). Within the Gatlin mansion were the Governor's daughter Katie (Missie Gold), his cook Reys Kraus (Inga Swenson), his secretary Marcy (Caroline McWilliams), his aide Taylor (Lewis J Stadlen), his later aide Clayton (René Auberjonois) who was also a property owner, and the Governor's press agent Pete (Ethan Phillips). More than 150 episodes were made, over which Benson rose from his humble butling to the post of Assistant Governor. They were shown at random across the ITV network after the initial episode.

Producers: Susan Harris, Paul Junger Witt and Tony Thomas.

BERYL'S LOT

YTV. First broadcast:26 October 1973

This comedy drama series of one-hour episodes was inspired by the true life story of novelist Margaret Powell, a cook who married a milkman and set about taking her 'O' and 'A' levels as she approached her sixtieth birthday. She was 61 when her first book was published. Carmel McSharry starred as Beryl, a charlady in her forties married to a milkman, Tom (Mark Kingston, later George Selway). They had three children, Rosie (Verna Harvey), Jack (Brian Capron) and Babs (Anita Carey). As Beryl surveyed the spoils of her life and contemplated the future, she determined to improve herself and better her station. To the surprise of all around her she registered for evening classes. Other

regular characters throughout the four seasons, which continued into 1977, were Trevor and Vi Tonks (Tony Caunter and Barbara Mitchell), Horace and Wullie Harris (Robert Keegan and Annie Leake), Fred Pickering (Robin Askwith), Charlie Mills (Norman Mitchell), Freda (Queenie Watts) and Wacky (Johnny Shannon).

Writers: Kevin Laffan, Bill MacIlwraith. Directors included Moira Armstrong and David Reynolds. Producers: John Frankau, Jacky Stoller, Derek Bennett.

BEST OF FRIENDS

ABC. First broadcast: 6 January 1963

Created and written by Brad Ashton, Bob Block and Gerry Maxin, this series starred Charles Hawtrey as Charles, an insurance clerk employed by his Uncle Sidney (Henry Longhurst). Much as Uncle Sidney would have liked to be rid of Charles, his hands were tied in that the business was controlled by family shareholdings. Next door to the insurance firm was a café run by Hylda (Hylda Baker). It was to Hylda that the wet and weak Charles would go for solace and motherly attention after exciting the wrath of Uncle Sidney. Hylda would often accompany Charles on his assignments. Caught up in their adventures was the glamorous Sheena (Sheena Marsh). Thirteen editions were screened.

Producer: Ernest Maxin.

THE BEST THINGS IN LIFE

ATV. First broadcast: 12 August 1969

Harry H Corbett starred as Alfred Wilcox, a hang-dog bachelor who valued his independence. His chief interests were the horses and the pub. He lodged with Mr and Mrs Pollard (Bob Todd and Pearl Hackney) and had been engaged to their daughter Mabel (June Whitfield) for 11 years. Alfred and Mabel worked at the same plastics factory where he was a salesman well-versed in all the wheezes and wangles of hire purchase. Mabel shared her frustration at failing to get Alfred to the altar with her best friend at work, secretary Yvonne Armitage (Pat Heywood). Carmel McSharry also appeared regularly as Pauline. The show, created by Bernard Botting, returned for a further series in 1970.

Writers: Botting, Adele Rose, Jack Trevor Story. Director: John Robins. Producer: Shaun O'Riordan.

THE BETTY WHITE SHOW

CBS (AMERICA) PRESENTED BY CHANNEL 4.
First broadcast (UK): 10 December 1984

The original pilot for this series was shown on Channel 4 as part of an MTM (Mary Tyler Moore) Productions evening and was repeated on 14 August 1985 with a series of 13 beginning the following week. Betty White played Joyce Whitman, an actress who won a role as a policewoman in a TV show of which her ex-husband John Elliott (John Hillerman) just happened to be the producer. Their Mexican divorce proved to be invalid. Joyce wisecracked her way through with Mitzi Meloney (Georgia Engel).
Producer: Bob Ellison. An MTM production.

THE BEVERLY HILLBILLIES

CBS (AMERICA) PRESENTED BY ITV.
First broadcast (UK): 1 February 1963

This creation by Paul Henning, who also produced the shows, has been one of the most popular in the history of the sitcom genre, although when it was launched in the USA in 1962 it was greeted with scant respect by critics who thought it either belittled hillbilly folk or ridiculed the lifestyle of America's west coast. Over the years it ran up 274 episodes and proved that critics are rarely the arbiters of public taste.

Britain first met the Hillbillies the following year and saw the nouveaux millionaires leave the Ozark mountains where they had struck oil and ride their flatbed truck, loaded with jugs of corn liquor, towards Beverly Hills. On board were widower Jed Clampett (Buddy Ebsen), the head of the family, and his crotchety old mother-in-law Granny Daisy Moses (Irene Ryan). The younger travellers were Jed's buxom, blonde daughter Elly May (Donna Douglas) and his tall, dark, handsome and bovine nephew Jethro Bodine (Max Baer Jr, son of the former heavyweight boxing champion). Also featured for the first couple of years was elderly cousin Pearl Bodine (Bea Benaderet) who was looking for a man and was in constant feud with Granny. Benaderet left the series when Paul Henning came up with a new show in which she starred in her own right, PETTICOAT JUNCTION.

The Clampett millions were deposited with their next-door neighbour and bank manager Mr Milburne Drysdale (Raymond Bailey) whose secretary Jane Hathaway (Nancy Kulp) had the unenviable task of keeping the country folk happy. Mr Drysdale's wife (Harriet MacGibbon) was an ordinary woman until she met the Clampetts . . . Her life was never to be normal again, especially when she discovered that Jethro's mongrel, Duke, had sired puppies by her pedigree poodle. The Drysdales had a son named Sonny (Louis Nye) who set his sights on Elly May. Granny, in particular, tried to perpetuate her Ozark lifestyle, creating vile-smelling concoctions and visiting food stores to try to buy ingredients like lizards' eggs and dried beetles. By the end of 1964 Jed had bought a film company and the jokes were wearing just a little bit thin. Stuntman Jerry Brutsche doubled for both Elly May and Granny!
Directors included Joseph Depew, Richard Thorpe and Richard Whorf. Executive producer for Filmways: Martin Ransohoff. The theme tune was sung by Earl Flatt and Lester Scruggs.

BEWITCHED

ABC (AMERICA) PRESENTED BY BBC.
First broadcast(UK): 22 October 1964

This series, created by Harry Ackerman and Bill Dozier, was first seen in 1964 and ran, in the USA, for seven seasons. Elizabeth Montgomery (daughter of actor Robert Montgomery and married to producer Bill Asher) starred as Samantha Stephens, the last in a long line of sorceresses. She married advertising executive Darrin (Dick York until 1969, then Dick Sargent) and on her wedding night she confessed to being a witch. Although he pleaded with her to abandon her powers, she merely had to twitch her nose to employ her witchcraft. On that wedding night, Samantha received the traditional visit from her mother Endora (Agnes Moorehead), who was appalled that her daughter should marry a mortal and was bent on destroying the marriage. Whenever Darrin annoyed her, which was often, Endora would cast spells upon him. Samantha was aided and abetted in her witchcraft by her clumsy Aunt Clara (Marion Lorne), who had a knack of forgetting her spells while in mid-spell, and by her lookalike cousin Serena (also played by Montgomery), who was always up to mischief. Samantha and Darrin had two children, Tabatha (a witch) and Adam (a warlock).

Fundamentally, Samantha was the good witch and Endora the baddie. The series made much use of special effects which were the creation of Dick Albain. He produced a remote-controlled vacuum cleaner and suitcases which packed and unpacked themselves. The first transmission in Britain was by the BBC and there were 252 editions, many of which were subsequently seen on ITV and Channel 4.

BIG BOY NOW
ATV. First broadcast: 30 May 1976

Leslie Crowther starred as Tony Marchant, a middle-aged bachelor tied to the apron strings of his widowed mother Heather (Fabia Drake). Tony ran an estate agency with his married brother Roy (Ronald Lewis). He envied Roy for having escaped and longed to leave home himself. When Captain Edgar Bingham (Derek Farr) started to pay romantic attention to Heather, Tony gave him every encouragement in the hope that they would marry and free him from his bonds. Roy's wife Marjorie (Alethea Charlton) made an occasional appearance, especially when she suspected her husband of having an affair with office secretary Mavis (Hilary Pritchard). For the second series starting 17 February 1978, Roy and Marjorie had gone away, leaving Tony as the only son around, tied even closer to his clinging, jealous mother.
Writer: Ronnie Taylor. Producer: Les Chatfield.

THE BIG BUSINESS LARK
BBC RADIO. First broadcast: 6 July 1959

Writer Lawrie Wyman, creator of THE NAVY LARK and THE EMBASSY LARK, set this new eight-programme lark in British United Plastics Ltd where the Chairman and Managing Director was Sir Charles Bonniface (Jimmy Edwards). He had a son Frank (Frank Thornton) who was also in the business and a secretary Mrs Edith Chalmers (Gwen Cherrell).
Producer: Alastair Scott Johnston.

BIG DEAL
BBC. First broadcast: 14 October 1984

Set in west London, this comedy drama charted the ups and downs of Robby Box (Ray Brooks) and his very tolerant girl-friend Jan Oliver (Sharon Duce). Robby was a total no-hoper, but brimfull of charm, who sought to earn his living playing poker. He had breezed his way through life for more than 20 years in pubs and betting shops, but suddenly he noticed his youth slipping away and he had nothing to show for the misspent decades. He began to have notions that stability might be attractive but, alas, those notions could not embrace the prospect of real work. Jan, who was the single parent of teenage daughter Debby (Lisa Geoghan), was his saviour as well as his lover, though she was attracted to him because he was still such a child. Her dilemma was whether or not she wished to change him from the very person to whom she was attracted. Geoff McQueen wrote two series, each of ten 50-minute episodes, which ended on 5 December 1985.
Directors: Jeremy Summers, Carol Wiseman. Producer: Terence Williams.

BIG JIM AND THE FIGARO CLUB
BBC. First broadcast: 8 July 1981

This began as a single pilot show in the autumn of 1979 and was followed by a series of five which began 18 months later on BBC2. Norman Rossington starred as Big Jim, a carpenter and the leader of a gang of mates, all in the building trade, who had been at sea together. Within their club, which they formed in the small seaside town on the South coast where they worked, they mused on all the anarchic and valiant things they would like to have done prior to the world turning sour. The sourest of all was the would-be dictator Harold Perkins (Roland Curram), the Clerk of Works, who derived great joy from spoiling their fun. Club members were Old Ned the drain digger (Gordon Rollings), Turps the painter (Sylvester McCoy), Chick the brickie (David Beckett) and the youngster Nimrod (David John) who was something of a surrogate son to Big Jim.
Writer: Ted Walker. Producer: Colin Rose.

BBC RADIO. First broadcast 14 February 1987

Six years later the idea was recycled for a six-part radio series. The cast was the same except for Harold Goodwin who stepped in to play Old Ned, Gordon Rollings having died. Bernard Cribbins set the scene as the storyteller.
Producer: Martin Fisher.

THE BIG NOISE
BBC. First broadcast: 2 October 1964

This weekly series of just four episodes was written and created by Frank Muir and Denis Norden, based on an original idea by Denis Goodwin. Bob Monkhouse starred as Bob Mason, a former shop-assistant on the wet-fish counter at the Co-op, who rose to fame and fortune as the number one disc-jockey personality in the country, the Big Noise. Norman Rossington portrayed Mason's manager, Kim Hunter, a former Cambridge Footlights member with an uncle in broadcasting. Thus he appeared to the Big Noise to have had an easy entry into show business. A variety of guest stars passed through the series including Irene Handl as Bob's Aunt Lily, David Hemmings as Mart Robins, Valerie Singleton as the station announcer, and Jimmy Savile and Peter Noble as themselves.

Music: Kenny Napper. Producers: Joe McGrath and James Gilbert.

THE BIG ONE

CHANNEL 4. First broadcast: 5 March 1992

This story of unexpected romance was written by Elly Brewer and Sandi Toksvig. Toksvig also starred as Deddie Tobert, an advertising agency executive with a profoundly feminist attitude and a razor-sharp tongue. She gave temporary lodging at her flat in Tooting to larger-than-life American author James Howard (Mike McShane) while he looked for a place of his own. Although they were cat and dog on the surface, they developed feelings for each other but both were reluctant to show them. There were seven episodes and at the end of the series James was left with just one last chance to show Deddie how he felt about her.

Director: John Henderson. Producers: Jimmy Mulville and Mary Bell for Hat Trick Productions.

BILLY BUNTER OF GREYFRIARS SCHOOL

BBC. First broadcast: 19 February 1952

Frank Richards began writing his stories of William George Bunter, the Owl of the Remove, in 1910 and was still writing them when he brought his 'fat boy' creation to the screen. The character had been immortalised in *The Magnet* comic with original drawings by CH Chapman. Casting Bunter was vital to the success of the series and Gerald Campion, who won the role, made a success of it despite being a full-grown man at the outset, continuing to be Bunter until the series was dropped in 1962.

Greyfriars was a boarding school where whackings and fagging were commonplace. Bunter waited eternally for a postal order from Bunter Court to keep up the supplies of tuck required to

maintain his gross shape. Bunter was a loner, mocked by the others, particularly the famous five: Harry Wharton (John Charlesworth, later Anthony Valentine, later Julian Yardley), Bob Cherry (Keith Faulkner, later Brian Roper, later Jeremy Bulloch), Johnny Bull (Barry Macgregor, later Colin Campbell, later David Coote, later Gregory Warwick), Frank Nugent (Michael Danvers-Walker, later Peter Marden, later Lawrence Harrington, later Michael Tennant) and Hurree Jamset Ram Singh (David Spenser, later Ronald Moodie, later Barry Barnett, later Hugh Ward). The Form Master of the Remove was the cane-swinging Mr Quelch (Kynaston Reeves, later Raf de la Torre, later Jack Melford).

When the series originated, it was shown twice on Tuesdays, once at 5.40 p.m. and again at 8.00 p.m., but in those days before video tape, the cast and production team had to do the whole thing twice live.

Writer: Frank Richards. Producers: Joy Harrington, Pharic Maclaren, Shaun Sutton, Clive Parkhurst.

BILLY LIAR

LWT. First broadcast: 26 October 1973

In the wake of its great success as a novel, a stage play and a movie, Keith Waterhouse and Willis Hall's creation came to the small screen. Jeff Rawle was cast as Billy, the famous dreamer, and his parents Geoffrey and Alice were played by George A Cooper and Pamela Vezey. They lived together with Gran (May Warden) in pleasant, semi-detached suburbia. Billy's flights of fancy left his mother bemused, and confused his employer, the saturnine Mr Shadrack (Colin Jeavons). By the second series in the autumn of 1974 Billy had acquired a fiancée, Barbara (Sally Watts).

Producer: Stuart Allen.

BIRDS OF A FEATHER

BBC. First broadcast: 16 October 1989

This creation by Laurence Marks and Maurice Gran notched up its 64th edition with the Christmas special transmitted on 25 December 1993. Two adopted sisters from North London, Sharon (Pauline Quirke) and Tracey (Linda Robson) married Chris (David Cardy, and after the first series Peter Polycarpou) and Darryl (Alun Lewis) respectively. One day the two men went off to work and never returned. They had been nicked for armed robbery and each received a 12-year sentence.

Sharon's Greek husband claimed he had no money and she lived in a grotty flat at Camelot House, Edmonton. Darryl, on the other hand, provided a neo-Georgian mansion in Chigwell, Essex, for Tracey and sent son Garth (Matthew Savage) to public school – all on the proceeds of his crimes of which Tracey was unaware. As a result, Sharon moved in with Tracey and, from her new posh address, sought new and exciting men while her husband remained banged-up in Maidstone prison. Visiting the boys was difficult and rarely successful for Sharon while Tracey couldn't wait for the next visit, but it became easier when they were moved to an open prison nearer to home in the 1993 series.

Next door to the girls lived man-mad Jewish 'princess' Dorien Green (Lesley Joseph), who had been married to boring accountant Marcus (Nickolas Grace, later Stephen Greif, then Grace again) for more than 20 years. Marcus was rarely seen but oft referred-to as Dorien sought to queen it in Chigwell and involved herself in a social power struggle with Melanie Fishman (Jan Goodman). She was ostensibly taking a degree but there was scant evidence of her ever studying seriously. The over-riding issues of the storylines were sex and money, the girls invariably being short of both.

Directors included Tony Dow, Nic Phillips, Sue Bysh, Charlie Hanson, Terry Kinane. Producers: Esta

While the boys are away . . . sisters Sharon (Pauline Quirke) and Tracey (Linda Robson) are BIRDS OF A FEATHER (Photo: © BBC)

Charkham, Nic Phillips, Candida Julian-Jones, Charlie Hanson for Alomo Productions.

BIRDS ON THE WING
BBC. First broadcast: 11 June 1971

Richard Briers starred as Charles Jackson, a wealthy man of dubious business who banked in Switzerland and had a need to travel by air a great deal. He had serious designs on the opposite sex, especially Elizabeth (Anne Rogers) who could play the game as well as he could. Elizabeth's defences were strengthened by Samantha (Julia Lockwood). Six episodes were screened.

Writer: Peter Yeldham. Producer: Graeme Muir.

A BIT OF A DO
YTV. First broadcast: 13 January 1989

David Nobbs adapted his own novels into two six-part series, the second six starting on 20 October of the same year. Set in a small Yorkshire town where everyone knew everyone else's affairs, the stories followed the births, marriages, deaths and extra-marital activities of two families, the inferior Simcocks and the snobby, superior Rodenhursts. The Simcocks were Ted (David Jason), Rita (Gwen Taylor) and their sons Elvis (Wayne Foskett) and Paul (David Thewlis). The Rodenhursts were dentist Laurence (Paul Chapman) who suffered premature death, his wife Liz (Nicola Pagett), their estate-agent son Simon (Nigel Hastings) and daughter Jenny (Sarah-Jane Holm) who, to her family's horror, was to marry not one but both of the Simcock sons! Liz carried Ted Simcock's baby, conceived during the wedding reception of Jenny and Paul, and Ted and Rita split up. Liz married widower Neville Badger (Michael Jayston) and Ted moved from social disaster to romantic and economic disaster. Ever present observers at every 'do' were Rodney and Betty Sillitoe (Tim Wylton and Stephanie Cole), middle-aged and comparatively wealthy, who took it in turns to get drunk. Other principal characters were Carol Fordingbridge (Karen Drury), barman Eric (Malcolm Hebden), waitress Sandra (Tracy Brabin), Gerry Lansdown (David Yelland), Corinna Price-Rodgerson (Diana Weston), Geoffrey Ellsworth-Smythe (Malcolm Tierney) and Lucinda Snellmarsh (Amanda Wenban). Each episode took place at a different town 'do', be it private or public.

Theme music sung by George Melly. Producer: David Reynolds.

BLACKADDER

BBC. First broadcast: 16 June 1983

Four series and one Christmas special amounted to 25 episodes in all of this show which began as 'The Black Adder' and became successively 'Blackadder II', 'Blackadder the Third' and 'Blackadder Goes Forth'. The last programme was transmitted on 2 November 1989.

The ghastly Blackadder (Rowan Atkinson) journeyed through history from the 15th century, through the Elizabethan age, into Regency Britain and on to the First World War. On his vile and violent ways, the cowardly horseman with a deformed haircut and evil black tights was accompanied by his smelly, idiotic servant Baldrick (Tony Robinson). The *Radio Times* introduced the first episode with the description of Black Adder as 'the scummiest toe-rag in the great laundry basket of English history'. He mellowed into a more sympathetic character after the first series. Through the episodes there were many notable guest performances of historical characters including Richard III (Peter Cook), Richard IV (Brian Blessed), Princess Maria (Miriam Margolyes), The Moorhen (Patrick Allen), Elizabeth I (Miranda Richardson), Lord Melchett (Stephen Fry), Lord Flashheart (Rik Mayall), Prince Ludwig (Hugh Laurie), Dr Johnson (Robbie Coltrane), Captain Darling (Tim McInnery), Baron Von Richthoven (Adrian Edmondson) and Field Marshal Haig (Geoffrey Palmer). Others, too numerous to mention, contributed to the acclaim which these programmes received but the substantial slice of the credit should go to the writing team of Rowan Atkinson, Richard Curtis and, from Blackadder II, Ben Elton.
Directors: Martin Shardlow, Mandie Fletcher, Richard Boden. Producer: John Lloyd.

Captain Edmund Blackadder (Rowan Atkinson) Goes Forth with percussion maestro Private Baldrick (Tony Robinson) (Photo: © BBC)

BLANDINGS

BBC RADIO. First broadcast: 2 February 1985

Jeeves and Bertie Wooster were not the only comic creations of Pelham Grenville Wodehouse – his Lord Emsworth of Blandings (Richard Vernon), who had been created in 1913, came to radio 18 years after he had materialised on television in BLANDINGS CASTLE. The series also proved to be a swan song for veteran radio producer Bobby Jaye, who retired on its success after 40 years with the Corporation. He produced the first six-part series and there were 17 further editions produced by Martin Fisher which ended on 12 September

1989. Regular characters included Beach (Lockwood West, later Timothy Bateson), Lady Constance (Margot Boyd, later Elizabeth Spriggs and then Joan Sanderson) and the Hon. Galahad Threepwood (Ian Carmichael). All the episodes were adapted from the original Wodehouse stories by Richard Usborne.

BLANDINGS CASTLE

BBC. First broadcast: 24 February 1967

John Chapman adapted PG Wodehouse's 1913 stories of Clarence, 9th Earl of Emsworth (Ralph Richardson) into six half-hour episodes. The doddery Earl roamed around his castle, content in the rose garden or in his piggery where his favourite sow was the Empress, and appeared to live in a mild and dreamy world of his own. But he was not without cunning and those around him dared not drop their guard. They included his butler Beach (Stanley Holloway), son Frederick (Derek Nimmo), sister Lady Constance (Meriel Forbes), McAllister the gardener (Jack Radcliffe), Sir Gregory Parsloe-Parsloe (Jimmy Edwards) and Mr Eustace Chalfont (Fred Emney). The exterior scenes were shot at Penshurst Place, Kent, although Wodehouse originally set Blandings Castle in Shropshire.

Music: Ron Grainer. Producer: Michael Mills.

BLESS ME, FATHER

LWT. First broadcast: 24 September 1978

These stories by Peter De Rosa, a former priest who had written books under the name Neil Boyd, starred Arthur Lowe as Father Duddleswell, priest to the parish of St Jude's in the London suburb of Fairwater. In the first episode he was expecting the arrival of his new curate, the freshly ordained and rather shy Father Neil Boyd (Daniel Abineri). They went about the everyday affairs of the parish and were looked after by housekeeper Mrs Pring (Gabrielle Daye). Making an occasional appearance was Bishop O'Reilly (Derek Francis). The setting was the early 1950s. There were two further series starting 11 November 1979 and 5 July 1981, making 18 shows in total.

Producer: David Askey.

BLESS THIS HOUSE

THAMES. First broadcast: 2 February 1971

Created by Vince Powell and Harry Driver, this turned out to be one of the longest running sitcoms on British television. More than 70 episodes were made between 1971 and 1976.

The Abbott family, living in Putney, was consumed by battles of the sexes and by the problems of the generation gap. Sid James starred as Sid Abbott, head of the family in all but reality. His interests were simple as ABC – ale, birds and Chelsea FC. He was employed as a representative for a stationery firm. He considered himself to be 'with it' yet he was demonstrably without it. He was hounded by his wife Jean (Diana Coupland), who inevitably emerged from their confrontations as the winner. They had two children, Mike (Robin Stewart) and Sally (Sally Geeson), who attempted to indoctrinate their parents in the ways of the modern world. In 1971, Mike had just left school and was disinclined to look for a job, while Sally was in her final year at grammar school. Over the years came problems of boyfriends and girlfriends and an ever-growing distance from parental ideals. Other characters who appeared for at least a full season included neighbours Trevor (Anthony Jackson) and Betty (Patsy Rowlands) and Sid's office secretary sexy Sandra (Charlotte Howard).

Writers included Vince Powell and Harry Driver, Carla Lane and Myra Taylor, Dave Freeman, Bernie Sharp, Lawrie Wyman and George Evans, Adele Rose, Jon Watkins. Producer: William G Stewart.

BLOOMERS

BBC. First broadcast: 27 September 1979

This series of only five episodes takes on a poignant significance in that Richard Beckinsale played his last role before his untimely death on 9 April 1979. In fact, more than five months then elapsed before the first transmission of the show, which was set in a florist shop where Dingley (David Swift) offered out-of-work actor Stan (Beckinsale) a partnership. The other character involved was Lena (Anna Calder-Marshall), whose arguments and potential break-up with Stan precipitated his joining the flower business. The series was destined for an initial six editions but Beckinsale's death prompted the team to call it a day.

Music: Ken Jones. Writer: James Saunders. Producer: Roger Race.

BLOSSOM

USA PRESENTED BY CHANNEL 4.
First broadcast: 24 April 1992

Don Reo created this situation which starred Mayim Bialik in the title role as a 14-year-old girl growing up in an all-male household. She lived with her divorced father Nick Russo (Ted Wass) and her two older brothers, Joseph (Joey Lawrence) and Anthony (Michael Stoyanov). Blossom had a boyfriend Vinny (David Lascher) and a best girl-friend called Six (Jenna Van Oÿ). The stories tackled serious teenage subjects including sex and drugs. Blossom herself was something of a child prodigy and was very mature for her years. Brother Anthony, who was an ambulance driver, took himself to Las Vegas for a weekend, got drunk and woke up to find himself married to a black girl he had no recollection of ever having seen before! More than 60 editions were seen on Channel 4 and a new series began on 31 December 1993.

Producers: Paul Junger Witt, Tony Thomas and Don Reo.

BLOTT ON THE LANDSCAPE
BBC. First broadcast: 6 February 1985

This six-part series based on the novels of Tom Sharpe was adapted by Malcolm Bradbury. A not entirely honourable MP Sir Giles Lynchwood (George Cole), a likeable man when he got his own way but a thorough pig when he did not, lived at his country seat, Handyman Hall. A proposed motorway threatened his tranquil existence and that of his wife Maud (Geraldine James) and Blott, the handyman (David Suchet). The head of the household was Mrs Forthby (Julia McKenzie), possibly the only one who realised that Sir Giles made his several forays up to London to gratify his strange sexual desires. Totally befuddled in the plot was the troubleshooter despatched by the Ministry of the Environment (Simon Cadell).
Music: David MacKay. Director: Roger Bamford. Producer: Brian Eastman.

BLUEBIRDS
BBC. First broadcast: 5 October 1989

This six-part children's series was written by Angela Ince and Shirley Lowe. Barbara Windsor as Mabel and Sheila Steafel as Annie starred in a neighbourhood where there had been too many muggings and other crimes. They banded together to make their estate a better place in which to live. Other characters were Gertrude (Isabelle Lucas), Ivy (Pauline Delany), Proudfoot (Lance Percival), Cullen (Ron Pember), Alfred (Dennis Edwards), Dora (Beryl Cooke), Jennifer (Jo Warne) and Bill Parks (Sean Blowers).
Producer: Jeremy Swan.

THE BOB CUMMINGS SHOW
USA PRESENTED BY ITV.
First broadcast (UK): 18 September 1956

Film actor Robert Cummings moved into television in the mid-1950s and was one of the first imports by ITV to Britain. In this series he played Bob Collins, a fashion photographer who was hard put to evade the matrimonial intentions of the models who posed for him. His assistant and secretary was a plain girl by the name of Schultzy (Ann B Davis). She always wore her hair in a bun and dreamed of romance with Bob and becoming a glamour girl herself. Apart from Bob's belief in his powers to charm the ladies, his other priority was to protect his widowed sister Margaret MacDonald (Rosemary DeCamp) from all possible suitors, especially Paul Fonda (Lyle Talbot). Margaret had a son, Chuck (Dwayne Hickman), whose interests followed those of his uncle.

BOLD AS BRASS
BBC. First broadcast: 16 May 1964

These stories of the Briggs family were written by David Climie but were created by Ron Watson in a single half-hour play, *Man of Brass*, which was shown in November 1963. The series was first seen the following year and the six episodes were broadcast fortnightly. Jimmy Edwards starred as Ernie Briggs who played the double B-flat brass bass in the band of a North-Country town. His all-consuming musical passion was not shared by his wife Bessie (Beryl Reid) nor by his daughter Peggy (Jill Hyem). Other regulars in the shows, which had a variety element to them, were Ronnie Barker, Ronnie Brody and Ernest Arnley.
Musical director: Gordon Franks. Producer: Philip Barker.

BONEHEAD
BBC. First broadcast: 2 October 1960

This children's series was described by its creator Shaun Sutton as 'a weekly reminder that crime doesn't pay'. Colin Douglas starred as the title character, a lovable simpleton who was a member of a gang of three blundering, bumbling crooks. Their leader was the Boss (Paul Whitsun-Jones), a bulbous, fatuous enthusiast of gangster films from which he sought inspiration. The third gang member was the miserable Happy (Douglas Blackwell), a mournful old lag for whom all roads led to prison. There were two series, each of five episodes, ending 26 August 1961.
Writer and producer: Shaun Sutton.

BONJOUR LA CLASSE
BBC. First broadcast: 15 February 1993

Nigel Planer starred as Laurence Didcott, an idealistic but useless teacher of French who joined The Mansion School, a fee-paying independent establishment with a 235-year-old tradition. What he found on arrival was a school staffed with lunatic eccentrics under a headmaster who was driven by money rather than educational achievement. Didcott managed to irritate and alienate his colleagues, and furthermore, he was totally inept when it came to controlling a class of street-wise children. *Writers: Paul Smith and Terry Kyan. Director: John Henderson. Producer: Jamie Rix for Talkback productions.*

BOOTSIE AND SNUDGE

GRANADA. First broadcast: 23 September 1960

The producers of THE ARMY GAME, Peter Eton and Milo Lewis, had the bright idea to 'spin off' two favourite characters into civvy street. Private 'Excused Boots' Bisley (Alfie Bass) – Bootsie for short – and Sgt Major Claude Snudge (Bill Fraser) were the chosen pair. They were duly demobbed and just four episodes later were installed as boots boy and major-domo respectively in a seedy London gentlemen's club, The Imperial. The Rt Hon Secretary of this establishment was Hesketh Pendleton (Robert Dorning) and there was an 83-year-old waiter, Henry Beerbohm 'Old' Johnson, played in 1960 by 38-year-old actor Clive Dunn. They remained at the club for four seasons. In 1974, after a ten-year gap, producer Bill Podmore resurrected BOOTSIE AND SNUDGE but reversed their roles. While

Alfie Bass (left) and Bill Fraser, newly arrived in Civvy Street, as BOOTSIE AND SNUDGE (Photo: Granada Television)

Bootsie had always been the 'little man' under Snudge's bullying thumb, he had now won a million on the pools and Snudge had to do the creeping. They gave up their jobs to spend the fortune. There were 106 episodes.

Theme music: Peter Knight. Writers (1960–64) included Barry Took, Marty Feldman, John Antrobus, Peter Miller, James Kelly and Ray Whyberd (ventriloquist Ray Alan), and (1974) Ronnie Cass and David Climie. Producers included Peter Eton, Milo Lewis and Eric Fawcett and (1974) Bill Podmore.

BORN AND BRED

THAMES. First broadcast: 13 September 1978

Douglas Livinstone created and wrote these black comedy dramas which were built around two South London families and their clan members. The oldest member of the Benge family was Annie (Rose Hill), who had spent most of her life caring for sick and stray animals. In the first episode, the local newspaper organised a reunion of all her family members in her honour. The senior member of the Tonsley family was Tommy (Max Wall). Other regular characters were Frank Benge (James Grout), Ray Benge (Gorden Kaye), Dennis Tonsley (Trevor Peacock), and Molly Peglar (Joan Sims) who was the merry widowed licensee of the Crown and Sceptre, where the barman was Freddie Green (Milton Johns). Also weaving in and out of the stories were Iris (Susan Tracy), Jim (Niall Padden), Stephen (Richard O'Callaghan), Pamela (Susie Blake), Rose (Constance Chapman), Daphne (Gillian Raine), Marge (Kate Williams), Shirley (Helen Cotterill) and Christopher (Christian Bullock). There was a second series of six which began on 2 September 1980, making twelve 50-minute programmes in total.

Directors; Baz Taylor, Derek Bennett. Producers: Peter Duguid, Tim Aspinall.

BOTH ENDS MEET

LWT. First broadcast: 18 February 1972

Dora Bryan starred as Dora Page, a widow raising her young son Ronnie (David Howe) and trying to support her father-in-law Mr Page (Meadows White) without adequate income. In her efforts to make ends meet, she took a job in the Cannon's Family Sausages factory, run by Mr Julius Cannon (Ivor Dean). Her workmates included Glad (Pat Ashton), Flo (Deddie Davies), Maudie (Wendy

Richard) and Harry (John Lyons). Her neighbours were George and Hilda Rogers (Tim Bateson and Fanny Carby) and the rather snobbish Mrs Templeton-Smythe (Joan Benham). A second series was transmitted in the autumn of the same year but retitled DORA.

Writers included Brian Chasser, Len Downs, Mike Firman, Patrick Radcliffe. Producers: Philip Casson, Mark Stuart.

BOTTLE BOYS

LWT. First broadcast: 1 September 1984

This story of life on the milk rounds of Dave Deacon (Robin Askwith) and his colleagues at Dawson's Dairy was written by Vince Powell. Dave was hopeless but well-intentioned as he sought to serve his public to the best of his ability – unfortunately he was not gifted with much ability. His boss was Stan Evans (Richard Davies) and his mixed bag of fellow milkmen included Jock Collins (Phil McCall), Billy Watson (Dave Auker) and Joe Phillips (Oscar James). The female attraction at the dairy was Sharon Armstrong (Eve Ferret). The first series of six programmes was followed by seven more starting 13 July 1985.

Producer: Stuart Allen.

BOTTOM

BBC. First broadcast: 17 September 1991

The 'Bottom' of the title referred not to the anatomy but to the place in life's pile where the two lead characters found themselves. Adrian Edmondson and Rik Mayall wrote the shows and starred as Eddie and Richie, two repellent bachelors who shared an unsavoury bedsit complete with filthy fridge and who had missed out on all life's offerings and opportunities. As they festered, they fantasised about sex, one of life's joys which neither had experienced in years. There were twelve shows over two seasons ending 29 October 1992.

Producer: Ed Bye.

THE BOUNDER

YTV. First broadcast: 16 April 1982

Peter Bowles starred as suave and sophisticated conman Howard, who had just been released from prison where he had served a sentence for embezzlement. He lodged with his sister Mary (Rosalind Ayres) and his humourless estate agent brother-in-law Trevor (George Cole). He took a strong fancy

to the young widow living next door, Laura (Isla Blair). The first series of six episodes was followed by a further nine which began on 16 September 1983.

Writer: Eric Chappell. Producer: Vernon Lawrence.

BOWLER

LWT. First broadcast: 29 July 1973

Writers John Esmonde and Bob Larbey took the character Stanley Bowler (George Baker) from their own series THE FENN STREET GANG, where he had been Peter Craven's rather shady boss, and elevated him to his own series. Bowler was an arch spiv, a petty villain with a finger in any and every profitable pie. However, money could not buy that which he craved above all else – class! For much as he tried to acquire airs and graces, class eluded him. He had a right-hand man whom he called his valet, Reg (Fred Beauman), and he was estranged from his wife Doreen (Renny Lister). Bowler's Cockney mother was portrayed by Gretchen Franklin.

Producer: Philip Casson.

THE BOYS FROM THE BUSH

BBC. First broadcast: 25 January 1991

Tim Healy starred as Reg, a proud Londoner from Shepherd's Bush who lived in Melbourne and had done so for 20 years. He was a fervent trade unionist and a passionate Queen's Park Rangers fan. He was never comfortable with many aspects of Australian life, especially the people, the culture (or lack of same), the beer, the food, the sport, nor anything else he could find to whinge about. Chris Haywood co-starred as his business partner Dennis. The two of them had little in common other than a will to make money and they owned Melbourne Confidential, an agency which would tackle any undertaking. While Reg was football-daft, Dennis had an obsession with women. Other regular characters through the two series and 21 fifty-minute episodes, ending 14 July 1992, were Leslie (Mark Haddigan), who wanted to marry Arlene (Nadine Garner); Doris (Pat Thomson), Delilah (Kris McQaude) and Corrie (Kirsty Child). As and when required, some characters would return to England and the series was filmed in both locations.

Writer: Douglas Livingstone. Directors: Robert Marchand, Shirley Barrett. Producer: Verity Lambert for Cinema Verity.

BRADLEY

GRANADA. First broadcast: 21 March 1989

In this six-part children's series, the central character, Bradley (Paul Bradley), embarked on a sequence of misadventures which involved his own talking reflection (Peter MacQueen).
Director: James Wynn. Producer: Richard Morss.

BRASS

GRANADA. First broadcast: 21 February 1983

This much lauded tongue-in-cheek send-up of all the northern 'trouble at t' mill' dramas of the past was created and written by John Stevenson and Julian Roach. The stories were built around two families, the rich Hardacres and their poor employees, the Fairchilds. Bradley Hardacre (Timothy West) was a self-made mill owner, mine owner and munitions manufacturer who lusted after power and women. He had an embittered wife, the dipsomaniac, wheelchair-bound Patience (Caroline Blakiston), and a long-standing mistress Agnes Fairchild (Barbara Ewing), the wife of George Fairchild (Geoffrey Hinsliff) who gratefully worked for Bradley. The Hardacres had four children. There was ambitious Austin (Robert Reynolds) who longed to rule the empire, brilliant but immoral Morris (James Saxon), and innocent Charlotte (Emily Morgan) who liked to help out at the hospital where Dr Macduff (David Ashton) treated workers who had been injured and wounded by Bradley's cruel and callous working conditions. The fourth child was Isobel (Gail Harrison), a temptress who ultimately married Lord Mountfast (John Nettleton).

The Fairchilds had two sons in whom Agnes stoked a burning hostility towards their bosses, thus earning her the name Red Agnes. The sons were Jack (Shaun Scott), who fell in love with Charlotte Hardacre, and Matthew (Gary Cady). The action took place in the 1930s in the town of Utterley. The stories of loves, passions, greed and social injustices continued in a second 13-part series which started on 21 May 1984.
Director: Gareth Jones. Producer: Bill Podmore.

On 23 April 1990, six new editions began transmission, this time screened on Channel 4 and set in 1939 when Bradley expected to increase his fortune through his munitions operation and the marketing of inflatable air-raid shelters.
Director: Les Chatfield. Producer: Mark Robson.

BREAD

BBC. First broadcast: 1 May 1986

Carla Lane's saga of a Liverpool family and its battle against poverty ran for 68 editions, ending on 3 November 1991. The Boswells were held together by mum Mrs Boswell (Jean Boht) with no help from her errant husband Freddie (Ronald Forfar). With unemployment on Merseyside at a level that made finding a job all but impossible, the family of lovable rogues were bound by a deep sense of loyalty and a need to survive. The five grown-up Boswell children were Joey (Peter Howitt, later Graham Bickley), Jack (Victor McGuire), Aveline (Gilly Coman, later Melanie Hill), Adrian (Jonathon Morris) and Billy (Nick Conway). Adding to Mrs Boswell's trials were Grandad (Kenneth Waller), who lived next door in the terraced street and always seemed to be calling for his dinner, and Lilo Lil (Eileen Pollock), Freddie's bit on the side. Aveline married Oswald (Giles Watling), and other characters who featured, although not on a regular basis, included the DHSS clerk (Pamela Power), Billy's wife Julie (Caroline Milmoe, later Hilary Crowson), Shifty (Bryan Murray) and Celia Higgins (Rita Tushingham).
Directors: Susan Belbin, Robin Nash, John B Hobbs.
Producers: Robin Nash, John B Hobbs.

The Boswell family, 'making BREAD out of nothing but air' and visiting Rome for the 1988 Christmas special (Photo: Copyright © BBC)

THE BRIAN KEITH SHOW

NBC (AMERICA) PRESENTED BY ITV.
First broadcast (UK): 9 September 1974

American comedian Brian Keith played Dr Sean Jamison, a paediatrician based in Hawaii. Working alongside him in the hospital was his attractive daughter Dr Anne Jamison (Shelley Fabares). In the United States the show was also known as 'The Little People'. Other regular characters were Drucilla Gruber (Nancy Kulp), Puni Mialoha (Victoria Young), Dr Austin Chaffee (Roger Bowen) and Stewart (Sean Tyler Hall).

BRIDGET LOVES BERNIE

CBS (AMERICA) PRESENTED BY ITV.
First broadcast: 28 July 1973

Bernard Slade created this series which was set in New York, where wealthy Irish Catholic school teacher Bridget Fitzgerald fell in love with Jewish cab driver Bernie Steinberg. Meredith Baxter starred as Bridget and David Birney as Bernie. They had two major obstacles to surmount before the course of true love could run smooth, namely their respective parents, Walter and Amy Fitzgerald (David Doyle and Audra Lindley) and Sam and Sophie Steinberg (Harold J Stone and Bibi Osterwald). Lending sympathetic ears were Bernie's Uncle Moe (Ned Glass) and Father Michael (Robert Sampson). Baxter and Birney later married in real life.
Producers: Arthur Alsberg, Bob Nelson.

THE BRIGHT SIDE

CHANNEL 4. First broadcast: 9 May 1985

Paula Wilcox starred in this series of six programmes as Cynthia Bright, a woman struggling to live and make the most of her situation while her husband Lionel (Paul Copley) was in prison. Lionel shared a cell with Chadwick (Bill Treacher) and Humphries (Johnny Shannon), and Cynthia became friendly with Chadwick's wife (Madge Hindle). This helped her to cope with Lionel's mother (Hilda Braid) and the ever present Mr Lithgow (Geoffrey Hughes).
Music: Denis King. Writer: Willis Hall. Producer: William G Stewart for Regent Productions.

BRIGHTON BELLES

CARLTON. First broadcast: 7 September 1993

This ill-fated series was the British version of THE GOLDEN GIRLS. The original American concept by Susan Harris, and the American scripts, were adapted from Miami to a Brighton setting by Christopher Skala. The characters were reproduced as Frances (Sheila Hancock) for Dorothy, Bridget (Sheila Gish) for Blanche, Annie (Wendy Craig) for Rose, and Josephine (Jean Boht) for Sophia. The initial pilot show was screened as an edition of *Comedy Playhouse* on 9 March 1993. A series intended to run for six weeks started in the autumn that same year but, alas, was withdrawn before its conclusion by the newly installed ITV Network Centre controller, Marcus Plantin.
Director: James Cellan Jones. Producer: Humphrey Barclay for Humphrey Barclay Productions.

BRIGHT'S BOFFINS

SOUTHERN. First broadcast: 4 August 1970.

With much use of special effects and explosives, this children's series ran for a 13-week season each year for three years. Alexander Doré starred as Group Captain Bertram Bright, who directed a gang of mad scientists engaged in work for some long-forgotten government department. Given only a meagre grant and occupying a run-down establishment, Halfwit House, Bright's boffins were forced to cheat, lie and blackmail for their own security. He was assisted by Sergeant Thumper (Denis Shaw), Dogsears Dawson (Gordon Rollings), Marmaduke (Eddie Reindeer), Berk (George Moon), Molly McCrandle (Avril Angers), Professor and Julie Farthing (Bartlett Mullin and Belinda Sinclair), Catseyes Kavanagh (Dominic Roche), Peter Vincent (Anthony Verner) and Tippy (Johnny Briggs). There was an out-of-space creature called Oswald which was played by Sadie Corre. The boffins had an unseen benefactor, Sir Desmond Dark, but it was Molly McCrandle, in the double role of scientist and auntie who could cook, who looked after them. After Halfwit House burned down they set up headquarters in a railway yard.
Writers included Dominic Roche, Denis Goodwin and Keith Miles. Producer: Peter Croft.

BRINGING HOME THE BACON

BBC RADIO. First broadcast: 25 October 1945

Outsize Jewish comedian Max Bacon starred as Maxie, a character who professed to be an authority on the English language, a health specialist and a promoter of Shakespeare. He was assisted by his number one associate Fink (Horace Kenney) and pursued by Schnitzelpuss (Joe Lee), his constant creditor. Triss Henderson portrayed herself as a scatterbrain and other regular cast members were Neal Arden, Connie Clare and Fred Yule. Six editions were broadcast.

Writers: Julian Vedey and Walter Donaldson. Producer: David Porter.

THE BRITTAS EMPIRE
BBC. First broadcast: 14 February 1991

The new town of Whitbury had a local authority leisure centre where the manager was sanctimonious nerd Gordon Brittas (Chris Barrie), who took up his new post on the day of the first transmission. A loathsome idealist, Brittas strove for harmony, peace and perfection among his staff. He had a neurotic wife who turned up at every inconvenient moment, especially during her pregnancy which resulted in the birth of twin Brittases, Matthew and Mark. Her name was Helen and she was played by Pippa Haywood.

At the club, the deputy manager, without whom Brittas would have been in even deeper weekly water, was Laura Lancing (Julia St John) and the secretary was Julie (Judy Flynn). The receptionist Carole (Harriet Thorpe) was usually homeless, fraught with the problems of her three children, and her youngest, Ben, spent most of his infancy in a cupboard behind the reception desk. The incompetent general maintenance man was the Geordie loyalist to Mr Brittas, as he addressed him, Colin Wetherby (Michael Burns) who eventually was made a deputy manager. Of the fitness and sports coaches, only three were constant throughout the 29 episodes. They were Linda (Jill Greenacre), Tim (Russell Porter) and Gavin (Tim Marriott).

In the very last episode on 7 March 1994, Brittas had been fired from his job and lasted just five minutes as a petrol-pump attendant. When the leisure centre exploded in a ball of fire, he became a hero, rescuing two errant children who were trapped, as well as Carole's son Ben. He was awarded the George Medal.

Theme music: Frank Renton. Writers: Richard Fegen and Andrew Norriss. Producer: Mike Stephens.

BROGUE MALE
BBC RADIO. First broadcast: 30 December 1985

This four-part series by Paul Bassett Davies and John Gerald Collee starred film actor Richard Johnson as Sir Digby Spode, a compendium of the hero of so many 1930s films who was handsome, strong and totally devoid of sensitivity. He was accompanied on his adventures by his intrepid sidekick Hubert Carstairs (Royce Mills) as they pursued evil across the continents. Their greatest enemy was the dastardly Count Laszlo Stroganoff (Stephen Greif).

Producer: Alan Nixon.

BROTHERS
SHOWTIME (AMERICA) PRESENTED BY CHANNEL 4. First broadcast (UK): 29 November 1985

This pioneering comedy series, created and produced by Gary Nardino, was turned down by the major American networks before it found a home and an audience on cable.

On the eve of his wedding, Cliff Waters (Paul Regina) revealed to his brothers Joe and Lou (Robert Walden and Brandon Maggart) that he was homosexual. Cliff was the youngest of the three and Joe had been an important football star. The family fought to come to terms with Cliff's sexuality and needless to say, there was no wedding. Cliff was not portrayed as being in any way limp-wristed or camp, but rather as an anti-stereotype of homosexuals on screen. The setting was New York and the other principal characters in the ten episodes were Penny Waters (Hallie Todd) and Cliff's gay friend Donald Maltby (Philip Charles MacKenzie).

BROTHERS IN LAW
BBC. First broadcast: 17 April 1962

Richard Briers played his first leading role in a television series as young barrister Roger Thursby in this seven-part adaptation of Henry Cecil's book of the same title.

Thursby, intelligent and enthusiastic, faced up to his first cases and encounters with the protocol of the legal profession. His senior in chambers, Henry Blagrove (Richard Waring), and his master in chambers, the eccentric Kendall Grimes (John Glyn-Jones), leant him moral support.

The scripts, by Frank Muir and Denis Norden, stuck to legal truth but presented it in terms of light entertainment. Sharing his trials and wincing in sympathy from the public gallery as Roger faced judge and jury was his actress girlfriend, Sally

Mannering (June Barry). The Judge was played by Walter Hudd.

Music: Dennis Wilson. Producer: Graeme Muir.

BBC RADIO. First broadcast: 9 June 1970

Eight years after the television series Richard Waring adapted the writings of Henry Cecil into 39 Radio shows which ran over three seasons and ended on 17 July 1972. Richard Briers resumed his role as Roger Thursby as did Richard Waring himself as Henry Blagrove. John Glyn-Jones also returned as Grimes but the part of Sally Mannering was now played by Ann Davies. The role of Judge was portrayed by guest actors, the first being John Le Mesurier.

Producers: David Hatch, Trafford Whitelock.

THE BROTHERS McGREGOR

GRANADA. First broadcast: 4 September 1985

Julian Roach and John Stevenson created and wrote these shows which got off to a fine start, reaching number five in the weekly ratings in the opening week and never dropping out of the top 20 over the seven-week run. Strangely, 19 further episodes over the three new series all failed to make the top 20. The last show was transmitted on 25 August 1988. The brothers were, in fact, half brothers. Wesley (Paul Barber), whose father was a black West African missionary, and Cyril, whose father was white and uncertain, together ran a secondhand car dealership but separately harboured different ambitions. Cyril sang part-time in a nightclub and visualised himself as a budding Frank Sinatra. Wesley leaned towards matters more serious and recognised his prospects lay in the world of business and politics. To this end, he wrote to all world leaders so that they might acquaint themselves with his existence and be prepared for his coming. Their mother Dolly (Jean Heywood) had a hankering to see Wesley's father once more. Cyril had a fiancée Glenys Pike (Jackie Downey) who lived in eternal hope of marriage. All the characters lived, worked and played on Merseyside.

Producers: Bernard Thompson and Bill Podmore.

BRUSH STROKES

BBC. First broadcast: 1 September 1986

John Esmonde and Bob Larbey created and wrote the 40 editions of this series which ran until 8 April 1991. Karl Howman starred as Jacko, painter and decorator, who could not resist women. He en-joyed wining them and dining them but did not always get them into bed and, in fairness, that was not *always* his objective. He loved and lost most of the women who crossed his path until he finally made it down the aisle with Sandra (Jackie Lye) after a cliffhanger end to one of the series when he turned to best man Eric (Mike Walling) and said: 'I think I've made a terrible mistake.' The whole studio audience groaned. Much of the action took place in Elmo's wine bar. A huge man, Elmo (Howard Lew Lewis) was the opposite of Jacko and read sexual implications into virtually everything. The boss for whom Jacko worked was Lionel (Gary Waldhorn) who subsequently died and the business was taken on by his widow Veronica (Elizabeth Counsell). Lionel and Veronica had a daughter, Lesley (Erika Hoffman). Almost ever-present was Jacko's sister Jean (Nicky Croydon) who was married to Eric. The setting was Motspur Park.

Producers: Sydney Lotterby, Mandie Fletcher, Harold Snoad, John B Hobbs.

THE BUBBLEGUM BRIGADE

HTV. First broadcast: 2 May 1989

This children's series featured a gang which had as its motto: 'Broken hearts mended while you wait'. The brigade members who dealt with such troubles were William (Bill Oddie), Auntie Doodah (Veronica Clifford), Alph (Ian Kirkby), Bunny (Michelle Moore), Fuddle (James Hyden) and Jinx (Flora Fenton). There were six episodes.

Writers: Bill Oddie and Laura Beaumont. Producer: Pennant Roberts.

BUFFALO BILL

USA PRESENTED BY CHANNEL 4.
First broadcast (UK): 19 May 1984

Dabney Coleman starred in 13 episodes as Bill Bittinger, egocentric presenter of a local TV programme in Buffalo, New York. He was rude and demanding of those around him, especially his much-abused stage manager Woody (John Fiedler) and the station manager Karl Shub (Max Wright). The females involved in Bill's activities were Joanna White (Joanna Cassidy) and Wendy Killian (Geena Davis).

BULLDOG BREED

GRANADA. First broadcast: 19 September 1962

Created by Derek Granger, this series starred Donald Churchill as Tom Bowler, an amiable chap with a tendency to create panic and havoc. He lived in a semi-detached house, well within the smog-belt of a provincial town. He had a dizzy girlfriend, receptionist Sandra Prentiss (Amanda Barrie), and a best pal, Billy Broadbent (Geoffrey Whitehead). Billy inadvertently got swept up in most of Tom's disasters, much to the despair of Billy's parents Henry and Lillian Broadbent (Peter Butterworth and Betty Huntley-Wright).

Music: Johnnie Spence. Writers: Harry Driver and Jack Rosenthal. Director: Graeme McDonald. Producer: Derek Granger.

THE BURNS AND ALLEN SHOW
CBS (AMERICA) PRESENTED BY BBC RADIO AND TELEVISION.

The most successful husband and wife pairing ever to broadcast was George Burns and Gracie Allen. In 1929/30 they spent six months in London and guested numerous times on BBC radio but it is their American-made shows which are fondest remembered. It may be hard to believe today that George, lively and still working in his late nineties, was really just the feed to Gracie's scatterbrained character who could progress from the ridiculous to the totally absurd with what appeared to be logicality.

In the United States they switched networks on several occasions and their first regular slot was on ABC's Guy Lombardo Show which was sponsored by the General Cigar Company. The image of George Burns without a cigar is as smoke without fire. So began their incredible career over the airwaves on 15 February 1932.

In October 1950 they made the difficult and all-too-rarely successful transfer to the new medium of television, playing George and Gracie at home, but with the innovation that George would begin each show with a brief monologue to camera and, from time to time, employ the same technique to deliver an aside to the viewer. With them from radio came their original announcer Bill Goodwin (later Harry von Zell), a handsome and amorous man, and their neighbours Harry Morton (Hal March, later Larry Keating) and his wife Blanche (Bea Benaderet). The first words ever spoken on the TV series were by George direct to camera saying: 'Hello, everybody. I'm George Burns, better known as Gracie Allen's husband . . .' In later editions they introduced their real-life son Ronnie.

For the first two years the shows were transmitted live. They began recording them in 1952 and the BBC showed the first edition available on 16 September 1955. Out of a total of 299 shows, fewer than half were ever seen by British audiences. An interesting aside is that Burns was quoted as saying they were the first TV show to make use of cue cards.

Producer (TV): Fred de Cordova.

BUTTERFLIES
BBC. First broadcast: 10 November 1978

Carla Lane created this domestic series for BBC2 in which Wendy Craig starred as Ria Parkinson, a suburban wife and mother, married for almost 20 years and unappreciated by her family. She shared her humdrum life with her husband Ben (Geoffrey Palmer), a boring dentist who collected butterflies for a hobby. Though the marriage seemed always on the verge of crumbling, the eternally depressive Ben fought to hold it together while Ria could see life quickly passing her by. They had two teenage sons, Adam (Nicholas Lyndhurst) and Russell (Andrew Hall), whose behaviour, attitudes and manners did not conform to the standards which Ben expected. He was greatly irritated by their cynical, light-hearted approach to life and by their preoccupation with girls.

Ria met smooth, groomed and educated businessman Leonard (Bruce Montague) in a restaurant, thereby beginning a platonic affair of clandestine meetings and frustration. The series was innovative with its use of surreal dream sequences and its tackling of previously taboo subjects like adultery and teenage pregnancy out of wedlock. When it became clear to Leonard that Ria would never leave Ben, he emigrated to America, ostensibly for good. However, he returned for the final series and the tug-of-love ended with Ria making a tearful return to her family.

Other regular characters included the cleaning lady Ruby (Joyce Windsor) and Leonard's chauffeur Thomas (Michael Ripper). In the second series, the Parkinsons acquired new neighbours, the Conrads, portrayed by Milton Johns and Wendy Williams. The last of 28 episodes was screened on 19 October 1982.

Directors included Mandie Fletcher, Gareth Gwenlan, John B Hobbs and Sydney Lotterby. Producers: Gareth Gwenlan and Sydney Lotterby.

THE CABBAGE PATCH

CENTRAL. First broadcast: 29 July 1983

This six-part series looked at family life from the point of view of a 36-year-old wife and mother of two children. She was Janet (Julia Foster) and her harassed husband was Tony (Emlyn Price). They had two small daughters, Kate (Natasha Byrne) and Elizabeth (Amelia Lowdell). To compound Janet's difficulties of everyday life, she had an appalling mother, Lillian (Betty Marsden). Her saviours were her two friends, Ruth (Jill Benedict) and Susie (Belinda Lang).
Producer: Shaun O'Riordan.

CAMP RUNAMUCK

NBC (AMERICA) PRESENTED BY BBC.
First broadcast (UK): 18 October 1975

Two summer camps, one for boys, the other for girls, were just across a lake from each other. There was fierce rivalry between the two, leading to acts of sabotage and open warfare. Principal characters included Spiffy (David Ketchum), Wivenhoe (Arch Johnson), Pruett (Dave Madden), Mahala May (Alice Nunn) and Caprice (Nina Wayne). Though 26 episodes were made, the BBC screened just five, on Saturday mornings.
Producer: David Swift.

CAN WE GET ON NOW, PLEASE?

GRANADA. First broadcast: 2 June 1980

Writer Dennis Woolf set this series of six in a magistrates' court. Clerk to the Justices, Mr Pettigrew (Hugh Paddick), strove to run an efficient court but was beset by corruption all around and found himself at odds with the Chairman of the Bench, Mr Butterfield (Robert Dorning), and his fellow JPs, Mrs Pryor (Sheila Steafel) and Mr Skinner (Michael Barrington). The assistant clerk to the court, Miss Teesdale (Valerie Phillips), angered Mr Pettigrew by her repeated phone calls from the office to her boyfriend in Greece. The court usher was Mr Bailey (Charles Lamb).
Director: Eric Prytherch. Producer: Brian Armstrong.

CAP'N WULLIE

BBC RADIO. First broadcast: 18 July 1942

Veteran music-hall star Will Fyffe played Captain William Tulloch, old salt and retired captain of a coaster who had settled down on land. His wife (Grace McChiery) was a prim, devoted lady for whom Wullie was a constant source of anxiety. To give himself an interest, the Cap'n got together with two pals, Angus 'The Fluke' MacDonald (James Anderson) and Sandy Murdoch (Ian Sadler), to run a wee Merchant Sailors' club on Clydeside where each Saturday night they had a concert. Six shows were broadcast.
Writer: Moultrie R Kelsall. Producer: Eric Fawcett.

CAR 54, WHERE ARE YOU?

NBC (AMERICA) PRESENTED BY ITV.
First broadcast (UK): 9 April 1964

SERGEANT BILKO producer Nat Hiken created this cop show like no other previous cop show in 1961. Britain had to wait until 1964 to see the first of 22 episodes. Working the 53rd precinct in New York were patrolmen Gunther Toody (Joe E Ross) and Francis Muldoon (Fred Gwynne). Toody was fat, genial and stupid. He stood just 5ft 6in in contrast to his slightly more intelligent partner who towered above him at 6ft 5in. This pair of incompetent cops were the responsibility of the unfortunate Captain Martin Black (Paul Reed) and long-suffering Sergeant Sol Abrams (Nathaniel Frey) who had been in the force for 25 years. A fellow patrolman in the precinct was Leo Schnauzer, played by Al Lewis. Joe E Ross had played the part of Mess Sergeant Rupert Ritzik in SERGEANT BILKO, where his wife had been played by Beatrice Pons. She took on the same role in CAR 54, playing Toody's nagging wife Lucille. Muldoon was unmarried.

CARLISLE EXPRESS

BBC RADIO. First broadcast: 6 October 1940

In this fictitious train journey of 21 programmes the train never managed to get to Carlisle. The star of

the show was danceband vocalist Elsie Carlisle. She owned the railway company, which only had one train, and appointed a disastrous managing director, Bertie (Bobbie Comber), who insisted on driving the engine. At the end of the 13th programme he found himself unable to cope with the job and sold his interest in the CARLISLE EXPRESS to Mr Albatross (Fred Yule), whose only previous experience had been with a clockwork train set. The rest of the crew were Taffy the fireman (Percy Griffiths), Wear and Tear the porters (Wheeler and Wilson), Mr Event the guard (Charles Heslop), Spillover the restaurant car attendant (Charlie Clapham) and Fanny Flapjack the permanent passenger (Vera Lennox). They were later joined by an engineer (Horace Percival) and other regular passengers, Mr and Mrs Sydney Gobnuckle (Jack Train and Dorothy Summers) and Felicity Funfair (also played by Vera Lennox). Also on board, but kept in a box, was a mule named Prendergast. Guests and Miss Carlisle enjoyed the luxury of either the BBC Dance Orchestra or the Variety Orchestra travelling with them!
Writer: Loftus Wigram. Producer: Michael North.

CASANOVA

BBC. First broadcast: 13 September 1973

Leslie Phillips starred in seven episodes as Henry Newhouse, a modern libertine who worked in public relations and could not resist flirtations and dalliances with beautiful women. He was surrounded by disapproving though equally beautiful women in his wife Carol (Jan Holden), his secretary (Gail Grainger) and his goddaughter (Madeline Smith).
Writers: Ray Galton and Alan Simpson. Producer: Harold Snoad.

CHALK AND CHEESE

THAMES. First broadcast: 2 April 1979

This short series of just six programmes by Alex Shearer began when into a snobbish, gentrified street of bijou residences moved a pair of Cockneys, Dave and Rose Finn (Michael Crawford and Gillian Martell). They were not exactly welcomed by neighbours Roger and Amanda Scott (Robin Hawdon and Julia Goodman) but as both girls were pregnant, they found they had certain things in common.
Producer: Michael Mills.

CHANCE IN A MILLION

CHANNEL 4. First broadcast: 10 September 1984

Fate, coincidence or the lap of the Gods all governed the life of Tom Chance (Simon Callow), to whom the reverse of whatever was intended would happen. He went on a blind date and met a girl – not the one he should have met, however, but Alison Little (Brenda Blethyn). Thereby began a romance which took four series of six programmes each to get to the altar, ending on 1 December 1986. Alison's parents (Hugh Walters and Deddie Davies) spent much time trying to persuade their daughter that Tom might not be the right man for her. He had an odd manner of speech in which he began every sentence with a verb and omitted all articles, definite or indefinite. He continued throughout to make a hash of everything he touched.
Writers: Andrew Norriss and Richard Fegen. Producer: Michael Mills for Thames.

CHARGE!

BBC. First broadcast: 28 February 1969

Robert Morley starred as Herbert Todhunter who lived on a barge in the Hampton Court area with his friend Partridge (Robert Raglan). Todhunter was a mixture of prejudice and ignorance and was totally distrustful of people, but was always ready to admonish another as the self-proclaimed gladiator of right. Moreover, he was the last bastion of all things English and fought to make sure the rest of the world knew its place. Partridge was not just his friend but his brother-in-law, having married his late sister, Beatrice. There were five editions screened in which Todhunter aired his views on life.
Writers: Robert Morley and Jeremy Paul. Producer: Graeme Muir.

CHARLES IN CHARGE

CBS (AMERICA) PRESENTED BY BBC.
First broadcast (UK): 3 September 1985

Scott Baio, who had found fame as Chachi in HAPPY DAYS, was cast as student Charles who was employed as live-in helper to Jill and Stan Pembroke (Julie Cobb and James Widdoes). The Pembrokes lived very busy lives and entrusted their three children, Jason, Douglas and Lila (Michael Pearlman, Jonathan Ward and April Lerman), to Charles. The series was created by Barbara Weisberg and Michael Jacobs and had two other regular

The regulars and bar staff at CHEERS, where everybody knows your name: left to right, Norm, Carla, Rebecca, Woody, Sam, Frasier, Lilith and Cliff (Photo: Channel 4)

characters who figured strongly in Charles's life, Buddy Lembeck (Willi Aames) and Gwendolyn Pierce (Jennifer Runyon). The BBC screened the last of 23 editions on 21 April 1986.
Director: Alan Rafkin.

CHARLEY CONQUEST

BBC RADIO. First broadcast: 26 September 1962

David Lodge starred in the title role as an East End second-hand car dealer who circulated freely in the underworld. However, he had a strong belief in right and wrong and would help the police if he felt a crime had been a 'dirty' one. He had a criminal record himself and had served time in prison, but the listener was left unsure whether or not he had been guilty of the crime for which he was convicted. His partner and sidekick was Maxie Harris (Harry Towb), himself an East Ender but so in love with all things American that he assumed a Bronx accent and dreamed of owning his own ranch in Stepney. Keeping the boys on the straight and narrow for the 13 broadcasts, although not beyond a gentle little wangle himself, was Father Tracy, the priest of the parish, portrayed by Stephen Jack.
Writer: Gene Crowley. Producer: Jacques Brown.

CHARLEY'S GRANTS

BBC. First broadcast: 22 March 1970

Lord Charley (Willoughby Goddard) was an ebullient benefactor of the arts if it suited him, but he

also sought his own artistic experiences of various kinds and schemed to obtain grants from the Heritage Trust in general and from Miss Manger (Hattie Jacques) in particular. There were six episodes.
Writers: John Fortune, John Wells and NF Simpson. Producer: Ian MacNaughton.

CHARLIE
BBC RADIO. First broadcast: 6 February 1983

Roald Dahl's classic tale of 'Charlie and the Chocolate Factory' was adapted into this seven-part radio serial by David Wade. Charlie Bucket (Jason Littler), a lad who only got one bar of chocolate a year, won one of only five prizes which allowed the lucky winners to spend a day sampling all the delights of Mr Willy Wonka's (Derek Smith) factory.
Producer: Caroline Smith.

THE CHARLIE McCARTHY PROGRAMME
USA PRESENTED BY BBC RADIO.
First broadcast (UK): 20 August 1943

These programmes were recorded in America by special arrangement with the Special Service Division of the War Department of the USA. Ventriloquist Edgar Bergen had achieved the unthinkable and made his dummy, Charlie McCarthy, a radio star in the US in the mid-1930s. McCarthy was created as a slyly drawling little ruffian with a great contempt for his boss, Bergen. He had an asthmatic chuckle which emanated from his little round head and he shared his gags with his hick pal, Mortimer Snerd. In the 1944 season, Bergen introduced a frightening little personality named Effie Klinker who was older than Charlie and was rather severe. Her hair was drawn tightly back and she did not share Charlie's humour. Edgar Bergen was assisted by real-life people, notably Dale Evans and Ray Noble and his Orchestra. The BBC continued with the shows until after the end of the war, thus paving the way for the home-grown EDUCATING ARCHIE.

CHARTERS AND CALDICOT
BBC. First broadcast: 10 January 1985

The two cricket-loving old buffers were created by Frank Launder and Sidney Gilliat for Alfred Hitchcock's 1938 film *The Lady Vanishes* and were played by Basil Radford and Naunton Wayne. For this television series, Robin Bailey was cast as Charters and Michael Aldridge as Caldicot. They were perpetual schoolboys whose lack of tolerance of both women and foreigners was based on their inability to understand cricket. That they became entangled in criminal plots was usually accidental. Keith Waterhouse wrote six 45-minute episodes.
Director: Julian Amyes. Producer: Ron Craddock.

CHEERS
NBC (AMERICA) PRESENTED BY CHANNEL 4.
First broadcast (UK): 4 February 1983

One of the most popular and successful series in the history of television, CHEERS was the creation of Glen Charles, Les Charles and James Burrows. There were 275 episodes and Channel 4 showed the last on 13 June 1993. The series won 26 Emmy awards. Set in a friendly neighbourhood bar in Boston, the theme song 'Where Everybody Knows Your Name' summed up the atmosphere. It was based on a real Boston bar, the Bull and Finch, where the cast actually gathered together to watch the transmission of the final episode. The stories of love and heartache always left each series ending on a cliffhanger.

It is impossible to single out a principal character but continuity came from Sam Malone (Ted Danson), who originally owned the bar and served as barman. In the very first episode, Diane Chambers (Shelley Long) called in for a drink before flying off to Barbados with her fiancée to get married. When he opted to jilt her and return to his former wife, Sam gave her a job as a waitress. As romance blossomed between Sam and Diane, so too did hostility between Diane and Sam's long-serving barmaid and mother of many children, the hot-tempered Carla Tortelli (Rhea Perlman). The barman was Ernie Pantouso (Nicholas Colasanto), known as 'The Coach', who was Diane's only real friend. He was a former baseball star and had a grown-up daughter. Alas, Colasanto died after the third series. Before long, Diane had an affair with her analyst, Dr Frasier Crane (Kelsey Grammer). When she and Frasier went off to Europe to marry, Sam followed them and persuaded her against it. Sam, however, was a womaniser and kept a black book of phone numbers of available girls. Frasier returned and ultimately married Dr Lilith Sternin (Bebe Neuwirth), but towards the end of the series they separated. The closest Sam ever came to the altar was when Janet Eldridge (Kate Mulgrew) gave him an ultimatum.

A new bartender arrived in January 1985 (UK) in the form of Woody Boyd (Woody Harrelson), a dim-witted naif from the sticks of Indiana. He eventually found love and married rich girl Kelly (Jackie Swanson). In the meantime, Sam and Diane had set off for the altar but never made it. To recover, Sam went on a round-the-world sailing trip and returned six months later to find a new bar manager appointed, the efficient and profit-driven Rebecca How (Kirstie Alley). Her boss, and by then the owner of Cheers, was Evan Drake (Tom Skerritt) who had a yacht and a glamorous lifestyle. Rebecca eventually married Robin Colcord (Roger Rees), who lost all his money and ended up in prison. Towards the end of this marathon series, Rebecca accidentally burned down the bar and Sam had no insurance. In the very final episode, Diane returned and she and Sam once and for all declared their love for each other. It finished with yet another cliffhanger in that Sam was left deliberating whether or not to run off to California with her.

Equally as important as the staff of the bar were the regular customers: big, fat Norm Peterson (George Wendt) who hogged a beer, a barstool and a plate of nuts; Cliff Claven (John Ratzenberger), Norm's best friend and a master of weird trivia; and the aforementioned Frasier. There were many illustrious guest appearances including Emma Thompson, the Righteous Brothers, Serilyn Fenn, Senator Gary Hart and, in the final episode, Tom Berenger. The most famous of all, though, was John Cleese, who won an Emmy for his 1987 portrayal of marriage counsellor Simon Finch-Royce who concluded that Sam and Diane were unsuited.

CHEF!

BBC. First broadcast: 28 January 1993

Lenny Henry starred as Gareth Blackstock, flamboyant and zealous chef at Le Château Anglais, one of the smartest restaurants in Britain. He was loud and meticulous in gastronomic creativity and dreamed of owning his own place. He had a short fuse and his hot temper had his staff quaking. His permanently discontented wife Janice was played by Caroline Lee Johnson. Gareth had no morals when it came to paying the bills of his suppliers. As well as the seven-part series a one-off Christmas special was screened on 24 December the same year. *Writer: Peter Tilbury. Director: John Birkin. Producer: Charlie Hanson for APC/Crucial.*

CHELMSFORD 123

CHANNEL 4. First broadcast: 9 March 1988

Rory McGrath and Jimmy Mulville both wrote and starred in this history of life in Roman Britain, McGrath as Badvoc and Mulville as Aulus Paulinus. Other characters included Grasientus (Philip Pope), Functio (Robert Austin), Mungo (Noel Pearson), Blag (Howard Lew Lewis) and Gargamadua (Erika Hoffman). A first series of six was followed by five further episodes starting 9 January 1990.
Directors: John Stroud, Vic Finch. Producers: Adrian Bate and Denise O'Donoghue for Hat Trick Productions.

THE CHICAGO TEDDY BEARS

CBS (AMERICA) PRESENTED BY ITV.
First broadcast (UK): 25 August 1972

Set in the Chicago of the 1920s, Dean Jones starred as Linc McCray, the co-owner with his Uncle Latzi (John Banner) of a speakeasy, The Paradise Club. Linc's cousin Big Nick (Art Metrano) was the leader of the Chicago Teddy Bears, a team of would-be gangsters who made bungled and inept attempts to take the place over. The romantic interest in Linc's life was provided by Irene (Judy McConnell). Other leading characters in the 13-part series included Marvin (Marvin Kaplan), Duke (Mickey Shaughnessy), Dutch (Huntz Hall) and Leftie (Jamie Farr).

LAS CHICAS DE HOY EN DIA

SPAIN PRESENTED BY BBC.
First broadcast: 1 October 1990

Translated 'The Girls of Today', this was one of the few sitcoms to originate in Europe where the genre is hardly known. The show was about two girls sharing a flat in Madrid and looking for jobs. The BBC screened just one solitary episode as part of the DEF II strand.

CHICO AND THE MAN

NBC (AMERICA) PRESENTED BY BBC.
First broadcast (UK): 12 September 1974

The phenomenal success which this show enjoyed in the United States was not repeated when the BBC showed less than a third of the 75 episodes recorded, sporadic transmissions ending on 13 December 1975. Veteran actor Jack Albertson starred as Ed Brown, the 'Man' of the title. He was the bad-tempered, all-American owner of a garage in a Hispanic district of Los Angeles who was alternately helped and hindered by young Mexican–American Chico Rodriguez (Freddie Prinze). Chico developed a catchphrase, 'Looking' Gooood', and he became a hugely popular figure; but alas, Prinze found the adulation all too much and took his own young life while the series was still in its prime.

Music: José Feliciano. Producer: James Comack.

CHINTZ
GRANADA. First broadcast: 27 April 1981

Peg Lynch created this series of seven stories which were adapted by Alex Adams and Dilys Laye. Set in Cheshire, the situation was middle-class, middle-brow, almost middle-aged, bridge-playing lives centred on Kate and Rich Carter (Michele Dotrice and Richard Easton) and their neighbours Dottie and Fred Nelson (Dilys Laye and Christopher Benjamin).

Director: Eric Prytherch. Producer: Brian Armstrong.

CHRIS CROSS
CENTRAL. First broadcast: 18 March 1994

The setting for this children's serial in seven parts was Stansfield Academy, an international boys' boarding-school where Oliver Cross (Eugene Byrd) was the established kingpin among the students. When new boy Chris Hilton (Simon Fenton) arrived it was patently obvious that he would quickly win friends, so a rivalry with Cross was established. When the girls' school came to board at the academy the rivalry intensified. Among the girls was the headmaster's granddaughter Dinah McGee (Rachel Blanchard). The other two featured regulars were teacher Mr Rogers (Alan David) and an eccentric character called X (Timothy Douek).

Writer: DJ McHale.

CITIZEN JAMES
BBC. First broadcast: 24 November 1960

Sid James, fresh from his triumphs in HANCOCK'S HALF HOUR, starred in this series created by the same writing team, Ray Galton and Alan Simpson. Sid's character bore his own name and was a reformed fiddler who had become a doughty fighter of lost causes, the champion of the underdog who

invariably got bitten himself. Sidney Balmoral James was, at the same time, a self-employed parasite ever eager to punch authority on the nose, something of a middle-aged delinquent. In the first series of six programmes, Sid's sidekick and general factotum was William 'Bill' Kerr (Bill Kerr), who was much in awe of Sid and yearned to be an equal enemy of society. For many years, Sid had been engaged to Liz Fraser (Liz Fraser), the proprietress of a drinking club from which he had managed to skim off much of the profit. While Liz was fully aware of Sid's way of life, for some reason she remained anxious to marry him. Bill Kerr left the cast after the first series and when the second run of 12 began on 2 October 1961, the previously minor character of Charlie (Sydney Tafler), a fringe member of the bookmaking fraternity, was elevated to the post of Sid's henchman. A third and final run of 13 episodes got underway on 31 August 1962.

Music: Gordon Franks. Writers: Galton and Simpson, Sid Green and Dick Hills. Producers: Duncan Wood, John Street, Ronald Marsh.

CITIZEN SMITH
BBC. First broadcast: 12 April 1977

John Sullivan created Wolfie Smith (Robert Lindsay) from a character he had observed during the summer of 1968 in a pub called The Nelson Arms. Wolfie was the leader of the Tooting Popular Front, an army of half a dozen inept, would-be fascist political terrorists. Wolfie's battle cry was 'power to the people' and he was backed up by his best mate Ken (Mike Grady), who aspired to becoming a Buddhist monk. Wolfie's girlfriend Shirley was played by Lindsay's then wife, Cheryl Hall. Other army members included the violent Speed (George Sweeney) and the unfortunate Tucker (Tony Millan), who had a wife and nine children to support. Ken's girlfriend was Desiree (Anna Nygh). Shirley's hopelessly stupid mother was portrayed by Hilda Braid while no fewer than three actors, Artro Morris, Peter Vaughan and Tony Steedman, successively portrayed her father. Wolfie was forever in financial debt to the gangster landlord of the local pub, Harry Fenning (Stephen Greif). Aside from his political megalomania, Wolfie's other passions extended from the Beatles to Fulham Football Club. A pilot episode was screened first before a series of eight episodes began on 3 November 1977. Over four seasons there were 28 editions, the last one on 4 July 1980. There was also a Christmas

special on 31 December the same year.
Writer: John Sullivan. Producers: Dennis Main Wilson, Ray Butt.

CITY LIGHTS

BBC. First broadcast: 14 October 1986

Bob Black created and wrote this series which began on BBC Scotland and ran for 31 editions over five series ending on 4 April 1991. Gerard Kelly starred as Willie Melvin who worked in a bank but harboured dreams of becoming a writer. He was a totally respectable character, which was more than could be said for Chancer (Andy Gray), with whom he spent much of his time. Chancer always had some mind-boggling money-making racket on the go, one of which landed him with a short jail sentence. Willie's life at the bank was shared by Mr McLelland (John Bett) and Brian (Jonathan Watson). Other regulars floating through his world were his mum (Jan Wilson), widowed and on the lookout for a man; Irene (Elaine C Smith), who moved from one traumatic affair to another; and Tam (Iain McColl).
Director: Ron Bain. Producer: Colin Gilbert.

THE CLAIRVOYANT

BBC. First broadcast: 15 May 1986

Arnold Bristow (Roy Kinnear) was a used-car dealer who was knocked unconscious by a hit-and-run driver. When he came to, he had a previously dormant gift of clairvoyance. His business began to slump when he found his new powers made it difficult for him not to tell the truth. Those who endured the change which came over Arnold through this six-part series were Lily (Sandra Dickinson), Burma (Hugh Lloyd), Newton (Shaun Curry), Carmen (Carmel Cryan) and Dawn (Glynis Brooks).
Writer: Roy Clarke. Producer: Alan JW Bell.

CLANCY OF THE OUTBACK

BBC RADIO. First broadcast: 24 April 1963

This series of eight episodes was set in Australia at the time of the roaring gold rush days, the late 1850s. Dick Bentley starred as Clancy, a laconic character with a wry humour who became involved with all the types who followed the gold trail deep into the outback: cardsharps, publicans, dancing girls, blackmailers and cattle drovers. Clancy had a cheerful disdain for gold, recogni-

sing the heartbreaks it could bring and the restrictions on freedom that wealth would impose. Wallaby Creek was the town which was nearest to home for Clancy and from there he embarked on his adventures with Swaggy McCool (Reg Lye), a one-time shearers' cook. Clancy had a romantic attachment to Kitty Elliott (June Salter) who ran a small stage-coach company with her Ma (Margaret Christensen). The conflict for Clancy came in the guise of Sergeant Roper (David Nettheim) of the Wallaby Creek police who saw Clancy more as a threat to his own authority than as a help.
Writer: Michael Noonan. Producer: Charles Maxwell.

CLARENCE

BBC. First broadcast: 4 January 1988

Clarence Sale (Ronnie Barker) was a short-sighted and inept removal man and when he enlisted the help of ladies' maid Jane Travers (Josephine Tewson), his life was dramatically changed. They planned marriage but had a trial period living together and struggling to make ends meet. The bolster down the centre of the bed caused Clarence much sexual frustration. Six episodes were screened.
Writer: Bob Ferris. Producer: Mike Stephens.

CLASS ACT

CARLTON. First broadcast: 7 April 1994

Joanna Lumley, flavour of the first half of the 1990s, starred as Kate Swift in this comedy drama in seven hour-long episodes by Michael Aitkens. Kate was landed by her husband with debts and left to take the rap for his crooked activities. She was given a six-month jail sentence and while inside, she palled up with Australian cat burglar Gloria O'Grady (Nadine Garner). On release, they encountered wimpish and seedy tabloid journalist Jack Booker (John Bowe), whose evidence had helped to convict Kate in the first place. Kate, who formerly moved in high society circles, hated him on sight, but circumstance forced her into a volte-face and the three unlikelies teamed up in a struggle for survival. Richard Vernon played Kate's doddery old father, Sir Horace Mainwaring, and James Gaddas portrayed Det. Insp Latham.
Director: Jane Howell. Producer: Verity Lambert for Cinema Verity.

A CLASS BY HIMSELF

HTV. First broadcast: 13 September 1972

Richard Stilgoe created and wrote this series of six shows. Lord Bleasham (John Le Mesurier) was an eccentric and impoverished peer residing at his run-down seat in Somerset. All that remained of his former wealth was a Rolls-Royce and his chauffeur and butler, Clutton (Peter Butterworth). He also had a daughter, Joanna (Seretta Wilson). When they met a young student, Barnaby Locke (Richard Stilgoe), who was hitching a lift, he latched on to them and dreamed up various schemes intended to make money for the family.

Director: David Boisseau. Producer: Patrick Dromgoole.

CLAY'S COLLEGE

BBC RADIO. First broadcast: 13 June 1949

The college was billed as 'the fun and games academy' and the supervisor was Clay Keyes. The part of Polly the cook was played by Keyes' sister, Gladys Keyes, and the two of them were responsible for the script of the seven-part series. The old lodgekeeper was portrayed by Richard Goolden and the resident students were Hattie Jacques, Michael Moore, Hugh Morton and Deryck Guyler. Each week a guest star would be introduced as a 'new pupil'. There was a college orchestra under the direction of Frank Cantell.

Producer: Frederick Piffard.

THE CLIMBER

BBC. First broadcast: 20 January 1983

Harry Lumsdon (Robin Nedwell) had worked in a bakery for 16 years when he decided to take an IQ test. The resultant score of 166 encouraged him to apply his newly recognised brainpower to better himself and the company which employed him. Those who fell victim to his budding genius on a weekly basis for six editions were Ted (David Battley), Shirley (Jacqueline Tong) and Reg (David Williams).

Writer: Alex Shearer. Producer: Alan JW Bell.

THE CLITHEROE KID

BBC RADIO. First broadcast: 28 June 1957

Just 4ft 3in tall and weighing 5 stone, James Robertson Clitheroe became known to millions as the eternal naughty schoolboy Jimmy Clitheroe.

One of the all-time most popular radio shows, it ended after more than 280 editions on 13 August 1972. The earliest cast featured Jack Howarth and Violet Carson (both later to star in *Coronation Street*) with Judith Chalmers as Judith Clitheroe and Peter Sinclair as Grandad, a role he would play for many years. By the second year, Renée Houston had played a short run as Clitheroe's mother before Patricia Burke took over the part. Jimmy's sister Susan was first played by Judith Daugherty, then by Diana Day, and on 20 February 1961, Danny Ross joined the cast as Susan's gormless boyfriend, Alf Hall. Other important players were Leonard Williams who portrayed both family friend Theodore Craythorpe and neighbour Harry Whittle, and Mollie Sugden who took over as mother for a short while in 1964; and a variety of characters were interpreted over the years by Peter Goodwright, Tony Melody, Brian Trueman, Gordon Rollings, Deryck Guyler, Jack Watson, Joe Gladwin, Betty Alberge and Molly Weir. In the autumn of 1965 Mike Yarwood was a cast member.

Writers: Frank Roscoe, James Casey. Producers: Geoff Lawrence, James Casey.

CLOSE TO HOME

LWT. First broadcast: 1 October 1989

Brian Cooke created this series which starred Paul Nicholas as vet James Shepherd and Angharrad Rees as his ex-wife Helen. They had two children, Kate and Robbie (Lucy Benjamin and Andrew Read). Helen had married her second husband, the hot-blooded and often errant Frank de Angelo (Stephen Frost) whom she left from time to time. Other leading characters were James' assistant Rose (Jane Briers) and his colleague Tom (John Arthur), and the love interest in James' life came from Vicky (Pippa Guard) who had a farm. A first run of nine programmes preceded a second series beginning 16 September 1990.

Writers: Brian Cooke, Paul Minett, Brian Levison. Producers: Nic Phillips. Ian Hamilton.

CLUB NIGHT

BBC RADIO AND TELEVISION.
First broadcast: 1 September 1955

Although this show was first heard where it originated, in BBC North Region, in November 1951, it did not make it on to the national network until nearly four years later. The setting was a Northern working-men's club where the star was Middlesbrough comedian Dave Morris, who portrayed the irrepressible, loud-mouthed know-all who interfered in whatever activities members quietly pursued. He was also the club treasurer, officious and bossy from his portly frame, complete with cigar and straw hat. The stentorian club steward was played by Billy Smith and the secretary by Tom Harrison. The new member was Cedric (Joe Gladwin), whose favourite tipple was nothing stronger than a lemon-and-dash. Liverpool comedian Fred Ferris played 'The Wacker', a ubiquitous character who moved from room to room enquiring ''As 'e bin in?' of some mythical stranger who was never identified. In fact The Wacker's sole purpose was to scrounge a drink. With the ever loyal, simple-minded and bowler-hatted Cedric by his side, Morris had to take the insults of Snuffy Hargreaves (Frank Bass) and listen to the interminable, pointless stories of the old soldier from India, Pongo Bleasdale (Ronnie Taylor, later Geoffrey Banks, later Leonard Williams). Kenneth Connor appeared in several editions as 'Arry 'Awkins.

While the radio series ran for more than 70 editions until the autumn of 1958, the same cast moved to television where the club opened on 9 July 1957 for seven weeks and returned for a second season on 22 October the same year.

Writers included Dave Morris, Frank Roscoe, Rex Diamond, James Casey (writing as Cass James). Producers: John Ammonds, Ronnie Taylor.

COASTING
GRANADA. First broadcast: 26 October 1990

This series of seven one-hour comedy dramas starred Peter Howitt as streetwise Eddie Baker and James Purefoy as his banker brother Mike. They were both on the run following a business deal which had gone badly wrong. They landed in Blackpool where they took on an assortment of occupations and sought refuge with the Ryan family: Maria (June Barry), Danny (Barry Rutter), Julie (Sue Jenkins), Theresa (Sandy Hendrickse) and Seamus (Joe Marlow).

Writers: John Flanagan and Andrew McCulloch, Rod Beacham. Director: David Tucker. Producer: Verity Lambert for Cinema Verity.

COCKLES
BBC. First broadcast: 4 January 1984

Douglas Livingstone wrote this six-part comedy drama of 55-minute episodes. The setting was Cocklesea, a once thriving but since run-down resort to which Arthur Dumpton (James Grout) returned with memories of idyllic childhood holidays spent there. He found that his old boyhood pal Jacques du Bois (Norman Rodway) had failed in his bid to make a living as a landscape painter. Jacques was married to Gloria (Joan Sims), who ran the Sunnysides Guest House, and was something of a con-man, regularly deceiving Arthur as the latter tried to relive his lost youth. The reason for Arthur's return was that his wife had run off with his best friend and it later transpired that he and Gloria had been sweethearts many years earlier. Arthur was an amiable man of whom most Cocklesea residents took advantage.

Music: Marc Wilkinson. Director: Barry Davis. Producer: Ruth Boswell.

COLIN'S SANDWICH
BBC. First broadcast: 18 October 1988

By day Colin Watkins (Mel Smith) slaved for British Rail without appreciation. His alter ego was a writer by night. He was anti-yuppie and spurned his contemporaries who tried to goad him into joining their devil-may-care existence. Colin was university-educated but an arrogant under-achiever. He saw the world as utterly stupid and while he ranted and raved, he did nothing to effect any changes. This state of affairs prevailed throughout the first six-part series. A second run of six got underway on 12 January 1990 with Colin tasting fame through the publication of his first story. As he progressed in his career towards screenplays and the trappings of success, so his personal life moved along and girlfriend Jenny (Louisa Rix) ultimately became his wife. He duly swapped his sandwich for champagne and caviar.

Writers: Paul Smith and Terry Kyan. Producer: John Kilby.

COLONEL TRUMPER'S PRIVATE WAR
GRANADA. First broadcast: 15 September 1961

This six-part series was set in 1940. Dennis Price starred as Colonel Basil Trumper, one of the faceless, intrepid men who lurked in dark corners on behalf of Counter Intelligence. His close and furtive associate went under the name of Pan Malcov and was played by Warren Mitchell. Other officers

making a mockery of Intelligence were Lt Hastings (William Gaunt) and Private Hicks (George Tovey). As Britain stood alone in the summer of 1940, Colonel Trumper was her secret weapon.
Writers: Bill Craig, Barry Took, Dick Vosburgh and Hugh Woodhouse. Director: Stuart Latham. Producer: Peter Eton.

COME BACK MRS NOAH
BBC. First broadcast: 17 July 1978

Over a five-week period, Mrs Noah (Mollie Sugden) and Clive Cunliffe (Ian Lavender) and their fellow travellers were marooned in space aboard Britannia Seven and hurtling in orbit at 35,000 miles per hour. Frantic attempts were being made on Earth by the mission controller Garfield Hawk (Tim Barrett), his assistant Scarth Dare (Ann Michelle) and their technician (Jennifer Lonsdale) to bring them safely home. Alternately reducing and producing the hysteria of the circumstance were Carstairs (Donald Hewlett), Fanshawe (Michael Knowles) and Garstang (Joe Black). Meanwhile the world was kept abreast of events by the television reporter (Gorden Kaye).
Writers: Jeremy Lloyd and David Croft. Director: Bob Spiers. Producer: David Croft.

COME TO CHAR-LEE
BBC RADIO. First broadcast: 26 February 1953

Cheerful Charlie Chester starred in this 12-part series, ostensibly set in his flat where his valet was Cardew 'The Cad' Robinson. Michael Bentine played his eccentric neighbour Michael, a crazy historian who lived in the past. The love interest was supplied by Dora Bryan and Patricia Cutts, with Edna Fryer replacing Bryan for the last four editions. David Hughes and the Radio Revellers were on hand to provide the obligatory song. The last show was broadcast on 14 May 1953.
Writers: Pat Dunlop and Maurice Drake. Producer: Leslie Bridgmont.

COMING HOME
BBC. First broadcast: 27 February 1981

David Fitzsimmons was the writer of this six-part series. Donald Maddocks (Philip Jackson) was totally disorganised in his way of living and he was quite happy with it that way. Alas, his wife Sheila (Sharon Duce) did not share his contentment and matters regressed from bad to worse. Sheila's par-

ents were Muriel and Ted (Lynda Marchal and Roger Sloman).
Director: Martin Shardlow. Producer: Sydney Lotterby.

COMPANY AND CO.
BBC. First broadcast: 8 January 1980

Company and Co was a three-piece singing group comprising Samantha Company (Maria Aitken), Simon Company (Simon Williams) and Billy Hawkes (Philip Lowrie). Their manager was Barbara Harris (Isabel Dean). Between them all, they also ran a club and got into financial messes along the way. There were seven 50-minute programmes by various writers including John Peters and Carey Harrison.
Director: Douglas Camfield. Producer: John Sichel.

COMRADE DAD
BBC. First broadcast: 13 January 1986

In this seven-part series written by Ian Davidson and Peter Vincent, George Cole starred as Reg Dudgeon, a down-to-earth London opportunist who found himself living in 1999 in a city renamed Londongrad following a Russian coup, bloodlessly executed the previous year. The Dudgeon family comprised Treen (Barbara Ewing), Bob (David Garlick), Zo (Claire Toeman) and Gran (Doris Hare).
Producer: John Kilby.

CONFIDENTIALLY – THEY'RE OFF
BBC RADIO. First broadcast: 29 September 1957.

Taking the first word of the title from the signature tune of the star, Reg Dixon, this 12-part series by Eddie Maguire was set in a racehorse trainer's yard and described by the writer as 'a series of horse laughs!'.

Dixon himself was Reg, the stable lad who, though well-intentioned, got himself into various silly scrapes and situations. The other principal characters were Major Hunt the trainer (Francis de Wolff), his daughter Mary (Dilys Laye), Parker the head stable lad (Roger Snowdon), the Padre (T St John Barry), Ginger, an apprentice (Anthony Green) and Clara the cook (Patricia Hayes). A horse named Soapy and all other animals in the programmes were interpreted by Percy Edwards.
Producer: Alastair Scott Johnston.

CONJUGAL RITES

LWT. First broadcast: 16 April 1993

Gwen Taylor and Michael Williams starred as Gen and Barry, a couple married for 21 years, mature and sensible but feeling a need to reassess their matrimonial status. Gen was outraged when she learned that Barry had contemplated leaving her. Embroiled in the battle for survival were teenage children Philip (Stephen Moyer) and Gillian (Cordelia Bugeja), and Grandad (Alan MacNaughton). In the end they resorted to a marriage guidance counsellor (Chris Lang). Six episodes were transmitted in the first run and a second series began on 6 May 1994.

Writer: Roger Hall. Director: Mike Vardy. Producer: Humphrey Barclay for Humphrey Barclay Productions.

CONSTANT HOT WATER

CENTRAL. First broadcast: 10 January 1986

This series by Colin Pearson was a vehicle for Pat Phoenix to shrug off her role as Elsie Tanner in *Coronation Street*. She played the part of Phyllis Nugent, a very proper lady but a nosey old gossip who moved from inland to become the landlady of a Bridlington guest house. The landlady of the property next door, Miranda Thorpe (Prunella Gee), was not only much younger but had been there much longer. The pawns in their games of rivalry were Frank Osborne (Steve Adler), Norman Nugent (Roger Kemp), Jeff (Kevin Lloyd), Brian (Al Ashton), Paddy (Joe McParland) and Trevor (Mohammed Ashiq). Pat Phoenix died the same year as the six-part series began, on 17 September 1986.

Director: Bernard Thompson. Producer: Paula Burdon.

COPPERS END

ATV. First broadcast: 19 February 1971

Ted Willis created this send-up of a provincial police force. Bill Owen starred as Sgt Sam Short, a lazy, conniving copper who was more interested in making money than arrests. To that end, the one and only squad car was available for weddings, funerals and driving lessons. His colleagues at Coppers End strove to avoid everything from filling in forms to plodding the beat. They were PC Eddie Edwards (Richard Wattis), PC Chipper Collins (George Moon) and PC Dinkie Dinkworth (Royce

Mills). Oblivious to their schemes was Chief Superintendent Ripper (Kevin Brennan). Their world was suddenly turned upside down by the arrival of super-efficient policewoman Sgt Penny Pringle (Josephine Tewson).

Writers: David Cumming and Derek Collyer. Director: John Sichel. Producer: Shaun O'Riordan.

THE CORNER HOUSE

CHANNEL 4. First broadcast: 4 May 1987

Christopher Eymard and Robert Llewellyn wrote this six-part series as a starring vehicle for themselves. Gilbert (Eymard) and his assistant Dave (Llewellyn) ran a corner café which Sam (Martin Allen) of the fire brigade tried to close down for flagrant breaches of regulations. Regular characters were Dave's girlfriend Annie (Arabella Weir), delivery man and painter of nudes Pete (Aslie Pitter), Grace (Annie Hayes), Rosie (Rosy Fordham) and Mr Cobham (Howard Lew Lewis).

Director: Don Coutts. Producer: David Jones for RPM Productions.

CORRIGAN BLAKE

BBC. First broadcast: 25 April 1963

This series of six stories, created and written by Alun Owen, came from a single Owen play of the previous year, 'You Can't Win 'em All'. John Turner starred as Corrigan Blake and each story concerned his relationship with a different kind of girl, ranging from a Middle-East harem to the spectrum of social classes then to be found in London. Blake was a Cockney, a travelling man who had no regular occupation and no ties. He prized his freedom above all else and could never resist a pretty girl. He was joined on his adventures by aristocratic sidekick Wallace St John Smith (Paul Daneman). Among the girls who passed through Blake's life were Yootha Joyce, Geraldine Newman, Nyree Dawn Porter, Angela Douglas and Moira Redmond.

Director: James McTaggart. Producer: Elwyn Jones.

THE COSBY SHOW

NBC (AMERICA) PRESENTED BY CHANNEL 4.
First broadcast (UK): 20 January 1985.

With 208 editions over eight seasons, this is one of the all-time great success stories of the genre. Bill Cosby, master of the throwaway one-liner, starred as Dr Cliff Huxtable, a well-educated and seemingly wealthy paediatrician who with his loving family

Bill Cosby starred as Dr Cliff Huxtable in 208 editions of THE COSBY SHOW (Photo: Channel 4)

occupied a luxury home at 10 Stigwood Avenue, Brooklyn Heights, New York. His wife Clair (Phylicia Ayers-Allen for the first series, thereafter using her married name Phylicia Rashad) was a lawyer. The show charted the progress of their five children and the underlying longing of Cliff to have the house just for himself and Clair once more.

There were four daughters and one son. The eldest was Sondra (Sabrina Lebeauf), who married Elvin Tinderdale (Geoffrey Owens). Sondra, too, was a lawyer and Elvin a teacher. They presented the Huxtables with twin grandchildren, Winnie and Nelson. Huxtable son Theo (Malcolm-Jamal Warner) overcame dyslexia to study at New York University (Sondra had graduated from Princeton). Each time Theo took an apartment, circumstances financial or personal catapulted him back to the bosom of the family home. Second daughter Denise (Lisa Bonet) married Martin Kendal (Joseph C Philips), a divorced graduate of the naval academy who already had a small daughter Olivia (Raven-Symoné) by his first wife Paula. When Martin was posted abroad, Olivia became the ward of Cliff and Clair. Prior to her marriage, however, Denise had briefly attended Hillman College, which spawned the spin-off series A DIFFERENT WORLD. The real rebel among the Huxtable kids was Vanessa (Tempestt Bledsoe) who swept in and out of the home and relationships like a will o' the wisp, yet while rebellious was always loyal to family values. The baby of the family was daughter Rudy (Keshia Knight Pulliam), the absolute epitome of cheeky and cute Americana. Over the years she attracted many pre-teen admirers but her great protector and beau was friend and neighbour Kenny (Deon Richmond), who saw all the others off with aplomb. Midway through the series the Huxtables were joined by a distant cousin from the wrong side of the sticks, 17-year-old Pam Turner (Erika Alexander) who came to live with them. Other regular characters included Cliff's parents, Russell and Anna (Earle Hyman and Clarice Taylor).

Channel 4 began transmissions with the pilot show and the first of the subsequent series began on 15 February of the same year. The final show was seen on 2 January 1994 when Theo graduated and planned to fly to Singapore to take Olivia to join Denise and Martin. In that extended edition, Cliff finally but erroneously thought he had fixed the chimes of the doorbell.

Creators: Ed Weinberger, Michael Leeson and William Cosby Jr. Principal director: Jay Sandrich. Producers: Terry Guarnieri, Marcy Carsey, Tom Werner.

COUNTRY MATTERS

BBC RADIO. First broadcast: 27 April 1994

Dave (Jonathan Tafler) and Cathy (Lesley Sharp) opted to abandon their city life for the idyll of country pastures in the village of Drayton Warlock. Their expectations were different from the realities they encountered. There were six episodes.
Writer: Mike Coleman. Producer: Ann Jobson.

THE COURTSHIP OF EDDIE'S FATHER

ABC (AMERICA) PRESENTED BY ITV.
First broadcast (UK): 24 August 1973

Bill Bixby starred as widower Tom, whose precocious six-year-old son Eddie (Brandon Cruz) was on the lookout for a suitable new wife for his dad. They had a housekeeper, Mrs Livingstone (Miyoshi Umeki).
Music: Harry Nilsson. Producer: James Komack

COWBOYS

THAMES. First broadcast: 3 September 1980

This series, created and written by Peter Learmouth, concerned a building firm mismanaged by Joe Jones (Roy Kinnear). His workers were Geyser (Colin Welland), Wobbly Ron (David Kelly) and Eric (James Wardroper). They did not work for Jones by choice, nor did he employ them by choice. It was just that nobody else would employ them and nobody else would work for Jones. The first run of six episodes was swiftly followed by a second six starting on 20 November the same year. By this time Joe had got himself a personal assistant in the shape of Muriel Bailey (Janine Duvitski). A final series of six began on 8 December 1981.
Producer: Michael Mills.

CRIME, GENTLEMEN, PLEASE!

BBC RADIO. First broadcast: 26 February 1948

Max Kester wrote this comedy thriller in eight episodes in which Naunton Wayne and Basil Radford starred as sleuths Berkeley and Bulstrode, who set off as their usual impeccable English gentlemen down avenues swimming with red herrings. Other characters included Millie (Dora Bryan), Lettice (Roberta Huby) and Sam (Wilfred Babbage).
Producer: Vernon Harris.

CROOKS' TOUR

BBC RADIO. First broadcast: 23 February 1940

The characters Caldicot (Naunton Wayne) and Charters (Basil Radford) were first encountered in Alfred Hitchcock's 1938 film *The Lady Vanishes*. The writers of that film script, Frank Launder and Sidney Gilliatt, joined with radio writers John Watt and Max Kester to build a series around them. Caldicot and Charters were silly-ass, cricket-loving Englishmen travelling abroad. The first episode of six established the pair in the Arabian Desert on their way back to England from a world tour. Their charabanc broke down, they met a Sheikh (Alan Wheatley) who turned out to have been at school with them, and rode in triumph into Baghdad on camels. There they were mistaken for spies and their adventure began. There was a second series of six episodes starting in August the following year. That time the Sheikh was played by Douglas Young. See also CHARTERS AND CALDICOT.
Producer: Vernon Harris.

CROWTHER'S CROWD

BBC RADIO. First broadcast: 21 September 1963

Only three performers appeared in its 14 editions. They were students set on reforming the world: Leslie (Leslie Crowther) studying medicine, drama student June (June Whitfield) and Ronnie (Ronnie Barker) who was a trainee at a school for chefs. They met in the El Aroma coffee bar in Bloomsbury and tackled a different topic each week. Music was provided by Mickie Most and the Minute Men.
Writers: George Evans and Derek Collyer. Producer: Alastair Scott Johnston.

THE CUCKOO WALTZ

GRANADA. First broadcast: 27 October 1975

This series, created by Geoffrey Lancashire, began with recently married Chris and Fliss – short for Felicity – Hawthorne (David Roper and Diane Keen), poor but happy, living in their run-down home with a deckchair marked 'Property of Prestatyn UDC' and little else. When Chris' rich friend Gavin Rumsey (Lewis Collins) turned up fresh from a broken marriage with a vanload of expensive furniture, it seemed the ideal solution all round for him to move in as their lodger. With Chris rather doleful and unexciting and Fliss pretty and vibrant, it seemed only a matter of time before the dashing and handsome Gavin would sweep her into his king-size bed, but he never did. Gavin's financial flamboyance grated on Chris and Fliss, saddled with raising twins, as they scrimped and saved to afford modern essentials like a washing-machine.

The threesome continued through two further series in 1976 and 1977, at the end of which Chris hoped and prayed that Gavin would take his liberated ideas of sexual freedom off to Greece and marry his new girlfriend Arianna (Stassia Stakis). There then followed a break of two and a half years before a fourth and final series began in June 1980. This time the Hawthornes had a new lodger, Adrian Lockett (Ian Saynor), and Chris was working as a newspaper reporter. Although at first Chris thought it a big joke, matters grew in intensity as Adrian fell head over heels in besotted love for Fliss. Over the years, the couple shared their confidences with friends Connie Wagstaffe (Clare Kelly) and Austen Tweedale (John McKelvey).

Music: Derek Hilton. Writers: Geoffrey Lancashire, John G Temple. Directors: Bill Gilmour, Brian Mills, Douglas Argent. Producers: Bill Gilmour, Brian Armstrong, John G Temple.

CUFFY

CENTRAL. First broadcast: 13 March 1983

In this spin-off from SHILLINGBURY TALES, Bernard Cribbins continued his role as the incorrigible village tinker Cuffy, with a scruffy old coat and cap and a scent for mischief. He lived in a caravan. Other village characters in the six programmes included Jake (Jack Douglas), Mandy (Linda Hayden), Reverend Norris (Nigel Lambert) and Mrs Simpkins (Diana King).

Music: Ed Welch. Writer: Francis Essex. Producers: Chris Baker, Paul Harrison.

CURRY AND CHIPS

LWT. First broadcast: 21 November 1969

This controversial show, which ran for just one six-part series, was written by Johnny Speight. It was set in a factory called Lillicrap Ltd where the liberal-minded foreman was portrayed by Eric Sykes. Among the work force was Pakistani immigrant Kevin O'Grady, known to all as Paki-Paddy. He was played by Spike Milligan who blacked-up for the role. Alongside him as his bench-mate was a Cockney-born black man, played by Kenny Lynch, and Smellie (Sam Kydd). Others in the factory were portrayed by Fanny Carby, Geoffrey Hughes and Norman Rossington. Speight's use of what he called 'realistic' factory language drew as much public protest from unsuspecting viewers as did the issues of racial integration.

Producer: Keith Beckett.

Fliss (Diane Keen) looks thoughtful while Chris (David Roper) has time for both breakfast and the newspaper in THE CUCKOO WALTZ (Photo: Granada Television)

DAD'S ARMY

BBC. First broadcast: 31 July 1968

While most sitcoms rely on the interplay between two or four central characters, Jimmy Perry and David Croft are the British masters at creating and writing situations for ensemble playing. Their credits include IT AIN'T HALF HOT MUM, HI-DE-HI!, and YOU RANG M'LORD, but it is DAD'S ARMY which remains their finest achievement. They wrote 81 editions over ten seasons, ending on 13 November 1977.

The setting was the imaginary South Coast town of Walmington-on-Sea, not far from Eastbourne, during the Second World War. Local bank manager George Mainwaring appointed himself commanding officer of the town's Home Guard platoon with the rank of Captain. He was pompous, proud and pernickety. He had a wife, Elizabeth, who was never seen. His platoon was made up of a variety of unlikely fighting men, and his second-in-command, Sergeant Arthur Wilson (John Le Mesurier), was also his chief clerk at the bank. The softly-spoken Wilson issued commands like invitations and never quite lived up to Mainwaring's expectations. Third in the line of command was local butcher Lance-Corporal Jack Jones (Clive Dunn), an old soldier who had served in Africa and 'fought the Fuzzy-Wuzzies'. He had mastered the use of the bayonet and always advised Mainwaring that 'they don't like it up 'em'. Jones had his own style of drill and was always a fraction of a second behind the others. His butcher's van was converted for platoon manoeuvres and his catchphrase became 'Permission to speak, sir'. There were nudges and winks as to how rich widow Mrs Fox (Pamela Cundell) seemed invariably to have a little extra meat in her larder, but all was revealed in the last episode when she and 'Jonesie' married.

The Privates on parade ranged from 17-year-old Frank Pike (Ian Lavender) to the positively geriatric Charles Godfrey (Arnold Ridley). Pike was too young to be called up and he was a clerk at Mainwaring's bank. He always turned out wearing a muffler at the insistence of his mum, the redoubtable Mrs Mavis Pike (Janet Davies). Pike referred to Sergeant Wilson as Uncle Arthur although he was not really his uncle. Wilson clearly had a relationship with Mrs Pike and there was underlying suspicion that he might be Frank's father. Frank's naif manner led to his being called 'stupid boy' by Captain Mainwaring at each and every irritation. Private Godfrey, on the other hand, was really only in the platoon because the house he shared with his two rarely seen maiden sisters, Dolly and Cissy, was strategically placed should the enemy ever land. His frequent need to 'go to the lavatory' got on Mainwaring's nerves. Private James Walker (James Beck who died prematurely in August 1973) was a spiv and a jester who always managed to have a few black market 'extras' about his person. Through devious means he had avoided conscription into the forces proper and intended to keep it that way. The elderly village undertaker, Private Frazer (John Laurie), was a dour Scot who would pessimistically forecast the failure of every operation – 'We're

The last line of defence in Walmington-on-Sea, DAD'S ARMY. Left to right: Sergeant Wilson, Captain Mainwaring, Private Godfrey, Lance-Corporal Jones, Private Frazer, Private Pike (Photo: Copyright © BBC)

doomed, we're doomed' – usually to be followed by Jones' 'Don't panic, Mr Mainwaring!'.

For drill and strategic planning, the platoon assembled at the Church Hall which they were forced to share with the mild mannered, rather effeminate vicar (Frank Williams) and his more aggressive verger (Edward Sinclair). Most serious opposition to Mainwaring's authority came from chief ARP Warden Bert Hodges (Bill Pertwee), the Walmington-on-Sea greengrocer. He mocked and ridiculed the Home Guard's efforts and would often interrupt their tensest moments with his familiar cry: 'Put that light out!' Other characters who made lesser but nonetheless significant contributions included Welsh newspaper reporter Private Cheeseman (Talfryn Thomas), the rather podgy Private Sponge (Colin Bean) and the Colonel of the nearest Army post (Robert Raglan). The theme song, 'Who Do You Think You Are Kidding Mr Hitler', was written by Jimmy Perry, sung by Bud Flanagan and played by the Band of the Coldstream Guards.
Directors: David Croft, Harold Snoad, Bob Spiers. Producer: David Croft.

BBC RADIO. First broadcast: 26 January 1974

Perry and Croft's greatest TV creation was adapted for radio by Harold Snoad and Michael Knowles. The television cast replayed their roles in a first series of 20 episodes and a second series of 26 which got underway on 16 March 1976, ending on 7 September the same year.
Producer: John Dyas.

DANGER – MARMALADE AT WORK

THAMES. First broadcast: 12 March 1984

This was a nine-part sequel to the 1982 series EDUCATING MARMALADE. Having appeared before a Judge (Max Wall), the incorrigible Marmalade Atkins (Charlotte Coleman) was placed in the hands of social worker Wendy Wooley (Elizabeth Estensen) who found her a succession of jobs, not one of which she could hold for an episode.
Writer: Andrew Davies. Director: John Stroud. Producer: Marjorie Sigley.

DANGER – MEN AT WORK

BBC RADIO. First broadcast: 11 May 1939

This was probably the first attempt at surreal humour in British broadcasting and some claim it paved the way for THE GOON SHOW. Max Kester devised the series in which the dignified, statuesque and exceedingly large widow Mrs Ponsonby (Doris Nichols), battle-axe extraordinaire, hired a bunch of con-men to effect repairs at her various properties. With the ever-present assistance of the double-talking Greek Nikolas Ridikoulos (Jacques Brown), the first set of swindlers were comedians Van and Allen; in a second series starting 1 December 1939 they were played by Jack Train and George Moon; and the third series, from 2 April 1940, established the best-remembered crooked characters, Duckweed and Eggblow, played by Haver and Lee. A fourth run began on 5 June 1940. After the war, two attempts were made to get the show going again but it proved less successful. The last short series was heard from 25 March 1947. Eggblow had disappeared and Clay Keyes came in as Duckweed while the rest of the cast remained unchanged. A new character was Colonel Swivelhead (Charlie Irwin) and Mrs Ponsonby had a companion played by Susan Scott.
Producer: Max Kester.

THE DARLING BUDS OF MAY

YTV. First broadcast: 7 April 1991

Bob Larbey adapted the novels of HE Bates into the first series of six one-hour episodes. Thereafter, over two Christmas specials and two subsequent six-part series ending 5 April 1993, other writers including Richard Harris and Paul Wheeler shared the writing credits. The Larkin family lived in a Kent village (actually filmed in Puckley) in the early post-war years. Pop Larkin (David Jason) was a junk dealer with a heart of gold, married to the irrepressible Ma Larkin (Pam Ferris) and raising their family according to their own standards. Their adventures took them across the Channel to France for a holiday and had them raising hundreds of pigs and committing social gaffes at every turn. The eldest Larkin child, Mariette (Catherine Zeta Jones), fell in love with and married Inland Revenue worker Charley (Philip Franks). Other principal characters included Primrose (Julie Davies, later Abigail Romison), Petunia (Christina Giles), Zinnia (Katherine Giles), Victoria (Stephanie Ralph), Edith Pilchester (Rachel Bell), Ernest Bristow (Michael Jayston) and the Brigadier (Moray Watson).
Directors included David Giles, Robert Tronson, Rodney Bennett. Producers: Robert Banks Stewart, Peter Norris, Simon Lewis.

A DATE WITH NURSE DUGDALE

BBC RADIO. First broadcast: 21 April 1944

One of schoolmaster Arthur Marshall's female creations, Nurse Dugdale blew through hospital wards with her piercingly bright voice crying at one and all: 'Out of my way, dears, out of my way instantly!' In this six-part series she was in the company of Sister Parkinson (Marjorie Westbury) and in a sequel series, NURSE DUGDALE TAKES THE AIR, in November 1945, Dorothy Carless portrayed Probationer Nurse Muspratt.

Writer: Arthur Marshall. Producer: David Yates Mason.

THE DAYS AND NIGHTS OF MOLLY DODD

USA PRESENTED BY BBC.
First broadcast (UK): 15 July 1990

Molly Dodd (Blair Brown) was an attractive divorcée who led a hectic life as a real-estate broker in New York. Her former husband Fred Dodd (William Converse-Roberts) was a world-weary musician who was always around. Molly lived alone in a Manhattan apartment where she and the elevator man Davey (James Green) did not see eye to eye on anything. She had a nagging mother Florence (Allyn Ann McLerie) and a boss Steve Cooper (Peter MacNichol) who was madly in love with her. The shows were unusual for American sitcom in that they were made without an audience or canned laughter track. The writer, Jay Tarses, was also the director and producer and occasionally appeared himself as Molly's garbage collector.

DEAD ERNEST

CENTRAL. First broadcast: 15 February 1982

This series of seven shows was written by John Stevenson and Julian Roach. Andrew Sachs starred as Ernest Springer who celebrated a win on the football pools, got struck in the eye by a champagne cork and woke up to find himself in Heaven. His celestial colleagues were Archangel Derek (Ken Jones), who was henpecked by Archangel Doreen (Janet Rawson), and Cherub Fred (Harry Fowler). Ernest tried to get back to Earth, where Zena Walker played Edna Springer and Arthur and Alice were portrayed by Bill Waddington and Gretchen Franklin.

Director: Alan Wallis. Producers: Tony Charles and Allan McKeown.

DEAR DOTTY

BBC. First broadcast: 13 July 1954

These six programmes, shown fortnightly, starred Avril Angers as Dotty Binns. Dotty held a menial post on the staff of an upmarket magazine, *Lady Fare.* She found herself in all kinds of trouble in her quest to win promotion to journalist. Regular characters involved in her adventures were Mr Tibbett (Jack Melford), Ian Prendergast (Cecil Brock), Margo Fairfax (Naomi Chance) and William (David Kinsey).

Writers: Sid Colin and Talbot Rothwell. Producer: Bill Ward.

Schoolteacher John (right, Ralph Bates) at the 1–2–1 club with Kirk (Peter Blake), Kate (Belinda Lang) and Ralph (Peter Denyer) in DEAR JOHN (Photo: Copyright © BBC)

DEAR JOHN . . .

BBC. First broadcast: 17 February 1986

Ralph Bates starred as John, a schoolteacher who one day returned home to read a note from his wife telling him she had run off with his former best friend. Still in his mid-30s, John found himself living in a west London bedsitter, confused and indecisive and lacking the dynamism to get himself back on his feet. In a desperate move to find a soul mate, he joined the 1–2–1 club where he met a sequence of ghastly people, all pretending to be what they were not, and each a little if not a lot pathetic. While John was never a wimp, he did have feelings of inadequacy based on the fact that the best friend with whom his wife Wendy had cleared off was a 6ft 2in physical training instructor. A first series of seven programmes was followed by a second run of six which got underway on 7 September 1987. The final episode was a Christmas special seen on 21 December that year. There would possibly have been more had Ralph Bates not been ill and died on 27 March 1991. See also DEAR JOHN: USA.

Writer: John Sullivan. Producer: Ray Butt.

DEAR JOHN: USA

USA PRESENTED BY BBC.
First broadcast(UK): 4 June 1989

In a classic case of coals to Newcastle John Sullivan's format for DEAR JOHN was sold to America where the shows were remade and then sold back to the BBC. John Lacey (Judd Hirsch) was deserted by his wife who ran off with his best friend. To help him through the resultant trauma, he joined the One-To-One singles support group. Regular characters included Kate (Isabella Hofmann), Louise (Jane Carr), Ralph (Harry Groener) and Kirk (Jere Burns). Sullivan himself actually wrote some of the episodes.

DEAR LADIES

BBC. First broadcast: 15 March 1983

Patrick Fyffe and George Logan brought their character creations Dr Evadne Hinge and Dame Hilda Bracket to television after successful radio shows THE ENCHANTING WORLD OF HINGE AND BRACKET and THE RANDOM JOTTINGS OF HINGE AND BRACKET. Again they lived in their make-believe Suffolk village of Stackton Tressel (actually filmed in the Cheshire village of Great Budworth) with its olde world English charm,

cricket on the green, tea with cucumber sandwiches and musical soirées. There were three series, each of six programmes, ending on 3 November 1984.

Writer: Gyles Brandreth. Producer: Mike Stephens.

DEAR MOTHER – LOVE ALBERT

YTV. First broadcast: 15 September 1969

Rodney Bewes created, co-wrote and co-produced this series with Derrick Goodwin. Bewes also starred as Albert Courtney, a young man away from home who had just become a marketing consultant for a confectionery company. Each week he wrote a letter to his mother. The comedy came from the difference between the contents of the letter and the realities of his life. Garfield Morgan portrayed Albert's boss, Mr AC Strain, and the female interest was provided by Sheila White as Vivian McKewan and Geraldine Newman as Vivian's mother. The shows ran for a second series the following year. In the third series in 1971, Albert had moved into a new flat which he shared with two very attractive young girls, Frances Ross (Mary Land) and Leslie Willis (Luan Peters). This arrangement was not to the liking of his new fiancée, Doreen Bissel (Liz Gebhardt), nor his future mother-in-law (Amelia Bayntun). See also ALBERT.

Theme Music: Mike Hugg.

THE DEBBIE REYNOLDS SHOW

NBC (AMERICA) PRESENTED BY BBC.
First broadcast (UK): 10 January 1970

Film star Debbie Reynolds starred in this 26-part series created and produced by Jess Oppenheimer who had also been responsible for I LOVE LUCY. Reynolds played Debbie Thompson, a giddy housewife who trundled from one disaster to another as she tried to impress and surprise her long-suffering but ever-loyal husband Jim (Don Chastain). Debbie's sister Charlotte (Patricia Smith) and her inept brother-in-law Bob (Tom Bosley) lived next door, from which address their 11-year-old son Bruce (Bobby Riha) ran a community newspaper.

DEMOB

LWT. First broadcast: 15 October 1993

This six-part comedy drama was set immediately after the end of the Second World War and followed the story of two men from different backgrounds, Lance Cpl Ian Deasey (Griff Rhys Jones) and Captain Dick Dobson (Martin Clunes), who had teamed up as a comedy double-act while in the army. Having been a success in the Naafi canteen and survived all that Rommel could fire at them, they returned to Civvy Street to try and make the grade in show business. Initially they found a very austere London and briefly went back to their old jobs before the lure of the bright lights proved irresistible. In no time they were on stage at the Blue Parrot Club, a seedy Soho nightspot. Other principal characters included Janet Deasey (Amanda Redman), Rudy Lorimer (James Faulkner), Hedda (Samantha Janus), Marshall Gould (George Melly), Edith (Liz Fraser) and Alan Deasey (Luke Marcel). However, it is likely that the series may be best remembered for the final television appearance by Les Dawson, who was cast as entertainer Morton Stanley but died during a break in recording on 10 June 1993.

Writers: Dean Lemmon and Andrew Montgomery. Director: Rob Knights. Producer: Adrian Bate.

DESMOND'S

Channel 4. First broadcast: 5 January 1989

At the time of writing this was Channel 4's most successful home-grown sitcom. It was the creation of Trix Worrell who wrote most of the episodes and went on to direct several himself. The setting was a Peckham barber's shop presided over by Desmond Ambrose (Norman Beaton) and his wife Shirley (Carmen Munro). Desmond's was not just a place for a haircut. It was the meeting place for Peckham's West Indian philosophers like Porkpie (Ram John Holder). Indeed, little haircutting was seen as a variety of relations and ancillary characters passed through for tea or to gossip, or simply to pass the time of day. They put up with grumpy Desmond and loved his long-suffering wife who was always able to rustle up refreshment at any hour of the day. The principal characters included Matthew (Christopher Asante, later Gyearbuor Asante), Sean (Justin Pickett), Gloria (Kim Walker), Louise (Lisa Geoghan), Tony (Dominic Keating), Michael (Geoff Francis), Lee (Robbie Gee), Mandy (Matilda Thorpe) and Beverley (Joan Ann Maynard). Over five series to 20 December 1993 there were 58 episodes, with a sixth series commissioned.

Directors: Mandie Fletcher, Nic Phillips, Charlie Hanson, Trix Worrell, Jan Sargent, David Askey, Ian McLean. Producer: Humphrey Barclay for Humphrey Barclay Productions.

Fun and games for Norman Beaton and the DESMOND'S crew at the barber's shop in South London (Photo: Channel 4)

THE DETECTIVES

BBC. First broadcast: 27 January 1993

The unlikely pairing of Jasper Carrott and Robert Powell began as a series of sketches in CANNED CARROTT in 1990. They played two clumsy detectives, Bob Lewis and Dave Briggs, who botched every case they handled, to the exasperation of Superintendent Cottam (George Sewell). They were elevated to this full series in their own right which began with a six-week run and returned for a second series which ended on 6 April 1994.

Writers: Steve Knight and Mike Whitehill. Producer: Ed Bye for Celador.

DEVENISH

GRANADA. First broadcast: 15 July 1977

Dinsdale Landen starred as Arthur Prufrock Devenish, chief games deviser of Universal Passtimes Ltd, manufacturers of toys and games. Devenish had big ideas, especially about his own importance, but in actual fact he was an interfering busybody who irritated most of his colleagues. The chairman of the company was Admiral Wallow (Geoffrey Chater) and the managing director was Hugh Fitzjoy (Terence Alexander) who had a secretary Audrey Pilbeam (Doran Godwin). The company secretary was Neville Liversedge (Geoffrey Bayldon). On the side of Devenish were his own secretary Angela Nutall (Veronica Roberts) and his two henchmen, Wilf Braithwaite (Roger Kane) and Rog Box (John Kane). The series, created and written by Anthony

Couch, began a second run on 3 April 1978. There were 13 shows altogether.
Theme music: Johnny Pearson. Director: Brian Mills. Producer: John G Temple.

DIAL DORIS
BBC RADIO. First broadcast: 29 January 1941

Doris Hare starred in six episodes as a lady running a bureau which claimed to be able to answer or supply anything whatsoever. For a small fee, nothing was too much trouble. She was always willing but totally inept. She muddled – albeit with the best intentions – and stuck to her principle never to turn anything down, however bizarre the request. That her efforts ended in disaster was rarely her fault. In her bureau she had help from an assistant (Jack Train) and an office boy (Sonny Jenks).
Writer: Ted Kavanagh. Producer: Michael North.

DIANA
NBC (AMERICA) PRESENTED BY BBC.
First broadcast (UK): 23 October 1973

One wonders why Diana Rigg had to go to America to make her first sitcom? A critic, Jack Edmund Nolan, wrote: 'One marvels at American TV's capacity to reduce even the best to its level.' Diana Rigg played Diana Smythe, an English divorcée, who landed in New York to take up her career as a fashion illustrator. Her friends and colleagues in 13 episodes were Norman and Norma Brodrick (David Sheiner and Barbara Barrie) and Howard (Richard B Schull).

THE DIARY OF A 20TH CENTURY VAMPIRE
BBC RADIO. First broadcast: 29 October 1993

Writer Joe Turner chronicled the adventures of trainee vampire Eloise (Louise Lombard), her vampire teacher from Transylvania Auntie Lucretia (Joanne Kanska), and Eloise's boyfriend Wayne (William Ivory). Six episodes were heard.
Producer: Elizabeth Anstee.

DICK AND THE DUCHESS
MGM PRESENTED BY ITV.
First broadcast (UK): 30 April 1958

This series was produced at Britain's Elstree studios and starred Patrick O'Neal as Dick Starrett, an American insurance investigator based in London.

Starrett's wife Jane was the daughter of an English earl and he called her The Duchess. She was portrayed by Hazel Court. Jane was a nagger, a lousy driver, a nosey-parker, and had a tendency to overspend. Dick's work took him among the shady characters of the London underworld. Jane had a hankering for adventure and refused to be left out. In spite of her good intentions she always seemed to make a hash of whatever she touched. Richard Wattis played Dick's English colleague Peter Jamison.
Writers: Dennis Freeman, Harvey Bullock and Ray Allen. Producers: George Fowler and Sheldon Reynolds.

THE DICK VAN DYKE SHOW
CBS PRESENTED BY BBC.
First broadcast (UK): 4 July 1963

One of the fondest remembered comedy titles of the 1960s, this series was created by Carl Reiner and starred Dick Van Dyke as Rob Petrie, head scriptwriter of 'The Alan Brady Show'. Rob lived at home in New York with his wife Laura (Mary Tyler Moore), a former dancer, and their young son Richie (Larry Matthews) who was five years old when the series began. The comedy arose from both Petrie's domestic and professional situations. At work he had two other writers working with him, the tough-talking, man-chasing Sally Rogers (Rose Marie) and the wisecracking Buddy Sorrel (Morey Amsterdam). The producer of 'The Alan Brady Show' was Melvin Cooley (Richard Deacon). Brady himself made only infrequent appearances, but when he did, he was played by Carl Reiner and viewers only ever saw the back of his head. Other regular cast members were Ann Morgan and Jerry Paris, who portrayed the Petries' next-door neighbours. The series ran for 158 episodes in the USA from 1961 to 1966, picking up Emmy awards in 1964 and 1965.
Producers included Sheldon Leonard and Jerry Paris.

THE DICKIE HENDERSON SHOW
AR. First broadcast: 14 November 1960

One-time Hollywood child star Dickie Henderson, son of Yorkshire comedian Dick Henderson, starred as an amiable entertainer whose adventures fluctuated between his domestic life and the world of show business. The series notched up its 100th show in December 1963 and continued annually until 1968 when the last show was transmitted on 20 March. Dickie was married to Jane (June Laverick 1960–67, Isla Blair for the 12 programmes in 1968). They had a son, Richard (John Parsons 1960–62, Danny Grover 1963 onwards), who was eight years old in 1960. Dickie had a musical director throughout the series, the disorganised, sloppy and eternally late for appointments Jack Meadows, played by Canadian actor Lionel Murton. The shows made much use of guest stars.

Writers included Jimmy Grafton, Jeremy Lloyd, Stan Mars and Eric Newman. Producer: Bill Hitchcock.

A DIFFERENT WORLD

NBC (AMERICA) PRESENTED BY CHANNEL 4.
First broadcast (UK): 22 September 1988

In a spin-off from THE COSBY SHOW, Denise Huxtable (Lisa Bonet), second of the Huxtable children, went off to Hillman College for her sophomore year where she instantly clashed with her new room-mate, Jaleesa Vinson (Dawnn Lewis). Denise's parents, Cliff and Clair (Bill Cosby and Phylicia Rashad), made frequent visits – which was hardly surprising as Cosby's company owned the show! More than 100 episodes have been produced and are still being seen at the time of writing. After the initial series Denise failed to return to college thus allowing other characters to be moved into the forefront. Along with Jaleesa, the principal players became tutor Dwayne Wayne (Kadeem Hardison) and deep-drawling southerner Whitley Gilbert (Jasmine Guy). By 1991 Whitley was spending the holidays contemplating Dwayne's protestations of love and by the advent of the sixth series on 29 December 1993 (UK) they were returning from their honeymoon as newly-weds. Other significant parts as the story progressed were Stevie Rallen (Loretta Devine), JT Rallen (O'Shay), Maggie Lauten (Marisa Tomei), Freddie Brooks (Cree Summer), Ron Johnson (Darryl Bell) and Kimberley Reese (Charlene Brown).

Creator: William Cosby Jr. Producers: Marcy Carsey and Tom Werner.

DIFF'RENT STROKES

NBC (AMERICA) PRESENTED BY ITV.
First broadcast (UK): 2 September 1980

Widower Phillip Drummond (Conrad Bain), a white millionaire, fostered two orphaned black boys, Arnold and Willis Jackson (Gery Coleman and Todd Bridges). He took them from the ghetto to his own luxurious home. There he raised them alongside his own daughter Kimberley (Dana Plato). In this he was assisted by his housekeeper, Mrs Garrett (Charlotte Rae). The long-running series was created by Jeff Harris and Bernie Kukoff.

DISCORD IN THREE FLATS

BBC RADIO. First broadcast: 7 July 1962

This series was set in a large house in Kensington, 64 Cambridge Square, divided into flats. The landlord was solicitor Henry Ashford (Jack Hulbert). Occupying the flat above his own were Oscar and Katie Hendrick (Vic Oliver and Cicely Courtneidge), on the very top floor lived Ashford's fiancée, Miss Amanda Studd (Joan Benham), and in the basement were the caretaker (David Graham) and his daughter Patricia (Rosamund Knight). The eight shows invariably revolved around disharmony between landlord and tenants.

Writer: Bob Block. Producer: Alastair Scott Johnston.

DISHONEST TO GOODNESS

BBC RADIO. First broadcast: 22 September 1963

This series, created and written by Brad Ashton, starred Bernard Bresslaw and John Bluthal as two confidence-trickster brothers. So incompetent were they, however, that none of their elaborate and felonious schemes ever made them any richer. Other characters, where required, were portrayed by Bob Todd, Louis Mansi, Pamela Manson and others.

Producer: John Browell.

DIVIDED WE STAND

BBC. First broadcast: 10 November 1987

Maisie (Anna Keaveney) was fast running out of patience with her inconsiderate greengrocer husband Bert (Shaun Curry). His lack of consideration had finally broken her after 17 years and she built a dividing wall down the living room and established a rota for the use of other household facilities. The only thing they had in common was love for their daughter Susan (Michelle Holmes) who, anyway, lived in Spain. Sharing the rapid disintegration of the marriage over the six editions were Rita (Maggie McCarthy), Jack (Peter Childs) and Edna (Vivienne Martin).

Writer: Myra Taylor. Director: Sue Bysh. Producer: Harold Snoad.

DIZZY HEIGHTS
BBC RADIO. First broadcast: 18 February 1993

This series in seven parts was written by Robin Kingsland. The setting was a hotel in a seaside resort which was grossly mismanaged, and the theme was the resultant chaos caused by the Gristle family, Victor and Vera (Richard Robinson and Marie Philips) and Eustace (William Todd-Jones). In each edition Alan Heap and Mick Wall appeared as themselves.

DOCTOR AT LARGE
BBC RADIO. First broadcast: 12 June 1969

Following on from DOCTOR IN THE HOUSE the previous year, Ray Cooney adapted 13 more of Richard Gordon's stories. Richard Briers again played Simon Sparrow with Geoffrey Sumner as Sir Lancelot Spratt and Ray Cooney as Tony Benskin.
Producer: David Hatch.

DOCTOR AT LARGE
LWT. First broadcast: 28 February 1971

Following on from DOCTOR IN THE HOUSE, newly-qualified Michael Upton (Barry Evans) had a job in the ear, nose and throat department of St Swithin's. Also qualified were Paul Collier (George Layton) and Dick Stuart-Clark (Geoffrey Davies). They were working alongside newcomer Lawrence Bingham (Richard O'Sullivan). After three episodes, Upton and Collier left to join a general practice run by Dr Maxwell (Arthur Lowe) but the patients considered Upton looked too young to be a doctor. That, and the fact the Maxwell had a pretty daughter, Sue (Madeline Smith), forced Michael to leave after just six weeks. He then joined Stuart-Clark in a plush Harley Street practice run by Dr Whiteland (Fabia Drake). In a second 1971 series, Upton joined a practice run by Collier's uncle, Dr Griffin (Brian Oulton).
Writers included Graham Chapman, Bernard McKenna and Bill Oddie. Director: David Askey. Producer: Humphrey Barclay.

DOCTOR AT SEA
LWT. First broadcast: 21 April 1974

Following the sacking of Dick Stuart-Clark (Geoffrey Davies) from St Swithin's hospital, Duncan Waring (Robin Nedwell) resigned in pro-

test. They joined the medical staff aboard a cruise liner, the Begonia, and became DOCTORS AT SEA. They found themselves under the command of Captain Loftus (Ernest Clark). Also on the ship were the Nurse (Elizabeth Counsell), the Purser (John Grieve), the Chief Officer (John Drake), the Radio Officer (Desmond Stokes) and the Entertainments Officer (Bob Todd).
Writers included George Layton and Jonathan Lynn, Richard Laing, Bernard McKenna, Phil Redmond. Director: David Askey. Producer: Humphrey Barclay.

DOCTOR AT THE TOP
BBC. First broadcast: 21 February 1991

The young interns from St Swithin's hospital of the 1960s swapped channels for this series of seven episodes. Dr Duncan Waring (Robin Nedwell) had been appointed NHS consultant paediatrician at St Swithin's and was married to Geraldine (Georgina Melville) with five children. Dr Paul Collier (George Layton), unmarried, was consultant general surgeon with a private practice in Harley Street to top up his income. Dick Stuart-Clark (Geoffrey Davies) was Professor of Surgery, married to Emma (Jill Benedict) with a daughter Rebecca (Chloe Annett). The three of them more or less ran the hospital with 75-year-old Sir Geoffrey Loftus (Ernest Clark) in retirement.
Writers: George Layton, Bill Oddie. Producer: Susan Belbin.

DOCTOR DOWN UNDER
AUSTRALIA PRESENTED BY ITV.
First broadcast (UK):5 January 1980

For what seemed the final spurt of life in the series that began with DOCTOR IN THE HOUSE, only two of the previous cast limped home in this Australian thrash. The unfortunate doctor to receive our previous heroes was Professor Beaumont (Frank Wilson) and he was helped through his ordeal by Sister Potts (Mary Ann Severne). Over 13 programmes they had to make some medical sense of Duncan Waring (Robin Nedwell) and Dick Stuart-Clark (Geoffrey Davies), who did not freely adapt to antipodean customs and standards. Eleven years later they would crop up again in DOCTOR AT THE TOP.

DOCTOR IN CHARGE
LWT. First broadcast: 9 April 1972

A further 42 stories involving Richard Gordon's

characters. Dr Michael Upton (See DOCTOR IN THE HOUSE and DOCTOR AT LARGE) was no longer at St Swithin's but many of the regulars still formed the nucleus of the stories including Professor Loftus (Ernest Clark), Paul Collier (George Layton), Duncan Waring (Robin Nedwell), Dick Stuart-Clark (Geoffrey Davies) and Laurence Bingham (Richard O'Sullivan). Waring had a regular girlfriend, Nurse Sandra Crumpton (Sammie Winmill). His parents, PC and Mrs Waring, were played by Victor Platt and Mollie Sugden.

Writers included Graham Chapman and Bernard McKenna, George Layton and Jonathan Lynn, Phil Redmond, David Sherlock. Director: Alan Wallis. Producer: Humphrey Barclay.

DOCTOR IN THE HOUSE

BBC RADIO. First broadcast: 25 June 1968

Based on Richard Gordon's 1952 book, Ray Cooney adapted the stories of St Swithin's hospital into a 13-part radio series. Richard Briers starred as Simon Sparrow with Geoffrey Sumner as Sir Lancelot Spratt. The innocent Sparrow had a not-so-innocent pal in Tony Benskin who was played by Cooney himself. Other characters included the Secretary (Erik Chitty), the Sister (Beth Boyd) and the Padre (Michael Deacon).

Producer: David Hatch.

DOCTOR IN THE HOUSE

LWT. First broadcast: 11 July 1969

Twenty years after the book and 15 years after the movie, Richard Gordon's comedy of medical students made it to the small screen. The stories began when we learned that Dr Simon Sparrow (Dirk Bogarde in the movie) had left St Swithin's Hospital to go into general practice and Sir Lancelott Spratt (James Robertson Justice in the movie) had retired to the House of Lords. The new students included Michael A Upton (Barry Evans), Duncan Waring (Robin Nedwell), Paul Collier (George Layton), Huw Evans (Martin Shaw), Dave Briddock (Simon Cuff) and Dick Stuart-Clark (Geoffrey Davies). The establishment was represented by the Dean (Ralph Michael) and Professor Loftus (Ernest Clark). A second series of 13 programmes in 1970 introduced Jonathan Lynn playing Irish boxing captain Danny Hooley.

Writers included Graeme Garden and Bill Oddie. Directors: Bill Turner, David Askey. Producer: Humphrey Barclay.

DOCTOR KNOCK

BBC. First broadcast: 7 February 1961

This series originated through the translations by Harley Branville-Barker of the original stories by Jules Romains. It was recorded for broadcast to schools. Richard Wordsworth starred as Doctor Knock, who took over an ailing country practice in provincial France from Doctor Parpalaid (Felix Fulton) and his wife (Barbara Couper) and, within three months, had put an entire town to bed! The four episodes were transmitted for BBC Schools at 2.05pm on Thursdays and repeated the following Wednesday at 11.05am. Although as a doctor Knock was something of a tyrant and a little creepy, his patients attracted a cast of fine actors including Jean Anderson, Timothy Bateson, Peter Bowles, Graham Crowden, Neil McCarthy and Joan Young. He drove around the mountains in his little 1906 Renault at hair-raising speed, elevated himself to local governmental power and, on the way, acquired an elite fifth column played by Hilda Braid, Frank Finlay, Jeremy Geidt and Renée Houston.

Producer: Ronald Eyre.

DOCTOR ON THE GO

LWT. First broadcast: 27 April 1975

Following their stint afloat in DOCTOR AT SEA, Dick Stuart-Clark (Geoffrey Davies), Duncan Waring (Robin Nedwell) and Professor Loftus (Ernest Clark) returned to St Swithin's for this series. They were joined by new characters at the hospital including James Gascoigne (Andrew Knox), Andrew MacKenzie (John Kane) and Katherine Wright (Jacquie-Ann Carr).

Writers: George Layton and Jonathan Lynn, Bernard McKenna and Richard Laing. Directors: Bryan Izzard, Gerry Mill. Producer: Humphrey Barclay.

DOCTOR'S DAUGHTERS

ATV. First broadcast: 16 November 1980

This began life as a one-off pilot before making its debut as a series on 22 February 1981. Set in the Old Chapterhouse Surgery in the village of Mitrebury, it featured three elderly doctors, Carmichael (Jack Watling), 'Biggin' Hill (Richard Murdoch) and Fellows-Smith (Bill Fraser), who made way for new blood in the form of Doctors Lucy Drake (Lesley Duff) and Fay Liston

(Victoria Burgoyne). There were seven programmes in total.

Writers: Richard Gordon and Ralph Thomas. Producer: Stuart Allen.

DOG AND DUCK

BBC RADIO. First broadcast: 1 October 1959

A North-Country pub was the setting for this creation by James Casey and Frank Roscoe. The landlady was Thora Hird and the pub's best customer was Jimmy James. Unfortunately, Jimmy never seemed to have any money and while Thora had a soft spot for him, it rarely extended to giving him credit. Thora was a widow and Jimmy, himself a widower, tried his utmost to lead her to the altar but, by playing hard to get, Thora believed she could help him better himself. Jimmy usually overcame his lack of funds by sponging off his Irish pal Paddy, played by Tommy Quinn. There was little respite for Jimmy, even when Thora's eye was turned, as she employed a particularly aggressive barman (Harry Towb). Among the pub regulars in six editions were the buxom Bessie Fitch (Patricia Phoenix), an ex-Army major and Little Alfie Twigg, both played by Leonard Williams.

Producer: James Casey.

THE DOG COLLAR

BBC RADIO. First broadcast: 11 October 1959

One of the earliest attempts to extract laughs at the expense of the clergy, this series had four runs, each of six programmes, ending on 18 January 1965. David March starred as Father Robert Tressland who, in the first series, was the newly appointed curate at the Clergy House from which Father Vane (Duncan McIntyre) ministered to his parishioners. Other residents were Father Mike Leary (John Graham) and the housekeeper Mrs Bream (Ella Milne). Only Fathers Tressland and Leary continued through the subsequent years, first with new maid Rosie (Sheila Grant) and latterly with housekeeper Mrs Bennett (Marjorie Westbury).

Writer: Ursula Bloom Producer: Audrey Cameron.

DOGFOOD DAN AND THE CARMARTHEN COWBOY

BBC. First broadcast: 4 February 1988

Two long-distance drivers delivered tins of dog food along the same route but in opposite directions and for rival firms. Dan (Malcolm Storry)

worked for the Bona Fido company and drove the Hull to Carmarthen run. Aubrey (Peter Blake) delivered Doggy Dins from Carmarthen to Hull. They met up and discovered that they had a similar interest – not dog food but the chase of the fair sex. Their respective wives were Helen (Elizabeth Mickery) and Gwyneth (Arbel Jones). The two travelling Lotharios, at the end of their delivery, met enchanting girls. They happened to be each other's wives and, in true traditions of farce, none of the four was aware of the connection. All four pretended to their new acquaintance to be something and someone other than their true selves. Relationships were pretty steamy by the end of the six-part series.

Writer: David Nobbs. Producer: Alan JW Bell.

DON'T DO IT, DEMPSEY!

BBC. First broadcast: 4 April 1960

Just half a dozen of these comedies were written by Patrick Campbell and Vivienne Knight. The Dempsey in question was James Dempsey (Brian Reece), an Irish womaniser and drinker. He was something of a chameleon and only lapsed into his Irish accent if he thought it would serve his purpose. He was a cheerful optimist, unmarried and of no settled employment, yet he never appeared short of money to satisfy his expensive tastes.

Producer: John Harrison.

DON'T DRINK THE WATER

LWT. First broadcast: 22 July 1974

Writers Ronald Wolfe and Ronald Chesney took the character of the miserable inspector Cyril 'Blakey' Blake (Stephen Lewis) from ON THE BUSES, retired him and moved him to a small flat in Spain, to which he had emigrated with his spinster sister Dorothy (Pat Coombs). Blake did his best to make the most of his sunshine retirement but Dorothy hated it from the off, moaned and groaned and yearned for England. The hapless caretaker of the flats was Carlos (Derek Griffiths) and the other Spanish help was Carmela (Muguette De Braie). For a short while after the series began the Blakes found a couple of ex-pats to talk with occasionally, Bill and Beryl (Frank Coda and Christine Shaw), but by the time the second series hit the air, Dorothy was fully entrenched in her misery. Carmela had left and been replaced by Maria (Olga Lowe).

Theme music: Johnny Gregory. Producer: Mark Stuart.

DON'T FORGET TO WRITE

BBC. First broadcast: 18 April 1977

Charles Wood created and wrote this series about a none-too-successful playwright, Gordon Maple (George Cole), who had a dutiful and encouraging wife Mabel (Gwen Watford) and a close friend Tom Lawrence (Francis Matthews) who was a considerably more successful playwright than Gordon was himself. In a *Radio Times* article at the time of the first transmission, Sheridan Morley implied that because Charles Wood had lived in Bristol and had a friend there in Peter Nichols, the series might have been autobiographical. The stories developed in 50-minute episodes over two six-part series ending on 22 February 1979. Gordon suffered from writer's block from time to time and vicissitudes bounced him from wanting to be left alone and yearning company and appreciation.

Music: Anthony Isaac. Directors: David Askey, Alan Dossor, Christopher Baker. Producer: Joe Waters.

DON'T ROCK THE BOAT

THAMES. First broadcast: 5 January 1982

Widower Jack Hoxton (Nigel Davenport) ran a boatyard on the river. He met and fell in love with a girl half his age, Dixie (Sheila White). She was a theatrical and Jack's two grown-up sons, Les (John Price) and Billy (David Janson), were not impressed. Once Jack and Dixie married, the boys did all they could to put their step-mother down. The first series of six was followed by six more shows starting 12 July 1983.

Writers: John Esmonde and Bob Larbey. Producer: Mark Stuart.

DON'T TELL FATHER

A-R. First broadcast: 1 June 1959

This series of six episodes was set on a Thames barge where lived screen-writer Harry Dean (Colin Gordon) and his daughter Julia (Julia Lockwood). The comedy situations arose because Harry was inclined to get carried away by his own plots and start living them. Julia struggled to protect him from his own imagination and keep him out of trouble.

Music: Eric Spear. Producer: Pat Baker.

DON'T TELL FATHER

BBC. First broadcast: 26 April 1992

Vivian Bancroft (Tony Britton) was an eminent elderly actor who considered himself irresistible to women yet his only true love was himself. He was on his fifth wife, Natasha (Susan Hampshire), who was 20 years younger than him. Although other members of his family objected to his ruling the roost in a selfish and arrogant manner, they nonetheless adored him and liked to hang around him. The other Bancrofts were Kate (Caroline Quentin), Garth (Richard Ashton), Congreve (Nigel Williams) and Spirit (Jo-Anne Sale). Six episodes were screened.

Writer: Roy Clarke. Producer: Harold Snoad.

DON'T WAIT UP

BBC. First broadcast: 25 October 1983

Tom Latimer (Nigel Havers) was a doctor in general practice who had recently been divorced when the series started. His first reaction was one of shock when he learned that his parents were also contemplating divorce, and his father Toby (Tony Britton), a Harley Street dermatologist, moved in to share his flat. The stories over 38 episodes in six series followed Tom's relationship with his former wife Helen (Jane How) who later married a man named Kramer, Toby's relationship with his estranged wife Angela (Dinah Sheridan), Tom's relationship with Toby's secretary Madeleine (Susan Skipper) whom he eventually married and, most important of all, the relationship between father and son. The series was created and written by George Layton and it came to an end on 25 March 1990. Tom's partner in his practice was Charles Cartwright (Richard Heffer, later Simon Williams). *Producer: Harold Snoad.*

DOOGIE HOWSER MD

USA PRESENTED BY BBC.
First broadcast (UK): 5 September 1990

Boy genius Doogie Howser (Neil Patrick Harris) was 16 years of age and already a fully qualified doctor. He was in his second year as resident at the Eastman Medical Centre in Los Angeles. His father David (James B Sikking) was bemused by his son's extraordinary achievement but nonetheless devoted, as was his mother (Belinda Montgomery). Doogie's best friend was Vinnie (Max Casella).

Creator and producer: Steven Bochco.

Father and son doctors Toby and Tom Latimer (Tony Britton and Nigel Havers) at odds in DON'T WAIT UP (Photo: Copyright © BBC)

DORA

LWT

See BOTH ENDS MEET

THE DORIS DAY SHOW

CBS (AMERICA) PRESENTED BY ITV.
First broadcast (UK): 3 September 1969

In 128 episodes made in the USA, movie star Doris Day took her character Doris Martin through four different situations. She began as a widow running a small farm and had two children at school, Billy and Toby Martin (Philip Brown and Tod Starke). She was helped in her chores by Buck Webb (Denver Pyle), Aggie (Fran Ryan) and the accident-prone Leroy B Simpson (James Hampton). She then became a secretary in San Francisco before settling in the city with her children. Finally she worked as a writer for a magazine, responsible to editor Cy Bennett (John Dehner).
Producers included Richard Dorso, Bob Sweeney and Terry Melcher (Doris Day's son).

DOUBLE BEDLAM

BBC RADIO. First broadcast: 8 May 1946

Naunton Wayne and Basil Radford reprised their roles as Bentley Woolcott and Howard Spencer from FOOLS' PARADISE in this eight-part comedy thriller which whisked them off on another sleuthing adventure.
Writer: John Jowett. Producer: Vernon Harris.

DOUBLE CROSS

BBC. First broadcast: 12 April 1956

This six-part comedy thriller by Sid Green and Dick Hills starred Jimmy Jewel and Ben Warriss who each played two roles. Jewel was Jimmy Seymour and Smithers of MI5 while Warriss was Ben Wait and Carstairs of MI5. Privy to their inept muddles as the hunt for spies progressed were Irene (Tonia Bern), Walters (Del Watson), Betty Patterson (Jill Day) and Karl Peters (Gerard Heinz).
Producer: Ernest Maxin.

DOUBLE FIRST

BBC. First broadcast: 6 September 1988

This series by John Esmonde and Bob Larbey began with a one-hour introductory episode followed by six half-hours from the next week. Michael Williams starred as Norman Vernon 'NV' Standish who had been an outstanding Oxford graduate and sportsman, progressed to writing a highly-praised book, joined the diplomatic service and, at the time from which the series picked up, was working as a hamburger chef in the Home Counties. There he was found by the Webster sisters, Mary and Louise (Ann Bell and Jennifer Hilary), who wished to rehabilitate him. He switched jobs, including working in a book shop, and other characters who participated in his disturbed life were Louise's daughter Ellen (Holly Aird), Derek (Clive Merrison) and William (Peter Tuddenham).
Producer: Gareth Gwenlan.

THE DOUBLE LIFE OF HENRY PHYFE

ABC (AMERICA) PRESENTED BY ITV.
First broadcast (UK): 22 July 1969

This 1965 series from the USA did not reach British shores until 1969 and then stayed for just five episodes. Red Buttons starred as Phyfe, a meek and mild suburban clerk inadvertently plunged into the world of espionage. Fred Clark portrayed his mentor, Gerald Hannahan.

DOWN MANGEL STREET

BBC RADIO. First broadcast: 8 October 1942

The six editions of these stories of the Cockney family Ogboddy were written by Mabel Constanduros who starred herself as Mrs Ogboddy. Her husband was portrayed by John Rorke and all

The Globelink newsroom team, ready at a moment's notice to DROP THE DEAD DONKEY (Photo: Channel 4)

other parts were played by the resident company which comprised Phyllis Morris, John Turner, Gwen Lewis and Fred Yule.
Producer: Eric Fawcett.

DOWN OUR STREET

BBC RADIO. First broadcast: 1 October 1948

This eight-part series was the first solo series for Cockney comedienne Ethel Revnell whose partnership with Gracie West was a well-known act on the variety halls. Revnell, a specialist in child impersonations, played 'the Kid' as well as herself in the setting of her own home and surrounding community. She grappled with the everyday problems of herself and those of her friends and relations, who were portrayed, as and when required, by Ivor Barnard and guest actors.
Writers: Rex Diamond and Carey Edwards. Producer: Tom Ronald.

DOWN THE GATE

ATV. First broadcast: 23 July 1975

This series was written by Roy Tuvey and Maurice Sellar and based on an idea by Reg Varney. Varney starred as Billingsgate fish porter Reg Furnell. He was married to Irene (Dilys Laye) and his boss at the market was Mr Davies (Kevin Brennan). His market mates were Old Wol (Reg Lye), Len Peacock (Tony Melody) and Sid (James Appleby). The teagirl was Rosie (Helen Keating). When the show returned for a second run in July 1976, Reg had a new boss, Mr Preston (Percy Herbert), and added friends Harry (Peter Spraggon) and Wendy (Mela White).
Producers: William G Stewart, Alan Tarrant.

DREAM ON

USA PRESENTED BY CHANNEL 4.
First broadcast (UK): 9 August 1991

New Yorker Martin Tupper (Brian Benben) faced a mid-life crisis when his beautiful wife Judith divorced him and announced plans to marry an-

other man. With a son at school and friends trying to fix him up with new females, Martin took to living and reliving his experiences through flashbacks of old movies and TV shows. The last of 30 editions was seen on 28 February 1992.
Producer: John Landis.

DREAM STUFFING
CHANNEL 4. First broadcast: 6 January 1984

Jude and Mo (Rachael Weaver and Amanda Symonds) shared an undesirable flat in a tower block in London's East End. Their life was depressing and tough but they were able to laugh at their lot. Mo worked at the Glass Eye Factory until she was made redundant, while Jude languished in unemployment. The lack of quality of life was shared by friends, neighbours and relations of varied race and sexuality. Principal characters included May (Maria Charles) who had the launderette, pregnant Brenda (Caroline Quentin), Richard (Ray Burdis) and Bill (Frank Lee). Ten episodes were screened.
Writers: Paul Hines and Su Wilkins. Director: John Kaye Cooper. Producer: Humphrey Barclay for Limehouse Productions.

DRIVE INN
BBC RADIO. First broadcast: 1 April 1942

This eight-part series starred legendary pantomime dame George Lacy in the dual role of hotel manager Captain George de Courcy Chiseller and hotel hostess Lady Georgina Faggot-Trundle. Other hotel personnel were William Tell (Jack Melford), Mr Dillwater (Charles Harrison), Mr Carefree (Horace Percival), Miss Augusta Roper (Joan Young), Desiree (Gwen Lewis) and the switchboard girl (Phoebe Hodgson).
Writer: Loftus Wigram. Producers: Reginald Smith and Michael North.

DROP ME HERE, DARLING
BBC RADIO. First broadcast: 2 December 1982

In this 13-part series, Leslie Phillips and Jill Bennett starred as a divorced couple. Since their separation, he had fallen from his lofty position in the world and was broke; she had risen and become a business tycoon. The only job he was able to get was as her chauffeur, complete with cap and uniform, driving her Rolls-Royce.
Writer: Andrew Palmer. Producer: Edward Taylor.

DROP THE DEAD DONKEY
CHANNEL 4. First broadcast: 9 August 1990

Created, written and produced by Andy Hamilton and Guy Jenkin, this was the first sitcom to attempt to be topical up to the very last minute. The setting was the newsroom of Globelink News, a media outlet bought in the first episode by the never-seen Sir Royston Merchant, to the overall chagrin of the staff. Sir Royston installed his own executive, Gus Hedges (Robert Duncan), who, when faced with aggravation or problems, would pronounce 'I'm not here!' The editor was George Dent (Jeff Rawle) and his assistant was Alex Pate (Haydn Gwynne). Gambling cynic Dave Charnley (Neil Pearson) thought himself the office charmer and Damien Day (Stephen Tompkinson) was the smooth but ruthless news reporter. The news presenters were alcoholic Henry Davenport (David Swift) and whingeing, scatty Sally Smedley (Victoria Wicks). The production assistant was Joy (Susannah Doyle). To ensure the immediacy of the scripts, the shows were recorded less than 24 hours before transmission. A first series of ten was followed by 13 more editions beginning 26 September 1991. For a third run of 11 starting 7 January 1993, Alex was no longer on the team having been replaced by Helen Cooper (Ingrid Lacey).
Director: Liddy Oldroyd. A Hat Trick Production.

DUET
USA PRESENTED BY CHANNEL 4.
First broadcast (UK): 29 January 1991

The series was set in Los Angeles where Ben Coleman (Matthew Laurence), a writer of mystery stories, met Laura (Mary Page Keller) at a wedding reception where she was responsible for the catering. They fell in love and the ensuing episodes followed the progress of their affair and introduced Laura's sister Jane (Jodi Thelen) and their married friends Richard and Linda (Chris Lemmon and Alison La Placa). A run of 26 consecutive episodes was screened.

DUFFY'S TAVERN
USA PRESENTED BY BBC RADIO.
First broadcast (UK): 18 October 1944

In this American wartime series, the creator and writer Ed Gardner himself played the part of Archie, the manager of the tavern 'where the elite meet to eat'. In 1945 a movie was made with the same title and in 1956 the format was briefly anglicised by Frank Muir and Denis Norden as FINKEL'S CAFE.

THE DUKES OF HAZZARD
CBS (AMERICA) PRESENTED BY BBC.
First broadcast(UK): 3 March 1979

This creation by Guy Waldron was set in Hazzard County where the good guys became the outlaws and, through wild car-chases and spectacular stunts, baited the corrupt Sheriff Rosco Coltrane (James Best) and the evil Boss Hogg (Sorrell Booke). Fighting the system were country cousins Luke Duke (Tom Wopat), Bo Duke (John Schneider), Daisy Duke (Catherine Bach) and Uncle Jesse Duke (Denver Pyle). Boss Hogg fancied himself as a politician and always wore a white suit, but with much noise and plenty of gratuitous violence the Dukes would come out on top. The shows were produced on the American production-line basis and the BBC screened more than 100 episodes.
Producers: Joseph Gantman and Paul Picard.

Two couples together, purely through a sense of DUTY FREE: David and Amy (standing), Robert and Linda (Photo: Yorkshire Television)

THE DUSTBINMEN
GRANADA. First broadcast: 28 October 1969

Jack Rosenthal created this group of garbage collectors for a single play, 'There's a Hole in Your Dustbin, Delilah', which was seen on 30 September 1968. The following year the series proper began. Although the characters from the play remained, there were several cast changes. The leader of the gang was Bloody Delilah (Frank Windsor in the play, John Woodvine in the first series and Brian Wilde thereafter). The others were the Manchester City-mad Winston Platt (Graham Haberfield), 'Smellie' Ibbotson (John Barrett), Cheese 'n Egg, so called because his initials were CE and Church of England would have been inappropriate (Jack MacGowran in the play, Bryan Pringle thereafter), Heavy Breathing (Harold Innocent in the play, then Tim Wilton).

The first series of six programmes all went to number 1 in the ratings, a unique achievement. There were two further series, both in 1970. Jack Rosenthal broke new ground, much to the dislike of certain clean-up TV campaigners, with his use of gutter language.
Director: Michael Apted (the play), Les Chatfield. Producers: John Finch (the play), Jack Rosenthal, Richard Everitt.

DUTY FREE
YTV. First broadcast: 13 February 1984

David and Amy Pearce (Keith Barron and Gwen Taylor) went on a package holiday to Spain using David's redundancy money. There they met Robert and Linda Cochran (Neil Stacy and Joanna Van Gyseghem). David and Linda began an affair which involved much hiding in wardrobes and diving under beds. The hotel barman was played by Carlos Douglas and the manager by George Camiller. The first series of seven was followed by a second run of seven which began on 6 September the same year, ostensibly covering the second week of the holiday. In 1986, with Amy working but David still unemployed, they took a winter break to the same hotel where they were surprised to find that Robert and Linda had decided to do the same. The run was six weeks with the final programme on 12 February. At the end of the same year, both couples returned to the hotel once more for a one-off Christmas special.
Music: Peter Knight. Writers: Eric Chappell and Jean Warr. Producer: Vernon Lawrence.

E.R.

USA PRESENTED BY CHANNEL 4.
First broadcast (UK): 9 January 1987

Elliott Gould starred in nine shows as Dr Sheinfeld, a surgeon in the emergency room of a large inner city hospital. Though he was married, he was trying for a divorce and he was hotly pursued by women. He was always broke but that did not seem to affect his attraction to the opposite sex. Other regular characters were Dr Eve Sheridan (Mary McDonnell), Joan Thor (Conchata Ferrell), Maria Amarda (Shuko Akune), Julie Williams (Lynne Moody), Cory (Corinne Bohrer) and security officer Fred Burdock (Bruce Young).

EAST END – WEST END

A-R. First broadcast: 4 February 1958

This first solo vehicle for Britain's favourite South African Cockney, Sid James, was written by Wolf Mankowitz. Miriam Karlin played alongside James in a six-part series which was set in London's Jewish community of small-time operators and smart business dealers. Sid picked up a living as and when he could, never doing anything dishonest but always on the lookout for easy pickings.
Producer: Peter Croft.

EASY STREET

USA PRESENTED BY ITV.
First broadcast: 28 March 1987

Loni Anderson starred as widow LK McGuire who reluctantly shared her mansion with her snooty in-laws, Eleanor and Quentin Standard (Dana Ivey and James Cromwell). When she could take them no more, she invited her scruffy Uncle Bully Stevenson (Jack Elam) to visit, stay and ruffle their feathers. That he did with ease, and he and LK were assisted by their friend Ricardo (Lee Weaver).

EDUCATED EVANS

BBC. First broadcast: 2 October 1957

Charlie Chester starred as 'Educated' Evans, the eccentric little Cockney racing tipster created by Edgar Wallace and originally portrayed in a 1936 movie by Max Miller. It was dramatised into 18 half-hour television episodes by Sidney Nelson and Maurice Harrison, with some additional dialogue scripted by Bernard Botting and Charles Hart. Much of the action took place in the pub, where the barmaid was Gertrude (Myrtle Reed). Evans had a love–hate relationship with Det. Sgt Miller (Jack Melford), who enjoyed a flutter on the horses almost as much as he enjoyed hauling Evans up before the magistrates. Other regular characters included Mrs Wilkes (Mai Bacon), Old Sam (Leonard Sharp), Mrs Boltons (Dorothy Summers) and a mysterious chap without a name who was only ever referred to as 'the man in the pub', played by Michael Balfour. The last edition was seen on 10 June 1958.
Producer: Eric Fawcett.

EDUCATING ARCHIE

BBC RADIO. First broadcast: 6 June 1950

Ventriloquist Peter Brough took his lead from American Edgar Bergen and THE CHARLIE McCARTHY PROGRAMME whereby a talking doll could become a star of the air waves. Archie Andrews, eternal schoolboy, was first heard during the war in *Navy Mixture*, a variety show which paved the way for this, his own series. The show is particularly notable for the number of stars who were to graduate from it. In that first series, his tutor was Robert Moreton, and his girlfriend was Julie Andrews. Hattie Jacques was Agatha Dinglebody and Max Bygraves made a huge impression as the life-and-soul Cockney with two instant catchphrases, 'I've arrived, and to prove it I'm 'ere', and 'Big 'ead'. The writers were Eric Sykes and Sid Colin and the show won an instant National Radio Award. A series commencing 3 August 1951 introduced Tony Hancock as Archie's new tutor, with the catchphrase 'Flippin' kids'. Those who followed as tutor to Archie included Harry Secombe (1952), Ronald Shiner (1953), Bernard Miles (1954), James Robertson Justice (1955), Alexander Guage (1956), Jerry Desmonde (1957), Bruce Forsyth (1959) and Sidney James (1960). But it wasn't just the tutors who made an impact. With his talking mouth-organ, Ronald Chesney joined the cast in

Educating Archie Andrews, the first and only wooden star of British radio, is Peter Brough (Photo: Copyright © BBC)

1952, and Beryl Reid introduced her unforgettable Monica the next season. Funny voice men Graham Stark, Ken Platt, Dick Emery and Warren Mitchell had early opportunities to create characters that would stay with them through their careers, and in later editions Gladys Morgan as the cook and Bernard Bresslaw as her gormless nephew fresh from the Army made a significant impact. It was also through this show that Ronald Chesney met up with writer Ronald Wolfe and they would later go on to create shows including THE RAG TRADE.

When the show ended in 1960, there had been more than 200 editions. It must be true to say that no wooden character has before or since captured the imagination of the British public in the way that Archie Andrews did. In 1954 there was a brief attempt to break the format with a series called *Archie's The Boy*, but it swiftly reverted to the original title. One of the earliest contributors to the show – who is apt to be forgotten – was Gilbert Harding, who appeared as the cantankerous school inspector, a role that will not surprise those who remember the normal Harding persona. Benny Hill was another member of the team for one season as

were Alfred Marks, Pearl Carr and Shirley Eaton. *Writers included Sykes and Colin, Wolfe, Chesney, Marty Feldman, George Wadmore, Eddie Maguire, Pat Dunlop, David Climie. Producers: Roy Speer, Jacques Brown, Geoffrey Owen.*

A-R. First broadcast 26 September 1958

The problems of transferring Archie Andrews from radio to television were complex. Archie had not been built as a moving doll and the credit for designing the mechanics which would enable him to move freely on a set goes to a Rediffusion engineer, Woolf Goldberg, although there had been a previous attempt by BBC in the 1956 series HERE'S ARCHIE. After several experiments, Goldberg had Archie ready for television and Peter Brough was his voice. The series was made entirely on film and featured Irene Handl as Brough's housekeeper, Freddie Sales as a non-paying lodger, and Dick Emery as a Jack of all trades. *Writers: Ronald Chesney, Marty Feldman and Ronald Wolfe. Producer: Christopher Hodson.*

EDUCATING MARMALADE

THAMES First broadcast: 25 October 1982

Marmalade Atkins (Charlotte Coleman) was the worst child in the world and no school kept her for more than one of the 13 episodes of this children's series. She was the despair of her long-suffering parents (John Bird and Lynda Marchal), and the education officer Mrs Allgood (Gillian Raine) ran out of schools to which to send her after expulsions from everywhere including the local school, a convent, Eton and a Venice finishing school. The character returned the following year in a show called DANGER – MARMALADE AT WORK. *Writer: Andrew Davies. Directors: Colin Bucksey, John Stroud. Producer: Sue Birtwhistle.*

THE EGGHEADS

BBC. First broadcast: 13 July 1961

David Croft wrote and produced this series of seven episodes about a bunch of students lodging in rooms in Bloomsbury. Three males rented a flat: Peter (Peter Reeves), Bryan (Bryan Blackburn) and Canadian Bob (Robert Jackson). Vivien (Vivien Grant) had the flat next door. They all four shared a communal sitting-room and what was called a bath-cum-kitch. Engineering student Bryan found it impossible to set aside any time for study and the others fared little better. Their lives were one long round of coffee bars and parties. The occasional appearance of Bryan's mum was portrayed by Doris Hare. *Director: Vere Lorrimer.*

EIGHT BELLS

BBC RADIO. First broadcast: 16 April 1935

Created by Belfast producer Mungo Dewar, this show had first been heard, in Northern Ireland only, in 1932. After its first national airing, transmissions were irregular and it all but disappeared during the war. The shows had a Royal Navy setting in Belfast waters and were an excuse for music and song, but the comedy element remained strong with crew members Nobby Clark (Arthur Askey, later Tom Brandon), Shorty Sinclair (Fred Gwyn, later Harry Hudson), Lofty Delaney (John Rorke) and Leading Seaman Pincher Martin (Fred Yule, later Fred Gibson). The telegraphist Bill Jenkins was played by the drummer from the BBC Variety Orchestra, Styx Gibling. Originally the crew were aboard HMS Biatome but soon transferred to HMS St George. *Writer: Mungo Dewar. Producers: Sam Bulloch, Harry S Pepper.*

EL C.I.D.

GRANADA. First broadcast: 7 February 1990

Two former Scotland Yard policemen quit their jobs to make a new life on Spain's Costa Del Sol. Douglas Bromley (John Bird) severed all his ties and bought the yacht of the programme's title together with a bar near Marbella. Blake (Alfred Molina) approached the Spanish dream with more scepticism – and indeed only stuck it out for the first series of six editions. The bar was swiftly destroyed and the two men discovered a widespread criminal element at work along the Costa. They became private detectives and their number-one adversary was Gus Mercer (Kenneth Cranham) who, with his henchman Graham (Niven Boyd), plotted against them and Delgado (Simon Andreu) who ran the detective agency. With Molina out of the second series which came on to the screen on 27 January 1992, Bromley was joined on his boat and in the sleuthing business by his long-lost daughter Rosie (Amanda Redman), who turned up in the wake of being dumped by her boyfriend. Other significant characters included Metcalf (Donald Churchill), Frank (Tony Haygarth) and Mercedes (Viviane Vives). There were numerous writers and directors who contributed to the series. *Producer: Matthew Bird.*

THE EMBASSY LARK

BBC RADIO. First broadcast: 15 March 1966

Lawrie Wyman, creator and writer of THE NAVY LARK and THE TV LARK, came up with this creation chronicling the events in and around Her Britannic Majesty's Embassy to the Kingdom of Tratvia. The Ambassador was Sir Jeremy Crighton-Buller (Derek Francis), who with First Secretary Henry Pettigrew (Frank Thornton) had to cope with the slings and arrows of the blackmailing King Hildebrand III (Francis de Wolff). The Ambassador's wife, Lady Daphne (Charlotte Mitchell), dropped political bricks with gay abandon. Operating from next door and across the railway tracks respectively were the Russian Ambassador (Michael Spice) and the Chinese Ambassador (David Fallon). In one episode, the crew of HMS Troutbridge from THE NAVY LARK docked in Tratvia. The first series was in 13 parts and a new series of 15 episodes began on 5 March 1968. *Producer: Alastair Scott Johnston.*

EMNEY ENTERPRISES

BBC. First broadcast: 3 November 1954

Larger than life in both size and spirit, Fred Emney, complete with monocle and eternal cigar, was one of the first comedians to establish a television situation after the war. He was in his eighties when this series, which he also wrote, began. There were more than 30 editions, ending on 21 March 1957. He ran his enterprise business with the help of Edwin Styles as his general factotum and Deryck Guyler as his assistant. *Producers: Bill Ward, George Inns.*

EMPIRE

BBC. First broadcast: 11 May 1984

Patrick Macnee starred as Calvin Cromwell, chairman of multi-national corporation Empire Industries. The stories in the six-part series revolved around his Machiavellian personality and the politics of the boardroom. Other characters wrapped up in the plots and intrigues were Ben Christian (Dennis Dugan), Jack Willow (Richard Masur), Jackie Willow (Christian Belford), Roger Martinson (Howard Platt), Edward Roland (Michael McGuire), Arthur Broderick (Dick O'Neill), T Howard Daniels (Edward Winter), Meredith (Caren Kaye), Peg (Maureen Arthur) and Amelia

Lapidus (Francine Tacker), who was not only beautiful but had a company which Cromwell wished to acquire.

Writers: Lawrence J Cohen and Fred Freeman, George Zateolo, Dennis Danziger and Ellen Sandler, Jim Geoghan. Producer: Terry Hughes.

EMPIRE ROAD
BBC. First broadcast: 31 October 1978

Guyanese writer Michael Abbensetts made one of the first attempts to extract comedy from the racial tensions in the Midlands. The series initially starred Norman Beaton as Everton Bennett, the self-styled Godfather of the road. He returned after a six-month absence to find many changes in the community and his brother-in-law Walter Issacs (Joseph Marcell) in charge. West Indians, Asians and whites lived side by side through a first series of five episodes. The following year from 23 August, Rudolph Walker joined the cast as a sinister new landlord over ten episodes, but it remains one of those series that was just getting going when it was dropped.

Theme music: Matumbi. Producer: Peter Ansorge.

EMPTY NEST
USA PRESENTED BY CHANNEL 4.
First broadcast (UK): 18 August 1989

Susan Harris created this series which starred Richard Mulligan as Harry Weston, a paediatrician widowed for 18 months and pursued by a never ending stream of predatory Miami matrons. He had three daughters, policewoman Barbara (Kristy McNichol), Carol (Dinah Manoff) and Laverne (Park Overall). Helping him adjust to widowhood was his best friend, a large and scene-stealing dog named Dreyfuss, and a free-loading neighbour, Charley (David Leisure). There were two runs of seven programmes each, the second beginning on 29 October 1991.

THE ENCHANTING WORLD OF HINGE AND BRACKET
BBC RADIO. First broadcast: 27 February 1978

Drag artists Patrick Fyffe and George Logan set their creations Dr Evadne Hinge and Dame Hida Bracket in the imaginary Suffolk village of Stackton Tressel just beyond the village green towards Stackton Parva, an olde worlde existence in the Old Manse. They had a daily help Maud Print (Daphne

Heard) and had encounters with the Church organist, the Squire, the village policeman and others, played as and when required by Herbert Smith and John Savident. There were two 13-part series, the second ending 19 September 1979. See also THE RANDOM JOTTINGS OF HINGE AND BRACKET and DEAR LADIES.

Writers: Mike Craig, Lawrie Kinsley and Ron McDonnell. Producer: James Casey.

ENSIGN O'TOOLE
NBC (AMERICA) PRESENTED BY ITV.
First broadcast (UK): 22 September 1965

Dean Jones starred in the title role of this 1965 comedy in adventures with his buddies aboard the destroyer USS Appleby on duty in the Pacific. The stories were based on the novels by William J Lederer, *All the Ships at Sea* and *Ensign O'Toole and Me*. His shipmates were Chief Petty Officer O Homer Nelson (Jay C Flippen), Lieutenant Rex St John (Jack Mullaney), Commander Virgil Stoner (Jack Albertson), Seaman Gabby Dijulio (Harvey Lembeck), Seaman Howard Spicer (Beau Bridges) and Seaman Claude White (Bob Sorrells).

Producer: Hy Averback.

EVENING SHADE
USA PRESENTED BY CHANNEL 4.
First broadcast (UK): 10 February 1992

Burt Reynolds starred as former football hero Wood Newton who returned to his home town in Arkansas where he became High School coach. His wife Ava (Marilu Henner) had political ambitions. They had a baby daughter Emily and a much older, rebellious son Taylor (Jay R Ferguson). Other regular characters included Evan Evans (Hal Holbrook), Harlan Elldridge (Charles Durning), Freida Evans (Elizabeth Ashley) and Ponder Blue (Ossie Davies). Reynolds won an Emmy for Best Comedy Actor in 1991 for this series, which was first screened in Britain the following year. There were more than 50 editions, several of them directed by Reynolds himself.

Producers: Tommy Thompson and Don Rhymer.

EVER DECREASING CIRCLES
BBC. First broadcast: 29 January 1984

John Esmonde and Bob Larbey created and wrote this series which starred Richard Briers as Martin Bryce, a maddeningly well-organised fusspot with an obsession for upholding law and order. He was captain of the local tennis and cricket club and an avid committee member of just about every other club. His wife Ann (Penelope Wilton) displayed a remarkable patience as Martin set ever higher standards that were unattainable. The arrival of new next-door neighbour Paul Ryman (Peter Egan) brought an element of moderation into Ann's life with her insensitive husband. Smoothie Paul was just the right antidote, for know-all Martin manifested a passion for everything except his wife. The series ended after 27 editions on 24 December 1989. *Producers: Sydney Lotterby, Harold Snoad.*

EVERY SILVER LINING

BBC. First broadcast: 27 May 1993

Nat and Shirley Silver (Andrew Sachs and Frances de la Tour) were a Jewish couple who ran the Silver Diner café in London's East End. Shirley nursed wild ambitions to expand the business and to ensure that daughter Lorraine (Sarah Malin) was educated well and married well. Shirley herself longed to be better than just a sandwich maker and reverted to wearing mini-skirts and playing old pop records in a bid to recapture her own youth. Regulars at the café were Willie (Oscar Quitak), Leonard (David Yip) and Dean (Danny Swanson). *Writer: Simon Block. Director: Nick Bye. Producer: Richard Boden.*

Ann (Penelope Wilton) watches as Martin (Richard Briers) lays down the law to smoothie neighbour Paul (Peter Egan) in EVER DECREASING CIRCLES (Photo: © BBC)

EXECUTIVE STRESS

THAMES. First broadcast: 20 October 1986

George Layton created and wrote this series which took as its starting point the departure from the family home of the last of the five children of Donald and Caroline Fairchild (Geoffrey Palmer and Penelope Keith). Donald was an executive with Oasis Publishing. Caroline had also worked in published prior to raising their family. She was now determined to resume her career. Oasis was taken over by an American conglomerate, the Frankland Organisation and Donald was made sales and marketing director. To his great surprise and consternation, Caroline joined Oasis as editorial director and pretended never to have met Donald. They kept up their charade through the first run of seven episodes. There were some eyebrows raised in suspicion, particularly by Anthea Duxbury (Elizabeth Counsell) and by Edgar Frankland (Harry Ditson), the son of the tyrannical American magnate who owned the firm. During the second series their secret came out when Edgar was called back to the United States to work with the parent company. Donald and Caroline were made joint managing directors of Oasis and worked alongside each other through a third and final series of six which ended on 27 December 1988. There was much professional rivalry between them but no jealousy. Other principal characters at various intervals included Andrew Morgan (Ben Aris), Sylvia (Wanda Ventham), Gordon (Donald Pickering), and Peter and Valerie Davenport (Geoffrey Whitehead and Prunella Gee). *Producer: John Howard Davies.*

THE FAINTHEARTED FEMINIST

BBC. First broadcast: 10 March 1984

Jill Tweedie and Christopher Bond wrote these five programmes in which Lynn Redgrave starred as Martha who, saddled with a husband like Josh (Jonathan Newth), was only too keen to adopt the new principles of feminism. In this she was encouraged by the militant Mary (Sarah Neville) and Mo (Helen Cotterill). Martha refused to remain a house slave to Josh, her two teenage children and her baby, but events had a habit of conspiring to make it hard for her to put her new-found principles into practice.

Director: Mandie Fletcher. Producer: Zanna Beswick.

FAIRLY SECRET ARMY

CHANNEL 4. First broadcast: 22 October 1984

Geoffrey Palmer starred as retired Major Harry Kitchener Wellington Truscott of the Queen's Own West Mercian Lowlanders, a right-wing fanatic who formed his private army to safeguard the country against the loony left and all forms of decadence. His mission was to arrest the advance of wets, anarchists and feminists. Truscott would rant and rave, bully and coerce in Alf Garnett style. There were two series, each of six editions, the second beginning on 1 September 1986. Characters in and out of his army were Nancy (Diane Fletcher), Beamish (Jeremy Child), Doris Entwistle (Liz Fraser), Sgt Major Throttle (Michael Robbins), Crazy Colin Carstairs (James Cosmo), Stubby Collins (Ray Winstone), Jill (Diana Weston), Peg-Leg Pogson (Paul Chapman) and Ron Boat (Richard Ridings).

Writer: David Nobbs. Directors: Robert Young, Roy Ward Baker. Producer: Peter Robinson for Video Arts.

THE FALL AND RISE OF REGINALD PERRIN

BBC. First broadcast: 8 September 1976

David Nobbs adapted his own book *The Death of Reginald Perrin* into 21 episodes, the last of which was transmitted on 10 January 1979. Leonard Rossiter starred as Reginald Iolanthe Perrin, middle-aged suburbanite executive at Sunshine Desserts. At the outset of the story, he was on the brink of a nervous breakdown brought about by the sheer monotony of his life. What happened thereafter was told in serial form and involved many characters who themselves would undergo swingeing changes to their routine and be woven in and out of the misfortunes and ultimate fortunes of Reggie. At Sunshine Desserts, fast-talking Reggie had a loud-mouthed boss, CJ (John Barron), who boomed clear and often: 'I didn't get where I am today by . . .'. Reggie also had two colleagues, Tony Webster (Trevor Adams) and David Harris-Jones (Bruce Bould), who fawned 'Super' and 'Great' to whatever CJ said. Reggie's secretary was Joan Greengross (Sue Nicholls). On the domestic front

Reggie (Leonard Rossiter) contemplates his fluctuating fortunes in THE FALL AND RISE OF REGINALD PERRIN (Photo: Copyright © BBC)

he had a wife Elizabeth (Pauline Yates) and a militaristic brother-in-law, Jimmy (Geoffrey Palmer), who scrounged meals with his catchphrase, 'Bit of a cock-up on the catering front'.

Reggie's fall and rise included faking his own seaside suicide and reappearing in the guise of an old friend, Martin Welbourne. Divorced from Elizabeth, he remarried her in that new guise. He founded a company, Grot, which sold ludicrous objects at vastly inflated prices and made him a wealthy tycoon. When Sunshine Desserts went bust, he employed CJ, Joan, David and Tony but happiness still eluded him. In the final series he took them all away to set up a commune which was dedicated to world improvement. Other important characters included Prue Harris-Jones (Theresa Watson), Linda (Sally-Jane Spencer), Tom (Leslie Schofield) and Doc Morrissey (John Horsley). The American version was simply called REGGIE.

Music: Ronnie Hazlehurst. Producers: John Howard Davies, Gareth Gwenlan.

FAMILY AFFAIR

CBS (AMERICA) PRESENTED BY ITV.
First broadcast(UK): 10 July 1969

Although 138 episodes of this domestic series were made in the USA, viewers in Britain only ever saw a very small handful. Brian Keith starred as Bill Davis, engineer, millionaire and bachelor. Much to the dismay of his English manservant French (Sebastian Cabot), he took on the care and upbringing of his orphaned nephew and nieces. They were twins Jody and Buffy (Johnnie Whittaker and Anissa Jones) and their younger sister Cissy (Kathy Garver). They all lived together in his New York home.

Creator and producer: Don Fedderson.

THE FAMILY BRANDON

BBC RADIO. First broadcast: 19 April 1975

Disc jockey Tony Brandon had started his show business career as an impressionist and actor, and in this domestic series he swapped the radio turntables to revert to his comedy roots. His wife was played by Elizabeth Counsell and the Brandon family was completed by their two children Philip and Joanna, portrayed by Mark Hadfield and Ruth Dooner. There were two series, the first of six programmes and a second run of 13 which ended on 15 May 1976.

Writers: Mike Craig, Lawrie Kinsley and Ron McDonnell. Producer: James Casey.

FAMILY CRACKERS

BBC RADIO. First broadcast: 13 August 1941

This six-part domestic comedy series starred Harry Tate Jr, son of the famous music hall comedian. He was the father in a weird family, each of whose members purported to be crazier than the others. They were Mother (Doris Nichols), Dahlia (Betty Huntley Wright), Junior (Ronnie Beadle), Uncle Ned (Clifford Bean) and Odd Man Out (Frank Leslie). The show's catchphrase was 'How's your father?'.

Writers: Loftus Wigram and Harry Tate Jr. Producer: Eric Fawcett.

FAMILY TIES

NBC (AMERICA) PRESENTED BY CHANNEL 4.
First broadcast(UK): 10 August 1985

This series was made in the USA in 1982 but did not reach British screens until three years later. This explains how Michael J Fox was already a big movie star when Channel 4 snapped up the 80-odd episodes in which he played Alex P Keaton, the know-it-all son of Steve and Elyse Keaton (Michael Gross and Meredith Baxter-Birney). The parents were a liberal couple of former hippies who, twenty years on, still liked to swing and play young, while their children, Alex in particular, were arch conservatives. Alex found it hard to comprehend why his parents would wish to attend anti-nuclear rallies. He had an older sister Mallory (Justine Bateman) who was an object of desire for a much older man, and a younger sister Jennifer (Tina Yothers) who tolerated him while silently laughing at the way he took himself so seriously. In a few early editions Tom Hanks appeared as Elyse's brother Ned, who had embezzled millions of dollars. Alex hero-worshipped him.

Creator: Lloyd Garber. Producer: Gary David Goldberg.

THE FAMOUS TEDDY Z

USA PRESENTED BY BBC.
First broadcast (UK): 3 October 1989

Teddy Zakalokis (Jon Cryer) worked in the mailroom of the Unlimited Talent Agency in Beverly Hills. He was poised to quit the job and go to work in his uncle's bakery when he met actor Harland Keyvo (Dennis Lipscomb) and decided to become his personal agent. He found the parasitic life of taking a percentage of the movie actor's earnings to his liking and soon became famous for striking hard deals. The other regulars were Grandma Zakalokis (Erica Yohn) and Al Floss (Alex Rocco).

FANCY WANDERS

LWT. First broadcast: 24 October 1980

Sid Green wrote this series of six programmes in which Dave King starred as Fancy, an unemployed white tramp who palled up with a similar black character, Alastair (Joe Marcell). Alastair became caught up in the imaginings and wild dreams of Fancy, who had all the answers to the problems of the world.

Producers: Les Chatfield, Derrick Goodwin.

FARRINGTON OF THE FO

YTV. First broadcast: 13 February 1986

Dick Sharples created and wrote this series which starred Angela Thorne as Harriet Emily Farrington. The first run of six episodes began with Harriet newly posted as British Consul-General to an obscure South American banana republic. There she came head to head with the dyed-in-the-wool Major Willoughby-Gore (John Quayle) who did his utmost to discredit her. She was supported by the loyal Vice-Consul (admin) Annie Begley (Joan Sims), and the stalwart Fidel Sanchez (Tony Haygarth). A further run of seven programmes ended on 15 July 1987.

Music: Alan Parker. Producer: Ronnie Baxter.

FASTEN YOUR SEATBELT

USA PRESENTED BY ITV.
First broadcast (UK): 5 July 1963

Bob Cummings produced and starred in this series. He played Bob Carson, a pilot and adventurer with a taste for money, excitement and girls. He employed unorthodox means to ensure he always had plenty of all three. He drove a compact, two-seater fibreglass car which carried wings, a tail and fuselage in a built-in trailer. Consequently it could easily be converted into a light aircraft driven by a rear propellor. There were only two other regular actors in the 13 shows, Murvyn Vye as Lionel and Roberta Shore as Hank.

FATHER CHARLIE

CENTRAL. First broadcast: 28 February 1982

This series of six programmes was written by Vince Powell. Reverend Mother Joseph (Anna Quayle) requested the appointment of a chaplain for her Sisters of St Winifred convent. Bishop Larkin (John Savident) sent them Father Charlie (Lionel Jeffries), an eccentric late-in-life convert. He tried to bring a few modern improvements to the convent, like the provision of a television set. The sisters included Mercedes (Gillian Royale), Mary (Deddie Davies), Bernadette (Denyse Alexander), Lucy (Jamila

Daughters Anna and Karen flank Patrick, their FATHER, DEAR FATHER (Photo © Thames Television)

Massey), Anna (Annet Peters), Clare (Wendy Smith) Theresa (Jean Buik Morton) and Frances (Esther Byrd).
Producer: Stuart Allen.

FATHER, DEAR FATHER
THAMES. First broadcast: 5 November 1968

This series, created and written by Johnnie Mortimer and Brian Cooke, ran for seven series and 45 editions to 6 February 1973. It proved the ideal vehicle for stylish actor Patrick Cargill, who as Patrick Glover was ostensibly head of his family and was forced to fend off the attentions, demands, criticisms and eccentricities of a host of females. These included his two super-sophisticated, mini-skirted teenage daughters Anna (Natasha Pyne) and Karen (Ann Holloway). Patrick was divorced and his ex-wife Barbara (Ursula Howells) had married his best friend Bill (Patrick Holt). Initially, Barbara and Bill lived in Portofino, but it was not long before she returned to be yet another in his daily traumas. The older members of the female-dominated household were the housekeeper and nanny (Noël Dyson) and Patrick's dotty mother (Joyce Carey). His only male companion in his hopeless and harassed life was a St Bernard dog named HG Wells who spent most of his hours asleep on the settee. Professionally, Patrick was a writer of James Bond-type novels and at work he was equally hounded by his agent Georgie (Sally Bazely, later Dawn Addams). In the 1972 series, his pressures were marginally reduced when Anna married Tim Tanner (Jeremy Child). Barbara's husband Bill was now portrayed by Tony Britton and Karen, too, had a boyfriend, Howard (Richard O'Sullivan).
Producer: William G Stewart.

In 1977, a further seven episodes were made in Australia with just Cargill and Noël Dyson from the original cast. Australian actress Sally Conabère played the part of Elizabeth.

FATHER KNOWS BEST
CBS (AMERICA) PRESENTED BY ITV.
First broadcast (UK): 15 September 1956

This series began in the USA in 1954 and ran for 191 episodes. Robert Young starred as insurance executive Jim Anderson and Jane Wyatt played his wife Margaret. The stories concerned the parents' attempts to cope with the growing-pains of their three teenage children, Betty (Elinore

Donahue), Bud (Billy Gray) and pint-sized Kathy (Lauren Chapin). Quarrels were the norm for the Anderson family, but they were always able to sort out their differences to a happy and moral ending. The family reflected the comfort and attitudes of middle-class America at the time. The females of the household really did believe that kind, loving and worldly-wise Jim did know best.
Producer: Eugene B Rodney.

FATHER MATTHEW'S DAUGHTER
BBC. First broadcast: 11 May 1987

Terence Brady and Charlotte Bingham wrote this six-part series. Father Matthew (James Bolam) had been an agnostic jazz pianist prior to his call to Holy Orders and got the shock of his life when his sister died and specified in her will that her eight-year-old daughter Holly (Samantha Hurst), a naughty child, should be brought up by him. Fortunately for Father Matthew, his curate Father Charlie (Ray Winstone) had a sister Sharon (Gabrielle Lloyd) who had four sons and she volunteered to provide board and lodgings for Holly.
Producer: David Askey.

FATHER OF THE BRIDE
MGM PRESENTED BY ITV.
First broadcast (UK): 6 May 1966

Thirty-four episodes of this series, based on the novel of the same title by Edward Streeter, were made in 1961 but did not reach the UK until 1966. Leon Ames starred as Stanley Banks, a wealthy businessman married to Ellie (Ruth Warwick). Their daughter Kay (Myrna Fahey) announced her plans to marry Buckley Dunstan (Burt Metcalfe). Kay's younger brother Tommy was played by Ricki Sorenson. Buckley's parents Doris and Herbert Dunstan were portrayed by Lurene Tuttle and Herbert Sherman.
Writers included Katherine and Dale Eunson, Mathilde and Theo Ferro and Ken Fletcher. Director: Fletcher Markle. Producers: Rudy E Abel and Robert Maxwell.

FATHER'S DAY
CHANNEL 4. First broadcast: 17 April 1983

John Alderton starred as Lyall Jarvis, a husband who believed that women had had their own way for far too long and a father who endorsed the theory that children should be encouraged to play sport and take part in other activities rather than vegetate in front of the box. His wife was Dee (Rosalind Ayres in the first series, Karen Archer in the second). The children were Gemma (Dominique Barnes), Toby (Zac Nicholson) and Tasha (Kate Alderton). Lyall's own father was played by Paul Angelis. After a first run of six programmes a new series of seven returned on 8 July 1984.

Writer: Peter Spence. Director: Laszek Burzynski. Producer: Brian Eastman for Picture Partnership Productions.

FAWLTY TOWERS

BBC. First broadcast: 19 September 1975

Although only 12 half-hour episodes were ever made, this show remains one of the most revered sitcoms of all time. It was created and written by John Cleese and his then-wife Connie Booth. The setting was a small hotel near Torquay where Basil Fawlty (John Cleese) was a hotelier who hated guests. If he had to have them, he required them to be at least of the 'Country Life' class. He was manic, intolerant, insensitive and appallingly rude. He ran the terrible hostelry with his over-coiffeured, domineering wife Sybil (Prunella Scales), who was adept at gushing insincere charm to compensate for Basil's lack of same. The inept but eternally hopeful Spanish waiter Manuel (Andrew Sachs) came from Barcelona, a fact which Fawlty was often at pains to point out in the belief that it accounted for Manuel's incompetence. The only ray of sanity in the entire establishment came from the pert maid Polly Sherman (Connie Booth), who remained calm, collected and efficient, though much exasperated.

Throughout the programmes there was a constant flow of visiting victims on the receiving end of Basil's abusive invective. However, there were three permanent residents who managed to remain more or less impervious to his downpours of scorn: Major Gowen (Ballard Berkeley), Miss Tibbs (Gilly Flower) and Miss Gatsby (Renee Roberts), all of whom would sit stoically while disaster erupted all around them. Basil Fawlty's personification of snobbery based on ignorance was first seen on BBC2 in an episode entitled, appropriately, 'A Touch of Class'. The second and last series began, again on BBC2, on 19 February 1979.

Producers: John Howard Davies, Douglas Argent.

FEET FIRST

THAMES. First broadcast: 8 January 1979

John Esmonde and Bob Larbey wrote this series which ran for seven shows. Terry Prince (Jonathan Barlow) was a motor mechanic living and working in the Midlands and playing football in his local league at weekends. He was discovered by Harry Turnbull (Lee Montague), the manager of a First Division club, who signed him up and took him away from his familiar environment. His life changed under the influence of Turnbull, Mrs Viv Turnbull (Jacquie Cassidy) and the club's public relations officer Hamilton Defries (Doug Fisher).

Producers: Michael Mills, Mark Stuart.

THE FENN STREET GANG

LWT. First broadcast: 24 September 1971

When the shower from class 5C left school in PLEASE SIR, they went out into the cruel world determined to retain their friendships forged at school and preserve their group identity. In the first few programmes they were encouraged by the presence of their former teacher, Bernard Hedges (John Alderton), who had also left for pastures new. Frankie Abbott (David Barry) initially became a private detective, Maureen Bullock (Liz Gebhardt) trained to be a nurse, and schoolyard sweethearts Eric Duffy (Peter Cleall) and Sharon Eversleigh (now played by Carol Hawkins) drifted impecuniously towards marriage. In and out of jobs were Dennis Dunstable (Peter Denyer) and Peter Craven (Leon Vitali). The programme, created and for the most part written by John Esmonde and Bob Larbey, ran for three seasons.

Producers included David Askey, Graham Evans, Bryan Izzard, Howard Ross and Mark Stuart.

FFIZZ

THAMES. First broadcast: 9 September 1987

Jack Mowbray (Richard Griffiths) and Hugo Walker (Benjamin Whitrow) were directors of upper-crust wine merchants Mowbray and Crofts. Neither of them had a penchant for work and their first home was the cellar where they freely imbibed. Their financial irresponsibility led directly to the firm being on the point of collapse, to the extent that the bank sent in whizz-kid Alan (Robin Kermode) to sort out and try to save the business. Griselda (Felicity Montagu), employed by Jack and Hugo, did her best in spite of them and their best

'Clean the Windows!' Basil Fawlty (John Cleese) shows Manuel (Andrew Sachs) the way forward in FAWLTY TOWERS (Photo: Copyright © BBC)

customer was Lady Boughton (Phyllida Law). There was a second series of six, featuring the same characters which started its run on 25 July 1989. *Music: Denis King. Writers: Richard Fegan and Andrew Norriss. Producer: Derrick Goodwin.*

FIDDLERS THREE
YTV. First broadcast: 19 February 1991

In this 13-part series, Ralph Fiddler (Peter Davison) was tortured by having to hang on to his middle-management job for dear life. He came up with all sorts of schemes to advance his career but office procedure in the accounts department of the large company for which he worked was a bit beyond him. Though he tried to act tough, he was as soft as they come and came several croppers as a result. His wife Ros (Paula Wilcox) was a truly down-to-earth girl who had no qualms about going to his office or causing embarrassment to get him out of a scrape. The departmental boss was JJ Morley (Charles Kay) and others involved in the plots were Harvey (Peter Blake), Norma (Cindy Day) and Osborne (Tyler Butterworth).
Writer: Eric Chappell. Producer: Graham Wetherell.

FILTHY RICH AND CATFLAP
BBC. First broadcast: 7 January 1987

The title referred to three characters, Filthy Ralph (Nigel Planer), Richie Rich (Rik Mayall) and Eddie Catflap (Adrian Edmondson). Rich was a television comedian and presenter, but not in great demand. Catflap was his minder, while Filthy was his agent. The six-part series was written by Ben Elton. *Producer: Paul Jackson.*

A FINE ROMANCE
LWT. First broadcast: 8 November 1981

Bob Larbey created and wrote this series in which real life husband and wife Michael Williams and Judi Dench had an on–off–on romance. He played Mike and she was Laura. The matchmakers-in-chief were Laura's sister Helen (Susan Penhaligon) and her husband Phil (Richard Warwick). Mike's business was Selway Landscape Gardening, which he was inclined to neglect according to the health, or lack of same, of the romance. Lending a helping hand were Harry (Geoffrey Rose) and, occasionally, Laura's parents Mr and Mrs Dalton (Richard Pearson and Lally Bowers). Mike and Laura became lovers, then drifted apart but eventually, at the end of four seasons, Mike proposed. The final show was seen on 17 February 1984.
Producers: James Cellan Jones, Don Leaver.

FINKEL'S CAFE

BBC RADIO. First broadcast: 4 July 1956

Frank Muir and Denis Norden adapted the American radio series DUFFY'S TAVERN into Finkel's, 'the caff where the elite meet to eat'. As with Duffy, the proprietor Finkel never appeared. His cafe was managed by Eddie, an Irishman portrayed by Peter Sellers. Helping him run the business were Avril Angers, Sid James and Kenneth Connor. There was a Gypsy Tearoom band and a weekly guest star in six broadcasts.

Producer: Pat Dixon.

FIRE CRACKERS

ATV. First broadcast: 29 August 1964

Fred Robinson created this show which was set in the tiny village of Cropper's End (population 70). A bureaucratic oversight had allowed the local fire brigade to continue in existence, albeit in obsolescence. Manning their beloved fire engine, Bessie (c.1907), were Alfred Marks as fire chief Charlie, Joe Baker as Jumbo, Ronnie Brady as Loverboy, Sidney Bromley as the orange-bearded Weary Willie, and Cardew Robinson as Hairpin. (Robinson left before the 1965 series and was replaced by Clive Elliott as Tadpole). Their objective was to avoid any kind of fire and if ever an alarm sounded they would ring the neighbouring fire service, under the control of Station Officer Blazer (John Arnatt) and Leading Fireman Piggott (Norman Chappell). Charlie enjoyed a nice little credit arrangement with barmaid Rosie (Maureen Toal) at the Cropper's Arms, unless the boss George (Colin Douglas) was watching. The last of 14 programmes was seen on 20 February 1965.

Writers included Fred Robinson, John Singer and John Warren. Director: Josephine Douglas. Producer: Alan Tarrant.

FIRST OF THE SUMMER WINE

BBC. First broadcast: 3 January 1988

Roy Clarke, writer of LAST OF THE SUMMER WINE, took his principal characters from that series back to just before the war when they were young men and women. Peter Sallis played Mr Clegg, the father of Norman Clegg (David Fenwick), and Maggie Ollerenshaw was Mrs Clegg, Norman's mother. Wally Batty (Gary Whitaker) was trying to impress young Nora (Helen Patrick), and others included Compo (Paul Wyett), Foggy (Richard Lumsden),

Seymour (Paul McLain) and Ivy (Sarah Dangerfield). A 45-minute pilot was screened leading to a six-part series from 4 September the same year, and a second run of six began on 3 September 1989.

Producers: Gareth Gwenlan, Mike Stephens.

FISH

ABC (AMERICA) PRESENTED BY BBC.
First broadcast (UK): 1 April 1978

This spin-off from BARNEY MILLER in eight episodes again starred Abe Vigoda as Phil Fish, retired from the New York City Police, who with his wife Bernice (Florence Stanley) agreed to take on five underprivileged adolescent children from the nearby centre. They were Mike (Lenny Bari), Jilly (Denise Miller), Loomis (Todd Bridges), Diane (Sarah Natoli) and Victor (Cassisi).

Producer: Danny Arnold.

FLOGGIT'S

BBC RADIO. First broadcast: 17 August 1956

Elsie and Doris Waters' characters GERT AND DAISY were uprooted from Knothole Street in London's East End when Daisy's husband Bert's Uncle Alfred died, leaving them Floggit's Stores, a small general store in the picturesque village of Russett Green. With Bert temporarily employed, there was no alternative but for Gert and Daisy to take over the running of the shop. Russett Green boasted a pub with barmaid Emma Sneed (Joan Sims), Lord of the Manor Lord Russett (Ronnie Barker), local fuss-pot Mr Niggle (Hugh Paddick) and the ubiquitous Ma Butler (Iris Vandeleur). Gert and Daisy opened for business and ran successfully for three series. They later took on Mr Niggle's son Cyril (Harry Fowler) as errand boy.

Writers: Dave Freeman, John Junkin, Terry Nation. Producers: Alastair Scott Johnston, Bill Gates.

FLYING BLIND

USA PRESENTED BY CHANNEL 4.
First broadcast: 5 January 1994

Recent college graduate Neil Barash (Corey Parker) found post-college life a disappointment and was forced to take a job in a factory which made snack foods. On his first day the pace of his life multiplied several fold when he encountered Alice (Tea Leoni), an uninhibited wild child who whisked him to her downtown loft before he had a chance to delve into the world of junk food.

THE FLYING SWAN

BBC. First broadcast: 27 March 1965

This 13-part series belongs in the grey area between drama and sitcom and is probably more towards the former than the latter. Certainly its creator Donald Wilson and star Margaret Lockwood would see it in the drama department. However, there was much comedy, an on-going situation and regular characters. Lockwood played Mollie Manning, the widowed owner of the Flying Swan Hotel on the banks of the Thames, not far from Heathrow where her daughter Carol (played by real-life daughter Julia Lockwood) was based as an air hostess for Peregrine Airlines. Each episode was built around the quirks, shady dealings, peculiarities, lunacies or tragedies of a variety of guests. The regular staff included receptionist Prue (Wendy Hall), bar steward Fred Potter (Tom Watson), his girlfriend and barmaid Maisie (Nerys Hughes), and the Scottish general factotum Jessie McDonald (Molly Urquhart).
Theme music: Ron Grainer. Producer: Harold Clayton.

FLYING THE FLAG

BBC RADIO. First broadcast: 20 April 1987

Alex Shearer created and wrote this series about British diplomats abroad. Dinsdale Landon starred as Ambassdor Mackenzie, Her Majesty's bored and cynical representative in a poor, cold and small country behind the Iron Curtain. Other regular characters were William Frost (Peter Acre), Helen (Moir Leslie), Colonel Surikov (Christopher Benjamin) and US Ambassador Spiro (Stephen Greif). There were four series with a total of 28 broadcasts, the last on 4 August 1992.
Producers: Pete Atkin, Neil Cargill.

FOLLOW THAT DOG

SOUTHERN. First broadcast: 13 November 1974

Norman Rossington starred in this children's series as PC Fogg, a village bobby with a telepathic basset hound named Parry. The dog was able to transmit solutions to crimes through Fogg's dreams, so that he was able to baffle his battleaxe Sergeant Bryant (Patsy Rowlands) and the mild Inspector Bridges (Anthony Dawes). PC Fogg, who kept a mouse called Morrie in his helmet, was often assisted by two village children, Peter (Nigel Rhodes) and Rosie (Janet Finch).
Writer: Michael Nelson. Producer: Peter Croft.

FOLLOW THAT MAN

BBC RADIO. First broadcast: 2 November 1964

This was a most unusual series in that a different writer was invited to pick up and continue the story on a week by week basis. Edward J Mason kicked the nine-part series off with a broadcast in which he established the central character as Rex Anthony (played by disc jockey David Jacobs), a BBC entertainment producer who innocently became involved in international intrigue through the machinations of astrologer Professor Lemkin (Jeffrey Segal). Mason then handed over the development to Eddie Maguire, John P Wynn, Gale Pedrick, Lawrie Wyman, Philip Levene, Ted Willis, Bob Monkhouse and Denis Goodwin, Frank Muir and Denis Norden.
Producer: Edward Taylor.

FOOLS' PARADISE

BBC RADIO. First broadcast: 11 June 1945

Naunton Wayne as Bentley Woolcott and Basil Radford as Howard Spencer were quietly passing the time in their favourite way, watching cricket, when behind the pavilion was brewing a six-part adventure of spies, murders and comic intrigue. They were soon drawn into the plot. See also DOUBLE BEDLAM.
Writer: John Jowett. Producer: Vernon Harris.

FOR BETTER OR FOR WORSE

BBC RADIO. First broadcast: 11 February 1993

Bernard Pringle (Gorden Kaye) was engaged to Iris Bickerdyke (Su Pollard) in this series of eight episodes. Bernard lived with his father Wilf (David Ross) and worked for Mr Foley (Peter Wheeler) at Foley's Funeral Facilities. Also working there was Christabel (Julie Higginson), much to the displeasure of Iris and her mother Daisy (Paula Tilbrook) who named her 'Fancy Knickers'.
Writers: Mike Craig and Vince Powell. Producer: Mike Craig.

FOR THE LOVE OF ADA

THAMES. First broadcast: 20 April 1970

Vince Powell and Harry Driver created and wrote this love story of two 70-year-olds. It starred Irene

Handl as widow Ada Cresswell and Wilfred
Pickles as Walter Bingley, the grave-digger who
had buried her late husband. They began a love
affair and set up home together in Cemetery
Lodge. Their neighbours were Leslie and Ruth
Pollitt (Jack Smethurst and Barbara Mitchell). Leslie
was a fervent supporter of Manchester United,
Ruth was Ada's daughter. The series returned
later the same year for a second run with Walter
and Ada saving up to get married. Even though
Walter lost his job, the wedding took place on 26
October. The following year, Ruth gave birth to a
baby boy, Anthony, and they all lived happily ever
after!
Theme music: Ron Grainer. Producer: Ronnie Baxter.

FOREIGN AFFAIRS
BBC. First broadcast: 19 September 1966

Based on the conflicts of the time between the
British Foreign Office and the Soviet Embassy in
London, this six-part series starred Leslie Phillips as
Denis Proudfoot, personal assistant to the Admin-
istrator for Foreign Relations, Sir Hugh Marriot
(Austin Trevor). Dennis had a motherly secretary,
Miss Jessup (Dorothy Frere), and working as a
clerk in the mailroom was young Taplow (Richard
O'Sullivan). Over at the Russian Embassy lurked
Grischa Petrovitch (Ronnie Barker) who was as-
sistant to the Commissar, Serge Volchanivov (Joe
Melia). Grischa was slightly pro-British but on his
guard as secretary Irinka (Sonia Graham) worked
by the book.
*Writers: Leonard Samson, Johnnie Mortimer and
Brian Cooke. Producer: John Street.*

FOREIGN BODIES
BBC. First broadcast: 5 March 1987

Set in the troubled province of Northern Ireland,
this sitcom was the joint work of Ulsterman Graham
Reid and Dubliner Bernard Farrell, who came up
with two six-part series ending 8 June 1989. Two
Catholic nurses from Dublin, Roisin (Hilary
Reynolds) and Septa (Maeve Germaine), went to
work in a hospital in Belfast. There Roisin met
Protestant motor mechanic Tom (Dan Gordon),
who just happened to have a pal Alex (Colum
Convey), who courted trouble wherever he ventured. Though friendships were often stretched to
the limit, they set out to show that living in Belfast
could be a lot of fun.
Music: Ken Howard. Producer: Sydney Lotterby.

THE FOSDYKE SAGA
BBC RADIO. First broadcast: 2 October 1983

The Fosdykes had been a cartoon strip drawn by
Bill Tidy in the Daily Mirror, spoofing Galsworthy's
'Forsyte Saga' which the BBC had dramatised to
much acclaim in the late 1960s. Tidy and John
Junkin adapted the Fosdykes for this radio serial
which notched up 40 editions to 13 November
1985. In short, the Fosdykes were a North Country
family from a place called Griddlesbury, who had
eked out a life without sanitation or any other
creature comforts but who had risen to own a vast
tripe empire. This they had achieved in spite of the
evil intentions of Roger Ditchley (Christian
Rodska), who was jealous of any inroads made to
his father Ben's (Colin Douglas) long-established
tripe business. The Fosdykes were Rebecca
(Stephanie Turner), Josiah (Philip Lowrie), Victoria (Miriam Margolyes), Tom (David Threlfall)
and Albert (Enn Reitel).
Producer: Alan Nixon.

THE FOSSETT SAGA
LWT. First broadcast: 10 January 1969

This period comedy was created by one-time
policeman Dave Freeman. It ran for just one series.
Jimmy Edwards starred as James Wellington Fossett,
author of penny-dreadfuls, bon viveur and patron
of the arts in late Victorian London. He resided at
14, Old Cobblers Street where he retained his un-
paid valet and companion, Herbert Quince (Sam
Kydd). Quince was also a self-employed window
cleaner. Fossett enjoyed the Music Hall and
encountered Millie Goswick (June Whitfield), a
raunchy singer, and Khyber O'Malley (Paul
Whitsun-Jones), known as 'The Singing Dragoon'.
Fossett dreamed eternally of riches and planned the
expansion of the Empire. Quince, though servile,
proved a cunning side-kick.
Producer: David Askey.

THE FOSTERS
LWT. First broadcast: 9 April 1976

Britain's first all-black family show set out to por-
tray a typical immigrant family living in South
London. Samuel and Pearl Foster (Norman Beaton
and Isabelle Lucas) were the parents of artist son
Sonny (Lenny Henry), sexy 16-year-old daughter
Shirley (Sharon Rosita) and younger son Benjamin
(Lawrie Mark). Shirley shared her problems with

her old school friend and neighbour, unmarried Vilma (Carmen Munro). A first series of seven programmes was followed by a further 13 transmissions from 16 April the following year.

Writers: Jack Elinson, Norman Paul, Jon Watkins, Lou Derman, Bill Davenport. Producer: Stuart Allen.

FOUR IDLE HANDS

ATV. First broadcast: 26 March 1976

John Kane wrote this children's series which enjoyed a 13-week run. Mike Dudds (Phil Daniels) and Pete Sutton (Ray Burdis) were two school leavers in search of jobs. In the wake of their frustrated efforts, and encouraged by their respective fathers Mr Dudds (Royston Tickner) and Mr Sutton (Howard Goorney), they decided to start their own business; but with no qualifications between them, they were unsure what field they should explore. Their efforts were both encouraged and hindered by Emilio (George Innes).

Producer: David Foster.

FOXY LADY

GRANADA. First broadcast: 25 October 1982

Writer Geoffrey Lancashire set this series in the late 1950s. *The Ramsden Reminder*, the weekly local newspaper of a northern town, faced bankruptcy and a drastically low circulation. Following the death of the long-time editor, radical changes were called for and Daisy Jackson (Diane Keen) arrived as the new editor. The fortunes of the paper rose, but not for long and soon there were fresh crises. The principal characters were bank accountant Joe Prince (Geoffrey Burridge), feature writer JP Schofield (Patrick Troughton), sports editor Ben Marsh (Milton Johns), arts editor Tancred Taylor (Alan David), ladies' column writer Hector Ross (Gregor Fisher), print-room apprentice Owen Buckley (Steve Pinder) and Jack-of-all-trades Acorn Henshaw (Tom Mennard). There were two series and 13 episodes in total, the last one transmitted on 25 February 1984.

Directors: Richard Holthouse, Malcolm Taylor. Producer: John G Temple.

FRANK STUBBS PROMOTES

CARLTON. First broadcast: 12 July 1993

Simon Nye wrote these seven hour-long comedy dramas which starred Timothy Spall in the title role as a Soho ticket tout and would-be entertainments and ancillary activities promoter. Stubbs adopted as his inspiration the ruthless Dave Giddings (Nick Reding) but his own fundamental niceness meant he could never emulate his role model and, anyway, Giddings would have nothing to do with him. He went into many ventures with enthusiasm, reluctantly supported by his uneasy wife Petra Dillon (Lesley Sharp) and his glamorous niece Dawn Dillon (Danniella Westbrook). He tried his hand at promoting actresses to film director Ken (John Gordon Sinclair), a book by shady novelist Clive Riley (Hywel Bennett), the famous clairvoyant Molly Bramley (Dora Bryan), and even car-kit assembly packs. All came to naught. A second run began on 11 July 1994.

Director: Richard Standeven. Producer: Hilary Bevan Jones for Noel Gay Productions.

FRANK'S PLACE

USA PRESENTED BY CHANNEL 4.
First broadcast (UK): 24 August 1990

Boston professor Frank Parrish (Tim Reid) inherited a restaurant, The Chez, in New Orleans. When he made his first visit to see the place he found the employees hostile towards him, and they had a plan to try and buy the place for themselves. However, Frank quit Boston and took on the restaurant himself. The chef was Big Arthur (Tony Burton) and the general handyman was Cool Charles (William Thomas Jr).

FRASIER

NBC (AMERICA) PRESENTED BY CHANNEL 4.
First broadcast (UK): 20 April 1994

In this spin-off from CHEERS, Dr Frasier Crane (Kelsey Grammer) left Boston and returned to his home town, Seattle. There he hosted his own radio psychiatrist show on which he counselled listeners about their problems. His hopes for a quiet life were disrupted when his nuisance of a younger brother Niles (David Hyde Pierce) dumped their cantankerous dad (John Mahoney), a retired cop, and his dog Eddie on him. Even worse in Frasier's eyes was the ghastly chair which his father insisted on bringing with him. The home-help was dotty Daphne Moore (Jane Leeves) from Manchester, England, and Frasier's personal assistant at work was played by Peri Gilpin.

THE FRED ALLEN PROGRAMME

CBS (AMERICA) PRESENTED BY BBC RADIO.
First broadcast: 17 May 1943

Comedian Allen (1894–1956) remains a legend of American radio, discussed in the same breath as Jack Benny and Burns and Allen. In 1943, a series of radio shows was recorded in America by arrangement with the Special Service Division of the War Department of the USA, and Allen was first heard on the Forces network. He made much use of sound effects, believing that the listener had a fertile imagination capable of interpreting his or her own images from Allen's audio suggestions. He and Jack Benny engaged in a long-term feud of the airwaves, a feud of fiction but nonetheless a credible feud to the listeners. Allen's wit was caustic and satirical and focused on current events. He was supported by his real wife, Portland Hoffa, and by Al Goodman and his orchestra. There was a constant flow of guest stars.

FREDDIE AND MAX

THAMES. First broadcast: 12 November 1990

In this six-part series by Dick Clement and Ian La Frenais, Maxine Chandler (Anne Bancroft) was a fading Hollywood prima donna who had experienced several divorces and had become an ill-mannered bitch whose tantrums drove all and sundry to avoid her. She lived at London's Savoy Hotel. When she was contracted to write her autobiography, she hired as her researcher Freddie (Charlotte Coleman), who was down on her luck and in need of the work. Generous, warm-hearted Freddie was everything that egotistical, selfish Max was not, yet they managed to concoct a chemistry which was of benefit to both characters.
Producer: John Stroud.

FREEBIE AND THE BEAN

USA PRESENTED BY BBC.
First broadcast (UK): 27 July 1981

The 1974 movie of this title starred Alan Arkin and James Caan. This attempt to make a TV series about the two irresponsible cops lasted just half a season in the United States before it was cancelled. Nonetheless, the BBC bought and screened the eight episodes. Tom Mason was Freebie and Hector Elizondo was the Bean. Their boss was the San Francisco District Attorney (William Daniels).

FRENCH FIELDS

THAMES. First broadcast: 5 September 1989

In this sequel to FRESH FIELDS, William and Hester Fields (Anton Rodgers and Julia McKenzie) moved to live in northern France after he was headhunted for a job over there. Their limited Franglais and lack of knowledge of local ways and customs created several dilemmas. Other principal characters caught up in their lives included daughter Emma (Sally Baxter, later Karen Ascoe), Peter (Philip Bird), Madame Remoleux (Valerie Lush), Chantal Moriac (Pamela Salem), Monsieur Dax (Olivier Pierre) and Jill and Hugh Trendle (Liz Crowther and Robin Kermode). There were three series, each of six programmes, and in the final episode on 8 October 1991, William had been made redundant and he and his wife were contemplating whether or not to return to England.
Writers: John Chapman and Ian Davidson. Director: Mark Stuart. Producer: James Gilbert.

FRESH FIELDS

THAMES. First broadcast: 7 March 1984

Married for 20 years and comfortably off in Barnes, west London, William and Hester Fields (Anton Rodgers and Julia McKenzie) faced up to their future as the children had left home. Hester, scatty but youthful, opted to add occasional zip and spice to their lives and she looked for a part-time job. When she became the gruff but sensible William's secretary, they both found it hard to mix work and home. Whenever they found tranquillity it was inevitably shattered by their extremely nosey neighbour Sonia Barratt (Ann Beach) or Hester's mother Nancy Penrose (Fanny Rowe). There were 27 episodes, the last on 23 December 1986, over four series. In 1989 the Fields were moved to France for a sequel, FRENCH FIELDS.
Writer: John Chapman. Producer: Peter Frazer-Jones.

FRESH PRINCE OF BEL-AIR

NBC (AMERICA) PRESENTED BY BBC.
First broadcast: 14 January 1991

BBC2 screened this music-orientated series under the DEF II strand of youth programmes. The star was Grammy-winning rapper Will Smith who played a character with his own name. Will was from the poor area of downtown Philadelphia, a street-wise kid who was sent to stay with his extremely rich relations in their mansion in Bel-Air,

William and Hester (Anton Rodgers and Julia McKenzie) seem content enough here in their FRENCH FIELDS (Photo © Thames Television)

an exclusive residential area of Los Angeles. There he was under the eye of his larger than life Uncle Philip Banks (James Avery) and his snobbish Auntie Vivian (Janet Hubert). The Banks had three children of their own, Carlton (Alfonso Ribeiro) who was about the same age as Will, Hilary (Karyn Parsons) and Ashley (Tatyana M Ali). Hilary was vain, worked in a TV newsroom and lost her fiancée Trevor, who died while proposing during a bungee jump that went wrong. Will assumed the 'Prince' mantle as he fitted and flitted into his new surroundings. He worked in the coffee shop at the University of Los Angeles. Some of the best lines in the shows were uttered by the Banks' very English butler Geoffrey, played by Joseph Marcell. More than 50 editions of the series had been transmitted sporadically by the spring of 1994.
Producers: Deborah Oppenheimer, Werner Valian for Quincy Jones Entertainments.

FROM A BIRD'S EYE VIEW
ATV. First broadcast: 31 July 1971

This British-made series, one of ATV boss Lew Grade's assaults on the American market, concerned two rather dizzy air stewardesses on their travels around the globe. Millicent Martin was cast as English girl Millie Grover, and Patte Finlay played her American counterpart Maggie Ralston. They flew into hectic adventures from country to country, much to the hair-tearing irritation of their airline boss Mr Beauchamp (Peter Jones). The only other regular character was Millie's unmarried Uncle Bert, portrayed by Robert Cawdron.
Producers: Jack Greenwood and Sheldon Leonard.

FROM THE TOP
CENTRAL. First broadcast: 23 September 1985

Bill Oddie and Laura Beaumont created and wrote these stories set in the Jolly Theatre School. Oddie also starred as the stage-struck William Worthington who, at a mid-life, mid-forties crisis, abandoned his secure job and enrolled at the school as the only mature student among a group of kids. The school was run by Annie and Dolly Jolly (Moyra Fraser and Maggie Rennie) who strove for perfection through an initial series of six but who, by the final transmission on 14 December 1986, after six more struggles, were faced with such financial problems that the school faced closure. William's classmates included Polly Jolly (Joiese Waller), Wayne Layne (Michael Quill), Joyce (Erica Sheward), Leslie (Gavin Forward), Janis (Catherine Holman) and Humphrey (Scott Sherin).

Producer: Michael Dolenz.

THE FRONT LINE
BBC. First broadcast: 6 December 1984

This six-part series by Alex Shearer featured two half-brothers. Sheldon (Alan Igbon) was a Rastafarian who always tried to land his older and more responsible brother Malcolm (Paul Barber) in hot water. Though they maintained totally different lifestyles, they remained inseparable brethren, two black lads from the North who happened to live in Bristol. In the first edition Malcolm went on security patrol for a firm and met up with his pal Fraser (Christopher Bramwell), a policeman who encouraged him to join the force.

Producer: Roger Race.

FULL HOUSE
THAMES. First broadcast: 7 January 1985

Paul and Marsha Hatfield (Christopher Strauli and Sabina Franklyn) had been married for three years and lived with Paul's mum. They were desperate for a home of their own so jumped at the opportunity to share a roof and the attached mortgage commitments with Murray and Diana McCoy (Brian Capron and Natalie Forbes). By and large the arrangement worked with only minor stresses until Diana begame pregnant and gave birth to a baby. There were 21 episodes over three series, ending 19 November 1986.

Music: Harry Stoneham. Writers: Johnnie Mortimer and Brian Cooke, Vince Powell. Producers: Peter Frazer-Jones, Mark Stuart, Anthony Parker.

FULL STRETCH
CENTRAL. First broadcast: 5 January 1993

In these six hour-long comedy dramas by Dick Clement and Ian La Frenais, Baz Levick (Kevin McNally) was the proprietor of a luxury limousine-hire business with west London pretensions but actually operating from a run-down garage in north London. His clients, the guest stars (David Bowie in the first edition), formed the basis of each story. The company's wheelchair-bound administrator was Grace Robbins (Sue Johnston) and the drivers of the stretch limos were Tarquin Woods (Reece Dinsdale) and Tessa Knowles (Rowena King). Baz's wife was Tanya (Wendy Morgan) and the company name was Ivory Tower.

Director: Antonia Bird. Producer: Martin McKeand.

FURTHER ADVENTURES OF LUCKY JIM
BBC. First broadcast: 2 May 1967

Kingsley Amis created his Lucky Jim character in his 1954 novel which was made into a movie in 1957. Ten years later, Dick Clement and Ian La Frenais updated Jim into the Swingin' Sixties for this seven-part series. Keith Barron starred as Yorkshireman Jim Dixon, who fought his battles against the phoneys, bores and creeps of the world. He usually protested in silence, muttering obscenitites under his breath and making faces behind the protection of his hand. His adventures into the plastic world of the sexy fads and crazes of the day were embarked upon with his guard well up and his eyes sharply peeled.

Producer: Duncan Wood.

Fifteen years later Clement and La Frenais reincarnated the idea and cast Enn Reitel in the role of Jim. The setting remained the London 'scene' of the late 1960s to which Jim had returned following a year in Holland. The first of seven programmes went out on 1 November 1982.

Theme music: Alan Price. Producer: Harold Snoad.

THE FUZZ
THAMES. First broadcast: 8 September 1977

This short series of six programmes was created and written by Willis Hall. The stories were of a small but inept city police force led by Superintendent Allardyce (Colin Jeavons) with Det. Sgt Marble (Michael Robbins), PCs Cordwainer and Dickinson (Nigel Lambert and Mike Savage), WPC Purvis (Lynda Bellingham) and tea-girl Doris (Ena Cabayo).

Producer: Stuart Allen.

THE GAFFER

YTV. First broadcast: 9 January 1981

Bill Maynard starred as Fred Moffat, the Gaffer, managing director of a small light-engineering company which was always on the brink of disaster. He had a sardonic wit, which was directed especially towards his ever-loathing son Spencer (Chris Langham) and shop steward Harry (Russell Hunter). Fred became a local councillor where his arch rival in business, Joe Gregory (Alan Hockey), also had a seat. Among Fred's workers were Betty (Pat Ashton), Ginger (David Gillies), Charlie (Don Crann) and Henry (Keith Marsh). There were three series, each of seven programmes, concluding on 5 July 1983.

Writer: Graham White. Producer: Alan Tarrant.

GALLOPING GALAXIES!

BBC. First broadcast: 1 October 1985

Bob Block created and wrote this children's serial with the spaceship 'Voyager' being guided by a computer called SID (voiced by Kenneth Williams) as it hurtled through time warps, belts of asteroids and traffic lights with equal equanimity. At the helm was Captain Pettifer (Robert Swales) with officers Morton (Paul Wilce) and Webster (Nigel Cooke), and in pursuit was space pirate Murphy (Sean Caffrey, later Niall Buggy). In amongst disintegrating robots and extra-terrestrial happenings were some regular characters including Mabel and Elsie Appleby (Priscilla Morgan and Josie Kidd) and Mr Elliott (James Mansfield). There were two series, each of five parts.

Producer: Jeremy Swan.

A GENTLEMEN'S CLUB

BBC. First broadcast: 23 September 1988

Writer Richard Gordon set his fictional stately club in Pall Mall, London. Its former glorious plush, marble and brass had become gloomy and sombre and the building was slowly, like many of its members, crumbling. The six-part series starred William Gaunt as Aubrey and Richard Vernon as George.

Producer: Sydney Lotterby.

GEORGE AND MILDRED

THAMES. First broadcast: 6 September 1976

Writers Johnnie Mortimer and Brian Cooke took the dodgy landlords George and Mildred Roper (Brian Murphy and Yootha Joyce) from their basement flat in MAN ABOUT THE HOUSE and installed them in a new home on a modern housing estate in middle-class suburbia, 46 Peacock Crescent, Hampton Wick. Mildred settled like a duck to water but George, working-class and proud of it, hated his new environment.

Much of the antagonism between the Ropers came from sex, or rather the lack of it, as George would repeatedly claim to have a headache rather than indulge in sexual activity with his marital partner. Mildred was a social-climbing snob who falsely believed she had achieved a status equal to

Accidents will happen, and have done here to GEORGE AND MILDRED (Photo © Thames Television)

anyone in the neighbourhood. Their neighbours were Jeffrey and Ann Fourmile (Norman Eshley and Sheila Fearn). The toffee-nosed executive Jeffrey looked down with distaste on the unemployed, lazy George. The Fourmiles had a seven-year-old terror of a child, Tristram (Nicholas Bond-Owen). Adding to Mildred's concern for her status were her own sister Ethel (Avril Elgar) and brother-in-law Humphrey (Reginald Marsh) who only turned up when they had some new material acquisition to flaunt under Mildred's envious nose.

While George lost most of his battles with Mildred, he won most of his confrontations with Jeffrey, especially where Tristram was concerned. While Jeffrey sought to raise his son as a clone of himself, George delighted in instructing the little lad in undesirable pastimes like gambling. The series returned on 14 November 1977 and again on 7 September 1978. By this third series, the Fourmiles had a new baby, Tarquin, and George had palled up with a fellow layabout, Jerry (Roy Kinnear). There was a fourth series starting 13 November 1979 and the shows have been much repeated. In all there were 38 episodes, ending 25 December 1979. *Producer: Peter Frazer-Jones.*

GEORGE AND THE DRAGON
ATV. First broadcast: 19 November 1966

This series, created and written by Vince Powell and Harry Driver, began with Mrs Gabrielle Dragon (Peggy Mount) visiting an employment agency and being given the post of housekeeper to a country gentleman, Colonel Maynard (John Le Mesurier). On arriving at the Colonel's house she met his chauffeur, George Russell (Sid James). Sensing that George fancied himself as a ladies' man, Mrs Dragon swiftly warned him off and George was delighted to oblige. The two of them lived in open conflict with occasional interventions from the Colonel or the mild-mannered gardener, Ralph (Keith Marsh). There were 20 episodes, ending 17 February 1968. *Theme music: Tom Springfield. Producers: Shaun O'Riordan and Alan Tarrant.*

THE GEORGE BURNS SHOW
CBS (AMERICA) PRESENTED BY BBC.
First broadcast (UK): 4 January 1959

THE BURNS AND ALLEN SHOW came to an end when Gracie Allen retired from show business in 1958, leaving husband George to take centre stage alone. This new series saw George's character con-

centrate on trying to establish himself as a theatrical producer and promoter of great drama. Hangovers from the matrimonial series were Harry von Zell, who had been restricted to the role of announcer but in the new format professed serious acting ambitions, and Blanche Morton (Bea Benaderet) who was installed as George's secretary. The British transmissions confusingly ran parallel to the last few editions of THE BURNS AND ALLEN SHOW but George on his own was presented for 14 episodes.

GERT AND DAISY
A-R. First broadcast: 9 September 1959

Elsie and Doris Waters made their debut as a double act in 1923, so by the time they brought their radio and stage characters, Gert and Daisy, to television, they were already in semi-retirement. Gert and Daisy were a pair of Cockney gossips who chatted about the latest news of their husbands, the mythical Bert and Fred. For this television series, created for them by Ted Willis, Gert and Daisy were the proprietresses of a theatrical boarding house which provided a suitable excuse for the show to have different guests each episode.
Writer: Lew Schwarz. Producer: Milo Lewis.

GET BACK
BBC. First broadcast: 26 October 1992

Laurence Marks and Maurice Gran created this series and called it 'recession comedy'. Brothers Martin and Albert Sweet (Ray Winstone and Larry Lamb) grew up on a council estate in Finsbury Park where their dad Bernie (John Bardon) still lived. Both the boys had enjoyed success in business but when the economic recession began to bite, Martin's wealth was stripped away from him as the Thatcherite dream exploded. As his business crashed, so the bank called in his debts and Albert refused to bail him out. As a result, Martin and wife Loretta (Carol Harrison) and their daughters Joanna (Michelle Cattini) and Eleanor (Kate Winslet) were forced to sell their five-bedroomed home in Hatch End and squat with mean old Bernie in his grotty little flat. Martin began a gusty fightback while Bernie just wanted the rent and free beer. Albert appeared to enjoy continued prosperity with his wife Prudence (Jane Booker) as his unfortunate brother, who had once had his own clothes shop, was reduced to jobs like debt-collecting and selling dog-food. A first series of seven programmes was followed by eight more episodes from 27 September 1993.

Writers included Marks and Gran, Gary Lawson and John Phelps, Bernard McKenna. Directors: Graeme Harper, Terry Kinane. Producer: Bernard McKenna.

GET SMART

NBC (AMERICA) PRESENTED BY BBC.
First broadcast (UK): 16 October 1965

This spoof spy series was created by Mel Brooks and Buck Henry. Don Adams starred as Secret Agent 86, Maxwell Smart, working as a faithful servant of the top-secret Government department known as CONTROL. Smart and his associates were in eternal conflict with a sinister group of enemies known as KAOS. His closest colleagues were Agent 99 (Barbara Feldon) and a spy dog called Fang which operated under the code name K-13 and possessed one of the sharpest brains in the CONTROL organisation. They all worked to the Chief, portrayed by Edward Platt. The show produced a catchphrase for Adams, 'Sorry about that'. The headquarters of CONTROL was a music hall from which Smart operated under secret cover as a salesman of greetings cards. He had all the James Bond paraphernalia of an agent, including a telephone in one of his shoes. In 1970 ITV began screening some of the episodes. There were 138 in total.

Producer: Arne Sultan.

GET SOME IN

THAMES. First broadcast: 16 October 1975

Nineteen fifty-five in the RAF was the setting for this show. Three young men from different backgrounds received their call-up papers to report for national service to RAF Skelton. They were grammar-school boy Ken Richardson (David Janson), Teddy-boy Jakey Smith (Robert Lindsay) and vicar's son Matthew Lilley (Gerard Ryder). They came under the command of drill instructor Corporal Marsh (Tony Selby) who had a voice and temper like thunder and a pretty wife, Alice (Lori Wells). The three new recruits quickly became firm friends and a fourth, the rather backward Bruce Leckie (Brian Pettifer) who could not get the hang of drill, made up their tight circle. Occasional characters who drifted in and out of the shows included Min

the Naafi lady (Madge Hindle) and Squadron-Leader 'Sandy' Powell (Tim Barrett).

The first series, created and written by John Esmonde and Bob Larbey, was followed by two further series in 1976, at the end of which the squad and the Marshes moved to RAF Midham. The story was taken up in the fourth series which came to the screen in June 1977. At Midham they were all on the RAF medical training course where Flight-Sergeant Wells (George Innes) was the long-suffering instructor on the finer points of nursing. At the end of their training they were posted to Malta. Viewers rejoined them in April 1978 for a final seven programmes prior to the end of their service. They were then at RAF Hospital Druidswater where Corporal Marsh briefly found himself a patient. He recovered to join the hospital staff himself under Group Captain Ruark (Nigel Pegram).

Theme music: Alan Braden. Producer: Michael Mills.

THE GHOST AND MRS MUIR

NBC (AMERICA) PRESENTED BY ITV.
First broadcast (UK): 31 October 1970

The origins of this series are a novel by RA Dick and a 1947 feature film of the same title which starred Gene Tierney and Rex Harrison. The idea was resurrected for television by writer Jean Holloway and starred Hope Lange as young widow Carolyn Muir whose New England seaside cottage was haunted by the ghost of its former owner, the turn-of-the-century sea captain, Captain Gregg (Edward Mulhare). Carolyn had two children, Jonathan (Harlen Carraher) and Candy (Kellie Flanagan), and a housekeeper Martha (Reta Shaw). Living close to Gull Cottage was the Captain's descendant, Claymore Gregg (Charles Nelson Reilly). The Captain had supernatural powers and gradually he and Mrs Muir fell in love.

Music: Dave Grusin. Producers: Gene Reynolds, David Gerber.

THE GHOSTS OF MOTLEY HALL

GRANADA. First broadcast: 25 April 1976

Four-hundred-year-old Motley Hall was the ancestral home of the Uproar family. It had been empty for twenty years except for its ghosts. They were Sir George Uproar (Freddie Jones), a dyed-in-the-wool Victorian and the democratic leader of the ghosts; former footman Fanny (Nicholas Le Prevost),

Lady Carlton maintains her composure though surrounded by her GIRLS ON TOP (Photo: Central Television)

stable boy Matt (Sean Flanagan), Bodkin (Arthur English) and The White Lady (Sheila Steafel). The ghosts resented any intrusion from living people and were most alarmed if caretaker Mr Gudgin (Peter Sallis) showed any prospective purchasers around the premises. A first series of seven of these children's programmes was followed by a further seven, beginning 26 December 1976 and a final run of six from 29 January 1978.
Music: Wilfred Josephs. Writer: Richard Carpenter. Producer: Quentin Lawrence.

GILLIGAN'S ISLAND

CBS PRESENTED BY ITV.
First broadcast (UK): 15 April 1965

Created and produced by Sherwood Schwartz, this Robinson Crusoe situation marooned a variety of wealthy holidaymakers on a desert island and left them to fend for themselves. The skipper of their wrecked ship was played by Alan Hale and 1st mate Gilligan was portrayed by Bob Denver. Jim Backus was the rather vague, multi-millionaire Thurston Howell III, with Natalie Schaefer as his cynical wife. The other regulars were Tina Louise as Ginger, Russell Johnson as the Professor and Dawn Wells as Mary Ann. The comedy relied heavily on visual humour and revamped many of the classic sight gags from the silent films era. There were 98 editions.

THE GINGERBREAD GIRL

LWT. First broadcast: 9 April 1993

Janet Dibley starred in this seven-part series as Linda, a divorcée who struggled to bring up her daughter Kerry (Isabella Marsh). Making ends meet

was not made any easier by ex-husband Matt (John Diedrich), who was invariably behind with maintenance payments. Not only that but he remained possessive of Linda and got hot under the collar when she started seeing David (Dominic Guard). When Kerry started with behavioural problems, Linda sought advice from neighbour Eddie (Tyler Butterworth) but his remedial proposals went down like suet pudding.
Writer: Alex Shearer. Producer: Robin Carr.

THE GIRL WITH SOMETHING EXTRA

NBC (AMERICA) PRESENTED BY ITV.
First broadcast (UK): 21 June 1979

Young, newly-married Sally (Sally Field) had the ability to read minds. After just a short time, her powers got on the nerves of her husband John (John Davidson), to the point where he feared thinking thoughts. As a barrister, however, he found that rather difficult. Although 22 episodes were made, few ITV companies screened them all.
Creator: Bernard Slade. Producers: Bob Claver, Larry Rosen.

GIRLS ABOUT TOWN

ATV. First broadcast: 2 October 1969

This began as a single comedy, written by Adele Rose and produced by Ronnie Baxter, and starred Anna Quayle as Rosemary and Barbara Mullaney as Sylvia, two bored housewives suffering the seven-year itch, who joined an escort agency. The following year, on 9 March 1970, it returned as a series but with several changes. Julie Stevens played Rosemary Pilgrim, married to George (Robin Parkinson). Her co-conspirator was Brenda Liversedge (Denise Coffey) who was married to Harold (Peter Baldwin). The two women spent their every moment trying to inject some sparkle into their lives. There were two further series and by the end of 1971 Rosemary had had a baby boy and George's mother (Dorothy Reynolds) had moved in, supposedly to help out.
Writer: Adele Rose. Producer: Shaun O'Riordan.

GIRLS ON TOP

CENTRAL. First broadcast: 23 October 1985

Four girls with vastly different backgrounds and foregrounds came together to share an upstairs flat in a fashionable London house owned by eccentric aristocrat Lady Carlton (Joan Greenwood) who lived downstairs. The setting was Chelsea and Lady Carlton was also a writer of romantic fiction. Her outrageous tenants were brassy blonde, hypochondriac and pathological liar Candice (Tracey Ullman); bossy, fussy feminist Amanda (Dawn French) who worked for Spare Cheeks magazine; boring couch potato Jennifer (Jennifer Saunders) who made models from shells; and fourthly, loud and vulgar American Shelley (Ruby Wax). Shelley's rich parents had allowed her to visit Europe to pursue her aspirations to become an actress. Her handicap was an inability to act. The series originated with a run of seven programmes. A second series of six followed, beginning 30 October 1986, but after the first episode, Candice, who had a mail-order business, left for the States.

Writers: Dawn French, Jennifer Saunders and Ruby Wax. Director: Ed Bye. Producers: Paul Jackson, Trevor Walton.

GIVE US A BREAK

BBC. First broadcast: 22 September 1983

This seven-part comedy drama series was the work of one-time carpenter Geoff McQueen, who would later go on to create *The Bill*. The setting was the snooker saloons of London's East End, McQueen country, where the central character was Micky Noades (Robert Lindsay), a hustling, gambling wheeler-dealer whose survival would be less assured without girlfriend Tina Morris (Shirin Taylor). She hailed from Liverpool and when her younger brother Mo (Paul McGann) arrived in the big city, he received a frosty welcome from Micky until the latter found out that Mo was an ace snooker player – and in the East End, that spelt pound notes. Much of the action took place in the Crown and Sceptre where Tina worked and Micky drank. The landlord of the pub was Ron Palmer (David Daker).

Directors: David Reynolds, Christopher King. Producer: Terence Williams.

THE GLAMOUR GIRLS

GRANADA. First broadcast: 23 October 1980

In this series by David Nobbs, two girls with little in common other than a desire to leave their humdrum lives and find a little glamour and excitement joined a new sales promotion agency, Glamgirl Ltd,

opened by self-styled entrepreneur Ernest Garstang (Duggie Brown). The girls were Veronica Haslett (Brigit Forsyth) and Debbie Wilkinson (Sally Watts). Garstang had a young assistant Brian Frodsham (Tom Price) who saw himself as something of a whizz-kid. He shared a flat and a platonic relationship with Debbie. Brian's widowed mother (Rosemary Martin) had a romance with one of Glamgirl's clients, Dylan Meredith (James Warrier). A second run of six began on 23 February 1982.

Music: Derek Hilton. Director: Malcolm Taylor. Producer: John G Temple.

GLORIA

CBS (AMERICA) PRESENTED BY BBC.
First broadcast (UK): 29 October 1984

Archie Bunker's daughter Gloria (Sally Struthers) from ALL IN THE FAMILY had separated from husband Mike (Rob Reiner) and was spun-off into this series with her eight-year-old son Joey (Christian Jacobs). She moved away and took a job as assistant to veterinary practitioner Dr Willard Adams (Burgess Meredith). Gloria's life had never been a bed of roses and she found it hard to start over again. She was helped by friend and confidante Maggie Lawrence (Jo DeWinter). The show was created and produced by Dan Guntzelman and Bob Claver and 22 editions were screened.

THE GLUMS

BBC RADIO
See TAKE IT FROM HERE.

LWT. First broadcast: 11 November 1979

The Glums from radio's TAKE IT FROM HERE were brought back to life in a series of short sketches as part of *Bruce Forsyth's Big Night* which began on 7 October 1978. The original scripts by Frank Muir and Denis Norden were used and adapted and Jimmy Edwards recreated his original role as Mr Glum. The part of his gormless son Ron was played by Ian Lavender and Eth was portrayed by Patricia Brake. So popular did this revival prove that the Glums were given their own series of six half-hour shows. Mr Glum, his son and prospective daughter-in-law were played by the same actors as on *Big Night*. Their landlord Ted was played by Michael Stainton. Again the Muir–Norden scripts were used, with two stories per programme.

Director: John Reardon. Producer: Simon Brett.

GLYNIS

CBS (AMERICA) PRESENTED BY BBC.
First broadcast (UK): 24 September 1964

British actress Glynis Johns starred as Glynis Granville, a writer of mysteries who landed in perilous predicaments in her resolute search for plots. She was regularly rescued from such dire situations by husband Keith (Keith Andes) who, in between rescue missions, ran his own successful law practice. Glynis found a willing accomplice to her sleuth activities in retired policeman Chick Rogers (George Mathews) who had been appointed manager of the block of flats where the Granvilles lived. The last episode was screened on 8 October.
Producer: Jess Oppenheimer.

THE GNOMES OF DULWICH

BBC. First broadcast: 12 May 1969

Following HUGH AND I and HUGH AND I SPY, Hugh Lloyd and Terry Scott had another stab at working together in this series of six created by Jimmy Perry. It was Perry's fascination with garden gnomes that bore the idea and the shows were devised in such a way that humans were but voices-off, and the gnomes, therefore, were life-size. The proud British gnomes in one garden were Big, Small and Old (Scott, Lloyd and John Clive), all made of stout British stone. The plastic impostors in the adjacent garden were played by Leon Thau, Lynn Dalby and Anne de Vigier.
Producer: Graeme Muir.

GOING STRAIGHT

BBC. First broadcast: 24 February 1978

In this sequel to PORRIDGE, Britain's favourite criminal, Norman Fletcher (Ronnie Barker), was released from Slade Prison having resolved to go straight and never return. Fletch found life hard on the outside having adjusted so well to the confines of incarceration. His old cell-mate Lennie Godber (Richard Beckinsale) had been released before him and Patricia Brake also reprised her role as Ingrid. Fletcher's son Raymond was played by Nicholas Lyndhurst. There were just six editions.
Writers: Dick Clement and Ian La Frenais. Producer: Sydney Lotterby.

GOLDEN GIRL

BBC. First broadcast: 27 July 1960

Catherine Boyle starred in this six-part series in which she played a secretary, Katie Johnson, who through an unexpected inheritance became the richest girl in the world. Her money was placed in the hands of an investment manager (Francis Matthews) whose inability to answer awkward questions provoked his dismissal after the first series. Katie acquired her own secretary, Janet Turner (Faith Brook), and she appointed a lawyer, John Baker (Patrick Barr), to handle her affairs. Also featured on a regular basis were Catherine Boyle's own Pekinese dogs, Mi-tzi and Tai-Tai.
Writers: Michael Pertwee, Larry Forrester. Director: Robin Nash. Producer: Ronald Marsh.

THE GOLDEN GIRLS

NBC (AMERICA) PRESENTED BY CHANNEL 4.
First broadcast (UK): 1 August 1986

Susan Harris created this situation where four elderly ladies lived together in Miami. The house was owned by Blanche (Rue McClanahan), a faded Southern belle of a widow who remained man-mad and saw no reason why her sex life should be in any way diminished by the ageing process. Rose (Betty White) was also widowed and portrayed a naive innocence. She was always the last to see the joke. Her husband had died during the act of making love. Dorothy (Beatrice Arthur) was the central pivot of the household. Divorced from Stan (Herbert Edelman) and a retired school teacher, she was physically and vocally powerful and unforgiving, especially of Stan who had walked out on her after 38 years of marriage to set up with an air hostess. She did have vulnerability, however, and worried about her height and her attraction for the opposite sex. The fourth lady was Sophia (Estelle Getty), Dorothy's mother and a woman who would speak her mind, often with outrageous frankness. This series never shirked from tackling women's subjects which previously might have been considered taboo, and, in so doing, picked up numerous awards. Channel 4 transmitted the last of 175 editions on 7 April 1993. The final two episodes formed a two-part story entitled 'One Flew Out of the Cuckoo's Nest', in which Dorothy announced her plans to marry Blanche's Uncle Lucas (Leslie Nielsen). The other three ladies moved into a new situation, GOLDEN PALACE. See also BRIGHTON BELLES.
Directors included Terry Hughes. Producers: Susan Harris, Paul Junger Witt and Tony Thomas.

The spice of later life lived to the full by THE GOLDEN GIRLS (Photo: Channel 4)

GOLDEN PALACE

USA PRESENTED BY CHANNEL 4.
First broadcast: 14 April 1993

Creator of THE GOLDEN GIRLS, Susan Harris, solved the problem of Beatrice Arthur leaving the cast by giving the remaining three a brand new situation. Blanche (Rue McClanahan), Rose (Betty White) and Sophia (Estelle Getty) began a new life running a Miami hotel. The manager was Roland (Don Cheadle) and the chef was Chuy (Cheech Marin). The girls' dream of running a quiet little inn proved tougher than they imagined. Nineteen editions were shown.
Producers: Susan Harris, Paul Junger Witt and Tony Thomas.

THE GOLDEN PARROT CLUB

BBC RADIO. First broadcast: 28 September 1968

This hangover from wireless days recreated the format whereby a situation was established within which variety turns could be presented. The host was comedian Freddie 'Mr Parrot Face' Davies, who also played various character parts. Regulars in the club were Mr and Mrs Amos Bickerdyke (Colin Edwynn and Davies as Mrs), and the same two actors played the weekly complainers, Norman and Stanley. The barmaid was Daisy, portrayed by Barbara Mullaney, who would later make her mark as Coronation Street's Rita. Davies also created his alter ego, Samuel Tweet, later to surface in THE SMALL WORLD OF SAMUEL TWEET. Thirteen editions were heard.
Writers: Mike Craig, Lawrie Kinsley and Gary Knight. Producer: Geoff Lawrence.

GONE TO THE DOGS

CENTRAL. First broadcast: 29 November 1991.

Jim Morley (Jim Broadbent), Larry Patterson (Warren Clarke) and Larry's wife of 25 years Lauren (Alison Steadman) had all been at school together. Larry, self-satisfied and smirking, had made a few million out of a video business. Jim had just come out of prison and was a born loser. Jim's son, Little Jim (Harry Enfield), worked for Larry as a 'gofer' and helped in the kennels with his racing greyhounds. Jim used Little Jim as a means to reappear in Larry and Lauren's lives. He had always had a crush on Lauren and she did not rebuff his new advances. Jim also raced greyhounds and he dreamed of beating Larry not only on the track but also in his pursuit of Lauren. Six episodes were transmitted and a 1992 sequel, GONE TO SEED, followed.
Writer: Tony Grounds. Director: Sandy Johnson. Producer: Michele Buck.

GONE TO SEED

CENTRAL. First broadcast: 13 November 1992

This six-part follow-up to GONE TO THE DOGS had the same writer, Tony Grounds, and the same principal actors but the characters were changed. Alison Steadman, Jim Broadbent and Warren Clarke played triplets with the family name Plant. Monty (Broadbent) was a country and western singer who wanted to turn their garden in London's docklands into an oasis of flowers. Winston (Clarke) was an ambitious wrestler more interested in money than flowers and Hilda's (Steadman) chief passion was for Millwall Football Club, although she was into nature, hard work and commitment to gardening. The family business, a garden centre, which was ailing, was run by their mother Mag (Sheila Hancock) and the conman lurking to swallow up the property was Wesley Willis (Peter Cook).
Director: Sandy Johnson. Producer: Tim Whitby.

GOOD EVENING, EACH

BBC RADIO. First broadcast: 29 April 1958

This series only just qualifies as a sitcom in that it was one of those vehicles, much loved by the BBC, which provided an excuse to introduce variety acts. The stories were built around a Birmingham Palais-de-Danse which the men from the Ministry wanted to pull down for a road-widening scheme. Beryl Reid starred as three characters: Marlene, who had a crush on the Palais band-leader (Nat Temple); the schoolmistress Monica (from her earlier series *Starlight Hour*); and Mrs Shin-Bone, a gushing society do-gooder who repeatedly proclaimed, 'Shake off the shackles with Shin-Bone.' The landlord of the Palais was played by Ken Platt and the man from the Ministry by Derek Guyler. Thirteen editions were broadcast.
Writers: David Climie, Frank Roscoe and Ronald Wolfe. Producer: Roy Speer.

GOOD GIRL

YTV. First broadcast: 27 July 1974

These six comedy dramas were written by Philip Mackie and starred Julia Foster as Angie Botley, the young innocent daughter of Cyril Botley (Peter

Hughes) and man-hating Gwen Botley (Brenda Cowling). Angie met and was wooed by an older man, grumpy television executive Eustace Morrow (Peter Barkworth) who gave her a job. In spite of his powerful position at work, Morrow was over-dominated by his mother (Joan Hickson). He and Angie fell in love and faced the problems entailed. Their work colleagues were Henry Nutting (Brian Deacon) and Colin Peale (Peter Bowles).
Director: David Cunliffe. Producer: Peter Willes.

THE GOOD GUYS

LWT. First broadcast: 3 January 1992

Guy MacFadyean (Nigel Havers) lived in a flat in Richmond and had just lost his job when he met, by chance, Guy Lofthouse (Keith Barron) who arrived from Leeds after walking out on his job and his marriage. They became flatmates and followed a rather aimless pattern until they decided to start helping other people. Neither was able to cope with any form of modern technology and Lofthouse was bewildered by the South. Their joint activities led them into numerous predicaments and into the paths of many beautiful girls. The first eight-part series of these hour-long comedy dramas was followed by a second run of eight beginning on 8 January 1993.
Writer: John Bird. Directors: Simon Langton, Anthony Simmons. Producers: Andrew Montgomery and Michael Whitehall for Haverhall Pictures.

THE GOOD LIFE

BBC. First broadcast: 4 April 1975

John Esmonde and Bob Larbey created and wrote this series set in Surbiton. Tom and Barbara Good (Richard Briers and Felicity Kendal) opted to quit the rat race and become self-sufficient from the produce, animal and vegetable, of their suburban garden. To this end Tom gave up his steady job as a draftsman and the pair of them donned wellies, picked up a spade, dug and planted, and installed pigs, a goat and hens. It was all too much for one neighbour in particular, Margo Leadbeatter (Penelope Keith), who vacillated between abject horror at the Goods' activities and a profound conviction that they had gone totally insane. Margo's husband Jerry (Paul Eddington) worked as a designer of plastic novelties for cereal packets at the same advertising agency from which Tom resigned. He observed the Goods' new way of life with detached amusement and the odd suggestion of

Suburban smiles all round for a change as Surbiton's most famous residents, Margo (Penelope Keith), Tom (Richard Briers), Jerry (Paul Eddington) and Barbara (Felicity Kendal), enjoy THE GOOD LIFE (Photo: © BBC)

envy. Tom was resolute that they could seriously sustain themselves by growing a surplus and bartering for essentials which they could not produce themselves. Barbara's commitment was full but there was a feeling that she was really only doing it for him. She was the object of sympathy from the social snob Margo, who felt Tom had dragged Barbara into his bizarre new existence. The last of 30 editions went out on 10 June 1978.
Music: Burt Rhodes. Producer: John Howard Davies.

THE GOOD LIFE

NBC (AMERICA) PRESENTED BY BBC.
First broadcast (UK): 5 April 1974

Beset by high taxes and enormous bills, suburban couple Albert (Larry Hagman) and Jane (Donna Mills) opted for the comfort and lack of pressure from creditors of becoming butler and cook respectively to the household of millionaires Charles and Grace Dutton (David Wayne and Hermione Baddeley). The only other member of the staff was odd-job man Nick (Danny Goldman). Fifteen episodes were screened.
Creators: Lawrence J Cohen and Fred Freeman. Producers: Lee Rich and Claudio Guzman for Columbia.

GOOD PULL-UP FOR CYCLISTS

BBC RADIO. First broadcast: 10 September 1940

This began as a very occasional series and was devised by Ernest Longstaffe. The characters and their machines were billed as follows: Major Puffin, heavy roadster (Bobbie Comber); Clarry, light sports (Clarence Wright); 'Arry drop 'andles (John Rorke); Sophie Spoonbrake, second-hand bargain (Gwen Lewis); Tom, any old iron (Tommy Brandon); and both Helen and Betty, featherweight (Helen Clare and Betty Huntley-Wright). Five years later, the same format assumed a new title, THE WOBBLETON WHEELERS, again with Rorke, Brandon and Wright but with Mabel Constanduros as Miss Spoonbrake and Dick Francis as Major Puffin. The first of those broadcasts was on 12 September 1945.
Producer: Ernest Longstaffe.

GOODBYE MR KENT

BBC. First broadcast: 28 January 1982

Victoria Jones (Hannah Gordon) had been deserted by her husband and struggled to make ends meet while bringing up her daughter Lucy (Talla Hayes). She advertised for a female lodger but got landed with Travis Kent (Richard Briers), a dishevelled journalist of no fixed abode. He coaxed her into accepting him by protestations of being a good cook and turning on the charm. He brought both havoc and happiness to the household over the seven editions of the show.
Writers: Peter Vincent and Peter Robinson. Producer: Gareth Gwenlan.

GOODNIGHT AND GOD BLESS

CENTRAL. First broadcast: 12 April 1983

Ronnie Kemp (Donald Churchill) was a former Redcoat who had become a star as the genial host of a game show. However, off the screen he was not so genial as his viewers would believe. He was neurotic, wore a wig and drove around ostentatiously in his chauffeured Rolls-Royce. He was also mean and bad-tempered and a bit of an idiot in the eyes of his staff, Harry (Nick Stringer) and show hostess Debbie (Tracey Perry). Two people who hated his shows were his wife Celia (Judy Loe), who was half his age, and his father-in-law Geoffrey (James

Cossins), who was Ronnie's contemporary. Added to his list of non-admirers in this series of six programmes was his ex-wife Audrey (Rowena Cooper).
Writers: Donald Churchill and Joe McGrath. Producer: Alan Dossor.

GOODNIGHT SWEETHEART

BBC. First broadcast: 18 November 1993

Nicholas Lyndhurst starred in this time-warp comedy in six editions by Laurence Marks and Maurice Gran. Lyndhurst played TV repairman and engineer Gary, who was unhappily married to his demanding wife Yvonne (Michelle Holmes). One day he wandered into a pub, and found himself in the early 1940s and met the landlord's beautiful daughter Phoebe (Dervla Kirwan). Thereafter he was caught across the time divide and had to make decisions as to which period he wished to inhabit. Other featured characters were Eric (David Ryall), Ron (Victor McGuire) and PC Deadman (Christopher Ettridge).
Director: Robin Nash. Producer: John Bartlett for Alomo.

THE GOON SHOW

BBC RADIO. First broadcast: 22 January 1952

Though it is hard in this show to pinpoint any ongoing situation other than craziness, there is certainly continuity of characters and no book on broadcast comedy of any kind could fail to stretch its parameters to include it.

Following an experimental series in 1951 called *Crazy People*, the first Goon Show was broadcast at the start of the following year and starred Peter Sellers, Harry Secombe, Michael Bentine and Spike Milligan. By the start of the second series on 11 November of the same year, 1952, Bentine had departed. The last of more than 200 episodes was heard on 28 January 1960 with Spike Milligan th: re-after admitting that the show had cost him his sanity! He was, after all, the great creative force behind the Goons and bore the responsibility for most of the scripts.

The characterisations are legend: Major Denis Bloodnok, Henry Crun, Ernie Splutmuscle, Hercules Grytpype-Thynne and Bluebottle, all played by Sellers; Eccles, Minnie Bannister, Little Jim and Count Moriarty, all played by Milligan; and the pivotal character was often Neddie Seagoon, as portrayed by Secombe. There was always a stolid

Ever decreasing smiles from Goons (left to right) Spike Milligan, Peter Sellers and Harry Secombe (Photo: Copyright © BBC)

BBC announcer to go with the show. The first of these was Andrew Timothy but it is Wallace Greenslade, who joined the team for series three on 2 October 1953, who is forever associated with the Goons. In the music department, the Ray Ellington Quartet with Dick Katz on piano are synonymous with the show, as is harmonica player Max Geldray. The orchestra was first in the hands of Stanley Black and then Wally Stott. Guest appearances and occasional substitutions for the stars were made by Dick Emery, Graham Stark, Jack Train and Kenneth Connor. The Goons' mentor and script editor was Jimmy Grafton who continued to represent Secombe until his death.

There was a reunion to coincide with the Golden Jubilee of the BBC entitled THE LAST GOON SHOW OF ALL. It was broadcast on the radio on 5 October 1972 and shown on BBC television on 26 December 1972.

Producers: Dennis Main Wilson, Peter Eton, Pat Dixon, Charles Chilton, John Browell.

THE GOVERNOR AND JJ

CBS (AMERICA) PRESENTED BY BBC.
First broadcast (UK): 10 April 1973

Dan Dailey starred as State Governor Drinkwater who was widowed and lived with daughter JJ (Julie Sommars). The series of 39 programmes was created by Leonard Stern and contained some mild political satire. The other two regular characters were George (James Callahan) and Maggie (Neva Patterson).

Producers: Leonard and Arne Sultan.

GRACE AND FAVOUR

BBC. First broadcast: 10 January 1992

Jeremy Lloyd and David Croft relocated many of their characters from ARE YOU BEING SERVED following the closing-down of Grace Brothers' department store. Young Mr Grace had died leaving his vast fortune to charity and his loyal staff penniless, having spent their pension fund on an old manor house which he bequeathed to them. They decided to try to run the place as a country hotel. The familiar faces were Mrs Slocombe (Mollie Sugden), Mr Rumbold (Nicholas Smith), Captain Peacock (Frank Thornton), Miss Brahms (Wendy Richard) and Mr Humphries (John Inman). Newcomers were the country-bumpkin nearby farm tenant Maurice Moulterd (Billy Burden) and his pretty daughter Mavis (Fleur Bennett). Because staff accommodation was severely limited, the outrageously camp Mr Humphries was forced to share a bed with Mavis. Another new face was Miss Jessica Lovelock (Joanne Heywood) who had been nurse to the late Mr Grace and had nowhere else to go. She, too, settled into Millstone Manor. There were two series, each of six editions, ending 8 February 1993.

Producer: Mike Stephens.

GRANDAD

BBC. First broadcast: 3 October 1979

Actor Clive Dunn had been playing old men even when he himself was comparatively young, as all aficionados of DAD'S ARMY know well. In 1970 he made a novelty record, 'Grandad', which became the best-selling Christmas record of the time and topped the pop charts for three weeks. Almost ten years later, writer Bob Block had the bright idea to turn Dunn's Grandad character into a comedy series for children. It worked, and ran to four series, with the last of 22 editions screened on 1 February 1984. The Grandad of the series was Charlie Quick, the caretaker of Parkview Rehearsal Hall, who was known to all the dancing and acting students by his eponymous name.

Producer: Jeremy Swan.

THE GRAVY TRAIN

CHANNEL 4. First broadcast: 27 June 1990

These four one-hour comedy dramas, written by Malcolm Bradbury, were a send-up of the EC and its politics. Hans-Joachim Dorfmann (Christoph

Waltz) arrived in Brussels from Germany to work at the Directorate of Information and Culture. He unwittingly got involved in the biggest fraud in the Community's history and up to his neck in beautiful girls, corruption and a plum mountain which was to be despatched to Eastern Europe. The principal wheeler-dealers who pulled the strings in each direction were British diplomat Spearpoint (Ian Richardson) and the mysterious Milcic (Alexei Sayle).
Director: David Tucker. Producers: Ian Warren and Philip Hinchcliffe for Portman Productions.

THE GRAVY TRAIN GOES EAST

CHANNEL 4. First broadcast: 28 October 1991

Malcolm Bradbury's four-part sequel to THE GRAVY TRAIN again starred Ian Richardson as Michael Spearpoint, the bombastic and ingratiating British diplomat. The setting moved to the fictitious Balkan state of Slaka which had just been liberated after years of Communist control. A woman novelist, Katya Princip (Francesca Annis), had been elected president and she was determined that her country should join the European Community. The British, through spokesman Spearpoint, were violently opposed to the entry of Slaka. Poor dogsbody Hans-Joachim Dorfmann (Christoph Waltz) was sent east on a mission to discover the intricacies of the diplomatic barriers. He was swiftly expelled from Slaka but embarked on a new quest to find the country's missing secret fortune.
Director: James Cellan Jones. Producers: Ian Warren and Philip Hinchcliffe for Portman Productions.

GREEN ACRES

CBS (AMERICA) PRESENTED BY BBC.
First broadcast (UK): 3 April 1966

One hundred and seventy episodes of this show were produced and the BBC made intermittent transmissions. Successful big-city lawyer Oliver Wendell Douglas (Eddie Albert) moved himself and his luxury-loving wife Lisa (Eva Gabor) to the ramshackle old Haney Farm in Hooterville where they proposed to live out the rural daydream of the city slicker. She was both amazed and dismayed as they quit their smart New York apartment for the dubious delights of the valley. He bent his back to earn a living from the soil while she remained obdurate in her longing to return to the comforts of

the city. Their nearest neighbours were portrayed by Pat Buttram and Tom Lester.
Creator: Jay Sommers. Producer: Paul Henning.

GRINDL

NBC PRESENTED BY ITV.
First broadcast (UK): 10 August 1964

The fine comedy actress Imogene Coca (probably best remembered by those who saw the SID CAESAR SHOW) starred as the title character of this series. She was a Jill-of-all-trades who would try her hand at anything. That she was mistress of none was part and parcel of the character. The series began in the USA in 1963 and the following year in Britain. It is believed that the creator, David Swift, got the idea for the name while on holiday in Switzerland, presumably in Grindlwald. Grindl worked for an employment agency as a temporary anything. She was sent to numerous weird households by the agency boss Anson Foster (James Millhollin). Grindl was one of life's dreamers and Grindl was the only name she knew. There were 32 editions.
Producers included David Swift, Winston O'Keefe and Harry Ackerman.

GROWING PAINS

BBC RADIO. First broadcast: 14 March 1989

Ray Brooks and Sharon Duce, who starred together in BIG DEAL, teamed up again for this series in which they played Tom and Pat Hollingsworth, a childhood couple who opted to become foster parents. Raising other people's children brought its fair share of complications for the cheerful couple, especially as they shared their home with Pat's grandmother (Jean Heywood). A first series of six was followed by a second six ending 7 August 1990.
Writer: Steve Wetton. Producer: Lissa Evans.

THE GROWING PAINS OF ADRIAN MOLE

THAMES. First broadcast: 5 January 1987

Sue Townsend's six-part sequel to THE SECRET DIARY OF ADRIAN MOLE AGED 13¾ again starred Gian Sammarco as Adrian. The only significant change of cast was that Lulu replaced Julie Walters as Adrian's mother Pauline. Stephen Moore as Adrian's dad, Beryl Reid as Grandma and Lindsey Stagg as Pandora all reprised their roles as did Bill Fraser as Bert and Doris Hare as Queenie. This time, Adrian spent his 16th birthday alone as his pregnant mother and father had separated. Life as a later teenager appeared no better than that as an adolescent to Adrian.

Producer: Peter Sasdy.

THE GROWING PAINS OF PC PENROSE
BBC

See ROSIE

GROWING RICH
ANGLIA. First broadcast: 28 February 1992

Fay Weldon wrote this comedy drama of six hour-long episodes, which told the story of three girls from the Fenlands who failed their 'A' levels and were dropped into the grown-up world where they could see for themselves the horrors of pram-pushing and other tedious expected activities. They were Carmen (Rosalind Bennett), Laura (Caroline Harker) and Annie (Clair Hackett). All three were resolved to escape but there was a sinister plot to bring about their downfall by the local rogue and entrepreneur Sir Bernard Bellamy (John Stride) and the Devil (Martin Kemp) who was disguised as Sir Bernard's chauffeur. Annie's mother Mavis Horner (Jacqueline Tong) was a clairvoyant who looked into her crystal ball to see the future.

Director: Brian Farnham. Producer: Roger Gregory.

GRUEY
BBC. First broadcast: 24 February 1988

This children's series by Martin Riley was written in six parts. Gruey Grucock (Kieran O'Brien) was a Liverpool supporter and an enthusiastic schemer and dreamer who was unfortunately a walking disaster-area. All his adventures turned to frustration, often at the hands of his arch-enemy Nidgey Jackson (Scott Fletcher) and in spite of the stalwart support afforded him by his friends Wooly Woolsmith (Danny Collier) and Quidsy Rahim (Ayesha Hussain) and his parents (Paul Copley and Jane Lee).

Director: Roger Singleton-Turner. Producer: Paul Stone.

THE GRUMBLEWEEDS IN . . .
BBC RADIO. First broadcast: 26 October 1986

Yorkshire cabaret group The Grumbleweeds enjoyed 15 years of radio series but only three of those

were as sitcom. The rest were all sketch shows. The sitcoms reached a total of 18 editions ending on 1 November 1988. Set in Grumbleweed Towers, the zany characters included Uncle Rubbish (Graham Walker), whose house it was and who had a car named Flossie, the sound effect for which was made by an old sewing machine. Others were Rev. Claude Pod (Robin Colville), Melanie (Albert Sutcliffe) who was forever searching for her teeth, Uncle Nasty (Maurice Lee), Wilf 'Gas Mask' Grimshaw (Carl Sutcliffe), Sid Squeak (Robin), Fred Fibber (Graham) who lived next door, camp theatricals Ernest and Geoffrey (Robin and Graham), and Adolf (Maurice), husband of Freda Nattercan (Graham).

Writer and producer: Mike Craig.

GRUNDY
THAMES. First broadcast: 14 July 1980

Grundy (Harry H Corbett) had a corner newsagent's shop. He was a puritan, shattered by the break-up of his marriage and horrified by the permissive society. Then he met divorcée Beryl Loomis (Lynda Baron) on a train and came face to face with that very society, in a sort of prudery-meets-rudery situation. She turned his life upside down. Other regular characters in six shows were Sharon (Julie Dawn Cole) and Murray (David Janson).

Writer: Ken Hoare. Producer: Robert Reed.

GUESTWARD HO!
ABC (AMERICA) PRESENTED BY ITV.
First broadcast (UK): 7 February 1966

Although created in 1960 by the Desilu studio, this comedy western series was not seen in Britain until 1966. Its 38 episodes featured the Hooton family who forsook the big city to run a ranch way out west. Mark Miller starred as Bill Hooton, a former Madison Avenue executive, and Joanne Dru co-starred as his wife Babs, who had worked in New York as a top model. They had a son Brook, portrayed by Flip Mark. Their efforts to run the ranch were regularly hampered by a friendly but rather defensive Indian, Hawkeye, who was played by J Carrol Nash. Other regular characters were Lonesome (Earle Hodgins), Rocky (Tom Montenaro Jr), Pink Cloud (Jolene Brand) and Blossom (Janice Carroll).

Writers included Ronald Alexander, Arthur Julian, Bob Schiller and Bob Weiskopf. Directors included Fred de Cordova, Claudio Guzman and Sherman Marks. Producer: David Heilweil.

H

HAGGARD

YTV. First broadcast: 27 January 1990

Set in England in the 18th century, Keith Barron starred as Squire Haggard in stories by Eric Chappell based on the book *Squire Haggard's Journey* by Michael Green. Together with his dissolute son Roderick (Reece Dinsdale), the bawdy, boozy, lecherous and scheming Haggard roistered and swaggered his frock-coated way around the shires in search of an heiress who might repair his depleted fortunes. Regular characters included Grunge (Sam Kelly), Sir Joshua (Michael Jayston) and Fanny (Sara Crowe). The eccentric Georgian first came to the screen in a five-part series; five further episodes began on 18 July 1992.
Music: Robert Hartley. Producer: Vernon Lawrence.

HAIR IN THE GATE

BBC RADIO. First broadcast: 17 September 1993

This send-up of arts programming on TV and radio ran for six broadcasts. The spoof show for which the team worked was called 'Arting About' and the cast included Alistair McGowan, Geoffrey Whitehead, Forbes Masson, Lorelei King and Harriet Thorpe.
Producer: Paul Schlesinger.

HALLELUJAH

YTV. First broadcast: 29 April 1983

Firmly believing that the Yorkshire town of Brigthorpe was the worst remaining refuge of original sin, Salvation Army Captain Emily Ridley (Thora Hird) preached fire and brimstone that the sinners might repent. She had no intention of retiring from her work in spite of suggestions that she consider such a move from her fellow officers, Brother Benjamin (David Daker) and Brigadier Langton (Garfield Morgan). Together with Sister Alice Meredith (Patsy Rowlands) and Sister Dorothy Smith (Rosamund Greenwood), Emily ran the Paradise Street Citadel. Over two seven-part series, the second beginning on 2 November 1984, she failed to save a single soul.
Writer: Dick Sharples. Producer: Ronnie Baxter.

HANCOCK

ATV. First broadcast: 3 January 1963

Tony Hancock, revered star of BBC radio and television, thought he could do without his writers, Ray Galton and Alan Simpson, and his sidekick, Sid James. The result was this disastrous 13-part series, written by Terry Nation from an original idea by Ray Whyberd. The Hancock of HANCOCK'S HALF HOUR swapped East Cheam, his astrakhan-collared coat and black Homberg for a sheepskin jacket, soft felt hat and a job in a department store. The store manager was Mr Stone (Patrick Cargill) and other characters were Owen Bowen (Kenneth Griffith) and Uncle Bunny (Mario Fabrizi).
Producers: Alan Tarrant and Tony Hancock.

HANCOCK'S

ABC. First broadcast: 16 June 1967

In this, Tony Hancock's last television series, he was cast as the owner, singing waiter and mine host of an improbable nightclub set in the 'swinging' London of the summer of 1967. There was but a skeletal staff as Hancock had supposedly spent all the money on the fixtures and fitting and the hiring of an orchestra. June Whitfield played Esmeralda Stavely-Smythe, whose duties included being hatcheck girl, cigarette girl, bunny girl in fishnet tights and tail, and waitress. Joe Ritchie portrayed Toulouse, the head waiter, chef and washer-up. There were guest stars each week whom Hancock introduced as 'turns' booked to play the club. The ill-fated show ran to just four editions.
Music: Nat Temple. Writers: John Muir and Eric Green. Producer: Mark Stuart.

HANCOCK'S HALF HOUR

BBC RADIO AND TELEVISION.
First broadcast (radio): 2 November 1954

The prolific pens of Ray Galton and Alan Simpson wrote no fewer than 102 radio editions, the final show going out on 29 December 1959. Meanwhile the first of 63 television editions had been seen on 6 July 1956 and the last was transmitted on 30 June 1961.

The tragedy of Tony Hancock, who died in Sydney on 25 June 1968, has been well documented, yet greater love hath Britain for no comedian in retrospect than that still accorded Anthony Aloysius Hancock of 23 Railway Cuttings, East Cheam. His character was melancholy, slightly seedy and sad yet he was a cunning fool. Dressed in astrakhan-collared coat and black homberg hat, he found the perfect foil in Sid James as Sidney to share his world of outrageous fantasy. The disreputable Sidney was Hancock's flatmate whose obscene laugh and facial grimaces elevated him to almost equal status with Hancock himself. However, the beginnings of the above-mentioned tragedy occurred when Hancock the character began to overtake Hancock the man, and all the insecurities of the former manifested themselves in his personal behaviour. He thought he could do it all alone and for the final television series beginning 26 May 1961 Sidney was written out. Oddly enough, some of the best-remembered episodes come from that series, 'The Bedsitter', 'The Radio Ham' and 'The Blood Donor'. But disaster was round the corner when Hancock also thought he could dispense with Galton and Simpson and the BBC. In 1963 he moved to ATV and became his own producer for a best-forgotten series called simply HANCOCK.

Hancock and Sidney were assisted in their exploits by various fine comedy actors. Those who made their indelible mark on the radio version included Bill Kerr, Hattie Jacques, Moira Lister and Kenneth Williams, while for television Jacques and Williams survived only the early shows and John Le Mesurier, Hugh Lloyd and Johnny Vyvyan all made memorable contributions.
Radio producers: Dennis Main Wilson, Tom Ronald. Television producer: Duncan Wood.

THE HANDY GANG

A-R. First broadcast: 3 May 1963

This children's show involved much slapstick comedy with whitewash, soot and custard pies in its 13-week run. Three odd-job men lived in the boiler room of a block of flats. They were Johnny (Johnny Hutch), Dave (Dave Jackley) and Tiny (Bob Bryan). Johnny was lively and enthusiastic in his work, Dave was the self-appointed leader and Tiny was huge and daft. They took their orders initially from Mr Arkingshaw (Freddie Foss) and later from the Colonel (Reginald Marsh), who managed the flats. *Writers: David Edwards and Johnny Hutch. Producer: Pat Baker.*

Tony Hancock and Sid James do not impress the bus clippie (Joan Heal) in this HANCOCK'S HALF HOUR (Photo: Copyright © BBC)

HANGIN' WITH MR COOPER

USA PRESENTED BY CHANNEL 4.
First broadcast (UK): 16 July 1993

Mark Cooper (Mark Curry) was a newly-qualified primary school teacher who shared a flat and a platonic relationship with two girls, Vanessa Russell (Holly Robinson) and Robin Dumars (Dawnn Lewis). They shared the rent, the running costs and each other's problems, especially those relating to their love lives. There were 23 shows screened. *Creator: Jeff Franklin.*

THE HAPPIDROME

BBC RADIO. First broadcast: 9 February 1941

This was essentially a variety show built around three regular characters. Harry Korris played Mr Lovejoy, the proprietor of The Happidrome. Mr Lovejoy had previously been a music hall chairman, complete with large moustache and red handkerchief. Both vanished when he acquired the lease of The Happidrome and the jovial, rotund chap set about presenting the cheeriest entertainment for the public. He then sported a loud check suit, a bowler hat a couple of sizes too small for him, and smoked a fat cigar. He was assisted by his stage manager Ramsbottom (Cecil Frederick) and callboy Enoch (Robbie Vincent) who was threatened with the sack each week. The show was broadcast from a real theatre with an audience and all the artists were required to wear full stage costume and make-up. It was scheduled for a run of six pro-

grammes but actually ran for 52 continuous weeks. Another series began in March 1943 and it notched up its 100th edition in January 1944. Through the very darkest days of the war, the show's catchphrases, 'Let me tell *you*', 'If ever a man suffered' and 'Take him away, Ramsbottom' inspired national laughter. A post-war series began on 8 October 1945 and the last ever Happidrome was heard on 26 December 1947.
Producer: Ernest Longstaffe.

HAPPILY EVER AFTER
ABC. First broadcast: 12 February 1961

This series, also known as *The Dora Bryan Show*, co-starred Pete Murray as Dr Peter Morgan and Dora Bryan as his dumb-blonde wife Dora. She bewildered him with a sequence of wacky schemes which got them into various scrapes. There was obvious influence from I LOVE LUCY, even to having the next-door neighbours, Harry and Grace (Bryan Coleman and Audrey Noble), as foils. The first series of seven shows was followed by four more episodes from 10 May 1964.
Writers: James Kelly and Peter Miller. Producer: Philip Jones.

THE HAPPY APPLE
THAMES. First broadcast: 20 June 1983

Keith Waterhouse adapted an original play by John Pulman to create this seven-part series. The stories followed the fading fortunes of a small advertising agency, Murray, Maine and Spender. The future was looking downhill for Charles Murray (Nicky Henson), Freddie Maine (Jeremy Child) and Arthur Spender (John Nettleton) until secretary Nancy Gray (Leslie Ash) made herself into a one-girl market research unit and turned the company around. Other grateful employees were Bossington (Derek Waring), Kenilworth (Peter-Hugo Daly) and Miss Wheeler (Judith Paris).
Producer: Michael Mills.

HAPPY DAYS
ABC (AMERICA) PRESENTED BY ITV.
First broadcast (UK): 26 October 1977

The creator of this hugely successful series, Garry Marshall, deliberately set the action in the 1950s 'to take away the kids' anxieties. There were no drugs and the world was calmer.' In the United States there was a pilot episode in 1972 which inspired the 1973 movie *American Graffiti*, which in turn led to the series in 1974. There were a staggering 255 episodes, and the shows were still being re-run in 1994 on Channel 4.

Originally the two central characters were teenage school pals Richie Cunningham (Ron Howard) and Warren 'Potsie' Weber (Anson Williams), but during the second season the real star of the piece turned out to be a character named Arthur Fonzerelli (Henry Winkler), known to one and all as 'The Fonz' or 'Fonzie'. The young people lived the life of the Eisenhower era as students in Milwaukee at Jefferson High School. To bring Fonzie to the forefront, the writers had him move into an apartment above the Cunninghams' garage, as the Cunningham parents, Howard and Marion (Tom Bosley and Marion Ross), needed the money. The Fonz became a cult hero. He was a college drop-out but street-wise and a smooth operator with girls. He wore black leather, had slicked-back, duck-tailed hair and rode a motor-bike. He swaggered through life, delivering his pearls of wisdom in front of a studio audience which cheered and screamed at his every entrance.

Later some of the action moved to the University of Wisconsin and the Fonz ultimately became a teacher, although his lack of a degree gave him an inferiority complex alongside colleagues like Roger Phillips (Ted McGinley). Other principal characters included Ralph Malph (Donny Most), George

HAPPY DAYS for Henry Winkler as 'The Fonz' (Photo: Channel 4)

and Winnie McKinnie (Ned Wertimer and Sherry Hursey), Arnold (Pat Morita), Alfred (Al Molinaro), Lori Beth (Lynda Goodfriend), Laverne De Fazio (Penny Marshall) and Shirley Feeney (Cindy Williams), who had a spin-off series LAVERNE AND SHIRLEY; Joanie Cunningham (Erin Moran) and Chachi (Scott Baio), who also had a spin-off with JOANIE LOVES CHACHI. The character Mork (Robin Williams) made his first appearances alongside the Fonz before stepping into his own series, MORK AND MINDY. *Producer: Garry Marshall.*

HAPPY EVER AFTER
BBC. First broadcast: 7 May 1974

The partnership between Terry Scott and June Whitfield began in 1969 when June played in various sketches in a series called *Scott On . . .* which tackled different themes each week. In one such sketch they played husband and wife and it proved so popular that a half-hour show was written by John Chapman and Eric Merriman and transmitted as a single *Comedy Playhouse* under the title HAPPY EVER AFTER. They were Terry and June Fletcher and their family had fled the nest so that, for the first time in 23 years of marriage, they experienced freedom and its attendant problems. The first of five series amounting to 45 episodes began on 17 July 1974. There was one final transmission with a Christmas special on 20 December 1978. The two Fletcher daughters were Susan (Lena Clemo, later Pippa Page) and Debbie (Caroline Whitaker). Ever present was Aunt Lucy (Beryl Cooke) and a talking mynah bird. In October 1979 the couple returned to the screen as TERRY AND JUNE.
Writers included John Chapman, Eric Merriman, Christopher Bond, John Kane, Jon Watkins. Producer: Peter Whitmore.

HAPPY FAMILIES
BBC. First broadcast: 17 October 1985

Ben Elton wrote this six-part series in which Guy Fuddle (Adrian Edmondson), a total idiot, was sent on a mission by his dying grandmother (Jennifer Saunders) to locate his four sisters (all played by Saunders) and bring them home before she snuffed it. Those trawled into the resultant farce included the cook (Dawn French), Dr De Quick (Stephen Fry) and Flossie (Helen Lederer).
Producer: Paul Jackson.

HAPPY HOLLIDAY
BBC RADIO. First broadcast: 15 July 1954

The setting for this weekly, 15-part comedy with music was Littleham-on-Sea, a South Coast resort which the Mayor (Peter Sellers) was resolved to put firmly on the map. To this end he hired an upmarket and glossy entertainments officer, Major Denzil Pierce (Dennis Price). He in turn had an assistant, a Cockney and his former batman Charlie Unkers (Bill Owen). The Mayor had a daughter (Jean Brampton) and Peter Sellers also played the part of one of the town's landladies, Mrs Larkin, who also had a daughter (Elizabeth Larner). Several eccentrics found their way to the resort including Frederick Featherstonehaugh (Dick Emery) and, on a less regular basis, J Beerbohm Bloggs (Graham Stark) and Bart Underblast (Harry Secombe). The music came from Stanley Black and his Concert Orchestra and the George Mitchell Merrymakers.
Writers: Jimmy Grafton and Peter Griffiths. Producer: Dennis Main Wilson.

HARDLUCK HALL
BBC RADIO. First broadcast: 14 July 1964

This series, a rare comedy show broadcast on the Third Programme, marked the radio writing debuts of its creators, David Nobbs and Peter Tinniswood. Hardluck Hall was the stately pile and family seat of Sir Plantagenet Pickle (Valentine Dyall). Tired of the jeers and sneers which suggested he was incapable of running the Hall, Pickle advertised it as available to be let, complete with owner, and suitable for 'a happening or serious theatrical venture'. His offer was taken up by Tom Ology (Stephen Moore), whose slogan was 'In poverty integrity'; Robin Robot (Bryan Kendrick), a gadget-mad man of the future; queen of niceness Priscilla Houseproud (Marigold Sharman); Sir Sydney Servall (John Baddeley), a politician otherwise known as Brand X; and 18-year-old Doreen Nylon (Janet Milner). Each of the six episodes centred on the story of one of those characters.
Producer: Richard Thomas.

HARDWICKE HOUSE
CENTRAL. First broadcast: 24 February 1987

Hardwicke House was a school, an academic backwater presided over by the hapless, hopeless, whisky-tippling headmaster Mr RG Wickham (Roy

Kinnear). The deputy head Paul Mackintosh (Roger Sloman) had an unhealthy appetite for the more nubile among the sixth-form girls. The rest of the staff included French mistress Cynthia Grabbe (Pam Ferris), a tireless committee worker and the union representative; PE teacher Harry Savage (Tony Haygarth), by name and by nature; history master Dick Flashman (Gavin Richards), who had been a second-hand car dealer; Icelandic eccentric Erik Magnusson (Duncan Preston) who taught Maths and ate raw fish; strict disciplinarian Herbert Fowl (Granville Saxton), who taught English; and the three-months qualified geography teacher, Peter Philpott (Nick Wilton). The series began with a one-hour episode followed by six half-hours starting the next day and weekly thereafter.
Music: Peter Brewis. Writers: Richard Hall and Simon Wright. Director: John Stroud. Producer: Paula Burdon.

HARK AT BARKER
LWT. First broadcast: 11 April 1969

Ronnie Barker starred as Lord Rustless, an earl of the realm and a portly old lech living in his stately pile. The character had originally been created by writer Alun Owen in a single play, 'Ah – There You Are', transmitted in a series called *The Ronnie Barker Playhouse*, prior to the subsequent series of eight. Rustless, aside from his lechery, was an ageing innocent on the threshold of his second childhood. He smoked cigars and paraded around his estate in pyjamas and a smoking jacket. His staff were Badger the butler (Frank Gatliff), secretary Mildred Bates (Josephine Tewson), Dithers the gardener (David Jason), the cook (Mary Baxter), and maid Effie (Moira Foot). Barker himself portrayed many other characters as and when required. The show returned for a second series in the autumn of 1970. See also HIS LORDSHIP ENTERTAINS.
Writers included Peter Caulfield, Bernard McKenna, Chris Miller, Bill Oddie and Gerald Wiley (Barker himself). Director: Maurice Murphy. Producer: Humphrey Barclay.

HARRY AND THE HENDERSONS
USA PRESENTED BY BBC.
First broadcast (UK): 27 September 1991

Based on the movie *Bigfoot and the Hendersons*, this series was seen in two 13-week runs and the last programme was screened on 10 April 1992. The story began when the Henderson family was returning from a camping holiday and accidentally ran over the eight-foot tall, hairy creature whom they subsequently came to know as Harry (Kevin Peter Hall, later Dawan Scott). Harry moved into the family home with mother Nancy (Molly Cheek), father George (Bruce Davison) and the two Henderson children, Ernie (Zachary Bostrom) and Sarah (Carol-Ann Plante).
Producer: Lin Oliver for MCA.

HART OF THE YARD
NBC (AMERICA) PRESENTED BY ITV.
First broadcast (UK): 8 October 1980

Ron Moody starred in six editions as inept Det. Insp Hart of Scotland Yard who was sent on temporary attachment to the San Francisco Police Department. There, his partner was Jennifer Dempsey (Cassie Yates) and they worked under Lieutenant Vince de Gennaro (Michael Durrell).
An MCA production.

THE HATHAWAYS
ABC (AMERICA) PRESENTED BY ITV.
First broadcast (UK): 1 July 1963

This preposterous 26-part series starred Jack Weston and Peggy Cass as Walter and Elinor Hathaway. Living in Las Vegas where crazy things are taken for granted, the Hathaways adopted three chimpanzees and raised them as their own children. Walter was a real-estate agent but longed to escape if he could only get rich quick. The chimps were two males, Charley and Enoch, and a baby female, Candy. They were owned and trained by Gene Detroy who once played a season at the London Palladium with his most famous chimp, Marquis.
Writer: Bill Manhoff. Producers: Robert Sparks and Ezra Stone.

HAVE I GOT YOU . . . WHERE YOU WANT ME?
GRANADA. First broadcast: 3 June 1981

Philip Harland and Paul Harris wrote this six-part series. Dentist Tom (Ian Lavender) and teacher Valerie (Kim Braden) both lived in a village called Eastwood where they had been courting for ten years. They had often been on the brink of marriage but had never taken the plunge. Their friends were Monty (John Alkin), Jason (Jeremy Sinden), Vicky

(Susannah Fellows) and Vera (Joanne Zorian).
Director: Malcolm Taylor. Producer: Brian Armstrong.

HAVING A WONDERFUL CRIME

BBC RADIO. First broadcast: 28 December 1948

In this comedy thriller in eight episodes, Hargreaves (Naunton Wayne) and Hunter (Basil Redford) set off for a tranquil holiday fishing in Ireland. Instead of peace they found themselves embroiled in some very fishy business indeed. Other characters swept up in their escapades included Colonel Ryan (Colin Douglas), Moya Ryan (Josephine Crosbie), Spike Mulraney (Ian Sadler) and Mrs O'Shaughnessy (Mignon O'Doherty).
Writer: Max Kester. Producer: Vernon Harris.

HE AND SHE

CBS (AMERICA) PRESENTED BY BBC.
First broadcast (UK): 12 September 1968

The stories in this 26-part series charted the adventures of serious young cartoonist Dick Hollister (Richard Benjamin) and his daffy wife Paula (Paula Prentiss). Dick's boss, Oscar North, was portrayed by Jack Cassidy. The setting was suburban United States with a hint of sophistication.
Producer: Arne Sultan.

HE'S A WONDERFUL WIFE

BBC RADIO. First broadcast: 27 July 1977

Lenny Penfold (Ian Lavender) was quite content to play the domestic 'wife'; happily, as he saw it, sitting around the flat enjoying his records and occasionally donning the apron, while his wife Sally (Elizabeth Counsell) went out to work as the family breadwinner. The regulars who looked on their arrangement with some disdain were Mrs Grodzinski (Margery Withers) and Rigour Morton (Norman Bird). Ten programmes were broadcast.
Writer: Peter Spence. Producer: Simon Brett.

HEAD OF THE CLASS

USA PRESENTED BY BBC.
First broadcast (UK): 9 March 1987

Howard Hesseman starred as Charlie Moore, teacher of a class of gifted teenagers known as 12C. The class had its own computer, code-named Wilma,

and the school head was Dr Samuels (William G Schilling). Among Charlie's charges at Fillmore High were Bernadette (Jeanetta Arnette), Maria (Leslie Bega), Arvid (Dan Frischman), Darlene (Robin Givens), Jawaharlal (Jory Hussain), Simone (Khrystyne Haje), Alan (Tony O'Dell), Eric (Brian Robbins), Sarah (Kimberley Russell), Dennis (Dan Schneider) and Janice (Tannis Vallely). As well as being a teacher, Charlie was also the union representative. More than 60 episodes were screened.
Directors included Art Dielhenn, John Tracy, Lee Shallat and Frank Bonner.

HEALTH AND EFFICIENCY

BBC. First broadcast: 30 December 1993

One-time mathematics teacher Andrew Marshall created and wrote this series set in St James' General Hospital where the principal issue was one of cost-cutting. Gary Olsen starred as the beleaguered senior registrar Michael Jimson, who was forced into money-grubbing antics by the new market-oriented NHS. He had at one time been engaged to consultant Kate Russell (Felicity Montagu), who now used all her guile to try to restrain his schemes. The Unit Manager was Diana Ewarts (Deborah Norton), a brute of a woman who had her work cut out in trying to restrict the scalpel-happy incisions of surgeon Rex Regis (Roger Lloyd Pack), an old-timer who resented the recent reorganisations. Notwithstanding, the married Rex was having an affair with Diana. Other regulars in the six episodes included Phil Brook (Victor McGuire) and Beth (Adjoa Andoh).
Producer: Richard Boden.

THE HELLO GOODBYE MAN

BBC. First broadcast: 5 January 1984

Writer David Nobbs set this six-part series in the offices of Cookham's Cures where Denis Ailing (Ian Lavender) had just been appointed salesman. He had no previous experience and proved to be both hopelessly inadequate for the job and psychologically unsuited to the business of selling. Those who suffered his inept efforts were Jennifer Reynoldston (Mary Tamm), Ken Harrington (Paul Chapman), Glenn Harris (Dominic Guard) and Mr Cookham (Peter Russell), who gave Denis the job in the first place.
Producer: Alan JW Bell.

HELLO PLAYMATES
BBC RADIO. First broadcast: 31 May 1954

A short series of six began as what the BBC called a 'taster' to test public reaction. It proved favourable and a full run of 13 began on 16 December 1954. Arthur Askey as 5ft 4in brash and ebullient Arthur starred alongside 6ft 2in David Nixon as quiet, unassuming David. Both were eligible bachelors and Mrs Purvis, played by Irene Handl making her radio debut, did not mind which, provided that one of them would marry her daughter Nola (Pat Coombs). Each episode, Mrs Purvis would find fresh aspects of Nola's charms with which to dazzle the reluctant bachelors. The scripts were by Bob Monkhouse and Denis Goodwin who also played extraneous parts when required.
Producer: Leslie Bridgmont.

HELL'S BELLS
BBC. First broadcast: 9 June 1986

Derek Nimmo has played his fair share of clergymen in his career and this six-part series cast him as Dean Selwyn Makepeace of Norchester Cathedral (the film location was Hereford). There he enjoyed a quiet and trouble-free existence with his irritable sister Edith (Phyllida Law) and his young fiancée Maudie Mountjoy (Penelope Horner). He had a cosy routine until the arrival of new Bishop Godfrey Hethercote (Robert Stephens) and his wife Emma (Susan Jameson), who determined to move away from the cushy traditions of the Cathedral and create deeper involvement with the errant flock.
Writer: Jan Butlin. Producer: Mike Stephens.

HELP!
BBC. First broadcast: 2 September 1986

Three Liverpool youngsters, all unemployed but eternally optimistic, got the most out of the raw deal that life had given them thanks to a special sense of Merseyside humour. They were Lenny (David Albany), known as the poet because of his Grade 4 CSE in English; Davva (Jake Abraham), who was rumoured to have been born without a brain; and Tex (Stephen McGann), who was the entrepreneur of the group. There were two runs of six episodes but the second, beginning on 9 April 1988, was in a time-slot normally associated with children's programmes.
Writer: Joe Boyle. Directors: Mike Stephens, Tony Dow. Producer: Mike Stephens.

HELTER SHELTER
BBC RADIO. First broadcast: 19 November 1940

This wartime show featured Reginald Purdell and Frederick Burtwell as Reg and Gus, Cockney wardens of an air-raid shelter. Trying to keep some sort of order was the shelter marshall (Lionel Gamlin, later Hugh Morton and finally Jack Melford). The shelter canteen was run by Sally (Sylvia Marriott) and her assistant (Joan Gates). There was much bursting into song by them and the RAF officer (Jan van der Gucht) or the sailor (Clarence Wright), and Vera Lynn was a regular shelterer. Purdell also portrayed Gus's infuriating but oddly lovable Uncle Cecil and the final regular of the team was Miss Duck (Gwen Lewis). The format was devised by Francis Worsley and Jenny Nicholson. The final show was heard on 2 September 1941.
Producers: Reginald Purdell and Lionel Gamlin.

HEMSLEY'S HOTEL
BBC RADIO. First broadcast: 30 October 1949

Remarkable child impersonator and ventriloquist Harry Hemsley first broadcast in 1923. Over the years he created his own family of non-existent children who became firm favourites with listeners. He presented them in random sketches until, in 1947, he got close to an ongoing situation in a series called *Old Hearty* in which the children talked to the old longshoreman played by Fred Yule. However it was two years later that Hemsley's radio 'family' first broadcast in the hotel and his imaginary children were so authentic that the BBC received many complaints that children should not be allowed to stay up so late! The kids were Elsie, Winnie, Johnnie and baby Horace, whose incomprehensible babytalk could only be interpreted by Winnie. Equally confused were Pieface the Chef (Martin Benson), receptionist Miss Pillweed (Molly Lumley), head waiter Pierre (Norman Shelley) and the mysterious guest Madame Incognito (Cecile Chevreau).
Writers: Jill Allgood and Harry Hemsley. Producer: Audrey Cameron.

HER MAJESTY'S PLEASURE
GRANADA. First broadcast: 25 September 1968

This was the first British comedy series to be set in a prison. It was created by Peter Eckersley and Leslie Duxbury but did not achieve the same following as the later PORRIDGE, though it returned for a second and final run early the following year. The prison governor was played by Wensley Pithey in the first series and by Michael Barrington in the second. The supporting staff included officers Arnold Clissit (John Sharp) and Leslie Mills (Ken Jones). The long-term lags were Pongo Little (John Nettleton), Mushy Williams (John Normington), Sesame Ingram (Joe Gladwin) and 'grizzly bear' Smith (Tommy Mann). Pongo's wife, Freda, was portrayed by Kate Brown. The prisoners were united by their love of football above anything else. *Writers: Leslie Duxbury, John Stevenson. Directors included Michael Cox, June Howson and Mike Newell. Producer: Peter Eckersley.*

HERE COME THE DOUBLE DECKERS
BBC. First broadcast: 1 January 1971

In this 18-episode children's series, seven kids made their headquarters in a disused London Transport double-decker bus. They were Tiger (Debbie Russ), Brains (Michael Audreson), Scooper (Peter Firth), Sticks (Bruce Clark), Doughnut (Douglas Simmonds), Billie (Gillian Bailey) and Spring (Brinsley Forde). From the bus they hatched their adventures with the help of the only regular adult in the series, Albert (Melvyn Hayes).
Writers included Harry Booth, Jan Butlin, Glyn Jones. Directors included Harry Booth, Jeremy Summers. Producer: Roy Simpson.

HERE WE GO AGAIN
ABC (AMERICA) PRESENTED BY ITV.
First broadcast: 6 June 1973

Richard Evans (Larry Hagman) and Susan Standish (Diane Baker), both divorcees, met, fell in love and married. Their newly-wedded bliss was plagued by the over-friendly intrusions of their former spouses, Judy Evans (Nita Talbot) and Jerry Standish (Dick Gautier). The series of 13 shows was created by Robert Kaufman.
Producers: Lew Gallow, Steve Pritzker.

HERE'S ARCHIE
BBC. First broadcast: 27 May 1956

This was the first attempt by ventriloquist Peter Brough to present his famous dummy Archie Andrews on television. So that Brough did not have to work with the doll on his lap, a crude but ingenious attempt was made to electronically fit a remote control to Archie's movable parts. The supporting characters for the six editions included Mrs Twistle (Irene Handl), Mr Boner (Cyril Goodwin), Archie's tutor (Francis de Wolff), Brough's secretary (Jane Graham) and Ronnie (Ronald Chesney). See also EDUCATING ARCHIE.
Writers: Ronald Wolfe and John Waterhouse. Producer: John Warrington.

HERE'S HARRY
BBC. First broadcast: 11 October 1960

Harry Worth starred as himself, the bumbling confused ditherer who set himself up as a contemporary knight-errant with a trilby for a helmet, spectacles for a visor, umbrella for a lance and briefcase for a shield. He ventured forth from his semi-detached comfort in the Northern town of Woodbridge to wage battle with his arch-enemies red tape, officialdom and bureaucracy. The show ran to eight series ending in December 1965 when Harry had just left his roots to move to London. Along the way he had two housekeepers, Mrs Williams (Vi Stevens) and Mrs Benson (Doris Gambell), but the most influential person in his life was his never-seen auntie, Mrs Amelia Prendergast.

Harry Worth's famous shop window illusion from the opening titles of HERE'S HARRY (Photo: Copyright © BBC)

Those whom he vanquished in his battles against authority were regularly portrayed by Deryck Guyler and Leonard Williams while his pals Tommy and Alf were played by Reginald Marsh and Joe Gladwin. Prior to the final series Harry lived at 52, Acacia Avenue where he was devoted to his cat Tiddles and saw himself as a pillar of Woodbridge society.

Writers: Harry Driver, Vince Powell and Frank Roscoe, Ronnie Taylor. Producers: John Ammonds, John Street.

HERE'S LUCY
CBS (AMERICA) PRESENTED BY ITV.
First broadcast: 3 January 1972

Lucille Ball starred as widowed Lucille Carter, living and working in California as a secretary for an employment agency run by her uncle Harrison Carter (Gale Gordon). Her two children, Kim and Craig Carter, were portrayed by Lucille Ball's real children, Lucie Arnaz and Desi Arnaz Jr. The series made much use of guest stars in its 144 episodes including frequent visits from Jack Benny, George Burns and Milton Berle.

Producer: Gary Morton.

HEY JEANNIE
CBS (AMERICA) PRESENTED BY BBC.
First broadcast (UK): 1 December 1956.

Vivacious British actress Jeannie Carson starred as Jeannie MacLennan, a girl from Dunfermline, Scotland, who embarked on a chapter of adventures in New York after meeting a taxi driver of that city (Allen Jenkins). There were 32 editions in all.

HI-DE-HI!
BBC. First broadcast: 1 January 1980.

Jimmy Perry and David Croft created and wrote this series which took as its initial setting Maplin's Holiday Camp in the year 1959. Those who had visited the real-life camps of Billy Butlin or Fred Pontin would have recognised the similarity immediately, especially when they came to meet the staff responsible for Camp entertainment. The principal characters were entertainments manager Jeffrey Fairbrother (Simon Cadell), Camp host Ted Bovis (Paul Shane), senior 'Yellowcoat' and Radio Maplin broadcaster Gladys Pugh (Ruth Madoc) from Wales, chalet maid Peggy (Su Pollard) and comedian Spike Dixon (Jeffrey Holland). Others who

The staff at Maplin's greet a new bunch of campers with enthusiasm and a HI-DE-HI! (Photo: Copyright © BBC)

played significant roles in almost 70 editions to January 1988 included Barry Howard as Barry, Felix Bowness as Fred Quilly, Diane Holland as Yvonne, Nikki Kelly as Sylvia, Rikki Howard as Betty, Penny Irving as Mary, Susan Beagley as Tracey, Linda Regan as April, Laura Jackson as Dawn, and David Griffin as Sqn Ldr Clive Dempster DFC. The Yellowcoat boys were played by the Webb Twins and Chris Andrews. The boss of the Camp, Joe Maplin, was never seen.

Producers: David Croft, Mike Stephens.

HIGH AND DRY
YTV. First broadcast: 7 January 1987

Alan Sherwood and Michael Knowles wrote this series of seven programmes which was set in 1946 in a resort on the Yorkshire coast. Bernard Cribbins starred as Ron Archer who, with his son Trevor (Angus Barnett) and a handicap of not having any money, managed to acquire the decaying Midbourne pier. Along with local residents Richard Talbot (Richard Wilson) and Miss Baxter (Vivienne Morgan), a Friends of the Pier Association was

formed and restoration of the Victorian structure got underway.
Music: Neil Innes. Producer: Ronnie Baxter.

HIGH ST BLUES
LWT. First broadcast: 6 January 1989

Four small shopkeepers, whose premises were all in a row, fought to hang on to their respective businesses when Waverley's Supermarkets tried to acquire the site. They were cobbler Charlie McFee (Phil McCall), who worked with his young apprentice Bob Farthing (Chris Pitt); junk shop owner Chesney Black (Ron Pember); Mavis Drinkwater (Elizabeth Stewart), whose wool shop had been in the family for decades and whose niece Susan Drinkwater (Victoria Hasted) thought she was a dotty old spinster who ought to sell up; florist Rita Franks (Valerie Walsh), whose business was blooming but, as a good Jewish mother of Paula (Georgia Mitchell), was not totally averse to making a capital gain to secure their future. Waverley's Supermarkets were represented by the managing director (Shirley Dixon); the head of the 'dirty deeds' department, Valentine (Martin Turner); and their proud 'unacceptable face of capitalism' Sharpe (Johnny Shannon). There were six episodes.
Writers: Jimmy Perry and Robin Carr. Producer: Robin Carr.

HILARY
BBC. First broadcast: 10 December 1984

A pilot programme of this show written by Peter Robinson and Peter Vincent was shown prior to a six-week series beginning on 14 January 1985. Marti Caine starred as TV researcher Hilary Myers, who lived a life of frenetic chaos and worked to her boss Kimberley (Jack Smethurst). Hilary was a divorcée with a teenage son Wesley (Philip Fox) and a best friend Lyn (Carolyn Moody). She worked on a simple chat show but somehow she managed to complicate the simplicity. At home she had a mynah bird named Arthur, the sounds of which were made by veteran bird impersonator Percy Edwards.
Producer: Harold Snoad.

HIS AND HERS
YTV. First broadcast: 23 June 1970

Role reversal was the subject matter of this series by Ken Hoare and Mike Sharland. Rupert Sherwin (Ronald Lewis) was a freelance journalist with very little work. As a consequence, he stayed at home and ran the house. His wife Kay (Sue Lloyd), meanwhile, was a highly successful accountant in the City. She was the family breadwinner. Their new neighbours Toby and Janet Burgess (Tim Brooke-Taylor and Madeline Smith) found the Sherwin's domestic arrangement distinctly odd. Almost two years later there was a second series in which Barbara Murray played Kay and the Burgesses were no longer on the scene.
Producers: Graham Evans, Ian Davidson.

HIS LORDSHIP ENTERTAINS
BBC. First broadcast: 5 June 1972

Ronnie Barker starred in a six-programme series as Lord Rustless whose stately pile, Chrome Hall, had been turned into a hotel. His own inefficiency in hotel management was matched by that of his staff, Dithers (David Jason), Cook (Mary Baxter), Effie (Moira Foot), Bates (Josephine Tewson) and Badger (Frank Gatliff). See also HARK AT BARKER.
Writer: Jonathan Cobbald. Producer: Harold Snoad.

HITCH HIKE
BBC RADIO. First broadcast: 21 December 1942

Clifford Lewis wrote this series which originally starred Syd Walker as the lorry driver but, as a result of ill health, he was replaced by Fred Yule. The van boy, Ginger, was portrayed by Vera Lennox and other characters were played by the resident company which comprised Joan Young, C Denier Warren and Dick Francis. The show ran for 13 weeks.
Producer: Ernest Longstaffe.

THE HITCH-HIKER'S GUIDE TO THE GALAXY
BBC RADIO AND TELEVISION.
First broadcast (radio): 8 March 1978

Douglas Adams's serious but highly comic send-up of science fiction began quietly on the radio but by the time he adapted his own scripts for the six-part television series which began on 5 January 1981, it had already found a cult audience and spawned two books. The story on both media took off from the point when the central character Arthur Dent (Simon Jones) was rescued in the nick of time by his best friend Ford Prefect (Geoffrey McGivern radio, David Dixon TV), an alien from the planet

Betelgeuse (pronounced Beetlejuice), as the Earth was unexpectedly destroyed. Thus the great hitchhike got underway. The plots were complicated but explained by the voice of The Book (Peter Jones) and embraced a cornucopia of characters including Trillian (Susan Sheridan radio, Sandra Dickinson TV), Marvin (Stephen Moore) and Zaphod Beeblebrox (Mark Wing-Davey), who had two heads. The series was years ahead of its time in the way that it approached what came to be known as 'green' issues and was one of the first television series to make innovative use of computer-generated graphics. Arthur and Ford, after their galactic adventures, ended up on Earth prior to human civilisation.
Radio producers: Simon Brett, Geoffrey Perkins. Television producer: Alan J W Bell.

HMS PARADISE
A-R. First broadcast: 16 July 1964

Writer Lawrie Wyman enjoyed a long run of success on the radio with THE NAVY LARK and brought his nautical pen to television with this creation which ran for 26 consecutive episodes. The plot was comparatively complicated in that there was a fictitious island, Boonsey, somewhere off Portland, Dorset, a land base somewhere on Portland and HMS Paradise, one of the Navy's cushiest postings, patrolling somewhere between the two. Ostensibly, Paradise was carrying out oceanic research while protecting the fishing rights of the islanders of Boonsey. That there were no fishermen on Boonsey seemed to have escaped the notice of the Royal Navy. Head of the shore base was Captain Turvey (Richard Caldicot), known to all as 'Old Thunderguts'. Allegedly in command of the ship was Commander Fairweather (Frank Thornton), who much preferred angling to commanding. His Number One was the dashing but rather dizzy and lovesick Lieutenant Pouter (Robin Hunter). Chief Petty Officer Banyard (Ronald Radd) was a wide boy with the ability to fiddle most luxuries – tax free! He was unwittingly assisted in his misdemeanours by Able Seaman Murdoch, a Scotsman of little brain played by Angus Lennie. The small naval base on Boonsey itself was in the hands of Commander Shaw (Graham Crowden). While there was much lusting after whatever females happened to be in any of the locations, the resident fair sex interest was provided by the typist Wren Amanda (Priscilla Morgan).
Director: Bill Hitchcock. Producer: Sid Colin.

HOGAN'S HEROES
CBS (AMERICA) PRESENTED BY ITV.
First broadcast (UK): 5 January 1967

This series was so obviously based on the play *Stalag 17* that a successful action for plagiarism was brought in the US Courts. The producers paid up and the stories ran for six years. Bob Crane starred as Colonel Robert Hogan, the allied commander of a crazy Nazi prisoner-of-war camp known as Stalag 13. The German officers ostensibly in charge were the ridiculous Colonel Klink (Werner Klemperer) and the equally stupid Sgt Hans Schultz (John Banner). It was immediately clear that the prisoners were having a great time and running all sorts of operations and rackets from inside the camp. With Hogan were Lieutenant Carter (Larry Hovis), Sgt Kinchloe (Ivan Dixon), Louis LeBeau (Robert Clary) and Peter Newkirk (Richard Dawson). Other regular German characters included Langenscheidt (John Cedar), General Burkhalter (Leon Askin), Hilda (Sigrid Valdis) and Helga (Cynthia Lynn). The prisoners always emerged on top and were able to launch behind-the-lines attacks on enemy installations.
Producer: Ed Feldman.

HOGG'S BACK
SOUTHERN. First broadcast: 8 September 1975

Michael Pertwee created and wrote these children's stories of zany, absent-minded Dr Hogg (Derek Royle) who returned from retirement to re-open his practice at Belling-on-Sea. Though he was always well-intentioned, he got into all sorts of scrapes and comic mishaps. In the first series of 13 programmes he had a housekeeper, Pearl (Jacki Piper, later Wendy Richard). In the second series of 13 transmitted from June 1976, his housekeeper was Mrs Mac (Pat Coombs). Other seaside regulars in Dr Hogg's life were the vicar (Eric Dodson), General Balding (Robert Dorning), Mrs Biggle (Dorothea Phillips) and Mr Diehard (Gordon Rollings).
Producer: Peter Croft.

HOLD THE FRONT PAGE
THAMES. First broadcast: 16 January 1974

Actress Denise Coffey created this children's series about a team of reporters working for *The Weekly Bizarre*. The ace correspondent was R Hero (Roy Hudd), with Gloria Glamorsox (Denise Coffey),

Harriett Heedless (Lois Lane), racing and foreign reporter Harry Bracket (Andrew Robertson) and jack-of-all-trades Gerry (Gerry Marsden). The caustic catalyst of the copy desk was a cat named Vernon. The series made much use of graphics and cartoons by Jim Gask.
Producer: Daphne Shadwell.

HOLDING THE FORT
LWT. First broadcast: 5 September 1980

Laurence Marks and Maurice Gran created and wrote this series about young married couple Russell and Penny Milburn (Peter Davison and Patricia Hodge) and their baby Emma (Victoria Kendall). In role reversal, Penny returned to her old job in the army while Russell stayed home to look after the baby and set up his own brewery in the basement. In this he was not very ably assisted by his unkempt and unpredictable friend Fitz (Matthew Kelly). There was further conflict because while the Milburn income came from the army, Russell and Fitz were avowed pacifists. After the first series of six there were two further runs of six ending 22 August 1981. See also RELATIVE STRANGERS.
Producer: Derrick Goodwin.

HOLIDAY LODGE
CBS (AMERICA) PRESENTED BY ITV.
First broadcast (UK): 12 February 1963

This series, created and produced by Seymour Berns, ran for just one 13-week season in the USA in 1961. It starred Canadian comedians Johnny Wayne and Frank Shuster as the entertainment managers of the Holiday Lodge mountain resort. With them as members of an incompetent staff were Maureen Arthur as Dorothy, Charles Smith as Woodrow, and Justice Watson who played the manager of the lodge, JW Harrington.

HOLMES AND YOYO
NBC (AMERICA) PRESENTED BY BBC.
First broadcast (UK): 29 October 1976

Experienced but hopelessly inept police detective Alexander Holmes (Richard B Shull) had managed to land four partners in hospital during his bungled investigations. The research department attached to the force produced a new partner for him in the shape of Yoyo (John Schuck), an electronic robot with a human form. Thirteen editions were shown.
Producers: Leonard Stern and Jackie Cooper.

HOME AGAIN
BBC RADIO. First broadcast: 2 June 1980

This serial in six parts by Peter Tinniswood starred Robin Bailey as Fulton Jones who, twenty years previously, had said he was just slipping out to get a box of matches and had never been seen again. Much to the consternation of his wife (Doreen Mantle) he turned up on the doorstep out of the blue.
Producer: Griff Rhys Jones.

HOME AND AWAY
BBC RADIO. First broadcast: 30 March 1954

Theatre and film star Jack Buchanan starred as playwright Jack Fuller whose busy life often kept him away from his family. Fuller's wife Daffodil was portrayed by Buchanan's long-standing stage partner Elsie Randolph. The Fullers had three daughters, Billie (Josephine Crombie), Janet (Beryl Roques) and Hyacinth (Carole Shelley). The only other regular character was Tangent (David Hutcheson) who worked for Jack. Many guest stars were brought into the plots by writer David Climie, including David Jacobs as a boyfriend, Alfie Bass, Beryl Reid, Peter Sellers, Joan Sims and Eleanor Summerfield. There were 18 editions ending on 27 July.
Producer: Jacques Brown.

HOME IMPROVEMENT
USA PRESENTED BY CHANNEL 4.
First broadcast (UK): 4 February 1994

This show crossed the Atlantic with a fanfare of Channel 4 trumpets heralding it as the hottest new show of the year. It was greeted by British viewers and critics with equal indifference and serves as an ongoing reminder that comedy is the most fickle import–export commodity between the two countries. Tim Allen starred as Tim Taylor, Detroit-based husband, father of three sons and know-it-all presenter of a DIY cable-TV show called 'Tool Time'. He had a mania for power both to drive the tools on the show and in his own home. He used the cable show as a platform to flaunt his masculinity and lace his debate about the sexes with barbs and experiences from his own domestic life. Indeed the actuality of his domestic situation repeatedly propelled him back to reality. His wife was Jill (Patricia Richardson) and the three young sons were played by Jonathan Taylor Thomas, Taran Noah Smith

and Zachery Ty Bryan. Some of the better lines in the scripts went to Tim's cynical assistant on the show, Al (Earl Hindman). Tim sought philosophical guidance from a neighbour named Wilson who was always hidden behind a six-foot high garden fence when spouting his words of wisdom.
Producers: Carmen Finestra, Matt Williams and David McFadzean.

HOME JAMES
THAMES. First broadcast: 1 July 1987

This sequel to UP THE ELEPHANT AND ROUND THE CASTLE ran for four six-part seasons to 23 July 1990. Jim London (Jim Davidson) was forced to leave Railway Terrace when the demolition squad moved in on behalf of a property developer. He found employment as a delivery man for an electronics factory where his first boss was Wobbler Wainwright (Colin Farrell). He soon became personal chauffeur to the millionaire owner of the factory, Robert Palmer (George Sewell), and his duties came under the watchful eye of Wobbler's mate Henry Compton (Harry Towb). In his full chauffeur's livery, Jim set out to impress the girls, Sarah (Vanessa Knox-Mower) and Paula (Sherrie Hewson). Jim's responsibilities gradually increased and he became Robert's trouble-shooter until the business went bust and Robert lost his fortune. At that point Jim and Henry shared a room so that they could let out Henry's room for cash. They started a new business, Rent-a-Butler, which never got off the ground. In the meantime Robert was on the road to financial recovery and by the final series he was back on top with a consultancy operation. Jim was again his chauffeur and Henry became his butler. The secretary was Eleanor Hayward (Juliette Grassby).
Directors: Mark Stuart, David Askey. Producers: Anthony Parker, Martin Shardlow.

HOME TO ROOST
BBC RADIO. First broadcast: 19 August 1974

Anne Jones wrote this domestic series about the problems and daily nigglings when a man retires and is about the house for much of the day. Deryck Guyler and Mollie Sugden starred as Mr and Mrs Wheeler in just such a predicament. He felt she had no sense of humour, yet she knew he cracked the same jokes week in, week out. He looked for a little light job for an elderly gent, but to no avail. Regular characters through the 19 programmes over two

series which ended on 23 September 1975 were Jack Bailey (Norman Rossington) and Nev (John Baddeley).
Theme music: Alex Welsh. Producers: Richard Maddock and Peter Titheradge, Trafford Whitelock.

HOME TO ROOST
YTV. First broadcast: 19 April 1985

Henry Willows (John Thaw) had been divorced for seven years, lived alone, and was grumpy and set in his ways. He was used to his freedom, peace and tranquillity which were suddenly upset when his eldest son Matthew (Reece Dinsdale) arrived to live with him, having been thrown out by his mother when she realised he had inherited all his father's characteristics. The only domestic intrusion into Henry's world prior to Matthew's turning up had been cleaning lady Enid Thompson (Elizabeth Bennett). Father and son did much silent staring as the mirror image faced each of them, but they settled into a routine which came under threat when Matthew's sister Julie (Rebecca Lacey) announced her intention of moving in with them. There followed a swift dawning of the truth of the proverb that 'three's a crowd' and she was not encouraged to linger. The first series of seven programmes was followed by a second seven which got underway on 5 September 1986. By the time the third run of seven started on 14 October 1987, Henry and Matthew had a new cleaning lady, Fiona Fennell (Joan Blackham). There were six more episodes and in the final one on 19 January 1990, Matthew left to go to college. He was secretly hoping for some display of emotion from his father, but Henry had been planning for and looking forward to the day for some considerable time.
Music: Peter Knight. Writer: Eric Chappell. Producers: Vernon Lawrence, David Reynolds.

HONEY FOR TEA
BBC. First broadcast: 13 March 1994

Felicity Kendall starred in six episodes as Californian widow Nancy Belasco whose crook of a husband collapsed and died leaving her penniless. He had willed his vast fortune to his former college at Cambridge, St Maud's (pronounced Mud's), so it was to there that Nancy reluctantly repaired with her thick son Jake (Patrick McCollough) to seek employment for herself and an undergraduate place for him. Through guile and bravado she wormed herself in to see the dotty Master of the college, Sir Richard Hobhouse (Leslie Phillips), who, in between singing old rock songs at the piano, made her assistant bursar to the hostile, traditionalist Welshman Dr Basil Quinn (Alan David). The only friend she was able to find within the ancient, hallowed walls was English tutor Professor Simon Latimer (Nigel Le Vaillant), adjacent to whom she found she had been allocated rooms. Jake took a fancy to the Master's personal secretary, the Hon. Lucy Courtney (Caroline Harker), and Nancy bombasted her way past college porter Jarvis (John Rapley) who tried to work to the rule book.

Writer: Michael Aitkens. Producer: Gareth Gwenlan.

THE HONEYMOONERS
CBS (AMERICA) PRESENTED BY ITV.
First broadcast (UK): 6 July 1958

This show began in the USA in 1951 but only had its first British transmission seven years later. Jackie Gleason starred as bus driver Ralph Kramden who lived with his wife Alice (Audrey Meadows, later Sheila MacRae). Ralph was a loud-mouthed know-all, a forerunner of Alf Garnett and Archie Bunker, and indefatigable in his projects to get rich quick. His pride refused him to allow Alice to go out to work, yet they teetered always on the edge of being flat broke. They shared their tribulations with their best friends and neighbours from the apartment below their own, Ed Norton (Art Carney) and his wife Trixie (Joyce Randolph). Ed worked as a sewer cleaner. The series, of which 39 editions were made in black and white, still enjoys cult status in the USA where Ralph became something of a hero. It never caught on to the same degree in Britain either in the 1950s or when the BBC re-ran the shows as comedy classics from 16 June 1989. Gleason himself wrote, produced and directed several of the episodes.

HONOLULU BEACH
BBC RADIO. First broadcast: 20 February 1940

This comedy with music in a Hawaiian setting was written by its star, Jewish comic Joe Hayman, who played Jake Rosen, the proprietor of a tavern. Other characters included Plato the chef (Jacques Brown), Confucious the waiter (Sydney Keith), Kaloma (Evelyn Dove), Halima (Dorothe Morrow), Howard the beachcomber (Leslie Bradley) and gangster Spike McGee (Robert Wyndham).

Music: Peter Bernard. Producer: Roy Speer.

HOOP-LA!
BBC RADIO. First broadcast: 27 November 1944

Although basically a variety show, the setting was a fairground and there were several regular characters promoting 'All the Fun of the Fair'. Robb Wilton starred as the Complaints Manager with Polly Ward in the 'Pin-Up Parlour' and the ubiquitous Bert (Benny Lee). Max Wall was ever-present and created within this show the framework of what would become OUR SHED with Auntie (Doris Nichols) and Guy (Harold Berens). The catchphrase was Wall's 'Ack-tually', pronounced with a nasal toffee-sounding pretence. In a second series starting 9 February 1945, Jack Train joined the cast as 'Cheapjack Train from Petticoat Lane'.

Producers: Tom Arnold, Pat Dixon.

HOPE AND KEEN'S CRAZY HOUSE
BBC. First broadcast: 7 July 1971

Variety double act Mike Hope and Albie Keen starred in this children's series. The house was ostensibly a multi-storey mansion with different aspects of madness going on in its hundred different rooms. It also had a convenient guest room where 'turns' could do their party piece. Resident were ancient butler Crumple (Peter Goodwright) and Mrs Grapple the Cook (Ruth Kettlewell). There were six episodes. The following year, from 7 April, the same team were involved in six further shows but changed the setting from a house to a bus on the trail of some buried treasure.

Writers: Mike Craig and Lawrie Kinsley, David A Yallop and Harry Jones. Producer: Paul Ciani.

HOPE IT RAINS
Thames. First broadcast: 3 June 1991

Tom Bell starred as bachelor Harry Nash, a self-centred man rooted in his ways, who was landed with looking after his stroppy teenage god-daughter Jace (Holly Aird) when her parents died. Jace was something of a rebel and she disturbed the comfort of Harry's style. He ran a waxworks museum at a seaside resort with the help of his friend Dennis (Eamon Boland). Jace stayed in bed till noon, was rude and made the place a mess. The first series of six programmes ended with her sailing off on a yacht promising Harry she would be back in a fortnight. The second run

of six opened up on 24 June 1992 with Harry having heard not a word from her after six weeks. She returned in the first episode and they were able to resume hostilities.
Producer: John Howard Davies.

HOT METAL
LWT. First broadcast: 16 February 1986

Robert Hardy starred in a dual role in this send-up of the bottom end of the tabloid newspaper industry. He was press baron Terence 'Twiggy' Rathbone who owned Rathouse International, one of whose papers was the *Daily Crucible* which faced closure through drastic falls in circulation. He bore a striking facial resemblance to the new editor, Russell Spam (also played by Hardy) who brought in a new policy exposing sex and political scandals and providing readers with daily titillation on the third page. This outraged the managing editor Harry Stringer (Geoffrey Palmer) but boosted circulation beyond wildest dreams. Others involved with the fortunes of the rag were Greg Kettle (Richard Kane), Bill Tytla (John Gordon Sinclair), Max (Geoffrey Hastings) and, peripherally, Father Teasdale (John Horsley). Jack Watling made occasional appearances as the Prime Minister until, in the second series, the Crucible brought about the downfall of the government. Twiggy had courted the Tories through the first series of six episodes but with the arrival of a Labour government at the advent of series two, 6 March 1988, he swopped sides. Harry Stringer had mysteriously disappeared in a flying accident and a new managing editor was installed, Richard Lipton (Richard Wilson). There were 12 programmes altogether.
Writers: Andrew Marshall and David Renwick. Director: David Askey. Producer: Humphrey Barclay.

HOTEL MAJESTIC
BBC RADIO. First broadcast: 3 October 1957

Canadian actress Barbara Kelly starred as hotel public relations officer Sally O'Brien in this 13-part series. Each edition would present her with new complications which must not affect the other guests nor the smooth running of the hotel. Almost invariably she would have to ask the telephone operator (Christina Horniman) to call in Inspector Cosgrove (Carl Bernard). The manager was Mr Raub (Jack Melford).
Producer: Tom Ronald.

HOUSE CALLS
CBS (AMERICA) PRESENTED BY BBC. First broadcast (UK): 27 June 1981

Set in an American hospital known as Kensington Central, this serives was more concerned with the love lives of the staff than the administration and patients. Ann Anderson (Lynn Redgrave) arrived to take up a hospital management post and immediately caught the eye of playboy Dr Charley Michaels (Wayne Rogers). The two other featured doctors were Amos Weatherby (David Wayne) and Norman Solomon (Ray Buktenica). The series was loosely based on the 1978 movie of the same title which had starred Walter Matthau and Glenda Jackson. Fourteen episodes were shown in Britain ending 31 October 1981.

HOUSE OF WINDSOR
GRANADA. First broadcast: 15 May 1994

Launched at a time when the British press and public between them had developed a pronounced cynicism – but never indifference – about the activities of the Royal Family, this series added fuel to the fire of media hunger when it first hit the screen. Leslie Phillips starred as Lord Montague, Head of the Royal Household with the title Lord Chamberlain. A former Admiral, Montague was a traditionalist and resented with fervour the appointment of a Royal public relations man, Max Kelvin (Warren Clarke), a thinly disguised caricature of a one-time tabloid newspaper editor. Their backgrounds being from opposite ends of the social spectrum, the two men were incompatible. Both were pacified by the diplomacy of the Private Secretary, Sir Nicholas Foulsham (Neil Stacy). Others caught up in the politics of the Royal household included Giles Huntingdon (Jeremy Sinden), who was Montague's incompetent assistant; Caroline Finch (Serena Gordon), who worked in the press office with the despicable Kelvin; Lady Sharpcott (Margaret Courtney), elderly Lady in Waiting to the Queen; footman Ray (Sean Gallagher), a sharp rogue; camp footman Danny (Barry Howard) and maid Kate (Louise Germaine).
Director: Graeme Harper. Producer: Tony Wood.

HOW NOW, BROWN?
BBC RADIO. First broadcast: 6 July 1954

Arthur Hill starred as Arthur J Brown, a happy-go-

lucky chap who attracted trouble like a magnet. His friend was Joseph O'Leary (Robin Bailey) and the love interest in Arthur's life was Sally Cruncher (Denise Bryer). Sally's father was played by Francis de Wolff. Arthur Hill also wrote the eight-part series.
Producer: Jacques Brown.

HOW'S YOUR FATHER?
BBC RADIO. First broadcast: 10 April 1964

This series by Denis Goodwin starred Ted Ray as Father, a widower who lived with his son Robin, played by his real-life son Robin Ray. They had a domineering housekeeper, Mrs Bender (Thora Hird), who had a beautiful daughter Angela (Annette André) with whom Robin fell hopelessly in love. Completing the household was Ted's sister Ethel (Eleanor Summerfield), a candid woman who never held back her thoughts and observations on their situations. Friends and neighbours were portrayed by Pat Coombs and Terence Alexander.
Producer: Trafford Whitelock.

HOW'S YOUR FATHER?
GRANADA. First broadcast: 24 July 1974

John Stevenson wrote these stories of a double generation gap. The mug-in-the-middle was Eddie Cropper (Michael Robbins), who shared home with his beer-swilling father Ted (Arthur English), his wife Doreen (Barbara Young) and their two children, drop-out son Edward (Nicholas Hoye) and daughter Christine (Georgina Moon). Eddie's boss, Mr Winterbottom, was played by Reginald Marsh and Sheila Steafel appeared regularly as Ivy Watkins. The series returned for a second run the following February.
Producers: Bill Podmore, Brian Armstrong.

HOW'S YOUR FATHER?
YTV. First broadcast: 27 February 1979

Harry Worth starred as Harry Matthews, a recently widowed father of two teenage children. His son Martin (Giles Watling), aged 19, and daughter Shirley (Debby Cumming) found their father wildly out of touch with the modern world. Harry was a staid banker with old world principles. When Shirley announced she was planning to get engaged, Harry tried all in his power to stand in her way. He sought the help and

advice of friends and neighbours like Vera Blacker (Fanny Carby) and Mrs Simkins (Sonia Graham). The first series of six programmes was followed by a second run of six starting 18 July 1980.
Music: Denis King. Writers: Pam Valentine and Michael Ashton. Producer: Graeme Muir.

HUDD
BBC. First broadcast: 23 November 1965.

Roy Hudd starred in the title role as a clumsy character, ever anxious to please but prone to social disasters. He was the only regular in this series which was developed from an earlier half-hour *Comedy Playhouse*. There was also no permanent situation in that Hudd travelled around, be it to an unfortunate hotel in Brighton or to some other location where unsuspecting victims would be drawn into his disasters.
Writers: George Evans and Derek Collyer. Producer: John Paddy Carstairs.

HUGH AND I
BBC. First broadcast: 17 July 1962

Actor John Chapman created and wrote this series which ran until 1966. The saga of suburbia starred Terry Scott as the bachelor son of Mrs Scott (Vi Stevens), undutiful to his mother, unable to find a job to suit him and forever in search of quick and easy fortune. Hugh Lloyd co-starred as the lodger who provided the rent through his job at a local aircraft factory. Lugubrious Hugh became embroiled in Terry's schemes which were orchestrated in the Scott home, 33 Lobelia Avenue, Tooting. The neighbours of the Scotts were the Crispins, he loud-mouthed and truculent (Wallas Eaton), and she rather snobbish without cause (Mollie Sugden). The Crispins had a shapely and attractive daughter, Norma (Jacquie Wallis, later Jill Curzon), who was the object of the desire of both Terry and Hugh. The neighbours on the other side were the Wormolds. Arthur was elderly, deaf and a bit of a groper. He was portrayed by Cyril Smith, a veteran actor who first appeared on the stage in 1900 (later Jack Haig). Arthur's devoted wife Griselda was played by Patricia Hayes. The first series ran for eight episodes, and a further eight began 21 May 1963 followed by 14 more from 3 January 1964. By the end of the 13th and last programme of the fourth series, Hugh had won

£5,000 on the Premium Bonds and the pair had embarked on a cruise.
Theme music: Wally Stott. Producer: David Croft.

HUGH AND I SPY
BBC. First broadcast: 22 January 1968

As an extension to their long-running HUGH AND I series, Hugh Lloyd and Terry Scott embarked on six adventures away from their customary domesticity and into the world of espionage. The all-action shows were written by John Chapman.
Music: Wally Stott. Producer: David Croft.

HULBERT HOUSE
BBC RADIO. First broadcast: 2 March 1948

The Hulbert brothers, Jack and Claude, starred in this 13-week series. Debonaire Jack landed in odd troublesome situations which were always complicated by brother Claude's attempts to follow his example. The supporting players of whatever roles were required included Dick Francis, Jack Melford and Mary O'Farrell.
Writers: Max Kester and Jack Hulbert. Producer: Tom Ronald.

ITMA

BBC RADIO. First broadcast: 12 July 1939

This most famous of all radio comedies was essentially the product of three men: the star of the show, Liverpudlian funny man Tommy Handley; the scriptwriter, Ted Kavanagh; and the producer, Francis Worsley. Four programmes were broadcast in the summer of 1939 but the series proper was first heard at 8.30pm on Thursday, 19 September 1939.

The title was taken from the *Daily Express* headline 'It's That Man Again', used each time Adolf Hitler staked another territorial claim. Michael North wrote the signature tune:

> It's that man again, Yes that man again
> Yes sir, Tommy Handley is here.
> Mother's pride and joy
> Mrs Handley's boy,
> Oh, it's useless to complain –
> When trouble's brewing, it's his doing,
> That man, that man again.

Initially the programmes were set on a broadcasting ship from which Handley could transmit whatever he liked. He was aided by a secretary, Cilly (Celia Eddy), and a wild Russian inventor played by Eric Egan. The four shows in that run were not very successful and by the time the autumn series was prepared it had been decided that That Man should be a senior member of the ranks of officialdom – he became the Minister of Aggravation and Mysteries at the Department of Twerps. There he was aided by a new secretary, Dotty (Vera Lennox); the office charlady, Mrs Lola Tickle (Maurice Denham – 'I always do my best for all my gentlemen'); Vodkin, the Russian inventor (Maurice Denham); and Fusspot (Jack Train). Each programme contained a spoof of Radio Luxembourg in the form of Radio Fakenburg, with Maurice Denham as the announcer and Sam Costa as the singer of the commercials. As the BBC's variety department was moved from London to Bristol, so it was felt that the Office of Twerps should be evacuated out of the capital. The second programme of the series had produced Jack Train's character Funf, the ever-present German

spy who was the butt of Handley's jokes. With the move to the country, Train found a new character as Farmer Jollop.

The format established Handley as the Minister, constantly interrupted by this variety of people who knocked on the ITMA door. The series ended in February 1940 and would not return for almost 18 months. When it did come back, only Jack Train, Vera Lennox and Handley himself remained. The rest had been called up. The BBC Variety department was now in Bangor and new team members were recruited from the Variety Rep. Some of ITMA's best-recalled figures date from the second period, but the situation was totally changed. Briefly, the title was changed to ITSA (It's That Sand Again) as Handley became His Washup, the Mayor of Foaming-at-the-Mouth, a shabby and badly-run small resort. Among those figures were Handley's American henchman Sam Scram (Sydney Keith), the vendor of naughty postcards Ali Oop (Horace Percival), the Commercial Traveller who never sold anything (Clarence Wright), Lefty (Jack Train), the gangster, and Claude and Cecil (Percival and Train) who deferred exaggeratedly to each other: 'After you, Claude. No – after you, Cecil.' Percival also created the Diver, who reminded all who passed by his seaside pitch, 'Don't forget the Diver'. Also created at this time were the new foreign secretary to the Mayor, Signor So-So (Dino Galvani), who was playing havoc with the English language forty years before 'ALLO 'ALLO ('Let me cuss you on both cheeks'), and the classic Cockney charlady Mrs Mopp (Dorothy Summers). Mrs Mopp had been sent by 'the labour' to dust the Mayor's dado and soon her strong entrance line, 'Can I do you now, sir?', had become a national favourite. Her exit line 'Ta Ta For Now', shortened to TTFN, is still in use.

By 1942 ITMA had a regular listening audience of more than 16 million and the Royal Family were avid fans. One memorable edition was recorded at Windsor Castle at the express request of their Majesties. With the advent of a new series that autumn, Foaming-at-the-Mouth had acquired a war factory, managed by Handley. Funf made the occasional reappearance, always accompanied by Johann

Bull (Fred Yule), a hail and hearty spy who loved explosives and his little 'chokes'. Yule also was the voice for Norman the Doorman ('vicky-verky') while Jack Train added Bookham the variety agent, and Clarence Wright became the Man from the Ministry who irritatingly repeated the last word of his every sentence. Perhaps the best-remembered characterisation from that time is Jack Train's Colonel Chinstrap, who was to continue his dogged pursuit of liquid refreshment until the final broadcast in 1949. His catchphrase was, 'I don't mind if I do.'

From autumn of 1943 to the end in 1949, ITMA ceased to be a summer season and was broadcast for 35 or 40 shows each year. The factory was transformed variously into a spa, a hotel and a holiday camp. New characters emerged like Comical Chris (Bill Stephens) and Mr Whats'isname (Horace Percival). Jean Capra joined the team to play Poppy Poopah and Handley was established as the Squire of Much-Fiddling Manor. By the end of 1943 the shows were being recorded at London's Criterion theatre. In 1944 Jack Train, recovered from illness which had kept him out of some previous season's shows, returned and introduced Mark Time, who answered any question with 'I'll have to ask me Dad'. Diana Morrison joined as Handley's rather overpowering secretary, Miss Hotchkiss, named after a machine-gun. On 10 May 1945, ITMA broadcast its triumphant Victory edition. Post-war, Handley was appointed Governor of a far-distant country, Tomtopia. The team took two weeks to prepare and four weeks at sea to get there. On board ship the meals were made by chef Curly Kale (Carleton Hobbs) and eaten by George Gorge (Fred Yule) who had a voracious capacity for 'lovely grub'. Other travellers were Welshman Sam Fairfechan (Hugh Morton), Nurse Riff-Rafferty and Lady Sonely, both voiced by Mary O'Farrell. On Tomtopia, Handley met the polygamous chief Bigga Banga (Fred Yule) and the Oxford-accented Wamba M'Boojah (Hugh Morton). Others included Bigga Banga's daughter Banjeleo (Lind Joyce) and the Englishman who had lived there since the Boer war, Major Munday (Carleton Hobbs), and his daughter Naive (Jean Capra). Colonel Chinstrap had accompanied Handley to the island – as had Miss Hotchkiss – and headed straight for the Jungle Arms.

At the end of the ninth series Governor Handley sailed for Britain. He arrived in Scotland at Castle Weehouse where he encountered a new bane of his

Yes, it's That Man Again: Tommy Handley in one of the 310 editions of ITMA (Photo: Copyright © BBC)

life, Tattie Mackintosh and her mother, both played by Molly Weir. Handley was trying to organise a flight to the moon. Among the characters on hand to help and hinder were Dan Dungeon (Deryck Guyler) the castle guide, Colonel Chinstrap's nephew Brigadier Dear (Hugh Morton), and the gloomy laundrywoman Mona Lott (Joan Harben). The rocket was launched at the end of October 1946. It missed the moon and landed on Tomtopia! In autumn 1947 Handley was back in England as the Government's adviser on industrial and scientific affairs. Deryck Guyler had created Frisby Dyke, a Liverpudlian who had a weekly wordy dialogue with Handley. Fred Yule's new character was Atlas ('What, me? In my state of health?') and Hattie Jacques had joined as the larger-than-life schoolgirl Sophie Tuckshop. The final series began in October 1948 with Handley a permanent resident of Henry Hall, the tramps' guest house run by Miss Hotchkiss. On 28 October ITMA made its 300th broadcast. The show would run only ten more editions. Tommy Handley died suddenly of a cerebral haemorrhage on 9 January 1949.

Musical directors over the years were Billy Ternent, Jack Hylton, Charles Shadwell and Rae Jenkins. The ITMA singers included Paula Green, Kay Cavendish and the Cavendish Three, Denny Dennis and Lind Joyce. For a few programmes while Francis Worsley was confined to hospital, Ronnie Waldman assumed the duties of producer.

I DIDN'T KNOW YOU CARED

BBC. First broadcast: 27 August 1975

Peter Tinniswood created and wrote this saga about the war between the sexes in Northern England as seen through the eyes of the Brandon family, who first came to notice in a trilogy of books by Tinniswood. The family was dour and appeared to enjoy being miserable in comfort. There were 28 episodes over four series ending on 26 June 1979. At the outset, the Brandon household consisted of the moderately amiable Mr Brandon (John Comer), his matronly wife (Liz Smith), their dreamy but would-be executive son Carter (Stephen Rea, later Keith Drinkel), and seedy old misogynist Uncle Mort (Robin Bailey) who shuffled around in muffler and flat cap. Carter was engaged to Pat Partington (Anita Carey, later Liz Goulding), and despite all his chauvinism and attempts to avoid the altar, they married at the end of the first series and moved into the Brandon home at the start of the second. Her presence did little to lift the funereal atmosphere which Uncle Mort seemed so to relish. Other regular characters were Pat's mother Mrs Partington (Vanda Godsell), Uncle Stavely (Bert Palmer, later Leslie Sarony), Sid Skelhorn (Ray Dunbobbin, later Bobby Pattinson) and Linda Preston (Deirdre Costello).

Theme music: Ronnie Hazlehurst. Producer: Bernard Thompson.

I DREAM OF JEANNIE

NBC (AMERICA) PRESENTED BY ITV.
First broadcast (UK): 6 April 1972

Although made in the USA in 1965, this series was not shown in Britain until the early 1970s. Larry Hagman starred as astronaut Tony Nelson who was engaged to his CO's daughter Melissa Stone (Karen Sharpe). He was sent into space with fellow astronaut Roger Healey (Bill Daily) but their capsule crash-landed on a Pacific island. There Major Nelson found a bottle, inside which had been trapped Jeannie, a genie. He released her and from that point, he and Major Healey were transported on a sequence of adventures. Nelson and Jeannie married. She was very glamorous and did all she could to serve her master. The role of Jeannie was played by Barbara Eden. There were more than 100 episodes, created and, for the large part, produced by Sidney Sheldon.

I LOVE LUCY

CBS (AMERICA) PRESENTED BY ITV.
First broadcast (UK): 25 September 1955

Lucille Ball starred as Lucy Ricardo (née McGillicuddy), the lovable, infantile, scatterbrained wife of Cuban singer and bandleader Ricky Ricardo. Ricky was played by Lucy's real-life husband Desi Arnaz, who was, indeed, a Cuban singer and bandleader. She strove to play the role of supportive wife while her ambitions for a show-business career drove Ricky to weekly exasperation.

The couple had met in 1940 on the set of a movie *Too Many Girls* and the idea for I LOVE LUCY was born out of their true domestic friction. They were pioneers in as much as they produced a pilot show independently in a small Hollywood film studio using three cameras and recording sequentially. They found themselves a sponsor (Philip Morris cigarettes) and won the backing of two CBS executives, Harry Ackerman and Hubbell Robinson. The first of what would ultimately be 179 episodes was screened on the US network in October 1951. Another innovation was to film the series before a studio audience. Lucille and Desi set a new trend by forming their own production company, Desilu, and negotiating with CBS to retain the world distribution rights for the series. This was but one of many fights with CBS. The network was reluctant to have Desi in the show. They wished to bring in the man who had co-starred with Lucille on the radio series *My Favorite Husband*, Richard Denning. They lost. They did not want Desi to be the weekly producer. They lost. CBS wanted to record the series in New York (after all, it was set there), Lucille and Desi wished to make the shows in Los Angeles. CBS lost. Lucille wanted to have Desi's name in the title. CBS won.

The principal writers were Madelyn Pugh and Bob Carroll, who created situations of conflict between Lucy and Ricky which, for the most part, originated from Lucy failing to get what she wanted and then cheating and conniving to attain her goal. In this she was aided and abetted by her friend from the next-door apartment Ethel Mertz, portrayed by Vivian Vance. Ethel's irascible husband Fred, played by William Frawley, aligned himself with Ricky against the guiles and wiles of the women, although the schemes of Lucy and Ethel would always triumph in the end, with Lucy working her way into Ricky's act in various disguises.

When Lucille gave birth to Desi Jr her pregnancy and the baby were written into the series, but to satisfy the moral requirements of the time, the word expectant had to be used, rather than pregnant. Desi Jr did not appear in the show as himself. The role of Ricky Jr was played by Richard Keith. The series won Emmy awards in 1952 and 1953, but British viewers, and then only those in London, did not see the show until 1955. It has been repeated dozens of times round the globe and earned so much money for Desilu that they were able to buy the RKO studios. The couple divorced in 1960 with Desi selling his shares to Lucy.

Co-producer and co-writer: Jess Oppenheimer.

I, LOVETT
BBC. First broadcast: 24 March 1993

This series in six parts was written by Ian Pattison and Norman Lovett, who starred himself in the title role as an eccentric inventor. He shared the house in which he lived with a cynical talking dog named Dirk.

Director: Ron Bain. Producer: Colin Gilbert.

I MARRIED JOAN
NBC (AMERICA) PRESENTED BY BBC.
First broadcast (UK): 30 March 1956

Vaudeville veteran Joan Davis starred as Joan Stevens, the dizzy and clumsy wife of Judge Bradley Stevens (Jim Backus). The comedy was frantic and played at a pace which ultimately exhausted Davis, who died in 1961 at the age of 54. The last of more than 60 editions was screened by the BBC on 26 November 1957.

I OBJECT
BBC. First broadcast: 14 April 1965

Charlie Chester and Charles Hart devised this 12-part series in which members of the public were invited to raise an objection to some aspect of television. The case would then be argued for and

against by learned counsels Sir Charles Chester (Charlie Chester) and Sir Edward Ray (Ted Ray). The Judge was portrayed by Jimmy Edwards and he would sum up the pros and cons of the objection to a jury of 12 selected members of the studio audience.

Producer: Albert Stevenson.

I THOUGHT YOU'D GONE
CENTRAL. First broadcast: 27 July 1984

In the belief that their children had finally all left home, Gerald and Alice (Peter Jones and Pat Heywood) sold up in Croydon and moved to a small house in the country. However, when Tony (Ian Gelder) separated from Sandra (Yvonne Antrobus) and Sue (Rowena Roberts) gave up as a research chemist, they found they had a houseful again. Added to that, one of the offspring dumped a boat so that it blocked the garage entrance. Other regulars in the seven-part series were Justin (James Trelfa), Lucy (Charlotte Walker), Mandy (Louisa Haigh) and Ruby Pugh (Rosalind Knight).

Writers: Peter Jones and Kevin Laffan. Director: Paul Harrison. Producer: Shaun O'Riordan.

I WAS KITCHENER'S TREBLE
BBC RADIO. First broadcast: 18 April 1966

Lampooning the 1958 film *I Was Monty's Double*, this series in eight parts starred Dick Bentley as Kitchener's treble, a man purporting to be too physically large to be a double. He was a garrulous Australian and his counterpart was Richard Wattis, who assumed the role of a stuffed-shirt Englishman. Theirs was a running battle involving literature and history with interjections from Patricia Routledge, John Bluthal and the 'zither girl', Shirley Abicair.

Producer: Richard Dingley.

I WOKE UP ONE MORNING
BBC. First broadcast: 21 March 1985

Four alcoholics met in hospital while undergoing psychotherapy after drying out. They were Derek (Frederick Jaeger), a gentleman farmer driven to drink by his wife's affair with a farm hand; Danny (Peter Caffrey), an Irishman whose dreams of life as a bed of roses came to nought; Max (Michael Angelis), who could not cope with reality; and Zero (Robert Gillespie), with a failed marriage and a sense of having been washed out by life. There were twelve programmes over two series ending on 10 April 1986.

Theme music: Bill Lovelady and Mitch Dalton. Writer: Carla Lane. Producer: Robin Nash.

IF IT MOVES – FILE IT
LWT. First broadcast: 28 August 1970

This rare venture into comedy by dramatist Troy Kennedy Martin lasted for just one season. The stories of the Civil Service concerned two faceless ministry minions, Quick (John Bird) and Foster (Dudley Foster), who worked for M17 in the Ministry for Technology and Works. They called themselves experts although nobody could identify the subject of their expertise. The pair were constantly thwarted in their bid to run the department by their boss, Froggett (John Nettleton).

Director: Derek Bennett. Producer: Humphrey Barclay.

IF THE CROWN FITS
ATV. First broadcast: 29 April 1961

Robert Morley starred as King Rupert, the impecunious monarch of a small Mediterranean country called Grabnia. He ruled from the capital city, Grabnis, and the production was contemporary of its time. His daughter and heiress, Princess Amelia (Tracy Reed), was a beatnik who wore jeans and rode around on the back of a scooter driven by her boyfriend George (David Cole). The Court was presided over by Major Domos (Peter Bull) and his footman Stevens (Erik Chitty), who had been engaged to a lady named Prudence for 45 years. The Prime Minister of Grabnia was played by Miles Malleson and the Chancellor by Charles Lloyd Pack. The sentry who guarded the King's palace was portrayed by Richard Walter. In the first of six editions, the shortlived public relations man was Fred Potter, played by Robert Hardy.

Music: Max Harris. Producer: Alan Tarrant.

IF YOU SEE GOD, TELL HIM
BBC. First broadcast: 11 November 1993

David Renwick and Andrew Marshall joined forces to create these four 45-minute stories in which Richard Briers starred as wheelchair-bound widower Godfrey Spry, who was obsessed by television commercials and whose brain had a concentration span of just 30 seconds which ena-

bled him to watch and take in the adverts. Co-starring were Adrian Edmondson as Gordon Spry and Imelda Staunton as Muriel Spry.

Producer: Marcus Mortimer.

I'M DICKENS . . . HE'S FENSTER
ABC (AMERICA) PRESENTED BY ITV.
First broadcast (UK): 23 September 1964

Leonard Stern created and produced this show in 1962 and it was seen in Britain two years later. It concerned two carpenters, Harry Dickens (Jack Astin) and Arch Fenster (Marty Ingels), who were not only workmates but each other's best friend. Fenster was a girl-grabbing, gravel-voiced playboy while Dickens was rather more conservative. They could agree on absolutely everything except how to solve a problem. Arch was a bachelor but Harry was married to Kate (Emmaline Henry). The regular workmates at the wood-working shop were Mel Warshaw (Dave Ketchum), Bannister (Frank DeVol) and Mulligan (Henry Beckman). The 32 episodes involved much slapstick.

I'M KEN, HE'S BILL
BBC RADIO. First broadcast: 29 March 1972

Peter Cleall was Ken, Derek Seaton was Bill: a couple of unlikely young lads who were always broke and never could afford to treat the girls in their lives (Suzanne Kerchiss and Clare Sutcliffe). The other regular cast member was Patricia Hayes who played Mrs Platt. There was a different guest in each of the six editions.

Writers: Richard Matthews and John Davis. Producer: Edward Taylor.

IN FOR A PENNY
LWT. First broadcast: 7 July 1972

Bob Todd starred as Dan, the attendant of the Town Hall's Victorian lavatories. His overseer was Councillor Mr Bundy (Ivor Salter) who also ran a travel agency. Know-all Dan had all the answers to the problems of local government and was not backward in sharing his opinions. A regular visitor to Dan's domain was the Sergeant (Jack Woolgar), who was ever ready to trade philosophies. The lavatory cleaner was Ali (Kevork Malikyan). Six programmes were written by John Hawkesworth and John Whitney.

Producer: Mark Stuart.

IN LOVING MEMORY
YTV. First broadcast: 21 May 1979

Writer Dick Sharples and producer Ronnie Baxter originally made a one-off pilot of this show for Thames which was seen on 15 November 1969. Almost ten years later, they revived the format for this long-running series for Yorkshire Television. Set in 1929 in the Northern town of Oldshaw, a father and daughter, Jermiah Unsworth and Ivy (Edward Chapman and Marjorie Rhodes in the pilot), ran an undertaking business. When the series proper began, Jeremiah (Freddie Jones) died in the first episode and so Ivy (Thora Hird) took over the business with her gormless nephew Billy (Christopher Beeny). Over six series there were 36 episodes concluding on 27 March 1986. Billy lived with Ivy until he eventually married and even then, she accompanied him on honeymoon. Other characters who played leading roles for a substantial number of shows were gravedigger Tom Wrigley (Paul Luty), Miss Amy Jenkinson (Avis Bunnage), confirmed bachelor Ernie Hadfield (Colin Farrell) and Mary Braithwaite (Sherrie Hewson).
Music: Alan Parker.

IN SICKNESS AND IN HEALTH
BBC. First broadcast: 1 September 1985

Because of the great impact which Alf Garnett had in TILL DEATH US DO PART in the 1960s, it is all too easy to forget that writer Johnny Speight and actor Warren Mitchell extended the character as an OAP through 46 further brushings and bruisings with the Welfare State over seven years to 3 April 1992. The new series found Alf and wife Else (Dandy Nichols) living in a council maisonette close by his beloved West Ham football ground. Else was confined to a wheelchair which Alf pushed with graceless discontent as would be expected. Daughter Rita (Una Stubbs), unhappy in her marriage, made several appearances and Alf's drinking partner was Arthur (Arthur English). The second series (1986) began with Alf returning from Else's funeral. Thereafter he was looked after by Mrs Hollingbery (Carmel McSharry) and over the seasons they became engaged, the attraction to Alf being her cooking and her pension. Alas, she was to stand him up at the altar but they continued to be engaged and even visited her rich brother in Australia together. A regular character was Fred Johnson

(Ken Campbell) and in the final series Alf had a new boozing chum, Michael (James Ellis).
Producers: Roger Race, Richard Boden.

THE INCREDIBLE ADVENTURES OF PROFESSOR BRANESTAWM
THAMES. First broadcast: 10 July 1969

This children's series of eight programmes was adapted by Trevor Preston from the 1933 book by Norman Hunter. Jack Woolgar starred as the zany, mad inventor Prof Branestawm whose every endeavour went hopelessly wrong. He was absent-minded to boot, and could rarely find any of his five pairs of spectacles. He was aided and abetted by his close friend Colonel Dedshott (Paul Whitsun-Jones) and by his indomitable housekeeper Mrs Flitterswoop (Freda Dowie).
Director: Voytek. Producer: Pamela Lonsdale.

THE INCREDIBLE MR TANNER
THAMES.

See KINDLY LEAVE THE KERB

INSIDE GEORGE WEBLEY
YTV. First broadcast: 24 September 1968

Creators Keith Waterhouse and Willis Hall cast Roy Kinnear in the title role as a compulsive worrier – and when he worried, he made sure everyone else worried. If he swallowed a prune stone he expected certain death, or if he went away he had to return to check he had switched off the gas. Patsy Rowlands played his wife Rosemary, whose principal interests were eating and sleeping. The show returned for a second season in February 1970.
Producers included Bill Hitchcock, David Mallet and John Duncan.

INSIDE OUT
BBC. First broadcast: 12 February 1985

The six 50-minute episodes of this comedy drama were written by Simon Moore. Carla Yates (Lou Wakefield) and Polish prostitute Beverly Grabowski (Gwyneth Strong) had been cell-mates in prison. On release they formed the Excell Agency to help ex-cons find legitimate employment. Along

the zany way of the stories, Carla developed a meaningful relationship with probation officer Max Stratton-Jones (Michael Thomas), although she had a husband Lloyd Yates (Philip Sayer).
Theme music: Phil Collins. Directors: Tony Smith, Pedr James. Producer: Sally Head.

IRISH HALF HOUR
BBC RADIO. First broadcast: 22 November 1941

This series was originally created for Irish men and women serving in the wartime armed forces. The programme began with an all music edition headed by Count John McCormack on 15th November 1941. The following week was the comedy edition which is significant within these pages for it was on that show that Dublin comedian Jimmy O'Dea (pronounced O'Dee) first broadcast his characterisation of Mrs Mulligan, the Pride of the Coombe. Biddy Mulligan was to prove one of the most durable of radio creations, rarely off the air from then until 21st December 1948. O'Dea's long-time stage partner Harry O'Donovan wrote the scripts and played many of the smaller parts. Mrs Mulligan came from Ballygoback-wards and had a husband, Mick or Mickser as he was known, played by Joe Linnane. Other Mulligans, though not permanently featured, included Nora and Bridgit (both Maye Tipple), Sheila (Yolande Mageean) and Maureen (Maureen Potter). Events usually took place in either the Mulligan kitchen or in the pub and Biddy was fond of a tipple in either. The shows changed title over the seasons from *Monday At Mulligans* to *Over To Mulligans*, *At The Mulligan Inn* and *The Mulligan Menage* but the basic situation and character stayed the same.
Producers: Eric Fawcett, Pat Hillyard, Francis Worsley, James Mageean, Tom Ronald.

IT AIN'T HALF HOT MUM
BBC. First broadcast: 3 January 1974

Jimmy Perry and David Croft created this series about a Second World War Royal Artillery concert party based in India. In fact, the jungle sequences were shot in Norfolk and the desert sequences in Sussex. There were 56 episodes, the last transmitted on 3 September 1981. It fell to Sergeant-Major Williams (Windsor Davies) to try and train the rag-bag performers in simple exercises like the ancient ceremony of lowering the Union Jack or basic drill. Those

sweating in his wake included pint-sized Gunner 'Lofty' Sugden (Don Estelle) and Bombardier Beaumont (Melvyn Hayes), who 'dragged-up' as Gloria, an archetypal Hollywood film star, for the concerts. Michael Bates blacked-up to portray the character Rangi Ram, while the whole platoon came under the command of Colonel Reynolds (Donald Hewlett) and his second-in-command Captain Ashwood (Michael Knowles). In the early seasons, George Layton also starred as Bombadier Solomons.
Directors: John Kilby, Phil Bishop, Bob Spiers. Producer: David Croft.

IT STICKS OUT HALF A MILE
BBC RADIO. First broadcast: 13 November 1983

Three characters created by Jimmy Perry and David Croft for DAD'S ARMY were brought together for this series of six programmes written by Harold Snoad and Michael Knowles. The setting was Frambourne-on-Sea, three years after the end of the war, where Arthur Wilson (John Le Mesurier) had been made manager of Swallow's Bank. Frank Pike (Ian Lavender) had moved there with him but their peacetime was shattered when Bert Hodges (Bill Pertwee) turned up in the town with a business proposition to renovate the crumbling pier. A new character in their lives was Miss Perkins, played by Vivienne Martin.
Producer: Martin Fisher.

IT TAKES A WORRIED MAN
THAMES. First broadcast: 27 October 1981

The first six programmes were transmitted by ITV before the second run of six switched to Channel 4, beginning 16 October 1983. Peter Tilbury both wrote the series and starred as Philip Roath, a 35-year-old insurance salesman struggling to cope with a broken marriage and a job which he did not like. He moved from crisis to crisis as his confidence, both at work and with the opposite sex, waned. He paid numerous visits to his analyst (Nicholas Le Prevost), who failed to boost him to any worthwhile degree. His former wife was Ellen (Gaye Brown), his boss was Napley (Andrew Tourell), one of his colleagues was known simply as 'Old Man' (Christopher Benjamin), and the girls in his life were Ruth (Diana Payan) and Liz (Sue Holderness).
Producers: Douglas Argent, Anthony Parker.

IT'S A CRIME
BBC RADIO. First broadcast: 7 April 1958

Eddie Maguire wrote these 12 comedy thrillers which starred Brian Reece as British Intelligence agent Tony Meadows. With a carefree and resourceful spirit he journeyed far afield to track down his quarries, and in the first episode he was in Tangiers where he met and married Angela (Denise Bryer), who, thereafter, went everywhere with him. His fellow agent was Webster (Humphrey Morton) and they were responsible to Colonel Craig (Gordon Davies).
Producer: Vernon Harris.

IT'S A DEAL
BBC RADIO. First broadcast: 9 March 1961

Ronald Chesney and Ronald Wolfe created and wrote this situation as a starring vehicle for Sid James. He played Sid, a property developer who never managed to pull off a deal. His assistant was Pricey, played by Dennis Price. Pricey had been educated at public school and tried to turn a blind eye to the chicanery employed by Sid. Through Price, Sid acquired a secretary, Susan Corkindale (June Whitfield), who was born of gentry. The general manager of the office was Benson (Wallas Eaton), and the office boy Steve was played by Robin Ray. Thirteen weekly episodes were heard.
Producer: Tom Ronald.

IT'S A FAIR COP
BBC RADIO. First broadcast: 22 May 1961

This pairing of Eric Sykes and Hattie Jacques was written by John Junkin and Terry Nation. Eric was a new recruit to the Police Force and reported for duty to Blossom Hill police station, presided over by Sergeant Deryck Guyler. The happy and sympathetic home life required of a police officer was provided by Eric's sister, played by Hattie Jacques. Leonard Williams was the Superintendent at Blossom Hill where in Cell 1 there lived in comfort a more or less permanent prisoner, complete with armchair and television, in the form of Dick Emery. There were eight episodes ending 10 July.
Producer: Herbert Smith.

IT'S A GREAT LIFE
BBC RADIO. First broadcast: 23 June 1948

Bonar Colleano starred as himself in the role of a small-part actor under contract to Deadwood Film Studios. Each time it looked as though he might land a substantial role he lost out to a big star, which provided the excuse for a guest each week. The supporting players to Colleano included Benny Lee, Miriam Karlin, Joe Linnane, Paul Carpenter and Deryck Guyler. A first series of 14 was followed by a second run of 13 from 29 May 1950.
Writers: Sid Colin, George Wadmore. Producers: George Inns, Charles Chilton.

IT'S A LIVING
A-R. First broadcast: 11 October 1962

In this four-part series, created and written by Fred Robinson, Jimmy Jewel and Ben Warriss were partners in a general store. Ben and his wife Bertha (Fanny Carby) lived on the premises with their daughter Betty (Adrienne Poster, then 13 years old and who later changed her name to Posta). Jimmy was the lodger. Ben was eternally exasperated by Jimmy's stupidity (an extension of their variety act). One of Jimmy's principal failings was his gullibility. He was forever buying stock, usually in bulk, that the shop did not require and could not possibly sell. His main supplier of surplus rubbish was Foxy Flint (Lance Percival).
Producer: Peter Croft.

IT'S AWFULLY BAD FOR YOUR EYES, DARLING
BBC. First broadcast: 18 November 1971

Jilly Cooper and Christopher Bond wrote this five-part series about four upmarket girls who shared a squalid flat and each other's smalls in London SW3. Clothes were strewn all over the place and a week's supply of coffee cups gathered dust in the bedroom. The girls were Gillian Page-Wood (Jane Carr), known as Pudding; Virginia Watter (Jennifer Croxton), Clover Mason (Elizabeth Knight) and Samantha Ryder-Ross (Joanna Lumley). While they shared material things in the flat, the same generous spirit did not extend when it came to stealing boyfriends.
Producer: Leon Thau.

IT'S GARRY SHANDLING'S SHOW
USA PRESENTED BY BBC.
First broadcast (UK): 5 July 1987

The American comedian starred as himself as he moved into a new neighbourhood, leaving a trail of failed love-affairs behind him. He enjoyed basket-ball but his main obsession was his own hair, which he meticulously looked after. His best friend was Pete Schumaker (Michael Tucci) and other regular characters included Nancy (Molly Cheek) and the other Schumaker kids, Jackie and Grant (Bernadette Birkett and Scott Nemes). Much use was made of Garry's 'flashback machine'. Twenty episodes were screened.

Writers: Alan Zweibel, Jeff Franklin. Director: Alan Rafkin.

IT'S YOUR MOVE

NBC (AMERICA) PRESENTED BY BBC.
First broadcast (UK): 17 February 1986

Matthew Burton (Jason Bateman) was a fast-talking teenager who fancied himself as a bit of a con-artist. His main preoccupation was to destroy the relationship between his mother Eileen (Caren Kaye) and the impoverished writer Norman Lamb (David Garrison) who lived across the hallway. Matt's best pal was Eli (Adam Sadowsky), who fancied Matt's sister Julie (Tricia Cast). Unfortunately for Eli, Julie considered him to be the lowest form of life. Twenty-two editions were shown.

Creators: Ron Leavitt and Michael G Moye. Producers: Katherine Green and Fred Fox Jr for Embassy.

THE JACK BENNY SHOW

NBC (AMERICA) PRESENTED BY BBC RADIO AND
TELEVISION.
First broadcast (UK): 11 December 1942

Jack Benny was one of the first comedians to realise the potential of situation comedy. Most vaudevillians hitherto simply told gags on the radio and adapted their stage acts only slightly. For THE JACK BENNY SHOW, the listener was asked to believe that the broadcast was a rehearsal for a radio show held informally in the Benny home. As the characterisation developed and the familiarity of the audience grew, from 1934 for 20 years Sunday night at 7pm became a date kept by many millions of Americans.

The Benny character was that of a vain man, worried about his balding head and his age – he remained 39 years old throughout his career! The lasting memory, however, is of Jack the Miser, the cheapskate driving a wheezing, coughing and spluttering ancient Maxwell car. The wheezes, coughs and splutters were supplied by the voice of Mel Blanc. He furthered the image by failing to pay the members of the cast a living wage and hoarding his money in the sub-basement of the house, guarded by an Arctic polar bear named Clarence. Clarence's growl was again the voice of Mel Blanc. One day a gas inspector went down to the vault to read the meter. He was never heard from again.

Benny's humour involved much self-ridicule. He always came unstuck, in spite of his air of self-confidence. Benny realised there were more laughs to be had if his stooges got the better of him, thus flying against convention. His pretensions to being a virtuoso of the violin were mercilessly slapped down as was his larger-than-life ego. He was the master of timing. No performer knew better the value of a pause. He could extract side-aching laughter from silence. For example, when approached by a robber who demanded: "Your money or your life", Benny did not answer. After an eternity of frustration for the robber he once more snapped: "Quit stalling. I said your money or your life." Benny finally responded: "I'm thinking it over."

He was supported by characterisations equally as well-rounded as his own. His wife Mary invented Mary Livingstone from Plainfield, New Jersey, Jack's fictional secretary and girlfriend. She deflated his boasting with her wise-cracks and would embarrass him by reading aloud a letter from her mother who hated him. In real life Mary had been born Sadie Marks but she ultimately changed her name legally to Mary Livingstone. Rochester, portrayed by black actor Eddie Anderson, began on the 1934 series as an occasional Pullman porter but proved so popular that he was made the Benny family butler. Rochester had a fondness for gin, nightlife and women. Anderson became the highest-paid black performer of his time in America. He appeared on more radio and TV shows with Jack than did any other actor.

The role of radio announcer was taken by former football star Don Wilson. He was the butt of many gags about his expanding girth. Playing the dumb young kid who exasperated Benny was tenor singer Dennis Day. Bandleader Phil Harris appeared as a heavy-drinking, wild and brassy illiterate who addressed Benny as 'Jackson'. He was completely immoral and preened himself on his witty ripostes. Other members of the radio family were the voices of a team of versatile actors led by Blanc and including Sheldon Leonard (later to become the television producer of I Spy in the 1960s), Frank Nelson and Artie Auerbach, who provided a succession of Jewish prototypes including Mr Kitzel, a frankfurter seller with the cry: "Get your hot dogs vit de peeckle in de meedle an' de moostard on top – just de vay you like 'em an' dey're all red hot." From 1945, although not on every show, film star Ronald Colman and his English wife Benita appeared as Benny's next-door neighbours. In all, the Colmans were featured on more than fifty shows.

On radio THE JACK BENNY SHOW was initially sponsored by Jell-O and later, in the 1940s, by Lucky Strike cigarettes. Numerous writers were employed, significant among them Sam Perrin, George Balzer, Ed Beloin, Neil Morrow and John Tackaberry. In November 1948 Jack Benny's company was acquired by CBS for a substantial fee. On 28 October 1950 he made his TV debut for the network with the same characters who were still running weekly on the radio, including an authentic Maxwell car. On television much use was made of Hollywood star guests and the shows ran until 1963. They were produced by Fred De Cordova. In 1964 he returned to NBC for one final season but poor ratings spelt the end of the show. He died in December 1974.

He was first heard on BBC radio on 15 May 1941 under the title *The Jack Benny Half Hour*. The first broadcast of THE JACK BENNY SHOW on BBC television was on 27 July 1956.

JACK OF DIAMONDS
BBC. First broadcast: 13 January 1983

Dick Emery starred in this comedy thriller in six parts by John and Steven Singer. Bernie Weinstock (Emery) was called in to trace the whereabouts of a substantial quantity of diamonds which a British soldier was believed to have hidden in Holland during World War II. He was assisted by Norman Lugg (Tony Selby). Dick Emery also cropped up in a succession of minor character roles, both male and female.
Producer: Stuart Allen.

JACK'S DIVE
BBC RADIO. First broadcast: 12 August 1943

Jack's Dive was a roadhouse owned by Jack Warner and established by money borrowed from his Auntie Sybil. Jack was also the waiter. He appointed as manager a retired army officer, Claud (Claud Allister), to whom Jack had once acted as batman. Claud was to bring a certain polish to the dive. Warner also played the French chef who was assisted by two kitchen maids (Doris Nichols and Vivienne Chatterton). Although the roadhouse was hardly five-star, it did manage to stage first-class cabaret each week! There were eight editions.
Writers: Jack Warner and Rex Diamond. Producer: Leslie Bridgmont.

JACKSON PACE: THE GREAT YEARS
GRANADA. First broadcast: 11 October 1990

This six-part children's series was written by Daniel Peacock and told the story of tousle-haired explorer Jackson Pace (Keith Allen) and his quest to beat the evil Daken (Nic D'Avirro) in the search for the treasure of Kinard. Other principal characters involved in the ultimate destiny of the treasure included Ryveeta Tusk (Josie Lawrence), Roger Whibley (Daniel Peacock), Lord Taggon (Hugh Paddick), Princess Layme (Cory Pullman), Prince Filo (Gian Sammarco) and Lord Layta (Paul B Davies).
Director: Alistair Clark. Producer: Mark Robson.

JEEVES AND WOOSTER
GRANADA. First broadcast: 22 April 1990

PG Wodehouse's celebrated characters, the bumbling Bertie Wooster (Hugh Laurie) and his gentleman's gentleman Jeeves (Stephen Fry), were dramatised by Clive Exton into four series, each of six programmes and coming to a close on 20 June 1993. Trouble for Wooster, certainly in London, came from his Aunts Agatha (Mary Wimbush, later Elizabeth Spriggs) and Dahlia (Brenda Bruce). Set in the 1930s, several of the episodes were filmed in New York where Bertie liked to escape from imbroglios at home.
Directors: Robert Young, Simon Langton, Ferdinand Fairfax. Producer: Brian Eastman for Picture Partnership Productions.

JENNINGS
BBC RADIO AND TELEVISION.
First broadcast: 16 October 1948

Schoolmaster Anthony Buckeridge created 12-year-old schoolboy Jennings, first in books and then for the wireless. He wrote more than 75 episodes, the last of which was heard on 26 September 1975. The setting was Linbury Court School where Jennings usually reduced the smooth running of the educational establishment to chaos and confusion. He was portrayed by a succession of young actors including David Page, Glyn Dearman, Hugh Janes and Glenn Campbell. His best pal Darbishire was portrayed by Louis Somerville, Henry Searle, Adrian Walker and Timothy Bleecker among others. The adult actors re-mained the same for most of the years with Geoffrey Wincott as Mr Carter (John Dadlish in the final series) and Wilfred Babbage as form-master Mr Wilkins (Anthony Buckeridge himself in the final series).
Producers included David Davis and Graham Gauld.

On 5 September 1966 a series of six began on BBC television. The cast changed completely with new actors for Jennings (David Schulten), Darbishire (Robert Bartlett), Mr Carter (Ian Gardiner) and Mr Wilkins (John Moore).
Producer: Johnny Downes.

JIM THE GREAT

BBC RADIO. First broadcast: 26 March 1977

Jimmy Edwards in the title role romped through two series, bestowing his greatness whether as a patron of the arts or wherever else he felt he was needed. Helping him on his regal way were Julian Orchard, Joan Sanderson and John Baddeley. The 12th and final programme was broadcast on 14 October 1979.

Writer: Andrew Palmer. Producer: Edward Taylor.

THE JIMMY STEWART SHOW

NBC (AMERICA) PRESENTED BY ITV.
First broadcast (UK): 15 October 1971

Film star James Stewart starred as James K Howard, professor of anthropology, married to Martha (Julie Adams). They lived in a small town with their eight-year-old son Teddy (Dennis Larson). However, James also had a 29-year-old son, PJ Howard (Jonathan Daly), married to Wendy (Ellen Geer).

When their house burned down, PJ and Ellen moved in with James and Martha, bringing with them their own eight-year-old son, Jake (Kirby Furlong). There were 24 episodes in total.

Producer: Hal Kanter.

JOAN AND LESLIE

ATV. First broadcast: 17 September 1956

One of ITV's earliest shows, this began in 1955 as a 15-minute slot under the title *Leslie Randall Entertains*. He established a regular sketch with his real wife, Joan Reynolds, which grew into the half-hour sitcom. Leslie was a freelance writer who wrote an agony column under the pen name of Dorothy Goodheart. Joan played his wife. Leslie's pal and neighbour, Mike Kelly, was played by Harry Towb and Noël Dyson portrayed the charlady, Mrs

Stephen Fry (right) and Hugh Laurie as JEEVES AND WOOSTER (Photo: Granada TV)

Henshawe. By 1958 Leslie had abandoned the Dorothy Goodheart column and he and Joan were often seen out of the domestic situation as they travelled around. The title again changed to *The Randall Touch* and Towb and Dyson made only occasional appearances. It did not survive beyond 1958.

Writers included Bill Craig, John Law, Gerald Kelsey and Dick Sharples. Producers: Hugh Rennie and Alan Tarrant.

JOANIE LOVES CHACHI
ABC (AMERICA) PRESENTED BY ITV.
First broadcast (UK): 7 January 1983

Producer Garry Marshall spun this series off his earlier smash-hit HAPPY DAYS. The Delvecchio family, Alfred (Al Molinaro), Louisa (Ellen Travolta) and their son Chachi (Scott Baio), moved from Milwaukee to Chicago where they ran an Italian restaurant. With them went Joanie Cunningham (Erin Moran) and the two teenage sweethearts formed a band and sang duets in the restaurant. They were helped in the day-to-day running of the place by Uncle Rico (Art Metrano). Varying numbers of episodes were seen around the ITV regions.

JOEY
BBC RADIO. First broadcast: 4 March 1966

A single play by Terence Dicks, 'The Lonely Hearts', was broadcast in 1965 and turned by its author into this six-part series. Joey Green (Harry Fowler) was an East End wide-boy who lived more by his wits than work. Much of the action took place in a café presided over by kindly, philosophical Jewish proprietor Hymie Rosen (Alfie Bass). Joey had a girlfriend Mary (Valerie Kirkbright) who laboured in vain to pin him down to a wedding date.
Producer: John Bridges.

JOHN BROWNE'S BODY
ATV. First broadcast: 3 April 1969

This comedy thriller series of seven programmes by René Basilico starred Peggy Mount as Virginia Browne, a bungling sleuth, with Naunton Wayne as Fitzroy. The body of John Browne rolled out of a vehicle into the gutter, right beside a troupe of buskers. The resultant problems involved the widow Browne in matters foreign to her, like probate, PAYE and insurances. She was reluctantly forced

to become a business executive. Other regular characters were Kiki (Trisha Mortimer), French (Philip Stone), Spiro (Eric Kent), Gilberts (Kevin Stoney), Skeets (Harold Lang) and Felicity Cordon (Zulema Dene).
Producer: Shaun O'Riordan.

JOINT ACCOUNT
BBC. First broadcast: 26 January 1989

Don Webb wrote this series which began with a six-week run and returned for ten further editions on 19 March 1990. In a story of role reversal, Hannah Gordon and Peter Egan starred as Belinda and David Braithwaite. While she was a high-flying bank manager, he stayed home as the house-husband and did a little charity work. The other regular characters were Ned Race (John Bird), Jessica (Ruth Mitchell) and Louise (Lill Roughley).
Producer: Mike Stephens.

JOKING APART
BBC. First broadcast: 14 January 1993

Steven Moffat's bitter comedy about divorce began life as a one-off play in a strand of *Comic Asides* on 12th July 1991. That was repeated on 7th January 1993 with a six part series starting the following week. Mark Taylor (Robert Bathurst) was a scriptwriter who found his life being overtaken by his work. In a whirlwind romance he met and married Becky Johnson (Fiona Gillies) but she left him just as quickly accusing him of paying her too little attention. Mark's friends Robert and Tracy (Paul Raffield and Tracie Bennett) offered him shelter and comfort and through misunderstandings, Mark and Tracy ended up in bed together. Becky found a new man, Mark found a new woman and Tracy left Robert and much carnal swapping resulted in complications for all.
Directors: John Kirby, Bob Spiers. Producer: André Ptaszynski for Pola Jones productions.

JOLLYOLIDAY
BBC RADIO. First broadcast: 1 July 1942

The idea of this series of eight shows was to support the government directive to families to spend their annual holiday at home rather than go to the seaside. The stories centred on Mr and Mrs Twistle (Bill Stephens and Marion Dawson) and starred Albert Modley as their young son Oswald. Yorkshire comedian Modley specialised in playing small-boy parts and this was his first radio series. Other regular players were Percy Garside and Charles Penrose.

Writers: Arthur Mertz and Russell Medcraft. Producer: Ernest Longstaffe.

JOSSY'S GIANTS
BBC. First broadcast: 23 April 1986

Better known as the Geordie darts commentator who can mathematically calculate quicker than the average viewer, Sid Waddell turned his hand to writing for this programme which ran for two five-episode series ending on 8 April 1987. Though they were intended and slotted for children's viewing, many dads lived their schooldays vicariously as school coach Jossy Blair (Jim Barclay), so badly injured in his first game as a professional footballer that he could never play in the top rank again, took over the gang of 13-year-olds known as the Clipton Grasshoppers.

Director: Edward Pugh. Producer: Paul Stone.

JULIA
NBC (AMERICA) PRESENTED BY ITV.
First broadcast (UK): 3 July 1970

In the USA this series was highly controversial when it arrived in 1968, but it hardly raised an eyebrow when first shown in Britain. Its theme was racial integration. Diahann Carroll starred as Julia Baker, a widowed nurse living in comfortable middle-class suburbia and raising her small son from a mixed marriage, Corey (Marc Copage). Corey endeavoured to matchmake for his mother. The multiracial characters included Earl J Waggedorn and his wife Marie (Michael Link and Betty Beaird), Dr Morton Chegley (Lloyd Nolan), Hannah Yarby (Lurene Tuttle), Eddie Edson (Eddie Quillan) and Carol Deering (Alison Mills). Black America criticised the show heavily because Julia's problems and lifestyle were not those relevant to most of the black community.

Producer: Hal Kanter.

JULIE
USA PRESENTED BY CHANNEL 4.
First broadcast: 21 December 1993

British-born Julie Andrews starred in six editions as big-time singer Julie Carlyle, who found her celebrity status less than fulfilling and quit the bright lights of Broadway when she married a vet, Sam

McGuire (James Farentino). She moved to Iowa to live with him and his two children, Alice (Haley Tyrite) and Adam (Rider Strong).

Producer: Blake Edwards.

JUST A GIGOLO
CENTRAL. First broadcast: 8 April 1993

Tony Slattery starred as Nick Brim, a schoolteacher in the depths of depression having lost his job and for whom life took on new meaning and a whole new career opened up when a woman mistakenly believed he was her paid escort that she had booked through an agency. Nick had a problem in that he was deeply in love with Natalie (Rowena King) but his own impecunious brother Simon (Paul Bigley) encouraged him to exploit his attractions through the escort needs of lonely ladies. Seven editions were screened.

Writers: Carl Gorham, Michael Hatt and Amanda Swift. Director: Martin Dennis. Producer: Paul Spencer.

JUST DENNIS
CBS (AMERICA) PRESENTED BY ITV.
First broadcast (UK): 15 April 1960

One hundred and forty-six episodes of this series were made between 1959 and 1963. The characters were based on those created by Hank Ketcham in his cartoon comic-strip 'Dennis the Menace'. Jay North starred as Dennis and dressed exactly like the small boy in the cartoon in horizontally striped tee-shirt and a pair of oversized overalls. His parents, Henry and Alice Mitchell, were portrayed by Herbert Anderson and Gloria Henry. However, it was the Mitchell's next-door neighbours, the Wilsons, who bore the brunt of Dennis's menace. Joseph Kearns portrayed the long-suffering, bumbling, short-sighted Mr George Wilson, and Sylvia Field was Mrs Wilson. In later episodes George Wilson was replaced by John Wilson, played by Gale Gordon. When the series began, Dennis's best pal was Joey (Gil Smith) but he was swiftly replaced by Tommy (Billy Booth). Although in Britain ITV screened the series as JUST DENNIS, it was always known in the USA as *Dennis The Menace*.

Writers included William Cowley and Peggy Chantler. Directors included William D Russell. Producer: Jim Fonda.

Vince and Penny (Paul Nicholas and Jan Francis) drink to a rare moment of romantic harmony in JUST GOOD FRIENDS (Photo: Copyright © BBC)

JUST FANCY

BBC RADIO. First broadcast: 11 January 1951

Master of radio comedy Eric Barker created, wrote and starred in these shows which notched up a 100th edition on 15 December 1961 during the ninth and final series. Barker set the situations in the mythical resort of Westbourne-on-Sea and in particular, prior to its being closed down, in the Cranbourne Towers Hotel. There Barker and Deryck Guyler lived out the endearing reminiscences and contemporary observations of two old men who never had names but who were permanent residents, garrulous and spiced with enough incident to flavour the springtime of their senility. Stories were also woven around the romances and intrigues of the Lillian Forsdyke trio who played at the local tea rooms until their services were no longer required. Barker charted the decline of the resort as so many real resorts were sliding down the

same slippery slope. His wife Pearl Hackney appeared with him, and those involved over the seasons included Desmond Walter-Ellis, Patricia Gilbert, John Warrington, John Stevens, Freda Bamford, Ruth Porcher, Kenneth Connor, Charlotte Mitchell and Denise Bryer.
Producer: Charles Maxwell.

JUST GOOD FRIENDS

BBC. First broadcast: 22 September 1983

John Sullivan created and wrote this series which starred Paul Nicholas as Vince Pinner and Jan Francis as Penny Warrender. Their romance took a rocky road, mainly because Vince had an overwhelming desire to steer clear of marriage. He once left Penny standing at the altar, but still, albeit some time later, she took him back into her life and her bed. There was a class difference between them which made for a good deal of turbulence in their relationship. Vince was a bookie and totally irresponsible in his personal life. His was a working-class background which contrasted with the middle-class prissiness of Penny. There were elements of tragedy within the comedy framework of the love story, which writer John Sullivan developed from a letter which he read in an agony column from a jilted woman who once more had come face to face with the culprit. Penny's parents were Daphne (Sylvia Kay) and Norman (John Ringham) and Vince's parents were Rita (Ann Lynn) and Les (Shaun Curry). There were 22 editions over three seasons.
Producer: Ray Butt.

JUST JIMMY

ABC. First broadcast: 29 November 1964

Diminutive comedian Jimmy Clitheroe had long been established as a radio star in THE CLITHEROE KID when ABC transferred a similar format to television. Jimmy was the perennial naughty Lancashire schoolboy who was the exasperation of his mother (Mollie Sugden). Jimmy had an unseen pal who was the subject of much of his conversation, named Billy Jackson. Living with the Clitheroes was Jimmy's cousin, the gormless Danny (Danny Ross) who had a motorbike and thoughts for nothing but dancing and girls. Most of the shows were written by Ronnie Taylor although there were contributions from Fred Robinson, Frank Roscoe and Alick Hayes. The last of more than 90 editions was transmitted on 20 September 1966.
Producer: Ronnie Baxter.

JUST KIDD-ING

BBC RADIO. First broadcast: 23 September 1941

The setting for these nine broadcasts was the Goode Shippe Catastrophy where the pirates were led by the Chief cut-throat (Bobbie Comber), with the cook (Joan Young), the bottle-washers (Bennett and Williams), the joiner (Trefor Jones) and the halyard girl (Helen Hill).
Writer: Loftus Wigram. Producer: Tom Ronald.

JUST LIZ

THAMES. First broadcast: 1 September 1980

In this six-week series by John Esmonde and Bob Larbey, Liz Parker (Sandra Payne) was left behind when her fiancé Nigel went to Bahrain to earn sufficient money for them to get married. While Nigel was away, her colleague at work Reg Last (Rodney Bewes) took it upon himself to protect her but his over-zealous efforts gave people the wrong idea, especially Liz's neighbour Mr Chatto (Gorden Kaye) and other friends, Jessie Worth (Avril Angers) and Mr Dalyell (Terence Alexander).
Producer: Robert Reed.

JUST OUR LUCK

ABC (AMERICA) PRESENTED BY ITV.
First broadcast (UK): 10 January 1985

A television meteorologist, Keith Burrows (Richard Gilliand), found he had acquired and was able to command a mischievous black genie, Shabu (TK Carter). Ellen Maxted also starred as Meagan. ITV screened five episodes.
Producers: Lawrence Jordan and Ronald Frazier.

JUST PERFICK

BBC RADIO. First broadcast: 4 November 1969

John Esmonde and Bob Larbey adapted HE Bates' saga of the Larkin family for an initial 12 radio half-hours, with 13 further episodes starting on 14 April 1971. Larbey would return to the same subject 20 years later to write THE DARLING BUDS OF MAY for Yorkshire Television. Bernard Miles starred as Pop Larkin and Betty Marsden as Ma as they established their Utopia in the heart of the Kentish countryside. Their eldest daughter Mariette (Alexa Romanes) became engaged to be married to Charley Charlton (Michael Harbour).
Producer: Alastair Scott Johnston.

JUST THE JOB

BBC RADIO. First broadcast: 3 October 1971

Bernard Cribbins and Donald Sinden starred as two odd-job men who tackled a different challenge in each of the eight episodes.
Writers: Colin Marks, Lawrie Wyman and George Evans. Producer: Edward Taylor.

JUST WILLIAM

BBC RADIO. First broadcast: 30 October 1945

Richmal Crompton adapted her own stories for broadcasting in association with Rex Diamond and Alick Hayes. The programme ran over several series until the end of 1952. (For characterisations, see LWT below.) The role of William was originated by John Clark and subsequently played by Julian Denham, David Spenser and Andrew Ray. Father and mother were originally portrayed by Gordon McLeod and Betty Bowden, then by Bruce Belfrage and Enid Trevor, with Ruth Dunning taking over as Mrs Brown in 1952. William's best pal Ginger was originated by Billy Nicholls, then played by Tony Stockman followed by Maxwell Longmuir, Derek Rock and finally (I kid you not) Patricia Hayes. Violet Elizabeth Bott was first played by Olive Kirby, then by Jacqueline Boyer, Valerie Jene, Anthea Askey and Patricia Fryer. Charles Hawtrey featured in the early episodes as errand-boy Hubert Lane.
Music: Leighton Lucas. Producers: Alick Hayes, Audrey Cameron.

LWT. First broadcast: 6 February 1977

Author Richmal Crompton created her awful schoolboy with a vivid imagination, William Brown, in 1917. Keith Dewhurst adapted the stories into two 13-part series, the second of which began on 23 October of the same year. Adrian Dannatt played the part of William, and his gang – the 'outlaws' – were Douglas (Tim Rose), Ginger (Michael McVey) and Henry (Craig McFarlane). William's parents were played by Hugh Cross and Diana Fairfax and he had a sister Ethel (Stacy Dorning) and a pompous, girl-chasing bore of a brother, Robert (Simon Chandler). In the opposite social corner to the Browns were the family Bott, who lived at the manor hall. Mr and Mrs Bott (John Stratton and Diana Dors) had a lisping daughter Violet Elizabeth (Bonnie Langford), who set her heart on marrying William.
Producers: John Davids and Stella Richman.

KYTV

BBC. First broadcast: 3 May 1990

The team who had enjoyed radio success with **RADIO ACTIVE** brought their anarchic talents to the screen to present a mock television company and its representative programming. Theirs was a satellite station with Anna Daptor (Helen Atkinson Wood), Martin Brown (Michael Fenton-Stevens), Mr Hartford (Philip Pope), Mike Flex (Geoffrey Perkins) and Mike Channel (Angus Deayton). There were two further series, again of six episodes each, beginning 17 March 1992 and 17 September 1993. *Writers: Angus Deayton and Geoffrey Perkins. Directors: John Kilby, John Stroud. Producer: Jamie Rix.*

KATE AND ALLIE

USA PRESENTED BY CHANNEL 4.
First broadcast (UK): 17 February 1986

Two divorced women, Kate McArdle (Susan Saint James) and Allie Lowell (Jane Curtin), shared a house in order to lighten their respective financial and emotional burdens. Kate had a daughter Emma (Ari Meyers), and Allie a son Chip (Frederick Koehler) and a daughter Jennie (Allison Smith). Although the kids were all around the same age they did not always hit it off. On the surface Kate and Allie had little in common. Kate was a liberal from the swinging sixties with a high energy-drive, while Allie was a much quieter traditionalist. However, together they made a formidable team. Their former husbands, Charles Lowell (Paul Hecht) and Max McArdle (Harley Venton), made occasional appearances. More than 100 editions of the show were made.

KEEP IT IN THE FAMILY

THAMES. First broadcast: 7 January 1980

This series, created by Johnnie Mortimer and Brian Cooke, ran to a total of 31 programmes over five series ending on 19 October 1983. The stories of the Rush family, cartoonist Dudley (Robert Gillespie), his wife Muriel (Pauline Yates) and their two teen-age daughters Susan (Stacy Dorning) and Jacqui (Jenny Quayle, later Sabina Franklyn), became an upstairs-downstairs of family life when the girls took over the ground-floor flat of their parents' home. The only other regular member of the cast was Glyn Houston who played Dudley's boss, Duncan Thomas. By the final series he, too, had moved in with the Rush family.
Writers included Mortimer and Cooke, Alex Shearer, Dave and Greg Freeman. Producers: Mark Stuart, Robert Reed.

KEEP IT IN THE FAMILY

YTV. First broadcast: 21 September 1971

James and Yvonne Bannister (Tim Barrett and Vivienne Martin) thought it would be a good idea to have her father, Des (Jack Haig), and his mother, Norah (Joyce Grant), come and live with them. After all, they reasoned, they could keep each other company. The idea did not work out so simply. The family problems were increased by the generation gap between the grandparents and the Bannisters' son, Val (Tony Maiden).
Writers: David Nobbs and Peter Vincent. Producer: Ian Davidson.

KEEPING UP APPEARANCES

BBC. First broadcast: 29 October 1990

This series by Roy Clarke was built around one central character, the social-climbing Hyacinth Bucket (pronounced Bouquet and played by Patricia Routledge), and her family. She was preoccupied to the point of obsession with her social standing and her ideas of etiquette. She went to absurd extremes to impress those whom she considered important in her neighbourhood, which was distinctly middle-class suburbia, though she would never admit it. She firmly believed that she was both famous and respected for her candlelight suppers and that her very presence at other people's events would raise both their profile and hers within the community. However, the truth was that neighbours like Elizabeth and Emmet (Josephine Tewson and David Griffin) and the vicar (Gerald Sim) would cower in horror in anticipation of her company. Emmet's great dread was that Hyacinth would sing at him.

Her mild little husband, Richard (Clive Swift), lived a life of resigned exasperation as Hyacinth's demands, plans and schemes for social aggrandisement increased in their outrageousness. She expressed devotion to her Daddy, although she could not possibly have him live with them, and to her son, Sheridan, who only ever telephoned when he needed money. Hyacinth had two sisters and a brother-in-law who shared a house on a council estate not far enough away to spare her the acute embarrassment of their appearance and behaviour. The elder of the sisters, Daisy (Judy Cornwell), was an unkempt slut who would lie in bed bemoaning the lack of sexual attention she received from her big, fat slob of a beer-guzzling husband, Onslow (Geoffrey Hughes), who was more interested in snooker. Onslow, rarely seen, to Hyacinth's great chagrin, in anything more than a vest, occasionally led Richard astray, getting him drunk and helping him vaguely remember the joy of having fun. The youngest of the three sisters was Rose (Shirley Stelfox in the first series, thereafter Mary Millar). She was man mad and dressed tartily in the shortest of skirts and vulgar outfits. Daddy (George Webb) also lived in their house, imagining he was still in the war. There was another, unseen sister, who lived in 'the big house on the hill'. The writing, as in other Roy Clarke creations, introduced many visual stunts to complement the dialogue. The 1993 Christmas special was the 31st edition. *Producer: Harold Snoad.*

THE KIDS FROM 47A
ATV. First broadcast: 23 January 1974

This children's series was written and created by John Kane. It concerned four orphans. The eldest, and as such responsible for the welfare of the others, was the disaster-prone but nonetheless sensible Jess (Christine McKenna). Her task was not made any easier by her brothers and sister. Most provocative among them was the rather villainous, telly-mad usurper of authority, George (Russell Lewis). His brother Willy (Nigel Greaves) was just a little less mischievous, while sister Binny (Gaynor Hodgson), initially a bit of a book-worm, gradually developed a heightened awareness of boys. While anchored in comedy, the shows also tackled some serious subjects in a realistic manner. *Director: Jonathan Wright Miller. Producer: Richard Bramall.*

Hyacinth (Patricia Routledge) ensures that her husband (Clive Swift) will be KEEPING UP APPEARANCES (Photo: Copyright © BBC)

A KIND OF LIVING

CENTRAL. First broadcast: 19 February 1988

Schoolteacher Trevor Beasley (Richard Griffiths) and his wife Carol (Frances de la Tour), with their cherubic new baby Og (Christopher Ravenscroft), left Bolton for London where Trevor had a new job and the family a new home. Behind them they left Trevor's dad (Robin Bailey) and friends Brian Thompson (Tim Healy) and Brian's sister Linda (Anita Carey). In the first series of six episodes, down-trodden Carol seemed to be weathering the matrimonial ride with chauvinistic Trevor and the christening of the baby passed off smoothly, even with the attendance of Carol's mother, Mrs Bennett (Elizabeth Spriggs). Trevor and his ideals were rooted firmly in the past and during a second run of seven starting 11 November 1988 the marriage began to disintegrate. In the end, Carol left Trevor in order to follow her own career motivations. A third series of 13 episodes got underway on 25 March 1990. Trevor, living alone, returned to Bolton to bury his father – and to bury the hatchet with Brian and Linda. Linda had a baby son, and love blossomed between her and Trevor and they finally decided to marry.
Music: Philip Bird. Writer: Paul Makin. Director: Paul Harrison. Producer: Glen Cardno.

KINDLY LEAVE THE KERB

LWT. First broadcast: 21 May 1971

Writers Johnnie Mortimer and Brian Cooke created this series of six. Peter Butterworth as Ernest Tanner and Peter Jones as Sidney Pratt formed one of the oldest busking partnerships on the streets of London. Sidney assumed the role of manager and spieler for Ernest's escapology act. They were always strapped for cash and never really could afford the right equipment for a proper act. They barely scraped enough money from the cinema queues to keep body and soul together and buy a cuppa from the seedy café run by Archie (Meredith Edwards). In 1981, on 19 February, the same writers resurrected the format, this time for Thames Television and retitled THE INCREDIBLE MR TANNER. Brian Murphy was Ernest and Roy Kinnear was Sidney. Tony Melody played Archie and female interest was added with Prudence (Rosie Collins). Again, six episodes were recorded.
Producer: Derek Bennett (1971). Peter Frazer-Jones (1981).

KING STREET JUNIOR

BBC RADIO. First broadcast: 25 March 1985

Jim Eldridge wrote these stories about a tough junior school set in what the Government described as a social priority area. There were 51 editions over six series to 28 May 1992. In the first seven editions Peter Davison starred as idealistic new teacher Eric Brown, but thereafter Karl Howman fulfilled the same ideal as Philip Sims. The battle-scarred headmaster was Mr Beeston (James Grout) and the deputy head was Mr Holliday (Tom Watson). The school secretary was Mrs Stone (Margaret John) and others on the staff were Mrs Rudd (Vivienne Martin), Mr Long (Paul Copley), Miss Lewis (Marlene Sidaway) and Mrs Patterson (Deirdre Costello).
Producer: John Fawcett Wilson.

KINVIG

LWT. First broadcast: 4 September 1981

Nigel Kneale wrote this seven-part series in which Tony Haygarth starred as Des Kinvig, an electrical repairman. Married to a doting wife, Netta (Patsy Rowlands), he spent his leisure hours with his pal Jim Piper (Colin Jeavons) who was obsessed with spaceships and alien inter-planetary movement. Kinvig was ambivalent to Jim's preoccupation until he met Miss Griffin (Prunella Gee), who whisked him off to the planet Mercury where he met the 500-year-old Buddo (Simon Williams). There he was made aware of the threat to Earth from the hostile Xux tribe and he joined the fight for preservation of our planet.
Producer: Les Chatfield.

KIT CURRAN

CHANNEL 4. First broadcast: 21 July 1986

Following on from ITV's 1984 series THE KIT CURRAN RADIO SHOW, the title character, played by Denis Lawson, moved to Channel 4 for this new show of six episodes. Curran quit the local radio station where he had been a disc jockey and established Curran Associates Inc in Brentford. He tried many enterprises, from double-glazing to a dating agency, but really his ambition was to start his own radio station. His main handicap lay in the fact that he had no money. Pamela Scott (Lindsay Duncan) tried to keep him on the straight and narrow along with former colleagues who were inveigled into his new enterprise, Damien Appleby (Clive Merrison) and Les Toms (Paul Brooke). *Writers: Andy Hamilton and Guy Jenkin. Producer: Anthony Parker for Thames.*

THE KIT CURRAN RADIO SHOW

THAMES. First broadcast: 2 April 1984

Andy Hamilton created and wrote this series of seven episodes. Denis Lawson starred as Kit Curran, a greedy, callous disc jockey at local station Radio Newtown. He was indifferent to his listeners but besotted with himself. His harassed station boss was Roland Simpson (Brian Wilde) and others forced to tolerate Curran's arrogance were Sally Beamish (Debbi Blythe), Damien Appleby (Clive Merrison) and Les Toms (Paul Brooke). *Producer: Derrick Goodwin.*

KNIGHT AND DAYE

USA PRESENTED BY BBC.
First broadcast (UK): 7 June 1992

Hank Knight (Jack Warden) and Everett Daye (Mason Adams) had both been radio presenters in the 1940s. They had developed a feud which was still raging more than 30 years later. Hope Lange appeared as Everett's wife Gloria. Seven shows were screened.

KNOW YOUR PLACE

BBC RADIO. First broadcast: 16 June 1983

Roy Dotrice was the caretaker and Patricia Hayes the cleaner in these eight downstairs stories by Andrew Palmer and Nell Brennan. Other players wrapped up in the saga included Pat Coombs, John Graham, James Taylor, Frances Jeater and Joe Dunlop. *Producer: Edward Taylor.*

L FOR LESTER

BBC. First broadcast: 8 October 1982

Brian Murphy starred in six episodes as Lester Small who ran his own School of Motoring in a West Country town. As the town's driving instructor he was a chapter of accidents, especially where Mrs Davies (Hilda Braid), the wife of the bank manager (Richard Vernon), was concerned. Lester developed a deep and on-going feud with Chief Inspector Rodgers (James Cossins). Amanda Barrie played Sally Small, Colin Spaull was milkman Bert and John Forgeham appeared as Alf Bayley.

Writer: Dudley Long. Director: John B Hobbs. Producer: Dennis Main Wilson.

THE LABOURS OF ERICA

THAMES. First broadcast: 13 March 1989

Brenda Blethyn starred as Erica Parsons who, as her 40th birthday approached, decided to do something about her life. To this end she drew up a list of adventures and experiences which had hitherto eluded her and set about experiencing all that she had missed. To her son Jeremy (Paul Spurrier) her behaviour was odd and grew increasingly odder. The men in her world were Clive Bannister (Clive Merrison) and Dexter Rook (Geoffrey Davies). When Dexter professed his love for Erica she politely explained that she had further ambitions on her list and consequently no time for romance. A first run of six programmes was followed by a second series of six starting 5 March 1990.

Writers: Richard Fegan and Andrew Norriss. Director: John Stroud. Producer: James Gilbert.

LADIES' MAN

USA PRESENTED BY ITV.
First broadcast (UK): 12 October 1981

Lawrence Pressman starred as Alan Thackeray, single parent of Amy (Natasha Ryan) and the only male writer on a women's magazine. His researcher was Gretchen (Simone Griffeth) and his journalist colleagues included Holstein (Louise Sorel), Betty (Karen Morrow), Susan (Allison Argo) and Andrea (Betty Kennedy), who fell in love with him. Thirty episodes were shown.

THE LADY IS A TRAMP

CHANNEL 4. First broadcast: 17 February 1984

Johnny Speight wrote this series of seven programmes. Old Pat (Patricia Hayes) and Lanky Pat (Pat Coombs) were a pair of tramps who lived in, and were very possessive of, a back yard somewhere in London. Each week they would encounter some fellow vagrant in their territory.

Directors: Dennis Main Wilson, Douglas Argent. Producer: William G Stewart for Regent Productions.

LAME DUCKS

BBC. First broadcast: 22 October 1984

This series by Peter J Hammond, a dramatist who was making his first stab at comedy, began with a non-comedic situation in which Drake (John Duttine) had been hit by a lorry and, while languishing in hospital, was told by his glamorous wife (Primi Townsend) that she wanted a divorce. However, he resolved to sell up and use the proceeds to escape to a country cottage. He had, unfortunately, a habit of picking up people along his way. In the hospital he had met reformed pyromaniac Tommy (Patric Turner) and they were joined by hitch-hiker Angie (Lorraine Chase) and ball-walking postman Maurice (Tony Millan). They all settled neatly into a cottage at Scar's Edge with private detective Ansell (Brian Murphy). A first series of six was followed by a second run of six which got underway on 17 September 1985.

Producer: John B Hobbs.

A LANCASHIRE LAD IN LONDON

BBC RADIO. First broadcast: 7 January 1938

These six 15-minute shows were George Formby's only venture into broadcast situation comedy, in which he played his usual gormless Northern misfit lost with his wife (Beryl Formby) in the maelstrom of the capital.

Writer: Howard Thomas. Producer: Max Kester.

LANCE AT LARGE
BBC. First broadcast: 13 August 1964

This was the first television series to be written by former *Sheffield Star* reporters David Nobbs and Peter Tinniswood. It starred Lance Percival, for whom the writers had contributed material on *That Was The Week That Was*. Percival played the part of Alan Day, described as 'an ordinary chap' who, in the course of an ordinary day, got involved in other people's lives. The writers eschewed the conventional situations of the period – office, house or factory – and took Alan Day out and about, making much use of film. Guest stars included Eric Barker, Bernard Bresslaw, Fred Emney and Millicent Martin. Six editions were screened.

Producer: Dennis Main Wilson.

LAND OF HOPE AND GLORY
THAMES. First broadcast: 24 June 1992

Sheila Ferguson (once of pop group The Three Degrees) starred in six episodes as Gloria Hepburn, a dynamic American appointed as business manager to Gerald Hope-Beaumont (Andrew Bicknell). Gloria's brief was to inject some US-style marketing into his stately home and its ancillary potential. Nanny Princeton (Joan Sanderson), who had known the house for years, was most disapproving of the prospective changes.

Writer: Simon Brett. Producer: Peter Frazer-Jones.

LANGLEY BOTTOM
YTV. First broadcast: 14 July 1986

Barry Cryer and John Junkin wrote this six-part series which was set in the village of the title, where time had stood still for years but where change, much of it unwelcome, was afoot. Bill Maynard starred as Seth Raven, a know-all with an opinion on everything. The one and only village 'bobby', PC Wren (Peter Martin), was to be transferred after upholding the law for 30 years. Other village characters were Mrs Wentworth (Elvi Hale), Rev. Dennis Claybourne (Tim Barrett), Hilda Howarth (Rhoda Lewis), Madge Howarth (Barbara Hicks),

Vernon Nobbs (Don Crann) and Mr and Mrs Patel (Kaleem Janjua and Jamila Massey) who kept the village grocery store.

Producer: Alan Tarrant.

THE LARKINS
ATV. First broadcast: 19 September 1958

Fred Robinson created and wrote this series in which Peggy Mount and David Kossoff starred as Ada and Alf Larkin, a Cockney couple who lived at 66 Sycamore Street, somewhere in suburbia. Ada was the archetypal battle-axe, loud of voice and short of temper, and with her hair swept up to create a menacing, fearsome and intimidating appearance, she totally dominated the family. Her put-downs would arouse the indignation of the ineffectual Alf who, in spite of his attempts to fight back, was securely under the thumb. Alf worked in the canteen of a plastics factory. Ada had never had a job. They had a son Eddie (Shaun O'Riordan) who had been in and out of jobs and was virtually unemployable. However, he was assistant scout-master to the local pack. Making up the household were daughter Joyce (Ruth Trouncer) and her American husband Jeff Rogers (Ronan O'Casey). Jeff had been a writer of cowboy stories for a comic called The Bullet until he was fired and became unemployed. Joyce had been a secretary prior to getting married.

Living next door to the Larkins were the Prouts, Sam and Hetty (George Roderick and Barbara Mitchell). Sam, who occasionally went missing without explanation, did no work and Hetty had been a clippie before marrying Sam. They had a daughter Myrtle (Hilary Bamberger) who was in love with Eddie. The other regular character was the local vicar (Charles Lloyd Pack). A 1960 film, *Inn For Trouble*, had Ada and Alf as landlords of a country pub. By autumn 1963, Sycamore Street had been bulldozed and Alf had been made redundant. Eddie disappeared to make his fortune, and Jeff and Joyce had moved to America. With the money from the house and Alf's golden handshake, the Larkins bought a café with a couple of rooms which they could let. It was not far away so they kept their friends and went to the same pub. Their lodger on a more or less permanent basis was Osbert Rigby-Soames (Hugh Paddick).

Producers included Bill Ward and Alan Tarrant.

THE LAST OF THE BASKETS

GRANADA. First broadcast: 10 May 1971

John Stevenson created and wrote this series which was set in Little Clogborough-in-the-Marsh, somewhere in the rural North. The 12th Earl of Clogborough (Richard Hurndall), in his 93rd year, opted to abandon his stately pile and mountain of debts and bid adieu to his last remaining servant, butler Redvers Bodkin (Arthur Lowe). However, before his plan could be executed, it was necessary to find the heir to the title, and the 13th Earl, Clifford Basket (Ken Jones), was duly located living in sublime ignorance with Mrs Basket (Patricia Hayes). Their lives would never be normal again as the faithful Bodkin assumed responsibility for their welfare. The initial series ran for six programmes and a second run was screened in 1972.
Music: Derek Hilton. Producer: Bill Podmore.

LAST OF THE SUMMER WINE

BBC. First broadcast: 4 January 1973

The Christmas special transmitted on 27 December 1993 was the 125th edition of this creation by Roy Clarke which was first seen as a single edition of *Comedy Playhouse*. The first series got underway on 12 November 1973.

The whimsical stories were set in the Yorkshire Pennines where three old men whiled away their hours by sharing memories of the past, trials and troubles of the present and ambitions for the future through a spectrum of emotion spanning pathos to out-and-out farce. The two permanent characters who were ever-present over the two decades were Compo (Bill Owen), the disgustingly scruffiest and uncleanest of all who lusted tirelessly after Nora Batty (Kathy Staff) both before and after she was widowed, and Norman Clegg (Peter Sallis), the laconic friend who tended to get carried along. Their first companion was Blamire (Michael Bates), a retired bachelor who had been a sergeant in the Royal Signals and who seemed an unlikely pal for the smelly Compo and widower Clegg, who had spent his working life with the Co-op furniture department.

When Michael Bates became ill and left the show (he died in 1976), his place was taken by Brian Wilde who portrayed another former military man,

Foggy Dewhurst, who had been an army sign-writer. There was much publicity surrounding the fact that Owen and Wilde did not see eye to eye and when Wilde left, Michael Aldridge joined the cast as retired schoolteacher Seymour Utterthwaite, who fancied himself as an inventor. In 1990, casting aside personal differences, Aldridge left and Wilde returned, thus restoring the most loved of the triumvirates.

Clarke created many popular characters over the long period including Sid (John Comer), café proprietress Ivy (Jane Freeman), Nora's husband Wally (Joe Gladwin), Wesley Pegden (Gordon Wharmby) the mechanic married to Edie (Thora Hird); Howard (Robert Fyfe), married to Pearl (Juliette Kaplan) but always trying to get away to spend time with his brassy mistress Marina (Jean Fergusson); the almost blind Eli (Danny O'Dea) who walked into things; Smiler (Stephen Lewis), the reluctant lodger of the harridan Nora Batty; Edie's daughter Glenda (Sarah Thomas), married to Barry (Mike Grady); and Howard's Auntie Wainwright (Jean Alexander), a junk dealer who would buy and sell anything. See also FIRST OF THE SUMMER WINE.
Producers: James Gilbert, Bernard Thompson, Sydney Lotterby, Alan JW Bell.

Left to right: Clegg, Foggy and Compo in LAST OF THE SUMMER WINE (Photo: Copyright © BBC)

THE LAST SONG

BBC. First broadcast: 3 November 1981

Leo Bannister (Geoffrey Palmer) was separated from his wife Alice (Caroline Blakiston) and wanted to live a quiet life. He was 50 years of age when Liz (Nina Thomas), aged just 24, moved into his life and placed him in a quandary. In the first series of six episodes, Liz wanted to marry him after his divorce but Alice, finding the separation hard to cope with, made increasing demands on Leo and forced him to face up to the watershed in his life. His daughters Jane (Hetty Baynes) and Alison (Gay Wilde) added to his heartache with their own problems, thereby putting Liz's nose out of joint. When a second series of seven editions got underway on 18 February 1983, Liz had disappeared and Leo and Alice tried to get by accepting that disharmony was their norm.

Writer: Carla Lane. Producer: Sydney Lotterby.

LATE EXPECTATIONS

BBC. First broadcast: 7 April 1987

Middle-aged parents of three, Ted and Liz Jackson (Keith Barron and Nanette Newman) had been married for 23 years and went on a second honeymoon. On their return, Liz discovered she was pregnant. As the six-part series progressed, it was revealed that she was expecting twins! The grown-up children were Suzie (Caroline Mander), Polly (Sara Griffiths) and George (Paul McCarthy). Keeping an eye on the development of the pregnancy was Dr John Anderson (James Grout).

Writer: John Gleeson. Producer: John B Hobbs.

THE LAUGH TRAIL

BBC RADIO. First broadcast: 12 February 1941

This six-part series starred black American comedians Harry Scott and Eddie Whaley who arrived in England in 1909 and never returned to the United States. They first broadcast from Savoy Hill in 1926. In THE LAUGH TRAIL they played two detectives, Cuthbert and Pussyfoot, known as the 'human bloodhounds'. While they were adept at picking up the scent, the subsequent trail would be a series of blunderings and mishaps. The two characters were an extension of Scott and Whaley's cross-talk routine which had been a popular feature of the *Kentucky Minstrels* radio show.

Writer: Con West. Producer: Harry S Pepper.

LAURA AND DISORDER

BBC. First broadcast: 19 February 1989

Wendy Craig starred as Laura Kingsley in this six-part series. Following her divorce, she returned to England after ten years living in California. Her daffy personality ensured her life was one long chapter of chaos.

Writers: Jonathan Marr and Ross Bentley. Producer: John B Hobbs.

LAVERNE AND SHIRLEY

ABC (AMERICA) PRESENTED BY BBC.
First broadcast (UK): 11 January 1988

This spin-off from HAPPY DAYS was made in 1976 but not shown in Britain until 12 years later, and then at 8.30 in the morning! Penny Marshall as Laverne De Fazio and Cindy Williams as Shirley Feeney starred as two working-class girls in the 1950s who worked in a Milwaukee brewery where their tedious daily routine involved putting tops on beer bottles. Shirley in particular was trying hard to hold on to her virginity as the first signs of the permissive society crept slowly west. The BBC stripped 35 editions each weekday morning.

Producer: Garry Marshall.

LAW AND DISORDER

BBC RADIO. First broadcast: 4 October 1960

In his first film, *Brothers in Law* (1957), Eric Barker played the part of managing clerk in a barrister's chambers. In the wake of that film he created and wrote this series for himself. He played Mr Trodd, the managing clerk of a firm of solicitors, Cheetham and Drabbe, whose office was set in a small market town. There was no surviving Drabbe so the two partners were Aubrey Cheetham (Austin Trevor) and his son Stephen (Terence Alexander). As neither was particularly bright, it fell upon Mr Trodd to extricate them from potential disasters. To compound the firm's troubles, Stephen had little interest in the law and was, anyway, diverted by the social ambitions of his wife, Angelina (Ambrosine Phillpotts). Thirteen editions were recorded.

Producer: Charles Maxwell.

LAW AND DISORDER

CENTRAL. First broadcast: 17 January 1994

Penelope Keith starred in six editions as widowed barrister Phillippa Troy, who was also a writer of children's books and had created a character called

Prickly Peter the Hedgehog. She faced the jury to defend a variety of accused and her opponent in Court was Gerald Triggs (Simon Williams). They mooted their cases before Judge Wallace (Charles Kaye). Instructing solicitor was Arthur Bryant (Eamon Boland) and Phillippa's clerk in chambers was Steven (John Junkin), with junior Susan (Emma Davies).

Writer: Alex Shearer. Producer: John Howard Davies.

LAZARUS AND DINGWALL

BBC. First broadcast: 1 February 1991

Lazarus (Stephen Frost) and Dingwall (Mark Arden) were undercover cops with the Really Serious Crime Squad. The six-part series was a pastiche of television macho cop pairings in the Starsky and Hutch mould. Their chief was portrayed by Peter Bland.

Writers: Kim Fuller and Vicky Pile. Producer: Bob Spiers.

LEAVE IT TO CHARLIE

GRANADA. First broadcast: 13 July 1978

Charlie Fisher (David Roper) was a well-intentioned, benevolent but luckless and accident-prone insurance salesman. He worked for the Bolton-based company Lancastrian Assurance, where his immediate boss was Arthur Simister (Peter Sallis). Charlie was keen at work but things had a habit of going wrong for him. Other regular characters were Arthur's wife Alice (Gwen Cherell), managing director Mr Ffolliott (John Horsley), office caretaker Harry Hutchins (David Ross), secretary Jennifer Padgett (Sally Kinghorn) and Charlie's landlady Florence McGee (Jean Heywood). After the first series of seven shows there were two further series starting in January 1979 and February 1980.

Music: Derek Hilton. Writer: HV Kershaw. Producer: Eric Prytherch.

LEAVE IT TO ME

BBC RADIO. First broadcast: 16 September 1952

Cicely Courtneidge starred as the proprietor-manager and principal shareholder of a company which claimed to solve everyone's problems of whatever nature. Thorley Walters played her secretary and assistant. Unusually for the period, this was pure situation comedy without the usual incumbrance of singers and musicians. The seven programmes were broadcast weekly.

Writers: Sid Colin and David Climie. Producer: Audrey Cameron.

LEAVE IT TO THE BOYS

BBC RADIO. First broadcast: 21 November 1947

The boys were comedians Michael Howard and Monte Rey, who ran a firm that purported to be able to do anything at any moment. Each week they would be issued with a new order by the imprudent Lady Bird (Gwen Lewis) who, despite calamity upon calamity, remained resolutely optimistic that the boys could actually deliver. They were hindered and hampered in their efforts by the dumbest of dumb blondes, Ann Twirp (Ann Lancaster), and any other characters were played as required by Peter Butterworth and Dick Francis. Petula Clark was on hand for the then-obligatory song. The series ended on 16 January 1948.

Writer: Talbot Rothwell. Producer: Eric Spear.

LEAVE YOUR NAME AND NUMBER

BBC RADIO. First broadcast: 28 April 1950

Canadian husband and wife Bernard Braden and Barbara Kelly starred as two young performers doing the rounds of auditions while trying to make the grade on the English stage. Miriam Karlin was one of the supporting players. There were 14 editions.

Writer: Eric Nicol. Producer: Ian C Messiter.

LEAVING

BBC. First broadcast: 25 July 1984

Carla Lane wrote these stories of Martha and Daniel Ford (Susan Hampshire and Keith Barron) who, in spite of having a 'nice' life with family, house and friends, wished to separate without acrimony. They went through the formalities of divorce but both found it difficult to embark on a new life. Throughout their turmoil, their children Gina and Matthew (Lucy Aston and Gary Cady) fought to retain some normality, with occasional help from Granny Ford (Elizabeth Bradley). There were two six-part series, the second ending on 25 April 1985.

Producer: John B Hobbs.

LEGACY OF MURDER
BBC. First broadcast: 16 February 1982

This six-part light comedy thriller by John and
Steven Singer was filmed entirely on location. Dick
Emery played no fewer than six roles; Lord Algrave,
Bernie Weinstock, Joe Galleano, Monica Danvers-
Crichton and Mrs Oldfield. Weinstock was a small-
time detective employed to trace six people who
had not been seen for 30 years. Others in the cast
included Richard Vernon, Michael Robbins and
Barry Evans.
Producer: Harold Snoad.

LEGAL, DECENT, HONEST AND TRUTHFUL
BBC RADIO. First broadcast: 7 February 1984

The setting for these 12 programmes was an adver-
tising agency where Ken (Martin Jarvis) and Sandy
(Christopher Godwin) were encouraged to believe
that a career in advertising would lead to happiness.
They found out otherwise over two series, the last
broadcast being on 11 November 1986. Other regu-
lar characters included Mr Cheater (James Griffiths),
Freddie (Lockwood West), Deborah (Rosalind
Ayres) and Ambrose (Paul Jesson).
*Writers: Guy Jenkin and John Canter. Producer:
Pete Atkin.*

LENIN OF THE ROVERS
BBC RADIO. First broadcast: 13 February 1988

Almost hidden away in the late-night schedule was
Alexei Sayle who starred as Ricky Lenin, midfield
supremo of Communist football club Felchester
Rovers. Alongside him played Stevie Stalin (Andrew
McClean) and Terry Trotsky (Keith Allen). Former
football commentator Kenneth Wolstenholme
played the role of Frank Lee Brian. There were
guest appearances from John Sessions, Donald
Hewlett and Ballard Berkeley. The last of eight
programmes was heard on 22 April 1989.
*Writers: Marcus Berkmann and Harry Thompson.
Producer: Harry Thompson.*

THE LENNY HENRY SHOW
BBC. First broadcast: 27 October 1987

Comedian Lenny Henry starred as Brixton's larger-
than-life disc jockey Delbert Wilkins who used
street-talk and was highly conscious of his fashionable image. His attitude to life was often irrespon-

The Crucial FM experience in the 'wicked'
hands of Delbert Wilkins (Lenny Henry, right)
and Winston (Vas Blackwood) (Photo:
Copyright © BBC)

sible but his pal Winston (Vas Blackwood) was
always there to look after him. In the first six-part
series Delbert's radio station was a pirate operation, but by the second run of six from 15 September 1988, Brixton Broadcasting Corporation was
legally on the air and for life-in-the-fast-lane Delbert
some of the excitement had gone. His girlfriend
Claudette (Nimmy March) became pregnant which
threw him into a quandry: whether to do a runner
or stay and face his responsibilities. Other regular
characters were Julie (Gina McKee), Alex (Michael
Mears), Wazim (Naim Khan), Rose (Ellen
Thomas), Sgt Lillie (Malcolm Rennie) and PC
Monkhouse (Pip Torrens).
*Music: Joe Dworniak. Writers: Stan Hey and Andrew
Nickolds. Producer: Geoff Posner.*

LES AND ROBERT
BBC RADIO. First broadcast: 13 March 1993

Les (Robin Driscoll) and Robert (Tony Haase)
set off from Lancing in Sussex to make their
way to India. They never got further than the
sinister Wiltshire village of Crapploak where
they became stranded and penniless. Les fell in love
with village maiden Dotty Turner (Sally Grace)
while Robert was mistaken for the long-lost son of
wealthy Mrs Rothchild (Hilda Braid). In the final
part of the four-part serial, Mrs Rothchild had
killed herself and Les and Robert were charged
with her murder.
*Writers: Robin Driscoll and Tony Haase. Producer:
Louise Coats.*

LES DAWSON – MAN OF FICTION

BBC RADIO. First broadcast: 26 February 1970

Comedian Dawson starred as a disaster-prone assistant in a public library in this series of six programmes. Other librarians and members of the public were portrayed by the resident company of Robert Dorning, Joe Gladwin, Sandra Gough and Daphne Oxenford.
Writers: James Casey and Frank Roscoe. Producer: James Casey.

LES GIRLS

CENTRAL. First broadcast: 15 May 1988

These seven comedy dramas centred on provincial model agency Maggie's Models, run by Maggie (Annie Lambert). Seventeen-year-old schoolgirl Amanda (Sadie Frost) was determined to break into the tough world of modelling and at Maggie's she found herself in competition with Veronica (Rachel Fielding), Susan (Janet McTeer) and Polly (Arabella Weir). Jo-Ann (Debbie Bishop) was looked down upon by the others because she did 'glamour' work. In one episode, Amanda Donohoe appeared as posh London model Camilla. The males in the show were Mervyn (Gerard Horan), Reg (Thomas Wheatley) and Conrad (Tom Georgeson).
Writers: Margaret Phelan, Linda Kernan. Director: Anthony Garner. Producer: Patrick Harbinson.

LET THERE BE LOVE

THAMES. First broadcast: 4 January 1982

Johnnie Mortimer and Brian Cooke created and wrote this series which starred Paul Eddington as Timothy Love, a smoothie who enjoyed his freedom, money and fair share of girls. Then he met Judy Morrison (Nanette Newman) and fell in love with her. At first he was unaware that she was a widow with three children, Charles (Stephen Nolan), Edward (Ian Morrison) and Elizabeth (Claudia Gambold). Once he made that discovery, the prospect of such responsibility and the gentle sound of wedding bells filled him with alarm. Timothy confided his fears to his colleague Dennis (Henry McGee) at the advertising agency where he worked. The first series of six shows was followed by a second run of six starting on 10 March 1983. Timothy and Judy had now married and they all lived together in one house with just one bathroom.
Producer: Peter Frazer-Jones.

THE LIFE AND TIMES OF HENRY PRATT

GRANADA. First broadcast: 9 November 1992

David Nobbs adapted his own novel into four hour-long episodes of comedy drama which charted the journey of Henry 'Eee, I am daft' Pratt through the British class system from his birth in Yorkshire in 1935. Pratt was portrayed at his smallest by Andrew Nicholson, as a schoolboy by Robert Nicholson, as a young lad by Bryan Dick and as a young man by Jack Deam. He was beset by tragedy: his mother died, and his father committed suicide in the outside privy. Not the bare bones of comedy, but with the pen of Nobbs and his eccentric characters there was much to laugh at with Henry. He journeyed through his own sexual frustrations, an unpleasant brush with homosexuality and being passed around relations of differing moral standards. Cousin Hilda (Dinah Stabb) took in gentlemen lodgers and was a prude, Auntie Doris and Uncle Teddy (Maggie O'Neill and Alun Armstrong) were quite the reverse, and Henry was uncomfortable with Daphne (Tilly Vosburgh) because he could not stand Geoffrey Porringer (Andrew Seear). Others who influenced Henry's life to a greater or lesser degree included Miss Candy (Julie T Wallace), Ezra (Jeff Rawle), Paul Hargreaves (Christopher Haley), Nattrass (Edward Holmes), Diana (Sophie Chaumette), Belinda (Amy Simnett) and Tony Preece (Peter Wight).
Director: Adrian Shergold. Producer: Jenny Reeks.

LIFE BEGINS AT FORTY

YTV. First broadcast: 13 June 1978

After 17 years of marriage, Chris and Katy Bunting (Derek Nimmo and Rosemary Leach) learned that they were to become parents for the first time at the age of 40. This was the cue for some feverish activity in their well-set, middle-class lives involving Chris's mother (Fanny Rowe), their friends Gerry and Jill Simpson (Michael Graham Cox and Rosemary Martin, later Anna Dawson), Badger White (Tim Barrett) and Horace the milkman (Gordon Rollings). The baby duly arrived in spite of the incompetent ditherings of Chris, and when the time came for the christening, Katy's sister Gertie (Moira Lister) arrived to add to the confusion. The first series of seven programmes was followed by a second run starting 8 February 1980.
Writer: Jan Butlin. Producer: Graeme Muir.

LIFE IS WHAT YER MAKE IT
BBC RADIO. First broadcast: 8 September 1971

Ronald Fletcher played himself, reporting on topical issues as seen and heard through the eyes and ears of a typical family comprising Dad (Michael Robbins), Mum (Pat Coombs), Beryl (Liz Gebhardt) and Len (Frank Abbott). Thirteen editions were broadcast.
Writers: Tony Bilbow and Mike Fentiman. Producer: Martin Fisher.

A LIFE OF BLISS
BBC RADIO AND TELEVISION.
First broadcast: 29 July 1953

This long-running series was originally tailored by writer Godfrey Harrison to fit David Tomlinson who first played the part of David Alexander Bliss. Later that year, from 9 September and because of Tomlinson's film commitments, George Cole slipped into the role and stayed there until the final episode on 3 March 1969. Throughout, Harrison had no collaborator in creating the life and loves of amiable, shy and bewildered bachelor Bliss, who meandered through life with his sole constant companion Psyche the dog, whose voice was provided by Percy Edwards. David always had a married sister and brother-in-law who were played by, amongst others, Nora Swinburne and Esmond Knight, Phyllis Calvert and James McKechnie, and Diana Churchill and Colin Gordon, with Isabel Dean replacing Churchill in the 1960 television series. David's girlfriends included Penny Gay (Petula Clark) who ditched him at the altar, Shirley Summers (Moira Lister), Georgina Jay (Lana Morris), Joy Joel (Noelle Middleton), Zoe Hunter (Sheila Sweet) and Tina (Muriel Pavlow). For many years Gladys Henson portrayed David's charlady Mrs Griffin and his parents were played by Gladys Young and Ernest Jay (later Carleton Hobbs).

The show moved to television on 21 January 1960 where it began with Dean and Gordon in the roles of sister and brother-in-law, but by the next year they were replaced by Frances Bennett and Hugh Sinclair as Pam and Bob Batten. In the earlier years Donald Sinden used to intrude as Phil Bender with his wife Valerie (Gwen Cherell).
Radio producer: Leslie Bridgmont. Television producers: Graeme Muir, Godfrey Harrison.

THE LIFE OF RILEY
GRANADA. First broadcast: 6 January 1975

Bill Maynard starred as insurance agent Frank Riley, a widower with a roving eye. Into his bachelor life returned his 18-year-old, God-fearing, Welsh-speaking son Brian (Frank Lincoln), who had no job and nowhere to live. He quickly disapproved of his father's lifestyle and managed to crop up at inopportune moments and thwart Frank's romantic efforts. Brian himself had a nice, steady sweetheart, Janice Butcher (Susan Littler). Frank's friends and colleagues included Ethel Goodchild (Eileen Kennally), George Pollitt (John Comer) and Clifford Pringle (John McKelvey).
Writers: HV Kershaw, Brian Finch. Producer: Eric Prytherch.

THE LIFE OF RILEY
NBC (AMERICA) PRESENTED BY ITV.
First broadcast (UK): 19 August 1959

This began as a radio show in the USA in the 1940s and starred Hollywood tough guy William Bendix as the not very bright blue-collar worker Chester A Riley. When the transfer to television was first tried as early as 1949, Bendix was not available so the role went to Jackie Gleason. It was not a success and was soon taken off the network. However, in 1952 Bendix became available to re-create the character which he did until 1958. It was these Bendix shows which ITV broadcast in Britain. Riley and his wife Peg (Marjorie Reynolds) lived in reasonable contentment in Los Angeles at 1313 Blue View Terrace. They had a daughter Babs (Lugene Sanders) and a son Junior (Wesley Morgan). Riley was, in many ways, a gentle forerunner of Archie Bunker. He liked nothing better than to swill beer with his feet up in front of a ball game on television and set the world to rights. Chester and Peg spent much of their time with friends and neighbours Gillis (Tom D'Andrea) and his wife Honeybee (Gloria Blondell).
Producer: Tom McKnight.

LIFE WITH FATHER
CBS PRESENTED BY ITV. First broadcast (UK): 2 July 1963

This series of 26 episodes was based on a book by Clarence Day which chronicled the adventures of an upper middle-class New York family in the 1880s. The family had the author's name, Day. Leon Ames starred as the tyrannical father Clarence, who was equally tyrannised by his family. Lurene

Tuttle played the mother and their children were Clarence Junior (Steven Terrell), John (Malcolm Cassell), Whitney (BG Norman) and Harlan (Harvey Grant). Before it came to the small screen, a movie version of the story had been made in 1947 starring William Powell and Irene Dunne with Elizabeth Taylor.

LIFE WITH LORD CHARLES
BBC RADIO. First broadcast: 18 June 1967

In the wake of Edgar Bergen and Peter Brough, ventriloquist Ray Alan brought his dummy Lord Charles, 'last of the wooden-headed aristocracy', to radio stardom in this series of eight shows. His manservant was Withers (Deryck Guyler). Other parts, as and when required, were played by Brian Trueman, Barbara Mullaney, Colin Edwynn, Penny Morrell and Peter Wheeler.
Writers: Charles Hart and Peter Bishop. Producer: Geoff Lawrence.

LIFE WITH THE BURKES
BBC RADIO. First broadcast: 5 July 1958

Cyril Fletcher starred in two roles, head of the family Albert Burke and his small son 'Erbie, in this saga of domestic life written by Johnny Speight. Albert's wife was Emma (Margaret St Barbe West in the first of twelve episodes, Marjorie Rhodes thereafter). The other two occupants of the household were Sally (Nan Kenway) and Grandma (Gladys Dawson).
Producer: Alastair Scott Johnston.

LIFE WITH THE LYONS
BBC RADIO AND TELEVISION.
First broadcast: 5 November 1950

American film stars, husband and wife Ben Lyon and Bebe Daniels, had endeared themselves to British listeners before the war, but they won a special place in the esteem of the nation by staying in London when hostilities started and broadcasting their comedy show with Vic Oliver, *Hi Gang!*, until Lyon left to join the American 8th Army Air Force. After the war they settled in Britain to raise their family, Richard and Barbara, and shared the experience with listeners through this domestic comedy series, written in the main by Bebe herself. In their household they had a maid-housekeeper, Aggie Macdonald (Molly Weir),

and next door was nosey neighbour Florrie Wainwright (Doris Rogers) and her put-upon husband George (Ian Sadler). By way of an in-joke Ben's boss was called Mr Fox (Hugh Morton), as in real life at the time Lyon was an executive with 20th Century Fox. Apart from the family, the other regular was the rather vague Mr Wimple (Horace Percival). The shows came to an end after almost 150 editions over 11 series on 19 May 1961. On 29 June the cast began a television series on the BBC, but it is as wireless stars that they remain in the memory.
Writers: Bebe Daniels, Bob Block, Bill Harding, Ronnie Hanbury, Ray Sonin. Producer: Tom Ronald.

LIFE WITH THE LYONS
A-R. First broadcast: 17 September 1957

Ben Lyon and Bebe Daniels with their off-spring Barbara and Richard appeared in this series for ITV which began while the same title was still one of BBC's top radio shows. This is the earliest example of ITV 'poaching' from the radio, but it did not really work and lasted just one series. With the family were Molly Weir as Aggie the cook, Doris Rogers as Florrie, and their faithful dog Skeeter.
Writers: Bebe Daniels, Bob Block and Bob Ross. Director: John Phillips. Producer: Barry Baker.

LIFE WITHOUT GEORGE
BBC. First broadcast: 12 March 1987

Jennifer Russell (Carol Royle) lived with George Stanton for five years until he walked out on her for another, younger woman. She ran a dance centre and established a relationship with estate agent Larry (Simon Cadell) who was infatuated with her. Unfortunately for the relationship, Jenny seemed unable to get George out of her mind. Her friend was Amanda (Rosalind March, later Elizabeth Estensen) and Larry's friend and colleague was Ben (Michael Thomas). The role of Mr Chambers who worked at the studio was played by Ronald Fraser. A first series of six shows was followed by a second run of eight beginning 23 March 1989, when Jenny came to realise that Larry meant more to her than she had allowed herself to believe, and she eventually became pregnant.
Writers: Penny Croft and Val Hudson. Producer: Susan Belbin.

THE LIKELY LADS
BBC. First broadcast: 16 December 1964

Dick Clement and Ian La Frenais created this much-loved series which was first seen on BBC2. Bob Ferris (Rodney Bewes) and Terry Collier (James Bolam) were two ordinary lads living and working in the North East. They both worked in an electrical components factory where they earned around £12 per week to spend on the beer and birds that were an integral part of their irreverent lifestyle. Bob was the quieter and more serious-minded of the pair, with Terry the greater risk-taker and pioneering chauvinist, although he was protective towards his sister Audrey (Sheila Fearn). There were six editions in the first series followed by six more starting 16 June 1965. A third and final run of eight got underway on 4 June 1966 by which time the lads were feeling their age at 22. Bob had acquired a motor scooter to give him greater mobility around town. He was fired with ambition, both personal and at work, whereas Terry was comparatively contented with his lot. Veteran actor Wilfrid Lawson made a guest appearance in the third series as Terry's Grandad. The story of Bob and Terry was taken up again by the same writers and actors in WHATEVER HAPPENED TO THE LIKELY LADS.
Producer: Dick Clement.

BBC RADIO. First broadcast: 6 August 1987

James Bolam adapted the original scripts for THE LIKELY LADS television shows into half-hour radio programmes. He again played Terry Collier with Rodney Bewes as Bob Ferris and Sheila Fearn playing Terry's sister, Audrey. A first run of eight shows was followed by eight further editions ending 7 July 1968.
Producer: John Browell.

LIL
BBC. First broadcast: 13 April 1965

This six-part series by Elaine Morgan was first seen on BBC Wales and repeated on BBC1 for the rest of Britain from 7 July. Lil (Jessie Evans) lived alone in a small town in one of the valleys of South Wales. Much was stacked against her but with a mixture of courage, doggedness and guile she managed to overcome most of her everyday problems. Her friend in the series was Blod (Joan Newell), who shared a similar fate.
Producer: David J Thomas.

LITTLE ARMADILLOS
CHANNEL 4. First broadcast: 13 September 1984

Pete Richens and Colin Gibson created and wrote these seven programmes. The setting was the Seal Club in a particularly seedy area of London's docklands. The owners were Wayne and Donny Armadillo (Jim Sweeney and Steve Steen), identical twin psychopaths. Their evil intentions, however, were usually bungled.
Producer: Bob Spiers for TVS.

A LITTLE BIG BUSINESS
GRANADA. First broadcast: 8 August 1963

This first saw life as a single half-hour when David Kossoff starred as Marcus Lieberman, an elderly craftsman in the furniture-making business, who introduced his son Simon (James Maxwell) to the trade. The following year on 27 February it became a series, with Kossoff again playing Marcus but with Francis Matthews in the role of Simon. Marcus and his loyal friends, Lazlo (Martin Miller) and Charlie (Billy Russell, later Jack Bligh) were old-fashioned, dyed-in-the-wool craftsmen who were resigned to the onslaught of modern business methods introduced by the highly educated Simon. Simon's colleague Basil Crane was played by David Conville and his secretary Miss Stevens by Joyce Marlowe. Simon's wife Naomi was first portrayed by Diana Coupland and later by Constance Wake.
Writer: Jack Pullman. Directors included Cliff Owen and Milo Lewis. Producer: Peter Eton.

A LITTLE BIT OF WISDOM
ATV. First broadcast: 30 March 1976

In two series using this title, in 1974 and 1975, Norman Wisdom had starred in individual comedy plays with no continuity of characters or situations. However, in this seven-week series, Norman was given a permanent job as a clerk in a builder's office. His unfortunate boss was Albert Clark (Robert Keegan) whose attractive daughter Linda (Frances White) caught Norman's fancy. Away from the office he shared a flat with Alec Potter (Neil McCarthy).
Writers: Ronnie Taylor, Lew Schwarz, John Kane, Jon Watkins. Producer: Les Chatfield.

THE LIVER BIRDS
BBC. First broadcast: 14 April 1969

This long-running series was created by Carla Lane,

Flat-sharing LIVER BIRDS Beryl (Polly James) and Sandra (Nerys Hughes) (Photo: Copyright © BBC)

Myra Taylor and Lew Schwarz and began as a one-off *Comedy Playhouse* before a short series of three began the same year on 21 July. Two young, single girls shared a small flat in Huskisson Road, Liverpool. In those first four shows Pauline Collins played the rather prissy Dawn, but when the series began in earnest on 7 January 1971 Dawn had gone and the zany Beryl Hennessey (Polly James) was joined by the naive Sandra Hutchinson (Nerys Hughes). All their problems were related to money and boyfriends as they struggled to make ends meet and cling on to their virginity until marriage. There were also visits from parents to contend with, the most regular being Sandra's mother (Molly Sugden). Mr Hutchinson was played by Ivan Beavis and the Hennessey parents by Sheila Kay and Cyril Shaps. By the third season, Sandra and Beryl had moved to a smarter, three-bedroomed flat and Sandra had a boyfriend, Paul (John Nettles). At the end of the fourth run Beryl married a Londoner, Robert (Jonathan Lynn). With Beryl's departure, Sandra's new flatmate was Carol Boswell (Elizabeth Estensen) who wore loud, gaudy clothes and ludicrous platform shoes which contrasted with Sandra's conservative dress-sense. Carol had a brother Lucien (Michael Angelis) who kept rabbits, and a mother (Eileen Kennally, later Carmel McSharry) who had raised her family to be good Catholics. In the sev-

enth season Sandra went to work for a vet, Derek (Tom Chadbon). They fell in love and were married. Carol became their lodger and in the eighth and final run Sandra became pregnant. The last edition, the 80th, was seen on 5 January 1979.
Producers: Sydney Lotterby, Douglas Argent, Roger Race.

LIVING IT UP

A-R. First broadcast: 27 October 1958

Twenty years after **BAND WAGON**, this was a poor attempt to recreate the magic which Arthur Askey and Richard Murdoch had created on the radio. Whereas in 1938 the pair had shared an imaginary flat at Broadcasting House, the 1958 television version had them running a pirate TV station from a penthouse atop Television House, Rediffusion's Kingsway headquarters. Appearing with Askey and Murdoch in the six editions were Hugh Morton, Billy Percy and Danny Ross.
Writers: Sid Colin and Talbot Rothwell. Producer: Bill Hitchcock.

LIVING WITH BETTY

BBC RADIO. First broadcast: 12 December 1986

Arline Whittaker wrote these stories which were heard in three six-week series ending on 24 December 1989. Barbara Windsor starred as Betty who shacked up with long-distance lorry driver Bill (Glyn Edwards). He had a son Trevor (Simon Molloy) who was a dentist, and a daughter-in-law

Katherine (Diana Mather) who worked in a bank. Next door lived snobbish Muriel Cavanagh (Rosalind Knight) and her hen-pecked husband Harold (Peter Sallis).
Producer: Mike Craig.

LOLLIPOP LOVES MR MOLE
ATV. First broadcast: 25 October 1971

Jimmy Perry created and wrote this show which starred Peggy Mount and Hugh Lloyd as Maggie and Reg Robinson. Their pet names for each other are embodied in the title. Maggie was strong and forceful and she protected the obliging but vulnerable Reg from the cruel outside world. They lived in peace and harmony until Reg's brother Bruce (Rex Garner) and his wife Violet (Pat Coombs) returned from Africa to stay for an intended few days. They turned up on the doorstep with six cabin trunks and their short stay turned into an eternity. A second series was made in 1972 under the shortened title LOLLIPOP.
Director: David Askey. Producer: Shaun O'Riordan.

THE LONELYHEARTS KID
THAMES. First broadcast: 17 July 1984

School sweethearts Ken and Judy (Robert Glenister and Deborah Farrington) had lived together for several years. However, as Judy matured, her uncertainty about the relationship grew. She found Ken lagged behind and they gradually drifted apart. In the second episode of six, she left him. He did his crying on the shoulder of his sister Ros (Julia Goodman) and found an unexpected friend in his old school adversary Ray (George Winter).
Writer: Alex Shearer. Director: Douglas Argent. Producer: Anthony Parker.

LOOKING FOR TROUBLE
BBC RADIO. First broadcast: 2 May 1955

Jimmy Jewel and Ben Warriss starred as the trouble seekers who again teamed up with Betty Paul, who had played the girlfriend in UP THE POLE. For eight weeks they got themselves in and out of scrapes, and did so again from 11 April 1956.
Writers: Len Fincham and Lawrie Wyman. Producer: Jacques Brown.

LORD TRAMP
SOUTHERN. First broadcast: 1 August 1977

Hugh Lloyd starred in the one and only series of this show as a happy-go-lucky tramp, Hughie Wagstaff, who inherited a title, a large country estate and a fortune. However, it did not change his life for the better and he was weighed down with the responsibilities which came with the inheritance. He preferred his life as the simple tramp unencumbered by material problems. With the property came staff in the form of Miss Pratt (Joan Sims), Tipping (George Moon) and Lucy (Lally Percy). Jack Watling played the part of a duke who lived nearby.
Writer: Michael Pertwee. Producer: Peter Croft.

THE LOSERS
ATV. First broadcast: 12 November 1978

Alan Coren wrote this six-part series in which Leonard Rossiter starred as Sydney Foskett, a seedy wrestling manager. He was seeking a bad wrestler whom he could exploit for his ability to lose, and he duly discovered his perfect loser in the dim-witted Nigel (Alfred Molina). Foskett was assisted in his shabby exploits by Dennis Breene (Joe Gladwin).
Producer: Shaun O'Riordan.

LOVE AND KISSES
ATV. First broadcast: 4 November 1955

This is a unique entry in this book in that it was a stage play, presented at the Grand Theatre, Blackpool, by Jack Hylton, which was recorded in live performance at the theatre in the summer of 1955 and subsequently broken up into five episodes for screening as a situation comedy. Glenn Melvyn wrote the script and played the role of Wally Binns. The star was Arthur Askey as Bill Brown, with Lally Bowers portraying his wife Sal. They had a daughter, Rose, played by Askey's real daughter Anthea. Their son Percy was played by Ian Gardiner and Wally's wife Emma Binns was played by Barbara Miller. The gormless Alf Hall was portrayed by Danny Ross. All these characters had originally been conceived for Melvyn's play *The Love Match*. What little plot there was concerned Bill facing eviction if he failed to raise the money to pay off the brewery. He crashed his milk van into a car and tried to pin the blame on Alf. The wives went on strike and Bill and Wally sloped off to a football match.
Producer: Richard Bird.

THE LOVE OF MIKE

A-R. First broadcast: 20 April 1960

Michael Medwin, fresh from his triumph as Corporal Springer in THE ARMY GAME, starred in 30 consecutive episodes as dance-band trumpeter Mike Lane. He was always broke, never even able to pay the rent and spent his life chasing girls and easy money. He considered himself a man of style and fine taste, choosing to drape himself around the flat in a padded dressing gown and smoking from a long cigarette-holder. A bachelor roué, his tools of seduction were a record player, soft lights and a total absence of scruples which allowed him to take unfair advantage. However, though he thought he could shoot a great line, his ferocious chase never really got him far. Brian Wilde played his flat-sharing chum (later Bernard Fox), George Roderick was their hen-pecked neighbour who frequently escaped to the flat, and Carmel McSharry was the charlady.

Writers included Gerald Kelsey and Dick Sharples. Producers included Cyril Butcher, Bill Hitchcock, Ronald Marriott, John Phillips and Bill Turner.

LOVE, SIDNEY

USA PRESENTED BY CHANNEL 4.
First broadcast (UK): 19 January 1984

Tony Randall starred as Sidney Shorr whose former live-in girlfriend Laurie Morgan (Swoosie Kurtz) turned up on his doorstep with her young daughter Patti (Kaleena Kiff) and elected to stay. Patti was also Sidney's daughter but she was unaware of her father's identity. Laurie was an actress in a TV soap opera. Channel 4 screened 16 episodes.

LOVE THY NEIGHBOUR

THAMES. First broadcast: 13 April 1972

One of the more controversial sitcoms in the annals of British television history was launched on an unsuspecting public in the spring of 1972. The creation of Vince Powell and Harry Driver, it was the first comedy to test the touchy issue of race. Eddie and Joan Booth (Jack Smethurst and Kate Williams) were a white couple, he a staunch socialist. Their new next-door neighbours were a black couple, Bill and Barbie Reynolds (Rudolph Walker and Nina Baden-Semper). Bill was a true-blue Tory. The two men were antagonistic towards each other, prone to using offensive nicknames like 'chocolate

drop' and 'honky'. The wives were much better integrated and became good friends. Eddie's bigotry was highlighted in conversations at the local club where the company included Arthur (Tommy Godfrey), Jacko Jackson (Keith Marsh) and Nobby Garside (Paul Luty). The format proved highly popular and enjoyed a long run each year until 1976.

Writers included Powell and Driver, Lawrie Wyman and George Evans, Brian Cooke, Sid Colin, Johnnie Mortimer. Producers: Stuart Allen, Ronnie Baxter, Anthony Parker.

LOVEJOY

BBC. First broadcast: 10 January 1986

Ian McShane starred as the antiques dealer Lovejoy in this comedy thriller series developed by Ian La Frenais from the novels by Jonathan Gash, set in the Fenland district of East Anglia. Lovejoy pursued his own often shady dealings while protecting the unsuspecting from the criminal activities of those on the periphery of the trade. By the time (post writing of this book) the autumn 1994 series has been seen, there will have been 71 episodes. He had two constant and oft bewildered assistants, Tinker Deal (Dudley Sutton) and Eric (Chris Jury). Eric ultimately left to help run his uncle's pub at the coast and was replaced in the Lovejoy employ by eager novice Beth (Diane Parishe). The love interest for the central character was supplied by the aristocratic Lady Jane Felsham (Phyllis Logan) and, once she had left, by the initially stand-offish Charlotte (Caroline Langrishe). While the police always kept a detached eye on Lovejoy's activities, he moved with consummate ease in and out of the social classes finding time, now and again, to direct an aside to the viewers. From 1992 Malcolm Tierney joined the cast as Charlie Gimbert who had bought Felsham Manor and thereby found himself embroiled in the Lovejoy affairs.

Directors: Bill Brayne, Geoff Love, Francis Megahy, John Crome, Sarah Hellings, Baz Taylor. Producers: Richard Everitt, Emma Hayter, Robert Banks Stewart, Jo Wright and Colin Schindler for Witzend.

LOVELY COUPLE

LWT. First broadcast: 7 April 1979

This series of 13 programmes by Christopher Wood told the story of the romance between David Mason (Anthony O'Donnell) and June Dent

(Elaine Donnell). Initially they merely wished to go on holiday together, which brought howls of disapproval from parents on both sides, the bingo-loving widow Mrs Mason (Maggie Jones) and the Dents (David Lodge and Geraldine Newman). David and June became engaged and, much against June's wishes, had no choice but to live with David's mum after their wedding. There was constant conflict and both David and June sought solace with their respective friends, Allan Brown (Nick Edmett) and Carole Richards (Pauline Quirke).
Producer: Derrick Goodwin.

THE LOVERS

GRANADA. First broadcast: 27 October 1970

Jack Rosenthal created these stories of two Manchester teenagers, Geoffrey (Richard Beckinsale) and Beryl (Paula Wilcox). The gauche and gullible Geoffrey was desperate to lose his virginity while the naive but scheming Beryl desperately tried to

Geoffrey (Richard Beckinsale) and Beryl (Paula Wilcox) make a charming couple in Jack Rosenthal's THE LOVERS (Photo: Granada Television)

cling on to hers. She dreamed of marriage and he yearned for an opportunity to get her alone on the sofa. In the 'will they – won't they' scenario, Beryl was supported by her mother (Joan Scott) and Geoffrey by his pal Roland (Robin Nedwell). The first series, written by Rosenthal, ran for six weeks. A second series of seven, written by Geoffrey Lancashire, was made the following year.

Theme music: Derek Hilton. Director: Michael Apted (1970). Producers: Jack Rosenthal (1970), Les Chatfield (1971).

LUCK'S WAY

BBC RADIO. First broadcast: 26 July 1949

Cockney comedienne Ethel Revnell starred as Ethel Wiggins in this ten-part series of domestic comedies. She also played the part of Angela, the ghastly child who drove them all mad. Ethel's father was Mr Wiggins (Wilfred Babbage), her sister was Ruby (Cecile Chevreau) and her sister-in-law was Ivy (Doris Rogers). They had a lodger, Mr Stead (Hal Stead), and a neighbour, Mrs Higginbotham (Clarice Clare).

Writers: Leslie Julian Jones, Carey Edwards and Aubrey Danvers-Walker. Producer: Tom Ronald.

LUCKY FELLER

LWT. First broadcast: 2 September 1976

Terence Frisby wrote this seven-part series in which David Jason starred as Shorty Mepstead who lived at home in South-East London with his mother (Pat Heywood) and brother Randolph (Peter Armitage). The two brothers ran a small plumbing business. Shorty's problem was that he was very shy with girls but his new girlfriend, Kathleen Peake (Cheryl Hall), gradually coaxed him out of his shyness. Her parents (Glynn Edwards and Maggie Jones) were at constant war with each other, in contrast to the tranquility of the Mepstead home.

Director: Gerry Mill. Producer: Humphrey Barclay.

THE LUCY SHOW

CBS (AMERICA) PRESENTED BY BBC.
First broadcast (UK): 27 December 1962

Following her divorce in 1960 from Cuban musician Desi Arnaz, Lucille Ball created a new television persona for herself, that of Lucy Carmichael, a widow living in Danfield, Connecticut with her two young children, Chris (Candy Moore) and Jerry (Jimmy Garrett). The Carmichaels shared an apartment with another widow, Vivian Bagley (Vivian Vance), and her young son Sherman (Ralph Hart). Both families were always in financial difficulties and Lucy was the bane of the life of Theodore J Mooney (Gale Gordon), the president of the bank where she worked. (In the first series Lucy's boss, Harry Connors, was played by Dick Martin.) For the final series, Mr Mooney thought he had escaped Lucy when he was transferred by the bank to California but she and her son Jerry also moved there, leaving her daughter and the Bagleys back east. There were 156 episodes and the BBC screened the last on 27 March 1966.

Producers: Lucille Ball and Gary Morton (her new husband).

LUV

BBC. First broadcast: 9 March 1993

Harold Craven (Michael Angelis) was a Liverpudlian from a working-class background who made good and became a millionaire. All he ever wished to do thereafter was his best for his wife Terese (Sue Johnston) and their three adopted children. They were unemployed Darwin (Stephen Lord); Hannah (Sandy Hendrickse), whose choice in boyfriends left much for moralist Harold to desire; and Victor (Russell Boulter), who was gay. Sadly, most of Harold's family efforts failed to work out since he omitted to realise that money was not everything. He gave them material possessions at will but he blindly did not see that his wife needed other attentions. During the first series of nine episodes, Harold had a brief but stormy affair with Eden (Julie Peasgood), who went to work at his plastic-flowerpot factory. By the end of that series Terese had left him and moved in next door. When a second run of eight programmes came to an end on 20 April 1994, they were struggling again with their relationship and Harold's factory had slid deep into debt. The Rolls-Royce and his chauffeur Lloyd (Peter Caffrey) had to go, and the battle for survival was underway. As bankruptcy threatened, Harold was forced to try and sell the factory. Hannah, meanwhile, had married her Italian boyfriend Antonio (Zubin Varla) and presented the Cravens with a grandchild. Eden disappeared after being rejected in her bid to seduce Darwin.

Writer: Carla Lane. Producer: Mike Stephens.

M*A*S*H*

CBS (AMERICA) PRESENTED BY BBC.
First broadcast (UK): 20 May 1973

It is a tribute to the writing, acting and production talents involved that a situation rich in comedy could be created from a real war in which more than two million people lost their lives. The stories came from an original novel by Richard Hooker which was dramatised by Ring Lardner Jr for a 1970 movie directed by Robert Altman. The subsequent television series was the creation of producers Gene Reynolds and Burt Metcalf, together with writer Larry Gelbart who eventually wrote more than a third of the 251 episodes.

Set in Korea during the war which began in June 1950 and ended in July 1953, MASH was an acronym for Mobile Army Surgical Hospital, a frontline unit responsible for patching-up soldiers and returning them to the battle. The characters in this series belonged to MASH 4077. At the time the series was launched in the United States on 17 September 1972, Americans were questioning the morality of wars, the government and the President in the wake of Vietnam. Within months America was again to be rocked by the Watergate scandal. So M*A*S*H*, with its anti-war and anti-establishment attitude, was perfectly timed.

At the outset the principal characters were two anarchic surgeons, Captain Benjamin Franklin 'Hawkeye' Pierce, played by Alan Alda, and Captain 'Trapper John' McIntyre, portrayed by Wayne Rogers, who worked excessively long hours in the huts which served as wards, operating theatres and living quarters. Rogers left the cast and was replaced by Mike Farrell as Captain BJ Hunnicutt. M*A*S*H never held back from exposing the horrors of war and exploited with often vicious humour the irony of nursing men back to strength only to return them to the fighting. Neither did the writers shirk from the inevitable frustrations, both medical and sexual, of such a surgical unit. The original commanding officer of 4077 was Lt Colonel Harry Blake (McLean Stevenson), who was later replaced by Colonel Sherman Potter (Harry Morgan). Hawkeye faced overt disapproval for his ideals and actions, notably from Major Frank Burns

(Larry Linville), chief nurse Major Margaret 'Hot Lips' Houlihan (Loretta Swit) and the music-loving Major Charles Emerson Winchester III (David Ogden Stiers). Among the lower ranks were the naive country-boy Corporal Walter 'Radar' O'Reilly (Gary Burghoff) who grew older and wiser as the war progressed, and Corporal Maxwell Klinger (Jamie Farr), who took to wearing women's clothing in a desperate bid to obtain a Section 8 discharge on grounds of insanity.

M*A*S*H* ran for ten years and the characters developed and grew with their experiences. Several of the actors contributed to the writing and among the mountain of awards which the series collected, Alan Alda won Emmys for acting, writing and directing. The final episode, 'Goodbye, Farewell and Amen', was a two-and-a-half hour special which ended in a group suicide pact. It was shown in the UK on 27 December 1984.

McHALE'S NAVY

ABC (AMERICA) PRESENTED BY BBC.
First broadcast (UK): 22 July 1963

This long-running show (138 editions) owed its origins to a single one-hour straight drama, *Seven Against The Sea*. It starred Ernest Borgnine as Lt Commander Quinton McHale and the crew of a Patrol Torpedo boat of the US Navy on duty in the Pacific during the Second World War. Studio executives thought it would make a comedy series and turned the idea over to writer and producer Edward Montange who developed McHale and his team of incompetent sailors. Borgnine stayed with his role and was joined by Joe Flynn as the hapless flotilla commander, Captain Wallace Binghamton. In order to try to get some discipline aboard McHale's craft, PT 73, Binghamton assigned a keen young Ensign, Charles Parker (Tim Conway), as their Executive Officer. However, rather than raise the men to his level, Parker was swiftly reduced to theirs. Generally the activities centred around and on the island of Taratuta. Other regular characters included Torpedoman Lester Gruber (Carl Ballantine), Gunner's Mate Virgil Edwards (Edson Stroll) and Lieutenant Carpenter (Billy Sands).

McKAY THE NEW
BBC RADIO. First broadcast: 19 November 1991

Michael Fenton Stevens starred as John McKay, the impoverished laird of Castle McKay, who battled to keep his stately pile together and gain the loyalty of his unfaithful staff. The stories embraced sex, disease, music and the threat of the castle being turned into a theme park. Characters included cook Flora (Denise Coffey), Angus (John Grieve), Emma (Leni Harper) and Andy (Jon Glover). Six episodes were broadcast.
Producer: Neil Cargill.

MAGGIE AND HER
LWT. First broadcast: 13 January 1978

Leonard White created and wrote these shows which starred Julia McKenzie as divorced schoolteacher Maggie, who lived alone in a flat. Her peace was persistently interrupted by 'her', the good-natured but extremely nosey neighbour Mrs Perry (Irene Handl). Maggie met and fancied several men but failed to land one, often as a result of Mrs Perry's interference. In the second episode, even Maggie's escape route was cut off when Mrs Perry landed a menial job at the school where she taught! A second series followed in May 1979 making 14 programmes in all.
Theme music: Laurie Holloway. Producers: David Askey, John Reardon, Simon Brett.

THE MAGNIFICENT EVANS
BBC. First broadcast: 6 September 1984

Ronnie Barker starred as Plantagenet Evans, a Welsh photographer with his eye and lens on the ladies and who also dabbled in woodburning stoves and antiques of doubtful origin. He was a flamboyant character, driven by money and lust. His assistant Rachel (Sharon Morgan) was also his long-suffering fiancée, while the ever-devoted Willie (Dickie Arnold) traipsed around carrying equipment and sandwich-boards at Evans's behest. Six episodes were shown.
Writer: Roy Clarke. Producer: Sydney Lotterby.

MAID MARIAN AND HER MERRY MEN
BBC. First broadcast: 16 November 1989

Tony Robinson wrote this children's series and starred in it himself as the Sheriff of Nottingham.

His writing purveyed Robin Hood (Wayne Morris) as a wimp and all the men of Sherwood Forest were terrorised by Maid Marian (Kate Lonergan). Indeed, the traditional disciples were replaced by an odd bunch which included Barrington (Danny John-Jules), Rabies (Howard Lew Lewis) and Little Ron (Mike Edmonds). The role of King John was played by Forbes Collins. There were 18 editions over three series, ending on 11 February 1993. The first two series were directed by David Bell.
Producer: Richard Callanan.

MAJOR DAD
USA PRESENTED BY BBC.
First broadcast (UK): 8 January 1990

Polly Cooper (Shanna Reed) was a reporter for the *Oceanside Chronicle* and was sent to cover a story on the Marine Corps. While there, she met Major John D MacGillis (Gerald McRaney). They fell in love but their path to the altar was not made easy by friends of the conservative career-soldier, nor by Polly's two daughters Elizabeth (Marisa Ryan) and Robin (Nicole Dubuc). Six editions were shown.
Producer: Will MacKenzie.

MAKIN' IT
ABC (AMERICA) PRESENTED BY ITV.
First broadcast (UK): 12 April 1979

This teen comedy created by Mark Rothman and Lowell Ganz followed the adventures of Italian-American high school student Billy Manucci (David Naughton) and the trials and tribulations resulting from growing up in his generation. These were shared by his brother Tony (Greg Antonacci) and sisters Tina (Denise Miller) and Dorothy (Ellen Travolta). A total of nine shows were made.
Producers: David Duclan, Deborah Leschin.

MAKING FACES
BBC. First broadcast: 25 September 1975

Sixteen years in the life of Jewish girl Zoya (Eleanor Bron) were covered in Michael Frayn's six half-hour episodes. Her very urbane introspective on her own meanings of life were shared with boyfriend – and later husband – Stuart (Tim Preece) and a variety of new characters each week. Each new person Zoya met made her feel a different person in herself.
Director: Gareth Gwenlan. Producer: Robert Chetwyn.

MAKING OUT
BBC. First broadcast: 6 January 1989

Based on an idea by Franc Roddam, the 24 episodes, each of 50 minutes' duration, were written by Debbie Horsfield. They spanned three series, ending on 12 November 1991. The setting was the Manchester factory of New Line Electronics, a converted mill where a gang of girls assembled modern components and shared their 'men problems' as they struggled to make ends meet. The cast was large but the principals by and large stayed the course. The boss for the first two series was sexy Rex (Keith Allen), the object of desire for glamorous granny Carol May (Shirley Stelfox) who had marriage problems. The girls' shop steward was Pauline (Rachel Davies) who had aspirations of gentility, but the true spiritual and practical leader was Queenie (Margi Clarke) who enjoyed nothing better than pitching into battle on behalf of one of the others. She was married to layabout petty criminal Chunky (Brian Hibbard). Rex's secretary was Norma (Tracie Bennett) who rose from her mousey existence to climb the management ladder, forging ahead of middle manager Bernie (Alan David). Donna (Heather Tobias) longed for motherhood and finally achieved it, and newcomer to the factory Jill (Melanie Kilburn), who had a family to feed, got herself involved with Irish Manchester United star Gavin (John Lynch). Klepto (Moya Brady) always had to evade the strictures of her all-male orthodox Greek family in order to pursue her enthusiasm for life and love. She was an avid Mills and Boon fan. Other regular characters included Simon (Gary Beadle), Ray (Tim Dantay), Rosie (Jane Hazlegrove) and Frankie (John Forgeham).
Directors: Chris Bernard, Richard Spence, Carol Wilks, Noella Smith, John Woods. Producers: John Chapman, Carol Wilks.

MALCOLM
BBC RADIO. First broadcast: 22 February 1978

Mike Goddard starred as Malcolm Atkinson, a well-intentioned but unemployable lad as successive employers found out over the six weeks of the show. Paula Tilbrook played Malcolm's mother who shared her exasperations with Mrs Ross (Cynthia Michaelis). The series was set in the Northern borough of Gawthorpe.
Writer: Terry Gregson. Producer: Bob Oliver Rogers.

MAMA MALONE
CBS (AMERICA) PRESENTED BY CHANNEL 4.
First broadcast (UK): 18 February 1984

English actress Lila Kaye starred as Italian matriarch Mama Malone who had her own TV cookery show in New York. While preparing her dishes she also undertook to solve people's problems. She had a son Dino (Don Amendolia), a divorced daughter Connie (Randee Heller) and a grandson Frankie (Evan Richards). Thirteen episodes were shown.
Producers: Paul Bogart and Terrence McNally.

MAN ABOUT THE HOUSE
THAMES. First broadcast: 14 August 1973

When it began, this series by John Esmonde and Bob Larbey was rather daring in that it was not common-place at the time for mixed sexes to share a home. The setting was Earl's Court, London, where Chrissy (Paula Wilcox) and Jo (Sally Thomsett) shared a flat. They were looking for a third girl to share with them but ended up with Robin Tripp (Richard O'Sullivan) whom they found asleep in the bath after a party. He was a trainee chef and he was permitted to move in on the understanding that he would cook, carry coal and observe that the girls' bedroom was strictly out of bounds. The landlords, Mr and Mrs Roper (Brian Murphy and Yootha Joyce) who occupied the basement, took a dim view of the arrangement, as did Chrissy's mother (Daphne Oxenford) who, in the second episode, arrived to stay the night just as Robin had installed himself in the spare room. Money was always a problem and they had to pull out all the stops to pay the rent to the weak-willed but mean-minded Mr Roper. By the third series, in October 1974, Robin had failed his catering examinations and had palled up with a lecherous chap named Larry (Doug Fisher). There was a romantic spark between Chrissy and Robin which grew slowly but steadily. However, they never did get married, even when the wedding bells were ringing in the sixth series.
Producer: Peter Frazer-Jones.

THE MANAGEMENT
CHANNEL 4. First broadcast: 27 January 1988

Gareth Hale and Norman Pace developed their stand-up characterisations, the Two Rons, into six full half-hour episodes which they wrote and in which they played the starring roles. The Two Rons inherited a nightclub in an unenviable part of

London from their late Uncle Arthur. They then had to recruit their management team to run the operation. The nucleus of their manpower to support their own menacing stewardship was provided by Mr and Mrs Crusty (Bryan Pringle and Vilma Hollingbery), chef Typhus Los Bentos (Andy Linden) and Aunty Vicky (Barbara Windsor) who established a shop within the club. The glamorous front was provided by Fiona (Serena Evans) and Naomi (Kate McKenzie).

Director: John Gorman. Producer: Charlie Hanson for LWT.

MANN'S BEST FRIENDS

CHANNEL 4. First broadcast: 15 April 1985

Hamish James Ordway (Fulton Mackay) retired from the Water Board and moved into lodgings where the landlords were the free-and-easy Mr and Mrs Henry Mann (Barry Stanton and Barbara Hicks). Ordway's fellow tenants included Doll (Patricia Brake), Duncan (Bernard Bresslaw) and Irvin (Clive Merrison). The relaxed atmosphere of the building did not suit Ordway, who was a nosey-parker and an extreme fusspot. He resolved to put the house in order. Six editions were screened.

Writer: Roy Clarke. Producer: Derrick Goodwin for Thames.

THE MANY WIVES OF PATRICK

LWT. First broadcast: 4 September 1976

Patrick Cargill starred as Patrick Woodford, a wealthy antique dealer who had been married six times and had nine children and several grandchildren. The first series began with Patrick trying to divorce wife number six, Helen (Elizabeth Counsell), so that he might remarry wife number one, Elizabeth (Ursula Howells). Surveying the many intricacies of his wife troubles was his mother (Agnes Lauchlan), who gave her advice freely. Patrick's assistant at his antiques shop was Harold (Robin Parkinson). The show, created and written by Richard Waring, returned for a second season on 11 June 1977.

Producer: William G Stewart.

MARBLEHEAD MANOR

USA PRESENTED BY CHANNEL 4.
First broadcast (UK): 17 January 1989

The setting for the 24 editions of this show was the smart estate of highly eccentric millionaire Randolph Stonehill (Bob Fraser) and his wife Hilary (Linda Thorson). They were surrounded by an oddball assortment of servants including Rick the gardener, (Michael Richards), Albert Dudley (Paxton Whitehead), Jerry Stockton (Phil Morris), Dwayne Stockton (Rodney Scott Hudson) and Lupe (Dyana Ortelli).

MARJORIE AND MEN

ANGLIA. First broadcast: 28 June 1985

Patricia Routledge starred as happy-go-lucky divorcée Marjorie Belton who, in spite of her meddlesome mother, Alice Tripp (Patricia Hayes), managed to date a different man each episode during the six-week run. Marjorie worked in a bank where her colleagues included Henry Bartlett (James Cossins) and Sid Parkin (Ronnie Stevens).

Writer and director: John Gorrie. Producer: John Rosenberg.

MARRIAGE LINES

BBC. First broadcast: 16 August 1963

Writer Richard Waring, who had acted with Richard Briers the previous year in BROTHERS IN LAW, created this vehicle specially for Briers' talents. Briers was cast as George Starling, with Prunella Scales as his young bride Kate. The stories, which began as the couple returned from their Paris honeymoon, dealt with the difficulties and adjustments encountered in early married life. Anything adrift from perfect harmony gave rise to serious fears of incompatibility. George was a junior and lowly-paid City clerk and, in the first series, they set up home in a furnished flat in Earl's Court. Initially they had friendly neighbours, Peter and Norah (Ronald Hines and Christine Finn), but they soon left for a better address, leaving the Starlings discontented with their lot. By the second season, they, too, were looking to make a move. They averaged in the region of three rows per week, often as a result of George seeking out his old pals at the pub while Kate remained stuck at home. Money was in desperately short supply and repossessions of goods on hire-purchase took place. As George earned only £12 a week, Kate had to face the prospect of going out to work. Then she became pregnant. The third series began with the imminent arrival of 'The Cuckoo', as George referred to the unborn child. He was miffed that pregnancy had robbed him of his social life and multiplied his domestic chores,

not to mention all the floor space being occupied by maternity gear. Kate gave birth to a daughter, Helen. The last of 43 editions was seen on 3 June 1966.
Producer: Graeme Muir

BBC RADIO. First broadcast: 21 May 1965

In an unusual move, a series of 13 editions of this title began on radio while the television version was still in production. Richard Waring again wrote the scripts while Richard Briers and Prunella Scales reprised their roles as George and Kate Starling. However, their neighbours Norah and Peter were portrayed by Heather Chasen and Geoffrey Matthews. A run of 13 more shows ended 11 June 1966.
Producer: Charles Maxwell.

MARRIED
USA PRESENTED BY BBC.
First broadcast (UK): 27 April 1980

Richard and Libby Chapin (Beau Bridges and Helen Shaver) were a well-off, modern married couple with two children, Dylan and Nicky (Rossie Harris and Justin Dana). Just one subject sparked off their frequent rows – money! Six editions were screened.
Producer: Larry Gelbart.

MARRIED WITH CHILDREN
USA PRESENTED BY ITV.
First broadcast (UK): 8 January 1990

After 16 years of married life, the flame of love had died for Al and Peggy Bundy (Ed O'Neill and Katey Sagal), who now lived a life of compromise in which both suffered equally. They had two children, Bud and Kelly (David Faustino and Christina Applegate), and a family dog named Buck. Al had a shoe store. Their neighbours were Steve and Marcy (David Garrison and Amanda Bearse). The first series of 26 editions was followed by second run of 26 beginning on 9 June 1991.

THE MARSHALL CHRONICLES
USA PRESENTED BY CHANNEL 4.
First broadcast (UK): 11 July 1991

Marshall Brightman (Joshua Rifkind) attended high school where he appeared to be the only honest, all-round good egg in a dishonest world. Marshall's opposite was the school hoodlum Johnny Parmetko (Gabriel Bologna) whose girlfriend Melissa Sandler

(Nile Lanning) was Marshall's dream girl. Both boys had sisters, Cynthia Brightman (Jennifer Salt) and Donna Parmetko (Karen Medak). Hovering in the middle was Leslie Barash (Meredith Scott Lynn). Seven episodes were screened.

MARY
CBS (AMERICA) PRESENTED BY CHANNEL 4.
First broadcast (UK): 3 November 1986

Mary Tyler Moore starred as Mary Brenner, a divorcée who joined a third-rate newspaper, the *Chicago Eagle*, as agony aunt. Her work environment was shared by her boss, Frank DeMarco (James Farentino) and the paper's drama critic Ed LaSalle (John Astin). Other regulars included Tully (David Byrd) and Jo Tucker (Katey Sagal). Channel 4 dotted the shows sporadically through the schedule.
Created and produced by David Isaacs and Ken Levine for MTM.

THE MARY TYLER MOORE SHOW
CBS (AMERICA) PRESENTED BY BBC.
First broadcast (UK): 13 February 1971

Mary Tyler Moore starred as Mary Richards, unmarried and in her thirties, who said adieu to a four-year romance and walked into a new career as an associate producer in the newsroom of her local TV station, WJMTV, in Minneapolis St Paul. Her boss at work was Lou Grant (Edward Asner) and her colleagues were the wisecracking Murray Slaughter (Gavin MacLeod) and the vain and not very intelligent Ted Baxter (Ted Knight). Mary's home life was taken up with her friends and neighbours: New York Jewess Rhoda Morgenstern (Valerie Harper), also in her thirties and unmarried so they were able to panic together; Phyllis Lindstrom (Cloris Leachman), whom Mary later hired as her newsroom assistant; and Sue Ann Nivens (Betty White). Over a seven-year period 120 episodes were recorded in front of a live studio audience. See also RHODA and PHYLLIS.
Creators: James Brooks, Allan Burns and Grant Tinker. Music: Sonny Curtis. Director: Jay Sandrich. An MTM production.

MAUDE
CBS (AMERICA) PRESENTED BY ITV.
First broadcast (UK): 26 February 1976

Beatrice Arthur starred as Maude Findlay, a middle-class woman living happily in the New York

suburb of Tuckahoe with her latest husband, Walter (Bill Macy). Nearby lived her divorced daughter, Carol (Adrienne Barbeau), the product of one of Maude's unsuccessful marriages. Maude had a belief that she was able to cope with life and all its stresses yet, in reality, her ability so to cope was often found wanting. The Findlay's neighbour, Arthur Harmon, was played by Conrad Bain. Walter was an alcoholic and stifled Maude's ambition to seek public office. Over the 140 episodes made in the USA, the series tackled various serious issues involving feminist causes but never lost sight of the comedy objective. Only a handful of the total product was screened in the UK.
Producer: Norman Lear.

MAY TO DECEMBER
BBC. First broadcast: 2 April 1989

Paul A Mendelson created and wrote this saga of the generation gap which followed the meeting, courtship and marriage of late middle-aged solicitor Alec Callender (Anton Rodgers) and very much younger Zoe Angell (Eve Matheson, later Lesley Dunlop). The action took place either in Alec's home, into which Zoe moved even before their marriage, or in the offices of the family firm of solicitors, where he was senior partner over his son from his first marriage, Jamie (Paul Venables). Working in the office with them were the very prim and proper Miss Vera Flood (Frances White), who to everyone's surprise, including her own, became Mrs Tipple, and the deliciously unprim and suggestively improper Hilary (Rebecca Lacey). The characters were constant until the 1994 series when Hilary left for the Isle of Wight where she would be able to see more of her boyfriend, who happened to be a guest of Her Majesty's in Parkhurst. She was replaced in the office by Rosie MacConnachy (Ashley Jensen). Alec's daughter Simone, again from his first marriage, was played by Carolyn Pickles and Zoe's mother Dot was portrayed by Kate Williams. Zoe gave birth to a baby girl whom they named Fleur (Charlotte Perry). There had been 41 episodes when the sixth series ended on 27 May 1994.
Directors: Sydney Lotterby, Paul Harrison, John Kilby. Producers: Sydney Lotterby, Sharon Bloom for Cinema Verity.

ME AND MY GIRL
LWT. First broadcast: 31 August 1984

John Kane created this format which ran to 37 editions over six series. Richard O'Sullivan starred

as irresponsible widower Simon Harrap who was trying to bring up his young teenage daughter Samantha (Joanne Ridley). Following the death of his wife, Simon's mother-in-law Nell Cresset (Joan Sanderson) moved in to lend a hand, although by series three they also had a housekeeper, Isobel McCluskey (Sandra Clarke). Simon worked at an advertising agency called Eyecatchers where his best friend and partner was Derek Yates (Tim Brooke-Taylor). The secretary was Liz (Joanne Campbell). Derek was married to the fearsome Muriel and had a daughter Emma, but viewers never met them. Simon's main problem was to divert Samantha's interest away from boys and towards her school work. The last programme was seen on 5th November 1988.
Writers: John Kane, Bernard McKenna, Colin Bostock-Smith. Producer: John Reardon.

ME AND THE MISSUS
BBC RADIO. First broadcast: 4 July 1971

Bill Fraser was Me and Patricia Hayes was The Missus in this seven-part domestic comedy series. Robert Dorning played neighbour Mr Harris.
Writers: David Cumming and Derek Collyer. Producer: Trafford Whitelock.

ME MAMMY
BBC. First broadcast: 27 October 1969

Milo O'Shea starred as bachelor Bunjy Kennefick who worked as a top executive with a large company in London's West End. He had a luxury flat in Regent's Park and drove a sports car. He was the envy of all his married friends but he was still Mammy's boy. His mother Mrs Kennefick was played by Anna Manahan and his secretary Miss Argyll was portrayed by Yootha Joyce. There were eight shows in the first series. From the second series starting 7 August 1970, David Kelly joined the regular cast as Cousin Enda. The last of 22 episodes was seen on 4 June 1971.
Writer: Hugh Leonard. Producers: James Gilbert, Sydney Lotterby.

ME, YOU AND HIM
THAMES. First broadcast: 30 July 1992

Mark (Steve Punt), John (Nick Hancock) and Harry (Hugh Dennis) had been school friends and later gone on to college. When this six-part series began, they were experiencing difficulties in adapting to

life after college. As they emerged into the real world, they found it hard to put aside childish things. Harry had spent three years abroad, so it was a testing time for the durability of friendship. Punt, Hancock and Dennis also wrote the shows.
Producer: John Stroud.

MEET CHRISTOPHER BLAZE

BBC RADIO. First broadcast: 5 July 1951

Jack Hulbert starred in the title role. When his elderly aunt died, he inherited the ownership of *The Sentinel* newspaper. A condition of the bequest was that he give up his position as a Scotland Yard detective inspector. He complied without a second thought and arrived in Fleet Street to find *The Sentinel* in dire straits with deadly-dull editor Mr Meek (James Thomason) relegating crime stories to the back page. With the cooperation of crime reporter Smithy (Hamilton Dyce), Blaze set out to sensationalise the paper and turn its fortunes around. Although Blaze came under threat from the crooks he subsequently exposed, their menace was nothing to that which he endured from his dragon of a housekeeper Mrs Gimble (Elizabeth Maude). There were eight editions broadcast.
Writer: Edward J Mason. Producer: Martyn C Webster.

MEET THE CHAMP

BBC. First broadcast: 22 September 1960

Sid Colin created and wrote this series of six editions which starred Bernard Bresslaw as a gormless boxer and Jimmy James as his manager. Bernie's girlfriend, played by Vilma Ann Leslie, felt Bernie should become a park attendant or some other honest worker but Jimmy saw him as potential champion material and a provider of pound notes. Also in on the boxing act was Peter Butterworth as the trainer.
Producer: G.B. Lupino.

MEET THE HUGGETTS

BBC RADIO. First broadcast: 2 July 1953

Joe and Ethel Huggett (Jack Warner and Kathleen Harrison) were first introduced to the British public in the 1947 movie *Holiday Camp*. The idea for the typical Cockney couple came from Godfrey Winn, and a formidable team of writers contributed to the screenplay including Muriel and Sidney Box, Ted Willis, Peter Rogers and Mabel and Denis Constanduros. Three further films followed: *Here Come the Huggetts*, *Vote For the Huggetts* and *The Huggetts Abroad*. Six years after the original film, scriptwriter Eddie Maguire took the same two characters and the same two actors and created MEET THE HUGGETTS for radio. The series ran for nine years and Maguire wrote more than 150 half-hour episodes.

Joe was retired from the police force, although for the first two years he remained a special constable. He was deeply suspicious of all things new and had a fondness for bacon and sausages. He occupied many of his leisure hours tending his strawberry patch adjacent to the dustbin. Ethel spent her days worrying about everyone except herself. She was an avid reader of her daily horoscope, the portents of which could make or mar the next 24 hours. The Huggetts had a son, Harry, who was away in the forces. He never appeared through the nine seasons. They also had a teenage daughter Jane (1953 Joan Dowling, 1954 Vera Day, 1955 Valerie Jean, 1956–57 Marian Collins, 1958 Cynthia Bizeray, 1959–61 Alanna Boyce) and a younger son Bobby (1953–55 Anthony Green, 1956 Christopher Saunders, 1957–58 George Howell, 1959 James Langley, 1960 Michael Hammond, 1960–61 Malcolm Ranson).

In 1953 the Huggetts had two featured neighbours, attractive policewoman Peggy Cartwright (Mary Mackenzie) and the North-Country Bert Oakroyd (Sidney Vivian). However, from episode 11 of the 1954 series they vanished and were replaced by Fred Stebbings (Charles Leno). All other characters required for Maguire's stories were played by Kenneth Connor (1953–57), John Cazabon (1958, 1961), Warren Mitchell (1958–60) and Bill Pertwee (1961).

The Huggetts was an attempt to portray the typical family of post-war Britain. They lived in a little house in a little street in a big city. They had the problems of everyman: a lost wage-packet, spring-cleaning or laying a concrete path, making ends meet or getting along with each other.
Producers: Peter Eton (1953–56) and Jacques Brown (1957–61).

MEET THE REV

BBC RADIO. First broadcast: 8 July 1947

Gale Pedrick wrote these 15-minute shows which were set in an East End club for boys. Hugh Morton starred as Rev. Simon Cherry with Roy Plomley (of

'Desert Island Discs' fame) as Charlie Banks, pub landlord at The Lovers' Knot. Eleven editions were broadcast.
Producer: Audrey Cameron.

MEET THE WIFE
BBC. First broadcast: 14 April 1964

Writers Ronald Wolfe and Ronald Chesney created the characters Thora and Freddie Blacklock (Thora Hird and Freddie Frinton) for a *Comedy Playhouse* entitled 'The Bed' which was screened on 28 December 1963. This one-off half-hour, produced by John Paddy Carstairs, concerned the couple shortly after their silver wedding. Their matrimonial bed was lumpy and bumpy and Thora yearned for new twin beds.

Viewers were quick to identify with Thora and Freddie and the subsequent series, MEET THE WIFE, ran for three series. The last of 23 editions was screened on 19 December 1966. The comedy never descended into farce but strove to represent the reality of so many middle-aged married couples. That their marriage would not survive was never contemplated. They lived in modest comfort in a nice little home with a car, a telly and the odd quarrel. Theirs were the everyday ups-and-downs of married life.
Theme music: Russ Conway. Producers included: John Paddy Carstairs, Graeme Muir and Robin Nash.

MELLORS AND SELLERS
BBC RADIO. First broadcast: 5 January 1977

This comedy thriller was written by Alan Melville and broadcast in four 45-minute episodes. During Parliament's summer recess, two MPs found themselves holidaying at Royal Lytham St Anne's Golf Club and became jointly involved in a chain of mysteries. They were Conservative Vincent Mellors (Edward Hardwicke) and Labour Arnold Sellers (Robert Lang).
Producer: John Tydeman.

MELODY AND CO
BBC RADIO. First broadcast: 30 May 1940

This variety format starred Irish comedian Jimmy O'Dea as himself, a comedian with enthusiasm, ideas and a good show, but no money to enable him to play anywhere. He met a backer, a rich young man who needed a job in order to induce his

girlfriend, a reporter, to marry him. He agreed to finance Jimmy but one of the conditions was that the show must always play in a place where the girl was sent on newspaper jobs. This resulted in Jimmy's having to play run-down or fit-up venues. The characters were Mike (Jack Melford), Penny (Patricia Leonard), Angel (Marion Wilson), Roddy (Sam Costa) and the poor old props man (Jacques Brown) who spent long days in railway luggage vans. Nine editions were broadcast.
Writers: Aubrey Danvers-Walker and Harry O'Donovan. Producer: Vernon Harris.

MEN BEHAVING BADLY
THAMES. First broadcast: 18 February 1992

Simon Nye adapted his own novel of the same title into a six-part series which starred Harry Enfield as Dermot and Martin Clunes as Gary. They shared a flat which was always a mess and shared lurid sexual fantasies about their neighbour Deborah (Leslie Ash). They both had problems with girls, ditching some and falling in love with unattainable others. They used locker-room language and behaved in a generally rowdy way. When a second series of six programmes came to the screen on 8 September the same year, Dermot had left to travel round the world and Gary had a new flatmate, Tony (Neil Morrissey), who was no more concerned about the washing-up or leaving dirty socks lying around than Dermot had been. Other regular characters included Gary's girlfriend Dorothy (Caroline Quentin), and the series returned for a third run in 1994, on the BBC.
Director: Martin Dennis. Producer: Beryl Vertue.

THE MEN FROM THE MINISTRY
BBC RADIO. First broadcast: 30 October 1962

Edward Taylor created and produced this very long-running series which finally came to an end after 15 seasons on 22 August 1977. The actual ministry was not specified but the action took place within the General Assistance Department of the Civil Service which existed to help any other overloaded section. The operatives could be passed around various ministries. The head of the department was Roland Hamilton-Jones (Wilfrid Hyde White) and his assistant was the muddled and confused Richard Lamb (Richard Murdoch). The Permanent Under-Secretary, a wild character named Sir Gregory Pitkin, was portrayed by Roy Dotrice. Office efficiency came from secretary Diana (Diana Olsson) and, from

1966, Mildred Murfin (Norma Ronald). Wilfrid Hyde White ultimately left the cast and the new head of department was Mr Lennox-Brown (Deryk Guyler). Dotrice also left after four years.
Writers: Edward Taylor, Johnnie Mortimer and Brian Cooke.

MEN OF AFFAIRS
HTV. First broadcast: 3 October 1973

Michael Pertwee created and wrote this six-part series in which Warren Mitchell starred as government minister Sir William and Brian Rix as his Parliamentary Private Secretary, Barry Ovis MP. They worked closely together, although rarely to good effect.
Director: Derek Clark. Producer: Wallace Douglas.

MEN OF THE WORLD
BBC. First broadcast: 14 March 1994

David Threlfall starred as Lenny Smart, a cynical know-all in his mid-30s who managed a branch of Tymans Travel in Greater Manchester. His assistant in the agency, Kendle Bains (John Simm), was also his lodger. Kendle was ten years younger than Lenny, and Lenny saw it as his mission in life to save his young charge from a fate similar to his own: he had been deeply hurt when his wife left him, and had reverted to macho juvenile behaviour with scant respect for women. Kendle, on the other hand, was romantic and full of optimism. The six-part series was written by Daniel Peacock who also played the part of Gilby Watson, a dopey window-cleaner and mate of Lenny's.
Director: Terry Kinane. Producers: Laurence Marks, Maurice Gran and Claire Hinson for Alomo.

MERRY-GO-ROUND
BBC RADIO

This wartime title was a mixture of music and gags and is included only because it gave birth to STAND EASY, MUCH-BINDING-IN-THE-MARSH and WATERLOGGED SPA.

THE MERRYMART
BBC RADIO. First broadcast: 26 November 1945

This was originally intended as a vehicle for Cockney comedian Alf Goddard, but he fell ill just hours before the recording of the first programme. Dick Francis stepped in to assume the role of Mr Jolly,

the manager of The Merrymart store. His two assistants were Miss Fitt (Audrey Wayne) and Basil (Alfie Dean, one half of the variety act Collinson and Dean). As was the fashion at the time, there were weekly guests who made the store a setting for what was basically a variety show.
Producer: Ernest Longstaffe.

MESS MATES
GRANADA. First broadcast: 28 June 1960

The SS Guernsey was known to its odd crew as 'The Old Cow'. Their commander was Captain Biskett (Archie Duncan) and he was joined aboard the little coastal vessel by Mate 'Tug' Nelson (Victor Maddern), the bosun 'Croaker' Jones (Sam Kydd), Willie McGuinness (Fulton Mackay) and 'Blarney' Finnigan (Dermot Kelly). For the second series, which began 12 September 1961, Captain Biskett had a new command, the MV Continuity. Only Croaker Jones from his former crew remained with him. New recruits were engineer 'Twinkle' Martin (Michael Balfour), 1st Mate 'Dapper' Drake (Ronald Hines), and the ship's cook 'Fry Up' Dodds (Frank Atkinson). These stayed with Biskett for his third command, the MV Jersey Lily.
Writers: Talbot Rothwell and Lew Schwarz. Producers: Kenneth Carter, Eric Fawcett, Graeme McDonald.

MICKEY
USA PRESENTED BY ITV.
First broadcast (UK): 21 February 1966

Former child film-star Mickey Rooney (he was Huckleberry Finn in the 1939 movie) starred in this series of ten episodes as happy-go-lucky landlubber Mickey Grady who inherited a floating hotel, known as a boatel, on the California coast. Mickey had a wife Nora (Emmaline Henry) and two sons. The eldest, Tim, was played by Rooney's real-life son Tim Rooney, and the younger son, Buddy, was played by Brian Nash. The boatel situation gave adequate scope for the introduction of guest stars who were met by the crafty, but good-natured manager Sammy Ling (Sammee Tong).
Director: Richard Whorf. Producer: Selig J Seligman.

MIKE AND ANGELO
THAMES. First broadcast: 14 September 1989

This children's series is, at the time of writing, playing its sixth season after more than 70 episodes.

Divorced American writer Rita King (Shelley Thompson) had arrived in London to start a new life with her son Mike (Matt Wright, later Michael Benz). In the house which she bought, Michael explored the ramshackle rooms and in an old wardrobe discovered Angelo (Tyler Butterworth, later Tim Whitnall), a rather inept alien with the ability to walk up walls and across ceilings. Mike and he became pals and Angelo lived as part of the family. Other regular characters included Mr Pinner (John Levitt) and Philippa (Alessia Gwyther), and occasional characters included Mike's dad Tony (Jeff Harding), Rita's mum (Libby Morris) and Angelo's dad (Ron Moody).
Producer: Charles Warren.

MIKE AND BERNIE

THAMES. First broadcast: 14 December 1971

Mike and Bernie Winters' brief sortie into sitcom was scripted by Vince Powell and Harry Driver and lasted just one series. They more or less played themselves, a double act trying to forge a career in show business. Bernard Spear played their agent Lionel Ross, 'the Lew Grade of Lewisham'.
Producer: Stuart Allen.

MIND YOUR LANGUAGE

LWT. First broadcast: 30 December 1977

Barry Evans starred as Jeremy Brown who was a teacher of English to mature foreign students. The principal of the college where he taught was the dragon-like Miss Courtney (Zara Nutley), who heaped much criticism on Jeremy's classes. Among his students were Danielle Faure (Françoise Pascal), Ali Nadim (Dino Shafeek), Jamila Ranjha (Jamila Massey), Juan Cervantes (Ricardo Montez), and Anna Schmidt (Jacki Harding), who at one point was advised to marry an Englishman in order to stay in the country. She picked Jeremy Brown as a likely candidate. Others were Giovanni Cupello (George Camiller), Chung Su-Lee (Pik-Sen Lim), Taro Nagazumi (Robert Lee) and Maximillian Papandrious (Kevork Malikyan). The series was created and written by Vince Powell, and there were further series starting October 1978 and November 1979. In 1986 the formula was resurrected for 13 more episodes, starting 4 January, and the former caretaker Sid (Tommy Godfrey) had been replaced by Henshawe (Harry Littlewood).
Producer: Stuart Allen.

MIND YOUR OWN BUSINESS

BBC RADIO. First broadcast: 22 December 1987

Bernard Cribbins starred as Jimmy Bright, boss of Brightco International. He was a tycoon with fingers in many pies and his principal aides were Nan Forbes (Annette Crosbie), accountant Russell Farrow (Frank Thornton) and his assistant Sue Plant (Annee Blott). Kenneth Connor was occasionally heard as Jenks, the gateman. The last of 25 editions over four series was heard on 14 June 1991.
Writer: Andrew Palmer. Producer: Edward Taylor.

MINDER

THAMES. First broadcast: 29 October 1979

This creation by Leon Griffiths came to an end after nearly fifteen years when the 107th edition was transmitted on 17 March 1994. The two principal characters were used-car dealer Arthur Daley (George Cole), who also kept a lock-up in which he stored a variety of merchandise which happened to fall off the backs of lorries, and his 'minder' or bodyguard, thick Cockney Terry McCann (Dennis Waterman) who had served a brief prison sentence and wished to keep out of further trouble. Daley, a cigar-smoking spiv with expensive tastes in clothing, coined two catchphrases, the first, 'a nice little earner', related to his dodgy business schemes, and the second to his never-seen wife to whom he referred as "Er indoors'. The police were represented by the droll but dogged Det. Sgt Chisholm (Patrick Malahide) who was weekly on the trail of some petty crime, or, in his absence, Sgt Rycott (Peter Childs).

Daley conned and underpaid Terry and steered him into dangerous predicaments while managing to distance himself from most trouble spots. The serious business of business and drinking took place in The Winchester where the landlord was Dave (Glyn Edwards). In 1991 Waterman opted to quit the show and in an inspired piece of crafting and casting, Daley was given a new 'minder', his nephew Ray Daley portrayed by Gary Webster. Ray was the antithesis of lager-swilling Terry. He was bright, had a couple of 'O' levels and sipped non-alcoholic drinks. His character proved equally popular as Terry, often funnier, and the series maintained its position as one of the most revered in the annals of British television. Other significant participants remembered by devotees include Des (George Layton), Maurice (Anthony Valentine), Yorkie (Brian Glover) and Whaley (Roy Kinnear).

Many writers and directors contributed over the ten seasons.

Producers: Verity Lambert, Johnny Goodman, Lloyd Shirley, George Taylor, Ian Toynton for Euston Films.

THE MISFIT

ATV. First broadcast: 3 March 1970

Roy Clarke created and wrote these six one-hour stories about 50-year-old rubber planter Basil 'Badger' Allenby-Johnson (Ronald Fraser), who returned from Malaya to find a very changed England. In the first episode, 'Badger', a man of staunch Edwardian standards and the complete misfit in his Panama hat, was unable to comprehend the permissive society. His son Ted (Simon Ward) and his liberal daughter-in-law Alicia (Susan Carpenter) sent shock waves through him by their open-mindedness and casual behaviour. More shocks awaited 'Badger' when he was forced to travel North in a vain search for suitable employment. A second series was made in 1971.

Director: James Gatward. Producer: Dennis Vance.

MISFITS

YTV. First broadcast: 5 June 1981

Eric Chappell wrote this six-part series in which Mrs Liz Ridgway was living a peaceful existence in middle-class rural Yorkshire until Skinner and Oscar (Enn Reitel and Kevin Lloyd) burst into her life and turned it upside down. Anne Stallybrass starred as Mrs Ridgway and her two supposedly temporary lodgers were allegedly on their way to Katmandu. In the opening episode a gold cigarette case went missing and fingers of suspicion pointed at the young travellers. Mrs Ridgway's friend, Monica Forbes, was played by Marcia Ashton.

Producer: Ronnie Baxter.

MISLEADING CASES

BBC. First broadcast: 27 June 1967

AP Herbert's stories were adapted for television by Alan Melville, with additional scenes written by Henry Cecil and Christopher Bond. Roy Dotrice starred as Albert Haddock, the stickler for litigation who tried to introduce a modicum of common sense into the Common Law, often with the subtle connivance of Mr Justice Swallow (Alastair Sim). Haddock was indefatigable in his pursuit of justice and was usually opposed by Sir Joshua Hoot QC (Thorley Walters). The long-suffering Mrs Haddock was por-

trayed by Avice Landon. The last of 20 programmes over three series was on 10 September 1971.

Producers: Michael Mills, John Howard Davies.

MISS JONES AND SON

THAMES. First broadcast: 18 April 1977

Richard Waring created and wrote these daring – for their time – shows which cast Paula Wilcox as unmarried mother Elizabeth Jones, who was left by her man after a four-year relationship when she had every expectation of wedding bells. In episode three of the first series of six shows she gave birth to her son, Roly. She was totally unprepared for the realities of parenthood, having applied too late for supplementary benefit, failed to make the necessary provisions which would satisfy the health visitor, and failed to come to terms with the fact that her income would be reduced to the point where she could not manage. She was stalwartly supported by her mum and dad (Charlotte Mitchell and Norman Bird) who eventually came round to accepting their grandchild, although initially they had been too embarrassed and ashamed to place a notice of the birth in the *Daily Telegraph*. She had two loyal friends, Rose Tucker (Cass Allen) and her protective but platonic next-door neighbour Geoffrey (Christopher Beeny). Roly (Luke Steensil) was christened Roland Desmond Geoffrey Jones.

The series returned for a second six-week run on 9 January 1978 with Elizabeth's mother now played by Joan Scott. In the first episode of this second series, Geoffrey had to leave for business reasons. His vacant flat was taken by widower David (David Savile), who had a daughter Penny (Catherine Kirkwood). He was a writer, Elizabeth was an artist and he invited her to illustrate his latest book. Their friendship slowly developed and the series ended with three dots . . .

Theme music: Roger Webb. Producer: Peter Frazer-Jones.

MRS MULLIGAN

BBC RADIO

See IRISH HALF HOUR

MRS THURSDAY

ATV. First broadcast: 14 March 1966

In the first episode of this comedy drama series created by Ted Willis, wealthy George Dunrich lay on his deathbed while his four ex-wives gathered like vultures below. But it was for his long-serving charlady Alice Thursday (Kathleen Harrison) that the property tycoon sent, and with his dying breaths he told her she was to inherit his empire, his mansion and his Rolls-Royce. He duly expired and Alice borrowed a horse and cart to move her battered old furniture and possessions from the Mile End Road to Mayfair. Mrs Thursday was a lovable, golden-hearted Cockney but totally ignorant of the ways of business. In this she depended on Richard B Hunter (Hugh Manning) to keep predators at bay, but she learned, gradually, to sort her friends from the leeches. The shows, of 55-minute episodes, ran for two long seasons.

Writers included Ted Willis, Julian Bond, Gerald Kelsey, Diana Morgan, Lew Schwarz, Bruce Stewart, Martin Worth. Directors included William G Stewart, Robert D Cardona, John Cooper, James Ormerod, Alastair Reid. Producer: Jack Williams.

MR AITCH
A-R. First broadcast: 5 January 1967

Dick Clement and Ian La Frenais created Harry Aitch (Harry H Corbett) who, as a baby, had been found in a bag at Harrod's. More than money, Harry sought status. He enjoyed a get-up-and-go outlook on life and had girlfriends galore. His principal asset was half an old house on a bomb site in the centre of London's Bloomsbury area. From this he derived an income of £40 per week by using the land as a car park. However, he would never sell the plot as the idea of making capital was abhorrent to him. He had a couple of sidekicks: Albie, (Norman Chappell) who acted as his chauffeur and valet, and Loftie (Gordon Gostelow).

Theme music: Glen Mason and Keith Miller. Other writers included Dave Freeman and John Junkin. Directors: Christopher Hodson, John Robins and Bill Turner. Producer: Peter Eton.

MR AND MRS NORTH
BBC RADIO. First broadcast: 4 August 1950

This comedy thriller in eight parts was written by husband-and-wife team Richard and Frances Lockridge and starred husband-and-wife team Bernard Braden and Barbara Kelly in the title roles. *Producer: Ian C Messiter.*

MR BIG
BBC. First broadcast: 7 January 1977

Peter Jones and Christopher Bond wrote this series in which Jones also starred as Eddie, the head of a family of small-time crooks who shared a London squat. Eddie had dreams of becoming an underworld king but his dreams and schemes came to nothing. The lady in his life was Dolly (Prunella Scales), who found shop-lifting – but only from the quality shops – easier and more rewarding than messing about with social security. The younger members, who spent much of their time in bed, were layabout and scrounger Ginger (Ian Lavender) and dizzy Norma (Carol Hawkins). A first run of six was followed by seven further editions ending 4 August 1977.

Directors: Dennis Main Wilson, Ray Butt. Producer: Dennis Main Wilson.

MR DEEDS GOES TO TOWN
ABC (AMERICA) PRESENTED BY BBC.
First broadcast (UK): 7 August 1974

The theme of the 1936 movie of the same title was taken up for this 17-episode series which starred Monte Markham as Longfellow Deeds, a small-time newspaperman from a hick town who inherited a multi-million dollar New York business empire. Helping him through the labyrinths ahead was Tony Morris (Pat Harrington). The series was made in 1969 but only began on the BBC five years later. *Producer: Harry Ackerman.*

MR DIGBY, DARLING
YTV. First broadcast: 6 January 1969

Ken Hoare and Mike Sharland created and wrote this rather daring show which enjoyed two runs in 1969. Peter Jones starred as Roland Digby, a married man who was boss of a pesticide firm called Rid-O-Rat. Although home was where his wife was, peace and quiet, warmed slippers and cooked breakfast were all served at the office by his secretary, Thelma Teesdale (Sheila Hancock). She was obsessively protective and ambitious for him. Her efforts on his behalf were often frantic and hairbrained. Other regular characters included Mr Trumper (Brian Oulton), Olive (Beryl Cooke), Mr Bailey (Peter Stephens), Norman Stanhope (Michael Bates) and Joyce (Janet Brown). *Producers: Bill Hitchcock, Christopher Hodson.*

MR DON AND MR GEORGE
CHANNEL 4. First broadcast: 25 August 1993

Jack Docherty and Moray Hunter created, wrote and portrayed two characters, Donald McDiarmid and George McDiarmid, for a series of sketches which were part of the series *Absolutely*. They were then given their own six-part show. Though they shared the same surname, Mr Don and Mr George were not related. They were just good but highly eccentric friends who together explored a highly eccentric world.

Producer: Alan Nixon.

MR ED

CBS (AMERICA) PRESENTED BY ITV.
First broadcast (UK): 2 July 1962

In 1950, Donald O'Connor starred in a movie, *Francis*, as an Army private who befriended a talking mule called Francis. This was based on a novel of the same title by David Stern. By 1967 O'Connor had followed-up with six sequel pictures, and there was a seventh with Mickey Rooney in O'Connor's role. In 1960 the director of *Francis*, Arthur Lubin, had transferred the concept to civilian suburbia, changed the mule to a palomino horse and cast English-born actor Alan Young as Wilbur Post, the owner of the horse Mr Ed. The talking horse would talk to nobody other than Wilbur and in no other person's presence. However, he would answer the telephone in the stables if no-one else was around. The voice of the horse (Allan 'Rocky' Lane) projected Wilbur into all sorts of situations which forced him into clumsy explanations of his behaviour, especially to his wife Carol (Connie Hines). Equally confused by Wilbur's apparent eccentricities were the neighbours, Mr and Mrs Addison (Larry Keating and Edna Skinner). The Addisons were featured in the first 78 episodes but following the death of Keating the Posts acquired new neighbours, Colonel Gordon and Winnie Kirkwood, played by Leon Ames and Florence MacMichael for a further 65 episodes. Mr Ed had highbrow tastes with a wide knowledge and appreciation of music and the arts. He did enjoy television, although he refused to watch Westerns as so many of his relatives got killed! The show ran for six years.

Writers included William Burns, Lou Derman, Bob O'Brian, Norman Paul and Ben Starr. Producers included Arthur Lubin and Al Simon.

MR JOHN JORROCKS

BBC. First broadcast: 23 July 1966

Michael Voysey dramatised some of the stories of Robert Smith Surtees into eight television episodes. Surtees created his character for the *New*

Sporting Magazine in the 1830s. Jimmy Edwards, minus moustache, starred as Jorrocks, who gave up his job in a City counting-house to become Master of Foxhounds at Handley Cross. With him went his wife (Angela Baddeley), a townee who was utterly bewildered by country society. Her Cockney speech and ways were treated with disdain by the rural gentry led by Lady Barnington (Moyra Fraser) and the Duke of Donkeyton (Michael Bates). The Jorrocks household included his eligible niece Belinda (Heather Bell), his servant Benjamin (Alan Baulch) and huntsman James Pigg (Walter Carr), who had a tendency to get even more drunk than his master.

Director: Peter Dews. Producer: David Conroy.

MR MUDDLE – PRIVATE DETECTIVE

BBC RADIO. First broadcast: 22 April 1946

Comedian Robb Wilton wrote the 15-minute scripts and starred in this eight-part series. Helping Mr Muddle relive some of the pages from his casebook were his wife (Phoebe Hodgson) and Charlie Evans (Reginald Purdell), a character Wilton had created in his wartime monologues.

Producer: Michael North.

MR MUDDLECOMBE JP

BBC RADIO. First broadcast: 9 January 1937

Robb Wilton's most famous characterisation made his first broadcast in a single 15-minute programme. From a series beginning 28 January that same year until the last of almost 100 editions on 29 November 1948, Muddlecombe was one of the most popular shows on the wireless. He was Chairman of the Nether Backwash Rural District Council and Chairman of the Bench in the Court of 'Not-So-Common, Please', where he bungled and confused the course of justice with regularity. Sitting on the Bench with him was Mr Battersburn (Ernest Sefton), who developed a catchphrase, "Ee-what-a-to-do". Their adversary in and out of Court was usually Major Todd (Maurice Denham). A series in 1939 was called **PUBLIC FUTILITIES**, in which Muddlecombe concerned himself more with Council matters. For a 1941 series, he opened an office to practice as a solicitor with an unwilling, unhelpful and untrustworthy assistant, Adolphus (Laurie Lupino Lane), under the title **OFFICE HOURS**. In 1942 he was heard at home when wife Agnes (Marion Dawson) first entered the stories. For

most of the wartime series he was also an ARP warden, making Nether Backwash Hitler-proof. The original idea for the character was credited to Barry Bernard.
Writers: Adrian Thomas, Robb Wilton, Max Kester. Producers: Max Kester, Michael North.

MR WILLOW'S WIFE
BBC RADIO. First broadcast: 16 November 1971

Moira Lister starred in six episodes as Felicity Willow, the scatty but strong wife of businessman Paul Willow (Terence Alexander). The other regular character was Nanny, played by Doris Hare.
Writers: Ray Cooney and John Chapman. Producer: David Hatch.

THE MISTRESS
BBC. First broadcast: 17 January 1985

Maxine (Felicity Kendal) lived alone, ran a flower shop and kept rabbits. She was the mistress in an eternal triangle that had her having an affair with Luke (Jack Galloway) who was married to Helen (Jane Asher). Maxine was liberated and generally happy to be the mistress as she flitted from the shop to her cosy pink flat where most of the seduction took place. In later editions Peter McEnery took over the part of Luke.
Writer: Carla Lane. Producer: Gareth Gwenlan.

MIXED BLESSINGS
LWT. First broadcast: 3 March 1978

These stories by Sid Green centred on the racially-mixed marriage of two university graduates, white Thomas Simpson (Christopher Blake) and black Susan Lambert (Muriel Odunton). Neither had informed their respective parents, bank manager Edward and Annie Simpson (George Waring and Sylvia Kay) and William and Matilda Lambert (Stefan Kalipha and Carmen Munro), all of whom ultimately expressed their disapproval. It was left to Tom's Aunt Dorothy (Joan Sanderson) to show the young couple any encouragement and she allowed them to set up home in her basement. Thomas had failed to find a job and they were forced to exist on Susan's salary as a social worker. Susan had a younger brother, Winston, who was portrayed by Gregory Munroe, the real-life son of Carmen Munro, although he elected to spell his name differently. The first series of seven programmes was followed by two more series, by which time the couple had

had a baby, in October 1979 and April 1980. Thomas eventually secured a job as an engineer working for a Mr Huntley (Ernest Clark).
Producer: Derrick Goodwin.

MIXED DOUBLES
BBC RADIO. First broadcast: 18 June 1956

Bob Monkhouse and Denis Goodwin created this show as a vehicle for two real-life married couples, Cyril Fletcher and Betty Astell and Michael Denison and Dulcie Gray, to play each other's neighbours. Unfortunately, Astell fell ill and Fletcher began playing opposite Anne Crawford. Tragically, Crawford died and that first series was concluded by Jean Kent stepping into the breach. After nine editions, a communal production sigh of relief greeted the news that Betty Astell would be fit for the second series of 14 shows starting 14 June 1957. Their neighbourhood situation was Wimbledon Avenue somewhere in South London. Also in regular featured roles were Anthea Askey and Pat Coombs.
Producer: Leslie Bridgmont.

MOG
CENTRAL. First broadcast: 26 May 1985

This 13-part series was written by Dick Clement and Ian La Frenais and based on a novel by Peter Tinniswood. Mog (Enn Reitel) was a petty thief who took refuge in the Briardene mental home. Each time he thought it safe to venture out, circumstances contrived to keep him within the walls of the institution. While safely harboured, his company was FK Henderson (Tim Wylton), Captain Greenaway (Alan Shearman), Oliver (Christopher Villiers), Earl (Malcolm Frederick), Mrs Mortensen (Catherine Schell) and Mrs Williams (Toni Palmer).
Director: Nic Phillips. Producers: Glen Cardno and Allan McKeown.

MOLESWORTH
BBC RADIO. First broadcast: 23 March 1987

The character of Nigel Molesworth was created by Geoffrey Willans and Ronald Searle and adapted into this four-part radio series by Simon Brett. Molesworth (William Rushton) was an overgrown schoolboy who had once attended an educational establishment known as St Custard's. His post-school life had been devoted to getting by with the minimum of effort and the maximum of beer. In his pursuit of this idyll, he was helped and hindered by Grimes (Clive Swift), Louise (Penelope Nice), Gillibrand (Robert Harley), Peason (Bob Sinfield), Fotherington-Thomas (Phil Nice), and Arabella and Lucinda (both played by Chrissy Roberts). *Producer: Mark Robson.*

THE MOLLY WOPSIES
THAMES. First broadcast: 17 March 1976

This 13-part children's series by Ron Smith was set in 1940 in an Oxfordshire village where the local ghost was named Molly Wopsy. The name was assumed by a gang of village kids led by Dinkey Dunkley (Ben Forster) who wrought local havoc for the baffled policemen, PC Berry (Aubrey Morris) and Sergeant Needler (George Innes). Other gang members included Alan Musgrove (Phil Daniels), Norman Yates (Matthew Whiteman) and Dottie Minton (Julie Taylor). As well as the police, they also harassed Reverend Braithwaite (Frank Gatliff) and Farmer Brown (Patrick Barr). *Director: Stan Woodward. Producer: Ruth Boswell.*

THE MONKEES
NBC (AMERICA) PRESENTED BY BBC.
First broadcast (UK): 31 December 1966

Inspired by the Beatles' film *A Hard Day's Night*, American TV producers Bob Rafelson and Bert Schneider had the idea to cash in by manufacturing a similar group. To this end they placed an advert in the showbiz paper *Variety* which read: 'MADNESS: Wanted, a quartet of hip, insane, folk-orientated rock 'n rollers, 17 to 21, with the courage to work.' From the hundreds of responses they selected three Americans, Micky Dolenz, Peter Tork and Mike Nesmith and Manchester lad Davy Jones. Director Jim Frawly moulded them for three months and, with clever marketing and records made by real musicians in their name, the Monkees enjoyed sensational success with their zany adventures in a high-tech (for the time) series. They were introduced to the British public on New Year's Eve 1966 and retired 52 editions later on 20 April 1968.

MONKEY
NTV (JAPAN) PRESENTED BY BBC.
First broadcast (UK): 16 November 1979

The 16th-century writings of Wu Ch'eng-en were adapted for this Japanese series and David Weir wrote an English screen-play which put together the original pictures with English text, with the help of director Michael Bakewell. The adventures were of a priest, Tripitaka (Masako Natsume), who blundered hopefully through life with his own innocent foolishness and three supernatural travelling companions. They were the outrageous and indestructible God-King Monkey (Masaaki Sakai), a clown and troublemaker; Pigsy (Toshiyuki Nishida), a greedy little sex-maniac; and Sandy (Shiro Kishibe), a manic-depressive philosopher. The first run of 16 editions was followed by a further 11 starting on 31 October 1980. *Producer: Kokusai Hori.*

MOODY AND PEGG
THAMES. First broadcast: 29 July 1974

This series of six comedy dramas was written by Julia Jones and Donald Churchill. Following the end of an affair with her boss, unmarried Daphne Pegg (Judy Cornwell) left Bolton for London to find a flat. At about the same time, recently-divorced Roland Moody (Derek Waring) was also looking for a new flat. They both stumbled upon the same flat, both appeared to have a valid lease and, for expediency but with reluctance, they agreed to share. Roland was an antique dealer, Daphne was a civil servant. There was a permanent undercurrent of antagonism as each regarded the other more or less as a squatter. The only other regular character in the shows was George, a fellow flat-dweller who was a full-time student of the cello. There was a second series in 1975 when Roland's daughter Rowena (Lea Dreghorn) made an appearance. *Directors: Richard Martin, Jonathan Alwyn, Baz Taylor. Producer: Robert Love.*

MOONLIGHTING
CBS (AMERICA) PRESENTED BY BBC.
First broadcast (UK): 29 May 1986

Glenn Caron created and produced this phenomenally popular series which ran for more than 60 editions of 50 minutes' duration. Maddie Hayes (Cybill Shepherd) was a former model whose money had been embezzled by a fraudulent accountant. A small private detective agency, which she had once bought as a tax write-off, became the focus of her life as she determined to turn it into a success. The Blue Moon Agency was run by David Addison (Bruce Willis), a swaggering sleuth who resented her interference. They hated each other to such an extent that viewers knew it must be love, and they did in fact get between the sheets in the 1987 series, if only to explain Miss Shepherd's later expanding waistline in a real-life pregnancy. In the end Maddie broke David's heart when she married a man on a train, but David was not one to beaten at any cost. The shows were played at frenetic pace with the jokes often coming so thick and fast one was apt to forget what the crime was! The scatty girl who worked at the agency was Ms Agnes Dipesto (Allyce Beasley).

THE MORE WE ARE TOGETHER
YTV. First broadcast: 30 January 1971

In this middle-aged battle of the sexes, Victor Brooks and Betty Marsden starred as Wally and Norma Dunk (Kenneth Watson replaced Brooks as printer Wally mid-series). Wally's pal and the Dunks' lodger, Frank Wilgoose, was played by Roy Barraclough. He had a roving eye which let on the Dunks' neighbour, Doris Tingle (Avril Angers). The only other regular in the household of conflict was Doris' cat, Entwistle.
Writer: Robert Storey. Director: Mike Bevan. Producer: Ian Davidson.

Best of friends, MORK (Robin Williams) AND MINDY (Pam Dawber) (Photo: Channel 4)

MORK AND MINDY
ABC (AMERICA) PRESENTED BY ITV.
First broadcast (UK): 4 January 1979

The extra-terrestrial Mork (Robin Williams) from the planet Ork landed in the USA in 1978 and was quickly brought to the UK. Mork had first materialised in an edition of HAPPY DAYS and the creator of that show, Garry Marshall, was on the ball to spot the potential of his new character. In a reciprocal gesture, Henry Winkler as the Fonz from HAPPY DAYS appeared in the first episode of MORK AND MINDY to offer Mork lessons in human romance. A total of 95 programmes were recorded.

Mork landed in Boulder City and was immediately befriended by Mindy (Pam Dawber), who was the only human being to know his true origin. Mork had an extensive knowledge of the planet Earth and the social behaviour of humans as a result of old movies transmitted by US networks which were picked up on Ork. He was a zany guy and, as played by Williams, capable of some crazy comedy. He put his time stranded on Earth to good use and

at the end of each episode came forward in a bright-red pyjama suit and delivered a sermon to Orson on Ork about human frailties, jealousy, compassion, prejudice – a homily each week on some social issue. This soliloquy was delivered head-on and would always end with his cry 'Na-no Na-no'.

Other more or less regular characters included Mindy's grandmother Cora Hudson (Elizabeth Kerr), Frederick (Conrad Janis), Remo and Jean DaVinci (Jay Thomas and Gina Hecht), and Mr Bickley (Tom Poston).
Music: Percy Botkin Jr. Producers included Garry Marshall, Bruce Johnson, Dale McCraven.

MORRIS MINOR'S MARVELLOUS MOTORS
BBC. First broadcast: 8 April 1989

Mrs Plugg (Una Stubbs) put Morris Minor (Tony Hawks) in charge of her garage in Normalton. He was assisted by her son Sparky Plugg (Andy Serkis)

Dora Bryan starred as Kitty Flitcroft whose total domination of her 51-year-old son Leslie (Roy Barraclough) turned him into MOTHER'S RUIN (Photo: Granada Television)

and his pal Sedgefield (Carl Gorham). Scheming to either destroy or take over their garage business was restaurateur Angus Head (Tony Haase) with his henchman Martin (Philip Herbert). By a quirk of coincidence, Head's daughter Sonia (Camille Coduri) went to work at the garage as a trainee. Six editions were screened.
Music: Morris and the Minors. Writers: Tony Hawks and Neil Mullarkey. Director: Juliet May. Producer: Nick Symons for Noel Gay Television.

THE MOST LIKELY GIRL
ATV. First broadcast: 23 September 1957

Robert Bishop wrote and created this vehicle for Beryl Reid, who starred as Arethusa Wilderspin. Arethusa was to be groomed as the most likely girl to succeed in society and marry a lord. The task of turning her into this most likely girl fell to the wisecracking, sophisticated Eve Edwards (Noele Gordon). Helping and hindering was Madge Dresswell (Barbara Couper). Each of the six episodes featured a guest star as 'victim of the week'. *Producer: Cecil Petty.*

MOTHER AND SON
AUSTRALIA PRESENTED BY CHANNEL 4.
First broadcast (UK): 9 April 1986

Two series, each of seven shows, ran until 6 May 1987. Elderly widow Maggie Bruce (Ruth Cracknell) lived with her divorced son Arthur (Garry McDonald). Her other son Robert (Henry Szeps) lived close by. Arthur met, courted and finally married Deirdre (Suzanne Roylance) but was soon divorced from her and back with mother.

MOTHER'S RUIN
GRANADA. First broadcast: 29 May 1994

John Stevenson created and wrote these six programmes in which Dora Bryan and Roy Barraclough starred as mother and son, Kitty Flitcroft and Leslie Howard Flitcroft. Kitty had been a child star of

British movies, the British Shirley Temple of her day, and her day had well passed. She dominated Leslie Howard to the extent that she had ruined his career and his marriage. She had a fondness for gin and evening primrose, which was in plentiful supply from their health-food shop, Nurse Nature, where Leslie's assistant was Brucella Pashley (Julia Deakin). His girlfriend was neurotic divorcée Wendy Watson (Kay Adshead) who kept him in a permanent state of sexual frustration. Her usual excuse was the need to set a good example to her 16-year-old son Clive, whom she reduced to a quivering wreck by her neuroses. Thus was Leslie always denied. Kitty strove to break up the relationship and push Leslie in the direction of plain Brucella. *Director: John Stroud. Producer: Antony Wood.*

THE MOTOR WAY

BBC RADIO. First broadcast: 25 June 1962

Writer Lawrie Wyman set this series of eight programmes in a motor mechanic's garage after years of paying bills himself. Jack Warner starred as Jack Turner, proprietor of Turner's Garage, Established 1922. He employed two staff to work with him, his nephew Peter Turner (Peter Byrne), who was learning the trade, and the foreman Crocker (Deryck Guyler). Turner's was a small garage but when plans for a town bypass were proposed, the possibility of expansion reared its head. *Producer: Geoffrey Owen.*

THE MOTORWAY MEN

BBC RADIO. First broadcast: 2 February 1972

There were eight editions of this show, written by Peter Child and Peter Matthews. The three labourers working on motorway construction and maintenance were Steve (James Beck), Irish (Milo O'Shea) and Randy (Richard Davies). Their boss was Mr Fairfax (Richard Caldicot). *Producer: Alastair Scott Johnston.*

MOVING

THAMES. First broadcast: 9 January 1985

Stanley Price adapted his own West End play into this six-part series about the perils of moving house. Penelope Keith and Ronald Pickup starred as Sarah and Frank Gladwyn whose children had flown and who now found their house too large for just the two of them. They found an ideal flat but not a buyer for their house. Problems were compounded by their troublesome daughter Jane (Barbara Wilshere) and

Sarah's sister Liz Ford (Prunella Gee), who was hooked on Valium. Frank sought refuge with his friend Jimmy Ryan (Roger Lloyd Pack). *Music: Joseph Horowitz. Producer: Les Chatfield.*

MOVING STORY

CARLTON. First broadcast: 26 May 1994

Jack Rosenthal created the characters for this series in a single play, *The Chain*, in 1984. To his surprise, Carlton turned it into a comedy drama series which began with a 90-minute episode and was followed by five hour-long editions. Ken Uttley (Kenneth Colley) was the boss of Elite Removals, but after 30 years' service with the firm he allowed Bamber (Warren Clarke) to wear the guv'nor's white gloves and bowler hat and take charge of the team of removal men. Bamber nursed hopeless ambitions to be a contestant on *Mastermind*. In his employ were eternal bachelor Nick (Con O'Neill) who had fathered two children; Adrenalin (Philip Davis) whose name belied his spending most of the day on the phone fending off calls from his suspicious wife; and Asif (Ronny Jhutti), a naive 19-year-old Asian who was forced to make some speedy adjustments to his life. Their removal van was known unlovingly as 'The African Queen'. The business was just about kept afloat by Ken's secretary Patsy (Sheila Kelley), for whom Bamber carried a secret torch. *Theme music: Kirsty MacColl. Directors: Roger Bamford, Andrew Grieve. Producer: Linda Agran for Paravision UK.*

MUCH-BINDING-IN-THE-MARSH

BBC RADIO. First broadcast: 2 January 1947

The famous wartime RAF station in Laughter Command was first heard in MERRY-GO-ROUND. For its first peacetime broadcast under its own title, Squadron Leader Richard 'Stinker' Murdoch and Wing Commander Kenneth Horne converted the aerodrome into a country club with Murdoch as the manager and Horne as managing director. Sam Costa was the staff supervisor and Maurice Denham played Dudley Davenport, the clumsy washer-up with the catchphrase "I say, I am a fool!" Over the 177 editions, the last of which was heard on 23 March 1954, female characters included Hyacinth Meadows (Maureen Riscoe), Miss Plum (Dora Bryan) and several played by Diana Morrison. *Writers: Murdoch and Horne. Producer: Leslie Bridgmont.*

MUD

BBC. First broadcast: 17 February 1994

Daniel Peacock created and wrote this children's series which ran for seven weeks. Snobby Miss Palmer (Victoria Wicks) was the warden of an outdoor country activity centre who was dismayed at the prospect of playing hostess to three inner-city children from a council estate who won a holiday at the centre, Thelfont Heights. Her initial attempt to keep those kids segregated from the other 'posh' kids was swiftly frustrated when they fell down a disused well, and further disasters ensured that she, all the youngsters and her do-gooding colleague Miss Dudderidge (Susie Blake), a cheerful social worker, ended up to their necks in mud, or fighting, each edition.
Director: Claire Winyard. Producer: Christopher Pilkington.

MULBERRY

BBC. First broadcast: 24 February 1992

John Esmonde and Bob Larbey were the creators and writers of this series. Crotchety old spinster Miss Farnaby (Geraldine McEwan) hired a mysterious, but enigmatic and ultimately lovable character Mulberry (Karl Howman) as her manservant. Mulberry had much charm, and as he grew quite fond of the cantankerous old dear, so did she begin to soften towards him. He transformed her life. The house was a rambling old death-trap of a manor house, and when Mulberry arrived he found two surly and long-established servants already in place. They were Bert and Alice Finch (Tony Selby and Lill Roughley) and there appeared to be a manservant of no known origin called, simply, the Stranger (John Bennett). There were 13 editions, ending on 20 May 1993.
Producer: John B Hobbs.

MUM'S BOYS

BBC. First broadcast: 3 April 1968

Former chorus girl and conjuror's assistant Mrs Crystal Pallise (Irene Handl) had two sons, the products of two marriages: Leonard Pallise (Bernard Bresslaw), a dim-witted and failed actor, and Robin Fosdyke (Pete Murray). In the first episode Robin returned to his mother's terraced house, let off into flatlets, for the first time since his birth. His father was the Hon. Bertram Fosdyke and when the marriage was annulled, Robin had been taken and raised by his paternal grandparents. His reintroduction to his mother and half-brother spanned six episodes. *Music: Bill McGuffie. Writers: Jimmy Grafton and Jeremy Lloyd. Producer: Eric Fawcett.*

THE MUNSTERS

CBS (AMERICA) PRESENTED BY BBC.
First broadcast (UK): 9 October 1965

Writers and producers Joe Connelly and Bob Mosher created the Munster family in 1964 as a spoof of the Frankenstein and Dracula movies of the time. The BBC screened 70 episodes. The Munsters were ghouls. Fred Gwynne, outrageously tall and made-up as Frankenstein's monster, played head of the suburban family Herman Munster. He had a bolt through his neck and worked as a funeral director for Gateman, Goodbury and Graves. He wore green make-up (although the shows were made in monochrome) and was married to a vampire, Lily (Yvonne de Carlo), who had a white face and enormous fingernails. They had a werewolf son with pointed ears, Eddie (Butch Patrick), and a beautiful niece, Marilyn (Pat Priest). The show also starred Al Lewis who had played alongside Gwynne in CAR 54, WHERE ARE YOU?. Lewis portrayed the 378-year-old Grandpa who was a mad and dangerous scientist and driver of a super-charged coffin on wheels. He also possessed the power to turn himself into a bat.

In 1990, ITV began showing a new series, THE MUNSTERS TODAY. The first edition went out on 13 January featuring Herman (John Schuck), Lily (Lee Merriweather), Eddie (Jason Marsden), Marilyn (Hilary Van Dyke) and Grandpa (Howard Morton).

THE MUNSTERS TODAY

See THE MUNSTERS

MY BROTHER'S KEEPER

GRANADA. First broadcast: 7 September 1975

This series was written by and starred George Layton and Jonathan Lynn as non-identical twin brothers, Brian and Pete Booth, who had differing views and opinions on life and vastly opposite lifestyles. Brian was a policeman with stoic principles while Pete was a student with militant ideals. In spite of their overt differences, their blood tie remained strong. Hilary Mason played the boys' mother Mrs Booth, and Brian's superior Sergeant

Bluett was portrayed by Tenniel Evans. There was a second series beginning 10 May 1976.
Producer: Bill Podmore.

MY DEAD DAD
CHANNEL 4. First broadcast: 28 July 1992

The action of this series spread the events of just one day over the six-week run. Willie (Roy Hanlon) had been dead and buried for 14 years. His son Eck (Forbes Masson) had become a TV producer and Willie returned to haunt him, first materialising in a toilet cubicle wearing the flared suit and kipper tie in which he had been interred. They were attached to each other by an invisible umbilical cord so that for them to move more than a few paces apart caused Eck agonising stomach pains. In the final episode, Eck held a séance to try to have Willie returned to the dead.
Producer: Alan Nixon.

MY FAVORITE MARTIAN
CBS (AMERICA) PRESENTED BY ITV.
First broadcast (UK): 8 November 1963

Martin the Martian arrived on Earth in a flying saucer in 1963. He was portrayed by Ray Walston, previously best remembered for his role as Luther Billis in the film *South Pacific*. Martin could talk any language, read minds and disappear at will. He befriended a young newspaper reporter, Tim O'Hara (Bill Bixby). Tim was the only Earth person who could see Martin and the antennae which sprouted from the top of his head. Tim's landlady Mrs Brown was played by Pamela Britton, and her daughter Angela by Ann Marshall. The series ran until 1966 and there were 107 editions.
Producer: Jack Chertok.

MY GOOD WOMAN
ATV. First broadcast: 24 February 1972

Created and written by Ronnie Taylor, this show ran for five seasons. Leslie Crowther starred as the hapless husband, Clive Gibbons, whose wife Sylvia (Sylvia Sims) was a compulsive charity do-gooder. Clive tried to sway her to his opinion that charity should begin at home, but to no avail. He sought refuge in male company, initially with next-door neighbour Philip Broadmore (Keith Baron) and then in the last two series with his fellow darts player, bachelor Bob Berris (Glyn Houston). Throughout the shows much of Syvia's charitable

endeavour involved the local vicar, Rev. Martin Hooper (Richard Wilson).
Producers: Les Chatfield, William G Stewart, Ronnie Baxter.

MY HERO
NBC (AMERICA) PRESENTED BY ITV.
First broadcast (UK): 24 September 1955

Robert Cummings starred as Bob Beanblossom who worked in a real-estate office. The boss was a man named Thackeray (John Litel) whom Beanblossom saved from a murder plot in the first episode. Thereafter, he became 'my hero' to Thackeray's secretary Julie Marshall (Julie Bishop). The subsequent shows were concerned with domestic and office problems and romantic interludes. The series was originally made in 1952 and there were 33 editions.
Producer: Mort Green.

MY HONOURABLE MRS
BBC. First broadcast: 14 July 1975

With former actor Andrew Faulds MP acting as technical adviser, Richard Waring wrote this seven-part series in which Derek Nimmo starred as Henry Prendergast, whose wife Jane (Pauline Yates) nursed political ambitions. She was duly selected to be the candidate for the constituency of Brinkley in a by-election and was elected to the House of Commons. Henry was uncertain about living with a politician and while Jane was away on party business he found several other ladies ready to step into her place. Other regular characters included Trevor Chrichton (Aubrey Woods) and Eric Forbes (Alan Curtis).
Music: Dennis Wilson. Producer: Graeme Muir.

MY HUSBAND AND I
A-R. First broadcast: 20 July 1956

Real life husband and wife team Evelyn Laye and Frank Lawton starred in this domestic comedy, playing themselves against a background of home and the theatre. The six shows, transmitted fortnightly, were performed before a studio audience and afforded ample opportunity for the introduction of theatrical guests. Their regular back-up players were Linda Gray as Molly, Peter Collingwood as Jennings and Alicia Massy-Beresford as Jane.
Music: Cyril Ornadel. Producer: Eric Fawcett.

MY HUSBAND AND I
YTV. First broadcast: 9 January 1987

Pam Valentine and Michael Ashton created and

wrote this series which starred real-life husband and wife William Moore and Mollie Sugden as George and Nora Powers. Nora was head of personnel at Ashvale Advertising. George was unemployed until she found him a lowly job at Ashvale, but his attitude made her constantly ashamed of him. The chairman of Ashvale was Mr Withers (Graham Crowden), who rarely appeared. The day-to-day staff included Bambi Bamber (Deddie Davies), Tracy Cosgrove (Carol Hawkins), Mr Mundy (John Horsley), Samantha (Roberta Tovey), Pearl (Isabelle Lucas), Anita (Natasha Gray) and Henrietta (Jane Ashton). After the first run of seven programmes came a Christmas special on 18 December 1987 and a second series of seven starting 8 April 1988.

Music: Robert Hartley. Producer: Graham Wetherell.

MY MAN JOE

ATV. First broadcast: 24 February 1967

In its one and only run of six programmes, this series starred portly comedian Joe Baker as a hapless and helpless butler and valet, for whom all things went hopelessly wrong. He was in the employ of Lord Peregrine Hansford (Francis Matthews).

Writer: Godfrey Harrison. Director: Dennis Vance. Producer: Alan Tarrant.

MY MOTHER THE CAR

NBC (AMERICA) PRESENTED BY ITV.
First broadcast (UK): 8 November 1965

Jerry Van Dyke (brother of Dick) starred as suburbanite Dave Crabtree who spotted a 1928 jalopy on a used-car dealer's lot, bought it and discovered it was the reincarnation of his mother! On impulse, he flicked on the car radio and his mother's voice (Ann Sothern) said: "Hello Davey." Dave was a respectable lawyer married to Barbara (Maggie Pearce) and they had two children, Cindy (Cindy Eilbacher) and Randy (Randy Whipple). Their life was normal until Dave bought the car and his mother returned to dominate him. His mother had garish tastes – she demanded new leopard-skin seat covers and vulgar redecoration of the garage. She would gallivant around town, with or without Dave at the wheel. A great admirer of the old car was Captain Manzini (Avery Schreiber), who tried frequently but unsuccessfully to buy her. There were 26 episodes.

Writers included Phil Davis, Lila Garrett and Bernie Kahn. Producer: Rod Amateau.

MY NAME IS HARRY WORTH

THAMES. First broadcast: 22 April 1974

After his long run with the BBC in HERE'S HARRY, dithering comedian Harry Worth moved to ITV for this series of small-time adventures. When Harry moved into new digs with widowed landlady Mrs Maybury (Lally Bowers), he made an instant enemy of her brother George Bailey (Reginald Marsh), who resented Harry's intrusion and did all he could to get him out as soon as possible.

Writers: Ronnie Taylor, George Layton and Jonathan Lynn. Producer: William G Stewart.

MY OLD MAN

YTV. First broadcast: 3 May 1974

Clive Dunn starred as frisky old rascal Sam Cobbett who was forced to leave his home in Ironmonger Row when the demolition squad moved in. Playing Cobbett's daughter Doris was Dunn's real-life wife, Priscilla Morgan. Doris was married to Arthur (Edward Hardwicke) and they lived in a flat. Into this flat moved Sam, where nothing was right for him. He found the central heating inadequate, nowhere to put his own furniture and, in the absence of a garden, he yearned for an allotment. To add to the domestic strife, Sam did not see eye to eye with Doris and Arthur on the raising of children. The shows returned for a second series in March 1975.

Writer: Gerald Frow. Producer: Paddy Russell.

MY SAINTED AUNT

BBC RADIO. First broadcast: 3 September 1977

Trevor Bannister starred as out-of-work actor Richard Worthington who was penniless until his Aunt Lavinia died and left him a fortune. However, his inheritance was conditional on his finding a wife within 12 months. In his quest he was hindered considerably by the deceased aunt (Eleanor Summerfield), who was able to communicate her celestial views to him. A first series of nine preceded a further eight misadventures ending on 14 February 1979.

Writer: Colin Bostock-Smith. Producer: Martin Fisher.

MY SISTER AND I

ABC. First broadcast: 11 May 1956

Written and produced by Alick Hayes, the nine episodes followed the daily lives of two sisters,

Sally (Dinah Lee) and Jo (Jane Taylor), who had the capacity to think alike. Jack Howarth, later to star as Albert Tatlock in *Coronation Street*, played the girl's pigeon-fancying grandfather and Ethel Manners was the tea lady, Mrs Balfour. In a small supporting role, this series provided an early window for the talents of Ray Cooney, later destined to become a giant of stage farce.
Director: James George.

MY SISTER EILEEN

CBS (AMERICA) PRESENTED BY ITV.
First broadcast (UK): 4 November 1964

This series, made in the USA in 1960, was based on a book by Ruth McBinney and starred Elaine Stritch as Ruth Sherwood. Ruth was a freelance writer based in New York and she had to suffer the trials of her gorgeous, blonde younger sister Eileen, played by Shirley Bonne. They lived together in Greenwich Village. Stage-struck Eileen was the personification of innocence. Ruth spent much of her time extricating Eileen from trouble and potential danger. Their landlord, the greedy and intolerant Mr Appopolous, was portrayed by Leon Belasco. Raymond Bailey was the often helpful – but often not – Mr Beaumont, and Ruth's agent Marty was played by Stubby Kaye.
Producers: Oscar Rudolph and Dick Wesson.

MY SON REUBEN

THAMES. First broadcast: 8 September 1975

Vince Powell created and wrote this series about a smothering Jewish momma, Fay Greenberg (Lila Kaye), and her ageing bachelor son Reuben (Bernard Spear), who ran a dry-cleaning business. Next door lived Vera Clapham (Stella Tanner), a Jewess with a spinster daughter Ruth (Caroline Bernstein), who appeared to Fay to have all the right attributes to make a good wife for her son. However, Reuben was in love with a non-Jewish girl, Betty Smith (Jo Rowbottom). Helping to keep the peace was Rabbi Jackson (Christopher Benjamin).
Producer: Anthony Parker.

MY THREE SONS

ABC (AMERICA) PRESENTED BY ITV.
First broadcast (UK): 20 March 1961

Beginning in the USA in 1960, this Peter Tewksbury creation knocked up more than 350 episodes. Set in small-town, middle-class America in a place called Bryant Park, it starred Fred MacMurray as widower Steve Douglas, a beleaguered father of three and besieged by women who wished to marry him and mother the kids. The eldest son was Mike (Tim Considine), who was going steady with the girl next door. In the middle was Robbie (Don Grady), lead trumpeter in the school band, who had a large turnover of girls. The youngest, Chip (Stanley Livingston), showed more interest in space rockets than the opposite sex. They had a dog named Tramp. Self-appointed housekeeper and family guardian was grandfather William Francis 'Bub' O'Casey (William Frawley). He was gruff-voiced and irritable. He had a vaudeville background and kept rigid control of the family budget. He and Steve had violent disagreements about how the boys should be raised. Engineer Steve wished for Mike to follow in his footsteps but 'Bub' encouraged him towards a show business career. In later episodes, Bub was replaced by Uncle Charley (William Demarest). All five males realised that the home could benefit from a woman's touch, but could never agree on what constituted the perfect woman.
Producer: Don Fedderson.

MY TWO DADS

USA PRESENTED BY CHANNEL 4.
First broadcast (UK): 10 May 1990

Judge Wilbur (Florence Stanley) awarded custody of 12-year-old Nicole (Staci Keanan) to former college friends Michael (Paul Reiser) and Joey (Greg Evigan) when it was learned that either of them could have been Nicole's real father. They all set up home together. More than 50 episodes were screened.

MY WIFE AND I

A-R. First broadcast: 9 July 1958

Pamela Craig wrote this six-part domestic series which starred Rex Garner as David Finley and Mai Zetterling as his screwball wife Phyllis. David's complications with the opposite sex were doubled by his efficient secretary portrayed by Joan Benham.
Director: Eric Croall. Producer: Michael Westmore.

MY WIFE JACQUELINE

BBC. First broadcast: 30 July 1952

This domestic serial was written in six parts by AP Dearsley and was screened fortnightly. It starred Leslie Phillips as Tom Bridger with Joy Shelton as wife Jacqueline. Friends and neighbours were Trevor Matthews (Edward Dain) and Margaret (Anthea Holloway).

Producer: Dicky Leeman.

MY WIFE NEXT DOOR

BBC. First broadcast: 19 September 1972

Brian Clemens and Richard Waring created this series which ran for 13 weeks. John Alderton and Hannah Gordon starred as George and Suzy Bassett, a couple who had just been granted their decree nisi and, while waiting for the divorce to become absolute, each took a cottage in the country. On their separate arrivals they discovered to their horror that the cottages were adjacent. The resultant squabbles were as severe as when they had lived together under one roof. There was occasional parental interference from Suzy's mother (Diana King) and George's mother and father (Mollie Sugden and Ken Wynne). From time to time, it appeared as though there remained sufficient affection between George and Suzy for them to get together again, but it was not to be.

Music: Dennis Wilson. Writer: Richard Waring. Producer: Graeme Muir.

MY WIFE'S SISTER

GRANADA.

See OUR DORA

MY WORLD AND WELCOME TO IT

NBC (AMERICA) PRESENTED BY BBC.
First broadcast (UK): 24 December 1969

Based on the writings and drawings of James Thurber, this 26-part series starred William Windom as writer and cartoonist John Monroe, whose imagination lapsed him into fantasy mixing his cartoon characters with real people. His wife was Ellen (Joan Hotchkis), his daughter was Lydia (Lisa Gerritsen) and his boss was Hamilton Greeley (Harold J Stone). The series was created by Mel Shavelson.

Producers: Danny Arnold and Sheldon Leonard.

A tender moment for 'separated' couple George and Suzy Bassett (John Alderton and Hannah Gordon) in MY WIFE NEXT DOOR (Photo: Copyright © BBC)

9 TO 5
ABC (AMERICA) PRESENTED BY ITV.
First broadcast (UK): 15 October 1982

Bruce Gilbert, who produced the 1980 movie of the same title, and Jane Fonda, who was the star of the movie, created this TV spin-off. Three office girls, Violet (Rita Moreno), Judy (Valerie Curtin) and Roz (Jean Marsh), worked for the giant Consolidated Companies where they waged constant war with their boss, Franklin Hart (Jeffrey Tambor). He was an extreme chauvinist and the girls schemed to turn the tables on his overtly sexist attitudes. When Franklin Hart jr (Peter Bonerz) took over the corporate reins they found him to be a chip off the old block who resorted to employing an office spy to pass him advance intelligence of the girls' activities.

NANNY AND THE PROFESSOR
ABC (AMERICA) PRESENTED BY ITV.
First broadcast (UK): 29 June 1970

Juliet Mills starred as a nanny with magical powers to the children of widower Professor Everett (Richard Long). He had three kids, all of them young rascals in their own right: Hal (David Doremus), Butch (Trent Lehman) and Prudence (Kim Richards). Though Nanny was strange, she was nonetheless lovable and they all embarked on adventures together.
Creator: A J Carothers. Producer: David Gerber.

NATHANIEL TITLARK
BBC. First broadcast: 21 February 1956

Bernard Miles created this character which he portrayed in two series, each of six editions, ending on 8 May 1957. Titlark was a countryman who was at once poacher, poet, bird-spotter, philosopher and connoisseur of beers. He lived in an unspecified village in the Chiltern Hills with his wife Jessie (played in the first series by Megs Jenkins and in the second by Maureen Pryor). Titlark rebelled against authority, shied away from work and believed in man's right to freedom.
Writers: James Lansdale Hodson, Bill Naughton.
Producers: Adrian Waller, Andrew Osborn.

THE NAVY LARK
BBC RADIO. First broadcast: 29 March 1959

Radio's longest running comedy show was first heard on the light programme and ran for over 18 years. The stories were set aboard HMS *Troutbridge*, a naval vessel designed as a frigate and refitted in 1958 for the specific purpose of housing several undesirable elements of the Royal Navy on one ship, under careful watch. She was recommissioned as such and stationed just off Portsmouth.

HMS *Troutbridge* was under the command of Commander Povey (Richard Caldicot) and, for the first series only, his No. 1 was Lieutenant Price (Dennis Price), a too-smooth operator who never answered urgent signals from HQ. In subsequent series, the No. 1 was the equally untrustworthy Lieutenant Murray (Stephen Murray). Under them, in what became known as the 'Island Detachment', was Sub-Lieutenant Phillips (Leslie Phillips) of whom it was never certain whether he was naif simpleton or crook. However, there was no doubt about the shadiness of the actions and deals which took place in the ship's stores, where Chief Petty Officer Pertwee (Jon Pertwee) was in charge. To begin with, the only feminine interest aboard was provided by reluctant Wren Chasen (Heather Chasen), the Captain's secretary, but she was later joined by Wren Cornwell (Judy Cornwell) and Wren Heather (Jan Waters).

Whenever HMS *Troutbridge* was called upon to sail, the hazards of navigation were usually in the incapable hands of Lt Phillips whose technique was 'Left hand down a bit. Whoa!' His lookouts were AB Johnson (Ronnie Barker), a man with a passion for ships in bottles and who would say to Pertwee 'You're rotten, you are!', and AB Taffy Goldstein (Tenniel Evans). When required, Evans also played the part of the crusty old Admiral and, less frequently, the Governor, Sir Willoughby

Todhunter Brown. Ronnie Barker, too, had an alter ego playing Lieutenant-Commander Stanton. Very occasionally the Captain would endure the arrival of his wife, Mrs Povey, who was portrayed by Heather Chasen. Completing the regular cast was Michael Bates in the dual roles of Lieutenant Bates and AB Ginger. Week by week, any odd character required would be portrayed by this team of actors. The theme music, 'Trade Wind Horn-pipe', was written by Tommy Reilly and James Moody, and played on harmonica by Reilly.
Writer: Lawrie Wyman. Producer: Alastair Scott Johnston.

NEAREST AND DEAREST
GRANADA. First broadcast: 15 August 1968

Two music hall comedians, Jimmy Jewel and Hylda Baker, joined forces to portray Eli and Nellie Pledge, late middle-aged brother and sister, Lancashire born and bred, who had a natural antipathy towards each other and who suddenly found themselves the joint inheritors of a pickle factory. That the factory and the workforce were almost derelict did not make the inheritance any more palatable. The series was created by Vince Powell and Harry Driver and proved a huge hit with its gentle vulgarity, running for five seasons. The setting was north Lancashire, somewhere near Colne, where the Pledges' neigh-bours were the long-time married Walter and Lily (Edward Malin and Madge Hindle). Other regular characters were Stan (Joe Gladwin), Bert (Bert Palmer 1968, Leslie Sarony 1969) and Grenville (Freddie Rayner 1970–72).
Music: Derek Hilton. Writers included Powell and Driver, Tom Brennand and Roy Bottomley, John Stevenson. Producers included Peter Eckersley and Bill Podmore.

NELSON'S COLUMN
BBC. First broadcast: 17 February 1994

John Gordon Sinclair starred in six episodes as Gavin Nelson, a columnist on the *Herald*, a provin-cial newspaper. Each week Nelson struggled to spice up his copy with something of interest but he and his colleagues were inevitably scooped by rivals working for the *Courier*. Gavin strove in the pursuit of decency and truth in his professional capacity but in his private life and thoughts lusted after cub reporter Clare Priddy (Sophie Thompson). He even rented a room in the same house where she lived and was delighted at the prospect of being sent

on an assignment with her which meant their having to spend an overnight away from base. The strident editor was Jackie (Elizabeth Counsell) and Gavin's fellow reporter was Mike (Steven O'Donnell).
Writer: Paul Mayhew-Archer. Producer: Susan Belbin.

THE NESBITTS ARE COMING
YTV. First broadcast: 17 April 1980

The Nesbitts were a family of itinerant petty crooks who landed on the previously peaceful patch pa-trolled by the officers of Viaduct police station. Crime statistics went through the roof following the arrival of Mr and Mrs Nesbitt (Clive Swift and Maggie Jones) with Marlene (Deirdre Costello), Len (John Price) and Tom (Christian Rodska). Lined up against them were Det. Sgt Arnold Nixon (Ken Jones), Sgt Billy Machin (Tony Melody), PC Harris (John Clive), PC Crowther (Arthur White) and WPC Kitty Naylor (Patsy Rowlands). Six episodes were screened.
Producer: Ronnie Baxter.

NEVER A CROSS WORD
LWT. First broadcast: 27 September 1968

Donald Churchill created this situation for Nyree Dawn Porter to star as scatter-brained but intensely feminine Deirdre Baldock, a housewife married to Ronald (Paul Daneman). In the very first episode they had a lodger, Alf Hawkins (John Alderton), who subsequently moved on. They were in a rea-sonable income bracket and lived in suburbia near London. When Ronald was downgraded at work, Deirdre encouraged him to resign and she then became the breadwinner. Their lifestyle lost a little of its lustre and their muddles increased. In a sec-ond series the following year, Barbara Murray re-placed Nyree Dawn Porter as Ronald's wife. The Baldocks had left suburbia and moved to Chelsea's King's Road. Ronald had found a post in advertis-ing and Deirdre had a part-time job in an art gallery.
Writers: Donald Churchill, Michael Pertwee. Pro-ducers: Stuart Allen, David Askey.

NEVER MIND THE QUALITY, FEEL THE WIDTH
ABC. First broadcast: 18 February 1967

This very successful show, created and written by Vince Powell and Harry Driver, first saw the light of day as a single play in the *Armchair Theatre* strand. Frank Finlay starred as Irish Catholic trouser maker Patrick Michael Kevin Aloysius Brendan Kelly and John Bluthal as his Jewish partner Emmanuel 'Manny' Cohen, the jacket maker. They had a tailoring business in London's East End. When the first of the series reached the screen on 25 November that same year, Joe Lynch took the part of Kelly. Most of the comedy came from their differing religious beliefs: Cohen considered Kelly a bigoted Catholic and Kelly viewed Cohen as an ignorant heathen. However, they respected each other's tailoring skills and had worked together for 15 years. In many of the episodes their respective views were supported by Rabbi Levy (Cyril Shaps) and Father Ryan (Eamon Kelly). When ABC lost its franchise at the end of July 1968, Thames took up the show. There were 39 editions, the last one being transmitted on 14 September 1971.

Producers: Ronnie Baxter (1967–70), Stuart Allen (1971).

NEVER SAY DIE

CHANNEL 4. First broadcast: 16 November 1987

Jenny (Janette Legge), separated from her errant husband Dennis (Brian Cowper) and broke, took a job as warden to the elderly residents in the block of sheltered accommodation known as the Arthur Smuggins Flats. Among her charges were Sid (Arthur English), Jack (Tommy Eytle), Fred (Charlie Chester), Connie (Constance Chapman), for whom romance bloomed with Jack; Dorothy (Irene Handl), who had a spiritual guide named Chingascook (Christopher Malcolm); George (Peter Copley) and Joan (Margery Mason). Other regular characters were Mr and Mrs Danvers (Michael Atwell and Carole Hayman), Danny (Nicholas Delve), Soozie (Lusha Kellgren) and Gajmukhi (Zohra Segal). There were six programmes in the series.

Writer and director: Lou Wakefield. Producer: Humphrey Barclay for Humphrey Barclay Productions.

NEVER SAY DIE

YTV. First broadcast: 4 August 1970

This series, created and written by Peter Tinniswood, was set in the Emmott Robinson Ward of the Victoria Memorial Hospital somewhere in Yorkshire (the names of the characters suggest it might be Hebden Bridge). The unfortunate patients found their rights to make decisions for themselves seriously eroded and there was a constant tug of power between them and the staff. The inmates included Mr Hebden (Reginald Marsh), Mr Oliphant (Patrick Newell), Mr Finucane (Noel Purcell), Mr Bridge (Larry Noble), Corker (Teddy Green) and Albert (Wilfrid Brambell). Among the staff were Sister Ringstead (Ken Parry), Poniatowski (Hugh Walters) and Nurse Whitethroat (Mary Healey).

Director: Derrick Goodwin. Producer: John Duncan.

NEVER THE TWAIN

THAMES. First broadcast: 7 September 1981

There were 69 episodes of this Johnnie Mortimer creation over 11 series to 9 October 1991. Two feuding antique dealers, Simon Peel (Donald Sinden) and Oliver Smallbridge (Windsor Davies), failed to patch up their differences even when their respective offspring David Peel (Robin Kermode) and Lyn Smallbridge (Julia Watson) fell in love, married and gave them a grandchild, Martin (Ian Finnis). For much of the time, Simon and Oliver were rivals in love with Veronica Barton (Honor Blackman). When David and Lyn moved to Canada, Simon and Oliver visited them together but still managed to quarrel. With the children gone, the main peace-keeping forces were Simon's elderly Aunt Eleanor (Zara Nutley) and shop assistant and whipping boy Ringo (Derek Deadman).

Writers: Johnnie Mortimer, Vince Powell. Producers: Peter Frazer-Jones (1981–87), Anthony Parker (1988–91).

NEVER TOO LATE

BBC RADIO. First broadcast: 30 December 1980

A group of elderly citizens refused to allow age to stop them enjoying life to the full and taking on new challenges, be it venturing abroad or nearer to home. Thora Hird led the cast which included Avis Bunnage, Megs Jenkins, Pearl Hackney and Joe Gladwin. There were two series, a first of seven episodes and a second of eight which got underway on 29 December 1981.

Writer: Terry Gregson. Producer: Edward Taylor.

NEW ATTITUDE

USA PRESENTED BY BBC.
First broadcast (UK): 29 October 1990

Two sisters, Vicky and Yvonne St James (Sheryl Lee Ralph and Phyllis Yvonne Stickney), ran a Los Angeles hairdressing and beauty salon. The head stylist Lamarr was played by Morris Day. Lamarr had wild ambitions to be a rock star (and Day himself was once a member of Prince's band). Eight editions were transmitted.

THE NEW DICK VAN DYKE SHOW

CBS (AMERICA) PRESENTED BY ITV.
First broadcast: 16 September 1971

Dick Van Dyke became Dick Preston, an Arizona disc jockey and talk-show host. He was married to Jenny (Hope Lange) and their friends were Bernie and Carol Davies (Marty Brill and Mancy Dussault). Other regular characters were Mike (Fannie Flagg), the Preston's divorced daughter-in-law and her daughter Annie (Angela Powell) who was still at school. Seventy-two episodes were recorded.
Producer: Dick Van Dyke.

THE NEW PHIL SILVERS SHOW

CBS (AMERICA) PRESENTED BY ITV.
First broadcast (UK): 5 November 1963

Phil Silvers' eagerly awaited follow-up to SERGEANT BILKO was something of a disappoint-

Simon (Donald Sinden, left) and Oliver (Windsor Davies), ever at odds in NEVER THE TWAIN (Photo © Thames Television)

ment. He played the part of Harry Grafton, a fast-talking factory foreman whose chief interests were making money and creating nightmares for the management. Grafton was a civilian Bilko clone but lacked much of the fire and drive of the military character. Grafton assembled a competent team to assist his exploits and frustrate the boss, Mr Osborne (Douglas Dumbrille). They were Waluska (Herbie Faye), Roxy (Pat Renella), Lester (Jim Shane), Grabowski (Norman Grabowski) and Mr Brink (Stafford Repp). There were 30 editions.
Producer: Rod Amateau.

THE NEW STATESMAN

BBC. First broadcast: 12 September 1985

George Vance (Windsor Davies) was custodian of an agricultural museum somewhere near Aylesbury. It was as big a shock to him as to everyone else when he was elevated to the Peerage and had to take his seat in the House of Lords. He was a pompous Welshman who delighted in all things English and was not about to allow his ignorance and naivety to gag his performance on the new-found political stage. Vance was married to Enid (Anna Dawson) and they had two children, Clementine and Robert (Madeline Adams and Sean Chapman). Six episodes were transmitted.
Writer: Douglas Watkinson. Producer: David Askey.

THE NEW STATESMAN

YTV. First broadcast: 13 September 1987

Laurence Marks and Maurice Gran created this anarchic series which ran for 27 episodes over four seasons to 26 December 1992. Rik Mayall starred as Alan B'Stard, Conservative MP for the North Yorkshire constituency of Haltemprice. He was the youngest MP in the House and an out-and-out Thatcher follower. He was totally unscrupulous, arranging to maim opponents or to exploit others for financial gain. He was a self-styled manic country squire, wicked and avaricious. His wife Sarah (Marsha Fitzalan) was a lesbian who had inherited millions of pounds and whose only wish was to leave him. She stayed because he persuaded her that an MP should be seen with a wife. Alan's parliamentary scapegoat was the hapless Piers Fletcher-Dervish (Michael Troughton), who by the fourth series was poised to be made Chancellor of the Exchequer. Business adviser to B'Stard was the sex-changed Norman Bormann (Rowena Cooper, billed as RR Cooper). At the end of the second series B'Stard faked his own shooting which gave rise to a single special edition, a spoof cliff-hanger entitled 'Who Shot Alan B'Stard?' which was seen on 14 January 1990. As time progressed, B'Stard left Parliament and found himself a prisoner in a Russian gulag for two years before returning as a Euro MP. Other important characters were his hateful father-in-law Roland Gidleigh-Park (Charles Gray), Margaret Thatcher (Stephen Nallon), Neil Kinnock (Johnny More), Beatrice Protheroe (Vivien Heilbron), Sidney Bliss (Peter Sallis), Sir Stephen Baxter (John Nettleton) and Sir Greville (Terence Alexander). *Music: Alan Hawkshaw. Directors: Graeme Harper, Geoffrey Sax. Producers: David Reynolds, Tony Charles, Andrew Benson, Bernard McKenna.*

NEWHART

CBS (AMERICA) PRESENTED BY ITV.
First broadcast (UK): 11 March 1983

American comedian Bob Newhart starred as novelist, lecturer and television executive Dick Loudon who, with his wife Joanna (Mary Frann), bought an old, dilapidated Connecticut inn, The Stratford. They refurbished it to establish a business which they could run as a hobby. In their endeavours they were helped by Leslie Vanderkellen (Jennifer Holmes) and George Utley (Tom Poston). Neighbour Kirk Devane (Steven Kampmann) owned the nearby Minuteman Café. Mid-series, Kirk married Cindy Parker (Rebecca York). A colleague in tel-

Rik Mayall as Alan B'Stard MP, THE NEW STATESMAN (Photo: Yorkshire Television)

evision was Michael Harris (Peter Scolari), whose girlfriend Stephanie Vanderkellen (Julia Duffy) was hired by Dick to be the station's receptionist. More than 70 editions were recorded and were shown at various intervals across the ITV regions. *Producer: Sheldon Bull for MTM.*

NEWS AT TWELVE

CENTRAL. First broadcast: 22 February 1988

In this children's series, Kevin Doyle (Ewan Phillips) lived with his mother Doris (Julia Foster) at 13 Tindale Close, Biddlecombe. Each night he imagined his bedroom turned into a TV news studio and that he broadcast to the nation. He envisaged his mum and Uncle Norm Doyle (Walter Sparrow) as world superpowers, along with Arthur Starkey (Patrick Malahide), who between the three of them caused major diplomatic incidents. Also involved in Kevin's fantasies were his sister Sharon (Rebecca Lacey) and Granny Doyle (Constance Chapman). There were six programmes in the series. *Writer: Francis Sinclair. Director: Alex Kirby. Producer: Pamela Lonsdale.*

THE NICK REVELL SHOW
BBC RADIO. First broadcast: 25 January 1992

Stand-up comedian Revell created what he called 'sitcom for the Nineties' and, with just a first series of six programmes, picked up two prestigious awards. As star and writer, Nick Revell combined genuine issues and probabilities of the moment with surreal elements like Vince and Alvin, the talking geraniums, who were his constant companions. Other performers who contributed in a variety of parts included Alistair McGowan, Kate McKenzie and Doon Mackichan. A second run of six got underway on 3 June 1993.
Producer: Jon Magnusson.

NIGHT BEAT NEWS
S4C (WALES) PRESENTED BY CHANNEL 4.
First broadcast (C4): 5 March 1984

These 13 programmes centred on the chaotic activities of a news magazine programme at a TV station, Channel 9. The principal characters were the 'man on the spot', Owen Lewis (John Pierce Jones), backed up by Vicky (Nia Ceidiog), Monique (Carys Llywelyn), Simon (Dewi Morris), David (Dyfed Thomas), Greg (William Thomas), Freda (Christine Pritchard), Emlyn (Cadfan Roberts), Gareth (Robin Griffith), Annie (Lowri Anne Richards) and Derek (Lynn Rees).
Director: Jan Darnley-Smith. Producer: Peter Miller for WP Productions.

NIGHTINGALES
CHANNEL 4. First broadcast: 27 February 1990

Paul Makin created and wrote this series of black comedies about three highly unorthodox security guards, Carter (Robert Lindsay), Bell (David Threlfall) and Sarge (James Ellis). Their responsibility was to guard a building through the night. After the first series of six shows there was a long gap before a second run of seven programmes got underway on 30 December 1992.
Director: Tony Dow. Producers: Esta Charkham, Rosie Bunting for Alomo.

NIGHTS
CHANNEL 4. First broadcast: 10 February 1993

Five 15-minute films were screened over five consecutive nights as a prelude to a Channel 4 'Love Weekend' embracing St Valentine's Day in 1993. The story followed the love affair of Bob (Nick Hancock) and Carol (Lesley Sharp) from their first night together to their separation. There was disparity between their official account of events as recounted to friends and the actuality of those events as shown through animated models. Only through the models did the grim truth surface. Through flat-sharing, a holiday and a sad sex life, Bob and Carol maintained a front of contentment for the benefit of friends.
Writer and animator: Sarah Ann Kennedy. Director: Cindy Irving. Producer: Eleanor Stephens.

NINETEEN NINETY-FOUR
BBC RADIO. First broadcast: 23 March 1985

Writers Will Osborne and Richard Turner set this bleak comedic vision of Britain ten years on from George Orwell's classic book *Nineteen Eighty-Four*. Robert Lindsay starred in six editions as Edward Wilson, a thoroughly ordinary chap who was appointed Head of the Environment. He had a loyal home-help robot named Fletcher. Two years later, starting 28 March 1987, a further six editions were broadcast under the title NINETEEN NINETY-EIGHT. David Threlfall took over the role of Wilson, who was no longer in his position of responsibility but was heading for superstardom in other fields, with the faithful Fletcher alongside.
Producer: Nick Symons.

THE NINETEENTH HOLE
CENTRAL. First broadcast: 5 June 1989

Eric Sykes starred as Secretary of Prince's Hill Golf Club where the members and other officers made life difficult for Eric and for each other. In the first of seven episodes, a joker chose to denounce the Club in general and its Secretary in particular from atop the flagpole. Other characters were the President (Ivor Roberts), the Captain (Garfield Morgan), the Lady Captain (Charmian May) the Steward (Ronnie Brody), Woodley (John Quayle), Dennis (John Lyons), Bennett (Derek Newark) and Jack (Michael Redfearn). Most of the action took place in the club bar.
Writer: Johnny Speight. Producer: William G Stewart.

NO APPOINTMENT NECESSARY
BBC. First broadcast: 10 June 1977

Alf Butler (Roy Kinnear) was a greengrocer but he also owned a ladies' hairdressing salon which was

going rapidly downhill. He was kept on his toes trying to run between the two. The regular characters caught up in his business affairs were Penelope Marshall (Josephine Tewson), Beryl Armitage (Avril Angers), Colonel Marshall (Robert Dorning) and Sandra (Claire Faulconbridge). There were seven programmes in the series.
Writers: Peter Robinson and Hugh Stuckley. Producer: Harold Snoad.

NO COMMITMENTS
BBC RADIO. First broadcast: 9 January 1992

Simon Brett created and wrote this comedy drama in six parts. Anna (Rosemary Leach) had led a life which had seemed to be one long commitment to somebody or other without respite. Suddenly she found herself free and, for the first time, able to construct her own destiny. But her precious freedom was hardly born when her two demanding sisters, Victoria (Nicola Pagett) and Charlotte (Celia Imrie), arrived. In a second series Josie Lawrence took over the role of Charlotte, who was striving for a big break in her acting career. Victoria's daughter Emily (Lisa Coleman) was brought into the stories and, to Victoria's disapproval, came under Charlotte's influence.
Producer: Paul Schlesinger.

NO FRILLS
BBC. First broadcast: 5 September 1988

Kathy Staff starred as recently widowed Molly Bickerstaff. She opted to leave her native Oldham and move in with her daughter Kate (Belinda Sinclair) and granddaughter Suzy (Katherine Schlesinger) in London. Kate had been divorced for nine years and worked as an art lecturer. The trials of the three-generation household ran for seven episodes.
Writer: Janey Preger. Producer: Mandie Fletcher.

NO – HONESTLY
LWT. First broadcast: 4 October 1974

Terence Brady and Charlotte Bingham created and wrote this series of domestic comedies about a patient husband and his scatty wife. John Alderton and Pauline Collins starred, he as struggling actor Charles Danby, known to one and all as CD, and she as Clara, the daughter of an absent-minded peer, Lord Burrell (James Berwick). CD and Clara met at a ghastly party in Hampstead and, in spite of their very different backgrounds, they married. As a means to supplement CD's meagre earnings, Clara dabbled at being a writer. The same idea, with a change of cast, later became YES – HONESTLY.
Theme music: Lynsey De Paul. Directors: Bill Turner, David Askey. Producer: Humphrey Barclay.

NO JOB FOR A LADY
THAMES. First broadcast: 7 February 1990

Penelope Keith starred as newly elected Labour MP Jean Price who instantly found her political opponent in Tory Godfrey Eagan (George Baker). Jean was appalled at the hours MPs had to work and the cramped conditions at Westminster where she shared an office with Scottish MP Ken Miller (Paul Young). Her party whip was Norman (Garfield Morgan) and other colleagues included Geoff (Mark Kingston) and Harry (Nigel Humphreys). A second run of six episodes started on 7 January 1991 and George Baker left the cast for the third and final six-part series which ended on 10 February 1992.
Writer: Alex Shearer. Producer: John Howard Davies.

NO PLACE LIKE HOME
BBC. First broadcast: 13 December 1983

Arthur and Beryl Crabtree (William Gaunt and Patricia Garwood) had four children and looked forward to the new life which they planned once all had left the nest. Eldest daughter Lorraine (Beverley Adams) was married to the inept Raymond Codd (Daniel Hill) but soon discarded him and returned to her parents, although Raymond continued to hang around. The other Crabtree kids were Paul (Stephen Watson), Tracy (Dee Sadler) and Nigel (Martin Clunes, later Andrew Charleson), who all discovered that there really was no place like home. The neighbours were the shrieking, animal-loving Vera Botting (Marcia Warren, later Ann Penfold) and her husband Trevor (Michael Sharvell-Martin). Forty editions were transmitted, the last on 22 December 1987.
Writer: Jon Watkins. Producer: Robin Nash.

NO PROBLEM
CHANNEL 4. First broadcast: 7 January 1983

Channel 4 came on the air on 2 November 1982 and its initial sitcom output was limited to re-runs of tried and trusted favourites, I LOVE LUCY, THE ADDAMS FAMILY and GET SMART. The honour of being the channel's first original sitcom pres-

entation goes to this series, created and written by Mustapha Matura and Farrukh Dhondy for the Black Theatre Co-operative. After its debut run of seven shows it returned on 14 January 1984 for nine further episodes, and a final series of six ended on 8 June 1985. Set in Willesden, London, the Powell children and their friends had the run of the family home when their parents returned to Jamaica for an extended visit. The regulars were Toshiba (Chris Tummings) who ran a pirate radio station, Terri (Shope Shodeinde), Bellamy (Victor Romero Evans), Angel (Janet Kay), Sensimilia (Judith Jacob), Susannah (Sarah Lam) and Beast (Malcolm Frederick).
Producers: Michael Dolenz, Charlie Hanson.

NO SOAP, RADIO
USA PRESENTED BY BBC.
First broadcast (UK): 10 May 1983

A number of odd-ball characters centred around the Hotel Pelican where, among others, an underworld hit-man was in hiding, someone was plotting to buy the place, and a cereal packet contained terror! The principal screwballs included Roger (Steve Guttenberg), Mr Plitzky (Bill Dana), Tuttle (Stuart Pankin), Mrs Belmont (Fran Ryan) and Morris (Jerry Maren). Five editions were screened by the BBC.
Producers: Les Alexander and Dick Smith.

NO STRINGS
BBC. First broadcast: 16 April 1974

Originating as a single edition of *Comedy Playhouse*, this title swiftly went to series with the first of six episodes being screened on 4 October the same year. Derek (Keith Barron) was a tidy bachelor who lived in his own flat and enjoyed the ladies. When it became necessary for him to find a flatmate, he advertised and got Leonora (Rita Tushingham), who swiftly brought a feminine touch to his abode. Soon, however, Derek feared that Leonora's presence was cramping his style; but Leonora was lonely and the series ended with . . . .
Writer: Carla Lane. Producers: Roger Race (Comedy Playhouse), John Howard Davies.

NO STRINGS
YTV. First broadcast: 12 April 1989

Unknown to Sam Jessop (Edward Petherbridge) and Rosie Tindall (Jean Marsh), who had never met each other, their respective marital partners were engaged in an affair. When Sam and Rosie did chance to meet, they gradually fell in love. Sam had

two sons, Joe (John McAndrew) and Nick (Graham McGrath), and Rosie had a daughter, Sally (Amanda Waring). The part of Grandad was played by Robert Fyfe. There were seven episodes.
Writer: Jan Butlin. Producer: Ronnie Baxter.

NO – THAT'S ME OVER HERE
A-R. First broadcast: 17 November 1967

David Frost assumed the role of executive producer for this first solo starring vehicle for Ronnie Corbett. Corbett played the suburban little man who thought big, and Rosemary Leach portrayed his wife. Each morning, immaculate in three-piece suit, bowler hat, umbrella and briefcase, he would set off with his identically turned-out neighbour (Henry McGee) and head for the train to take him to his office in the City. Much of the comedy was visual. The other regular player was Jill Mai Meredith who was the mini-skirted office secretary. There were three series made, the last beginning 12 September 1970.
Writers included Barry Cryer, Graham Chapman and Eric Idle. Theme music: Mike Vickers. Producers: Marty Feldman and Bill Hitchcock.

NO TIME FOR SERGEANTS
ABC (AMERICA) PRESENTED BY ITV.
First broadcast (UK): 11 October 1964

Prior to this television series there had been both a stage production and a film presentation in 1958 based on Mac Hyman's novel. Executive producer William T Orr brought the concept to the small screen with 34 editions starring Sammy Jackson as Will Stockdale, the country bumpkin farm boy who joined a US Air Force base. Harry Hickox was cast as the unfortunate Sergeant King and Kevin O'Neal played the studious Ben Whitledge who considered himself privileged to serve in the Force. The obligatory fair-sex interest was provided by Laurie Sibbald who portrayed Millie Anderson, the sweetheart of the Post Exchange who was looked after by her grandfather, Jim Anderson (Andy Clyde). Other principal characters included Captain Martin (Paul Smith), General Thomas (Bill Zuckert), Wally Blanchard (Greg Benedict) and Will's bloodhound named Blue.
Directors included Leslie H Martinson and Charles R Rondeau for Warner Brothers.

NOBODY'S PERFECT
LWT. First broadcast: 28 September 1980

Elaine Stritch starred as American Bill Hooper, married for eight years to her English GP husband

Sam (Richard Griffiths). For both it was a second marriage. Sam had a divorced daughter, Liz (Kim Braden) who herself had a seven-year-old son Sammy (Simon Nash). Their neighbour, and Sam's best bolthole of escape from his strident wife, was Herbert Armstrong (Moray Watson). The Hoopers' daily help was Mrs Whicker (Ruby Head). A second series of six, making twelve shows in all, ended on 22 August 1982.

The only writing credit on these shows was 'adapted by Elaine Stritch'.
Director: Christopher Baker. Producer: Humphrey Barclay.

NORMAN

ATV. First broadcast: 2 April 1970

Norman Wisdom starred in the title role as an over-ambitious and under-talented musician who worked in an income tax office. One day, he threw his in-tray out of the window, stuck his fist through his hat and told his boss where to stick the job. He

A few of the 500 oddballs who make up the population of Cicely, Alaska in NORTHERN EXPOSURE (Photo: Channel 4)

sallied forth on a fruitless musical career. His landlady, Mrs Tate, was played by Sally Bazely. Six episodes were shown.
Writers: John Chapman and Ray Cooney. Producer: Alan Tarrant.

NORTHERN EXPOSURE
USA PRESENTED BY CHANNEL 4.
First broadcast (UK): 16 March 1992

Made in one-hour episodes, this comedy drama ran to a fourth series, which got underway on 21 February 1994. New Yorker Dr Joel Fleischman (Rob Morrow) agreed to go and work in Alaska for four years as repayment for the state having financed his medical school training. He expected to be posted to the city of Anchorage but instead he was assigned to the remote community of Cicely where the population numbered a mere 500 and most of those were eccentrics. On arrival he soon found basic comforts to be in short supply. The principal characters in Cicely included Maggie O'Connell (Janine Turner), who abandoned her wealthy lifestyle to become an air-taxi pilot. She had had five boyfriends, all of whom had met untimely deaths. Shelly Tambo (Cynthia Geary), 18-year-old beauty queen, left her husband to follow an older man to Cicely and then dumped him. That older man was Maurice Minnifield (Barry Corbin), ex-astronaut who nursed a dream to turn Cicely into a tourist riviera. Holling Vincoeur (John Cullum) became the new man in Shelly's life, thus making him an enemy of his former best friend Maurice. Chris Stevens (John Corbett) was the town's radio DJ and self-ordained minister. There were two Indians, Marilyn Whirlwind (Elaine Miles), who was Joel's assistant, and Ed Chigliak (Darren Burrows), an 18-year-old would-be arthouse film maker. Between them they made up a slightly surreal bunch of soul-searchers. A moose strolled down the main street during the opening titles.
Created and produced by Joshua Brand and John Falsey.

NOT IN FRONT OF THE CHILDREN
BBC TELEVISION AND RADIO.
First broadcast: 8 September 1967

Richard Waring wrote 35 editions of this show for television, ending on 9 January 1970. He also adapted 26 of his scripts for radio, beginning on 30 September 1969 with the last broadcast on 27 December 1970. Wendy Craig starred as Jennifer Corner,

mother in a solid middle-class family and married to Henry (Paul Daneman, later Ronald Hines and, on radio, Francis Matthews). The essence of the programmes was their frequent rows, invariably sparked off by the children, Trudi (Roberta Tovey), Robin (Hugo Keith-Johnston) and Amanda (Jill Riddick). For the final television series the role of Trudi was played by Verina Greenlaw.
Theme music: Ronnie Hazlehurst. Producer: Graeme Muir. Radio producer: Trafford Whitelock.

NOT ON YOUR NELLIE
LWT. First broadcast: 15 March 1974

Hylda Baker starred as Nellie Pickersgill, who left her native Bolton to help her father Jed (John Barrett) run the Brown Cow public house in Fulham. Nellie did not approve of drinking, and she *severely* disapproved of her father's lusty and lecherous behaviour and his patent addiction to beer and horses. She determined to keep one step ahead of the layabouts who hung around the pub, George (David Rayner), Charlie (Leo Dolan), Gilbert the dress designer (Roger Howlett) and Nigel Smallpiece (Ronald Chenery). There were three series altogether. A succession of barmaids included Beryl (Alexandra Dane), Doris (Wendy Richard) and Big Brenda (Sue Nicholls). By the final series Jed Pickersgill had had enough and gone back North to re-marry. Nellie was then joined at the Brown Cow by cousin Stanley Pickersgill (Jack Douglas).
Writers: Tom Brennand and Roy Bottomley. Producer: Bryan Izzard.

NOT WITH A BANG
LWT. First broadcast: 25 March 1990

Colin Garrity (Stephen Rea) and Brian Appleyard (Ronald Pickup) had nothing in common other than a fervent belief that they were the only two human survivors left on Earth. Janet and Graham Wilkins (Josie Lawrence and Mike Grady) also believed that they were the sole survivors. The four met up and formed a community. The responsibility for perpetuating the human race naturally fell on Janet, but it was doubtful whether her husband was up to the task. The series ran for seven programmes.
Writers: Tony Millan and Mike Walling. Producer: Robin Carr.

NOW AND THEN
LWT. First broadcast: 24 July 1983

John Esmonde and Bob Larbey created and wrote

these stories about middle-aged Peter Elston (Bernard Holley), married to Jill (Jill Kerman) with two children, Alan (Marc Gilbey) and Amanda (Polly Bell). As he watched the development of the rebellious Alan, he flashed back to his own childhood and adolescence. Peter as a child was played by John Alford. Other characters from 'then' were his parents, Norman and Bet (Sam Kelly and Marcia Warren), Gran and Grandad (Liz Smith and Arthur Lovegrove), his sisters Mary and Sonia (Tracy Hyde and Cindy O'Callaghan), and Aunt Sadie and Uncle George (June Brown and Barry Stanton). There were two series of six episodes, the second run beginning 8 July 1984.
Producer: Derrick Goodwin.

NOW LOOK HERE . . .
BBC. First broadcast: 15 November 1971

Ronnie Corbett starred as a bachelor in the small town of Bramley where he lived a semi-detached suburban life under the domination of his mother (Madge Ryan). Each day he trudged down the narrow garden path on his way to the office where he feigned a liberal and broad-minded attitude, but in reality he was in conflict with all around him, especially Keith (Richard O'Sullivan). When a second run of seven got underway on 24 January 1973 Ronnie had acquired a wife, Laura, played by Rosemary Leach. In 1981 Ronnie Corbett would again play a mother-dominated bachelor in SORRY, but before that, he and Laura would have further adventures in THE PRINCE OF DENMARK.
Writers: Graham Chapman and Barry Cryer. Producers: Bill Hitchcock, Douglas Argent.

NOW, TAKE MY WIFE . . .
BBC. First broadcast: 13 September 1971

Harry and Claire Love (Donald Houston and Sheila Hancock) were mortified parents of teenage daughter Jenny (Liz Edmiston) whose modern, liberated approach to life and boys in particular was beyond their understanding. They struggled to come to terms with a world of changing morals and ambitions for young girls. Twelve editions were screened.
Writer: Charles Laurence. Producer: Duncan Wood.

NURSE DUGDALE TAKES THE AIR
BBC RADIO

See A DATE WITH NURSE DUGDALE

NURSES
USA PRESENTED BY CHANNEL 4.
First broadcast (UK): 28 August 1992

Susan Harris created this series which was set in a hospital in Miami where a dedicated team of health care professionals faced the life and death pressures of their work. Nurse Sandy (Stephanie Hodge), a bitter and cynical divorcée, shared responsibility for the wards with the draconian supervisor Annie (Arnetia Walker) and Doctors Kaplan (Kenneth David Gilman) and Riskin (Florence Stanley). Other nurses were Julie (Mary Jo Keenen), Gina (Ada Maris) and Greg (Jeff Altman). Paco (Carlos Lacamara) was the junior porter. The head porter was Jack (David Rasche) and he was also the landlord of the slum which he rented to Paco. John Ratzenberger made a guest appearance as hospital administrator Mr Haffner. Channel 4 showed an initial run of six episodes and a further 20 from 6 August 1993.

THE NUTT HOUSE
USA PRESENTED BY BBC.
First broadcast (UK): 14 October 1989

Mel Brooks and Alan Spencer created this series set in a once-grand hotel, The Nutt House. Cloris Leachman starred as Ms Frick, a rigorous head housekeeper, and Harvey Korman co-starred as hotel manager Reginald J Tarkington. In spite of their outward calm, nothing went right for either guests or staff. Ten editions were screened by the BBC.

THE ODD COUPLE

ABC (America) PRESENTED BY ITV.
First broadcast (UK): 9 July 1971

Neil Simon's original play (turned into a movie in 1968 starring Jack Lemmon and Walter Matthau) was extended into a television series which ran for several years beginning in the USA in 1970 and in Britain the following year. Two men, both of whom had been left by their wives, lived together. They had widely differing temperaments and irritated each other beyond measure. Tony Randall was Felix, a fussy and rather prissy fashion photographer who compulsively cleaned and tidied. Jack Klugman played Oscar, a sports writer and commentator who was naturally untidy and disorganised. Felix would leave him notes of remonstration on his pillow. Nearby lived two sisters, Gwendolyn and Cicely Pigeon (Carole Shelley and Monica Evans), who in the early days were occasional girlfriends. Al Molinaro made regular appearances as Murray. There were more than 100 editions.
Producer: Garry Marshall.

ODD MAN OUT

THAMES. First broadcast: 27 October 1977

John Inman starred in this series of seven shows by Vince Powell. Inman played Neville Sutcliffe, a Blackpool fish and chip shop owner who had to travel to Sussex when he inherited a half share in his father's stick-rock factory which was located there. The other 50 per cent of the factory was left to his stepsister Dorothy (Josephine Tewson) who made it clear that his arrival was not welcomed. Neville discovered that his inheritance also included half a house and a huge overdraft. Other regular characters in the programmes were Ma (Avril Angers), Wilf (Peter Butterworth), Aunt Cissie (Betty Alberge), Percy (Jan Harding) and Marilyn (Vivienne Johnson).
Director: Anthony Parker. Producer: Gerald Thomas.

OFF THE RACK

CBS (AMERICA) PRESENTED BY ITV.
First broadcast (UK): 13 July 1986

Ed Asner starred as Sam Waltman, who assumed that following the death of his business partner he would be the sole proprietor of their garment firm. He had reckoned without the widow, Kate Halloran (Eileen Brennan), who not only took over her late husband's share but also became fully active in the day-to-day running of the business. The seven episodes were created by Dan Guntzelman and Steve Marshall.
Producer: Frank Badami II.

OFFICE HOURS

BBC RADIO

See MR MUDDLECOMBE JP

OH, BROTHER!

BBC. First broadcast: 13 September 1968

Derek Nimmo starred as the plum-voiced Brother Dominic, an accident-prone novice monk in Mountacres Priory, where he was to fully try the patience of Father Anselm (Felix Aylmer), the kindly old Prior, and the Master of the Novices (Colin Gordon). Other brethren were portrayed by Derek Francis, John Grieve and Patrick McAlinney. There were 19 editions over three series ending 27 February 1970. See also OH, FATHER!
Writers: David Climie and Austin Steele. Producers: Duncan Wood, Johnny Downes.

OH, FATHER!

BBC. First broadcast: 12 September 1973

This sequel to OH, BROTHER! again starred Derek Nimmo who was ordained Father Dominic in the first of seven episodes and left Mountacres to become curate to Father Harris (Laurence Naismith). He was just as prone to mishaps as he had been in his lesser monastic responsibility.
Writers: David Climie and Austin Steele. Producer: Graeme Muir.

OH HAPPY BAND

BBC. First broadcast: 3 September 1980

Writers Jeremy Lloyd and David Croft set this serial in six parts in the Northern town of Nettleby

where Harry Worth as himself was the conductor of the local brass band. Harry also found himself embroiled as leader of the opposition to proposals to build a new airport on the town's outskirts. The Man from the Ministry (Jeffrey Segal) came up against Harry and the other regular characters, who included Mr Herbert (Jonathan Cecil), Mr Braithwaite (John Horsley), Mr Sowerby (Billy Burden), Mr Pilgrim (Tom Mennard), Mr Giles (Tony Simpson), Mrs Draper (Jan Holden), Glenda (Moira Foot) and the Vicar (Harold Bennett).
Producer: David Croft.

OH MADELINE
ABC (AMERICA) PRESENTED BY CHANNEL 4.
First broadcast (UK): 18 September 1986

In this series created by Irma Kalish, Madeline Kahn starred in the title role as a very attractive woman in her mid-thirties who had been married to Charlie (James Sloyan) for several years. She was a woman of hard-hitting honesty who, when faced with the reality that her marriage was flagging, fought to save it. Her best friend was Doris (Jesse Welles) and, through little fault of her own, Madeline became innocently involved with Doris' husband (Louis Giambalvo). Channel 4 ran 12 episodes.
Producers: Marcy Carsey and Tom Werner.

OH MOTHER!
BBC RADIO. First broadcast: 20 April 1980

Christopher Sykes wrote two series of this show each of which ran for six editions, ending on 16 September 1982. Mollie Sugden was the mother and her daughter was Patricia Brake. In the first episode Ian Lavender played Patricia's boyfriend, but after having lunch with her and her mother he was never heard from again. There were other guest stars each week.
Producer: Martin Fisher.

OH NO! IT'S SELWYN FROGGITT
YTV. First broadcast: 4 February 1976

Alan Plater created the Froggitt character for a single play transmitted on 30 September 1974. Bill Maynard starred as Selwyn, a handyman with limited knowledge and talent but with a profound belief in his own ability. For the subsequent first series of six programmes the setting was Scarsdale, Yorkshire, where Selwyn had a labourer's job with

the Public Works department of the local council. He lived at home with his Mum (Megs Jenkins) and his social life revolved around Scarsdale Working Men's Club where he became secretary. Among those for whom he caused loud-mouthed havoc at work and play were Maurice (Robert Keegan) and Vera (Rosemary Martin, later Lynda Baron), who subsequently married; Ray (Ray Mort), Clive (Richard Davies), Jack (Bill Dean) and Harry (Harold Goodwin). The inept but fundamentally soft-hearted Selwyn returned for two further series in Scarsdale, in February 1977 and November of the same year, before changing his location for a 1978 series titled simply SELWYN.
Alan Plater wrote most of the episodes but there were contributions from HV Kershaw, Bernie Sharp and the team of Mike Craig, Lawrie Kinsley and Ron McDonnell. Producer: Ronnie Baxter.

OLD BOY NETWORK
CENTRAL. First broadcast: 16 February 1992

Dick Clement and Ian La Frenais created this seven-part series which starred Tom Conti as disgraced former MI5 double-agent Lucas Frye who returned home from exile in Moscow due to the thawing climate of the Cold War. On his return he confronted his old MI6 adversary Peter Duckham (John Standing) who had retired. They realised they both needed a job so they formed a private espionage agency. They were total opposites: Frye was an opportunist who could turn disaster to his advantage, while Duckham was more likely to create disaster out of an opportunity. The fact that Frye had at one time had an affair with Duckham's wife Sophie (Anne Lambert) was a wound which still festered. They had also been keen and deadly rivals at public school.
Producer: Sydney Lotterby.

THE OLD CAMPAIGNER
BBC. First broadcast: 6 December 1968

Terry Thomas starred as Jimmy Franklin-Jones, or FJ as he was known to his colleagues. He was a salesman for Balsom's Plastics and travelled the world on their behalf. His main preoccupation, however, was ladies. His wife Monica was played by Jean Harvey and he had a trainee assistant, Clancy (Jonathan Cecil). Other principal characters included Miss Pinto (Lois Penson), Isobel Benham (Janie Booth) and LB (Reginald Marsh). There were six editions.
Writer: Michael Pertwee. Producer: James Gilbert.

OLD MOTHER RILEY
BBC RADIO. First broadcast: 21 June 1941

Husband and wife stage and film stars Arthur Lucan and Kitty McShane brought their famous characterisations of Old Mother Riley 'and me darlin' daughter Kitty' to their first radio series which ran for eight weeks. The erring Kitty was always in hot water with her battleaxe of a mother who admonished her for staying out too late and never approved of her boyfriends. A second series of 10 came on the air on 6 June 1942 after which the couple concentrated on their film careers. They returned for a third series on 20 September 1948 with a couple of new departures. Old Mother Riley had had fierce arguments with one Mrs Ginnochie who had been oft quoted but never heard. In this series she was brought to life and played by Olivia Burley. Kitty, after her strings of boyfriends, was going steady with Danny (Willer Neil) who, conveniently, was a singer and able to sing Irish songs with her.

Writers: Arthur Lucan, Kitty McShane. Producer: Tom Ronald.

THE OLDER WOMAN
BBC RADIO. First broadcast: 12 January 1993

Roy Hitchcock (Martin Clunes) worked as a hack journalist on a provincial paper. His life was turned upside down when he met his former English teacher from school, Miss Jane Callaghan (Zoë Wanamaker), and he determined to win her at all costs and against the odds. Working with Roy at the newspaper office were tough sportswriter Elsa (Toyah Wilcox) and young would-be singer Dick (Geoff McGivern). Six programmes were heard.

Writer: Tony Bagley. Producer: Julian Westall.

ON THE BUSES
LWT. First broadcast: 28 February 1969

Although the critics treated it with initial contempt, this creation by Ronald Wolfe and Ronald Chesney found mass public approval and proved one of ITV's longest-running series of all time. The comedy was raucous and often healthily vulgar. The stories revolved around the employees of a bus company in a small Home Counties town and their home lives. Reg Varney starred as bus driver Stan Butler, a bachelor who lived at home with his widowed, over-devoted mother (Cicely Courtneidge in the first series, Doris Hare thereafter). Sharing the house were his homely sister Olive

Reg Varney stars as Stan Butler, ready to go ON THE BUSES (Photo: LWT)

(Anna Karen) and his bone-idle brother-in-law Arthur (Michael Robbins). Sharing Stan's working hours at the Luxton Bus Company were his conductor Jack (Bob Grant) and the miserable Inspector Blake, known as 'Blakey' (Stephen Lewis). Stan's usual route was the number 11 which went to the cemetery gates. Over four years, 73 programmes were made. By the 1973 series, Olive and Arthur were set to divorce, much to Mum's delight. Stan had a romantic interest in Sandra (Sandra Bryant) and the depot had a new clippie, Jessie (Yootha Joyce). The last episode went out on 6 May 1973. *Writers included Wolfe and Chesney, Bob Grant and Stephen Lewis, George Layton and Jonathan Lynn. Producers: Stuart Allen, Bryan Izzard.*

ON THE HOUSE
YTV. First broadcast: 24 September 1970

The building firm of Thomas Clackwood and Sons was contracted to construct a bijou housing estate. The principal problem to be overcome lay in the company's own employees, whose leader, Gussie (Kenneth Connor), sought any excuse to down tools. He was pitted against the site foreman, Charlie Cattermole (John Junkin), who had good reason to believe the world was against him. As the job fell further and further behind schedule so Charlie's extra-mural activities, namely the pursuit of girls, had to be curtailed. A second series was screened the following year ending 27 May, and among the so-called workers who spanned the project were

Fred (John Normington), Arnold (Tommy Godfrey), Derek (Derek Griffiths) and long-haired layabout Harvey Micklethwaite (Robin Askwith) whose thoughts rarely strayed from scheming to impress his girlfriend (Paula Wilcox). There were 12 editions altogether.

Writer: Sid Colin. Producer: David Mallet.

ON THE ROCKS

TYNE TEES. First broadcast: 8 July 1969

In this children's series, the stories revolved around a supposed television station, Seaview Television, which transmitted from a lighthouse to the residents of Mumbling Bay and Kipper Cove. (The actual lighthouse used for the series was St Mary's, located between Blyth and Whitley Bay.) The dotty producer was played by Billy McComb, and Arthur Mullard portrayed his right hand man and Jack-of-all-trades. Keeping the nearest to order possible was the producer's girl Friday and station singer, Pip Hinton. Bryan Burdon appeared as the local milkman turned comedian. The lighthouse keeper was played by Anthony Kenyon.

Writers: Larry Parker, Guy Rowston. Producer: Penny Wooton.

ON THE UP

BBC. First broadcast: 4 September 1990

East Ender Tony Carpenter was a self-made millionaire whose troubles stemmed from his marriage to his socially superior wife Ruth (Judy Buxton). Dennis Waterman starred as Tony who had all the trappings of success, including the big house in Surrey, membership of the golf club and faithful staff. The infidelity came from Ruth who was frequently walking out on him, and in the end divorce seemed inevitable. The housekeeper and cook was Mrs Wembley (Joan Sims) and the butler and chauffeur was Sam (Sam Kelly). Tony's loyal secretary Maggie (Jenna Russell) was in love with him. His mum (Dora Bryan, later Pauline Letts) wanted nothing to do with his snobby new status and lifestyle and remained firmly entrenched in her Cockney roots. There were 19 editions over three series ending on 2 November 1992.

Writer: Bob Larbey. Producer: Gareth Gwenlan.

Grumpy Victor Meldrew (Richard Wilson) and wife Margaret (Annette Crosbie) made ONE FOOT IN THE GRAVE the nation's favourite sitcom (Photo: Copyright © BBC)

ONCE UPON A TIME IN THE NORTH

BBC. First broadcast: 3 May 1994

Bernard Hill starred as Len Tollit who was made redundant and invested all his pay-off to set up Len Tollit Cellphones. Though he was an optimist, he overlooked the fact that the only supplier of cellphones for miles around was his old school rival Bob Carling (Bill Stewart). By the last of the six episodes, Len's business had collapsed and he had moved into landscape gardening. Sharing his home in Sutton Moor, a semi-rural Northern town, and his vacillating fortunes were his sensible but unfulfilled wife Pat (Christine Moore), boy-hungry feminist daughter Siobhan (Susan McCardle) and football-mad son Sean (Andrew Whyment). Living in the annexe of their home was Mr Bebbington (Bryan Pringle) and his revolting dog Pablo. Len, who drove the family's battered camper van for both business and pleasure, had a black-sheep brother Morris (Bob Mason), a truck-driver driven himself by a spiritual guide named Geronimo.

Writer: Tim Firth. Producer: Philip Partridge for Philip Partridge productions.

ONE FOOT IN THE GRAVE

BBC. First broadcast: 4 January 1990

David Renwick created and wrote this series in which Victor Meldrew (Richard Wilson) lived in cantankerous retirement in suburbia with his wife Margaret (Annette Crosbie), whose inexhaustible

patience was sorely tried by the irascible curmudgeon. Meldrew grumbled and groaned his way through 28 editions up to and including the 90-minute Christmas special in the Algarve, Portugal, which was transmitted on 26 December 1993. The series became a fashionable cult and Meldrew's frequent outburst of incredulity – "I don't believe it!" – became a catchphrase. Others to feel the barbs of his tongue were Mrs Warboys (Doreen Mantle), neighbours Patrick and Pippa (Angus Deayton and Janine Duvitski) and Nick Swainey (Owen Brenman).
Theme music: Eric Idle. Producer: Susan Belbin.

ONE MAN'S MEAT
BBC RADIO. First broadcast: 28 June 1964

Eddie Maguire created and wrote these 11 shows, broadcast on the Home Service on Saturday evenings. Terry Scott was cast as Terry Binks, the general manager of a flourishing cooked-meat factory. The poison was provided by his brother-in-law Brian Singleton (Brian Rix). Terry was married to Brian's sister Joyce (Elspet Gray). When the owner of the meat factory died suddenly, his will revealed that Terry's expectations of inheriting the business were not to be realised. The factory had been bequeathed half to Brian and half to Joyce. Thereby began a battle for supremacy between the owners and the general manager.
Producer: Alastair Scott Johnston.

ONE OF THE BOYS
CBS (AMERICA) PRESENTED BY ITV.
First broadcast (UK): 12 October 1982

Senior citizen Oliver Nugent (Mickey Rooney) was living in a retirement home when he was visited by his grandson Adam Shields (Dana Carvey), a student. Adam realised that his grandfather had too much life in him to waste away in the home, so he took him to live with himself and fellow student Jonathan Burns (Nathan Lane). In later episodes, Oliver found another old boy to make pals with, played by Scatman Crothers. The series was created and produced by Saul Turtletaub and Bernie Orenstein. Varying numbers of shows were screened in the different ITV regions.

ONLY FOOLS AND HORSES
BBC. First broadcast: 8 September 1981

John Sullivan's much-revered creation notched up its 55th edition with the 85-minute special shown on 25 December 1993, and along the way, this show became one of the few in history to break the 20-million viewer barrier.

Set in Peckham, the series began as a story of three men of three different generations, all without a woman in their life. David Jason starred as Derek 'Del Boy' Trotter, a wheeler-dealer with aspirations of great wealth but saddled with the responsibility of a not very bright younger brother, Rodney (Nicholas Lyndhurst). Del had that working-class upbringing that taught the moral value and necessity of family solidarity and, while he would sell any old load of rubbish to any punter foolish enough to buy it, he would protect Rodney from his own dim-witted follies with his life, even if he did consider Rodney to be a 'plonker'. The third character was Grandad played by Lennard Pearce, a bit of a whiner, capable of deep sulks but nonetheless lovable. When Pearce died in December 1983 the Grandad character died with him and Sullivan wrote in Uncle Albert (Buster Merryfield), who moved into the Trotter household after a life at sea.

Del's business was conducted either from home, from his three-wheeler Robin Reliant with its 'Trotter's Independent Trading Company' sign, or in the Nag's Head pub. Within the pub lurked characters who contributed to the show on a regular basis. The barman was Mike (Kenneth MacDonald), a laid-back, dry cynic who was surprised at nothing. His customers included the gangster spiv Boycie (John Challis), resplendent in camel coat with velvet collar, a wad of money and his wife Marlene (Sue Holderness). The pub thicky was Trigger (Roger Lloyd Pack) and others included lorry driver Denzil (Paul Barber) and Mickey Pearce (Patrick Murray). Love and marriage did eventually enter the lives of the Trotter brothers with Cassandra (Gwyneth Strong) for Rodney and Raquel (Tessa Peake-Jones) for Derek. Other characters included Alan (Denis Lill), Sid (Roy Heather) and corrupt policeman Roy Slater (Jim Broadbent).
Directors included Ray Butt, Martin Shardlow, Mandie Fletcher, Susan Belbin, Tony Dow, Gareth Gwenlan. Producers: Ray Butt, Gareth Gwenlan.

ONLY WHEN I LAUGH
YTV. First broadcast: 29 October 1979

Eric Chappell created and wrote this series in which three hospital patients, Figgis (James Bowlam), Glover (Peter Bowles) and Norman (Christopher Strauli), were incarcerated in a hospital ward, seemingly for ever, where their fates were in the hands of irascible Doctor Gordon Thorpe (Richard Wilson) and his male nurse Gupte (Derrick Branche). Apart from Matron (Brenda Cowling) and Cook (Pamela Cundell), the stories involved a floating population of doctors, nurses, patients and the four principal characters, their complaints about the visiting hours and their dissatisfaction with the hospital radio service. In all, 41 episodes were made and the show made the number one position in the ratings in 1979 and 1980, dropping only as low as number two in its third season.

Producer: Vernon Lawrence.

OPEN ALL HOURS
BBC. First broadcast: 20 February 1976

Roy Clarke's stories of a corner shop in a Yorkshire street began quietly with a six-episode run on BBC2. The shows were repeated on BBC1 in 1979 and found the audience that would ultimately carry the title to the very top of the ratings. Ronnie Barker starred as the stammering shopkeeper Arkwright whose threefold philosophy involved the extraction of as much money as possible from his customers, getting as much slave-labour as possible out of his assistant Granville (David Jason), who was rather dim and just happened to be his nephew, and the constant lusting after Nurse Gladys Emmanuel (Lynda Baron), a buxom wench who lived across the road and drove an old Morris Minor. Arkwright was a bully and rooted in the past. He refused to instal a modern till and boasted of his double-entry book-keeping. Other residents of the locality who became regular customers included Mrs Featherstone (Sephanie Cole) and Mavis (Maggie Ollerenshaw). Over four series there were 25 editions ending 6 December 1985.

Music: Max Harris. Producer: Sydney Lotterby.

THE OTHER 'ARF
ATV. First broadcast: 30 May 1980

Lorraine Chase starred as Cockney model Lorraine Watts whose love affair with upper-class Tory MP Charles Lattimer (John Standing) began when they met by chance in a restaurant. At the time, Charles had a fiancée, Sybilla Howarth (Patricia Hodge), and Lorraine had a boyfriend, Brian Sweeney (Steve Adler). Both Sybilla and Brian hung around making the path of true love far from smooth for Charles and Lorraine. Other regular characters were Lorraine's father George Watts (John Cater) and Charles's friend Lord Freddy Apthorpe (James Villiers), who eventually went abroad to get mar-

ried. By the final series in 1984, Lorraine and Charles were living together at his home, Dormer House, but he was out of politics and very hard-up, to the point where they were forced to take in paying guests. The administration of the house was assisted by Bassett (Richard Caldicot) and Mrs Lilley (Sheila Keith). Central took over the production from 1982 and the last of a total of 24 shows was screened on 30 March 1984.

Writer: Terence Howard. Directors: John Kaye Cooper, Alan Wallis. Producers: Tony Charles, Allan McKeown.

THE OTHER ONE
BBC. First broadcast: 11 November 1977

This series by John Esmonde and Bob Larbey followed bachelors Ralph (Richard Briers) and Brian (Michael Gambon) who, in the first series of seven adventures, went to Spain on holiday and to seek out the opposite sex. When the show returned for another six-part run on 23 February 1979, they were back in England with Brian launching a new career as a rep. Both their lives turned into an exhausting hard sell on the road, with Brian yearning for peace and quiet at home and Ralph planning for a hectic escape to Paris.

Music: Ronnie Hazlehurst. Producers: John Howard Davies, Roger Race.

OUR DORA
GRANADA. First broadcast: 18 September 1956

Created and written by Reuben Ship, this series starred Dora Bryan as Dora, the widow of a former GI who had died after they had gone to the United States to set up home. She had returned to England to the household of her sister Clara Hackett (Helen Christie), with whom she had once been part of a second-rate variety act. Clara was married to bad-tempered businessman Charlie Hackett (Martin Wyldeck) who had no time for his sister-in-law. Try as she would to be helpful, Dora succeeded in bringing nothing but trouble to the Hackett home. Dora Bryan left the show after the first four episodes. However, the characters of Clara and Charlie were retained and Eleanor Summerfield was brought in to play the part of Clara's sister. The sister's name was changed to Ellie Martin and the show was given a new title, MY WIFE'S SISTER. It began under its new name on 16 October and ran until 11 June the following year.

Producers included Henry Kaplan, Guy Nottingham, Milo Lewis.

OUR ELIZABETH

BBC RADIO. First broadcast: 26 August 1940

Novelist Florence Kilpatrick had established the character of Elizabeth in several of her books, and she adapted her into six weekly radio shows starring Hermione Baddeley. Elizabeth was a perky little Cockney girl who was barmaid at the local pub, The Clutch and Spanner. All other characters were portrayed, as and when required, by Ernest Jay, Hugh Morton, John Rorke and Fred Yule. *Producer: Tom Ronald.*

OUR HOUSE

ABC. First broadcast: 11 September 1960

Nine people met in an estate agent's office and realised that, by pooling resources, they could all live in one big house. Although all the residents did not appear in every episode, we were introduced to them all in the first edition. They were public librarian Georgina Ruddy (Hattie Jacques); local council rating-officer Simon Willow (Charles Hawtrey); the more unemployed than employed Daisy Burke (Joan Sims); retired merchant navy captain and his French violinist wife Captain and Mrs Iliffe (Frank Pettingell and Ina de la Haye); artists and newly-weds Stephen and Marcia Hatton (Trader Faulkner and Leigh Madison); law student Gordon Brent (Norman Rossington) and bachelor bank clerk Herbert Keene (Frederick Peisley). For the second series, which began on 16 September 1961, Jacques, Hawtrey, Madison and Peisley were joined by Bernard Bresslaw as William Singer, Harry Korris as an old ship's captain, Hylda Baker as his sister Henrietta, Eugenie Cavanagh as the dim and dizzy Marina, and Johnny Vyvyan as a rather mysterious, lonely bachelor.
Writers: Norman Hudis, Brad Ashton and Bob Block. Producer: Ernest Maxin

OUR HOUSE

USA PRESENTED BY BBC.
First broadcast (UK): 13 September 1987

Gus Witherspoon (Wilford Brimley) had a simple and peaceful existence until he decided to take in his widowed daughter-in-law Jessie Witherspoon (Deidre Hall). She arrived complete with her three children, Kris (Shannen Doherty), David (Chad Allen) and Molly (Keri Houlihan). Gus had to adapt his routine to take in the needs of his new family. His neighbour was Joe Kaplan (Gerald S

O'Loughlin). The BBC showed 16 editions over two series ending 20 August 1989.

OUR KID

YTV. First broadcast: 8 April 1973

When Ma Buslingthorpe died, she left the house, 59 Spring Street, Halifax, and her youngest son Bob (Barrie Rutter) in the care of her eldest son Ben (Ken Platt). Ever after, Ben had been the housekeeper and, ultimately, Bob had taken a job in a local factory. Their fraternal bond was naturally strong but when Lynda (Sylvia Brayshaw) fixed her eye on Bob, Ben felt the bond was under threat.
Theme music: Johnny Pearson. Writers: Keith Waterhouse and Willis Hall. Producer: Ian Davidson.

OUR LES

BBC RADIO. First broadcast: 8 December 1971

Les Dawson starred as a window-cleaner by day and as a turn in the working men's clubs of the North by night, without a deal of success at either. In a first series of eight broadcasts, Les was supported in a variety of roles by Colin Edwynn, Joe Gladwin, David Mahlowe and Jacqueline Clark. A further run of nine ended on 25 February 1973 with Mahlowe joined by Barbara Mullaney and Alison Steadman.
Writer and producer: James Casey.

OUR MAN AT ST MARK'S

A-R. First broadcast: 25 September 1963

Writers James Kelly and Peter Miller created these stories about incidents in the daily life of a country vicar. The parish of St Mark's was set in the village of Felgate. Leslie Phillips starred in the first series as Rev. Andrew Parker who arrived in Felgate in the opening episode. Parker was a rather eccentric vicar, especially in the eyes of his housekeeper, Mrs Peace (Joan Hickson). He drove a mini and had a girlfriend Anne Gibson (Anne Lawson). Mrs Peace was much relieved when Rev. Parker left for pastures new and the new vicar, Rev. Stephen Young (Donald Sinden), arrived with his Scottie dog, Mr Robertson on 16 April 1964. In the 1965 series beginning 26 April, Rev. Young took on a sexton and gravedigger named Harry the Yo Yo (Harry Fowler), so known because he had spent most of his life in and out of prison. The final edition was screened on 2 August 1965.

Directors included Christopher Hodson, Richard Doubleday and Bill Turner. Producer: Eric Maschwitz.

OUR MAN HIGGINS
ABC (AMERICA) PRESENTED BY ITV.
First broadcast (UK): 31 January 1963

Producer Paul Harrison created this television comedy from an American radio series called *It's Higgins, Sir*. It starred Stanley Holloway as a very English butler to American businessman Duncan MacRoberts (Frank Maxwell) and his wife Alice (Audrey Trotter). The MacRoberts family had been living a very ordinary, middle-class suburban life when they inherited a Scottish family fortune – and Higgins. Although Higgins behaved in a proper and dignified manner for most of the time, a little petty larceny was in his soul and he had a light-hearted approach to his position. Duncan and Alice had two sons, Tommy (Ricky Kelman) and Dinghy (KC Butts), and a daughter, Joanie (Regina Groves). There were 34 editions.
Writer: Alvin Sapinsley.

OUR MR MEREDITH
BBC RADIO. First broadcast: 11 July 1949

John Jowett wrote these 12 comedy thrillers which starred Edwin Styles as Charles Meredith who sleuthed his way through the stories. In close proximity to Meredith throughout were Joy Bannister (Violet Loxley), black-hearted Ada (Dorothy Summers), Inspector Sydenham (Sebastian Cabot) and Sergeant Marrow (John Sharp).
Producer: Vernon Harris.

OUR SHED
BBC RADIO. First broadcast: 17 July 1946

Max Wall wrote and starred in this series which began life as a segment of HOOP-LA! in 1944. Two years on it was given its own slot in its own right and ran for 11 weeks. The featured characters, who were billed as a trained troupe of performing zombies, included Ma (Doris Nichols), who had a fondness for milk stout, Mr Mosseltoff (Harold Berens), who busied himself with the black market, and The Voice (Arthur Rigby). Other characters including Handymen Guppy and Fogg, the Duchess and Humphrey were portrayed by the above-named and Kenneth Blain, Patricia Hayes, and Marian Pola.
Producer: Pat Dixon.

OURS IS A NICE HOUSE
LWT. First broadcast: 10 October 1969

Created and written by Harry Littlewood, this series starred Thora Hird as Thora Parker, proprietress of a North Country boarding house. She had two teenage children, Vera (Caroline Dowdeswell) and Alan (Leslie Meadows). Also in residence was Gran (May Warden), and neighbour Elsie Crabtree (Ruth Holden) regularly popped in to beg and borrow. Thora's residents came and went, some on a week-by-week basis, but among those who made their presence felt over the two series that the show ran were Mrs Orpington-Hunt (Beatrix Mackey), Alf Whittle (Harry Littlewood), Lottie Bottomley (Damaris Hayman) and retired ballet dancer turned nightclub manager Dudley Banks Smith (Ray Fell).
Producer: Stuart Allen.

OUT OF THIS WORLD
USA PRESENTED BY ITV.
First broadcast (UK): 25 March 1991

Just eight episodes of this series were stripped Monday to Thursday and then Tuesday to Friday of the following week. Evie (Maureen Flannigan) was a half-alien who became a clairvoyant after an electric shock, much to the consternation of her mother (Donna Rescow). Uncle Beano (Joe Alaskey) reverted to childhood while Lindsay (Doug McClure) was left straddling the middle ground trying to make sense of all of them.

OUTSIDE EDGE
CENTRAL. First broadcast: 24 March 1994

Writer Richard Harris based this series around two couples whose only common denominator was that the men both played for the same village cricket team. Roger Dervish (Robert Daws) was the team's obsessively pompous prig of a captain who was far from being as bright as he thought he was. He bullied and ranted at his simpering but loyal wife Mim (Brenda Blethyn), who all but disintegrated when an overt pass was made at her by elderly lothario Dennis Bradley (Denis Lill). The other couple were slobby, overweight Kevin Costello (Timothy Spall), who fancied himself as a gourmet cook, and his sex-mad wife Maggie (Josie Lawrence), who fancied anything wearing a pocket handkerchief but especially Kevin. Roger looked down on the Costellos as his social inferiors but

Bombastic Roger (Robert Daws, left) and slobby Kevin (Timothy Spall), cricketers and husbands both in OUTSIDE EDGE (Photo: Central Television)

common-as-muck Maggie hit it off all right with mousey Mim.

Director: Nick Hurran. Producer: Paula Burdon.

OVER THE GARDEN WALL
BBC RADIO. First broadcast: 10 February 1948

Rochdale comedian Norman Evans created his gossipy female character Fanny Fairbottom as the mainstay of his variety act and she was subsequently transferred to the airwaves. Evans had a rubber face, a gurner's dream, with spectacles atop Fanny's red nose beneath her wild red wig and dustcap. Fanny was the openly admitted inspiration for Les Dawson's similar creation 30 years later. On stage, Fanny's neighbour, before whom she heaved her more than ample bosom while sounding off on items of local disinterest, was never seen, but once she was introduced to an audience on the wireless she was a real Mrs Higginbottom, portrayed initially by Ethel Manners. Then, in the third series, Betty Jumel appeared as Betty Butterworth, Fanny's new neighbour. Other characters were Grandpa (Percy Garside, later Herbert Smith) and Little

Willie (Peter Broadbent). The whole thing for Evans was an extension of his finely-honed portrayal of a pantomime dame which was so well established on the halls. Under this title there were three series amounting to 18 broadcasts.

Writers: Ronnie Taylor and Eddie Maguire. Producer: Bowker Andrews.

OVER THE RAINBOW
MERIDIAN. First broadcast: 11 July 1993

Dick Clement and Ian La Frenais wrote this eight-episode story about four young people trying to make headway in the music business. In the first episode Neil (Peter Sullivan) married Finnoula (Angeline Ball). During the reception, he and best man Spencer (Ian Targett), known as Spence, blew up a safe in a robbery attempt. Spence got away and Neil got twelve months. When he was released, he discovered his wife shacked up with Spence in a room above her Uncle Roddy Lenehan's Brighton pub, The Rainbow. The result was that she would have neither of them, and Spence and Neil had to share a room while Finn moved in with her friend and singing partner Michelle (Bronagh Gallagher). Uncle Roddy (Eamon Morrissey) was not Finn's real uncle and indeed he lusted after her; it was just that he had married her aunt, but it did not stop him pursuing her. He, Finn and Michelle were all Irish. Michelle fancied just about anyone and was as sexually frustrated as Neil and Spence who, jointly and severally rebutted by Finn, adopted an attitude of casual indifference. The girls formed a band, Wicked Cleavage, and the boys wrote some great songs until it was discovered that they were all knocked-off from old albums! In the final episode they set off on what was supposed to be a world tour, organised by Neil, Spence and Uncle Roddy.

Director: Declan Lowney. Producers: Bernard McKenna and Allan McKeown for Selec TV.

OVER TO YOU
BBC RADIO. First broadcast: 30 September 1951

This successor to MUCH-BINDING-IN-THE-MARSH again starred Richard Murdoch and Kenneth Horne supported by Sam Costa, Maurice Denham and Diana Morrison. Apart from the title, there was little that had changed in this 13-week run.

Writers: Murdoch, Horne, Anthony Armstrong and Talbot Rothwell. Producer: Leslie Bridgmont.

PC 49
BBC RADIO

See THE ADVENTURES OF PC 49

PACIFIC STATION
USA PRESENTED BY CHANNEL 4.
First broadcast (UK): 27 July 1993

Late of SOAP and BENSON, Robert Guillaume starred as Det Bob Ballard, a veteran of the force who was a stickler for playing things according to the book. His partner Richard Capparelli (Richard Libertini) adopted a more casual and modern approach to the fight against crime. Their beat was the notorious Venice Beach area of Los Angeles. Capparelli's instinct to trust to luck was a source of much irritation to Ballard, but it seemed to get results. Eleven editions were screened.
Producer: George Suga for KTMV Productions.

PALACE HILL
CENTRAL. First broadcast: 5 January 1990

This children's series set out to spoof the younger members of the Royal Family. Set at Palace Hill Comprehensive School, the first series had a Princess Beatrice (Phoebe Wood) among the pupils who also included Mandy (Alison Dury), Maggie (Tessa Harrison), Nick Knuckle (Oliver Hawker), Chelsea Bun (Ian Kirkby), Jimmy (Steven Ryde), Binky Spoon (Gail Kemp) and Cilla Cone (Semone Rhone). For the second series starting 17 April 1991 there were two new pupils, Charles (Mark Dexter) and Di (Dantelle Tilley).
Writers: Peter Corey and Bob Hescott. Director: David Crozier. Producer: Sue Nott.

PAPER MOON
ABC (AMERICA) PRESENTED BY BBC.
First broadcast (UK): 24 September 1974

Taking the theme of the 1973 movie of the same title which had starred Ryan O'Neal and his daughter Tatum, this 13-part series set in the 1930s starred

Chris Connelly as Moze, a bible-selling confidence trickster who teamed up with smart little girl Addie (Jodie Foster). They conned their way across America's Mid-west in a rickety old Model-A Ford.

PAPERS! PAPERS!
BBC RADIO. First broadcast: 7 May 1942

Harry Fowler and Leslie Adams played two Cockney newspaper boys whose adventures and mishaps filled a 12-part series.
Writer: Cyril Campion. Producer: Jacques Brown.

PARADISE ISLAND
THAMES. First broadcast: 21 April 1977

Sole survivors of a shipwreck in the Pacific, Rev. Alexander Goodwin (Bill Maynard) and entertainments officer Cuthbert Fullworthy (William Franklyn) found themselves marooned on a desert island. While Fullworthy was anxious to construct a raft for their escape to Australia, Goodwin was quite content with the peace and tranquility of the island. There was just one series of six programmes.
Writers: Michael Haley, John Junkin, Vince Powell, Bernie Sharp. Producer: William G Stewart.

PARDON MY GENIE
THAMES. First broadcast: 10 April 1972

This children's series was created and written by Bob Block. A plumber's shop assistant, Hal Adden (Ellis Jones), polished an old watering-can and released a genie (Hugh Paddick). Being 4000 years old, the genie's magic was pretty rusty to begin with and he got Adden into various scrapes which usually involved an appearance by PC Appleby (Joe Dunlop). The shop was owned by Mr Cobbledick (Roy Barraclough) and his wife Patricia (Lynette Erving). Other regular characters were Dr and Mrs Hockridge (William Abney and Joyce Grant). In a second series launched in January 1973, there was a new genie played by Arthur White.
Director: Robert Reed. Producer: Daphne Shadwell.

PARDON THE EXPRESSION

GRANADA. First broadcast: 2 June 1965

At the time of writing, Leonard Swindley (Arthur Lowe) was the first and only character from *Coronation Street* to be spun-off into a self-contained series. Within the Street, Swindley's conversation often contained the phrase 'If you'll pardon the expression', which naturally formed the title of his post-Street adventures. He left Gamma Garments, a small shop in Weatherfield, to take the post of assistant manager at a branch of Dobson and Hawks, a national chain-store. With 35 employees, Swindley assumed an exaggerated air of importance, even buying a new suit. However, the store manager Ernest Parbold (Paul Dawkins) was a man for an easy life and was content to pass the buck for any problems or irregularities and deposit the blame on Swindley. For the 1966 series beginning 10 January, there was a new store manager, Walter Hunt, portrayed by Robert Dorning. Other regulars were the staff manageress Miss Sinclair (Joy Stewart) and the canteen manageress Mrs Edgeley (Betty Driver). Thee were 32 episodes ending 30 May 1966.

Writers included Harry Driver, Jack Rosenthal and Christopher Bond. Directors included Walter Butler and Michael Cox. Producers included Harry Driver, Derek Granger and HV Kershaw.

PARENTHOOD

USA PRESENTED BY BBC.
First broadcast (UK): 4 June 1993

Based on the 1989 movie of the same title which starred Steve Martin, this series starred Ed Begley Jr as Gil Buckman, married to Karen (Jayne Atkinson) and raising their three children as well as looking after the needs of Grandma (Mary Jackson). There were 12 episodes.
Producer: Ron Howard.

PARSLEY SIDINGS

BBC RADIO. First broadcast: 5 December 1971

Jim Eldridge wrote this 10-part series about life on a run-down and badly neglected railway station where Arthur Lowe was the station master and Kenneth Connor played the dual role of porter and signalman. Other regulars in the cast were Liz Fraser and Ian Lavender.
Producer: Edward Taylor.

PARTNERS

BBC. First broadcast: 29 January 1981

Richard Waring wrote this serial in six parts about the partnership, both business and matrimonial, of Rupert and Diana Bannister (Derek Waring and Mel Martin). Trade was at an all-time low when Rupert was offered the chance of a financial injection into the firm which would provide the necessary capital for expansion. As his bad luck would have it, the offer came on the day of the hearing for his and Diana's divorce. He tried to retrieve the shares in Bannister Bathroom Fittings which he had given her on their wedding night, but Diana got wind of the deal and realised the true value of her holding. As such, they remained partners, which was just as well since Diana proved better at solving problems and issues like redundancies than Rupert. In the final episode there seemed a real chance that they could get their marriage back together. However, the decree was due to become absolute in 24 hours. Other regular characters were Brenda (Jacqueline Clarke), George Gilkes (Derek Francis), Pamela Heslop (Elizabeth Counsell) and Mr Matheson (Derek Farr).
Producer: Harold Snoad.

THE PARTRIDGE FAMILY

USA PRESENTED BY BBC.
First broadcast (UK): 2 September 1971

Film star Shirley Jones starred as Mrs Shirley Partridge who had five children, all of whom were music-crazy. She set out to steer them on a successful career. In fact her real-life son David Cassidy, who played the eldest child Keith, soon emerged as the star of the show and for a short while became the biggest teenage idol in the world. The other children in the family were Laurie (Susan Dey), Danny (Danny Bonaduce), Chris (Jeremy Gelbwaks) and Tracy (Suzanne Crough). Helping Shirley in her weekly exploits was Reuben Kincaid (David Madden).

THE PARTY PARTY

BBC RADIO. First broadcast: 16 May 1987

This anarchic six-week series was set in the future in the year 1992. The face of British politics was changed when Action Man, the leader of the Party Party, was asked to form a government and the people of Microcosm were taking acting lessons to appear in the resultant sitcom known as the Cabinet. The writers and participants were Morwenna Banks, Robin Driscoll, Robert Glenister, Hugh Laurie, Clive Mantle and Rory Bremner. *Producer: Jamie Rix.*

THE PATTY DUKE SHOW

ABC (AMERICA) PRESENTED by ITV.
First broadcast (UK): 15 October 1964

Patty Duke played the parts of two look-alike cousins, Patty and Cathy, in this series created by Sidney Sheldon. Patty was an all-American high school girl, a gum-chewing kid who loathed classes and loved rock 'n roll. Her cousin Cathy was a Scot who came to stay with the family. Cathy was studious and had a strong sense of decorum. Patty's parents were Natalie Lane (Jean Byron) and Martin Lane (William Schallert). Patty also had a younger brother, Ross (Paul O'Keefe). There were 104 editions. *Producer: William Asher.*

THE PAUL LYNDE SHOW

ABC (AMERICA) PRESENTED by ITV.
First broadcast (UK): 29 August 1973

American comedian Paul Lynde starred as attorney Paul Sims, married to Martha (Elizabeth Allen) with two daughters, Barbara (Jane Actman) and Sally (Pamelyn Ferdin). One day he returned home from his office to learn that he had a son-in-law. Barbara had married an unemployed layabout with a genius IQ. His name was Howie (John Calvin) and he and Barbara moved into the Sims basement. Paul grew increasingly harassed and frustrated and dreamt up a variety of schemes to get them out and to find Howie a job. The show was created by Sam Clark and Ron Bobrick from an original stage play entitled 'Howie'. *Producers: Harry Ackerman and William Asher.*

PEOPLE LIKE US

A-R. First broadcast: 7 October 1957

There were only three episodes of this title which was set in a boarding house in a small provincial town. The stars were variety comedians Reg Dixon and Sally Barnes. *Writers: Sid Colin and Talbot Rothwell. Producer: Kenneth Carter.*

PERFECT SCOUNDRELS

TVS. First broadcast: 22 April 1990

The idea for this series came from the two stars: Peter Bowles, who played Guy Buchanan, and Bryan Murray, who played Harry Cassidy. Buchanan and Cassidy were both confidence tricksters who met up at the funeral of a master of their ilk. They formed a partnership working as latter-day Robin Hoods, picking on deserving victims and being lovable rogues. This status quo obtained for the first dozen one-hour stories in two series of six the second beginning on 6 April 1991. However, a third run of six starting 25 April 1992 came under the wing of new producer Tony Virgo who removed all the lighter elements which had afforded the comedy; he sharpened the stories into heavier and sinister drama. Instead of only the greedy being conned, the victims began to include the pitifully innocent. Sian Phillips portrayed Cassidy's aunt, Mother Aloysius of the Convent of the Bleeding Cross in Ireland. *Writers included Ray Connolly, Kieran Prendiville, Anthony Couch, Barry Devlin and Peter J Hammond. Directors: Ian Toynton, Jan Sargent, John Gorrie, Graham Theakston. Producers: Tim Aspinall, Graham Benson, Terence Williams, Tony Virgo.*

PERFECT STRANGERS

USA PRESENTED BY BBC.
First broadcast (UK): 26 June 1989

Bronson Pinchot starred as Balki Bartokomous, an immigrant to the USA from a peasant background in a backward mid-European country. He inflicted himself on his cousin Larry Appleton (Mark Linn-Baker) who quickly learned that Balki was ill-equipped to cope with the facilities of contemporary America and set out to educate him over the eight episodes. The girls in the series were Mary Ann (Rebeca Arthur) and Jennifer (Melanie Wilson). *Producer: Joel Zwick.*

PET PALS

BBC. First broadcast: 21 May 1965

This children's show, based on an idea by James Green, ran for seven weeks. Jim Dale starred as the animal-crazy manager of a pet shop who loved his furry friends so much that he was reluctant ever to sell them. As a result the shop never made a profit and became increasingly like a zoo. Special animal sounds were made by Percy Edwards. *Writers: George Evans and Derek Collyer. Producer: GB Lupino.*

THE PETER GOODWRIGHT SHOW

BBC RADIO. First broadcast: 18 March 1963

Comedian and impressionist Goodwright starred as bachelor Peter who shared a flat with Anton (Anton Rodgers) in Chorlton-cum-Hardy, a Manchester suburb. Their troubles began with next-door neighbour Arnold Potter (Joe Gladwin) and followed them on adventures, whether in pursuit of the opposite sex or on a mission to film the Loch Ness monster. Anton proved to be the more successful with the girls. A first series of 13 shows was followed by a further run of 13 ending 21 June 1964. *Writers: Vince Powell and Harry Driver. Producer: Geoff Lawrence.*

PETTICOAT JUNCTION

CBS (AMERICA) PRESENTED BY ITV.
First broadcast (UK): 8 January 1964

Having played the role of Blanche Morton on US radio's BURNS AND ALLEN SHOW for more than twenty years and then the part of elderly cousin Pearl Bodine in THE BEVERLY HILLBILLIES, actress Bea Benaderet was taken by writer and producer Paul Henning and cast in this, her own starring show. She was Kate Bradley, proprietress of the Shady Rest Hotel where she lived with her three daughters, Billie Jo (Jeannine Riley), Bobbie Jo (Pat Woodell) and Betty Jo (Linda Kaye). It was set around 1890. The hotel lay at the end of a single railway line and was serviced by one elderly steam train, The Hooterville Cannonball. A railway executive, Homer Bedloe (Charles Lane), made repeated threats and did all in his power to close the line down. But all Kate's friends rallied as she fought her battles and fended off Homer. She was also supported by the other railway employees including the train conductor Charley Pratt (Smiley Burnette) and the fireman Floyd Smoot (Rufe Davis). However, her most stalwart support came from her daughters and from Uncle Joe (Edgar Buchanan), who lived with them. In spite of the rural setting, the show was studio-made and ran in the United States for five seasons. There were 148 episodes made.

PHENOM

USA PRESENTED BY CHANNEL 4.
First broadcast (UK): 8 March 1994

Teenage tennis prodigy Angela Doolan (Angela Goethals) was the object of a tug of interests between her coach Lou Della Rosa (William Devane) and her mother (Judith Light). Lou's cold and cruel method was designed to breed a killer loathing for opponents into his pupils and he drove Angela to focus all her pent-up venom on to the court. To compensate, Mrs Doolan smothered her daughter with warmth to prevent her becoming one of the emotional wrecks of the tennis circuit. Angela had an older brother Brian (Todd Louiso) who lacked confidence and considered himself an all-round failure. Her younger sister Mary-Margaret (Ashley Johnson) was quite the reverse, with a precocious self-confidence and the maturity to act as Angela's confidante. *Producer: Huckson Hidman for Gracie Films.*

THE PHENOMENON SQUAD

BBC RADIO. First broadcast: 3 October 1987

Roy Kinnear starred in a five-episode series as Superintendent Brabazon, hand-picked by his boss (Simon Cadell) to lead an undercover squad of trouble-shooters. However, Brabazon was a bungling incompetent, as were the others in his squad, Justine (Susie Blake) and Sigalov (Royce Mills). *Writer: Michael Snelgrove. Producer: Paul Mayhew-Archer.*

THE PHIL SILVERS SHOW

CBS (AMERICA) PRESENTED BY BBC.
First broadcast (UK): 20 April 1957

In the annals of television comedy, few shows are treated with greater reverence than this 1950s series created by Nat Hiken, starring Phil Silvers as Master Sergeant Ernest T Bilko 15042699 of the 3rd Platoon, Transport pool of the US Army base at Fort Baxter, Roseville, Kansas. Bilko was self-dedicated to the pursuit of riches and tried, always in vain, to bend and manipulate the rules of the Army in order to acquire money. Though he always failed, he had a loyal bunch of eccentric believers who followed and participated in his schemes. These included compulsive gambler Mess Sergeant Rupert Ritzik (Joe E Ross), slobby and gormless Private Duane Doberman (Maurice Gosfield), Private Fender (Herbie Faye) who had little faith in Bilko's get-rich-quick plans and was later promoted to Corporal, and Corporal Rocco Barbella (Harvey Lembeck). The camp commander was Colonel John 'Melon Head' Hall (Paul Ford). Other important characters included Mrs Hall (Hope Sansberry), Sergeant Joan Hogan (Elizabeth Fraser), Paparelli (Billy Sands) and Henshaw

(Allan Melvin). Over four years 138 episodes were made and at the time of writing, the shows were still being screened regularly around the world, often under alternative titles YOU'LL NEVER GET RICH and SERGEANT BILKO.

PHONEY ISLAND

BBC RADIO. First broadcast: 14 May 1940

With the benefit of the ITMA team of writer Ted Kavanagh and producer Francis Worsley, this series starred Dicky Hassett as the Cockney boss of an amusement park, inviting guests to 'roll up, roll up' for all the fun of the fair. Hassett, whose catch phrase was 'large lumps', worked with a team of regulars who included Frederick Burtwell, Arthur Chesney, Dick Francis, Vera Lynn and Dudley Rolph, who played a variety of characters and were liable to burst into song since the BBC Variety Orchestra under Charles Shadwell was also in residence.

PHYLLIS

CBS (AMERICA) PRESENTED BY ITV.
First broadcast (UK): 18 October 1976

This series, created and produced by Ed Weinberger and Stan Daniels for MTM Productions, was a spin-off of a character from THE MARY TYLER MOORE SHOW. Cloris Leachman starred as Phyllis who, on the death of her husband, was left penniless and was forced to move with her daughter Bess (Lisa Gerritsen) to San Francisco. There they lived with her unsympathetic in-laws, Jonathan and Audrey Dexter (Henry Jones and Jane Rose). She took a job where her boss was Leo Heatherton (Richard Schaal) and formed a friendship with Julie Erskine (Barbara Colby).

PIE IN THE SKY

BBC. First broadcast: 13 March 1994

Ten 50-minute episodes of this comedy drama created by Andrew Payne were screened, starring Richard Griffiths as Henry Crabbe, a Detective Inspector in the police force who was looking forward to retirement and then to the achievement of his life's ambition to open his own restaurant, 'Pie In The Sky'. Crabbe was a large man who lived to cook and eat traditional British home fodder. His wife Margaret (Maggie Steed) was a cautious accountant and, while she tolerated and generally supported her husband, was anxious that he did not squander the nest egg he had accumulated.

Crabbe was a respected investigator but had not progressed to the top of the force because he had not always toed the line, unlike his one-time friend Assistant Chief Constable Freddy Fisher (Malcolm Sinclair). Crabbe knew and understood that truth was rarely a factor on which to rely when it came to justice and by a quirk of fate which demonstrated that belief, Fisher was able to blackmail Crabbe into stalling his retirement plan and being available for police work at his behest. Notwithstanding, Crabbe installed his chickens in the garden and opened the restaurant with the help of ex-con Steve Turner (Joe Duttine) as co-chef, Margaret manning the till, Linda (Alison McKenna) the waitress and John (Ashley Russell) the waiter. Fresh vegetables for the restaurant were grown and supplied by Henderson (Nick Raggett). As Fisher continued to pressure Crabbe, so the latter was alerted to his every new scheme by astute young WPC Cambridge (Bella Enahoro).

Writers: Andrew Payne, Richard Maher, Paul Hine, John Milne, John Flanagan and Andrew McCulloch. Directors: Colin Gregg, George Case, Martin Hutchings, Lawrence Gordon Clark. Producers: Jacky Stoller and David Wimbury for Witzend.

THE PIG AND WHISTLE

BBC RADIO. First broadcast: 17 January 1938

Set in an imaginary rural village pub, these programmes were written by Charles Penrose of 'The Laughing Policeman' fame. He also played the appropriate part of village 'bobby' Sergeant Evergreen. Once war had broken out, the Pig and Whistle became a favourite haunt for members of the Home Guard. The landlady was Rosie Jones (Miriam Ferris) and other regular characters included Old Granfer (Charles Wreford), Jimmy Larkin (Sidney Burchall), Egbert Ullage (Peter Penrose), Rosie's cousin 'Erb (John Rorke), and Billy Potter, the village postman (Fred Yule). Yule also played Farmer Greenacre and made the relevant noises for Sammy, the pub cat. Popular comedian of the time Syd Walker appeared as himself under the assumption that it was his local. The last broadcast from the pub was on 19 October 1944.

Producer: Ernest Longstaffe.

PIG IN THE MIDDLE

LWT. First broadcast: 27 January 1980

Terence Brady and Charlotte Bingham created and wrote these stories of the eternal triangle, only in this case the would-be adulterer remained celibate. Bartholomew 'Barty' Wade (Dinsdale Landen) lived with his elegant and practical wife Susan (Joanna Van Gyseghem) in East Sheen. She nagged him incessantly that he watched too much TV and that he ate too much. At one of their parties, Barty met Nellie Bligh (Liza Goddard). She loved picnics and all the fun things which Barty felt he was denied. Nellie schemed to make their relationship more romantic and less culinary. The web grew increasingly tangled. When Barty eventually left Susan, he and Nellie did not live together but as next-door neighbours. The shows enjoyed three runs of six ending 8 April 1983.

Music: Francis Lai. Producer: Les Chatfield.

THE PIGLET FILES

LWT. First broadcast: 7 September 1990

Nicholas Lyndhurst starred as Peter Chapman whose simple and ordinary life as a happily married college lecturer was thrown into chaos when he was recruited by Major Maurice Drummond (Clive Francis) and Major Maxwell (John Ringham) to work as a spy for MI5. One of the demands of his new job was total secrecy which meant he was unable to tell his wife Sarah (Serena Evans) what he was up to. The all-action series in which Chapman bumbled and bungled his way through sex, violence and espionage ran to a second series, which came to the screen on 3 May 1991, and there were 14 episodes in total.

Writers: Paul Minett and Brian Leveson. Producer: Robin Carr.

PINKERTON'S PROGRESS

BBC. First broadcast: 18 May 1983

Set in Lyttleton Old School, the action took place mostly in the staff-room where newly appointed deputy headmaster Pinkerton (Geoffrey Whitehead) arrived to find the school being run entirely for the benefit of the masters to the detriment of the pupils. Pinkerton resolved to make changes which would ensure the place was run for his benefit. The principal characters were the Headmaster (Derek Farr), Miss Shilling (Eleanor Bron), Clifford (Andrew Robertson), Davies (Clive Merrison), Renfrew (Michael Elwyn), Parsons (David Sibley), Beech (Derek Francis), Flax (Alan Parnaby) and the Bursar (Paul Hardwick). There were six episodes.

Writer: Charles McKeown. Director: John B Hobbs. Producer: Gareth Gwenlan.

PLAZA PATROL

YTV. First broadcast: 15 July 1991

Double act Cannon and Ball made a brief excursion into sitcom land with this six-part series. They played security officers Bernard Cooney (Tommy Cannon) and Trevor Purvis (Bobby Ball) whose responsibility was a shopping plaza.

Writers: Richard Lewis and Louis Robinson. Producer: Graham Wetherell.

PLEASE SIR

LWT. First broadcast: 8 November 1968

Bernard Hedges (John Alderton) arrived as a newly qualified teacher at Fenn Street Secondary Modern school in a rough area of London. The toughest class, 5C, immediately nicknamed him 'Privet'. He soon assessed his new position after meeting the weak headmaster Cromwell (Noel Howlett), the assistant head Doris Ewell (Joan Sanderson), a would-be tyrant who smarmed her way around Cromwell, and the rest of the staff including Welshman Price (Richard Davies) and Smith (Erik Chitty). However, Hedges was quick to learn that the everyday power behind the throne of the school's running was vested in the hands of the caretaker, Potter (Deryck Guyler).

Hedges developed a special affinity with 5C and its leading protagonists Peter Craven (Malcolm McFee), Eric Duffy (Peter Cleall), Sharon Eversleigh (Penny Spencer), Frankie Abbott (David Barry), Denis Dunstable (Peter Denyer) and Maureen Bullock (Liz Gebhardt). Maureen had a serious crush on Hedges. By 1970, much to Maureen's chagrin, Hedges had acquired a fiancée, Penny Wheeler (Jill Kerman). This was to be the final term for 5C, although the series continued until the wedding. The pupils left to form THE FENN STREET GANG but PLEASE SIR ran to one further series in 1971. Hedges and his wife remained for the first three programmes but his teaching post was soon handed over to a Mr Dix (Glynn Edwards), who proved unsuitable and was replaced by David Ffitchett-Brown (Richard Warwick), a rather classy chap who drove a sports car. His lot was to come to terms with a new 5C which included Gobber (Charles Bolton), Des (Billy Hamon), Daisy (Rosemary Faith), Celia (Drina Pavlovic) and Terry Stringer (Barry McCarthy). Alas, Ffitchett-Brown lacked the necessary staying power and even new teachers, Hurst (Bernard Holley) and Miss Petting (Vivienne Martin), could not carry on to further series.

Created and written by John Esmonde and Bob Larbey. Producers: Mark Stuart, Phil Casson (1971).

PLEASURE BEACH

BBC RADIO. First broadcast: 4 July 1946

This new and luxurious holiday camp was presided over by Claude Hulbert and Fred Emney. It featured a resident orchestra under the baton of Stanley Black and the permanent staff and holidaymakers were portrayed by Sally Browne, Lyle Evans, Hugh Morton, Brian Reece, Enid Trevor and Arthur Young.
Writer: Rodney Hobson. Producer: Roy Speer.

THE PLUMS

BBC RADIO. First broadcast: 4 October 1937

From an idea by Sonny Miller, Max Kester wrote the stories of the Lancashire Plum family who were first heard in a series of 12 broadcasts, each of 15 minutes' duration. Mr Augustus Plum (Foster Carlin) was reasonably well off and was an enthusiastic player of the cornet. His wife Aggie (Minnie Raynor) was not Lancastrian but Cockney born and bred, and her exasperation which concealed a heart of gold was the perfect foil to Gus' eternal optimism. They had a daughter, Victoria Plum (Audrey Cameron), who was grown-up but chose to reside with her parents until she married. Completing the household was doddering old Uncle Ed (Clifford Bean) who cluttered up the hearth with indifference to all around him. When the series was revived on 1 January 1942 for 12 further editions, Britain was deep into the war. Only Clifford Bean remained from the original cast. Augustus (Wylie Watson) was no longer rich and was back in the mills manufacturing khaki. Aggie (Beatrice Varley) was, for some reason best known to the writer, no longer a Cockney but a Lancashire lass who busied herself with the home and was helped by 16-year-old maid Ruby (Gabrielle Daye). Victoria (Paula Green) worked in munitions while her husband was away in the Army.
Producer: Max Kester.

POLICE SQUAD

ABC (AMERICA) PRESENTED BY ITV.
First broadcast (UK): 10 March 1983

Po-faced Lieutenant Frank Drebin (Leslie Nielsen), of a big city police division's trouble-shooting squad, was continually thwarted in his aim to bring law and justice to the streets by bizarre circumstances. His friend and mentor was Captain Ed Hocken (Alan North). The police scientist was Ted Olsen (Ed Williams) and Drebin made much use of a street-wise character known as Johnny the Shoeshine Boy (William Duell) who was his main informer. Six episodes were shown on ITV.
Producer: Bob Weiss for Paramount.

POOR LITTLE RICH GIRLS

GRANADA. First broadcast: 12 July 1984

When cousins Kate Codd (Maria Aitken) and Daisy Troop (Jill Bennett) met for the first time in years, they discovered that each had been much married and was trying to survive without men and on little money. Together they took a basement flat and explored ways of making a fortune. Both were from wealthy backgrounds, and both discovered they still had the ability to twist men round their little fingers. Joan Hickson played the role of Lady Harriet. Seven programmes were shown.
Writer: Charles Lawrence. Director: Nicholas Ferguson. Producer: Pieter Rogers.

PORRIDGE

BBC. First broadcast: 5 September 1974

Dick Clement and Ian La Frenais created and wrote this series, set in Slade Prison, and the story was developed from an earlier play called 'Prisoner and Escort'. Ronnie Barker starred as old lag Norman Stanley Fletcher, banged-up once more for a five-year stretch for robbery. His cell-mate was the much younger Lennie Godber (Richard Beckinsale) who was rather naive and impressionable while workshy Fletcher cleverly and cynically exploited the system. Treating all prisoners with equal contempt was Chief Officer Mackay (Fulton Mackay) and the rather milder side of authority was Warden Barrowclough (Brian Wilde). The Governor of the gaol was played by Michael Barrington. Other prisoners included Blanco (David Jason), Ives (Ken Jones), Lukewarm (Christopher Biggins), Gay Gordon (Felix Bowness), Warren (Sam Kelly), McLaren (Tony Osoba), Harry Grout (Peter Vaughan), Harris (Ronald Lacey), Heslop (Brian Glover) and Rawley (Maurice Denham). There were 20 editions over three seasons ending on 25 March 1977. Ronnie Barker again starred in the sequel GOING STRAIGHT in 1978.
Producer: Sydney Lotterby.

PORTERHOUSE BLUE
CHANNEL 4. First broadcast: 3 June 1987

Malcolm Bradbury adapted Tom Sharpe's novel into four one-hour comedy dramas which provided the platform for David Jason to win the BAFTA best actor award for his portrayal of head porter Skullion at Porterhouse, the most archaic and reactionary of Cambridge colleges. He was the custodian of college traditions when they came under threat with the appointment of the new Master, Sir Godber Evans (Ian Richardson), who manifested his determination to drag Porterhouse into the modern world. This culminated in Skullion being dismissed after 45 years of service. As the plot developed, significant characters emerged including the Dean (Paul Rogers), the Senior Tutor (John Woodnutt), the Bursar (Harold Innocent), the Praelector (Ian Wallace), Professor Siblington (Willoughby Goddard), Sir Cathcart (Charles Gray), Mrs Biggs (Paula Jacobs), Lady Mary (Barbara Jefford), old Porthusian Cornelius Carrington (Griff Rhys Jones) and student Lionel Zipser (John Sessions) who, in one scene, was required to dispose of several thousand condoms.
Theme music by Rick Lloyd, sung by The Flying Pickets. Director: Robert Knights. Producer: Brian Eastman for Picture Partnership Productions.

POTTER
BBC. First broadcast: 1 March 1979

Redvers Potter (Arthur Lowe) had spent his working life with the family firm, Potter's Mints, and much of that career had been as the boss. He faced retirement but his lively and bombastic personality would not allow him to do so quietly. He devoted himself to minding everyone else's business, whether they sought his involvement or not. He believed himself to be the saviour of the trampled-upon minority and sought to ensure that all around him were fulfilled. His patient and caring wife was Aileen (Noël Dyson), his neighbour was 'Tolly' Tolliver (John Warner), an antiques dealer, and his friend and drinking companion was the Vicar (John Barron). Lowe starred in two series, the first of six episodes and the second of seven, starting on 27 February 1980. Following Lowe's death in 1982, the series returned for seven further editions on 17 July 1983. Robin Bailey assumed the role of Redvers Potter and all the aforementioned players continued in their parts.
Theme music: Ronnie Hazlehurst. Writer: Roy Clarke. Producers: Peter Whitmore, Bernard Thompson.

POTTER'S PICTURE PALACE
BBC. First broadcast: 13 September 1976

Brian Finch wrote this seven-part children's series. On the death of his Aunt Mattie, Peter Potter (Eden Phillips) expected to inherit her cinema but he reckoned without cousin Reggie Turpin (David Lodge) who set out to find and destroy her Will and take it over for himself. Reggie's right-hand man was Frank Plank (Colin Edwynn) and others involved in each edition were Melvyn Didsbury (Melvyn Hayes), Sidney Bogart (John Comer), Joan Biddle (Angela Crow) and The Kid (Bruce Watt).
Director: Tony Harrison. Producer: John Buttery.

A PRESENT FOR DICKIE
THAMES. First broadcast: 31 December 1969

Dickie Henderson starred in this extension of THE DICKIE HENDERSON SHOW. Dickie's wife Jane (June Laverick) was absent in Australia until the final programme of the series of six, the first of which found Dickie living at home with his mother-in-law, Mrs Upshott-Mainwaring (Fabia Drake). The 'present' in the title was delivered to Dickie and came from India. It was a live elephant, Mini, which came complete with elephant trainer Abdul (Jerry Ram). Other regular characters were West

Country handyman William (Billy Burden) and Parker (Dennis Ramsden).
Writers: Jimmy Grafton, Johnny Heyward, Stan Mars. Producers: Peter Frazer-Jones, Stuart Hall.

PRESS GANG

BBC RADIO. First broadcast: 26 March 1941

Stage star Stanley Lupino played the only reporter on a small country newspaper in six 40-minute episodes. The owner of the newspaper was played by the original *Me and My Girl* girl, Teddie St Denis. Stanley was in love with Teddie and tackled challenging projects to impress her and win her hand. They always went wrong.
Writer and producer: Max Kester.

THE PRINCE OF DENMARK

BBC. First broadcast: 10 April 1974

Having struggled free of his mother's apron strings in NOW LOOK HERE . . . by marrying Laura (Rosemary Leach), Ronnie (Ronnie Corbett) found that his new wife had inherited a pub, The Prince Of Denmark, which gave him ample space to sound off in his role of male chauvinist piglet. However, he had his work cut out to keep himself at peace with both the customers and the brewery. Six episodes were transmitted.
Music: Denis King. Writers: Graham Chapman and Barry Cryer. Producer: Douglas Argent.

PRIVATE BENJAMIN

CBS (AMERICA) PRESENTED BY ITV.
First broadcast (UK): 6 January 1982

Don Reo is credited with having turned the 1980 movie of the same title into 39 half-hour sitcoms. Lorna Patterson starred as Judy Benjamin, the well-heeled young Jewish widow who gave up her rich and spoilt life to join the Army. She did not find Army life as easy as she would have liked. Eileen Brennan recreated her movie role as Captain Lewis, and other regulars in the show included Sgt Ross (Hal Williams), Pte Glass (Joan Roberts), Pte Winter (Ann Ryersson), Pte White (Joyce Little) and Gianelli (Lisa Raggio).
Producers: Madelyn Davis and Bob Carroll Jr.

PRIVATE SCHULZ

BBC. First broadcast: 6 May 1981

This series of six 50-minute episodes by Jack Pulman

was set during the Second World War. Private Schulz (Michael Elphick) was a confused and bemused German soldier who was recruited by his crazed boss Major Neuheim (Ian Richardson) to flood Britain with forged £5 notes and thereby destroy the economy. Bizarre as the plot appeared to him, Schulz stoically gave it his best, if farcical, endeavours, even though his conscription into the SS was due to his prior civilian existence as a somewhat cowardly thief. Equally wrapped up in the ambitious plot was Bertha Freyer played by Billie Whitelaw.
Director: Robert Chetwynd. Producer: Philip Hinchcliffe.

PRIVATE SECRETARY

CBS (AMERICA) PRESENTED BY ITV.
First broadcast (UK): 27 September 1957

Film star Ann Sothern produced this series with her own production company. It began in the USA in 1952 and ran for 104 episodes. Sothern herself starred as Susie McNamara, a razor-sharp private secretary. Her boss Peter Sands (Don Porter) was the slightly crazy, disorganised head of a big-time talent agency. Susie fought to bring sense and stability to his business life. The result was that she was able to wield more power than he was.

A PROPER CHARLIE

BBC RADIO. First broadcast: 17 April 1956

Charlie Chester starred in this creation by Bernard Botting and Charles Hart which was set in the imaginary new town of Biddingfold. Charlie was an entrepreneur whose carefully laid plans invariably came to grief. Being a new town, there were plenty of contracts to be won but their award was dependent upon how well the applicant knew and treated the Alderman (Deryck Guyler). Charlie not only pursued the contracts but also the Alderman's beautiful and talented daughter (Mary Law). A first series of seven programmes was followed by another 20 editions, for which Bill Pertwee joined the cast, from 6 April 1958.
Producer: Leslie Bridgmont.

A PROPER CHARLIE

BBC RADIO. First broadcast: 3 November 1985

Vince Powell wrote this eight-part series. Charlie Garside (Jack Smethurst) worked in a factory where he was a strong union man but spent most of his time in the pub. He was married to Vera (Madge Hindle) and they had a daughter Linda (Jane Hazlegrove), who was anxious to go on the Pill, and a son Terry (Jason Littler). Their gossipy neighbour was Ivy (Betty Alberge). Charlie's mates at the pub were Taffy (John Jardine) and Cyril (David Ross). *Producer: Mike Craig.*

THE PRUITTS OF SOUTHAMPTON
ABC (AMERICA) PRESENTED BY ITV.
First broadcast (UK): 4 January 1967

Lawrence J Cohen and Fred Freeman created this series from a novel *House Party* by Patrick Dennis. Phyllis Diller starred as Phyllis Pruitt, an elderly socialite living in Southampton, Long Island. The Pruitts owed ten million dollars to the taxman, who did not dare to take them to court for fear of precipitating another Wall Street crash. Phyllis was constantly at war with her social rival, Regina Wentworth (Gypsy Rose Lee). Richard Gardner played Uncle Ned Pruitt, Pam Freeman was Stephanie Pruitt and Lisa Loring was Suzy Pruitt. Grady Sutton portrayed Sturgis the butler. The harassed tax collector, Mr Baldwin (Richard Deacon), was aided and abetted by Sheriff Peterson (Larry Lanter). There were 30 editions. *Producers: Everett Freeman and David Levy.*

PUBLIC FUTILITIES
BBC RADIO.

See MR MUDDLECOMBE JP

PULL THE OTHER ONE
CENTRAL. First broadcast: 15 June 1984

Grandma (Lila Kaye) lived with Sidney and Sadie Mundy (Michael Elphick and Susan Tracy) and their family. One day they set off for Cornwall and Grandma appeared to die en route. They laid her out on the roof rack and went to find a phone box. When they returned, the car and Grandma had been stolen. She was found in hospital where an insulin coma was diagnosed. She made a complete recovery and returned to dominate the household, even to the point of holding keep-fit classes in the front room. There were six episodes. *Music: Dave MacKay. Director: Peter Ellis. Producer: Joan Brown.*

PULL UP AT DAVE'S
BBC RADIO. First broadcast: 11 November 1952

Comedian Dave Morris changed location but not character from CLUB NIGHT as the 'Know-All' became proprietor of a transport café somewhere on the Great North Road where the knives and forks were chained to the tables and there was positively no credit. With Morris from the earlier show were Joe Gladwin as Cedric, Fred Ferris as 'The Wacker' who continued to ask 'As 'e bin in?', and Tom Harrison who had previously been the secretary. The café closed after 24 editions on 5 May 1953. *Writers: Dave Morris and Rex Diamond. Producer: Alick Hayes.*

PUNCH DRUNK
BBC. First broadcast: 4 January 1993

Set in the boxing world of Glasgow, this six-part series by Clayton Moore featured hard-up boxing manager Vinnie (Kenny Ireland), who took newcomer Hance (John Kazek) under his wing to groom him for stardom in the ring. His plans met fierce opposition from Vikki Brown (Diana Hardcastle) who headed an organisation called Doctors Against Boxing. *Director: Ron Bain. Producer: Colin Gilbert.*

PUNKY BREWSTER
NBC (AMERICA) PRESENTED BY ITV.
First broadcast (UK): 14 February 1987

Punky Brewster (Soleil Moon Frye) was a seven-year-old girl, abandoned by her parents, who lived with her puppy, Brandon, in an abandoned Chicago apartment until she was found by the crusty, grouchy old manager of the block, Henry Warnimont (George Gaynes). In spite of his grumpy disposition, Henry took a shine to the child and had her placed in care. She was desperately unhappy in care and ran away. He then became her guardian and she lived with him and housekeeper Mrs Cooper (Susie Garrett). She made a close friend of her own age, Cherie Johnson, played by an actress of the same name. In one episode pop star Andy Gibb portrayed Punky's piano teacher, Tony Glenn. There were in excess of 50 shows. *Producer: David W Duclon.*

QUANTUM LEAP

NBC (AMERICA) PRESENTED BY BBC.
First broadcast (UK): 5 November 1991

This time-warp comedy starred Scott Bakula as Sam Beckett who, because of an experiment in time travel which went wrong, found himself transported into the body of a total stranger each episode. His only companion in his transmutations was hologram Al (Dean Stockwell), a cigar-smoking womaniser who was invisible to all but animals, children and blondes. Together they travelled through time and space, always trying to do some good and with a power to change the past. More than 50 episodes were screened.

QUEEN OF ROMANCE

BBC RADIO. First broadcast: 19 November 1992

Lesley Joseph starred as romantic novelist Angela Temple, who had been married seven times. Her publisher Donald Bone (Gordon Reid) had a son, Conrad (Matthew Byam Shaw), who had been a journalist and fancied himself as a writer of fiction. However, he found it impossible to get his work published and was wildly jealous of Angela. She employed an elderly, rheumatoid-arthritic house-keeper, Mrs Delilah Partridge (Pat Coombes), a widow with an eye for eligible elderly men. Angela's doctor was the unorthodox Dr Cruickshank (Geoffrey Whitehead). There were two series, each of six programmes, the last episode was heard on 6 January 1994.

Writer: Stephen Sheridan. Producer: Caroline Leddy.

QUEENIE'S CASTLE

YTV. First broadcast: 5 November 1970

This series, created and written by Keith Waterhouse and Willis Hall, starred Diana Dors, complete with Northern accent, as the fire-breathing dragon of Buckingham flats, Queenie Shepherd. She lived there with her three sons, Raymond (Freddie Fletcher), Douglas (Barrie Rutter) and Bunny (Brian Marshall). Also in residence, albeit illegally, was her brother-in-law Jack (Tony Caunter). Money was a constant worry in the Shepherd household and Queenie's problems were exacerbated by her arch enemy and fellow flat-occupier, Mrs Petty (Lynne Perrie). The landlord of the flats was was played by Bryan Mosley. There were two further series, each of six programmes, and the final transmission was on 5 September 1972.

Producers: Graham Evans, Ian Davidson.

RAB C NESBITT

BBC. First broadcast: 31 December 1989

Rab C Nesbitt (Gregor Fisher) was first seen in the sketch show *Naked Video* and graduated to his own 45-minute special on New Year's Eve 1989. A series began on 27 September 1990 and there had been a total of 21 editions up to 23 December 1993. Nesbitt was a ranting Scottish philosopher, resplendent in string vest, and – for those able to penetrate the thickest of accents – he spouted a stream of foul-mouthed, sexist opinion from his disgusting living-room and other unsalubrious locations. His wife was Mary (Elaine C Smith) and his revolting children were Bernie (Eric Cullen) and Gash (Andrew Fairlie). His mate Jamesie Cotter was played by Tony Roper.

Writer: Ian Pattison. Producer: Colin Gilbert.

RADIO ACTIVE

BBC RADIO. First broadcast: 8 September 1981

Purporting to be Britain's first local radio station to broadcast on a national network, this anarchic show continued for 52 editions over seven series ending on 2 January 1988. The principal characters were Anna Dapter (Helen Atkinson-Wood), Mike Channel (Angus Deayton), Uncle Mike Stand and Martin Brown (both played by Michael Fenton-Stevens), Mike Flex (Geoffrey Perkins) and Nigel Pry (Philip Pope). Deayton and Perkins were responsible for most of the writing and Pope for the music. See also KYTV.

Producers: Jamie Rix, Jimmy Mulville, David Tyler.

RADIO BOOST

BBC RADIO. First broadcast: 1 January 1941

This early satire of commercial radio was created at a time when many BBC stars had defected to Radio Luxembourg. Six programmes were broadcast. Sir Samuel Nightingale (Dick Francis) was the manufacturer of Nightingale's Natty Nightshirts. He had two offspring, daughter Birdie (Betty Driver), a talented singer, and infant prodigy son Cyril (John Morris). Nightingale consulted the advertising agency Bragg and Bellow who took him to Radio Boost, where his campaign was masterminded by station manager 'Plug' Murphy (Arthur Riscoe). Murphy was assisted in his wild schemes by his secretary Polly Poppet (Phyllis Stanley). The Radio Boost Mighty Orchestra and singers were under the direction of Billy Cotton.

Producers: Bill MacLurg and Howard Thomas.

RADIO CARS

BBC RADIO. First broadcast: 18 April 1991

Angela (Harriet Walter) inherited a London minicab business and discovered she was the proprietress of a smoke-filled seedy office peopled by seedy males, led by tricky Eddie (Gary Waldhorn), a charmer who was used to having things all his own way. The drivers were a bunch of rascals on the make and included Nicco (Neil Dudgeon), Frenchie (Terence Edmond) and Gringo (Paul Gregory). Their regular customer was Mrs Corfton-Browne (Maxine Audley, later Anne Stallybrass). A first series of five was followed by six further episodes starting 4 November 1993.

Writer: Jennifer Phillips. Producer: Richard Wortley.

THE RAG TRADE

BBC. First broadcast: 6 October 1961

Writers Ronald Wolfe and Ronald Chesney set this series in a dressmaker's workshop at Fenner Fashions where the women workers were pitted against their male bosses. Peter Jones was the hapless Mr Fenner and Reg Varney played his foreman, Reg. The women were marshalled by machinist shop-steward, Paddy (Miriam Karlin) whose militant rallying call 'Everybody Out!' became a popular catchphrase. She was ably supported by shop treasurer Carole (Sheila Hancock) and Little Lil (Esma Cannon), the assistant button-hole hand and tea-maker in chief. Mr Fenner was unscrupulous and up to all manner of dodges while his workforce looked for any opportunity to scrounge a few extra pounds for their wage packets. Others in the workroom for the first series were Judy Carne, Barbara Windsor, Ann Beach, Toni Palmer and Rita Smythe.

In a second run the following year, those five were replaced by Gwendolyn Watts, Wanda Ventham, Jan Williams, Julie Samuel and Elaine Kagan. For the third series beginning 5 January 1963, Wanda Ventham was rejoined by Barbara Windsor and newcomers were Amanda Reiss, Sheena Marshe, Stella Tanner, Pat Denys, Claire Davenport and Carmel Cryan, but Esma Cannon and Sheila Hancock had left the cast. The role of Reg's mum was occasionally played by Irene Handl. There were 35 episodes and in the last one on 30 March 1963 it looked as though Reg and Judy (Barbara Windsor) were contemplating marriage.

Music: Gordon Franks. Producer: Dennis Main Wilson.

LWT. First broadcast: 10 September 1977

When London Weekend Television revived this format only Miriam Karlin as Paddy and Peter Jones as Mr Fenner remained from the BBC cast of the early 1960s. They were joined by several new characters including Tony (Christopher Beeny), Olive (Anna Karen, recreating her role from ON THE BUSES), Kathy (Diane Langton), Lyn (Gillian Taylforth), JoJo (Lucita Lijertwood) and Mabel (Deddie Davies). There were 22 editions over two seasons.

Writers: Ronald Wolfe and Ronald Chesney. Producers: Bryan Izzard, William G Stewart.

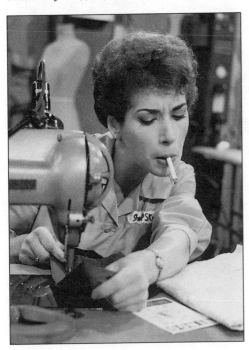

RANDALL AND HOPKIRK DECEASED

ATV. First broadcast: September 1969

These 50-minute comedy dramas, created by Dennis Spooner, explored the fantasy world of ghosts. Marty Hopkirk (Kenneth Cope), a partner in a firm of private detectives, was killed in a hit-and-run incident while working on a case. He reappeared as a ghost to his partner Jeff Randall (Mike Pratt), the only human being who could see him. Together they continued in business. Marty's bewildered widow Jean (Annette André) was subjected to several psychic phenomena as her late husband tried to make contact with her. The only other regular character was bad-tempered policeman Inspector Large (Ivor Dean). A total of 26 filmed episodes were made and the first one was shown in various regions on different days during the fourth week of September.

Writers included Ray Austin, Mike Pratt, Ralph Smart, Tony Williamson, Ian Wilson. Directors included Ray Austin, Paul Dickson, Cyril Frankel, Leslie Norman, Jeremy Summers, Robert Tronson. Producer: Monty Berman.

THE RANDOM JOTTINGS OF HINGE AND BRACKET

BBC RADIO. First broadcast: 9 April 1982

Patrick Fyffe and George Logan, creators and interpreters of Dr Evadne Hinge and Dame Hilda Bracket, more or less took over where they had left off in THE ENCHANTING WORLD OF HINGE AND BRACKET. Their life rolled on in the Suffolk village of Stackton Tressel where their fantasy world embraced their own home, the Old Manse, with daily help Maud (Daphne Heard, later Jean Heywood) and a variety of village characters including the Major (Anthony Sharp) and Peter and Mandy Moore (Chris Emmett and Frances Jeater). Dame Hilda did the jottings in the belief, belittled by Dr Evadne, that her diaries would one day carry literary importance. There were 67 programmes broadcast to 16 April 1989. See also DEAR LADIES.

Writer: Gerald Frow. Producers: John Dyas, John Fawcett Wilson.

Shop steward Paddy (Miriam Karlin) is easily distracted from work in between strikes in THE RAG TRADE (Photo: Copyright © BBC)

RAY'S A LAUGH

BBC RADIO. First broadcast: 4 April 1949

This, one of radio's longest-running series, starred Ted Ray with a variety of characters spanning more than 250 programmes to 13 January 1961. The first series alone ran for 65 weeks. The stories revolved around Ray in his different jobs and at home, where his wife was played by Australian actress Kitty Bluett (apart from the 1955 series when Diane Hart took over – Bluett returned the following year). There were many memorable creations, particularly two old dears, Mrs Hoskin and Ivy (Bob Pearson and Ted Ray). Mrs Hoskin would say: "I've sent for young Dr Hardcastle," and Ivy would reply: "He's luvely, Mrs Hoskin . . . he's luuuv . . . ley!" Bob Pearson, who sang in many of the shows with his brother Alf, also played a tiny little girl called Jennifer. To list all the creations would require too much space but the creators included Peter Sellers, Fred Yule, Graham Stark, Patricia Hayes, Jack Watson, Charles Leno, Charles Hawtrey, Alexander Guage, Pamela Manson, Laidman Browne, Pat Coombs and, worthy of special note, Kenneth Connor as the ghastly Sidney Mincing and as Ted's brother-in-law Harold. Among the catchphrases which stuck were 'It's agony, Ivy' and 'If you haven't been to Manchester, you haven't lived'.

Writers: Ronnie Hanbury and George Wadmore, Ted Ray and Eddie Maguire, Sid Colin and Talbot Rothwell, Bernard Botting and Charles Hart, George Inns. Producers: George Inns, Roy Speer, Leslie Bridgmont.

Outer space creation the RED DWARF and crew (Photo: Copyright © BBC)

RED DWARF

BBC. First broadcast: 15 February 1988

Rob Grant and Doug Naylor created this fantasy of 36 programmes over six series ending 11 November 1993. A spaceship of the 24th Century lost all its crew but one, Dave Lister (Craig Charles), who was left stranded aboard with no better company than the ship's computer Holly (Norman Lovett), which was nothing more human than a voice and a face on a screen; a hologram of his former bunk-mate who had died, Arnold Judas Rimmer (Chris Barrie); and a descendant of Lister's former pet cat known only as Cat (Danny John-Jules). By the fourth series in 1991 Hattie Hayridge had taken over from Lovett as Holly.

The characters were forced to co-exist in the confined space of the craft and as such there was much friction and conflict. In the second season they picked up a distress signal from another space vehicle and they encountered the robot Kryten (David Ross, later Robert Llewellyn). Hallucinations and fantasies gave adequate scope for the authors to introduce cameo guest characters including Christine Kochanski (Clare Grogan), who was Lister's ideal of a travelling mate. By the advent of series six, they had been in suspended animation for 200 years since the end of series five; their starship had been stolen and after the best part of three million years, Lister seemed to be in with a chance of real romance. However, they still had to contend with the menace of the newly encountered and dangerous Psirens. That their ship had been stolen suggested a major alien force at work, for the vessel was six miles in length. Also appearing as Psiren's Dr Manet was Jenny Agutter.

Directors: Ed Bye, Juliet May, Andy de Emmony. Producers: Paul Jackson for Paul Jackson Productions, Hilary Bevan Jones and Justin Judd for Grant-Naylor Productions.

THE REFUGE

CHANNEL 4. First broadcast: 21 September 1987

Because of the plights of her old university friend Julia (Julia Hills) and her own mother Helen (Caroline Blakiston), radio broadcaster Dee Dee (Lou Wakefield) turned her flat into a refuge for unwanted and abused women. They made it a policy not to allow men to cross the threshold, placing a sign on the door announcing 'Refuge – No Men'. Adding authority to their territorial claim was WPC Bollard (Carole Hayman) and they afforded sanctuary to a variety of women who briefly passed through including Jackie (Helen Lederer) and Bella-Donna (Denise Coffey). After a first run of seven there were seven more editions starting on 22 June 1988. By the end of that second series the refuge was in serious financial difficulties and facing closure.

Music: Peter Skellern. Writers: Sue Townsend and Carole Hayman. Director: Les Chatfield. Producer: Vernon Lawrence.

REGGIE

USA PRESENTED BY CHANNEL 4.
First broadcast: 14 September 1984

This was the American version of David Nobbs' format for THE FALL AND RISE OF REGINALD PERRIN. Perrin became Reggie Potter (Richard Mulligan), a 48-year-old man who fantasised about a different way of life away from business and his wife Elizabeth (Barbara Barrie). He was surrounded by a bevy of eccentric characters including secretary Joan (Jean Smart), CJ (Chip Zien), Mark (Tim Busfield), Linda (Dianne Kay), Tom (Timothy Stack) and Debra (Lisa Freeman). Six editions were screened.

RELATIVE STRANGERS

CHANNEL 4. First broadcast: 14 January 1985

Creators Laurence Marks and Maurice Gran took the character Fitz (Matthew Kelly) from their ear-lier series HOLDING THE FORT for this run of 12 programmes. Fitz was a happy-go-lucky loner, free of all responsibilities until his previously unheard-of teenage son John (Mark Farmer) turned up on the doorstep to live with him. It transpired that John was the result of one night's passion at a Butlin's holiday camp 18 years previously. Fitz worked at a shop owned by Percy Fisher (Bernard Gallagher) where John also worked for a spell. Father and son had their many differences but grew to be firm friends. The only other regular character was fellow worker Gerald (David Battley). A second series of seven shows ended on 9 March 1987.

Writers: Marks and Gran, Gary Lawson and John Phelps. Directors: John Kaye Cooper, Nic Phillips. Producer: Humphrey Barclay for Humphrey Barclay Productions.

THE RELUCTANT ROMEO

BBC. First broadcast: 2 August 1966

This creation of George Evans and Derek Collyer was first seen as a one-off *Comedy Playhouse* presentation. That show was repeated on 8 May 1967 followed by a series of eight new episodes. Leslie Crowther starred as the irresistible Thomas Jones, who struggled to shake off all the pursuing women. Though he had a fiancée, Sally (Margo Jenkins), he had other dalliances to keep at bay in true farce tradition like the sizzling Gina Darletti (Eunice Gayson) and Geraldine Woods (Amanda Barrie). His life became one hopeless tangle and involved Messrs Copthorne and Blazer (Geoffrey Sumner and Keith Pyott) in trying to extricate him.

Theme music: Ron Grainer. Producer: Eric Fawcett.

RENT

BBC RADIO. First broadcast: 6 May 1993

Richard and Maria (Patrick Barlow and Barbara Flynn) were contentedly married, childless, and lived in a house in dire need of repair. They took in students and the age gap forced them to realise they were not as young and trendy as they had previously imagined. The household members were Amy (Linda Polan), Ruby (Diane-Louise Jordan) and Paul (Toby Longworth). There were six broadcasts.

Writer: Lucy Flannery. Producer: Liz Anstee.

RENTAGHOST

BBC. First broadcast: 6 January 1976

Lost in the unsung schedules of children's television, this series by Bob Block ran for 58 episodes

over nine series to 6 November 1984. The story began when three Spirits from different centuries opened a business called Rentaghost, having all three returned to Earth. They were recently deceased Fred Mumford (Anthony Jackson); Hubert Davenport (Michael Darbyshire), a fussy Victorian ghost; and Timothy Claypole (Michael Staniforth), who was a mischievous medieval poltergeist. They were managed by an earthly agent, Mr Meaker (Edward Brayshaw), who had a wife Ethel (Ann Emery). She, at one point, was turned into a Cocker Spaniel. By 1980, Jackson and Darbyshire had left the cast but new arrivals included Molly Weir as Hazel the McWitch; Hal Dyer and Jeffrey Segal as Rose and Arthur Perkins; and a year later, Sue Nicholls as Nadia Popov and Christopher Biggins as Adam Painting. Queen Matilda arrived in the form of Paddie O'Neil and between them all, the Spirits created havoc.
Producers: Paul Ciani, Jeremy Swan.

REP

GRANADA. First broadcast: 9 July 1982

Digby Wolfe and Ray Taylor wrote this six-part series in which JC Benton (Iain Cuthbertson) was the proprietor of a shabby seaside repertory company in the 1940s. He bullied and cheated his actors, Royston Flagg (Stephen Lewis), Dudley Blake (Clive Carter), Flossie Nightingale (Patsy Rowlands), Violet Littlejohn (Clare Kelly), Wyndham Carter (Richard Hurndall), Angela Soames (Caroline Mortimer) and Dr Crombie (John Fraser).
Producer: Bryan Izzard.

THE RETURN OF SHELLEY

THAMES. First broadcast: 11 October 1988

Hywel Bennett again starred as SHELLEY who returned to England after five years teaching English in the USA and the Arab Emirates. He was horrified by the Americanisation of Britain which he felt had taken place during his absence. His former wife Maggie had changed and moved away to create her own life. He settled into accommodation where his landlords were Carol and Graham (Caroline Langrishe and Andrew Castell). With his eloquent observations, Shelley opened up a whole new world of understanding and freedom of thought for Graham, but Carol was not so receptive to his philosophies. The last of 19 episodes was transmitted on 9 January 1990. After that, the stories reverted to the original title SHELLEY.
Writers: Andy Hamilton, Guy Jenkin. Producer: Anthony Parker.

RHODA

CBS (AMERICA) PRESENTED BY BBC.
First broadcast (UK): 19 November 1974

Mary's friend in THE MARY TYLER MOORE SHOW, Rhoda Morgenstern (Valerie Harper), was spun-off into her own husband-seeking series set in New York. Rhoda was a Jewish girl who worked as a window-dresser and worried endlessly about her hip measurement and her attractiveness. She lived alone in an apartment where the voice of the unseen doorman was laden with doom. She had a mother of archetypal Jewish possession and emotion, Ida (Nancy Walker), and a sister Brenda (Julie Kavner) who was less screwed-up than the others. Early into the 110-episode series, Rhoda married Joe Gerard (David Groh) but the marriage was destined for swift failure. New men entered Rhoda's life including Gary Levy (Ron Silver) and Jack Doyle (Kenneth McMillan). The BBC screened the shows sporadically until 2 September 1981.
Music: Billy Goldenberg. Producers: James L Brooks and Allan Burns for MTM.

RICH TEA AND SYMPATHY

YTV. First broadcast: 5 July 1991

Julia Merrygrove (Patricia Hodge), divorced mother of two teenagers, accidentally locked trolleys in a supermarket with widower George Rudge (Denis Quilley), the head of Rudge Brothers biscuit factory. From that humble beginning grew an entanglement of the two families with a double helping of romance. As Julia and George fell in love, so, to their mutual shock, did her mother Granny Trellis (Jean Alexander) and his father Grandpa Rudge (Lionel Jeffries). Granny was snooker-crazy, Grandpa was sex-mad, George was a chauvinist and Julia was liberated. With five selfish children, John and Samantha Merrygrove (Jason Flemyng and Claudia Bryan) and Warren, Karen and Tracey Rudge (Chris Garner, Lorraine Ashbourne and Sara Griffiths), the fight was on for family survival. Also embroiled in the pull-and-push struggles were Julia's brother-in-law Steve Merrygrove (Ray Lonnen), Colin Pink (James Warrior) and Sally

(Anne Reid). The six-part series was created and written by David Nobbs.
Producer: David Reynolds.

THE RIFF RAFF ELEMENT
BBC. First broadcast: 2 April 1993

Debbie Horsfield's comedy drama of class barriers was critically hailed. The story began when retired diplomat Roger Tundish (Ronald Pickup) advertised the annexe of his country residence as available to be let to suitable tenants. He added, 'the riff raff element need not apply'. And so it came to pass that the ragamuffin Belcher family moved in to the Tundish residence and started a sequence of adultery, unplanned pregnancy and murder. The principal characters on the upper-crust side included Phoenix (Pippa Guard), Mortimer (Richard Hope), Joanna (Celia Imrie), Alister (Greg Wise) and Boyd (Nicholas Farrell), while at the bottom of the pile were Acky (Trevor Peacock), Maggie (Susan Brown), Petula (Mossie Smith) and Declan (Cal Macaninch). A second series of hour-long episodes began on 19 April 1994, and caused much angst when Alister was killed-off.
Producer: Liz Trubridge.

RINGS ON THEIR FINGERS
BBC. First broadcast: 13 October 1978

Sandy Bennett (Diane Keen) and Oliver Pryde (Martin Jarvis) had lived together for the best part of six years without the formalities of wedlock when this series began. She wanted to marry but he did not, and the political feminists of the time heaped scorn on the show but failed to prevent it becoming a hit. It did not pass without the critics' notice that the writer Richard Waring, the producer Harold Snoad and both the stars had all been divorced. Within a few episodes Sandy and Oliver were married, honeymooned in Brighton and embarked on a life of marital squabble. There were 19 editions over three seasons ending 27 November 1980 with pregnancy and all the trappings of a family. Sandy's parents were played by John Harvey and Barbara Lott.
Theme music: Frank Barber.

RISING DAMP
YTV. First broadcast: 2 September 1974

This much-loved and oft-repeated series began screen life as a single pilot. Yorkshire Television's Duncan Wood was quick to assess the potential and writer Eric Chappell delivered scripts so the series could begin on 13 December of that same year. The central character was Rigsby (Leonard Rossiter), the penny-pinching, egregious landlord of a squalid, decaying house which had been divided into bedsits. Rigsby himself lived downstairs with his cat, Vienna. His tenants were university administrator Miss Ruth Jones (Frances de la Tour), the spinster who was the object of his seedy lust; inept long-haired medical student Alan More (Richard Beckinsale); and mature student Philip Smith (Don Warrington), a prince in his native Africa. Rigsby was bitter, ignorant and repulsive, and he reviled the sex-starved Alan as though he were his social superior. That Philip was a prince made little impression on Rigsby for black meant inferior to him, no matter what the title. He was possessed of an acid tongue which spat out one-line jokes at everybody's expense. The show ran 28 episodes over four seasons to 9 May 1978.
Music: Dennis Wilson. Producers: Ian MacNaughton, Ronnie Baxter, Len Lurcuck, Vernon Lawrence.

THE RITZ
BBC. First broadcast: 24 April 1987

John Godber wrote this comedy drama in six 50-minute episodes. Eric (Richard James Lewis) and Veronica (Kate Layden) sunk all his redundancy money into buying The Ritz disco. The series covered the first six nights as Eric was forced to dream up wild and wonderful ploys in a desperate bid to attract the punters. The root of their troubles was rival disco owner Mad Mick (Richard Ridings), so Eric was forced to rely on his team of bouncers: Kenny (Andrew Livingston), who lived with his mother; Chike (Paul Rider), a university drop-out abandoned by his wife; and Skodge (Andrew Dunn), who was hard drinking and amorous. With depressive disc jockeys, frustrated catering manageress and lonely cocktail waitress, there were sometimes more staff than customers.
Directors: Martin Shardlow, John Godber. Producer: Chris Parr.

THE RIVER
BBC. First broadcast: 20 October 1988

This series in six parts by Michael Aitkens starred pop singer David Essex as Davey Jackson, canal lock-keeper at Chumley-on-the-water. Davey had

been a Cockney wideboy, a cheerful enough individual who had formed a rapport with nature while
a guest of Her Majesty in an open prison. The
romantic interest came to pass when bargee Sarah
MacDonald (Katy Murphy) broke her propellor
and sought shelter in Davey's cottage. Love bloomed,
in spite of Davey's live-in Aunt Betty (Vilma
Hollingbery) and the local snob, Colonel Danvers
(David Ryall). Not much support came Davey's
way but Tom Pike (Shaun Scott) was rarely far
away from the plot.
Producer: Susan Belbin.

ROBBING HOOD
BBC RADIO. First broadcast: 21 July 1992

Norman Wisdom starred in six editions as inveter-
ate jailbird Norman Hood, whose vow to go straight
was foiled on his first day of release when he teamed
up with refined and genteel con-woman Natalie
Matthews (Moira Lister).
Producer: Leslie Lawton.

ROBERT'S ROBOTS
THAMES. First broadcast: 12 November 1973

Bob Block created and wrote this children's series
about eccentric inventor Robert Sommerby (John
Clive), who built robots which looked and behaved
like humans. Robert lived with his Aunt Millie
(Doris Rogers) and he received a government grant
towards his work as Whitehall had spotted the
potential of his brilliance. The show's robots included Eric (Nigel Pegram), Katie (Brian Coburn),
Grimble (Richard Davies), Marken (Leon Lissek)
and Angie (Jenny Hanley). They were joined in a
second series at the end of 1973 by Desiree (April
Olrich), Plummer (David Pugh) and George
(William Lawford).
Producer: Vic Hughes.

ROBIN'S NEST
THAMES. First broadcast: 11 January 1977

Writers Johnnie Mortimer and Brian Cooke created this second spin-off (see GEORGE AND
MILDRED) from MAN ABOUT THE HOUSE.
Robin Tripp (Richard O'Sullivan), now a fully
qualified chef, was unemployed but harboured an
ambition to open his own bistro. He lived with his
girlfriend Vicky Nicholls (Tessa Wyatt), an air
hostess, above a Chinese restaurant in Notting Hill.
Vicky's father, James Nicholls (Tony Britton),

Robin (Richard O'Sullivan) seems quite at
home in his Nest with girlfriend Vicky (Tessa
Wyatt) (Photo © Thames Television).

frowned upon their living in sin and made his
opinions openly known. However, he was intrigued
and attracted by the potential of Robin's bistro and
became his partner. He also fancied his talents as a
waiter. James, separated from Vicky's mother
Marion (Honor Blackman), had a wandering eye
and thought the clientele of a bistro might afford
some good outlets for his libido. By the second
episode, ROBIN'S NEST was all set to open. It
was to be an all-family affair with the sole exception
of the washer-up, Albert Riddle (David Kelly),
whose job was made more difficult by the fact that
he had only one arm. He also had a criminal record.

The first six programmes were followed by a
new series of six which began on 23 February 1978.
The final programme of that run saw Robin and
Vicky marry. There were further series in September 1978, February 1979, January 1980 when the
occasional appearance of Marion Nicholls was portrayed by Barbara Murray, and January 1981 by
which time Vicky had had twins and there was a
new, familiar face at the bistro, Gertrude (Peggy
Aitchison).
*Writers included Mortimer and Cooke, Bernard
McKenna, Dave Freeman, George Layton, Adele
Rose. Producer: Peter Frazer-Jones.*

ROGER DOESN'T LIVE HERE ANYMORE

BBC. First broadcast: 24 September 1981

Roger Flower (Jonathan Price) was a musician and composer, impoverished and right in the throes of a particularly acrimonious divorce from Emma (Diane Fletcher). Emma had wealth in her own right but such was her loathing for Roger that she would neither help him financially nor paint anything other than a totally damning portrait of his character to their children Arabella (Alice Berry) and Charles (Benjamin Taylor). Roger was thereby forced to work doubly hard with the kids to try to ease them through the trauma of the break-up and retain a worthwhile relationship with them. He found some solace in the arms of Rose (Kate Fahy) but on the day Roger's divorce came through, she married a wrestler called Stanley (Michael Elphick). She justified this to Roger by saying she was turned-on by adultery. Six programmes were transmitted.

Writer: John Fortune. Director: John B Hobbs. Producer: Dennis Main Wilson.

ROLL OVER BEETHOVEN

CENTRAL. First broadcast: 25 February 1985

Created and written by Laurence Marks and Maurice Gran, and screened in 13 consecutive episodes, Belinda Purcell (Liza Goddard) was a rather mousy piano teacher living a dull life in a small village with her old-fashioned father Oliver (Richard Vernon). He was a retired headmaster who fervently believed the world came to an end with the Beatles. When a rock 'n roll legend, Nigel Cochrane (Nigel Planer), retired to the village, Oliver was horrified. Worse was to come when Nigel went to Belinda for piano lessons. Love bloomed, Belinda's life changed and so did that of Oliver. Nigel briefly emerged from retirement to go back on the road, and during his absence Belinda wrote pop songs with his friends, Marvin (Emlyn Price) and Lem (Desmond McNamara). In the end Belinda recorded an album and Oliver wanted a slice of the music business.

Director: Derrick Goodwin. Producers: Tony Charles and Allan McKeown.

THE ROLLING STONES

ABC. First broadcast: 30 January 1960

This creation by Tom Espie and Stanley Myers was a short-lived vehicle for the Braden family from Canada. Bernard Braden played Sandy Stone, who worked as a producer/cameraman for a company making travelogues. Where he went, so went his wife Barbara (Barbara Kelly) and their three real-life children, Chris, Kelly and Kim. Bernard suffered from acute absent mindedness while Barbara's practicality and methodical approach enabled her to cut through the red tape and officialdom which regularly threatened to hinder Sandy's work.

Music: Paddy Roberts. Producer: Anthony Finigan.

ROMANY JONES

LWT. First broadcast: 15 February 1972

This began as a single play and the subsequent series with the same cast commenced on 1 June 1973. Set in a caravan park, it featured workshy Bert Jones (James Beck) and his wife Betty (Jo Rowbottom) who lived in a scruffy, broken-down van that crawled with ants. Living in the adjacent caravan were Wally and Lily Briggs (Arthur Mullard and Queenie Watts). During the summer of 1973, James Beck died at the age of 42 but not before they had recorded a second series which was transmitted that autumn. For series three, which began in August 1974, the Briggs had new neighbours, the distinctly upper-class Jeremy and Susan Crichton-Jones (Jonathan Cecil and Gay Soper), and so it remained through a fourth series in the summer of 1974.

Theme music: Roger Whittaker. Writers included Chris Boucher, Peter Denyer, Jon Watkins, Ronald Wolfe and Ronald Chesney. Producer: Stuart Allen.

A ROOF OVER MY HEAD

BBC. First broadcast: 5 April 1977

Barry Took adapted Michael Green's book *The Art of Coarse Moving* into six episodes, the first of which was shown as a one-off *Comedy Special* with the series of five following from 3 August the same year. The story was of the disasters that befell James (Brian Rix) and Sheila (Lynda Baron) when they tried to buy a house. In their weekly path was Jack Askew (Peter Bowles in the first show, then Francis Matthews). Other regulars were Sir Phillip Comer (Richard Hurndall in the first show, then Dennis Ramsden), Flamewell (Alfie Bass), Gaye (Gail Harrison), Maureen (Deborah Watling, later Louisa Rix), Bert (Michael Stainton) and Mrs Bagworth (Sheila Keith).

Producer: Douglas Argent.

ROOM AT THE BOTTOM

ABC. First broadcast: 7 June 1964

Writer John Antrobus and director Dick Lester created this brief series which starred Lionel Jeffries as light-entertainment television producer Nesbitt Gunn, who should have been put out to grass years earlier. His incompetence brought his executive producer, the cigar-chewing Mr Hughes (Dick Emery), to the studio floor to placate various guest performers who suffered at the hands of Gunn's misdirection. Mr Hughes enjoyed throwing his weight around and saw off the production secretary (Wendy Craig) and a small-time entertainer (Monty Landis). The show ran just one series in 1964 but was revived over 20 years later (see below).

YTV. First broadcast: 9 November 1986

Adapted and written by Ray Galton and John Antrobus, this series was set at Megla Television where the tyrannical owner was Kevin Hughes (Keith Barron). One of his first acts was to sack drama producer Nesbitt Gunn (James Bolam) from his post and move him to the quiz department. In protest, Gunn barricaded himself inside his office and even girlfriend Celia (Deborah Grant) seemed unable to prise him out. When he at last emerged, he reluctantly took up his new post. Even in the lowly quiz department his job was under constant threat from Hughes. Other major characters included the Director General (George Baker), the Chaplain (Richard Wilson) and the new Head of Drama (Oliver Cotton). A second series of six started on 15 May 1988.
Producer: David Reynolds.

ROOM AT THE BOTTOM

BBC. First broadcast: 14 June 1966

This, the first series by writers John Esmonde and Bob Larbey, began as a single Comedy Playhouse presentation. The eight-part series that followed got underway on 14 March 1967. The setting was Saracens Manufacturing Company where the protagonists were the main-tenance men led by Gus Fogg (Kenneth Connor). His disciples were Happy Brazier (Gordon Rollings), Mr Salisbury (Brian Wilde) and Horace Robinson (Kenny Lynch). The object of their combined energies was to plot the extinction of newly-appointed Internal Security Officer Cyril

Culpepper (Patrick Newell). Caught between them and only wanting a quiet life in a seemly manner for one and all was Personnel Director Mr Powell (Deryck Guyler).
Producer: David Askey.

ROOM SERVICE

THAMES. First broadcast: 2 January 1979

Jimmy Perry created this seven-part series which was set in the 5-star Prince Henry Hotel in London. The three room-service waiters were, in order of seniority, Charles Spooner (Bryan Pringle), Aldo de Vito (Freddie Earlle) and Horace Murphy (Chris Gannon). The remainder of the hotel staff included Mrs McGregor (Jeillo Edwards), Dick Sedgwick (Matthew Kelly), Mr Morris (Basil Lord), Marlene Barry (Penelope Nice), Freda (Judi Maynard), Fedros (Michael Petrovitch), Ahmed (Neville Rofailla), Tin Tin (Ric Young) and the washer-up (Tony Allef).
Producer: Michael Mills.

ROOT INTO EUROPE

CENTRAL. First broadcast: 17 May 1992

William Donaldson created the character of Henry Root by writing letters in his name to various eminent people and, in 1980, publishing a book of the letters and their replies which became a bestseller. Donaldson himself turned his creation into this five-part comedy drama series, sending Henry (George Cole) and his long-suffering wife Muriel (Patricia Heywood) away from 139 Elm Park Mansions, London SW10, on his domineering way to meet men and women of eminence on a whistle-stop tour of Europe.
Producers: Mark Chapman and Justin Judd.

ROOTS

ATV. First broadcast: 11 September 1981

The title, by Laurence Marks and Maurice Gran, was a double play on words incorporating their hero's trade as a dentist and his Jewish origins. Melvin Solomons (Allan Corduner) was a successful dentist with a glittering career in front of him. When he announced his intention to give it all up in favour of pursuing his artistic bents, his parents Harry and Nettie (Stanley Meadows and Joy Shelton) threw up their hands in horror. His position was not eased by the fact that he had a married sister, Melanie Goldblatt (Lesley Joseph), who had found a suitable man in Howard (John Levitt). Notwithstanding, Melvin forged ahead with his rebellious ideals. There were six shows screened. *Producer: Keith Farthing.*

ROSEANNE
USA PRESENTED BY CHANNEL 4.
First broadcast (UK): 27 January 1989

Despite an endless stream of rumours concerning back-stage hostilities and wholesale purges of the 10-strong writing team, this series created by Matt Williams proved one of the biggest hits of all time on both sides of the Atlantic. Set in Lanford, Illinois, Roseanne Barr and John Goodman starred as Roseanne and Dan Conner, blue-collar parents of Becky (Lecy Coranson, later Sarah Chalke), Darlene (Sara Gilbert) and DJ (Sal Barone, later Michael Fishman). Both Roseanne and Dan were grossly overweight Jumbos, she slovenly but fun and he a pot-bellied independent building-contractor who relaxed over a beer and a game of poker. Roseanne had a few jobs but spent much of her life hunting for work. The family was poor. The children whined and whinged and eventually Becky eloped at the age of 17 and went off to live in south Minneapolis. Roseanne had an unmarried sister, Jackie Harris (Laurie Metcalf), who was desperate to find a man.

Roseanne Barr married Tom Arnold and by the fourth series, seen in Britain in 1992, she was billed as Roseanne Arnold. Tom Arnold himself became joint co-producer with his wife and also appeared in several episodes as the Conners' family friend Arnold. With more than 100 editions already in the can, a sixth series began on 4 February 1994 (UK) with Darlene who, among the children, had always had the sharpest lines, leaving to go to college in Chicago and thus making only occasional visits to the parental home. DJ moved closer to centre stage as he entered adolescence with all its ancillary worries and problems. With the help of some money invested by their mother, Roseanne and Jackie were able to run a diner called The Lunchbox.
Producers included Maxine Lapidus, Al Lowenstein, Brad Isaacs, Chuck Lorre, Rob Ulin for Carsey-Warner.

ROSIE
BBC. First broadcast: 2 September 1975

The first series of this Roy Clarke creation went out with the title THE GROWING PAINS OF PC PENROSE but after those initial seven episodes the four subsequent series took Penrose's nickname, Rosie, as the title. There were 34 editions in total, the last one transmitted on 30 October 1981.

For those first seven editions, the keen but very innocent Constable ME Penrose (Paul Greenwood) was a probationer posted away from home to a station under the command of Sergeant Flagg (Bryan Pringle). Thereafter he was returned on compassionate grounds to his home town where his life was dominated by women and, to his great embarrassment, he was known as Rosie to friends and colleagues alike. His superiors in the force did not share his belief that he was outstanding police material and his invalid mother Millie (Avril Elgar, later Patricia Kneale) and his Aunt Ida (Lorraine Peters), who packed his lunches, hounded him with their fears that he would be stabbed in the back any day. Only his Uncle Norman (Allan Surtees) offered him encouragement to escape the overpowering female influences in his life. Rosie had a fiancée, Gillian (Frankie Jordan), who would be speaking to him one day and not the next. Rosie's great friend was PC Wilmot (Tony Haygarth) and in the final series he left his mother's home and moved in with Wilmot.

Other characters included Chief Inspector Dunwoody (Paul Luty), WPC Brenda Whatmough (Penny Leatherbarrow), Gillian's parents Bill and Glenda (Don McKillop and Maggie Jones), and Merv (John Cater), a short-sighted police informer. Rosie stayed firmly rooted at the bottom of the force and the divorced Wilmot got him into all manner of schemes and scrapes, much to the disgust of Gillian.
Producers: Douglas Argent (series one), Bernard Thompson.

THE ROUGH WITH THE SMOOTH
BBC. First broadcast: 16 July 1975

Tim Brooke-Taylor and John Junkin together wrote this six-part series as a starring vehicle for themselves. They were two bachelor flatmates, Richard Woodville (Brooke-Taylor) and Harold King (Junkin). The sum total of their aims and pursuits was the opposite sex, and different guest actors and actresses appeared in each episode.
Producer: Harold Snoad.

Lanford's favourite heavyweights, the Conners (Roseanne Arnold and John Goodman) take nothing lying down (Photo: Channel 4)

ROUND AND ROUND
BBC. First broadcast: 25 June 1984

Spanning the years from 1958 to 1972, this six-part series by John Fortune followed the life of Maureen (Bernadette Short) from her first real love, Robert (John Gordon Sinclair), through her first sexual experience, Patrick (Nicholas Lyndhurst), to marriage with Francis (James Lister), the resultant children and divorce and a chance meeting with Malcolm (Tony Haygarth) in a florist's, from which love bloomed again. Throughout her trials, Maureen was supported by parents Mum and Dad Stevens (Eileen Kennally and Dave King).
Director: Peter Hammond. Producer: Ray Butt.

ROUND THE TWIST
AUSTRALIA PRESENTED BY BBC.
First broadcast: 6 April 1990

Following the death of their mother, three children, Linda (Tamsin West), Pete (Sam Vandenberg) and the baby of the family Bronson (Rodney McLennan) moved with their Dad (Richard Moir) into their new home, a lighthouse. The family name was Twist and they had the usual problems of adolescence and relationships. Other regular characters were Fiona (Daisy Cameron), with whom Pete fell madly in love, Rabbit (Stuart Atkin), Miss James (Robyn Gibbs), Mr Snapper (Esben Storm), Mr Gribble (Frankie J Holden) and Matron Gribble (Judith McGrath). There were 14 editions transmitted.
Writer: Paul Jennings. Producer: Antonia Barnard.

ROY'S RAIDERS
BBC. First broadcast: 20 July 1991

Michael Aitkens wrote this six-part series in which Roy (James Grout) ran a firm which specialised in providing motorbike couriers for the gentry. In truth, he employed a collection of oddballs, misfits and fantasists, and had his work cut out to protect himself and his riders from rival firm Bailey's Comets. Regulars involved in the complications of business and romance were Jill (Rebecca Stevens), Winco (Milton Johns), Henry (William Vanderpuye), Bazza (Shane Withington), Chris (Edward Tudor-Pole), would-be actress Daisy (Sara Crowe), and Jack (Mark Adams). The boss of Bailey's was Gavin (Des McAleer).
Theme song: David Essex (sung by William Vanderpuye). Director: Sue Longstaff. Producer: Susan Belbin.

RUDE HEALTH
CHANNEL 4. First broadcast: 16 March 1987

In a small town doctors' surgery, the tyrannical Dr Charles Sweet (John Wells) assumed control after the passing of kindly old Dr Crabbe. He was money-motivated and spent much of his energy in trying to persuade the town's wealthiest inhabitants to become private patients. He particularly targeted Sir Nigel Toft (Moray Watson) and his family, Lady 'Pig' Toft (Yvonne Manners) and daughters Caroline and Leonie (Judy Gridley and Susie Ann Watkins). Sweet was married to Veronica (Gay Soper) and his colleagues were Dr Andrew Putter (Paul Mari) and the unorthodox Dr Peter Pink (John Bett). In the first series of seven shows the receptionist was Mrs Thorpe (Josephine Tewson). For the second run of seven beginning 4 January 1988, she was replaced by Mrs Joy (Liz Fraser).
Writers: Phil Gould and Quentin Brown. Director: David MacMahon. Producers: Alan Janes and Greg Smith.

RULE BRITANNIA
THAMES. First broadcast: 8 October 1975

Four shipmates had made a solemn promise to each other to meet 25 years after they disembarked and went their separate ways. When the day came, the happily-married George Bradshaw (Tony Melody) and his wife Lil (Jo Warne) were visited by Jock McGregor (Russell Hunter) from Scotland, the stony-broke Paddy O'Brien (Joe Lynch) from Ireland, and Taffy Evans (Richard Davies) from Wales. Their reunion lasted for the entire series and the hapless George, to the disgust of Lil, was led ever further astray down a path of drink and punch-ups. Vince Powell created and wrote the programmes which ran for just one series.
Producer: Anthony Parker.

RUN BUDDY RUN
CBS (AMERICA) PRESENTED BY ITV.
First broadcast (UK): 21 October 1967

This series was a spoof on a 'fugitive' situation and starred Jack Sheldon as Buddy Overstreet, a book-keeper on the run from the underworld after he inadvertently became privy to secret information. Other regular characters were Harry (Gregg Palmer), Devere (Bruce Gordon), Junior (Jim Connell) and

Wendell (Nick Georgiade). Sixteen episodes were produced.

Director: Gene Reynolds. Producer: Jack Elinson.

RUNNING THE HALLS

USA PRESENTED BY CHANNEL 4.
First broadcast (UK): 17 March 1994

Set in Middlefield Academy, a co-ed boarding school in New England, this series was created by Steve Slavkin. Spoilt rich-kids ran around in smart designer clothes with the boys led by McBain (Richard Hayes) in pursuit of or in conflict with the girls led by Holiday (Lackey Bevis). The most evident teacher was Miss Karen Gilman (Pamela Bowen), while senior pupil Shark (Richard Sleight Jr) set his sights on spoiling the fun for the others.

Producer: Greg Gorden.

RUNNING WILD

LWT. First broadcast: 6 March 1987

Ray Brooks starred as Max Wild who suffered a mid-life male menopausal crisis and walked out on his working wife Babs (Janet Key) and grown-up daughter Stephanie (Michelle Collins) to search for his lost dreams of youth. He moved into a flat but tried to have the best of both worlds by keeping in touch with the family. He straddled the fence through the first run of six editions and by the time a second series got underway on 23 April 1989, he had tired of his grotty flat and lonely life and realised the folly of his actions. He sought a reconciliation but Babs had forged ahead in the interim and now had a successful life in public relations. She had managed just fine without Max and intended to continue that way. At one point Stephanie moved in with her father, but not for long as they failed to see eye to eye over her boyfriend Rob (Peter Amory). There were 13 programmes altogether.

Writer: Philip Trewinnard. Director: Vic Finch. Producers: Marcus Plantin, Derrick Goodwin.

RUTLAND WEEKEND TELEVISION

BBC. First broadcast: 12 November 1976

Eric Idle, late of *Monty Python's Flying Circus*, created and starred in this send-up of television's self-importance which ran for seven weeks. Rutland, Britain's smallest county prior to being summarily wiped off the map, was the location for the nation's smallest television network where Idle played the Programme Controller. The output of the fictional station included 'The History of the Entire World' and excerpts from the work of The Rutles, a thinly disguised parody of The Beatles. Idle was assisted in no small way by David Battley, Terence Bayler, Neil Innes, Gwen Taylor and several others.

Director: Andrew Gosling. Producer: Ian Keill.

SADIE, IT'S COLD OUTSIDE

THAMES. First broadcast: 21 April 1975

Sadie and Norman Potter (Rosemary Leach and Bernard Hepton) had been married for 23 years. Norman was a man of lost dreams, content to vegetate while staring at the television. Sadie took a long look at her own life and concluded that there must be more than just cooking, cleaning and sleeping. As middle-age set in so Sadie became increasingly aware that life had more to offer. This creation by Jack Rosenthal ran for six episodes.
Producers: Les Chatfield, Mike Vardy.

SALE THIS DAY

BBC RADIO. First broadcast: 5 November 1941

Variety stars Murray and Mooney (both first names Harry) starred as auctioneer's touts, or assistants, George Grabbit and Dan Droppit, in this six-part series. The auctioneer was Mr Bidgood IOU, played by a stalwart of BBC variety repertory, Dick Francis. Somehow writer Dick Pepper and producer Ernest Longstaffe managed to get a song from Donald Peers into the first episode.

ST ELSEWHERE

NBC (AMERICA) PRESENTED BY CHANNEL 4.
First broadcast (UK): 18 April 1983

This mix of drama and black comedy could be classified as soap opera or situation comedy. Its fusion of pathos, tragedy and romance was set in Boston's St Eligius Hospital which was nicknamed St Elsewhere by the staff. The principal characters included Doctors Donald Westphall (Ed Flanders), Ben Samuels (David Birney), Mark Craig (William Daniels), Annie Cavanero (Cynthia Sikes), Jack Morris (David Morse), Peter White (Terence Knox), Philip Chandler (Denzel Washington), Wayne Fiscus (Howie Mandel), Victor Ehrlich (Ed Begley Jr), VJ Kochar (Kavi Raz), Auschlander (Norman Lloyd), psychiatrist Dr Hugh Beale (GW Bailey) and Nurse Helen Rosenthal (Christina Pickles). When the sixth and final series got underway

on 11 September 1989, the hospital had been refurbished after a large conglomerate corporation had rescued it at the last minute from the threat of demolition. More than 80 episodes were screened. *An MTM production.*

SAM AND JANET

BBC RADIO. First broadcast: 12 January 1966

In this eight-part series David Kossoff played Sam and Joan Sims was Janet. They had been married for 19 years and lived in suburbia with their children, a car and a garden. Sam ran his own business manufacturing plastic table-mats. Janet coped with the hopes and fears of the long-suffering housewife and with Sam's violent temper. The following year, the series transferred to television (see below).
Writer: David Cumming. Producer: Bill Worsley.

ATV. First broadcast: 27 June 1967

John Junkin and Joan Sims starred as Sam and Janet Marshall, a comfortably-off married couple with a talent for complicating their everyday lives. He liked a pint or six and she concerned herself with world affairs, with the result that they were constantly at war with each other. When the show returned for a second and final run in January 1968, Vivienne Martin replaced Joan Sims as Janet.
Writer: David Cumming. Director: Paul Bernard. Producer: Alan Tarrant.

SAVED BY THE BELL

NBC (AMERICA) PRESENTED BY CHANNEL 4.
First broadcast (UK): 9 January 1993

Sam Bobrick created this series which was set at Bayview High School, Los Angeles, where a collection of beautiful young people played hard and worked little. They shared sporting and musical ambitions and were much encouraged by school principal Mr Belding (Dennis Haskins). The featured pupils included AC Slater (Mario Lopez), Zach (Mark-Paul Gosselaar), Jessie (Elizabeth Berkley), Lisa Turtles (Lark Voorhies) and Kelly Kapowski (Tiffani-Amber Thiessen). Much of the comedy came from the one character who was not born with the classic California beach-boy looks, the skinny, gawky and very popular Samuel 'Screech' Powers, played by Dustin Diamond. The first series of 13 was transmitted on a weekly basis and then, over the school holidays from 5 July the same year, 39 more episodes were stripped each weekday morning.

Music: Scott Gale and Richard Eames. Producers: Frank E Bario and Peter Engel.

SCOTT FREE

BBC. First broadcast: 22 July 1957

This, Terry Scott's first solo starring series, was set in the forgotten seaside resort of Bogmouth, where nothing ever happened and nothing ever would. Out-of-work actors Terry and Norman (Norman Vaughan) were sent by a desperate theatrical agent to take over the hopeless task of entertainment officers for the summer season. Their attempts to liven the place up were hindered by bungling Councillor Bland (Henry Longhurst), whose only saving grace was that he had a very pretty daughter (Marcia Ashton). A spectator to the efforts of Terry and Norman was local 'old salt' Gribble (Wallas Eaton), who always managed to trick the hapless pair into parting with their money. Six episodes were screened.

Writer: Lew Schwarz. Producer: Harry Carlisle.

SCREAMING

BBC. First broadcast: 15 March 1992

This six-part series by Carla Lane charted the effects that one man, Ralph (Tim Berrington), had on the lives of three women who set up house together, all of whom had had an affair with him. They were Annie (Gwen Taylor), Beatrice (Penelope Wilton) and Rachael (Jill Baker). Carla Lane was quoted at the time as saying: "It demonstrates how love is a great equaliser – and how it can make fools of us all." The three women were all intelligent and fundamentally different. Rachael worked as a keep-fit trainer for psychiatrically disturbed women and, when faced with Ralph's deceit, pretended he was dead. Annie was moving towards divorce, had a teenage daughter and remembered Ralph for the joy of sex. In between was Beatrice, whose difficult childhood as the only child of elderly parents left her inexperienced but witty and wise. Her affair with Ralph had been clandestine. Six episodes were transmitted.

Producer: Mike Stephens.

SCULLY

CHANNEL 4. First broadcast: 14 May 1984

Alan Bleasdale wrote this series about football mad Franny Scully (Andrew Schofield), a young Liverpudlian with dreams of being a professional player. His idol was Kenny Dalglish, who appeared in several episodes as himself, as did Ian St John and Bob Paisley in the final story. In the world of reality, Scully was surrounded by an assortment of Scouse characters including his parents (Joey Kaye and Val Lilley), his brother Arthur (Jimmy Gallagher), a sickeningly model child; piña colada-swilling Gran (Jean Boht), and Henry (Elvis Costello) whose headphones played train sounds. Scully's cheerful pal at school was Mooey (Ray Kingsley). Other colourful associates included Mad Dog (Mark McGann), Snotty Dog (Richard Burke), Puppy Dog (Lucinda Scrivener) and Tony the Great Pretender (Peter Christian). Scully fancied Joanna (Cathy Tyson) while Marie Morgan (Gilly Coman) fancied Scully. There were six half-hour episodes and a final one-hour edition on 18 June.

Theme music: 'Painting the Town Red' by Elvis Costello. Director: Les Chatfield. Producer: Steve Morrison for Granada.

SEAVIEW

BBC. First broadcast: 5 October 1983

Chris Barlas wrote this children's series which ran for three six-part seasons ending on 17 April 1987. Mr and Mrs Shelton (David Gooderson and Maggie Ollerenshaw) ran the Seaview Private Hotel. They had teenage children Sandy and George (Yvette Fielding and Aaron Brown) and a new baby. Other teenagers involved in the stories were James (Chris Hargreaves) and Petra (Carla Rogerson).

Director: Marilyn Fox. Producer: Paul Stone.

SECOND THOUGHTS

BBC RADIO. First broadcast: 1 November 1988

Before LWT picked up this format for television (see below), writers Jan Etherington and Gavin Petrie had committed their own experiences to paper for this radio series. The middle-aged lovers trying to make domestic harmony were Bill (James Bolam) and Faith (Lynda Bellingham). They were surrounded by Liza (Belinda Lang), Hannah (Kelda Holmes, later Emma Gregory, later Julia Sawalha)

and Joe (Mark Denham). There were four series altogether with the last of 29 editions broadcast on 23 July 1992.
Producers: Pete Atkin, Paul Schlesinger.

LWT. First broadcast: 3 May 1991

James Bolam and Lynda Bellingham again starred as Bill Macgregor and Faith Grayshot, living together and trying, against all the odds, to establish a relationship after failed first marriages. Faith had two teenage children, Joe (Mark Denham) and Hannah (Julia Sawalha) and a family dog called Defor. Her ex-husband was safely out of the way in Florida. Bill was a cartoonist who had been promoted to art editor at the magazine where he worked. Unfortunately his ex-wife Liza (Belinda Lang) worked as a design consultant at the same place. In Faith's eyes, Liza was the villain of the piece and she suspected Bill was still in love with her in spite of Liza having affairs left right and centre, including one with the married editor Richard (Geoffrey Whitehead). Faith also had to cope with her growing children and the discovery that Hannah was sleeping with her boyfriend. There were four series with a total of 43 episodes ending 17 December 1993.
Producers: David Askey, Robin Carr.

SECOND TIME AROUND

BBC. First broadcast: 23 October 1974

Michael Craig starred as Harry, a divorcé for ten years who, shortly after his 50th birthday, became smitten by Vicki (Patricia Brake) who was less than half his age. He aroused the understandable disgust and disapproval of those around him including Connie (Patricia Driscoll), Ronnie (Gerald Flood) and Maggie (Jacqueline Clarke). A first series of seven was followed by a second series of six ending on 14 February 1975.
Theme music: Alan Braden. Writer: Richard Waring. Producer: Graeme Muir.

SECONDS OUT

BBC. First broadcast: 6 June 1981

In a total of 13 rounds over two series ending 21 January 1982, Pete Dodds (Robert Lindsay) embarked on a professional boxing career, became British middleweight champion and challenged for the European title. His manager was Tom Sprake (Lee Montague) and his trainer was Dave Locket (Ken Jones).
Writer: Bill MacIlwraith. Producer: Ray Butt.

THE SECRET DIARY OF ADRIAN MOLE AGED 13¾

THAMES. First broadcast: 16 September 1985

Sue Townsend adapted her own book of the same title into this six-part series which charted the adolescence, through his own diary, of Adrian Mole (Gian Sammarco), a bespectacled youth beset by ordeals of sexual, spiritual and worldly development. His role models, both good and bad, were his mother and father Pauline and George Mole (Julie Walters and Stephen Moore) and Grandma (Beryl Reid). He befriended the elderly Bert Baxter (Bill Fraser) and lusted immaturely after Pandora (Lindsey Stagg). His every experience of life only served to increase his insecurity as his parents' marriage began to crumble. In 1987 a sequel, THE GROWING PAINS OF ADRIAN MOLE, was made.
Producers: Peter Sasdy and Lloyd Shirley.

THE SECRET LIFE OF KENNETH WILLIAMS

BBC RADIO. First broadcast: 14 July 1971

Outrageous camp comedy actor Williams starred as himself, the only man capable of saving his mother country England from the perils of revolution and anarchy. In a first series of eight and in 13 further editions ending 26 June 1973, Williams was aided and hindered in his rallies to the flag by Sir Charles Prattle (Richard Caldicot), Miss Gibbs (Caroline Blakiston), Maisie (Josephine Tewson) and Tomkins (Leslie Heritage). The part of 'Big Brother' was played by Aubrey Woods.
Writer: RD Wingfield. Producer: Keith Williams.

SEINFELD

USA PRESENTED BY BBC.
First broadcast (UK): 6 October 1993

Stand-up comedian Jerry Seinfeld turned his well-honed routine into this series about his life in New York as a single man. He did not hold with long-lasting or binding relationships and believed his spirit should be free to enjoy the carnal and material joys which were on offer. On a regular basis he dragged into the stories his former girlfriend Elaine (Julia Louise-Dreyfus), his odd-ball neighbour Kramer (Michael Richards) and his best friend George (Jason Alexander). Twelve episodes were screened in its first season. In the first edition of a second series on 23 April 1994, Seinfeld and Elaine established some new ground rules before having sex for the 38th time. She was the one who'd been counting!

Creator: Larry David.

SELWYN
YTV. First broadcast: 5 September 1978

Selwyn Froggitt (Bill Maynard) (see OH NO! IT'S SELWYN FROGGITT) was uprooted from his Yorkshire home in Scarsdale to become entertainments officer at the Paradise Valley holiday camp at a seaside resort on the East coast where the unfortunate manager was Mervyn Price (Bernard Gallagher). The series consisted of seven programmes.

Writers: Mike Craig Lawrie Kinsley and Ron McDonnell, Richard Knight. Producer: Ronnie Baxter.

SEMI-CIRCLES
BBC RADIO. First broadcast: 1 March 1982

Simon Brett wrote this radio series in six parts which starred Paula Wilcox and David Wood as Helen and Ben who moved into a neighbourhood that was on the up and contributed to its improving times. They turned what had been neglected into a desirable residence. Friends and neighbours in-

cluded Alastair (Bruce Alexander), Mrs Kelly (Pat Heywood) and Mr Juke (Arthur English).
Producer: Pete Atkin.

SEND FOR DOCTOR DICK
BBC RADIO. First broadcast: 23 October 1940

This series, created and written by Ted Kavanagh, concerned the adventures of the quack Doctor Dick (Dick Francis) and his nimble-witted assistant (Sonnie Hale). Neither of them had any qualifications and unsuspecting patients were subjected to all kinds of kill 'em or cure 'em remedies. They were assisted in their phoney practice by their glamorous and unfailing secretary, played by Patricia Leonard. There were only seven programmes in total and, as was usual at the time, the situations were always stretched to accommodate some musical interlude.
Producer: Vernon Harris.

SEND FOR SHINER
BBC RADIO. First broadcast: 21 September 1948

Film star and Cockney comedian Ronald Shiner played the title role in this eight-part series. Shiner was a reporter for a news agency whose mean

Ted (Russ Abbot, right) and Billy (Michael Williams) sample the sights of Blackpool in SEPTEMBER SONG (Photo: Granada TV)

Scottish editor Macintosh (Ian Sadler) forever haggled over his expenses.

Writer: Eddie Maguire. Producer: Charles Maxwell.

SEPTEMBER SONG

BBC RADIO. First broadcast: 28 February 1991

Before Granada picked up on the idea in 1993 (see below), this series by Ken Blakeson started on the radio with a run of seven half-hours. The stories were inspired by Northern comedian Tom Mennard who, in his later years, became well known to the nation as Sam Tindall in *Coronation Street*. Mennard was one of those unsung but very funny variety turns who had flogged himself through ups and downs across the remnants of the variety circuit. Mennard's alter ego was Billy Balsam (Geoff Hinsliff) who palled up with Ted Fenwick (James Greene), a lonely divorcé. They set forth on their adventures together in spite of different backgrounds and ideals. Although the credited writer was Blakeson, Mennard was also credited with additional material.

Producer: Susan Hogg.

GRANADA. First broadcast: 1 March 1993

Picking up from the BBC radio series Ken Blakeson's stories began a run of seven televised editions. It was the first acting role for slapstick comic Russ Abbot who played recently-widowed teacher Ted Fenwick. His drinking pal and fellow adventurer, would-be comedian Billy Balsam (Michael Williams), got a short-lived engagement as compère at the Magic Cat Café, Blackpool. They shared many of each other's heartaches and disappointments but at the end of the first series, Billy suffered a heart attack which Ted, in part, felt he might be responsible for. The second series of seven which began on 1 March 1994 saw them on a cruise to Greece as part of Billy's convalescence and there Ted bumped into a former girlfriend, Katherine Hillyard (Diana Quick). Love blossomed but not without a great many hurdles and in the end Ted was torn between returning to his native Manchester or starting a new life with Katherine in Cambridge. Diane Keen was also a regular member of the second series cast, playing Connie French, while Billy's new Greek pal Yannis Alexiou was portrayed by George Savides. When Billy wasn't getting drunk he was usually to be found trying to mend emotional fences with Connie. In the final story, Billy had turned up at Ted and Katherine's idyllic Cambridge abode, but disap-

peared again. Ted traced him to the Magic Cat, Blackpool.

Director: David Richards. Producer: Gareth Morgan.

SERGEANT BILKO

CBS (AMERICA) PRESENTED BY BBC

See **THE PHIL SILVERS SHOW**

SERVICE WITH A SMILE

BBC RADIO. First broadcast: 8 July 1957

Lancashire comedian Ken Platt starred in these adventures of a hotel porter. Platt played the junior porter, a gormless incompetent who sorely tried the patience of the head porter, portrayed by Dick Emery. Adding to the inefficiency of the hotel were chambermaid Daisy (Betty Alberge, later to play Florrie Lindley in *Coronation Street*) and the laundryman Hoo Flung Soo (Herbert Smith). Most other roles when required were voiced by Emery and Smith. Resident hotel cabaret artists were the Coronets. Eleven editions were heard.

Writers: Frank Roscoe and Ken Platt. Producer: John Ammonds.

SHARE AND SHARE ALIKE

BBC RADIO. First broadcast: 24 July 1978

To share was the very last thing on the minds of brothers Leslie (Hugh Paddick) and Jack (Michael Robbins) who were devastated when the solicitor (Deryck Guyler) announced that they had been left £50,000 between them on condition that they resided together harmoniously over a prescribed period. They had nothing in common and clashed head-on at home and at work. In the ninth and final episode of their disharmony, Jack set up a phoney séance to contact their mother in a last-ditch attempt to get their hands on the money.

Writers: Harold Snoad and Michael Knowles. Producer: John Dyas.

SHARON AND ELSIE

BBC. First broadcast: 27 January 1984

Set in the premises of James Blakes and Sons, a North Country firm of printers and greetings-cards manufacturers, there was much trouble at t' mill in these two six-part series which ended on 26 July 1985. Elsie Bancroft (Brigit Forsyth) found her working life disrupted by Sharon Wilkes (Janette Beverley) but gradually they became friends, working together for

their rights and playing together in their free time. Other regular characters involved in their exploits were Stanley (John Landry), Tommy Wallace (John Junkin) who was Sharon's uncle, Ivy (Maggie Jones), Ike (Gordon Rollings) and Mrs Tibbett (Paula Tilbrook).
Writer: Arline Whittaker. Producers: Roger Race, Mike Stephens.

THE SHARP END
BBC. First broadcast: 12 April 1991

Roy Clarke created and wrote this series of eight 50-minute episodes. Gwen Taylor starred as Celia Forrest who inherited her father's debt-collection agency and found herself in the cut-throat world of business where she struggled to keep it going. Both her mother (Clare Kelly) and daughter Wendy (Rachel Egan) voiced serious reservations but Celia was a resolute woman, and with help from secretary Crystal (Gaynor Faye) she set about the task in hand. Her rival was Andy Barrass (Philip Martin Brown), who believed

Hywel Bennett as the one and only SHELLEY (Photo © Thames Television)

debt-collecting to be a man's game.
Directors: Brian Parker, David Penn. Producer: Fiona Finlay.

A SHARP INTAKE OF BREATH
ATV. First broadcast: 20 February 1978

Peter and Sheila Barnes (David Jason and Jacqueline Clarke) had been married for seven years when the series began. The stories were woven around their on-going attempts to first of all understand, and then beat, 'the system'. Peter was a firm believer in freedom of choice and his escapades invariably implicated and involved some innocent third-party. The supporting cast of Alun Armstrong and Richard Wilson played different roles in each episode and continued to do so through two further series beginning 19 February 1979 and January 1980. Their appearances ceased to be regular in a fourth series beginning 11 January 1981. Much use was made of cartoon drawings by Mel Calman.

Theme music: Ken Jones. Writers included Leslie Duxbury, Ronnie Taylor, Kenneth Cope, Vince Powell. Producers: Les Chatfield, Stuart Allen.

SHELLEY

THAMES. First broadcast: 12 July 1979

Created and written by Peter Tilbury, this series got off to an unfortunate start when, after the first four programmes had been transmitted, ITV went on strike and the remaining programmes had to be held over until the following year. Nonetheless, it remains one of the most durable of ITV's creations in the sitcom field.

Hywel Bennett starred as university graduate Shelley, a young man with an attitude problem, from a working-class background but striving to improve his social and economic standing without resorting to work. He looked down on those less educated than himself. His partner was Frances Smith (Belinda Sinclair), who moved into a bedsit with him in Pangloss Road, North London, where their landlady was Mrs Edna Hawkins (Josephine Tewson). Shelley was in eternal conflict with the taxman, the building society and Fran's father, Gordon (Frederick Jaeger). At the age of 28 and with his degree in geography behind him, James Shelley was unprepared for the world. In the second season, beginning 17 April 1980, Shelley and Fran married. She rejected his first-choice best man, the undesirable Ned (David Pugh), so he had to settle for Paul (Warren Clarke). Shelley's mother Isobel (Sylvia Kay) attended the wedding. Shelley got a short-lived job as a copywriter in an advertising agency but was sacked. The third season, starting on 29 December 1980, saw Shelley find employment in the pastime of sitting around and waiting for the world to discover him. It was as late as this third season that the programme really caught on, but once the viewing public had found it, they could not get enough. It reached second place in the weekly ratings.

For the fourth series commencing 18 February 1982, there were new writers including Andy Hamilton, Colin Bostock-Smith and Bernard McKenna who found Shelley employment at the Foreign Office where, once again, he did not last long. Fran, meanwhile, gave birth to a daughter, Emma, but by the next run, beginning 4 November 1982, Fran had

given Shelley his marching orders and she refused to have him back unless he found a job that would adequately provide for her and Emma. He found shelter under Paul's roof where he developed a hostile relationship with the porter responsible for the flats, Desmond (Garfield Morgan). Shelley paid several visits to the 'Easy Job' agency but made no progress. When Mrs Hawkins enquired of Fran whether Shelley had a problem in bed, she replied: 'Yes. He can't get out of it!' At the end of the run, in spite of efforts by his mother to effect a reconciliation, Shelley emigrated to the United States. He re-emerged in 1988 in THE RETURN OF SHELLEY. However, there were to be still more episodes made just under the title SHELLEY: a new series started on 24 September 1990 in which he had a new landlord, Ted (David Ryall). He moved in with a community of old people and the last programme was transmitted on 1 September 1992.

Producer: Anthony Parker.

SHILLINGBURY TALES

ATV. First broadcast: 17 May 1981

This series by Francis Essex developed out of a single play *The Shillingbury Blowers* which had been shown on 6 January 1980. The blowers were members of the village brass band and by anybody's standards it was a pretty poor outfit. They had for years been conducted by Old Saltie (Trevor Howard) who disappeared after pop musician Peter Higgins (Robin Nedwell) moved into the village and put some musical life into the band. When the six-part series began, Peter had married Sally (Diane Keene), the daughter of Major Langton (Lionel Jeffries) and he was a respected member of the community. The same could not be said for Cuffy the Tinker (Bernard Cribbins) who lived in an eyesore of a caravan. This character was later spun-off into his own series CUFFY, along with other Shillingbury residents including Jake (Jack Douglas), Harvey (Joe Black), Mrs Simpkins (Diana King), Mandy (Linda Hayden) and Rev Norris (Nigel Lambert).

Music: Ed Welch. Director: Val Guest. Producer: Greg Smith.

SHINE A LIGHT

YTV. First broadcast: 1 April 1970

Essentially a two-hander, this series was set on Bachelor Rock, miles out at sea where Senior

Lighthouseman Wally Trott (Timothy Bateson) was stuck with Junior Lighthouseman Les Robinson (Tony Selby). There should have been a third person but they had failed to find anyone to take the job. Their only human contact was with the captain of the supply ship, Taffy Lewis (Howell Evans). The show ran for just one season.

Writers: David Nobbs, David McKellar and Peter Vincent. Director: Bill Hayes. Producer: John Duncan.

SHINE ON HARVEY MOON
CENTRAL. First broadcast: 8 January 1982

This series by Laurence Marks and Maurice Gran got underway with six half-hour episodes. Three subsequent series were each made up of programmes of one hour's duration. The final show of a total of 29 was transmitted on 23 August 1985. Set in Hackney, the time-span covered November 1945 to April 1948. Corporal Harvey Moon (Kenneth Cranham) returned home after an undistinguished war as a RAF stores clerk in India to find no house, no wife Rita (Maggie Steed) and no children Maggie (Linda Robson) and Stanley (Lee Whitlock). When he found them, Rita had no desire to return to him and 17-year-old Maggie was seeing his old friend Lou Lewis (Nigel Planer), much to Harvey's disgust and that of Nan (Elizabeth Spriggs). Before the war Harvey had been a professional footballer. Rita had several lovers and it was not long before Harvey took a shine to Stanley's headmistress, Harriet Wright (Fiona Victory). Harvey lived in a prefab and the Moons were a divided family. Harvey got a job in a factory, became active within the Labour party and was elected a local councillor. In July 1946 his home was destroyed by an unexploded bomb and he had to move into lodgings where his landlord was Eric Gottlieb (Leonard Fenton) and his sister Freida (Suzanne Bertish). By the end of the final run, Harvey and Rita had got back together but their relationship remained fragile.

Director: Baz Taylor. Producers: Tony Charles, Allan McKeown.

SHIRLEY'S WORLD
ATV. First broadcast: 6 November 1971

Shirley Maclaine's brief flirtation with sitcom cast her as Shirley Logan, a globe-trotting photographer with strong feminist principles. Her assignments got her into a variety of scrapes and adventures. She was responsible to her editor Dennis Croft (John Gregson). There were 17 episodes.

Writers: Frank Tarloff and Melville Shavelson. Producers: Barry Delmaine, Sheldon Leonard.

THE SHUTTLEWORTHS
BBC RADIO. First broadcast: 11 October 1993

This highly unusual series in four parts was broadcast on consecutive nights to 14 October. It was written by Graham Fellows who had a top ten hit record in 1978 under the name Jilted John. In the Shuttleworths, he played every part himself. John Shuttleworth was an aspiring songwriter living in semi-detached comfort in Sheffield. His wife was school dinner-lady Mary, and he had an agent and a next-door neighbour, Ken. Fellows recorded the shows in his own garden shed.

Producer: Paul Schlesinger.

SIDE BY SIDE
BBC. First broadcast: 27 April 1992

Incompatible neighbours were created by Richard Ommanney for this series. Vince Tulley (Gareth Hunt) was a plumber who had a successful business, was happily married to Stella (Julia Deakin) and lived in a nice house on which he applied his DIY skills. Next door lived newly-widowed Gilly Bell (Louisa Rix), who was irritated by many of Vince's home improvements, particularly the Grecian acropolis which he constructed in the garden. Gilly had many problems including daughter Katie (Mia Fothergill) who had a heavy metal musician, Terry Shane (Alex Walkinshaw), for a boyfriend. Vince was always guaranteed to add to Gilly's anxieties unless he was away at his time-share in Ibiza. The series was set in Kingston-upon-Thames and there were 13 programmes over two seasons ending on 1 April 1993.

Directors: Nic Phillips, Sue Bysh. Producers: Nic Phillips, Martin Fisher.

SILK, SATIN, COTTON, RAGS
BBC. First broadcast: 10 May 1952

This early television comedy drama in six parts was written by MA Lonsdale and charted the downward spiral of Miss Stella Graham (Cecile Chevreau). Witnesses through the episodes were Nick Nicholson (Barry K Barnes), Geoffrey Masters QC

Kenneth Cranham and Maggie Steed as husband and wife Harvey and Rita in SHINE ON HARVEY MOON (Photo: Central Television)

(Anthony Ireland), Sir William Heyward (Clive Morton), Max Rollo (Richard Murdoch) and Phipps (Gladys Henson).
Producer: Douglas Moodie.

SIMON'S BUG

BBC RADIO. First broadcast: 4 March 1989

Richard Quick wrote this comedy drama in four parts. Simon Webb (Hywel Bennett) suspected wife Joanna (Alison Steadman) of conducting an affair. When he planted some borrowed bugging equipment in his own telephone, he found out family goings-on beyond his wildest suspicions.
Producer: Paul Spencer.

SINGLES

YTV. First broadcast: 27 January 1988

This series of intrigue, lies and deception was created and written by Eric Chappell and Jean Warr about four individuals who met in a singles' bar and

embarked on a pattern of cross, inter and extra relationships. They were bachelor Malcolm (Roger Rees); recently separated Pamela (Judy Loe); Jackie (Susie Blake), with one failed marriage behind her; and Clive (Eamon Boland), who had been left by his wife to raise three children alone. The barmaid, Di, was played by Gina Maher. After a first series of seven programmes there were seven more editions starting 23 January 1989. For a third run of seven shows starting 10 July 1991, Roger Rees left the cast and was replaced by Simon Cadell as failed thespian Dennis Duval.
Music: Johnny Pearson. Producers: Vernon Lawrence, Nic Phillips, Graham Wetherell.

SINK OR SWIM

BBC. First broadcast: 4 December 1980

This series by Alex Shearer starred Peter Davison and Robert Glenister as brothers Brian and Steve Webber. Brian bought a leaky narrow boat in Bristol, on which they had every intention of living. In spite of the damp and primitive conditions on board, they managed to navigate the canal system as far as London. The idea was then to obtain a bank loan, renovate the boat and take tourists along England's waterways. However well-meaning

Brian's ideas were, they always turned to disaster. Steve, on the other hand, abhorred the conditions, hated being penniless and was obsessed by sex. Their bickering was not softened by Brian having a girlfriend, Sonia (Sara Corper), who was heavily into ecology and considered them to be a couple of boorish Northern clods. The naif Brian fought to improve himself and his lot while his cynical younger brother was forthright in his opinion that nothing mattered beyond carnal satisfaction. A first run of seven programmes was followed by six further editions starting 22 October 1981. By the launch of the third and final six-part series on 9 September 1982, they had arrived in Newcastle-upon-Tyne where Brian was studying computer sciences at the University and living in a hall of residence. Sonia shared a flat with another student, Charlotte (Briony McRoberts), but Steve was forced to look for work and digs.

Music: Ronnie Hazlehurst. Producer: Roger Race.

SIR YELLOW

YTV. First broadcast: 20 July 1973

Set in days of yore, Jimmy Edwards starred in this six-part series as cowardly knight on horseback Sir Yellow, who combed the country in search of wine, women and easy wealth. He and his comrades Gregory (Melvyn Hayes) and Cedrick (Michael Ripper) were pursued by the Black Knight, Sir Griswold (Alan Curtis).

Writer: Johnny Heyward. Director: Ian Davidson. Producer: Bill Hitchcock.

THE SIT-CROM

BBC RADIO. First broadcast: 6 October 1990

Sue Limb wrote this series in six parts. The setting was the English Civil War and Joss Ackland starred as Sir John Firebasket with Denise Coffey as his wife Lady Anne. In stories of love and hate, friends and enemies, other featured characters included Mercy alias Melissa (Miriam Margolyes), Tobias Thinne (Clive Merrison), Fr Francis (Nickolas Grace), Posthumous (Nicky Henson), Slow Ned (Chris Emmett) and Gazebo Fogg (Jack Klaff).

Producer: Jonathan James-Moore.

SITTING PRETTY

BBC. First broadcast: 19 November 1992

Annie Briggs (Diane Bull) came down to earth with a bump when her husband died unexpectedly. Sud-denly her opulent lifestyle was over and she was forced to return to her east London roots. In the 1960s she had been known as 'the Jackie Onassis of Bethnal Green'. Since then she had tasted the good life and lived in mock-Tudor splendour in London's stockbroker belt, but her new impecunious state forced her to go and live with her dreary sister Sylvie (Heather Tobias) on the run-down chicken farm of their parents, George and Kitty (John Cater and Vilma Hollingbery). Annie, who hinted at times that she might have had a tarty past, had a medical student daughter, Tiffany (Alison Lomas), whom she referred to as 'Dumpling'. After a first series of six episodes, six new editions got underway on 24 November 1993.

Writer: John Sullivan. Directors: Susan Belbin, Angela de Chastelai Smith. Producer: Susan Belbin.

THE SKYLARKS

BBC. First broadcast 11 July 1958

This 16-part series by Trevor Peacock and Gavin Blakeney concerned the misadventures of a Royal Navy helicopter crew aboard the aircraft carrier HMS *Aerial* (actually *Ark Royal*). AE Matthews starred as Vice-Admiral Sir Godfrey Wiggin-Fanshawe who believed the way to get around an aircraft carrier was by bicycle. The Captain of the ship was Crocker-Dobson (William Mervyn) and the chopper crew was made up of Lt Gilmore (Anton Rodgers), Lt Copper (Roland Curram), Radio Officer Reynolds (John Southworth) and Lt Stannard (Robert Chetwyn). Fabia Drake appeared as Lady Wiggin-Fanshawe. Much of the action was filmed in and around the Mediterranean.

Producer: John Warrington.

THE 'SLAP' MAXWELL STORY

USA PRESENTED BY BBC.
First broadcast (UK): 21 January 1989

Dabney Coleman starred as sportswriter Maxwell, a man with a talent for writing but none whatsoever for human relationships. Impatient and bad-tempered, he was estranged from his wife Annie (Susan Anspach) and had a part-time girlfriend, Judy (Megan Gallagher). His sports column was for *The Ledger* newspaper and carried the byline 'Slap Shots'. His editor was Nelson Kruger (Brian Smiar). BBC showed the last of 20 episodes on 27 September 1990.

Producer: Jay Tarses.

SLINGER'S DAY

THAMES. First broadcast: 3 September 1986

Following the death of Leonard Rossiter it was no longer possible for Thames to continue with TRIPPER'S DAY. Creator Brian Cooke kept the situation, Supafare Supermarket, but installed a new manager, Cecil Slinger (Bruce Forsyth), to replace Norman Tripper. Of the old staff, only Mr Christian (Paul Clarkson) and Hardie (Philip Bird) remained. They were joined by Fred (David Kelly), Shirley (Jacqueline De Peza), Colin (Charlie Hawkins) and Miss Foster (Suzanne Church). There were two series, each of six programmes, and the final edition was seen on 14 October 1987.
Writers: Brian Cooke, Vince Powell. Producer: Mark Stuart.

SLOE COACHES

BBC RADIO. First broadcast: 8 July 1986

Uriah Sloe (Roy Kinnear) was the sole proprietor of the tinpot transport firm of the title of this series of six broadcasts. His principal driver was Gerhardt (Andrew Sachs) and others involved in the financially crippled company were Jason (Clive Panto) and Josephine (Chrissy Roberts). The rival firm was Gallop Coaches.
Writers: Charlie Adams and Jon Lea. Producer: Andy Ayliffe.

THE SMALL INTRICATE LIFE OF GERALD C POTTER

BBC RADIO. First broadcast: 9 March 1977

Basil Boothroyd wrote this six-part series which starred Ian Carmichael in the title role as an optimistic but not very successful author, the contents of whose briefcase revealed a preoccupation with the titillation of undemanding, sexually-oriented rubbish novelettes. Charlotte Mitchell co-starred as his wife.
Producer: Bobby Jaye.

A SMALL PROBLEM

BBC. First broadcast: 26 January 1987

Tony Millan and Mike Walling wrote this series which had the BBC's switchboards jammed with complaints after the first of six episodes was transmitted. It was set in a Britain of the future where prejudice had reached such proportions that all adults under five feet tall were cocooned in highrise ghettos south of the Thames, had to keep a curfew and were denied basic rights. In this world, jubilant parents held 'coming-of-height' parties. Roy Pink (Mike Elles) was 5ft 0¾ in tall, but when the new EEC regulation height of 1.55m was adopted, he was reclassified and herded off. A Small Liberation Front was formed by Howard (Christopher Ryan) which lobbied the Height Tribunal.
Producer: David Askey.

THE SMALL WORLD OF SAMUEL TWEET

BBC. First broadcast: 5 June 1975

Freddie 'Parrot Face' Davies starred as Tweet in this six-part children's series. Set in Chumpton Green, Tweet worked in the local pet shop and took part in all aspects of life in the tiny village. Other characters included Lord Chumpton (Cardew Robinson), Russell Chumpton (Norman Turkington), Sandra Jones (Prue Clarke) and PC Wicketts (Colin Edwynn). When money was short and the bank put pressure on Lord Chumpton, his nephew Russell proposed certain changes at the pet shop which put Samuel Tweet's home and living at risk.
Writer: Gary Knight. Producer: Tony Harrison.

SNAKES AND LADDERS

Channel 4. First broadcast: 17 October 1989

This creation of Laurence Marks and Maurice Gran ran for seven editions. Set in 1999, the only barrier left in Europe was that between North and South represented by Scotsman Gavin (John Gordon Sinclair) and Londoner Giles (Adrian Edmondson). Gavin moved South where, under his boss Haverty (Christopher Godwin), he made progress up the professional and social ladders. Other principal characters were Gavin's mum and dad (Phil McCall and June Watson), Mr Pym (Ron Donachie), Mr Lambie (Roger Sloman), Donald and Ronald (Tony Meyer and David Meyer), the upper-class Serena (Lynsey Baxter) and the Nurse (Celia Imrie) at the psychiatric hospital for political detainees to which Giles was committed.
Producer: Baz Taylor for YTV.

SNIBSON'S CHOICE

BBC RADIO. First broadcast: 27 May 1942

Lupino 'Nipper' Lane recreated the persona of Bill Snibson which he had made famous on the London stage in *Twenty To One* and *Me and My Girl*, both by L Arthur Rose with music by Noel Gay. In this six-part series Snibson became involved in comedy

thriller stories written by Cyril Campion and Max Kester with specially written music by Noel Gay and played by Mantovani and his orchestra. Although each episode was self-contained, Snibson was never without his girl, Polly, who was portrayed by Marjery Wyn.
Producer: Max Kester.

SO HAUNT ME

BBC. First broadcast: 23 February 1992

Creator and writer Paul A Mendelson had worked in advertising and given up his job to concentrate on writing. So, too, had his character in this series, Pete Rokeby (George Costigan), who by this decision was forced to move downmarket into a less desirable district. He took with him his wife Sally (Tessa Peake-Jones) and family Tammy (Laura Simmons) and David (Jeremy Green). They were not long in residence before they discovered they were sharing their home with Jewish ghost Yetta Feldman (Miriam Karlin). It was the lingering smell of chicken soup that gave the game away. The 20th edition was screened on 13 February 1994.
Directors: John Stroud, Sylvie Boden. Producers: Caroline Gold, Sharon Bloom for Cinema Verity.

SO I'LL TELL YOU

BBC RADIO. First broadcast: 31 March 1958

Lawrie Wyman created and wrote these stories of events in the life of antique-shop owner Matthew Soames (David Kossoff), who voiced his cynical opinions with an acid tongue, yet retained a sentimentality for his subject and was able to spin a tale for each and every object in his emporium. His willing but dead-loss of an assistant was Gilbert Catchpole (Jeffrey Segal), who was forever a target of fun and ridicule for Soames, but in spite of that there was a deep and warm friendship between the two men. After a first series of six programmes, the show returned after a long gap on 26 February 1962 for a further run of six, and a further series of seven ended 20 October 1964. Following yet another gap, a final run of seven ended on 14 October 1968.
Producer: Norman Wright.

SO YOU THINK YOU'VE GOT TROUBLES

BBC. First broadcast: 17 October 1991

Laurence Marks and Maurice Gran wrote this six-parter in which Warren Mitchell starred as Jewish widower Ivan Fox, manager of a small tobacco factory in north London. When the firm relocated to Belfast, Ivan reluctantly had to uproot and move to the trouble-torn capital of Northern Ireland. Though his personal faith veered towards the agnostic, he found himself swept into the small Jewish community and embroiled in the religious passions of the Province. The subject matter was so delicate that Marks and Gran claimed they took 16 months and several efforts to write the first episode and came close to abandoning the project. Other characters featured were Charley and Anna Adamson (James Ellis and Linda Wray) and George Nathan (Harry Towb).
Director: Mike Holgate. Producer: Tara Prem.

SOAP

ABC (AMERICA) PRESENTED BY ITV.
First broadcast (UK): 26 November 1978

By the time the first of 80 episodes was screened in Britain, the series had already taken a year's flak in the USA where several attempts to have it banned had been undertaken. Susan Harris created the stories of two families who between them explored every sexual deviancy, social stigma and possibility of relationship.

Basically, the show was a spoof on all of that genre known as 'soap opera', told through two sisters, the rich Jessica Tate (Katherine Helmond) and the poor Mary Campbell (Cathryn Damon), and their respective families. Jessica, who had a string of lovers and ultimately went on trial for the murder of one such – and a step-nephew at that – was married to bent stockbroker Chester (Robert Mandan), who would bed anything in a skirt and ultimately confessed to the murder. Their daughter Eunice (Jennifer Salt), in keeping with parental example, went to bed with anything in trousers and even managed to seduce a Catholic priest. The other Tate daughter Corinne (Diana Canova) was magnetically attracted to her mother's lovers, usually at the same time. The Tate's son Billy was more normal, but obnoxious with it. They had a caustic, irritable, sardonic black butler, Benson (Robert Guillaume), who specialised in insults and refused to cook the family's requests if he did not fancy it himself. He was later given his own series, BENSON. The Tate house was also home to Jessica's father Major Gatlin (Arthur Peterson), a veteran of the First World War who had failed to realise that hostilities had ceased.

Mary Campbell's husband was Burt (Richard Mulligan), a manic depressive who had killed her first husband. At one point Burt was carried off in a space craft while an alien stayed and inhabited his body. The alien discovered the joys of human sex, as did Mary who for years had been forced to live with her husband's impotence. The Campbells had three sons. Danny (Ted Wass) married a daughter of a Mafia boss in a shotgun wedding and worked for the Mob. He also had an affair with Jessica. Jodie (Billy Crystal) was a professional football player and a homosexual. When his mother once caught him trying on her dresses, she said: "I've told you a hundred times. That dress fastens at the back." The youngest child was Chuck (Jay Johnson), a ventriloquist with a dummy named Bob. The dummy went everywhere with him and Chuck insisted that Bob be treated on an equal footing with everyone else. Robert Urich portrayed Peter, with whom both Jessica and Corinne had a simultaneous affair. The fans of the show claimed that it treated issues of sex, race and insanity with a healthy innocence; its detractors brought charges of gratuitous immorality.

Producers: Susan Harris, Paul Junger Witt and Tony Thomas.

SOB SISTERS

CENTRAL. First broadcast: 26 May 1989

Two very different sisters lived together in a dismal flat. They were Liz (Gwen Taylor), a poverty-stricken assistant to a vet, and Dorothy (Polly Adams) who was newly widowed and had to come to terms with the fact that she was no longer rich nor would she enjoy again the high life she had shared with her husband. Other principal characters were Leo (Freddie Jones), Charlie (Philip Bird) and Edna (Beryl Cooke).

Writer: Andrew Marshall. Director: Ray Butt. Producer: Christopher Walsh.

A SOFT TOUCH

ATV. First broadcast: 31 July 1978

Jack Holmes (John Flanagan) was something of a layabout, dreaming of a career in show business. He lived in cloud cuckoo land as he had no talent to back his aspirations. His young, talented and loyal wife Alison (Maureen Lipman) hoped and encouraged him to find a proper job to no avail. Six programmes were screened.

Music: Peter Skellern. Writer: Connor Fraser. Producer: Les Chatfield.

SOLO

BBC. First broadcast: 11 January 1981

Felicity Kendal starred as Gemma Palmer, a 30-year-old who on the surface had it all: independence, her own flat, a steady job and a live-in boyfriend, Danny (Stephen Moore). When she discovered that Danny had had a physical affair with her so-called friend Gloria (Susan Bishop), she made a swift reappraisal of her circumstances and opted to quit the job, dismiss Danny, cut off Gloria and go SOLO. Although not a heavy and verbose feminist, Gemma was not prepared to be pushed around by all and sundry and, at the time the series was launched she picked up the popular flow that a woman was free to make her own destiny. Danny had double standards when it came to sex and believed that a fling now and then was the acceptable norm for a male in his prime. Gemma had an overlying desire to retain control of her own life but she fell into many traps and still retained some feelings for Danny. She struggled against the obvious trials of life as a single woman. Throughout she was supported by her mother (Elspet Gray). By the second series she had managed to cast Danny aside and was truly solo. The final edition of a total 13 was seen on 17 October 1982.

Writer: Carla Lane. Producer: Gareth Gwenlan.

SOME MOTHERS DO 'AVE 'EM

BBC. First broadcast: 15 February 1973

The ultimate accident-prone, maladroit Frank Spencer was the joint creation of writer Raymond Allen and the actor who played him, Michael Crawford. In a series of ultimates, Michele Dotrice portrayed the ultimate long-suffering wife, Betty Spencer. Frank, in his beret and knitted tank-top or raincoat or pyjamas, got into predicaments that were not only very funny but often extremely dangerous. It is well documented that Crawford performed all his own stunts which were meticulously planned and executed. Notwithstanding, he suffered some fortunately minor injuries, though he took some quite alarming risks. His soft, almost infantile manner of speech, his nervous twitches of face and shoulders together with a proclivity to drop malapropisms, made him the bread and butter of every impressionist of the day, and that day began with the first of the 22 episodes which were screened. A second series came in November of the same year

Married to disaster-prone Frank Spencer (Michael Crawford), Betty (Michele Dotrice) knows only too well that SOME MOTHERS DO 'AVE 'EM (Photo: Copyright © BBC)

(1973) during which Frank and Betty had a baby daughter, Jessica (Emma Ware). Apart from two Christmas specials (1974 and 1975) the series was off the screen until 11 October 1978 when an older but little wiser Frank returned for a final run of seven shows.
Producer: Michael Mills.

SOMETHING TO SHOUT ABOUT
BBC RADIO. First broadcast: 5 July 1960

This series, created by Myles Rudge and written by him with Ronald Chesney, celebrated its 50th edi-

tion on 29 January 1962. Set in the world of advertising, Michael Medwin starred as Michael Lightfoot, an accounts executive with small agency Apsley, Addis, Cone, Barbican, Blythe, Giddy and Partners. Lightfoot's style was hectic and his world tended to centre round the golf course. His secretary Janet, who was more interested in him than the job, was played by Fenella Fielding. Maggie Tufnell (Eleanor Summerfield) was responsible for the company's TV adverts. She was highly efficient and had also taken a shine to Michael. The leading copywriter was Adrian Beales (Nicholas Phipps), who spent his hours dreaming up slogans like 'A Fridge In Every Igloo'. The floating shorthand-typist was Mavis Willis (Joan Sims) and in later episodes extra secretarial help was provided by Shirley (Sheila Hancock). All other characters required from week to week were the responsibility of Warren Mitchell. A serious concern for the producers, first John Simmonds then Eric Miller, was that every brand name in the script had to be meticulously cleared lest there should be a real product bearing the same name.

SON OF CLICHÉ
BBC RADIO. First broadcast: 28 August 1983

Writers Rob Grant and Doug Naylor created this surreal Space series for radio four and a half years before they would do a similar thing for television with RED DWARF. Both were to star Christopher Barrie. The first series in six parts won a Sony Radio Award in 1984 and the show returned for nine new editions on 3 November that year. Also starring were Nick Maloney and Nick Wilton and the adventures followed the exploits of Captain Invisible; his trusty sidekick The See Thru' Kid; Dave Hollins – Space Cadet; and weird occasionals like Transparo, the invisible goldfish.
Producer: Alan Nixon.

SON OF THE BRIDE
BBC. First broadcast: 6 June 1973

Terry Scott starred in this six-part series by John Kane as a grown-up son who was firmly tied to the apron-strings of his mother (Mollie Sugden). The ties, however, worked both ways and he made it difficult for his widowed mother to develop any new relationship. The other regular characters were Stan (George A Cooper), Miss McDowdie (Josephine Tewson) and Angela (Olivia Hamnett).
Producer: Peter Whitmore.

SORRY

BBC. First broadcast: 12 March 1981

Ronnie Corbett as Timothy Lumsden was tied to the apron-strings of his mother (Barbara Lott) for 43 episodes to 10 October 1988. Timothy, in his mid-forties, lived at home with his mother and father (William Moore) and worked during the day as a librarian. Mother Phyllis refused to accept the fact that he was a grown man and treated him as an eternal adolescent yet, while she ruled him, he was not a wimp. He had a sense of humour, was well-read and confident – except when it came to girls and then he got tongue-tied. Phyllis had delusions of grandeur beyond her station and no girl was good enough for Timothy. The setting was a quiet town in the Thames valley where retired Mr Lumsden tended his garden and trailed muddy boots through his wife's spotless kitchen. As well as being chief librarian, Timothy was also active in the local amateur dramatic society. Roy Holder appeared in many editions as Frank.

Writers: Ian Davidson and Peter Vincent. Producer: David Askey.

The apron strings cannot be far away as Timothy (Ronnie Corbett) enjoys the attentions of Mother (Barbara Lott). William Moore stars as Mr Lumsden (Photo: Copyright © BBC)

SORRY, I'M A STRANGER HERE MYSELF

THAMES. First broadcast: 15 June 1981

Created and written by David Firth and Peter Tilbury, this series starred Robin Bailey as henpecked librarian Henry Nunn who lived in Datchet with his nagging wife Sybil (Pamela Manson). On his 60th birthday, Henry learned that he had not only been left a fortune by an uncle but also the house in which he had been raised. He upped himself and Sybil from Datchet and moved to the inherited house in the Black Country. He had not, however, prepared for his neighbours. On one side he had loud-mouthed union convenor Tom (David Hargreaves) and his nosey-parker wife Doreen (Diana Rayworth), and on the other was immigrant Mumtaz (Nadim Sawalha), who cooked endless curries and permeated the village of Stackley with the smell. To compound their troubles, on arriving at the house the Nunns found it came complete with squatter, long green-haired Alex (Christopher Fulford). The first series was of seven shows. When a second seven-part run began on 13 April 1982, Sybil had retreated to Datchet but Alex was still in residence, giving Henry a new lease of youth.
Producer: Anthony Parker.

SORRY I'M SINGLE

BBC. First broadcast: 1 August 1967

Derek Nimmo starred as David, an eternal student who lived in a flatlet in a converted house in Hampstead. The other tenants were three females: Brenda (Gwendolyn Watts) had been recently divorced and had her eyes open for a next potential husband; she ran an on-going feud with Karen (Elizabeth Knight), and caught in the middle was Chinese girl Suzy (Pik-Sen Lim). They all occupied single rooms and shared the kitchen and bathroom. Nine episodes were seen.
Writers: Ronald Wolfe and Ronald Chesney. Producer: John Street.

SOUTH OF THE BORDER

YTV. First broadcast: 30 August 1985

Brian Glover starred as Edgar Rowley, a dyed-in-the-wool Yorkshireman who had worked as a miner all his life since leaving school. With the closure of the pit, he was forced to join the migration south in search of work. Dragging their heels behind were his wife Ellen (Belinda Sinclair),

Nan (Maggie Jones), Billy (Robin Parkinson), Anita (Mossie Smith) and Quentin (Christopher Godwin) as Edgar tried to adapt to an alien culture and way of life. Peter Tinniswood wrote the seven-part series.

Music: Ken Jones. Producer: Derrick Goodwin.

THE SPAMFRITTER MAN
BBC RADIO. First broadcast: 29 May 1978

Bryan Pringle starred as Wilfred Hargreaves in this eight-part serial. He owned a chip shop and was proud of it, indeed so proud that he fought to represent his town in the Chip Shop of the Year Contest. He was also proud of his home and his new lino, his wife Molly (Betty Alberge) and his daughter Doreen (Kay Adshead). His pal was Albert Bates (Peter Wheeler).

Writer: Andrew Lynch. Producer: Bob Oliver Rogers.

SPARE A COPPER
BBC RADIO. First broadcast: 27 August 1965

John Esmonde and Bob Larbey created this series to star one-time Old Vic actor Kenneth Connor as PC Albert Hereward Lamp, a zealous but rather confused bastion of the law. He was persistent both in his endeavours and his errors, to the consternation of Inspector Jolly (Deryck Guyler) and his other colleagues Sergeant James (Graham Stark) and WPC Ashley (Joan Benham). There were 16 editions ending on 8 August 1966.

Producer: Edward Taylor.

SPATZ
THAMES. First broadcast: 28 February 1990

Spatz was one of a chain of fast-food restaurants whose parent company was based in Canada. The London manager was Karen Hansson (Jennifer Calvert) and her assistant was young Canadian TJ (Paul Michael), who exasperated her at every turn. The staff included Debby (Stephanie Charles), Lilly (Ling Tai), Vince (Joe Greco), Dexter (Vas Blackwood) and Stanley (Jonathan Copestake). In the final programme of the first series of 12, TJ was promoted back to Canada, much to the delight of Karen. However, her joy was short-lived as, when the second run of 14 started on 3 January 1991, TJ was back in the London branch. Moreover, his girlfriend Julie (Catherine Russell) also worked at Spatz. A third and final series of seven ended on 10 April 1992.

Creator: Andrew Bethell. Writers: Lou Pressman and Grant Cathro, Jim Eldridge. Directors: Baz Taylor, Stan Swan. Producers: Carol Commisso and Alan Horrox.

SPLIT ENDS
GRANADA. First broadcast: 7 June 1989

Anita Dobson starred as Cath, the owner of a hair salon who felt the time was right for her to marry and settle down. There were two men in her life, American businessman Clint (Harry Ditson) and her womanising senior stylist David (Peter Blake). She enjoyed her moments with both but committed herself to Clint only to tell him it was off again in the final programme of six. The salon staff included Ruth (Barbara New), Herbie (Robin Davies), Lee (Lee Whitlock) and Aretha (Nimmy March).

Writer: Len Richmond. Director: Alan JW Bell. Producer: James Maw.

SPOKEN IN JEST
BBC RADIO. First broadcast: 7 June 1957

There were two series of this domestic comedy which took as its weekly starting point a well-known quotation or proverb. Yvonne Arnaud and Vic Oliver starred as Margot and Charles Marlow and Hugh Morton and Gwen Lewis played their neighbours, Mr and Mrs Stitchmore. The first run of 12 programmes was followed by a second run of 16 which got underway on 30 May 1958.

Writer: Carey Edwards. Producer: Tom Ronald.

SPOONER'S PATCH
ATV. First broadcast: 9 July 1979

Ray Galton, most famed for his writing partnership with Alan Simpson, which partnership spawned HANCOCK'S HALF HOUR and STEPTOE AND SON, joined forces with Johnny Speight of TILL DEATH US DO PART fame to create this spoof police series. The stories revolved around the day-to-day activities of Woodley police station, a metropolitan outpost under the command of manic Inspector Spooner (Ronald Fraser). On his staff were the out-and-out fascist PC Goatman (Norman Rossington), the laissez-faire PC Killick (John Lyons), and DC Bulsover (Peter Cleall) who modelled himself and his methods on every TV cop he had ever seen. Also in Spooner's employ, but unof-

ficially, was the local grass, Kelly (Dermot Kelly). Spooner himself lived in a flat above the police station. There was much connivance and corruption. For the second series which began on 4 September 1980 and the final series which began 15 April 1982, Donald Churchill replaced Ronald Fraser as Spooner. He got rid of Goatman but, in return, was saddled with a cantankerous traffic warden, Mrs Cantaford, played by Patricia Hayes. Kelly had left and Spooner had found a new informer, Jimmy the Con (Harry Fowler). There were 20 episodes in total.
Producer: William G Stewart.

SPRING AND AUTUMN

THAMES. First broadcast: 23 October 1972

This series by Vince Powell and Harry Driver began as a single play in which pensioner Tommy Butler (Jimmy Jewel), a cantankerous and awkward 70-year-old widower, was forced to leave his home and his friends in Sheffield and move in with his daughter and son-in-law, Betty and Joe Dickinson (Gaye Brown and Larry Martyn). By the time the idea became a series, starting 16 July 1973, Harry Driver had died and Vince Powell was writing alone. Jimmy Jewel continued as Tommy Butler but his daughter and son-in-law had become Vera and Brian Reid (June Barry and Larry Martyn). Nothing was right for Tommy. He complained about lack of space to put his own chattels, which included a stuffed parrot and a chamber pot, and he bemoaned the absence of a garden in the high-rise flat. The saviour for Tommy was a new, close friendship which he forged with 12-year-old local lad Charlie Harris (Charlie Hawkins). Charlie's mother, Betty Harris, was portrayed by Jo Warne. Tommy became a father figure for Charlie who had not seen his real father for seven years. Charlie was mad about football and his young enthusiasm for so much of life was often enough to divert Tommy from his daily hypochondria. Altogether there were five series.
Producers: Stuart Allen, Ronnie Baxter, Mike Vardy, Anthony Parker.

SQUARE DEAL

LWT. First broadcast: 3 September 1988

Richard Ommanney created and wrote these 14 programmes in two seven-part series, the last of which was screened on 13 October 1989. Timothy

Bentinck and Lise-Ann McLaughlin starred as upwardly-mobile young married couple Nigel and Emma Barrington. Nigel was an unscrupulous and devious estate agent and Emma had her own café. Into their lives came a young man in a hurry, Sean (Brett Fancy), who had written his autobiography and become a tenant of Nigel's. As Emma discovered piece by piece all Nigel's bad character points, so there developed a love triangle as she fought in vain to suppress her growing feelings towards Sean. While Nigel and Emma went through a messy divorce, Sean became a rock 'n roll singer and a new neighbour arrived in the shapely form of Geraldine (Georgina Melville), whom Nigel was quick to proposition.
Producer: Nic Phillips.

THE SQUARE LEOPARD

HTV. First broadcast: 12 August 1980

In this children's series, written and produced by Peter Miller, John Leyton starred as struggling solicitor Gerald Parish who rented the ground-floor flat in a smart house owned by Mary Lampert (Janet Key). She was the widowed mother of five children, Adela (Jessica Turner), Joanna (Jane Tottman), Toby (Toby Waldock), Bill (Marcus D'Amico) and Richard (Mark Evans). Gerald and the children took an instant dislike to each other. He was irritable and intolerant until the unexpected arrival of his father Henry (Raymond Huntley) suddenly transformed him into a model of kindness. Thirteen episodes were screened.

SQUARE PEGS

CBS (AMERICA) PRESENTED BY CHANNEL 4.
First broadcast (UK): 16 April 1983

Created and produced by Anne Beatts, these stories took place at Weemawee High School where girls chased boys and boys chased girls to the mutual detriment of their education. The principal characters were the shy and naive Patty Greene (Sarah Jessica Parker) and her best friend, assertive and extrovert Laura Hutchinson (Amy Linker). The rebel was Johnny Slash (Merritt Butrick) and his friend was Marshall Blechtman (John Fernia), the school clown. The final pairing of friends was super-cool Jennifer DiNuccio (Tracy Nelson) and Jewish rich-kid Muffy Tepperman (Jami Gertz). There were 22 editions transmitted.

THE SQUIRRELS
ATV. First broadcast: 8 July 1974

This programme began as a single transmitted pilot. Creator Eric Chappell turned it into a series which began on 18 July the next year, 1975. The setting was the accounts department of International Rentals, a TV hire company. Bernard Hepton starred as the boss Mr Fletcher, and the workers who shared in his misadventures were Rex (Ken Jones), Susan (Patsy Rowlands), Harry (Alan David), Burke (Ellis Jones) and secretary Carol (Susan Tracy in the pilot, Karin MacCarthy in the series). The show ran for three seasons.
Writers included Eric Chappell, Kenneth Cope, Alan Hackney, Richard Harris. Producer: Shaun O'Riordan.

STAND AT EASE
BBC RADIO. First broadcast: 22 February 1941

There were only three editions of this burlesque of Army life which took the form of a revue with book and lyrics by Edward J Mason and music by Basil Hempseed. Their collaboration is surprising since Hempseed joined up at the outbreak of war with the rank of Captain and Mason was posted to the same company as a private. However, this brief send-up starred husband and wife – at the time – Sonnie Hale as Private Hale and Jessie Matthews as Volunteer Matthews. Also involved were Major Bagley Poonah (Alan Robinson), Sergeant Bunk (Godfrey Baseley) and Mrs Pomeroy-Flushing (Dorothy Summers).
Producer: Martyn C Webster.

STAND EASY
BBC RADIO. First broadcast: 11 February 1946

The Army crew from MERRY-GO-ROUND were demobbed and launched in Civvy Street with this show. The star was Charlie Chester who also wrote all the scripts for the 150-plus editions. A featured character was Whippit Quick the cat burglar whose voice belonged to Ken Morris. Chester was strongly supported by Arthur Haynes, Len Marten and Louise Gainsborough, and later Edwina Carol and Terry Scott joined the team. In 1951 the format changed and the title became *Keep Smiling*.
Producers: Leslie Bridgmont, Ian C Messiter, Frank Hooper.

STANLEY AND THE WOMEN
Central. First broadcast: 28 November 1991

This four-part black comedy drama was based on the 1984 novel of the same title by Kingsley Amis. John Thaw starred as Stanley Duke, an ordinary man with a good job in a newspaper's advertising department and an attractive and intelligent second wife Susan (Penny Downie). One day the doorbell rang and he found his son in a deeply disturbed condition and learned that he was suffering from schizophrenia. The women in his life were Susan, who was rather vain; his self-centred and weak first wife Nowell Hutchinson (Sheila Gish); his son's psychiatrist Dr Trish Collings (Geraldine James); and one of his former girlfriends Lindsey Lucas (Sian Thomas). Son Steve (Samuel West) had lived with Nowell and her hard-drinking husband Bert (Michael Elphick).
Writer: Nigel Kneale. Director: David Tucker. Producer: Chris Burt.

STARRING LESLIE WILLEY
BBC RADIO. First broadcast: 29 December 1987

Ray Cooney and John Graham wrote this story in six parts about the production of a play from the inception: from the finding of the financial 'angels' and the casting to the rehearsals and finally, the performance. Leslie Phillips starred in the title role with Eric Sykes as George Pigden. It was broadcast on consecutive days.
Producer: Jonathan James-Moore.

STAY LUCKY
YTV. First broadcast: 8 December 1989

Geoff McQueen's stories of a most unlikely couple began with just three one-hour episodes. The next season began with a two-hour edition on 23 September 1990 followed by a series of six one-hours from 29 September. Seven further hour-long editions followed from 4 June 1993. Thomas Gynn (Dennis Waterman), a Cockney wide-boy on the run, met recently-widowed Sally Hardcastle (Jan Francis) at a service station on the M1. She was a headstrong Northern business lady. Thomas journeyed all the way to Newcastle where he drove minicabs while Sally had a narrow boat charter company in Yorkshire. However their paths were destined always to cross and their lives to mingle. Other characters embroiled in their adventures included Kevin (Chris Jury), Lively (Niall Toibin) and Pippa (Emma Wray).

By the time the 1993 series got underway, Thomas had served a prison sentence and Sally had moved well away. Thomas was sorely in need of support from friends past and present including Samantha (Susan George) and his former cell-mate Franklyn Bysouth (Ian McNeice). His affair with Samantha was short-lived but he landed lucky yet again in a brief affair with a girl played by Waterman's real wife Rula Lenska; and in the final three editions Thomas found romantic contentment with Jo (Leslie Ash). In the last programme on 6 August 1993, he and Jo were offered a trip to Tuscany by Franklyn.

Directors: David Reynolds, John Glenister, Lawrence Gordon Clark, Keith Washington. Producers: David Reynolds, Andrew Benson, Matthew Bird.

STEP BY STEP

USA PRESENTED BY ITV.
First broadcast (UK): 23 May 1994

Set in Port Washington, Wisconsin (pop. 9,338), this starred Patrick Duffy as Frank Lambert and Suzanne Somers as Carol Foster. Both were single parents when they met, fell in love and married. The ensuing domestic chaos was brought about by the respective kids' hostility towards each other. Frank's offspring were JT (Brandon Call), a smart teenager into sport and girls; Al (Christine Lakin), a tough adolescent girl who was learning to play the drums; and Brendan (Josh Byrne), the baby of the family. The Fosters were Dana (Staci Keanan), the eldest and given most of the best lines; her younger sister Karen (Angela Watson), who giggled her silly way through life; and Mark (Christopher Castile), a physical wimp but well-versed in philosophy. Frank had a nephew, Cody (Sasha Mitchell), who was besotted by Dana and immune to the sarcastic put-downs which she threw at him. Frank had his own construction company and Carol ran a beauty salon, annexed to the house, with her overweight, man-mad younger sister Penny (Patrika Darbo) and their mother (Peggy Rea).

Creators and producers: William Bickley and Michael Warren.

STEPTOE AND SON

BBC. First broadcast: 5 January 1962

Ray Galton and Alan Simpson's creations Albert Steptoe (Wilfrid Brambell) and his son Harold (Harry H Corbett) were first seen in a one-off half-hour play entitled 'The Offer' as part of the *Comedy*

The same old Christmas decorations are greeted with disgust by Harold (Harry H Corbett) and delight by Albert (Wilfrid Brambell) in the very last edition of STEPTOE AND SON (Photo: Copyright © BBC)

Playhouse strand. Such was the immediate impact of the two rag-and-bone men that 57 editions were produced.

Albert was a miser, unhygienic and generally disgusting. His ageing son had social ambitions but lived with the reality that he would never be able to break free from his father's possessive clutch. Their full names were Albert Edward Ladysmith Steptoe and Harold Albert Kitchener Steptoe and together they lived at The Mews Cottage, Oil Drum Lane, Shepherd's Bush. The house and backyard were cluttered with junk and they had a horse, Hercules, until he died in the episode shown on the 6 March 1970. Harold yearned for a woman and sophistication, registering shame at his own lack of education and disgust at his father whom he called, 'You dirty old man'. Any attempt by Harold to forge a steady relationship with a member of the opposite sex was immediately thwarted by Albert's resolve to let nobody come between him and his son. He would feign a heart-attack at a convenient moment if it suited his purpose and broke Harold's date. Albert kidded himself that he was a hero of the First World War and never missed a chance to don his medals. His role in the house was to prepare meals but his culinary talents rarely extended beyond shoving a pork pie in the oven. Harold would return exhausted after his round only to be faced with cleaning-up some mess or other that Albert had created.

The last programme of the eight series was transmitted on 26 December 1974 and the episodes which have survived in the BBC archive have been much repeated. A few editions thought to be lost for all time were discovered and shown again in 1994. Fifty-one episodes were adapted for radio broadcast by Gale Pedrick beginning on 3 July 1966. The format transferred to America where it was retitled Sanford and Son. The theme music was by Ron Grainer and called 'Old Ned'.

Producers: Duncan Wood, John Howard Davies, David Croft, Douglas Argent.

THE STRANGE WORLD OF GURNEY SLADE

ATV. First broadcast: 22 October 1960

Created by Anthony Newley at a time when situation comedy was firmly rooted in domesticity, this whimsical series was far ahead of its time. Newley himself starred as the title character, the name coming from the village in Somerset called Gurney Slade, through which Newley once drove and decided it would suit the role. Although this series began in stereotype domestic format with a family seated round a table, Slade walked out into a world of his own imagination where he talked to things animal, vegetable and mineral which sprang to life and talked back to him. In the first episode, Una Stubbs played a girl on an advertisement hoarding who was willed to step down and dance with Gurney Slade. Slade lived the life of someone who could do exactly as he pleased. There were just five editions.

Music: Max Harris. Writers: Sid Green and Dick Hills. Producer: Alan Tarrant.

STREETS APART

BBC. First broadcast: 24 October 1988

The principal characters in this series were cab driver Bernie (James Hazeldine), a widower with two children, and Sylvia (Amanda Redman), a high-flying literary agent. They had shared childhood together but Dame Fortune had taken them along different paths, though there still remained an attraction. Their new relationship was rocky and, despite how they felt about each other in private, their social circles were incompatible. Sharing their ups and downs were Jenny (June Barry), Lyn (Lesley Duff), Cliff (Desmond McNamara) and Rene (Diane Langton). A first series of six was followed by a second run ending 9 October 1989.

Writer: Adrienne Conway. Producer: Sue Bysh.

STRUGGLE

CHANNEL 4. First broadcast: 27 November 1983

Created and written by the political correspondent of The Guardian, Peter Jenkins, this series of six starred Tim Pigott-Smith as Steve Marsh, leader of the left-wing council in South Ham, London. He had around him a small clique of comrades known as 'the Caucus'. His political opposition was led by right-wing, working-class knight Sir Bert (Ray Smith), a former barrow boy who had worked his way up to owning a chain of greengrocers.

Producer: Graham Evans for LWT.

SUCH ROTTEN LUCK

BBC RADIO. First broadcast: 16 September 1989

Tim Pigott-Smith starred as Woodhouse, described in the show's publicity blurb as 'a second-class writer'. He attended a class for creative writing to advance his dream of finding fame and fortune through his literature. His other interest was jazz and with friend Seamus (Stephen Rea) he aspired to create the perfect jazz duo. The impressive supporting cast included Zoë Wanamaker, Maxine Audley, Miriam Karlin, Celia Imrie, Nickolas Grace, Timothy Bateson and Benjamin Whitrow. A second run of six started on 21 December 1991 and ran each day that week barring Sunday.

Music: Elizabeth Parker. Writer: Ronald Hayman. Producer: Paul Schlesinger.

SUPERGRAN

Tyne Tees. First broadcast: 20 January 1985

Jenny McDade adapted the books by Forrest Wilson into two 13-part series ending 1 June 1987. Gudrun Ure starred as Supergran, the saviour of Chisleton, a gentle old lady accidentally endowed with magical powers which equipped her to foil the schemes of the villainous Scunner Campbell (Iain Cuthbertson). The regular characters were Inventor Black (Bill Shine), The Muscles (Alan Snell and Brian Lewis), Inspector Muggins (Robert Austin), PC Leekie (Terry Joyce), Eddison (Holly English), Tub (Lee Marshall) and Willard (Ian Towell).

Theme music: Billy Connolly and Phil Coulter. Director: Anthony Simmons. Producer: Keith Richardson.

SURGICAL SPIRIT

GRANADA. First broadcast: 14 April 1989

Peter Learmouth created this series set at The Gillies Hospital. The stories charted the love lives of acid-tongued surgeon Dr Sheila Sabatini (Nichola McAuliffe) and Yorkshireman Dr Jonathan Haslam (Duncan Preston). Sabatini was a married woman with a teenage son but once her divorce was through, hospital administrator Joyce Watson (Marji Campi) played matchmaker to them. Sabatini and Jonathan became engaged but following too much to drink at the engagement party, she spent the night with an Italian restaurateur named Paco and he spent the night at the flat of one of the nurses. She broke off the engagement and they hurled invective at one another across the operating table. Other key players in the everyday chaos of hospital life were George Hope-Wynne (David Conville), Neil Copeland (Emlyn Price), Simon Field (Lyndam Gregory), Giles Peake (Simon Harrison) the registrar, and Sister Cheryl Patching (Suzette Llewellyn) who lived with Dr Michael Sampson (Beresford LeRoy). Forty-three editions spanned six series ending on 11 March 1994.

Writers included Peter Learmouth and Graeme Garden. Directors: John Kaye Cooper, David Askey. Producer: Humphrey Barclay.

SYKES AND . . .

BBC. First broadcast: 29 January 1960

Eric Sykes and Hattie Jacques first worked together on **EDUCATING ARCHIE** in 1952. Their first sitcom was called *Sykes and a Telephone* and subsequently each episode had a different title. They played twin brother and sister living together at 24 Sebastopol Terrace and the partnership continued until Hattie Jacques died on 6 October 1980. Sykes struggled to better himself from his little corner of suburbia and for the first

Eric Sykes and Hattie Jacques as twin brother and sister in SYKES AND . . . (Photo: Copyright © BBC)

three series he was generally put down by pompous, interfering neighbour Mr Brown (Richard Wattis) before he decided to emigrate. Eric laboured under the mistaken belief that he was always protecting his sister from life's realities whereas in truth she was mothering and affording her own protection for him.

Richard Wattis returned to the series and Deryck Guyler was a regular as Corky, the friendly village policeman. One of the last shows on 19 October 1979 in which Eric and Hattie were planning a holiday to the West Country was seen by a staggering 22.4 million viewers (although ITV was on strike at the time).

Writers: Johnny Speight, Eric Sykes. Producers: Dennis Main Wilson, Sydney Lotterby, Philip Barker, Roger Race.

THE TV LARK
BBC RADIO. First broadcast: 25 January 1963
....
Although the title might lead to confusion, this show really was radio. The crew from THE NAVY LARK were taken ashore by writer Lawrie Wyman to begin their new careers running the Troutbridge Commercial Television station, a small local operation sending out a pathetically weak signal to the inhabitants of Troutbridgshire. Retired from the Navy, or rather rendered redundant, the former crew members were merely Misters in their new occupation. Deputy Controller of Programmes was Henry Povey (Richard Caldicot), the producer was Stephen Murray, the director was Leslie Phillips, and Jon Pertwee was the floor manager. Michael Bates ran the design department, the production secretary was Janet (Janet Brown), on camera one was Fatso Johnson (Ronnie Barker) and on camera two Taffy Goldstein (Tenniel Evans). Ten shows were heard.
Producer: Alastair Scott Johnston.

THE TAB HUNTER SHOW
NBC (AMERICA) PRESENTED BY BBC.
First broadcast (UK): 5 January 1961
....
Tab Hunter, who had two top ten records in Britain in 1957, starred as cartoonist Paul Morgan whose greatest talents were the pursuit of girls and the avoidance of matrimony. He drew and wrote a daily comic strip, 'Bachelor at Large', based on his own adventures. His boss at Comics Inc was John Larsen (Jerome Cowan). Morgan had a very rich playboy pal, Peter Fairfield III (Richard Erdman), a highly eligible bachelor with whom he shared his wanderings. Each of the 32 episodes was constructed around a beautiful female guest star.
Producer: Norman Tokar.

TAKE A LETTER, MR JONES
SOUTHERN. First broadcast: 12 September 1981
....
Ronald Wolfe and Ronald Chesney wrote this seven-part series. Mrs Warner (Rula Lenska) was the UK head of an American company specialising in leisure activities. In a role reversal of the times, she had a male secretary, Graham Jones (John Inman). He was possessive, especially when an executive from the Australian division of the company, Rod Newton (Bruce Berry), took a shine to her.
Producer: Bryan Izzard.

TAKE IT FROM HERE
BBC RADIO. First broadcast: 12 March 1948
....
In the annals of British radio history this show ranks among the most innovative for its time. It began with what was planned to be a six-week run but was extended and, due to the sudden death of ITMA star Tommy Handley, found itself promoted to the coveted Saturday lunchtime slot. It was the first major vehicle for its stars, Jimmy Edwards, Dick Bentley and Joy Nichols, as well as for its writers, Frank Muir and Denis Norden. TIFH, as it soon became known, was a sketch show and its relevance to sitcom did not begin until November 1953 when Joy Nichols left the cast and June Whitfield joined. It was during that run that THE GLUMS were created, considered by many to be a watershed in comedy. They certainly pushed back the barriers of what had been allowed on the air, as loud-mouthed boor Mr Glum (Edwards) would impose some lewd misunderstanding as he burst in on his gormless idiot of a son Ron (Bentley) wooing his fiancée Eth (Whitfield) on the settee. Eth tried all manner of persuasion to get Ron to the altar or get him a job or interest him in almost anything, but always to no avail. THE GLUMS remained a part of TIFH until the last of more than 300 editions on 3 March 1960 when they were about to emigrate to Australia. Mrs Glum was never featured but sometimes heard making the odd noise in the background. Those noises were provided by the show's singer, Alma Cogan. The 13th and last series was written by Eric Merriman and Barry Took.
Producers: Charles Maxwell, Charles Chilton.

TAKE MY WIFE

GRANADA. First broadcast: 17 January 1979

Yorkshire comedian Duggie Brown was cast in eight shows as Harvey Hall, a struggling comic working the Northern clubs. His wife Josie (Elisabeth Sladen) was understanding of him but had scant comprehension of the demands of show business. His mother-in-law Mabel Norrington (Joan Benham) considered Harvey a class or two below the Norringtons and looked with disdain on his low-brow lifestyle. His agent, Maurice Watkins, was played by Victor Spinetti and his assistant, Doreen Underhill, by Toni Palmer.

Writer: Anthony Couch. Director: Gordon Flemyng. Producer: John G Temple.

TAKE THREE GIRLS

BBC. First broadcast: 17 November 1969

When this series of 50-minute comedy dramas began, the three girls sharing a flat in SW3 were Kate (Susan Jameson), Avril (Angela Down) and Victoria (Liza Goddard). Kate was a failed actress whose husband had upped and left her with a baby and the bills. Avril was in her first job and making progress up the ladder, finally moving to Paris at the end of the 12-part series. Victoria was a born loser whose every endeavour came unstuck, largely because of her mean father, Mr Edgecombe (David Langton). There were four stories centred on each of the girls. For a second series of six beginning 24 March 1971, only Victoria remained. She was joined in the flat by Jenny (Carolyn Seymour), a journalist, and Lulie (Barra Grant), an American psychology graduate with romantic problems. Out of their debby, mod lifestyle, Victoria found herself with a catchphrase, 'too silly'.

Writers included Hugo Charteris, Julia Jones, Terence Brady and Charlotte Bingham. Directors included Mark Cullingham, John Matthews, Tristan De Vere Cole. Producer: Michael Hayes.

TAKE UMBRIDGE

BBC RADIO. First broadcast: 15 April 1941

Charles Heslop wrote and starred as Professor Umbridge in what he described as six unfortunate incidents from the Professor's disreputable career. Umbridge was a phoney teacher of music and voice-production who made great efforts to extort money from unsuspecting and innocent people. His assistant was Henry Horatio Pibberdy (Richard Goolden). Other regular characters were Mrs Termigan (Doris Nichols), John (Guy Verney), Marjorie (Marjorie Westbury) and Victor (John Singer).

Producer: Gordon Crier.

TAKING THE FLOOR

BBC. First broadcast: 4 March 1991

Set in the Midlands, this series by Paul Makin followed the fortunes of working-class Brian Wheeler (Matthew Cottle), a competition ballroom dancer, and his spoiled and pampered dancing partner Karen Tranter (Barbara Durkin). Brian's parents were played by Janet Dale and Timothy Kightley, his brother Colin by Dean Gatiss and Karen's father by Christopher Godwin. Six episodes were screened.

Producer: Derrick Goodwin for Alomo.

TAKING THE WATERS

BBC RADIO. First broadcast: 5 July 1962

Set in Arcadian Grove, Putney, Elsie and Doris Waters starred as their Cockney alter egos GERT AND DAISY in this 13-part series. Staying with them as permanent residents were their nephew and ward Michael (David Spenser) and his fellow student Ronnie (Ronald Wilson), a distant cousin from Australia. The neighbours were Griff (Bruce Wightman) and Mrs Griffiths (Katherine Parr).

Writers: Marjorie and Antony Bilbow. Producers: Alastair Scott Johnston, Jacques Brown.

TALES FROM THE POOP DECK

THAMES. First broadcast: 7 April 1992

This six-part children's series starred Helen Atkinson Wood as the swashbuckling pirate and scourge of the King's navy, Blackheart. Her ship was the Sea Cow and her arch enemies, including Captain Stallion (Nicholas Pritchard) and Petty Officer Coleridge (Paul Shearer), were led by Admiral De'Ath (Charles Gray) aboard the navy's 17th-century galleon.

Writers: Lenny Barker and Vicky Stepney.

TANDOORI NIGHTS

CHANNEL 4. First broadcast: 4 July 1985

Farrukh Dhondy created this series about two rival Indian restaurants in London. Both were named after TV dramas of the moment, the upmarket Jewel in the Crown and the further downmarket Far Pavilions. Both were in the same street in Ealing. The main character was Jimmy (Saeed Jaffrey) who had begun his career as a restaurateur in Brick Lane almost 15 years previously. His was a story of success and the Jewel in the Crown his final glory. He had a daughter Asha (Rita Wolf) and a cook named Alladin (Tariq Yunus). The other principal characters were Gran (Zohra Segal), Bubbly (Shelley King), Noor (Andrew Johnson) and Rashid (Badi Uzzaman). In one episode, Jimmy's niece Sweetie (Sneh Gupta) returned from India to put in an appearance. The first series of six was followed by a second six-part run which ended on 11 November 1987.

Writers: Dhondy, Meera Syal, HO Nazareth. Directors: John Amiel, Christopher Menaul. Producers: Malcolm Craddock and Peter Ansorge. A Picture Palace production.

TAXI

BBC RADIO. First broadcast: 3 January 1942

Created during the war by writer Cyril Campion, this long-running series revolved around the adventures of Shorty (Jerry Verno), a London cab-driver whose weekly passenger remained a mystery until just before the end of the show. After an extensive run the show quietly disappeared only to resurface on 29 January 1946. The programmes were only 15 minutes in length.

Producer: Jacques Brown.

TAXI

BBC. First broadcast: 10 July 1963

Sid James starred as Sid Stone, a London 'mush' (taxi driver who owned his cab), with Bill Owen as his partner Fred Cuddell; 24-year-old actor Ray Brooks played journeyman driver Terry Mills. The three of them shared rooms in an old London house converted into flats. Sid was an adventurer with the knack of becoming embroiled in other people's business and problems. In the first series of eight 45-minute editions, written by Ted Willis, the female interest for Sid was Madeleine (Vanda Godsell). The second run was for 13 weeks and ended on 27 June 1964. Those shows were written by Harry Driver and Jack Rosenthal, and Bill Owen had left the cast, as had Vanda Godsell who was replaced by Diane Aubrey as Sandra. This series also introduced the couple from the upstairs flat, Bert and

Dolly Stoker (Toke Townley and Clare Kelly) and their daughter Jean (Janet Kelly).
Directors included Douglas Argent and Robin Nash. Producers: Michael Mills, Harry Carlisle, Douglas Moodie.

TAXI

ABC (AMERICA) PRESENTED BY BBC.
First broadcast (UK): 17 April 1980

The Sunshine Cab Company was set in New York City where the boss was the tyrannical, crude and heartless Louie de Palma (Danny De Vito), who goaded and deployed the staff at his whim and was also not averse to treating customers with a firm rudeness which belied his pint-size stature. The leading cabbie was Alex Rieger (Judd Hirsch) who was the receptacle of most of the problems of the others. The sole woman driver was Elaine Nardo (Marilu Henner), who had to try to fit two jobs into her life to enable her to bring up her child. The men were Tony Banta (Tony Danza), a failed boxer; Bobby Wheeler (John Conaway), who hoped to be an actor although he seemed to lack talent; John Burns (Randall Carver); and spaced-out, former hippie Reverend Jim Ignatowski (Christopher Lloyd) who joined in the second series. The pop-eyed mechanic with the sing-song voice and fractured English was Latka Gravas (Andy Kaufman). The shows were created and produced by James L Brooks, Allan Burns and Grant Tinker. The BBC showed the last of more than 100 editions on 23 December 1985.

TEARS BEFORE BEDTIME

BBC. First broadcast: 29 March 1983

Anne and Geoffrey Dickens (Geraldine McEwan and Francis Matthews) had three children, Giles, Vicky and Simon (Nigel Greaves, Amanda Bairstow and Anthony Calf). When they reached the ages of 18, 19 and 20 they became impossible to live with, so Anne and Geoffrey quit the family home and moved 70 miles away to escape their music, manners, friends and fashions.
Writer: Richard Waring. Producer: Harold Snoad.

TEENAGE HEALTH FREAK

CHANNEL 4. First broadcast: 21 May 1991

Daniel Peacock adapted the best-selling novel *Diary of a Teenage Health Freak* into three six-part series which ended on 29 March 1993. Peter Payne (Alex

Langdon) was a perfectly fit and healthy 15-year-old but, having read the doom and gloom reports of the break-up of the world's ozone layer, he believed he had contracted skin cancer as a direct result. Writer Peacock played Peter's rough and ready father while his neurotic mother, who was either in bed or playing with her dolls' house, was portrayed by Tilly Vosburgh. Peter's younger sister was played by Sukey Fekkes. At school Peter was besotted by his classmate Amanda Jeffs (Liza Walker). The Headmaster was played by Tony Robinson, and quirky art student Jo, who drove a beaten-up Mercedes, was portrayed by Samantha Edmonds. In the final series, Mum had a breakdown, Dad started drinking too much, Peter was forced to pose in the nude for Jo in order to borrow her camera and he acquired a criminal record, all thanks to Amanda.

Directors: Metin Huseyin, Peter Cattaneo. Producer: Adrian Bate for Limelight Productions.

TELL IT TO THE MARINES

A-R. First broadcast: 23 September 1959

Ted Willis devised this series which exploited the traditional rivalry between the Royal Navy and the Royal Marines. Leading seaman White (Alan White) led the Navy lads against the Marines where his principal opponent was Corporal Surtees (Ronald Hines). Other regular characters were Lieutenant Raleigh (Henry McGee), Petty Officer Woodward (John Bascombe), Tactical Communications Operator Kilmartin Dalrymple (Ian MacNaughton), Whittle (Ian Whittaker), Commander Walters RN (Ian Colin) and Marine Major Howard (Jack Allen). There were 29 editions.

Producer: Milo Lewis.

THE 10%ERS

CENTRAL. First broadcast: 18 April 1994

Created by Rob Grant and Doug Naylor, this title was seen as a one-off *Comedy Playhouse* in 1993 before the launch of the seven-part series. Eden Management was a West End talent agency (*they all take 15% in the experience of the author!*) headed by slimy Dominic Eden (Clive Francis), whose staff included self-centred egotist Joan (Elizabeth Bennett), loud-mouthed American Tony (Colin Stinton), obsequious Helen (Gabrielle Cowburn) and heart-throb Atin (Benedict Taylor). The elderly receptionist/secretaries were Gloria (Irene Sutcliffe) and Enid (Hilda Braid).

Producer: Marcus Mortimer for Grant-Naylor productions.

TENSPEED AND BROWN SHOE

ABC (AMERICA) PRESENTED BY ITV.
First broadcast (UK): 15 October 1981

A black hustler, EL Tenspeed (Ben Vereen), teamed up with a young stockbroker, Lionel 'Brown Shoe' Whitney (Jeff Goldblum), to form a private detective agency. The shows were created and produced by Stephen J Cannell. Thirteen episodes were screened.

THE TERRIFIC ADVENTURES OF THE TERRIBLE TEN

AUSTRALIA PRESENTED BY ITV.
First broadcast (UK): 9 November 1962

This children's series was bravely made by producer Roger Miram who used his own money and cast his own kids and those of friends. The youngsters constructed their own town, built from packing cases and whatever else was at hand, with their own laws, police and fire service and where they were free to fight with treacle, soot and water to their hearts' content. They encountered spies and made contact with outer space along the way. Miram was also the writer.

TERRY AND JULIAN

CHANNEL 4. First broadcast: 11 September 1992

Camp comedian Julian Clary joined the sitcom bandwagon with this six-part spoof of TERRY AND JUNE. He even managed to coax June Whitfield into appearing in one of the episodes. Julian played a homeless Channel 4 celebrity who turned up to share a flat with a rough and ready South London lad, Terry (Lee Simpson), and after some decorating and exchange of sordid innuendo, they settled down to live happily ever after.

Writers: Julian Clary, Paul Merton and John Henderson. Director: Liddy Oldroyd. Producer: Toni Yardley.

TERRY AND JUNE

BBC. First broadcast: 24 October 1979

This sequel to HAPPY EVER AFTER again paired Terry Scott and June Whitfield in the ups and downs of suburban matrimonial existence over 65 episodes to 31 August 1987. Terry and June Medford lived in Purley in a comfortable middle-class envi-

ronment in which Terry did most of the talking and June existed in the chintz comforts that he provided. Terry's ultimate boss at work was Sir Dennis Hodge (Reginald Marsh) and there was much dusting and preparation if he was coming round for dinner. His immediate superior at work was portrayed successively by Terence Alexander, Tim Barrett and John Quayle. The secretary was Miss Fennel (Joanna Henderson). The Medfords' neighbour Beattie was played by Rosemary Frankau.
Writers included John Kane, Jon Watkins, Dave and Greg Freeman, Colin Bostock-Smith. Producers: Peter Whitmore, John B Hobbs, Robin Nash.

THANK YOU, MRS FOTHERGILL

BBC RADIO. First broadcast: 7 June 1979

This six-part series featured the goings-on of the Cloughbottom Ladies Evening Guild. The participants were Alice Foster (Sheila Hancock), Phyllis Middleton (Pat Coombs), Peggy Fielden (Clovissa Newcombe) and Mrs Fothergill (Avis Bunnage).
Writer: Keith Parry. Producer: Bob Oliver Rogers.

THAT BERYL MARSTON . . .

SOUTHERN. First broadcast: 24 July 1981

Jan Butlin created and wrote this six-part series in which the lady of the title, known as the sex goddess of East Sussex, was never seen. Georgie Bodley (Julia McKenzie) owned and ran a Brighton curiosity shop. Her husband Gerry (Gareth Hunt) was a company executive. Their lives were perfect in every way but one. They had success, money and social status but their marriage was a disaster. Matters were brought to a head by Gerry's affair with Beryl Marston. The couple were only kept from coming to physical blows by their mutual friends Harvey and Phil (Peter John and Jonathon Morris), a gay couple who ran a health-food store. However, neither they nor the Bodley daughter Jane (Jayne Stevens) could prevent their ultimate divorce.
Producer: Bryan Izzard.

THAT CHILD

BBC RADIO. First broadcast: 12 April 1926

This is the earliest known domestic situation comedy and, though the six episodes were each only 10 minutes in length, it occupies a historic place in the establishment of the genre. Florence Kilpatrick

wrote the scripts in which mother Netta (Mabel Constanduros) and father Henry (Michael Hogan), struggled to cope with their awful daughter (Lorna Hubbard).

THAT'S LOVE

TVS. First broadcast: 19 January 1988

Terence Frisby created and wrote the 26 episodes which spanned four series ending 24 March 1992. The stories concerned the domestic problems of a young married couple, lawyer Donald (Jimmy Mulville) and his forceful wife Patsy (Diana Hardcastle), a designer. They were happily married until Donald learned some secrets from Patsy's past. In time Donald had an affair with rich widow Laurel Manasotti (Liza Goddard) but in a last-ditch attempt to patch up their marriage in the final series, he and Patsy sought the counsel of marriage-guidance consultant Tristan Beasley (Tony Slattery), a flirt who fell hopelessly in love with Patsy. The series ended with them coming to terms with the probability that their marriage would soon be over.
Director: John Stroud. Producer: Humphrey Barclay.

THAT'S MY BABY

BBC RADIO. First broadcast: 2 March 1950

Naunton Wayne as Fothergill and Basil Radford as Fanshawe starred in this comedy adventure in eight episodes by Max Kester. As always in the partnership between these two actors, they were uppercrust Englishmen who got caught up in the misadventures of others. This particular title also involved Barbara Murray as Bobbie Trevelyan.
Producer: Vernon Harris.

THAT'S MY BOY

YTV. First broadcast: 23 October 1981

A domestic employment agency had been terrorised by the demands of Ida Willis (Mollie Sugden) until they found her a post as housekeeper to Dr Robert Price (Christopher Blake) and his model wife Angie (Jennifer Lonsdale). Robert's mother Mrs Price (Clare Richards) had adopted him as a baby. Unknown to all, at least initially, was the fact that Ida was the real mother who had given him up for adoption at birth. On learning the truth, she became possessive and jealous of Mrs Price. The first series of six was followed by a run of nine from 7 January 1983 and a further seven from 27 April

1984. By the time the 1985 series of six began on 18 January, Robert had got a job in Yorkshire, so the whole family had to move. Ida found it difficult to settle but in the final run of seven beginning 21 February 1986, she had been joined by her brother Wilfred Willis (Harold Goodwin) and had made friends with Miss Parfitt (Deddie Davies).

Writers: Pam Valentine and Michael Ashton. Producer: Graeme Muir.

THAT'S YOUR FUNERAL

BBC. First broadcast: 15 January 1971

Bill Fraser starred as bombastic, cantankerous Basil Bulstrode, an undertaker who first appeared in March 1970 in a single *Comedy Playhouse* entitled 'Last Tribute'. Writer Peter Lewis, then theatre critic for the *Daily Mail*, turned it into this seven-part series set in the North of England. The undertakers wore full frock coats, wing collars and bowler hats, and abided by funereal traditions. The boss was Emanuel Holroyd (Raymond Huntley) who disapproved of Basil's non-stop talking and boasting. The junior was Percy (David Battley).

Producer: Douglas Argent.

THEM

BBC. First broadcast: 27 July 1972

Johnny Speight wrote this five-part series about two gentlemen of the road, an Irish tramp who wore half a dozen layers of coats and was played by Cyril Cusack, and a Cockney vagrant with battered homburg, morning coat and monocle, played by James Booth.

Director: Harold Snoad. Producer: Dennis Main Wilson.

THERE COMES A TIME . . .

YTV. First broadcast: 20 February 1985

Tony James (Andrew Sachs) embarked on a nightmare search for the ultimate meaning of life after being told by Dr Harry Eaton (Alan David) that his condition was such that he was poised to create medical history. More than that Tony did not know, but his wife Vanessa (Judy Cornwell) shared certain secrets with the doctor. Tony and Vanessa had a son, Peter (Robert Daws). The series ran for seven episodes.

Writer: Wally K Daly. Producer: Ronnie Baxter.

THERE'S ONE BORN EVERY MINUTE

BBC RADIO. First broadcast: 26 August 1966

Dick Sharples wrote this nine-part series after actress Thora Hird revealed her idea to play a rural district nurse. The character he created for her was Lizzie Oldshaw, a woman from the North who encountered all sorts of characters on her rounds. Her unlikely friend was local rascal and poacher Sam Gudgeon (Bill Owen).

Producer: Trafford Whitelock.

THICK AS THIEVES

LWT. First broadcast: 1 June 1974

Dick Clement and Ian La Frenais created and wrote this series which cast Bob Hoskins as Dobbs, a comic crook who was released from prison only to go home and discover his wife Annie (Pat Ashton) domestically ensconced with his best friend Stan (John Thaw). They settled into a *ménage à trois* but from time to time Annie would walk away and leave them to get on with it. For a couple of episodes life's complexities increased with the arrival on the doorstep of Tommy Hollister (Trevor Peacock), an escaped prisoner and pal of Dobbs' who insisted on staying. In her more fraught moments, Annie confided in her friend Daphne (Nell Curran).

Producer: Derrick Goodwin.

THICKER THAN WATER

BBC. First broadcast: 17 February 1969

Jimmy Jewel starred in this seven-part series as Jim Eccles, father of three daughters, Janet (Carolyn Moody), Carol (Jill Kerman) and Vicki (Roberta Rex). Co-starring with Jewel was Jean Kent as next-door neighbour Aggie Plunkett. Jim trod a fine line in order to make ends meet but was devastated when middle daughter Carol announced her engagement to Robert Bean (Gerald Moon) – Bean drove a television detector van and Jim did not have a licence!

Writer: Peter Robinson. Producer: Douglas Argent.

THICKER THAN WATER

YTV. First broadcast: 28 April 1981

Dick Sharples wrote this seven-part series in which Joss Ackland starred as widower Joseph Lockwood living with his two bachelor sons, Alan and Malcolm (Colin Farrell and Peter Denyer). Alan had a dance

band known as Al Lockwood's Syncopated Serenaders in which his brother played the bass. Joseph's pal was Harry Fishwick (David Battley).
Producer: Ronnie Baxter.

THINGS COULD BE WORSE

BBC RADIO. First broadcast: 15 September 1976

Harry Worth starred as his usual accident-prone bumbling character in a series of 13 adventures written by David McKellar and David Renwick. Helping Harry into and out of hot water were John Baddeley, John Graham and Miriam Margolyes.
Producer: Simon Brett.

THINGUMYBOB

LWT. First broadcast: 2 August 1968

The first of six episodes was transmitted on the first night that London Weekend Television went on the air. Stanley Holloway starred as Bob Bridge and Rose Hill as his wife Fay. Their neighbours were Bert and Monica Ryding (John Junkin and Kate Williams). The comedy was gentle and focused on Bob's retirement and life as a pensioner. The Bridges had a dog named Storm and a son and daughter-in-law, Ron and Jean Bridge (William Maxwell and Peta Vernon-Till), who were recently returned from Australia.
Theme music: Paul McCartney. Writer: Kenneth Cope. Producer: David Askey.

THIRD TIME LUCKY

YTV. First broadcast: 6 August 1982

Jan Butlin wrote this tangled web in which a couple who had married and divorced, had remarried and divorced their respective second partners and planned to marry each other again. George Hutchenson (Derek Nimmo) and Beth (Nerys Hughes) had had 11 years of marriage and the series began seven years on from their divorce. During those intervening years Beth married and divorced Bruce Jenkins (Clifford Earl) and George married and divorced Millie (Angela Douglas). Millie had subsequently married Henry King (Gerald Flood). George and Beth had two children, Jenny and Clare (Lorraine Brunning and Debbie Farrington). Six episodes wer screened.
Theme music: Peter Skellern. Producer: Graeme Muir.

THIRTY MINUTES WORTH

BBC RADIO. First broadcast: 23 September 1963

The record for the longest gap between series belongs to this title. Harry Worth was the star and after 20 years almost to the day, on 25 September 1983, the second series started. Returning with Worth was the original writer Vince Powell who had created the first series with Frank Roscoe. The 1963 team of supporting actors included Deryck Guyler, Anthony Sharpe, Edwin Apps and Brian Trueman. In 1983 the team was Jacqueline Clarke, Charles Collingwood, Julie Higginson and Sandra Dickinson. Both teams were equally confused by Harry's wittering and dithering.
Producers: James Casey, Mike Craig.

THIS IS DAVID HARPER

CHANNEL 4. First broadcast: 2 November 1990

Tony Slattery starred as David Harper, a newshound off to cover a different story each week through the six episodes. No other characters were constant.
Writer: Tony Sarchet. Director: Graham Dixon. Producer: Mary Bell for Hat Trick Productions.

THIS'LL BE A LESSON TO YOU

BBC RADIO. First broadcast: 10 December 1943

Revered revue artist and Tommy Handley's partner in their 'Murgatroyd and Winterbottom' sketches, Ronald Frankau wrote and starred in these six broadcasts. He cast himself as Principal of the Universal University, an academy for everyday education. He was assisted in his lunacy by Anne Lenner, Phoebe Hodgson, John Rorke and others.
Producer: Max Kester.

THOSE KIDS

ABC. First broadcast: 9 June 1956

This series for children, written and produced by Patricia Latham, starred Peter Butterworth as Mr Oddy with Totti Truman Taylor as his sister, Aunt Agatha. The pair of them were led into a variety of comedy situations by the kids, Henry (George Howell), Maisie (Lynn Grant), Robert (Christopher Sandford), Sally (Shandra Walden) and Al (Peter Soule). Thirteen episodes were screened.

THREE LIVE WIRES
A-R. First broadcast: 15 May 1961

James Kelly and Peter Miller created and wrote this series which starred Michael Medwin as the Cockney foreman in a television sales and repair shop. His repair mates, Malcolm and George, were played by Bernard Fox and George Roderick who had both been with Medwin in THE LOVE OF MIKE. Later in the run they were joined by a fourth repair man, Higgenbottom (Derek Benfield). All of them were equally ham-fisted and workshy. The pompous, self-opinionated shop manager, Mr Farnum, was portrayed by Deryck Guyler. There were 26 episodes.
Producer: Christopher Hodson.

THREE PIECE SWEET
BBC RADIO. First broadcast: 5 November 1979

Jill Hyem and Jennifer Phillips wrote this six-part series in which widow Rita Simmons (Patricia Routledge) lived with her daughter Phoebe (Paula Wilcox) in Richmond. To make ends meet, they had converted the top floor into a self-contained flat where the new incumbent was Alistair Proudfoot (Christopher Good). Neither Rita nor Alistair's mother (Margot Boyd) saw things with the same freedom as did their young.
Producer: Glyn Dearman.

THREE ROUSING TINKLES
BBC. First broadcast: 7 May 1966

In this surreal series of just three episodes by NF Simpson, Edwin Apps and his real-life wife Pauline Devaney starred as ordinary suburban couple Bro and Middie Paradock, who returned from shopping to their semi to discover that the spare room had been taken over by someone they had never seen before (Bryan Pringle). Gradually their home was infiltrated by strange people and objects.
Producer: Stuart Allen.

THREE TOUGH GUYS
ATV. First broadcast: 24 June 1957

This short-lived series of six shows was written and created by John Law and Bill Craig. Harry Green, Warren Mitchell and Peter Welch were the 'tough' guys, a criminal trio with their hearts set on larceny. Their avowed intent was to keep on the wide and crooked. For some reason the show had a theme

tune entitled 'Chicken Noodle', and the broadcasts were fortnightly.
Producers: Cecil Petty and Hugh Rennie.

THREE UP, TWO DOWN
BBC. First broadcast: 15 April 1985

Richard Ommanney created and wrote this war of class between snobby Daphne (Angela Thorne) from Cheltenham and Cockney oik Sam (Michael Elphick) from south London. Both were widowed. They came together when her plummy daughter Angie (Lysette Anthony) married his photographer son Nick (Ray Burdis). With money tight, the young couple had a baby and wished to let out the downstairs flat. Both Sam and Daphne had designs on the flat and ended up sharing it. Though they fought like cat and dog, often over their relative importance vis-à-vis the new grandchild, it was soon apparent that Sam fancied Daphne and the series created an ongoing cliffhanger as to whether or not they would marry. The tantalising middle-age romance was sustained over four seasons ending on 18 June 1989.
Directors: Mandie Fletcher, John B Hobbs. Producers: David Askey, John B Hobbs.

THUD AND BLUNDER
BBC RADIO. First broadcast: 31 October 1958

Naunton Wayne starred as Henry Coote in this eight-part comedy serial. Coote was the archetypal correct English gentleman, although not particularly clever. He had the knack of finding trouble and he was accompanied through this adventure by his nephew Willoughby Lamprey (Philip Guard), his butler Baines (Deryck Guyler), Pigg-Nettleford of the FO (Brian Hayes) and secretary Priscilla Wedgwood (Peggy Cameron). Businessman Mr Minford (Dudley Rolph) and foreign agent Zedwitz (Alan Keith) were objects of Coote's interest.
Writer: John Jowett. Producer: Vernon Harris.

TILL DEATH . . .
ATV. First broadcast: 17 May 1981

After years of success at the BBC with TILL DEATH US DO PART, writer Johnny Speight impudently took his characters across to the opposition for this seven-part series which set Alf and Else Garnett (Warren Mitchell and Dandy Nichols)

into retirement in Eastbourne. Alf's mate Bert had died and Bert's widow, Min (Patricia Hayes), had moved in with them as a permanent lodger. The Garnetts received frequent visits from their daughter Rita (Una Stubbs).
Producer: William G Stewart.

TILL DEATH US DO PART
BBC. First broadcast: 22 July 1965

Johnny Speight's creation of Alf Garnett (Warren Mitchell), the most bigoted, foul-mouthed, right-wing extremist on television, was launched on an unsuspecting British public as a single show broadcast under the banner of *Comedy Playhouse*, when the family name was Ramsey and not Garnett. The role of Alf's long-suffering wife was played by Gretchen Franklin. By the first edition of the subsequent series on 6 June 1966, the family name was Garnett and Else, Alf's 'silly moo' wife, was portrayed by Dandy Nichols. Sharing their house were daughter Rita (Una Stubbs) and her layabout husband Mike (Anthony Booth), who to Alf was a 'randy Scouse git'.

Alf would rant and rave at them all and on any subject, thereby exposing his racist and chauvinist beliefs. He was an avid supporter of West Ham United and a staunch monarchist. His wife, daughter and son-in-law were a captive audience for his tirade of vitriol. He was opposed to anything and

'Listen, you Scouse git,' demands Alf (Warren Mitchell) of son-in-law Mike (Anthony Booth) in TILL DEATH US DO PART (Photo: © BBC)

everything that they were for. Alf was a Tory, and Mike a socialist with long hair. Rita protested at her father's bigotry yet maintained an affection for him while never failing to encourage Mike to needle him. They all lived together in disharmony at the far eastern end of Wapping High Street in London's dockland. There were few other characters on a regular basis. John Junkin occasionally turned up as Wally the milkman and, in later series, the Garnetts' neighbours were Bert and Min (Alfie Bass and Patricia Hayes). The format transferred to America as ALL IN THE FAMILY in which Alf Garnett metamorphosed into Archie Bunker.

Till Death ran for seven series in a total of 54 episodes, the last of which was seen on 17 December 1975. There was also a 45-minute Christmas special on 26 December 1972. There followed a sequel series, IN SICKNESS AND IN HEALTH, and ATV tried a revival, TILL DEATH . . . in 1981. With the failing health of Dandy Nichols, she was missing from the last two series having ostensibly gone to Australia to visit her sister.
Producers: Dennis Main Wilson, David Croft.

TIME AFTER TIME
LWT. First broadcast: 18 March 1994

From a 1993 pilot entitled *Outside Chance*, this series was developed and written by Paul Minett and Brian Leveson. East London comedian Brian Conley starred as Kenny Conway, a car thief paroled from prison who returned to his family of crooks and horrified his mother Ma Conway (Kate Williams), herself a criminal, by announcing his intention to go straight. Ma was proud that there had never been a straight Conway and Kenny's

Kenny Conway (Brian Conley) and Gillian Walcott (Samantha Beckinsale): proof that opposites attract, TIME AFTER TIME (Photo: LWT)

father, Charlie, was locked up at the time. Kenny's 15-year-old brother Robbie (David Shane) harboured criminal ambitions but Kenny tried to steer him away from that path and out of the influences of friends like Jake Brewer (Richard Graham), a stolen-car dealer. He emerged from prison to be told he was engaged to the dizzy Donna (Georgia Allen) but it was his new probation officer, Gillian Walcott (Samantha Beckinsale), who captured his romantic imagination. She worked with the dreaded man of the probation service, the tough and austere Mr Tredwell (Neil McCaul).
Producer: John Kaye Cooper.

TIME OF MY LIFE
BBC. First broadcast: 18 March 1980

Ken Archer (Mark Kingston) was made redundant after 33 years' service with his firm and on the very same day his wife of 23 years' standing left him for a man 20 years his junior. With things at rock bottom, they proceeded to get catastrophically worse as his cheques began to bounce, he was mugged, committed to an asylum, arrested and taken hostage. Throughout his traumas, wife Jean (Amanda Barrie) pushed relentlessly for divorce and all the marital possessions. Seven programmes were transmitted.
Music: Ronnie Hazlehurst. Writer: Jim Eldridge. Director: Martin Shardlow. Producer: Dennis Main Wilson.

TIME OUT FOR PEGGY
ABC. First broadcast: 30 March 1958

Californian Budd Grossman created and wrote this series which ran for three seasons. Billie Whitelaw starred as scatter-brained Peggy Spencer who inherited a run-down boarding house complete with a few uncomfortable chairs, a menacing stag's head on the stairway, and water taps that caused the whole house to shake. Peggy's greatest drawback in her attempts to run the place was a total inability to cook. Her friend who tried to help her, Norma Burke (Diana King), ran a matrimonial agency. Among the residents were the perennial complainer Mrs Johnson (Grace Arnold), who was ever on hand to tell Peggy that her food was uneatable; Clarence Brothers (Anthony Howard for the first two series, then Bethell Horton), who mysteriously worked by night and slept all day though he was prone to regular sleep-

walking; and a vague but charming scientist, Mr Kirby (Christopher Steele). His great scientific delight was to create explosions. There were several guest visitors to the boarding house, the most frequent of which was the lovesick Quentin Beers (Desmond Walter-Ellis).
Music: Eric Spear. Producer: Philip Dale.

TO THE MANOR BORN
BBC. First broadcast: 30 September 1979

Penelope Keith had proved herself a hugely popular purveyor of snobbery in THE GOOD LIFE and in this series she was cast as upper-class Audrey fforbes-Hamilton, a widow living in Grantleigh Manor in the Somerset village of Cricket St Thomas. Unfortunately for her, widowhood soon revealed that debts and death duties necessitated her giving up the house. It was taken over by *nouveau riche* grocery tycoon Richard DeVere (Peter Bowles) who transformed and modernised the place. Eating the humblest of humble pies, yet retaining her dignity and belief in

More verbal sparring from Audrey (Penelope Keith) and Richard (Peter Bowles) in TO THE MANOR BORN (Photo: Copyright © BBC)

her superiority, Audrey moved into a small lodge on the estate. Thus began a love-hate relationship between the two, fuelled at intervals by Richard's Czech mother Mrs Polouvicka (Daphne Heard) and Audrey's best old schoolfriend, the mousey Marjory Frobisher (Angela Thorne). Audrey took with her from the stately home her aged butler Brabinger (John Rudling), even though there was hardly room to swing a cat inside the lodge. However, over the 21 programmes which spanned three series to 29 November 1981, love bloomed between Audrey and Richard, and his social gaffes and her social fall seemed likely to make an alliance. The series was created by Peter Spence.

Music: Ronnie Hazlehurst. Writers: Peter Spence, Christopher Bond. Producer: Gareth Gwenlan.

TOM, DICK AND HARRIET
THAMES. First broadcast: 20 September 1982

Thomas Maddison (Lionel Jeffries), his son Richard (Ian Ogilvy) and daughter-in-law Harriet (Brigit Forsyth) all lived together under the same roof. The ménage provoked the usual generation conflicts which increased with Harriet's pregnancy and Tom's room being needed for a nursery. The first series of six programmes was followed by a second run of six from 13 January 1983.

Writers: Johnnie Mortimer and Brian Cooke. Producer: Michael Mills.

THE TOM EWELL SHOW
CBS presented by ITV. First broadcast (UK): 4 July 1963

Produced by the star himself in the late 1950s, this show had crumple-faced actor Ewell playing long-suffering estate agent Tom Potter, who was completely surrounded and dominated by women. They were his wife Fran (Marilyn Erskine), his mother-in-law Irene Brady (Mabel Albertson), and his three daughters Debbie (Sherry Alberoni), Cissy (Eileen Chessis) and Carol (Cindy Robbins). Even the family dog and the budgie were female. The 26 stories all stemmed from Tom's harassment by the ladies.

Producer: Richard Kinon.

TONY'S
BBC RADIO. First broadcast: 21 October 1979

Set in a London-Italian barber's corner shop, Victor Spinetti starred in the title role as proprietor but under the domination of his doting Mama (Norma

Ronald). The two other hair-stylists were Hector (John Lawrie) and Maisie (Deborah Watling). The situation allowed scope for guests to arrive for haircuts in each of the six episodes.

Writer: Jim Eldridge. Producer: John Fawcett Wilson.

THE TOP SECRET LIFE OF EDGAR BRIGGS
LWT. First broadcast: 15 September 1974

David Jason starred as Edgar Briggs who, by clerical error, was transferred to Counter Espionage at the Ministry of Defence. He was appointed assistant to the Commander (Noel Coleman). However, although Briggs was a mistake and by any standards was stupid and unsuitable for the job, he managed to achieve the best results in the entire department. His colleagues could only look on with raised eyebrows of wonderment. They included Buxton (Michael Stainton), Spencer (Mark Eden) and Cathy (Elizabeth Counsell). Edgar's wife Jennifer was played by Barbara Angell.

Writers: Bernard McKenna and Richard Laing. Director: Bryan Izzard. Producer: Humphrey Barclay.

TOTTERING TOWERS
THAMES. First broadcast: 20 October 1971

This children's series was set in the stately home of the 43rd Duke of Tottering (William Mervyn), a brilliant inventor whose manor was the village of Tottering Sideways near Sumweir-on-Thames. He had huge debts, and two teenagers made it their goal to help him. They were the Duke's American cousin Daffy (Stacey Gregg), and Dick (Tom Owen), who was the nephew of the Duke's housekeeper Mrs Pouncer (Avice Landon). However, the house was reputed to contain a valuable secret and this was the objective of a gang of crooks. Characters in the series included PC Poppy (David Lodge), a ghost named Marmaduke (Robert Gillespie), Miss Twitty (Patsy Rowlands), Gabbige (David Stoll), Geko (Leon Lissek), 'Fingers' Fish (Louis Mansi), Benny the Nose (Vic Wise), Joe the Creep (also played by Robert Gillespie), Prayer-book Perce (Talfryn Thomas), 'Soapy' Cyril (Tim Barrett) and Hairy O'Hara (Harry Towb). The housemaid Mimi was played by Magda Miller. The last of 13 episodes was seen on 12 January 1972.

Writers: Milo Cortese, Max Oberman. Producers: Adrian Cooper, Vic Hughes.

A TOUCH OF SPICE
BBC. First broadcast: 9 March 1989

Victoria Morrison (Julia Watson) was commis-chef and Dawn McKenzie the waitress at a restaurant. Though from vastly different backgrounds, they were firm friends and shared a flat. They both hated the restaurant and left to start their own catering company, A Touch of Spice. Love-life was fairly hectic and Dawn's affairs were complicated by her family of petty crooks. Other featured characters were Victoria's mother Helen (Virginia Stride) and Clive (Martin Jacobs). Six episodes were transmitted.

Writer: Francis Gregg. Producer: Sue Bysh.

THE TRAIN NOW STANDING
LWT. First broadcast: 20 May 1972

Burberry Halt was one of the few rural railway stations to escape the axe of the infamous Dr Beeching. At the time of this series, Burberry Halt was host to three stopping trains each day. The stationmaster, resplendent in his old Great Western uniform, was Hedley Green (Bill Fraser). He worked by the 1933 rule book and insisted that his assistant, Peter Pringle (Hugh Walters), did the same. The harassed area manager was Mr Potts (Denis Lill). Other regular characters from the village included George (Norman Mitchell), Rosie (Pamela Cundell), Fred (Arthur White), Bill (George Waring) and Charlie (Geoff L'Cise). A second series began in the summer of 1973.

Theme music: Ron Grainer. Writers: Jon Watkins and John Swallow, Ian La Frenais. Producer: Derrick Goodwin.

THE TRAVELS OF JAMIE McPHEETERS
ABC (AMERICA) PRESENTED BY ITV.
First broadcast (UK): 25 July 1964

This comedy western series was based on the Pulitzer prize-winning novel of the same title by Robert Lewis Taylor. The setting was the California gold rush of 1849 and the stories followed the travels of Dr Sardius McPheeters (Dan O'Herlihy), an eternal optimist dreaming to make his fortune, and his son, the adventurous Jamie (Kurt Russell). Jamie spent much of his time protecting his father from his own fallibilities and impracticalities. They rode the Oregon trail with a wagon train led by Buck Coulter (Michael Whitney), with whom Dr McPheeters had a running feud. Other regular characters were Jennie (Donna Anderson), a pretty girl heading west in search of a husband, and the Hon. Henry Coe (Hedley Mattingley), a former British officer. James Westerfield and Sandy Kenyon portrayed a pair of inefficient villains. In later episodes there was a new wagonmaster, Linc Murdock (Charles Bronson). The stories were 50 minutes in length.

TRIPPER'S DAY
THAMES. First broadcast: 24 September 1984

Leonard Rossiter, in his last role before his untimely death on 5 October 1984, starred as Norman Tripper, manager of the Supafare Supermarket. Tripper was a fan of American TV cop shows and briefed his staff in similar style to that of an American police chief. He was having an affair with the canteen manageress, Hilda Rimmer (Pat Ashton). Other unfortunates on his staff were security officer Alf Battle (Gordon Gostelow), Mr Christian (Paul Clarkson), Hardie (Philip Bird), Laurel (David John), Higgins (Andrew Paul), Marlene (Charon Bourke), Sylvia (Liz Crowther) and Dottie (Vicky Licorish). Six shows were screened and the format was revived in 1986 as SLINGER'S DAY.

Writer: Brian Cooke. Producer: Anthony Parker.

TROUBLE FOR TWO
BBC. First broadcast: 12 May 1958

Although scheduled for six episodes, this pairing of Jacqueline Mackenzie as a reporter and Lorrae Desmond as an Australian entertainer notched up only four editions. They were bachelor girls sharing a flat in London and had a male char played by Donald Churchill.

Writers: Johnny Whyte and Jacqueline Mackenzie. Producer: Ronald Marsh.

TROUBLE IN MIND
LWT. First broadcast: 24 February 1991

This six-part series by Colin Bostock-Smith told of the trials and tribulations of successful psychiatrist Adam Charlesworth (Richard O'Sullivan), after his wife Julia (Susan Penhaligon) took on a new job as a garden designer.

Director: Terry Kinane. Producer: Al Mitchell.

THE TROUBLE WITH HARRY

BBC. First broadcast: 1 January 1960

Comedian and ventriloquist Harry Worth's first TV situation comedy was the brainchild of producer John Ammonds, who cast aside his variety personae and turned him into a well-meaning but ineffectual author who was dominated by the forceful aunt who would later play such a strong out-of-vision role in HERE'S HARRY. The series was in six parts and actors in support included Noel Hood, Paddy Edwards, John Blythe, Sam Kydd and Jack Woolgar.
Writer: Ronnie Taylor.

THE TROUBLE WITH TOBY

BBC RADIO. First broadcast: 18 July 1957

Richard Lyon, son of Ben Lyon and Bebe Daniels with whom he had starred in LIFE WITH THE LYONS, played Tobias T Trodd, a teenager growing up in the late 1950s. Elizabeth Allen and Claude Hulbert played his parents and Sheila Sweet was his girlfriend. Other regular cast members in the 11 editions included Andrée Melly, Hugh Paddick and Nan Marriott-Watson. A second series of eight began on 26 November 1957.
Writer: Ted Taylor. Producer: Bill Gates.

THE TROUBLE WITH YOU, LILLIAN

BBC RADIO. First broadcast: 28 September 1967

Writer Jennifer Phillips had two radio series before this format was taken up by London Weekend Television. The two elderly ladies who shared accommodation were Madge (Beryl Reid) and her lodger Lillian (Patricia Hayes). The 13th and final radio broadcast was on 10 November 1969.

Producer: Keith Williams.

LWT. First broadcast: 2 July 1971

This six-part story again concerned the relationship of two elderly ladies living together. The house belonged to Madge (Dandy Nichols) who was rather crotchety and a bit of a bully. Lillian (Patricia Hayes) was her paying lodger as well as being her best friend. Lillian required a great deal of diplomacy to enable them to sail on an even keel.
Writer: Jennifer Phillips. Producer: Howard Ross.

TROUBLES AND STRIFE

CENTRAL. First broadcast: 11 November 1985

A young, handsome and single new vicar arrived to take up his post at St Anselm's parish church. He was the Rev. Clifford James (Steven Pacey) and his arrival had a devastating effect on many of the wives in the area including Annette (Liz Gebhardt), Mary (Maureen Beattie), Christine (Annette Badland), Cherry (Patricia Brake), Sophie (Victoria Williams) and Fiona (Diana Weston). However, the real seat of power in the parish lay with the gin-swilling church caretaker Rosita Pearlman (Anna Karen) and warden Harry Price (Robert Blythe). Clifford did manage to carry out some normal duties including the wedding between Sophie and Christopher (Mike Grady). There were 13 shows in all, the last on 14 August 1987.
Writer: Joan Greening. Producer: Shaun O'Riordan.

TURN OUT THE LIGHTS

GRANADA. First broadcast: 6 January 1967

The characters Leonard Swindley (Arthur Lowe) and Walter Hunt (Robert Dorning) – see PARDON THE EXPRESSION – were sacked from Dobson and Hawks in July 1966. They reappeared on the screen with Hunt having had his horoscope read and confessing to Swindley that he was under the influence of his star sign, Aries the Ram. Swindley scoffed but changed his opinion following a meeting with Mr Merlin (Peter Wyngarde), a member of the Institute of Psychic Research. Swindley and Hunt, then engrossed in the subject, became amateur ghost-hunters, sleuths in a world of spooks and spirits.
Writers included Peter Eckersley and Kenneth Cope, John Finch, Stanley Hearn and Anthony Skene. Directors: David Boisseau and Michael Cox. Producer: Derek Granger.

TURNBULL'S FINEST HOUR

YTV. First broadcast: 17 November 1972

Ken Hoare and Mike Sharland created this short-lived series in which Major Clifford Turnbull (Michael Bates) was a retired army man living quietly until he met Sir Zachary Stein (Raymond Huntley) at a party. Stein was an executive with Pentagon Television, the ailing smallest and newest company in the ITV network. Stein persuaded Turnbull to head a rescue operation. Among the characters he encountered in his task were Bernard

Pratt (Blake Butler), Faye Bush (Liz Fraser), Roddy Cheever-Jones (Jonathan Lynn), Rex Rivoli (Roddy Maude-Roxby), Jellico Withers (Leonard Trolley) and Charlie (Alan Helm).
Music: Johnny Pearson. Producer: Bill Hitchcock.

TUTTI FRUTTI
BBC. First broadcast: 3 March 1987

Taking its title from Little Richard's 1956 American hit song, this series of six one-hour comedy dramas by John Byrne was built around fictitious rock group The Majestics, Scotland's 'Kings of Rock 'n Roll' who were celebrating their 25th anniversary at the top. Dismissing changes in musical trends over the years, The Majestics dressed and played in the original 1950s style. Moreover, their personnel had remained unchanged. The lead singer and guitarist was Big Jazza McGlone, but just before the story began he was killed in a car crash. Fortunately for the others and their manager Eddie Clockerty (Richard Wilson), the younger McGlone boy Danny (Robbie Coltrane), who bore a striking likeness to his late elder brother, came home from the USA after a seven-year absence and stepped in to fill the breach. The others were lead guitarist Vincent Diver (Maurice Roëves), drummer Bomba MacAteer (Stuart McGugan) and bass player Fud O'Donnell (Jake D'Arcy). Their roadie was Dennis Sproul (Ron Donachie). McGlone, something of a Glaswegian slob, fell in love with tough-girl singer and guitar player Suzie Kettles (Emma Thompson) who, among other shows of strength, had him sleep in the bath! In spite of very heavy Glaswegian accents, the series proved a huge hit.
Musical director: Zoot Money. Director: Tony Smith. Producer: Andy Park.

THE TWO CHARLEYS
BBC. First broadcast: 8 April 1959

Following their success together in Noël Coward's comedy of back-stage life *Red Peppers*, Charlie Chester and Eleanor Summerfield were again cast as a husband and wife double act working the halls in the dying days of Variety. In six shows they portrayed Charlie and Ethel Charles and their adventures took them from theatre to theatre, where they encountered different characters each episode.
Writers: Sheila Hodgson and Allan Prior. Producer: Dennis Main Wilson.

TWO D'S AND A DOG
THAMES. First broadcast: 6 July 1970

In this children's series by Jan Butlin, Dotty Charles (Denise Coffey) was left broke when her father died. Her only friend was Dingle Bell (David Jason), her late father's chauffeur. She also had a dog named Fido Dog. The stories were built around Dotty and Dingle's quest for work and money in order to survive.
Producer: Daphne Shadwell.

TWO IN CLOVER
THAMES. First broadcast: 18 February 1969

Sid Turner (Sid James) and Vic Evans (Victor Spinetti) were fed up with their humdrum existence as invoice clerks for an insurance company in the City. When they finally snapped under the monotony, they bought Clover Farm, a working farm in the country. With the business came Zsa Zsa the Jersey cow, Fanny the Friesian, and Anna the Aylesbury duck. They did not always find it easy to mix with the country set, especially as Sid's sporting activities were confined to the after-dark indoor type! The landlord of the local pub was portrayed by Victor Platt and the village policeman was played by Bill Pertwee. The series, which ran for two seasons, was written and created by Vince Powell and Harry Driver.
Theme music: Jack Parnell. Producer: Alan Tarrant.

THE TWO OF US
LWT. First broadcast: 31 October 1986

There were 29 episodes of this Alex Shearer creation over four seasons ending on 4 March 1990. Ashley (Nicholas Lyndhurst) and Elaine (Janet Dibley) lived together although they were not married. Ashley had proposed on several occasions but Elaine was quite content with their status quo and saw no reason to tie the legal knot. Their relationship survived, even when Elaine went away to work in India for six months, and after many years of trying to be conventional Ashley finally persuaded her to marry him. Other regular characters were Ashley's grandfather Perce (Patrick Troughton, later Tenniel Evans) and his parents Mr and Mrs Jennings (Paul McDowell and Jennifer Piercey).
Directors: John Gorman, Terry Kinane. Producers: Marcus Plantin, Robin Carr.

TWO PLUS TWO

BBC RADIO. First broadcast: 25 June 1964

Barry Took devised this series, sub-titled 'A Funny Thing Happened To Me on My Way To the Altar.' The first 'two' of the title were switchboard operator Maudie (Patsy Rowlands) and her out-of-work actor boyfriend George (Anton Rodgers). Maudie was left to wonder if she would ever manage to get George to the altar. The second 'two' were Maudie's switchboard colleague Louella (Barbara Windsor) and her husband Bernard (Norman Rossington), who was George's best friend. As a foursome they entangled themselves in the ordinary problems and ups and downs of everyday life. Arthur Howard portrayed the vicar. There were nine broadcasts.
Writers: David Cumming and Barry Took. Producer: Trafford Whitelock.

2POINT4 CHILDREN

BBC. First broadcast: 3 September 1991

Andrew Marshall created and wrote this series which played 21 editions up to the Christmas special transmitted on 20 December 1993. The stories centred on the Porter family whose lives were the normal chaos of any ordinary family coping with each other and the mortgage. Ben (Gary Olsen) was a central-heating engineer with a happy-go-lucky approach to life. His wife Bill (Belinda Lang) had a full-time job as a baker's assistant and another full-time job looking after Ben and their two children, Jenny (Clare Woodgate, later Clare Buckfield) and David (John Pickard). Bill felt she had missed out on much that life had to offer since she married and sought the true meaning of existence. During the 1992 series, she lost her job at the bakery and unemployment drove her mad. The only other regular character was Bill's friend Rona (Julia Hills).
Producer: Richard Boden.

TWO UP, TWO DOWN

BBC. First broadcast: 11 May 1979

Janey Preger wrote this six-part series which began

with a couple moving into their new house only to discover another couple already installed in the front bedroom. The pairings were Jimmy and Flo (Paul Nicholas and Su Pollard) and Stan and Sheila (Norman Tipton and Claire Faulconbridge).
Director: Roger Cheveley. Producer: Tara Prem.

TWO'S COMPANY

LWT. First broadcast: 30 October 1976

Elaine Strich played Dorothy McNab, a bestselling American author who moved to live in London and took on a very British butler, Robert (Donald Sinden). They developed an acerbic love-hate relationship in which subtle strategies were employed to exercise control of the house. Robert was uppity but realised he had a cushy job and felt threatened if Dorothy sought to employ any extra help. Cleaning ladies left them with alarming regularity and Dorothy was at a loss to understand the cause. The series, created and written by Bill MacIlwraith, returned for two further seasons in the winters of 1978 and 1979.
Director: John Reardon. Producer: Humphrey Barclay.

TYGO ROAD

BBC. First broadcast: 8 May 1990

This series in six parts was set in a community centre which, for the characters involved, was the last bastion against Thatcherism. The administrator was Adam Hartley (Kevin McNally) and those involved at the centre included Kate (Isobel Black), Leo (Steven O'Donnell), Lionel (Gordon Gostelow), who died and left £5,000 to the community; Gary (Vas Blackwood), Spinnij (Bill Bailey), Val (Leila Bertrand) and Selina (Alisa Bosschaert).
Writers: Richard Cottan and Christopher Douglas. Director: Bob Spiers. Producer: Andre Ptaszynski for Pola Jones Films.

THE UGLIEST GIRL IN TOWN
ABC (AMERICA) PRESENTED BY ITV.
First broadcast (UK): 18 October 1972

Peter Kastner starred as Timothy Blair, who worked for a Hollywood agent but in his spare time modelled as a female known as Timmy. He was first persuaded to model as a girl by his photographer brother, Gene (Gary Marshall). Timothy's fiancée was London-based British movie star Julie Renfield (Patricia Brake) and her associate was David Courtney (Nicholas Parsons). There were 20 editions.
Writer: Robert Kaufman. Producer: Harry Ackerman.

UKRIDGE
BBC RADIO. First broadcast: 21 December 1992

Julian Dutton adapted the stories of PG Wodehouse's character into this six-part series. Griff Rhys Jones starred as Ukridge, a man who always had some new money-making idea in his head.
Producer: Sarah Smith.

UNCLE JACK . . . AND OPERATION GREEN
BBC. First broadcast: 4 October 1990

Paul Jones starred in six episodes as Jack, a 'green' activist whose eccentric adventures unwittingly led to his possession of a formula for a deadly gas that turned human bones to jelly. Swept along in his wake were niece Kate (Helen Lambert) and nephew Michael (Guiseppe Peluso). Ruthless powers worldwide pursued the formula and Jack's most deadly adversary was Vixen (Fenella Fielding).
Writer: Jim Eldridge. Producer: Jeremy Swan.

UNDER AND OVER
BBC. First broadcast: 17 September 1971

Dublin singing group The Bachelors (Con Cluskey, Dec Cluskey and John Stokes) starred in six editions as three Irish navvies working on the Water-

loo Tunnel and digging their lives away when not pausing for a Guinness or two. The other regular characters were Lord Brentwood (Robert Keegan), their boss, and the pub landlord (Tommy Godfrey).
Writers: David Climie and Austin Steele. Directors: David Askey, Roger Race. Producer: Austin Steele.

UNDER ONE ROOF
BBC RADIO. First broadcast: 31 August 1947

This domestic comedy in eight parts starred British-born Roland Young, an actor who spent most of his professional life in America where he had lived since 1912. In this, his BBC debut, he played architect George Banter who had designed the house into which he and his wife (Sophie Stewart) moved. However, all his designs did not meet with Sophie's approval, nor with that of their family. The series also featured Roger Braban, Patsy Smart, Stephen Jack, John Warrington and Cecile Chevreau.
Writer: Mabbie Poole. Producer: Douglas Moodie.

UNION CASTLE
GRANADA. First broadcast: 19 April 1982

Trade unionist and self-made man Lord Mountainash (Stratford Johns) bought Runnymeade Castle in Wales where he lived with his daughter Annie (Lyndon Hughes) and his true-blue butler Wordsworth (Moray Watson). His Lordship's policies were in conflict with those of Wordsworth, who conspired against him with their upper-class neighbour Ursula, Lady Thaxted (Wanda Ventham). The Union's militant general-secretary was Elizabeth Steel (Carol Macready), known to one and all as Red Betty. There were seven programmes in the series.
Writer: Eric Paice. Director: Douglas Argent. Producer: Eric Prytherch.

UNNATURAL ACTS
BBC RADIO. First broadcast: 28 April 1987

'Zany' is a much-abused word when it comes to comedy but this series, written mostly by its actors, fits the description better than most, and the exploits and antics of Kit (Kit Hollerbach), Paul (Paul B Davies), Jeremy (Jeremy Hardy) and Caroline (Caroline Leddy) do not transfer easily to one paragraph. Suffice it to say that they all lived close by and got up to all sorts of crazy (their word) exploits. There were two series embracing 13 programmes which ended on 25 April 1988.

Other writers included Pete Sinclair, Steve Punt, Alison Renshaw. Producer: David Tyler.

UP POMPEII!

BBC. First broadcast: 17 September 1969

Frankie Howerd starred as Lurcio, the Roman slave who had charge of the household of his master Ludicrus Sextus (Max Adrian, later Wallas Eaton).

The comedy was smutty with much double meaning as evidenced in the names of the characters created by Talbot Rothwell: Ammonia (Elizabeth Larner), Erotica (Georgina Moon), Ambrosia (Lynda Baron), Nausius (Kerry Gardner) Plautus (Walter Horsbrugh, later William Rushton), Flavia (Mollie Sugden), Odius (John Junkin), Prodigus (David Kernan) and Senna the Soothsayer (Jeane Mockford). There were occasional guest appearances including Barbara Windsor as Nymphia, Bill Maynard as the money man Percentus, and George Baker as Jamesus Bondus. Lurcio would often speak straight to camera as a device for the Frankie Howerd stand-up comedian persona to nudge and wink his way through the script. There were 14 half-hour editions, the last on 26 October 1970. There was also a one-hour special on 31 March 1975 and a one-off revival by London Weekend written by Brian Leveson and Paul Minett on 14 December 1991. Both the specials bore the title *Further Up Pompeii*.

Writers: Talbot Rothwell and Sid Colin. Producers: Michael Mills, David Croft, Sydney Lotterby.

UP THE ELEPHANT AND ROUND THE CASTLE

THAMES. First broadcast: 30 November 1983

Jim Davidson starred as Jim London who became a first-time home owner when his Aunt Minnie died, leaving him 17 Railway Terrace in the Elephant and Castle. The joys of ownership were beset by an unseen sitting tenant who banged on the ceiling, then a squatter and a burglary. He was also troubled by Councillor Arnold Moggs (Nicholas Day). Other characters who drifted in and out of Jim's life included his mum and dad (Rosalind Knight and John Bardon); Wanda Pickles (Sue Nicholls), whose husband was in Parkhurst prison; his pal Arnold (Christopher Ellison), at whose wedding Jim was best man; Tosh Carey (Brian Capron), who was full of bright but impractical ideas; and Brian the Barman (Brian Hall). The last of 23 episodes was seen on 31 October 1985. A spin-off series, HOME JAMES, followed in 1987.

Writers: Spike Mullins, Tony Hoare, Colin Bostock-Smith, Jim Eldridge, Louis Ford. Producer: Anthony Parker.

'Oooh, no . . .' Frankie Howerd stars as Roman slave Lurcio in UP POMPEII! (Photo: Copyright © BBC)

Cheeky chappie Jim Davidson going UP THE ELEPHANT AND ROUND THE CASTLE (Photo © Thames Television)

UP THE GARDEN PATH
BBC RADIO. First broadcast: 7 November 1987

Writer Sue Limb first adapted her own novel of the same title into six episodes. She wrote eight new stories which got underway on 15 October 1988, then Granada stepped in to make a television series (see below) and the format did not return to radio until 17 November 1993 when six final editions started. Imelda Staunton starred as scatty but endearing teacher Izzy Comyn, whose life of chaos was not helped by two-timing TV producer Michael (Nicholas Le Prevost) and her wimp of a flatmate Dick (Mike Grady), who worshipped her. Her friend Maria was played by Marty Cruickshank. *Producer: Jonathan James-Moore.*

GRANADA. First broadcast: 2 May 1990

Sue Limb's series debuted on television with Imelda Staunton continuing her role as scatty school-teacher Izzy Comyn whose love life and domestic housekeeping were in turmoil. She lived in a scruffy flat, where she consumed far too much chocolate cake, and was in love with a married man, Michael (Nicholas Le Prevost). Her life was one of heartache and disappointment as she moved from man to

man including the upper-class Charles (David Robb) and stoic Bill (Neil McCaul). She even cast an eye in the direction of her former pupil Razers (René Zagger). Throughout the three six-part series ending 1 July 1993, Izzy was supported by Maria (Tessa Peake-Jones), Dick (Mike Grady), Louise (Susan Kyd) and Gwyn (Tom Mannion) as she felt her time for finding happiness was fast running out. *Director: David Askey. Producer: Humphrey Barclay.*

UP THE POLE
BBC RADIO. First broadcast: 20 October 1947

Sheffield-born cousins Jimmy Jewel and Ben Warriss starred in four series under this title. The first was set in the Arctic where they ran a trading post. Claude Dampier was Horace Hotplate, the Mayor of the North Pole, and Jon Pertwee was Mr Burp. After 12 editions in the Frozen North they were back in England for the next run beginning 1 November 1948 with the same team plus Betty Paul as their permanent girlfriend. As in their stage act on the variety halls, the mildly protesting Jewel was led towards trouble by know-all Warriss. In the third series beginning 21 November 1949, they were constables in a rural police station where Hotplate was the Superintendent and Burp was still up to no good. Bertie Hare joined the cast in various guises. The final series got underway on 20 June 1952 with Josephine Crombie replacing Betty Paul as the girlfriend. *Writer: Ronnie Hanbury. Producer: George Inns.*

UP THE WORKERS
ATV. First broadcast: 1 May 1974

Tom Brennand and Roy Bottomley wrote these shows based on an idea by Lance Percival. They were set in the Midlands factory of Cocker's Components Ltd and dealt with the confrontations and industrial relations between management and workers. The managing director was Dicky Bligh (Henry McGee) and the shop steward was Sid Stubbins (Norman Bird). Keeping those two at arm's length was labour relations officer Bernard Peck (Lance Percival). In the first series the other principal characters were chairman Sir Henry Carmichael (Ivor Dean) and workers Bert Hamflitt (Dudley Sutton), Mick Briggs (Charles Bolton) and Deirdre Hargreaves (Trudi Van Doorn). In a second series which began in February 1976 there was a new chairman, Sir Charles (Charles Lloyd Pack), and a new set of workers, Fred Hamflitt (Victor

Maddern), Mavis (Vivienne Martin), Andrea (Lesley Duff) and Fergy (Leon Vitali).
Producers: John Scholz-Conway, Alan Tarrant.

THE UPCHAT CONNECTION
THAMES. First broadcast: 24 October 1978

This series by Keith Waterhouse began with the explanation that Mike Upchat from THE UPCHAT LINE had gone to Australia, but before leaving he had raffled his key to the left-luggage locker at Marylebone station. The winner also inherited his address book, his name and his gift for chatting-up girls. The new Mike Upchat was played by Robin Nedwell. Over seven programmes he used his new-found talents but retained two platonic and understanding friends, Maggie (Susan Jameson) and Polly (Bernadette Milnes).
Producer: Robert Reed.

THE UPCHAT LINE
THAMES. First broadcast: 26 September 1977

In this series of seven programmes by Keith Waterhouse, John Alderton starred as Mike Upchat, the pen name of a little-known author who was more renowned for chatting-up any and every attractive girl in sight. There were no other regular characters but his procession of women included Alexandra Dane and Wanda Ventham. Upchat's only permanent abode was a luggage locker at Marylebone station. See also THE UPCHAT CONNECTION.
Music: Mike Batt. Producer: Robert Reed.

THE UPPER CRUSTS
LWT. First broadcast: 23 February 1973

Keith Waterhouse and Willis Hall created and wrote this series. Charles Gray and Margaret Leighton starred as Lord and Lady Seacroft whose drastically reduced circumstances landed them in a council flat. The late Lord had gambled away the family fortune, thus forcing them to make swingeing adjustments to their lifestyle and social circle. They had two children, Davina and Gareth (Lalla Ward and Martin Neil).
Producer: Mark Stuart.

THE UPPER HAND
CENTRAL. First broadcast: 1 May 1990

The format for this series was borrowed from the American show WHO'S THE BOSS? created by Martin Cohan and Blake Hunter. Former footballer Charlie Burrows (Joe McGann) had been forced into premature retirement through injury. He was a widower who, with daughter Joanna (Kellie Bright), left London for a new life at Henley-on-Thames as housekeeper to Caroline Wheatley (Diana Weston) and her snake-loving son Tom (William Puttock). Diana was an executive with advertising agency Blake and Hunter and was estranged from her wildlife documentary film producer husband Michael (Nicky Henson). Caroline drove a Jaguar while Charlie had a transit van emblazoned with Tottenham Hotspur and 'Honk If You Bonk!' stickers. In Diana's garage Charlie held keep-fit classes for local ladies. Caroline's mother was man-mad divorcée Laura West (Honor Blackman). Gradually, over 58 episodes and five seasons, the relationship between Charlie and Caroline changed from employer and employee to love, which sometimes threatened the smooth running of the household. The series ended on 23 December 1993.
Directors: Martin Dennis, Martin Shardlow. Producer: Christopher Walker.

US GIRLS
BBC. First broadcast: 27 February 1992

The conflicts of the culture gap between generations was the core of this situation which revolved around freelance journalist Bev (Joanne Campbell, later Nicola Blackman). Her attempts to forge an independent life were crushed by her teenage daughter Aisha (Marlaine Gordon) and Grandma and Grandad (Mona Hammond and Allister Bain) who, in the first series of six, lived with them. For the second run of six beginning 10 March 1993, the grandparents had moved into a house across the road but were still positioned to keep a watchful eye on Bev and Aisha.
Writer: Lisselle Kayle. Producer: David Askey.

Left, facing page: It was a classic 'will they, won't they' romance for Charlie (Joe McGann) and Caroline (Diana Weston) in THE UPPER HAND (Photo: Central Television)

VACANT LOT

ABC. First broadcast: 1 April 1967

Jeremy Lloyd and Jimmy Grafton wrote this series in seven parts. The setting was the works of Bendlove and Bodium who were builders, decorators, cabinet makers, funeral directors and private hire taxi drivers. The managing director was William Bendlove (Bill Fraser), a man given to bungling himself into scrapes and troubles and whose ineptitude was regularly covered up by his on-the-ball works foreman and brother-in-law Alf Grimble (Alfie Bass). Those in their charge at work were Stoker, Rock and Chippy who were played by Jack Haig, Nicky Henson and Arthur Mullard.

Producer: Milo Lewis.

THE VAGUELYS

BBC RADIO. First broadcast: 1 September 1947

Writer and producer Max Kester based these seven programmes, each of 15 minutes' duration, on the experiences which he endured with his family during a two-year search for their ideal home in the country. In search of their own rural retreat were Mr and Mrs Vaguely (Christopher Steele and Mary Jerrold) and their daughter Babs (Joan White).

VALENTINE PARK

CENTRAL. First broadcast: 19 June 1987

Life for the park's head gardener Tom (Ken Jones) was a bed of roses until he learned to his horror that a new employee was to be his wayward godson Max (David Thewlis). However, Tom took his godparental responsibilities seriously and arranged for Max to stay in his own digs where the landlady was Mrs Giles (Liz Smith). During the first series of six shows, Tom and Max drew quite close to each other and Max fell in love with Claire (Katy Newell). In the second run of six which began on 22 July 1988, life for Tom and Max was not so cushy under new parks manager Mr Smackley (Ellis Dale). Then Max was thrown out by Mrs Giles and his heart was broken when Claire announced she was going to college in London.

Writers: Nicholas Hyde and Glen Cardno, Mike Walling and Ian Whitwham. Director: Nic Phillips. Producer: Glen Cardno.

VALERIE

NBC (AMERICA) PRESENTED BY BBC.
First broadcast (UK): 27 October 1986

Valerie Harper starred as Valerie Hogan, a career woman whose domestic struggles outweighed those in her business life. The Hogan family was husband David (Jason Bateman), Willie (Danny Ponce), Mark (Jeremy Licht) and Michael (Josh Taylor). The BBC screened 13 episodes.

Producer: Ronny Hallin.

VERY BIG VERY SOON

CENTRAL. First broadcast: 19 July 1991

Paul Shane starred as the archetypal seedy theatrical agent Harry James, who made his parasitic living out of the hopefuls who worked the Northern club circuit. He made empty promises to no-hopers while he smoked his fat cigar and endeavoured to find them work. Those caught up in Harry's shady dealings were Beattie (Kate David), Ernie Chester (Tim Wylton), one of his oldest acts; Avril (Sheila White), Matthew Kite (Andrew Maclean), Vic (Shaun Curry) and Miss Birchall (Rosalind Knight), who was mad enough to entrust Harry with supplying the entertainment for her Ladies' Nights. There were six episodes.

Writer: Daniel Peacock. Director: Paul Harrison. Producer: Glen Cardno.

THE VERY MERRY WIDOW

BBC. First broadcast: 27 November 1967

The late Charles Villiers drowned off Cape Finisterre during a weekend yachting expedition. This left Jacqueline Villiers (Moira Lister) as a glamorous young widow up to her ears in debt. She had a daughter Jennifer (Sally Thomsett) at private school and was determined to keep her there, as she was to settle the debts. She took various jobs in her struggles for money including a meals-on-wheels service, acting as a companion to a batty old dowager, and selling fake china in Petticoat Lane. She also became a consultant for a consumer magazine. Much of her time was spent dodging the bookmaker, the wine merchant and the bank manager, who had been Charles' principal creditors. There were 19 editions over three seasons, the last screened on 11 July 1969. *Theme music: Burt Rhodes. Writer: Alan Melville. Producers: Robin Nash, Graeme Muir.*

A VERY PECULIAR PRACTICE

BBC. First broadcast: 21 May 1986

This peculiar series was peopled by peculiar persons who were installed at Lowlands University where the medical practitioners, for the first seven programmes at least, were wrapped up in the studies of venereal disease. The principal characters were bashful Dr Stephen Daker (Peter Davison), Dr Bob Buzzard (David Troughton) who considered VD to be 'a spot of tool trouble', and Dr Jock McCannon (Graham Crowden). From the female point of view came Dr Rose Marie (Barbara Flynn), Lyn Turtle (Amanda Hillwood) and the two nuns (Sonia Hart and Elaine Turrell). A second run of seven ended on 6 April 1988. *Writer: Andrew Davies. Director: David Tucker. Producer: Ken Riddington.*

A VERY PRIVATE MAN

BBC RADIO. First broadcast: 22 January 1981

This series in six episodes starred Rodney Bewes and Ann Bell as David and Helen Parkinson, a young couple tired of the modern frenzy of life who sought complete isolation in the serenity of the country. Other parts were played as required by Daphne Oxenford, Paula Tilbrook and Peter Wheeler. *Writer: Terry Gregson. Producer: Ron McDonnell.*

VERY TASTY – VERY SWEET

BBC RADIO. First broadcast: 12 May 1940

The title for this series of occasional broadcasts was the catchphrase of its stars, husband and wife team Nan Kenway and Douglas Young. They had become very popular on a revue programme, *Howdy Folks*, and VERY TASTY – VERY SWEET was developed from one of their sketches. It was set in a pub, the Startled Hare, where Kenway was the barmaid Mrs Yatton and Young was the partially-deaf main customer Mr Grice. Grice was the village food-hog and Sunday lunch was always at the pub. He had a cat named Tiddles. The pub featured entertainment with resident singers The Three In Harmony and Billy Ternent and his band. *Writer: Douglas Young. Producer: Reginald Smith.*

THE VICTORIA LINE

BBC RADIO. First broadcast: 2 August 1971

Terence Brady and Charlotte Bingham wrote this eight-part series in which Liza Goddard as Victoria and Yootha Joyce as Edna ran an agency that purported to be able to find and deliver whatever a client requested. They were assisted by a company of actors which included Caroline Blakiston, Olwen Griffiths and Basil Henson. *Producer: John Bridges.*

THE VITAL SPARK

BBC. First broadcast: 28 January 1966

The Vital Spark was a 'puffer' – not a train but the name given to the small cargo boats that plied between the Firth of Clyde and the Western Isles. The stories and characters were originally created by Neil Munro for the *Glasgow Evening News* in 1905. Roddy McMillan starred as Master Mariner Para Handy in a 1965 edition of *Comedy Playhouse* by Bill Craig which the author expanded into 19 episodes over three series ending 24 October 1974. Handy had a crew of three, Dougie the Mate (Walter Carr), engineer Dan Macphail (John Grieve), and cabin boy, cook and bottle-washer Sunny Jim (Alex McAvoy). The Spark was not seaworthy but all four loved her and lived their lives exclusively aboard her. The conflict arose whenever they came into contact with the conventional world where people lived according to rules and regulations. If the Spark became a laughing stock, which she often did, they would defend her honour. *Theme music: Ian Gourlay. Producer: Pharic MacLaren.*

THE WACKERS

THAMES. First broadcast: 19 March 1975

Vince Powell created the Clarkson family as a melting pot of Liverpudlian disharmony in which half were Catholic, half Protestant, half supported Everton and half cheered for Liverpool. Billy and Mary Clarkson (Ken Jones and Sheila Fay) had three children, Tony, Bernadette and Raymond (David Casey, Alison Steadman and Keith Chegwin). They lived in the Dingle area of Liverpool where their problems were compounded by Billy's mother Maggie Clarkson (Pearl Hackney) and Mary's father Joe Farrell (Joe Gladwin). Billy had recently been released from prison and his return to the family home upset the rhythm of life. His drinking pal was Charlie (Bill Dean).
Producer: Anthony Parker.

WAITING FOR GOD

BBC. First broadcast: 28 June 1990

Michael Aitkens created and wrote this very successful series – the special Christmas edition on 22

December 1993 was the 41st. The setting was the Bayview Retirement Home where most of the residents were quite happy to waste away their remaining days. However, the two central characters, Miss Diana Trent (Stephanie Cole) and Tom Ballard (Graham Crowden), had no such thoughts and set out to buck the system, scupper the devious schemes of crafty manager Harvey Bains (Daniel Hill) and goad the other residents out of their lethargy. Diana was the undoubted leader, a former globe-trotting photo-journalist whose waspish tongue saw her eventually elected into Europe as the representative of the elderly. Tom, a retired and widowed accountant, was the perfect eccentric foil in her frequent battles. Their companionship grew into a physical relationship and when money became tight for Diana, she moved in with him. Tom had a frightfully boring son, Geoffrey (Andrew Tourell), who in turn had a dipsomaniac and nymphomaniac wife, Marion (Sandy Payne). Harvey Bains had an assistant, Jane Edwards (Janine Duvitski), who was frightened to death of Diana and totally besotted by her awful boss. Unluckily, she was the original plain Jane. Other regulars were Basil (Michael Bilton), a resident, and Jenny (Dawn Hope), the waitress.
Producer: Gareth Gwenlan.

WALLY WHO?

BBC RADIO. First broadcast: 7 November 1982

Tony Brandon starred in ten episodes as Wally Thornton, an odd-ball failure in life who aspired to greater social whirls than living in a caravan in the corner of a scrapyard. His only friend was Eric (John Jardine), the landlord of the local pub, who listened to Wally's dreams and ambitions. Other characters were portrayed by Rosalind Knight, Chris Ellison and Nick Maloney.
Music: Debbie Katz. Writers: Rob Grant and Doug Naylor. Producer: Mike Craig.

The battling wrinklies, Tom (Graham Crowden) and Diana (Stephanie Cole) are not content just WAITING FOR GOD (Photo: Copyright © BBC)

Brenda (Emma Wray) and her Malcolm (Paul Bown) in WATCHING (Photo: Granada Television)

THE WALRUS AND THE CARPENTER

BBC. First broadcast: 14 December 1963

This began as a one-off *Comedy Playhouse*, and that programme was repeated on 23 February 1965 followed weekly by six new stories. Two old men were whiling away what time remained to them on Earth by trying to live it up. Gascoigne Quilt (Felix Aylmer) was a former school teacher whose career had been interrupted by an unfortunate dalliance with the headmaster's wife. Though he was intelligent and able, his life had been a mild disaster, even to being invalided out of the Royal Flying Corps in 1914 after breaking a hip while trying to climb into a cockpit. Luther Flannery (Hugh Griffith) was an illiterate ex-seaman from Swansea who had drunk his way around the world and left a woman married to him in every port. Quilt no longer had pupils and needed someone to teach. That someone was Flannery, who wished to die literate. They shared their musings and mutterings in public libraries, graveyards, hospital outpatient departments and cheap cafés.

Writers: Barry Took and Marty Feldman. Producer: Michael Mills.

WATCHING

GRANADA. First broadcast: 5 July 1987

Mismatched lovers Malcolm Stoneway (Paul Bown) and Brenda Wilson (Emma Wray) met in the first episode and their off-and-on romance carried them through seven seasons and 53 editions to 4 April 1993. Set on Merseyside, Malcolm's hobby was bird-watching in which Brenda joined, albeit reluctantly to begin with. Brenda had a sister Pamela (Liza Tarbuck) whose life progressed along much smoother lines. Pamela married David Lynch (John Bowler) and had a family. Brenda's mother Mrs Wilson (Noreen Kershaw) was always horrified each time the romance with Malcolm was back on, and Malcolm's mother Mrs Stoneway (Patsy Byrne) was equally critical of her son's behaviour. During one of their 'off' periods, Malcolm married Lucinda (Elizabeth Morton) who became pregnant. The marriage was doomed, though, and to the horror of all, he and Brenda met up again on a bird-watching weekend, and their progress towards marriage began once more. Other regular characters were friends Harold (Al T Kossy) and Cedric (Bill Moores).

Writer: Jim Hitchmough. Producer: Les Chatfield.

WATERLOGGED SPA

BBC RADIO. First broadcast: 17 September 1948

The naval edition of MERRY-GO-ROUND had been set aboard HMS Waterlogged at Sinking-in-the-Ooze and continued under that title until the change to WATERLOGGED SPA. The spa was known as the 'laughter resort for all' and the star, who also wrote the scripts, was Eric Barker. He was the manager of the resort and his real wife Pearl Hackney played the secretary. Regular characters included Lord Waterlogged (Richard Gray), Commander Highprice (Jon Pertwee), Flying Officer Kite (Humphrey Lestocq) and Herr Crow (George Crow). Some characters were never actually heard, merely referred to: Lord Waterlogged talked of the Honourable Phoebe, Kite recalled his old adjutant and Highprice was dominated by the mysterious 'He'. The show continued annually until 1950 after which Barker changed tack with JUST FANCY.
Producer: Leslie Bridgmont.

WE GOT IT MADE

NBC (AMERICA) PRESENTED BY BBC.
First broadcast (UK): 27 January 1984

Bachelors David Tucker (Matt McCoy) and Jay Bostwick (Tom Villard) shared a New York apartment. They decided to hire a live-in maid and got the shock of their lives – as did their respective girlfriends Beth (Bonnie Urseth) and Claudia (Stepfanie Kramer) – when young and fabulously attractive blonde Mickey (Teri Copley) turned up to take the job. There were 22 editions of the show, created by Gordon Farr.
Director: Alan Rafkin. Producer: Fred Silverman.

WELCOME BACK KOTTER

ABC (AMERICA) PRESENTED BY ITV.
First broadcast (UK): 21 January 1981

Gabe Kaplan, who co-created the show with Peter Myerson and Alan Sacks, also starred as Gabe Kotter, a Jewish teacher who returned to Brooklyn to teach at Buchanan High School, which he had previously attended as a pupil. Kotter found the pupils rather hot to handle and had frequent scrapes with the star student, Vinnie Barbarino (John Travolta). The school Principal was Mr Woodman (John Sylvester White) and Kotter's wife was called Julie (Marcia Strassman). Although 80 episodes were recorded in the USA they were not all screened in Britain.

Music: John B Sebastian. Producers: David Wolper and James Komack.

WELL ANYWAY

BBC. First broadcast: 24 September 1976

John Bird and John Fortune wrote and starred in this seven-part series. At the time, Fortune said, they wanted to call the show 'Desperation' but the BBC did not approve. They played two former Cambridge students who had known each other vaguely 16 years before the night when Fortune knocked on the door of Bird's scruffy Earl's Court flat, asked for a bed for the night and stayed for ever. They did not particularly like each other but other people liked them both even less. Bird scratched a living by doing a bit of this and a bit of that, while Fortune's character was a rather pathetic would-be conman and failed international jet-setter.
Producer: Dennis Main Wilson.

WE'LL THINK OF SOMETHING

THAMES. First broadcast: 1 September 1986

A Manchester couple, Les and Maureen Brooks (Sam Kelly and Marcia Warren), faced up to a life of unemployment following Les being made redundant. His pride would not allow him to sign on the dole. In this series of seven programmes they concocted various schemes to make money but, without exception, they collapsed.
Writer: Geoff Rowley. Producer: John Howard Davies.

WELSH RAREBIT

BBC RADIO. First broadcast: 12 June 1941

This show was devised in those cheerless days of 1940 to keep serving Welshmen and women in touch with their homeland. If it is remembered for nothing else, the signature music lives on, written by the show's two producers, Lyn Joshua and Mai Jones. Lyn wrote the words:

> We'll keep a welcome in the hillsides,
> We'll keep a welcome in the vales,
> This land you know will still be singing
> When you come home again to Wales.
> This land of song will keep a welcome
> And with a love that never fails,
> Will kiss away each hour of 'Hiraeth'
> When you come home again to Wales.

Mai Jones wrote the music. It was with this spirit and within this framework, 'Hiraeth' being an almost untranslatable form of nostalgia, that Caerphilly playwright E Eynon Evans created and wrote THE ADVENTURES OF TOMMY TROUBLE shortly after the series began on the national network. The part of Tommy was played by Lyn Joshua (later by Gunstone Jones and, in 1957 in a brief venture on to television, by George David). Evans himself played the part of Jimmy Jams and later a character called Willie the Whip. Other significant people in the early days of Tommy were Llewelyn (Tom Jones), Mrs Rees (Rachel Howell Thomas) and Willie (Philip Phillips). Willie was the stooge of the gang who fervently believed that busybody Tommy would one day solve everything instead of plunging headlong into disaster upon disaster.

WE'RE IN BUSINESS

BBC RADIO. First broadcast: 3 April 1959

This series was a resurrection of a character who had been a regular feature of another series, In All Directions (1952–55). Within that sketch show, Peter Ustinov and Peter Jones had invented a pair of deplorable spivs, Morrie and Dudley Grosvenor, whose devious minds were set on petty chicanery. In 1959, Jones took his character, Dudley Grosvenor, and found him a new partner in his quest for easy money. That new partner was Harry Worth (Harry Worth), a man with a private income which Dudley intended to exploit for his own interests and to further his bright ideas. Those ideas always miscarried. Their business headquarters was Syd's Café, run by Edie (Paddy Edwards), but for the second series starting 19 February 1960, they moved to a boarding house run by Miss Jubilee Boot (Irene Handl).
Writers: Peter Jones with (1959) George Evans and George Wadmore, and (1960) Barry Took and Marty Feldman. Producer: Charles Maxwell.

WEST END TALES

ATV. First broadcast: 16 February 1981

This seven-part series by Keith Waterhouse starred Robin Nedwell as Fiddler. The viewer saw aspects of Soho and Soho life through the eyes of this central character and his two mates, the bishop (Garfield Morgan) and Checkie (Larry Martyn). Their assembly point was Ma's (Toni Palmer) Café.

Other regulars were Tina (Susan Skipper) and Sergeant Dodds (Peter Childs).
Music: Laurie Holloway. Director: James Gatward. Producers: Colin Frewin and Keith Beckett.

WHACK-O!

BBC TELEVISION AND RADIO.
First broadcast: 15 November 1956

The hugely successful collaboration between writers Frank Muir and Denis Norden and comedian Jimmy Edwards which began with TAKE IT FROM HERE was continued with this long-running series. Set at Chiselbury school, motto 'They Shall Not Pass', Edwards was the blustering, grasping, semi-literate headmaster Professor James Edwards MA, Inter-PhD (Tangiers). He was a boozer who was not beyond forgery of the school accounts to pay the off-licence bill. He did not encourage traditional sports but rather encouraged his charges to grow vegetables, which he then sold from a stall outside the school gates. He displayed occasional affection for the boys of the school but the only true loyalty shown to him was from the devoted assistant head, Mr Pettigrew (Arthur Howard), who was the only regular through more than 40 programmes over the initial five years, the last programme of which was seen on 27 December 1960. Other teachers over that period included FD Price Whittaker (Kenneth Cope), SA Smallpiece (Norman Bird), RP Trench (Peter Glaze), Mr Halliforth (Edwin Apps) and Mr Proctor (Brian Rawlinson). The part of Matron was played first by Barbara Archer, then by Charlotte Mitchell. Ten years later, on 27 November 1971, the show re-

Jimmy Edwards as Headmaster has that crafty look about him in WHACK-O! (Photo: © BBC)

turned with Edwards for 13 further Muir and Norden editions. Julian Orchard played Pettigrew.

Television producers: Douglas Moodie, Douglas Argent (1971)

In the interim, the show had transferred to radio beginning on 23 May 1961 with the original Muir and Norden scripts adapted by David Climie. There were 45 editions ending on 22 July 1963. The cast changed frequently but Roddy Maude-Roxby played science teacher Aubrey Potter, Frederick Treves was 89-year-old junior classics master J St L Dinwiddie and the role of Matron was portrayed first by Joan Young and later by June Whitfield.

Radio producer: Edward Taylor.

WHAT HO, JEEVES!

BBC RADIO. First broadcast: 5 June 1973

The characters created by PG Wodehouse, Bertie Wooster and his manservant Jeeves, were adapted from his stories into 54 radio half-hours which spanned five series to 7 January 1981. Throughout, Michael Hordern played Jeeves and Richard Briers was Wooster. Vivian Pickles portrayed Aunt Dahlia. See also THE WORLD OF WOOSTER and JEEVES AND WOOSTER.

Adaptors: Chris Miller, Richard Usborne. Producers: David Hatch, Peter Titheradge, Simon Brett.

WHAT YOU LOOKIN' AT?

LWT. First broadcast: 7 August 1993

Created, written and directed by Trix Worrell, this seven-part series was set in a multi racial community youth centre, St Thomas's in inner London, where a young lady from rural Berkshire, Jane Wainwright (Trevyn McDowell), was coming to the end of a six-month probationary period as a youth leader and hoped for promotion to the job on a permanent basis. She had a free spirit which was opposed by the miserable caretaker, Colin (Bill Moody), who had more influence than he should. He was a dull cynic, treating Jane and the kids with equal disdain, referring to them as toe-rags. Though he was middle-aged, he lived with his mum and carried a stupid little dog named Pumpkin around with him. More supportive towards Jane was the older Mrs Williams (Angela Wynter). The principal young people were Trevor (Robert McKewley), Linford (Gary McDonald) whose namesake hero Linford Christie made a guest ap-

pearance in the final episode; Vanessa (Marcia Hewitt), Elaine (Kelly Marcel), Dawn (Caroline Watson), Jason (Elan Harris) and Darren (Jason Stracey), Trevor's younger brother. Trevor fancied Jane and the show was not light on sexual innuendo and double entendres. Much use was made of high-tech visuals and music to carry the stories along at great pace.

Producer: Humphrey Barclay for Humphrey Barclay Productions.

WHATEVER HAPPENED TO THE LIKELY LADS?

BBC. First broadcast: 9 January 1973

Dick Clement and Ian La Frenais, creators of THE LIKELY LADS, brought back Bob Ferris (Rodney Bewes) and Terry Collier (James Bolam) in this series. Terry returned home to Newcastle after five years in the Army serving abroad and having inadvertently married a girl whom he had left behind. Bob had been rejected by the Army because of flat feet and Terry discovered a vastly different best friend on his return. Bob had a house of his own, a car, and a pushy fiancée Thelma (Brigit Forsyth), the daughter of his boss. Bob had become a white-collar worker and was progressing up the middle management ladder. He believed that with his new status and his annual holiday on the Costa Brava he had climbed out of his working-class origins. Terry, however, saw through his pathetic ostentation and ridiculed his social posing. To add to Bob's discomfort, Terry took an instant dislike to the bossy Thelma who personified everything that he despised in women. Terry never allowed Bob to forget his past but a wander of rediscovery around their old haunts revealed much change and demolition in Newcastle. In the 13th and final episode of the first series, Bob and Thelma married. A second run of 13 began in January 1974 and the very final edition was an hour-long Christmas special on 24 December 1974.

Producers: James Gilbert, Bernard Thompson.

BBC RADIO. First broadcast: 30 July 1975

After the television show came to an end in 1974, John Browell adapted some of the stories into this 13-part radio series. James Bolam and Rodney Bewes again starred as Terry and Bob. Brigit Forsyth reprised her role as Thelma Chambers as did Sheila Fearn as Terry's sister Audrey.

Producer: John Browell.

THE WHITEHALL WORRIER

BBC. First broadcast: 13 January 1967

Alan Melville created The Rt Hon Mervyn Pugh (Robert Coote) for a 1966 edition of *Comedy Playhouse* and turned him into a six-part series. Pugh was a Cabinet Minister who fell into every booby-trap along the corridors of power. Moira Lister co-starred as his wife Janet. Mervyn's dogsbody and whipping-boy was Roger (Jonathan Cecil) and the pillars of the Civil Service which supported him were Miss Dempster (Nan Munro) and Mr Harrison (Arthur Howard). The Pughs had two grown-up children, David and Michele (Karl Lanchbury and Celia Hewitt), and a cook-housekeeper, Mrs Frome (Barbara Ogilvie).
Producer: Graeme Muir.

WHO IS SYLVIA?

ATV. First broadcast: 11 February 1967

Comedian Charlie Drake starred as Charles Rameses Drake, a man in search of the perfect mate. To this end he introduced himself to a marriage bureau where the secretary, Mrs Proudpiece (Kathleen Byron), took up the challenge over seven episodes.
Writers: Charlie Drake and Donald Churchill. Director: Shaun O'Riordan. Producer: Alan Tarrant.

WHO, SIR? ME, SIR?

BBC. First broadcast: 12 March 1985

Jenny McDade adapted the books by KM Peyton into this six-part children's series. The class of 2C at Gasworks Comprehensive School was peopled by non-achievers and hopeless athletes but when form teacher Sam (Ian Hastings) engaged them in battle on the sports field with local snob school Greycoats, they pulled out all the stops, with the encouragement of non-playing captain Nutty McTavish (Linda Frith).
Director: Colin Cant. Producer: Paul Stone.

A WHOLE NEW BALL GAME

BBC RADIO. First broadcast: 3 February 1993

Martin Davies wrote this black comedy in six parts. Following the death of her husband who had been a stalwart among the Roman Catholic community of St Andrews, Mrs Patterson (Brenda Blethyn) had to face the new challenges which life threw up at her. She had a headstrong daughter, Barbara (Charlotte Coleman), to cope with, and a son,

Robert (Paul Parris), who was suddenly faced with new responsibilities. The family was helped by Father Benedict (Desmond Barritt).
Producer: Lissa Evans.

WHOOPS APOCALYPSE!

LWT. First broadcast: 14 March 1982

Writers Andrew Marshall and David Renwick took sitcom into the future in these six programmes as they charted the events leading up to World War III. It was election year on both sides of the Atlantic and there was an international conspiracy in which the Quark bomb was calculated to restore Shah Mashiq Rassim (Bruce Montague) to power in Iran. Events went wrong and Israel was blown-up by mistake. Barry Morse played the US President, Johnny Cyclops, a former actor from Omaha. He had a fanatical security adviser known as the Deacon (John Barron) who had a hot-line to God. Other principal characters scattered around the world included Premier Dubienkin (Richard Griffiths), Commissar Solzhenitsyn (Alexei Sayle), Kevin Pork (Peter Jones), the Foreign Secretary (Geoffrey Palmer), the Chancellor of the Exchequer (Richard Davies), Jay Garrick (Ed Bishop) and Abdab (David Kelly). The most hunted terrorist in the world was Lacrobat (John Cleese).
Music: Nigel Hess. Director: John Reardon. Producer: Humphrey Barclay.

WHOOPS BAGHDAD

BBC. First broadcast: 25 January 1973

Frankie Howerd starred as Ali Oopla, a bond-servant in the service of the Wazir (Derek Francis). The Wazir's wife was Fatima (Josephine Tewson) and his two beautiful daughters were Saccharine (Hilary Pritchard) and Boobiana (Anna Brett). Other regular characters were the Captain of the Guard (Alan Curtis), Imshi (Norman Chappell), and Derti Dhoti (Larry Martyn). While the costumes and setting of the six episodes were different from UP POMPEII, the jokes remained the same.
Writers: Sid Colin, David McKellar and David Nobbs. Producer: John Howard Davies.

WHO'S THE BOSS?

ABC (AMERICA) PRESENTED BY ITV.
First broadcast: 2 June 1989

Martin Cohan and Blake Hunter created this format which was later anglicised into THE UPPER

HAND. However, ITV also screened the original American series and a varying number of episodes were seen across the regions. Widower Tony Micelli (Tony Danza) was forced to quit professional baseball through injury. Faced with raising his nine-year-old daughter Samantha (Alyssa Milano), he took a job as housekeeper to advertising executive Angela Bower (Judith Light) and her son Jonathan (Danny Pintauro). Also in the household was Angela's mother, Mona Robinson (Katherine Helmond).

An Embassy production.

WILD, WILD WOMEN

BBC. First broadcast: 6 January 1969

Creators and writers Ronald Wolfe and Ronald Chesney set this series of six programmes in the early years of the 20th century with girls working in a millinery basement sweat-shop where they churned out hats and plotted suffragette activity. It had its roots in a *Comedy Playhouse* of 1968. The hat-making girls were Millie (Barbara Windsor), Daisy (Pat Coombs), Blossom (Jessie Robbins) and Ruby (Toni Palmer). The owner of the business was Mr Harcourt (Paul Whitsun-Jones) and his assistant was Albert (Ken Platt).

Producer: GB Lupino.

WILDERNESS ROAD

BBC. First broadcast: 21 July 1986

Two young men, Cage (David Sibley) and Moon (Robin Driscoll), both unemployed and content to live that way, met up with Nancy (Veronica Quilligan), a stripper who was willing to pay the bills in exchange for a roof over her head. The landlord of The Sun public house, Arch (Leslie Sands), was prepared to let them have the off-licence and its flat adjacent to the pub. The villains were Keith and Alan (Gary Olsen and Peter Jonfield), a pair of heavies who enjoyed their work and had their ambitious eyes on The Sun. There were six episodes.

Writers: Richard Cottan and Bob Goody. Director: Susan Belbin. Producer: John Kilby.

THE WILL HAY PROGRAMME

BBC RADIO. First broadcast: 21 July 1944

After many years as a stage and film star, Will Hay turned to radio as his health began to fail and he sought less strenuous work. He broadcast a pilot show which proved to be of sufficient worth that a series got underway on the 18 August. The shows were subtitled 'The Diary of a Schoolmaster', for Hay's character was the mumbling, bumbling Dr Muffin of St Michael's school. Muffin's life was divided between his home, where his housekeeper was Mrs Potts (Beryl Riggs) with her tough little lamb of a son Alfie (Clarence Wright), and school, where his colleagues included Mr Brown (Dick Francis) and his pupils were the rude clever-dick Smart (Charles Hawtrey), know-it-all D'Arcy minor (John Clark) and stupid Beckett (Billy Nicholls). The first series lasted through eight editions followed by a special Christmas show on 20 December 1944 and then seven more programmes from 3 January 1945. A special programme was made for broadcast on 11 May 1945 called 'Victory At St Michael's' and a new series followed which featured most of the old cast plus Graeme Muir, who went on to produce scores of sitcoms for television, and Peter Byrne, who would later come to prominence as Andy Crawford in *Dixon of Dock Green*. The signature tune was 'Boys and Girls Come Out to Play'.

Writers: Max Kester and Con West. Producer: Alick Hayes.

WINK TO ME ONLY

BBC. First broadcast: 11 June 1969

This began life as a single presentation in the 1968 *Comedy Playhouse* season under the title 'View By Appointment' before writer Jennifer Phillips developed it into a six-part series. The stars were Beryl Reid and Hugh Paddick, who portrayed the only two regular characters, Rene and Sydney Jelliot, a married couple living just south of the Thames. Their incompatibility arose from Rene's out-going ebullience and love of entertaining which contrasted sharply with Sydney's shy reserve and loathing of domestic intrusion.

Producer: Douglas Argent.

WINNING WIDOWS

ATV. First broadcast: 9 September 1961

Peggy Mount starred as Martha and Avice Landon as Mildred, widowed sisters who lived together in a London suburb. Each had already had three husbands and, although neither was anxious to find a fourth, they both recognised the occasional use of a man about the house. Martha was a practical realist who found Mildred's romantic and impulsive ways irritating. Men had a habit of invading their lives when least wanted. There were 14 editions over two series ending 2 November 1962.

Music: Bob Sharples. Writers: Sid Green and Dick Hills. Producer: Alan Tarrant.

WINSTON

BBC RADIO. First broadcast: 26 April 1989

Peter Tinniswood originally created the character of Winston Hayballs (Bill Wallis) for an award-winning radio play 'The Village Fête' in 1987. He became the subject of 30 stories over five series which ended on 5 May 1994. These series were successively titled 'Winston', 'Winston Comes To Town', 'Winston In Love', 'Winston In Europe' and 'Winston Back Home'. Tinniswood described Winston as "the village poacher, with his fat, brown boozer's belly and his bits of fluff on the side". He had been kicked out by his wife and sought refuge at the Dower House where the Empsons were Father (Maurice Denham), Nancy (Shirley Dixon), Rosie (Liz Goulding) and William (Christian Rodska). Wherever the adventures went, so journeyed all the characters.

Producer: Shaun MacLoughlin.

THE WOBBLETON WHEELERS

BBC RADIO.

See GOOD PULL-UP FOR CYCLISTS

THE WOLVIS FAMILY

BBC. First broadcast: 4 May 1991

This comedy drama in seven parts was written by Tom Lubbock and Roger Parsons. Stuart Wolvis (Charlie Condou) had been an open, chirpy and outgoing child who had once appeared on a television game show with the rest of his family. Five years later he disappeared. He was found by West Byfleet Social Services living rough with his pal Spencer Hogg (Christopher Chescoe). Stuart was returned to his family but he did not speak. His parents Herbert and Sylvia (John Joyce and Janet Dale) sought help from therapist Dr Graham Wilcockson (Nicholas Woodeson) and agreed to soul-bearing sessions of the entire family in front of a television audience. The Wolvis daughter was Wendy (Honey Hazel).

Director: Roger Parsons. Producer: Kevin Loader.

WOMEN WHO DO

BBC RADIO. First broadcast: 4 May 1994

Arnold Evans wrote this serial in five 45-minute parts. Two contract cleaning ladies working for a firm called 'Spit and Polish' became involved with the private affairs of their clients as well as cleaning for them. They were single Liverpudlian mother Mitch (Kate Fitzgerald) and rather upper-crust Lucy (Sue Broomfield) who had taken to cleaning to help pay her way through medical school. Their class differences brought out much needling between the pair.

Producer: Jane Dauncey.

THE WONDER YEARS

USA PRESENTED BY CHANNEL 4.
First broadcast (UK): 20 August 1989

Channel 4 showed more than 100 episodes of this gentle comedy drama. Set in 1968, the story began with Kevin Arnold's (Fred Savage) first day at RFK Junior High School. The series reflected the politics and social issues of those times as seen with the benefit of narrated hindsight. Other principal characters were mum Norma (Alley Mills), dad Jack (Dan Lauria), brother Wayne (Jason Hervey), sister Karen (Olivia D'Abo), Kevin's girlfriend Winnie Cooper (Danica McKellar) and his Jewish friend Paul (Josh Saviano).

Producers included Bob Brush and Michael Dinner for New World Television.

THE WORDSMITHS AT GORSEMERE

BBC RADIO. First broadcast: 25 February 1985

Sue Limb wrote this spoof of the Lake District's poetical heritage. There was a first series of four broadcasts and then a further six were heard from 22 May 1987. The period was the turn of the 18th century and the thinly-disguised characters who might just be based on the Wordsworths of Grassmere included William Wordsmith (Geoffrey Whitehead), Dorothy Wordsmith (Denise Coffey), Samuel Tailor Cholericke (Simon Callow), John Sheets (Nicky Henson), Thomas de Quinine (Nickolas Grace), William Bloke (John Shrapnel), Stinking Iris (Miriam Margolyes) and Leechpedler (Chris Emmett).

Music: Stephen Oliver. Producer: Jonathan James-Moore.

THE WORKER

ATV. First broadcast: 27 February 1965

Charlie Drake's scourge of the labour exchange, the Worker, had never held a job for more than a day except once when he managed two days – the second being Good Friday. The clerk at the labour exchange, Mr Whittaker (Percy Herbert), had found him 980 jobs over 20 years. In the second and subsequent series, the clerk was Mr Pugh (Henry McGee), volcanically seething each time the Worker turned up at Weybridge Labour Exchange. After 12 programmes, to Mr Pugh's delight, he disappeared for three years, only to resurface on 29 December 1969 for two more series of hassle. He finally got rid of him on 9 September 1970. London Weekend Television revised the format within *Bruce Forsyth's Big Night* on 7 October 1978, again with Drake and McGee.

Writers: Lew Schwarz, Charlie Drake. Directors: Shaun O'Riordan, Paul Annett. Producers: Alan Tarrant, Shaun O'Riordan.

A WORLD OF HIS OWN

BBC. First broadcast: 22 January 1965

Dave Freeman created and wrote this series which began with a first run of six followed by six more editions starting 22 January 1965. Roy Kinnear starred as the day-dreaming Stanley Blake, a mild and seemingly ordinary husband yet lost in his own realms of fantasy. Anne Cunningham played his wife Helen, who was required to assume various characterisations in order to fit into Stanley's dream world, being a missionary one minute and harem dancer the next.

Theme music: Lionel Bart. Producers: David Croft, Graeme Muir.

THE WORLD OF WOOSTER

BBC. First broadcast: 30 May 1965

The short stories of PG Wodehouse were adapted for television by Richard Waring and Michael Mills. Set in the 1920s, Bertie Wooster (Ian Carmichael) bungled and fumbled his monocled way through life as an archetypal upper-class silly ass who was protected from self-inflicted catastrophe by his wise, imperturbable and efficient gentleman's gentleman, Jeeves (Dennis Price). A first series of six was followed by six more editions the following year and a final run of seven ending 17 November 1967.

Music: Sandy Wilson. Producer: Michael Mills.

WOULD THE LAST BUSINESSMAN . . .

BBC RADIO. First broadcast: 12 February 1978

And the title continued . . . to leave the Country please turn out the lights? Andrew Palmer wrote the scripts in the wake of the early and mid-1970s which had witnessed the introduction of VAT, the miners' strike and Edward Heath's three-day week. Leslie Phillips starred as the businessman who was concerned to protect his perks and fringe benefits from the VAT man, the taxman and all others who threatened his cosseted existence. The regular company supporting Phillips in his endeavours included Kenneth Connor, Hugh Paddick, Nell Brennan and Sue Holderness. There were two series, each of six programmes, the second ending on 31 May 1979.

Producer: Edward Taylor.

WRINKLES

BBC RADIO. First broadcast: 15 May 1980

This was the first original creation from writers Rob Grant and Doug Naylor who would later come up with RED DWARF. The setting was an old folks' home where Anthea Askey was the cook and Tom Mennard the general handyman. The voice of the matron was produced by violinist Baz Barker on his fiddle. The residents included Mr Pettigrew (David Ross), Winston (Ballard Berkeley), Arnold (Gordon Sallkilld) who was always going to die tomorrow, and Lewis (Nick Maloney) who shouted his every word as a direct result of having spent most of his life on a lighthouse. There were two runs, each of six, the second ending on 15 December 1981.

Producer: Mike Craig.

WYATT'S WATCHDOGS

BBC. First broadcast: 17 October 1988

Following the daylight robbery of the private house of his sister Edwina (Anne Ridley), retired army Major Wyatt (Brian Wilde) took the law more or less into his own hands and vowed to stem the rising tide of crime by forming a neighbourhood watch group. He adopted a preposterous self-importance and recruited the aforementioned sister, an upper-crust spinster, and burglar-alarm dealer Peter Pitt (Trevor Bannister), who was something of a ladykiller. Pitt was attracted to Wyatt's scheme by the prospect of meeting the local ladies and selling quantities of alarms. The Major and he could not abide each other. Six editions were transmitted.

Writer: Miles Tredinnick. Producer: Alan J W Bell.

XERXES

STV (SWEDEN) PRESENTED BY CHANNEL 4.
First broadcast: 3 August 1989

This subtitled series ran for six editions on Channel 4. Three young schoolfriends, Xerxes (Benny Haag), Tony (Joakim Borjlind) and Pekka (Kalle Westerdahl), left school and ventured forth into the big wide world. Xerxes found a job where he met girls more worldly experienced than himself who taught him lessons in love. He faced up to his family and announced his intention to find a home of his own, his sole object being to create a bachelor love-nest.

YANKS GO HOME

GRANADA. First broadcast: 22 November 1976

The setting for this series was 1942 in a Lancashire village where the USAAF had taken over a private airfield and the first GIs began to arrive. It was based on the true takeover by the Americans of the Lancashire airfield at Burtonwood. Stuart Damon starred as Corporal Vince Rossi, one of the first three dozen arrivals under the command of Colonel Ralph Kruger (Alan MacNaughton), along with Sergeant Gus Pulaski (Bruce Boa), Corporal Pasquale (Freddie Earlle) and Private Burford Pucket (Richard Oldfield). The next batch of arrivals included Colonel Irving (Lionel Murton) and Private Tutt (Jay Benedict). The rather startled villagers included Phoebe and Doreen Sankey (Meg Johnson and Catherine Neilson), Mr and Mrs Chambers (Norman Bird and Daphne Oxenford), Bert Pickup (Harry Markham) and Harry Duckworth (David Ross). By the second series beginning 8 August 1977, Doreen Sankey was engaged to be married to Private Tutt. There were a total of 13 programmes.

Writers included John Stevenson and Julian Roach, HV Kershaw, Michael Carter and Anthony Couch. Producer: Eric Prytherch.

YES – HONESTLY

LWT. First broadcast: 11 January 1976

Writers Terence Brady and Charlotte Bingham took the outline idea of their earlier series NO – HONESTLY, changed the characters and embarked on a new lease of life. Struggling songwriter Matthew Browne (Donal Donnelly) hired a typist, Lily Pond (Liza Goddard), little realising that she would become his wife. In the first series of 13 programmes, they became engaged on 15 February and married the following week. They lived in a permanently impecunious state and found it difficult to see eye to eye in both their working and private lives. They returned for a second series in March 1977. Lily's mother, Mrs Pond, was played by Eve Pearce and the Brownes' neighbours were June and Hayward (Georgina Melville and Ian Judge). Lily's friend and confidante was Georgina (Georgina Hale). During the second series the Brownes' resources were further stretched by the birth of a baby.

Theme music: Georgie Fame. Directors: Les Chatfield, John Reardon. Producer: Humphrey Barclay.

YES, MINISTER

BBC. First broadcast: 25 February 1980

Jonathan Lynn and Antony Jay created this satirical series. Political connivance and the Whitehall double-talk of Civil Servants were the everyday realities into which James Hacker MP (Paul Eddington), as newly appointed Minister of Administrative Affairs, found himself plunged. His ineptness afforded an opportunity for his Permanent Under-Secretary, Sir Humphrey Appleby (Nigel Hawthorne), to exert departmental control. Nervously hopping between them was Private Secretary Bernard Woolley (Derek Fowlds) who managed to quietly steer a moderating course. There were 22 editions over three series, the last one screened on 17 December 1984. A Christmas special edition in 1985 threw up the possibility of Hacker's becoming Prime

THE GUINNESS BOOK OF SITCOMS

Minister, thus paving the way for YES, PRIME MINISTER.
Producers: Sydney Lotterby, Peter Whitmore.

BBC RADIO. First broadcast: 20 October 1983

Radio producer Pete Atkin adapted 16 of the television scripts by Antony Jay and Jonathan Lynn into two eight-part series, the second of which ended on 27 November 1984. Paul Eddington, Nigel Hawthorne and Derek Fowlds all reprised their roles from the TV series.

YES, PRIME MINISTER
BBC. First broadcast: 9 January 1986

This sequel to YES, MINISTER was again written by Antony Jay and Jonathan Lynn and picked up as Jim Hacker (Paul Eddington) moved into No. 10 Downing Street with his faithful Sir Humphrey (Nigel Hawthorne) and Bernard (Derek Fowlds). It was Hacker's defiant stand against the Euro-sausage which catapulted him towards the highest office, together with a modicum of blackmail and backstabbing by Sir Humphrey Appleby! The stories steered a course through the twists, turns and minefields of bureaucracy, Whitehall and government. There were two series of eight, ending on 28 January 1987. The animated titles sequence was by Gerald Scarfe. This was one of the few British sitcoms to be sold in its original form to the United States.
Producer: Sydney Lotterby.

YOU MUST BE THE HUSBAND
BBC. First broadcast: 8 September 1987

Tom Hammond (Tim Brooke-Taylor) had always earned a modest living and supported his wife Alice (Diane Keane) and their grown-up twins. He worked in bathroom fittings for his boss, Gerald (Garfield Morgan), and she had kept house for 20 years. Then she wrote a steamy best-selling book and, almost overnight, became very rich indeed. Into Tom's life came doubts and questions about when, where and with whom Alice had carried out the necessary research; but, even more disturbingly, into his life came Alice's literary agent Miranda (Sheila Steafel), a hard-nosed woman who despised husbands and saw Tom as a threat to Alice's burgeoning career. A first series of seven transmissions was followed by a second run of ten which ended on 4 May 1988.

Writer: Colin Bostock-Smith. Directors: John Kilby, Richard Boden. Producer: John Kilby.

YOU RANG, M'LORD?
BBC. First broadcast: 29 December 1988

Created and written by Jimmy Perry and David Croft, this series began with a single 60-minute edition and was followed from 14 January 1990 by 25 episodes, each of 50 minutes' duration, over four series ending on 24 April 1993. The setting was the upstairs-downstairs of the stately home of Lord Meldrum (Donald Hewlett) who, though impoverished, did his best for all around him in spite of chicanery and devious love-affairs all around. The Meldrum family comprised the monocled Hon. Teddy (Michael Knowles), naughty and flighty Poppy (Susie Brann), androgynous Cissy (Catherine Rabett), and Lord Meldrum's dotty mother Lady Lavender (Mavis Pugh). Downstairs, the head of the household was James Twelvetrees, the object of Miss Poppy's lust and the dream lover of the maid Ivy Teasdale (Su Pollard). Although for a while it remained undisclosed to the staff, Ivy was the daughter of the scheming butler Alf Stokes (Paul Shane). Alf spent his time hatching plans to line his own pockets. The kitchen, where many of the scenes took place, was firmly ruled by cook Mrs Lipton (Brenda Cowling) with scullery maid Mabel (Barbara New) being thrown the odd tit-bit, usually to have it taken back from her at the last moment while Alf supped his Lordship's best wines. The boot boy was Henry (Perry Benson), a well-meaning youth who had his ears clipped no matter how hard he tried. A regular visitor to the kitchen who knew the prowess of Mrs Lipton's culinary skills was Police Constable Wilson (Bill Pertwee). Alas, it all came to a sad end when the Meldrums were forced to quit the hall and Ted and Ivy were last seen on a forlorn East coast beach pondering their future. Other regular characters included Sir Ralph (John Horsley) and promiscuous Lady Agatha (Angela Scoular).
Producer: David Croft.

YOU START, I'LL JOIN IN
BBC RADIO. First broadcast: 8 September 1987

This series in seven episodes starred George Layton as cynical piano player Mac with Vas Blackwood as ambitious drummer Trevor. Mac was 42, Trevor just 24. Neither of them had a regular job but Mac had a flat and a drum machine and between them they made much noise and little money.

Writers: David Bond and Paul Hawksbee. Producer: Pete Atkin.

YOUNG AT HEART

ATV. First broadcast: 14 April 1980

John Mills starred in this Vince Powell creation as Albert Collyer who, after fifty years working for the local pottery company, had to face the problems of retirement with his wife, Ethel (Megs Jenkins). When not getting under each other's feet, Albert and Ethel were to be found in the company of their neighbours, Norman and Barbara Charlton (David Neilson and Carol Leader). A high spot would be a visit to or from the Collyer daughter, Mary (Stephanie Fayerman), who lived in Manchester. There were three series of six programmes, the last two series produced by Central, ending on 29 October 1983.

Producer: Stuart Allen.

Left to right, Mike (Christopher Ryan), Rick (Rik Mayall), Neil (Nigel Planer) and Vyvyan (Ade Edmondson) enjoy the unique charm of shared squalor in THE YOUNG ONES (Photo: Copyright © BBC)

THE YOUNG ONES

BBC. First broadcast: 9 November 1982

Only 12 episodes were ever made of this influential series which gave many under-21s much to cheer about and left the establishment, as represented by the popular press, with everything to complain about. There were two seasons of six shows, the second starting on 8 May 1984. The regular cast were Nigel Planer as pathetically mournful hippy Neil, Rik Mayall as radical but stupidly silly Rick, Ade Edmondson as menacingly violent Vyvyan, and Christopher Ryan as the mild Mike. They shared a disgusting flat where the landlord was Jerzy Balowski (Alexei Sayle, who played several members of the Balowski family). Vyvyan and Rick hated each other, everyone hated Neil and the language, the crude and vulgar behaviour, and the anarchic attempts to debunk all that society held dear, sent shock waves across the nation. They lived in a world peopled with psychopaths, hostile students and neurotic self-deprecation. The list of actors who made guest appearances reads like a Who's Who of comedy from that point on, including Dawn French, Jennifer Saunders, Ben Elton, Robbie Coltrane, Gareth Hale, Norman Pace, Lenny Henry, Helen Lederer, Stephen Fry, Hugh Laurie, Emma Thompson, Dave Rappaport and several others.

Writers: Ben Elton, Rik Mayall and Lise Mayer (Alexei Sayle wrote his own contributions). Producer: Paul Jackson.

YOU'LL NEVER GET RICH
CBS (AMERICA) PRESENTED BY BBC.

See THE PHIL SILVERS SHOW

YOUNG, GIFTED AND BROKE
CENTRAL. First broadcast: 3 June 1989

Gary Lawson and John Phelps wrote these seven programmes based on an idea by Laurence Marks and Maurice Gran. Five teenagers on a Youth Training Scheme joined an electronics firm run by Frank (James Hazeldine), assisted by Linda (Mary Healey) and Paul (Simon O'Brien) who was in charge of the assembly line. The young trainees were Adrian (Mark Monero), Greg (Jason Rush), Tamsin (Elena Ferrari), Aysha (Cheryl Miller) and Bolton (Steven O'Donnell).
Director: Gerry Mill. Producer: Margaret Bottomley.

YOU'RE ONLY OLD ONCE
BBC RADIO. First broadcast: 1 June 1969

John Esmonde and Bob Larbey wrote this ten-part series as a starring vehicle for Clive Dunn who had specialised in the creation of old characters while still a young man himself. Helping prove that the elderly could have fun were Deryck Guyler, Patricia Hayes and Joan Sanderson.
Producer: Edward Taylor.

YOU'RE ONLY YOUNG ONCE
BBC RADIO. First broadcast: 20 June 1954

In a series of five half-hours on the Light Programme, Eric Morecambe and Ernie Wise ran the Morecambe and Wise Detective Agency. Pearl Carr was their secretary and Deryck Guyler portrayed the office boy, Battersby, who plodded his weary way around the corridors in search of mislaid information. Each week a guest star would arrive asking for help in some desperate situation. A second run of 12 weekly broadcasts got underway on the Home Service on 1 October the same year. The Agency had expanded and two assistant detectives joined the cast, played by Hattie Jacques and Herbert Smith. Although this was the first and only sitcom venture for Eric and Ernie, they had, in fact, made their first broadcast as a double act in 1942.
Writer: Frank Roscoe. Producer: John Ammonds.

YOU'RE ONLY YOUNG TWICE
ATV. First broadcast: 5 July 1971

Written and created by Jack Trevor Story, this series featured some very much alive residents of an old folk's home, Twilight Lodge. Matron (Adrienne Corri) had her work cut out handling residents like Peter (Peter Copley), Reg (Leslie Dwyer), Giulio (Vic Wise) and the reluctant newcomer, ex-detective Henry Armitage (Liam Redmond). On Matron's staff were Nurse Corrinna (Carmen Munro) and young Benny (Anthony Jackson).
Director: David Askey. Producer: Shaun O'Riordan.

YOU'RE ONLY YOUNG TWICE
YTV. First broadcast: 6 September 1977

This series, created and written by Pam Valentine and Michael Ashton, was set in Paradise Lodge, a superior retirement residence for elderly ladies. The ladies who resided there were far from senile and made life as difficult as possible for the proprietress Miss Milton (Charmian May), her assistant Miss Finch (Georgina Moon) and general factotum Roger (Johnny Wade). The ringleaders of residential disturbance were Flora Petty (Peggy Mount), Cissie Lupin (Pat Coombs), Dolly Love (Lally Bowers), Katy O'Rourke (Peggy Ledger) and Mildred Fanshawe (Diana King). The shows returned for further seasons in 1978, 1979 and 1981. There were 26 episodes in total.
Producer: Graeme Muir.

YUS MY DEAR
LWT. First broadcast: 10 January 1976

Writers Ronald Wolfe and Ronald Chesney took the characters Wally and Lily Briggs (Arthur Mullard and Queenie Watts) from their caravan site in ROMANY JONES to a new life in a council house. Wally had begun to earn good money working on a building site although he was hard pushed to hang on to his wages as both Lily and his parasitic brother Benny (Mike Reid), who lived with them, fought to get their hands on the spoils of his labour. In the first series of six programmes, Benny acquired a fiancée, Molly (Valerie Walsh). Although she lasted through the second series in September of the same year, she never managed to get him to the altar.
Producer: Stuart Allen.

INDEX

EPILOGUE

THE OFFICE OF MIKE CRAIG AND VINCE POWELL (sort of 'writers') IT IS MORNING, BRIGHT SUN SHINES THROUGH THE CRACKED DIRTY WINDOWS. VINCE SITS AT A MAKE-SHIFT DESK READING THE MORNING'S FINAL DEMANDS. OUTSIDE WE HEAR THE NOISE OF WORKMEN DEMOLISHING THE REST OF THE PREFABS.

Mike: (ENTERING EXCITEDLY) Vince, I think I've got it.

Vince: I'll get the pink ointment.

Mike: No, the title for our sitcom idea about those two labourers who work for the Highways Department of Cleckhuddersfax Council.

Vince: Come on then.

Mike: 'Any Road Up'!

Vince: Brilliant. Let's start on it now.

Mike: We can't.

Vince: Why not?

Mike: I've just had Guinness on the telephone.

Vince: It'll come off with a damp cloth.

Mike: They want us to write an Epilogue.

Vince: We could if we knew what it meant.

Mike: They want twenty-five words about this new book.

Vince: Which book?

Mike: This book. It's by Rod Taylor.

Vince: Oh! I can't stand him.

Mike: He once leant us a fiver.

Vince: I've always liked Rod Taylor. Are we mentioned?

Mike: Constantly!

Vince: Right, how about this? 'A brilliant, perceptive and all embracing work of genuine importance.' (PAUSE) Hang on, that's only one, two, three . . . er . . . seven, eight . . . that's only ten words, we've got fourteen left.

Mike: No problem. I'll give you fifteen words . . . 'Available for after dinner speeches, Barmitzvahs, supermarkets opened, yards cleared, cellars whitewashed – phone us on

Vince: You Wally! You've used all the words up.

Mike Craig and Vince Powell. August 1994.